The *Recorded Sayings* of Chan Master Zhongfeng Mingben

The *Recorded Sayings* of Chan Master Zhongfeng Mingben

Jeffrey L. Broughton
with
Elise Yoko Watanabe

OXFORD
UNIVERSITY PRESS

Oxford University Press is a department of the University of Oxford. It furthers
the University's objective of excellence in research, scholarship, and education
by publishing worldwide. Oxford is a registered trade mark of Oxford University
Press in the UK and certain other countries.

Published in the United States of America by Oxford University Press
198 Madison Avenue, New York, NY 10016, United States of America.

© Oxford University Press 2023

All rights reserved. No part of this publication may be reproduced, stored in
a retrieval system, or transmitted, in any form or by any means, without the
prior permission in writing of Oxford University Press, or as expressly permitted
by law, by license, or under terms agreed with the appropriate reproduction
rights organization. Inquiries concerning reproduction outside the scope of the
above should be sent to the Rights Department, Oxford University Press, at the
address above.

You must not circulate this work in any other form
and you must impose this same condition on any acquirer.

Library of Congress Cataloging-in-Publication Data
Names: Broughton, Jeffrey L., 1944- author. | Mingben, Shi, 1263–1323. | Watanabe, Elise Yoko.
Title: The recorded sayings of Chan Master Zhongfeng Mingben /
Jeffrey L. Broughton with Elise Yoko Watanabe.
Description: New York, NY : Oxford University Press, [2023] |
Includes bibliographical references and index. | English and Chinese.
Identifiers: LCCN 2023006050 (print) | LCCN 2023006051 (ebook) |
ISBN 9780197672976 (hardcover) | ISBN 9780197672990 (epub) | ISBN 9780197673003
Subjects: LCSH: Zen Buddhism—Early works to 1800. | Mingben, Shi, 1263–1323.
Classification: LCC BQ9258 .B76 2023 (print) | LCC BQ9258 (ebook) |
DDC 294.3/75—dc23/eng/20230213
LC record available at https://lccn.loc.gov/2023006050
LC ebook record available at https://lccn.loc.gov/2023006051

DOI: 10.1093/oso/9780197672976.001.0001

Printed by Integrated Books International, United States of America

For the "First Seat" at Shōfuku-ji (聖福寺) *in the late 1980s*

Nāgārjuna's *Root Verses on the Middle Way* (*Mūlamadhyamakakārikā* 17.33)

kleśāḥ karmāṇi dehāś ca kartāraś ca phalāni ca /
gandharvanagarākārā marīcisvapnasaṃnibhāḥ //

*Defilements, actions, and bodies, agents, and fruits,
are similar to the city of the gandharvas; they are like a mirage, a dream.*

—From Mark Siderits and Shōryū Katsura, trans.,
Nāgārjuna's Middle Way: **Mūlamadhyamakakārikā**
(Somerville, MA: Wisdom Publications, 2013), 191

***

Middle Treatise (*Zhong lun* 中論; Kumārajīva's Chinese translation of the above Sanskrit verse)

諸煩惱及業 作者及果報 皆如幻與夢 如炎亦如嚮

Defilements and actions, agents and karmic fruits are all like a phantasm [huan 幻] or a dream; they are like a blaze or an echo.

—T 1564.30.23c2–3

***

一切是幻。

Everything is a phantasm.

—From Zhongfeng Mingben's *House Instructions
for Dwelling-in-the-Phantasmal Hermitage*

Contents

Abbreviations ... ix

Introduction ... 1
    Linji Chan in the South During the Mongol Yuan Dynasty: Zhongfeng
        Mingben and Yuansou Xingduan ... 1
    Autobiography and *Huatou* Chan ... 7
    The Format and Underlying Theme of Zhongfeng's Autobiography ... 10
    The Confining Bureaucratic Chan Style of Mt. Tianmu Versus
        the Unencumbered Chan Style of a Vagabond Budai (布袋) ... 14
    Two Chan Records for Zhongfeng Mingben: *Zhongfeng*
        Extensive Record and *Zhongfeng Record B* ... 17
    Understanding the Phantasmal (*zhi huan* 知幻) ... 23
    Detaching from the Phantasmal (*li huan* 離幻): The *Huatou* ... 27
    Zhongfeng's *Great Matter of Samsara* (*shengsi dashi* 生死大事) ... 30
    Zhongfeng: "I Am Not Awakened" ... 32
    Entanglement of *Huatou* Chan and Pure Land *Nianfo* (*Nembutsu*):
        Zhongfeng and Tianru ... 35
    Zhongfeng and the "Nanzhao" (Yunnan) Pilgrim Xuanjian (玄鑒; d.u.) ... 38
    Zhongfeng and Japanese Zen ... 43
    Zhongfeng, Tianru, and Ming-Dynasty Linji Chan ... 55

Translation 1: Selections from *Instructions to the Assembly* in
Zhongfeng Extensive Record ... 63

Translation 2: Selections from *Dharma Talks* in *Zhongfeng
Extensive Record* ... 71

Translation 3: *Night Conversations in a Mountain Hermitage* in
Zhongfeng Extensive Record ... 83

Translation 4: *House Instructions for Dwelling-in-the-Phantasmal
Hermitage* in *Zhongfeng Extensive Record* ... 168

Translation 5: *In Imitation of Hanshan's Poems* in *Zhongfeng
Extensive Record* ... 179

Translation 6: *Song of Dwelling-in-the-Phantasmal Hermitage* in
Zhongfeng Extensive Record ... 212

Translation 7: *Cross-Legged Sitting Chan Admonitions* (with Preface)
in *Zhongfeng Extensive Record* ... 214

viii Contents

Translation 8: *Ten Poems on Living on a Boat* in *Zhongfeng Extensive Record* — 216

Translation 9: *Ten Poems on Living in Town* in *Zhongfeng Extensive Record* — 220

Translation 10: Selections from *Zhongfeng Dharma Talks* in *Zhongfeng Record B* — 225

Translation 11: *Instructions to the Assembly* from *Zhongfeng Talks* in *Zhongfeng Record B* — 245

Chinese Text for Translation 1: Selections from *Instructions to the Assembly* in *Zhongfeng Extensive Record* — 247

Chinese Text for Translation 2: Selections from *Dharma Talks* in *Zhongfeng Extensive Record* — 250

Chinese Text for Translation 3: *Night Conversations in a Mountain Hermitage* in *Zhongfeng Extensive Record* — 254

Chinese Text for Translation 4: *House Instructions for Dwelling-in-the-Phantasmal Hermitage* in *Zhongfeng Extensive Record* — 280

Chinese Text for Translation 5: *In Imitation of Hanshan's Poems* in *Zhongfeng Extensive Record* — 284

Chinese Text for Translation 6: *Song of Dwelling-in-the-Phantasmal Hermitage* in *Zhongfeng Extensive Record* — 294

Chinese Text for Translation 7: *Cross-Legged Sitting Chan Admonitions* (with Preface) in *Zhongfeng Extensive Record* — 295

Chinese Text for Translation 8: *Ten Poems on Living on a Boat* in *Zhongfeng Extensive Record* — 296

Chinese Text for Translation 9: *Ten Poems on Living in Town* in *Zhongfeng Extensive Record* — 298

Chinese Text for Translation 10: Selections from *Zhongfeng Dharma Talks* in *Zhongfeng Record B* — 300

Chinese Text for Translation 11: *Instructions to the Assembly* from *Zhongfeng Talks* in *Zhongfeng Record B* — 309

Bibliography — *311*
Index — *315*

Abbreviations

Broughton with Watanabe, *Chan Whip*
Broughton, Jeffrey L., with Elise Yoko Watanabe. *The* Chan Whip *Anthology: A Companion to Zen Practice*. New York: Oxford University Press, 2015.

Broughton with Watanabe, *Letters of Dahui*
Broughton, Jeffrey L., with Elise Yoko Watanabe. *The Letters of Chan Master Dahui Pujue*. New York: Oxford University Press, 2017.

CBETA
Chinese Buddhist Electronic Text Association. http://www.cbeta.org

Eigen Jakushitsu oshō goroku
Eigen-ji kaisan goroku kenkyūkai, ed. *Eigen Jakushitsu oshō goroku* 永源寂室和尚語録. 3 vols. Kyoto: Zen bunka kenkyūjo, 2016.
Translation and study of the Zen record of the medieval Japanese Rinzai monk Jakushitsu Genkō (寂室元光; 1290–1367).

Gozanban 9
Shiina Kōyū, ed. *Gozanban Chūgoku Zenseki sōkan 9: Goroku 4*. Kyoto: Rinsen shoten, 2013.
Contains Five-Mountains editions of *Zhongfeng Extensive Record* and *Zhongfeng Record B* (= *Zhongfeng Dharma Talks* and *Zhongfeng Talks*).

Heller, "The Chan Master as Illusionist"
Heller, Natasha. "The Chan Master as Illusionist: Zhongfeng Mingben's *Huanzhu Jiaxun*." *Harvard Journal of Asiatic Studies* 69, no. 2 (2009): 271–308.

Heller, *Illusory Abiding*
Heller, Natasha. *Illusory Abiding: The Cultural Construction of the Chan Monk Zhongfeng Mingben*. Cambridge, MA: Harvard University Asia Center, 2014.

Lauer, Calligraphy of Mingben
Lauer, Uta. *A Master of His Own: The Calligraphy of the Chan Abbot Zhongfeng Mingben (1262–1323)*. Stuttgart: Steiner, 2002.

Ming Chan Masters
Yunqi Zhuhong's (雲棲袾宏) *Abbreviated Collection of Famous Monks of the Imperial Ming* (*Huangming mingseng jilüe* 皇明名僧輯略; CBETA, X84, no. 1581, p. 358, c6).
Sayings of ten Chan masters of the Ming dynasty.

Noguchi and Matsubara, *Sanbō yawa*
Noguchi Yoshitaka and Matsubara Shinju, trans. *Chūhō Myōhon: Sanbō yawa yakuchū*. Tokyo: Kyūko shoin, 2015.
Annotated modern Japanese translation of the miscellany *Night Conversations in a Mountain Hermitage* in *Zhongfeng Extensive Record*

Noguchi, *Gendai Zen*
Noguchi Yoshitaka. *Gendai Zenshūshi kenkyū*. Kyoto: Zen bunka kenkyūjo, 2005.
Study of Chan in the Mongol Yuan period.

T
Takakusu Junjirō and Watanabe Kaigyoku, eds. *Taishō shinshū daizōkyō*. 100 vols. Tokyo: Taishō issaikyō kankōkai, 1924–1934.

Zhongfeng Dharma Talks
Tianmu Zhongfeng heshang Puying guoshi fayu (天目中峯和尚普応国師法語); first portion of *Zhongfeng Record B* in *Gozanban* 9, 501d–535c.

Zhongfeng Extensive Record
Tianmu Zhongfeng heshang guanglu (天目中峯和尚広録) in *Gozanban* 9, 99b–497c (also CBETA 2019.Q3, B25, no. 145, p. 687a1).

Zhongfeng Record B
Zhongfeng Dharma Talks and *Zhongfeng Talks* as a single volume in *Gozanban* 9, 499–562.

Zhongfeng Talks
Tianmu Zhongfeng Guanghui chanshi yu (天目中峯広慧禅師語); second portion of *Zhongfeng Record B* in *Gozanban* 9, 535c–561c.

Introduction

Linji Chan in the South During the Mongol Yuan Dynasty: Zhongfeng Mingben and Yuansou Xingduan

The Chan Buddhism of the Mongol Yuan dynasty (1271–1368) could be described as "cosmopolitan Chan." During the Yuan, Chan pilgrims came in substantial numbers from all over East Asia to train in the monasteries and hermitages of the region around Hangzhou, the former capital of the Southern Song dynasty (1127–1279). The state-sponsored system of "Five Mountains" (five great monasteries clustered in Hangzhou and Mingzhou in northern Zhejiang) and "Ten Monasteries" (lesser establishments spread over a larger geographical area of the Hangzhou region) served as a magnet.[1] This flourishing state of Yuan-dynasty Chan surely owed something to the Mongol creation of a multiethnic Chinese empire that engendered sustained cultural interaction over a vast geographical area.[2] Whereas the Southern Song

---

[1] Extant materials that speak of the establishment of the Five-Mountains system are scarce: one text is Song Lian's (宋濂; 1310–1381) *Record of Protecting the Dharma* (*Hufa lu* 護法錄; edited by Yunqi Zhuhong of the late Ming), a selection of materials related to Buddhism from Song's literary collection. The *Record of Protecting the Dharma* contains an inscription entitled *Stupa Inscription for Abbot Gufeng De Gong* [= Gufeng Mingde 孤峰明德; 1294–1372] *of Jingci Chan Monastery* (*Zhuchi Jingci chan si Gufeng Degong taming* 住持淨慈禪寺孤峰德公塔銘) which states: "In the past, the abbot of each monastery occupied the seat of his monastery to speak dharma, bringing benefit to sentient-beings. There were no ranks of 'high' and 'low.' At the tail end of the Song dynasty, Shi Weiwang [= Shi Miyuan 史彌遠; 1164–1233] submitted a proposal to the sovereign setting up the 'five mountains and ten monasteries.' This system is like a secular government office. [Abbots who] work as government employees within that system [at the beginning of their careers] must emerge into the world as teachers at small temples. Once their fame has spread, they are promoted in terms of grade. *If they can reach one of the five famous mountains, it is almost like serving as a general or senior minister*: in terms of human feelings, a glory that cannot be increased. Both monks and ordinary people frequently are envious of such a person. However, were their conduct not clearly beyond the standard, it would not have been easy for people's envy to have reached such a level." [古者住持。各據席說法。以利益有情。未嘗有崇卑之位焉。逮乎宋季。史衛王奏立五山十刹。如世之所謂官署。其服勞於其間者。必出世小院。俟其聲華彰著。然後使之拾級而升。其得至於五名山。殆猶仕宦而至將相。為人情之至榮。無復有所增加。緇素之人。往往歆豔之。然非行業夐出常倫。則有未易臻此者矣。] (CBETA 2019.Q3, J21, no. B110, pp. 623c26–624a3). Ishii Shūdō, "Chūgoku no gozan jissetu seido no kiso teki kenkyū 1," *Komazawa daigaku bukkyō gakubu ronshū* 13 (1982): 91 argues that the system seems to have begun during the Jiading era (嘉定; 1208–1224) of Emperor Ningzong (r. 1194–1224) due to the efforts of the Southern Song Grand Councilor Shi Miyuan. For a treatment of the five-mountains system, see Noguchi, *Gendai Zen*, 261–273.

[2] Endymion Wilkinson, *Chinese History: A New Manual*, 5th ed. (Cambridge, MA: Endymion Wilkinson, 2018), 869. Wilkinson remarks: "The Mongol legacy of a multi-ethnic Chinese empire was revived in a different form by the Manchus and inherited and refined by the Republic and the PRC."

was already a truncated empire by the time it was finally extinguished by the Mongols, the sprawling extent and multiethnic nature of the Mongol Yuan dynasty foreshadowed the Manchu Qing dynasty (and the People's Republic of China). The stabilizing influence of the *Pax Mongolica* facilitated travel and communication throughout East and Central Asia: Buddhist pilgrims benefitted. For instance, a steady stream of Japanese Zen monks and Korean Sŏn monks, who seem to have been "plugged in" to well-informed networks, were able to travel readily to specific Chan destinations in China and sojourn in China for many years, sometimes decades, before returning home and *recreating* what they had experienced.[3] This intensive cultural interchange during the fourteenth century led to the Five-Mountains (Gozan) Zen of medieval Japan; the late-Koryŏ Sŏn of T'aego Pou (太古普愚; 1301–1382), Naong Hyegŭn (懶翁慧勤; 1320–1376), and Paeg'un Kyŏnghan (白雲景閑; 1299–1375); and a Yunnan school of Chan.

Chan during the Yuan dynasty shows a division into two distinct geographical spheres: North of the Yellow River, and the coastal South (Zhejiang region).[4] The former centered on the monasteries of Dadu (present-day Beijing), the Mongol capital; the latter centered on the monasteries and hermitages of the Hangzhou region. In the North under the Jin dynasty (1115–1234), the Caodong school of Chan had flourished; and this continued to some extent into the Yuan period, with Caodong remaining a presence in Dadu. On the other hand, in the South during the Yuan, the Linji school predominated[5]: most of the abbots within the Five-Mountains system were Linji. In both the North and the South, out of the total number of Chan monks active in the Yuan, it is estimated that Caodong comprised less than four percent.[6]

The key figure of Yuan-dynasty Linji Chan in the southern Hangzhou sphere was Zhongfeng Mingben (中峯明本; 1263–1323). This book provides an introduction (from the perspective of Chan/Zen/Sŏn Studies[7]) to Zhongfeng's

---

[3] Enomoto Wataru, "Nichi-Chū kōryū shi no naka no chūsei zenshū shi," in *Chūsei Zen no chi*, ed. Sueki Fumihiko (Kyoto: Rinsen shoten, 2021), 57–59 surmises that, at any given time, there were about 140 to 230 Japanese Zen monks in Mongol China. He analyzes data for forty and finds that the average stay was about fourteen years, and the average age of setting out from Japan was about twenty-five.

[4] The following is based on Noguchi, *Gendai Zen*, 4–14.

[5] A preface to the *Yunwai Yunxiu chanshi yulu* (雲外雲岫禪師語錄) by Chen Sheng (陳晟) and dated 大德 4/1300 of the Yuan states: "Most of the people studying Chan put a high value on the Linji school, and the Caodong school has become a *lonely* school." [然學禪者流多宗臨濟。而曹洞為孤宗。] (CBETA 2019.Q3, X72, no. 1431, p. 168b9). Yunwai Yunxiu was a Caodong master active in the South.

[6] Noguchi, *Gendai Zen*, 13.

[7] On the present state of Chan/Zen/Sŏn Studies, see Albert Welter, Steven Heine, and Jin Y. Park, eds., *Approaches to Chan, Sŏn, and Zen Studies: Chinese Chan Buddhism and Its Spread throughout East Asia* (Albany: State University of New York, 2022). For a survey of Japanese scholarship on Chinese Chan, Japanese Zen, and Korean Sŏn, see Tanaka Ryōshō, ed., *Zengaku kenkyū nyūmon*, 2nd ed. (Tokyo: Daitōshuppansha, 2006). See also the bibliography of English, Chinese, and Japanese scholarship

Chan style (*chan feng* 禪風)[8] via translation of selected works in his Chan records, with close attention to such matters as Chan phrasing and terminology.[9] The texts selected from his Chan records include instructions to the assembly and dharma talks; his miscellany *Night Conversations in a Mountain Hermitage*; his one hundred poems in imitation of Hanshan (Cold Mountain); his admonitions on cross-legged sitting Chan; and so forth. His wider social world, cultural context, and idiosyncratic calligraphy are addressed only in passing.

Within the Yuan, Zhongfeng and Yuansou Xingduan (元叟行端; 1255–1341)[10] were two of the most well-known Linji Chan masters. They started off with much in common. They were close contemporaries (Zhongfeng was eight years younger than Yuansou). They were born less than two hundred kilometers from each other, Zhongfeng in Qiantang (Hangzhou in Zhejiang), and Yuansou in Linhai in Taizhou (in Zhejiang). The trajectories of their Chan careers and their Chan styles, however, were drastically different.

Yuansou's *yulu* (語錄) collection contains four "abbacy *yulu*," discrete records for each monastery at which Yuansou served as abbot.[11] Yuansou rocketed up the "bureaucratic" ladder of abbotships in the state-sponsored Five-Mountains system. He began by inheriting the dharma of Zangshou Shanzhen (藏叟善珍; 1194–1277) at Wanshou Monastery on Jingshan, the first of the Five Mountains. Later, his first abbotship was at the second of the Ten Monasteries; he was then promoted to the abbotship of the first of the Ten Monasteries; subsequently promoted to the second of the Five Mountains;

---

on Chan in Youru Wang, *Historical Dictionary of Chan Buddhism* (Lanham, MD: Rowman & Littlefield, 2017), 291–358.

[8] In Chan literature, the term *Chan style* (*chan feng* 禪風) usually refers to *the Chan school as a whole*. For instance, we find in the *Lingji chanshi yulu* (靈機禪師語錄; preface 1694) the following: "Recently, the Patriarchal Way has decayed, the Chan style has become thin and faint." [蓋緣邇來祖道衰微禪風澹薄] (CBETA 2019.Q3, J39, no. B448, p. 28c24). However, I use it to refer to the Chan style of an individual Chan master. It is sometimes used in this way in modern Chan/Zen Studies.

[9] In the following translations, certain Chan terms have been left untranslated. For instance, *huatou* (*phrase*) and *gong'an* (*case*) remain in *pinyin* transliteration. *Huatous* in English (such as **who is doing the nianfo** or **my original face**) are italicized and in bold. Also, given the pervasiveness of "intertextuality" in Chan literature, in the notes I have not tried to track down sources for innumerable "traces" or pieces of other Chan texts (which, in most cases, appear without any markers), nor have I given an encapsulation and source for every Chan story, particularly when it is not crucial for understanding Zhongfeng's point.

[10] For a thorough treatment of Yuansou, see Noguchi, *Gendai Zen*, 43–88. For a short entry, see Komazawa daigaku nai Zengaku daijiten hensanjo, ed., *Shinpan Zengaku daijiten*, 226. He was in the Dahui wing of the Linji line.

[11] *Yuansou Xingduan chanshi yulu* (元叟行端禪師語錄): "Fascicle One is the Huzhou Mt. Xiangfeng Zifu Chan Monastery *Yulu*. Fascicle Two is the Hangzhou Central India Wanshou Chan Monastery *Yulu*. Fascicle Three is the Hangzhou Lingyin Jingde Chan Monastery. Fascicle Four is the Hangzhou Mt. Jing Xingsheng Wanshou Chan Monastery *Yulu*." [卷一湖州翔鳳山資福禪寺語錄。卷二杭州中天竺萬壽禪寺語錄。卷三杭州靈隱景德禪寺語錄。卷四杭州徑山興聖萬壽禪寺語錄。] (CBETA 2019.Q3, X71, no. 1419, p. 514a8–15).

and finally reached the very pinnacle of the whole system: the abbotship of Jingshan, the first of the Five Mountains. Becoming the head of any one of the Five Mountains was akin to becoming a general or senior minister of the state. Promotion to the abbotship of the illustrious Jingshan was like becoming prime minister. Yuansou began his career with training at the top level of elite training halls; as a teaching master, he worked his way up the abbacy ladder of the system; and he ended his career as head of the top monastic complex.

In contrast, Zhongfeng started off studying with Gaofeng Yuanmiao (高峰原妙) at Gaofeng's Mt. Tianmu center (not one of the Five Mountains but well-known).[12] He became a main successor of Gaofeng, but he spent much of his career after Gaofeng's death avoiding major abbotships. The *Zhongfeng Extensive Record* contains neither "abbacy *yulu*" nor any formal talks in the Dharma Hall (*shangtang* 上堂). Zhongfeng only at the end of his life consented to become abbot of his teacher Gaofeng's Mt. Tianmu establishment (in this parallel to Yuansou's taking over his teacher's Jingshan). For most of his career, Zhongfeng secluded himself in mountain hermitages, and he also periodically lived on boats. (Houseboat living was not uncommon in the area: the famous Yuan-dynasty painter Ni Zan (倪瓚; 1306–1374) spent decades living in this manner.[13]) Portraits reinforce Zhongfeng's image of seclusion: they usually show him in a simple robe with minimal ornamental accoutrements. However, he did in fact have contact with many people, including Chan monks, scholar-officials, and even the imperial court: his autobiography systematically expunges this social aspect of his life. He was far from a total recluse, but he did consciously downplay conventional markers of success in favor of *seclusion*, which became the leitmotif of his Chan career. This is strikingly different from the very *public and official* career trajectory of Yuansou.

---

[12] Gaofeng's Chan style is rooted in his Three Essentials of Chan: "If you are thinking of engaging in genuine Chan practice, you absolutely must possess the Three Essentials. The first essential is having the faculty of *great confidence*. You know perfectly well that there is *this matter*: as if you are leaning against an unshakeable Mt. Sumeru. The second essential is the determination of *being greatly indignant*: as if you have encountered the scoundrel who killed your father, and you immediately want to cut him in two with one thrust of your sword. The third essential is having the *sensation of great uncertainty*: as if you have in secret committed an atrocious act, and this is the very moment when you are about to be exposed, but you are not yet exposed." [若謂著實參禪。決須具足三要。第一要有大信根。明知此事。如靠一座須彌山。第二要有大憤志。如遇殺父冤讎。直欲便與一刀兩段。第三要有大疑情。如暗地做了一件極事。正在欲露未露之時。] (*Gaofeng Yuanmiao chanshi yulu* 高峰原妙禪師語錄 [CBETA, X70, no. 1400, p. 687, b5-8] and *Gaofeng Yuanmiao chanshi chanyao* 高峰原妙禪師禪要 [CBETA, X70, no. 1401, p. 708, b5-8]).

[13] James Cahill, *Hills Beyond a River: Chinese Painting of the Yüan Dynasty, 1279–1368* (New York: Weatherhill, 1976), 114–115: "The last decades of his life he spent traveling in a houseboat around the T'ai-hu region and the San-mao Lakes district to the southwest, staying with friends or in Buddhist monasteries, living for a time in a humble dwelling that he called "Snail Hut."

Huatou practice in the style of the Song Linji master Dahui Zonggao (1089–1163) is another point of contrast between these two masters. In Dahui's method, the *huatou* is a single phrase (*yi ju* 一句) taken from a Chan story or non-Chan source. Throughout the twenty-four hours of the day—walking, standing, sitting, and lying down—the practitioner is to constantly *lift to awareness* the *huatou*/phrase and is severely cautioned not to engender any other thought beyond focus on the *huatou*. Eventually, a *sensation of uncertainty* about the *huatou* arises: the destruction of that *sensation of uncertainty* is tantamount to awakening. The *Recorded Sayings of Yuansou Xingduan* (*Yuansou Xingduan chanshi yulu* 元叟行端禪師語錄) shows no clear-cut examples of the typical Dahui vocabulary of *huatou* practice. Yuansou apparently eschewed it, even though he was in the Dahui wing of the Linji line, and *huatou* practice was common in his Chan environment. The *Zhongfeng Extensive Record* and *Zhongfeng Record B*, on the other hand, show Zhongfeng recommending *huatou* practice to many students, monastic and lay, and contain extensive discussion of the nature of the *huatou*.

However, the more interesting comparison between these two Chan teachers centers on how they carried themselves—their Chan "personas" or "styles." Later biographers refer to Yuansou's style as *angry* (*nu* 怒). A Qing-period collection entitled *Biographies of the Monk Treasures of the Southern Song, Yuan, and Ming Chan Forest* (*Nan Song Yuan Ming Chanlin sengbao zhuan* 南宋元明禪林僧寶傳) says of Yuansou:

> [Yuansou] was often angry, and as he got older it increased drastically. As he was sitting at his seat, throughout the day while people were serving his meals, he railed at them and cursed them. [At night,] after he entered his sleeping room, if somebody privately asked him the reason for this [railing and cursing], he would look around and say: "I'd like to tell you, but I've already forgotten." In the cases of both monks and laypeople, amid his angry cursing, those who apprehended the purport [i.e., awakened] were extremely numerous.[14]

Anger may have been part of the Chan style a younger Yuansou adopted, but read with modern eyes, this passage suggests the possibility that in old age he suffered some form of dementia.

---

[14] 復多怒。老益甚。每據坐。竟日傳餐訶罵。及入寢室。或竊問其故。乃左右顧視。欲舉已忘。故道俗於怒罵中。得旨者甚多。(CBETA 2019.Q3, X79, no. 1562, p. 627b12–14). This notion of "anger" appeared already in a stupa inscription written by a contemporary, the retired Yuan official Huang Jin (黃溍; *jinshi* degree during the Yanyou era/1314–1320): "The master scolded others in a loud voice, angrily reviling them—he thus compassionately guided his disciples." [*Yuansou Xingduan chanshi yulu* 元叟行端禪師語錄: 師以呵叱怒罵。為門弟子慈切之誨。] (CBETA 2019.Q3, X71, no. 1419, p. 547b4–5).

Yuansou's Chan monks often got a "hard time" from the forbidding master. The *Recorded Sayings of Yuansou Xingduan* (*Yuansou Xingduan chanshi yulu* 元叟行端禪師語錄) says:

> The Master [Yuansou] examined a newly arrived monk, saying: "From where has this sage come? What sort of deity is this?" The monk: "I approach the royal chopping-block!" The Master: "Hogwash-spouting Chan monks are like flaxseeds! [They're a dime a dozen!] Go put in your practice in the [Monks] Hall!" He examined another monk: "The stones on the chess board have chopped up your brain! The water in the bowl has leaked out and caused the soles of your feet to become inflamed!" The monk dithered in answering, and the Master immediately gave a shout. He examined another monk: "*Split in two the flowery mountains that reach to the heavens; release flow of the Yellow River that is clear through and through.* Let's put that [couplet] aside. Just give me an ordinary, everyday *phrase*!" The monk dithered as he opened his mouth. The Master immediately whacked him with the stick. His encounters [with students] were sharp and severe—most were of this type. The Master scolded them with a loud voice and subjected them to angry cursing. This was the compassionate guidance he gave his students.[15]

Zhongfeng's style, on the other hand, was said to be *calm and gentle* (*tanyi* 坦夷). The *Recorded Sayings of Chan Master Tianru Weize* (*Tianru Weize chanshi yulu* 天如惟則禪師語錄) says:

> The Master, when interacting with students, was calm and gentle. He considered a wink of his eye and the raising of his eyebrow to be his "stick and shout." He considered speaking while smiling to be his "needle and awl." When he acted for the sake of people in urgent situations, the knowers came to know on their own. He was like a medicine that counteracts [an illness]. For them he was like a change in the situation on the *weiqi* (*go*) board: subduing strong soldiers [i.e., strong formations of "stones"] without a fight and constituting a hanging thread for "dead [stones" to come back to life].[16]

As we might expect, Zhongfeng deemphasized the Linji-school stick and shout. Zhongfeng composed a set of rules for his own mountain hermitages

---

[15] 師嘗勘一新到僧云。何方聖者。甚處靈祇。僧云臨朕碪。師云。杜撰禪和。如麻似粟。參堂去。又勘一僧云。棋槃石。斫破你腦門。盆盂池。浸爛你脚板。僧擬答。師便喝。又勘一僧云。擘開華嶽連天秀。放出黃河徹底清。即且置。平實地上。道將一句來。僧擬開口。師便打。其機鋒峭峻。多此類。師以呵叱怒罵。為門弟子慈切之誨。(CBETA 2019.Q3, X71, no. 1419, p. 547a23–b5).

[16] 師即凹凸示之坦夷。以瞬揚為棒喝。以談笑為針錐。為人切處知者自知。如反攻之藥。如變局之棋。屈強兵於不戰。起絕命於懸絲。(CBETA 2019.Q3, X70, no. 1403, p. 829b10–c1).

(as opposed to the universal "purity-rules" texts in circulation): *Purity Rules for Dwelling-in-the-Phantasmal Hermitage* (*Huanzhu an qinggui* 幻住庵清規).[17] The "house style" (*jiafeng* 家風) prescribed in these rules explicitly eschews frequent use of the stick and the shout.[18] Whereas Yuansou snarled at students and freely applied both the stick and the shout, Zhongfeng, at least according to his most prominent disciple, gave a deafening shout by merely raising an eyebrow, and a slight smile on his face was akin to sticking an awl into the leg of a student to get him to move onward. These were two very different personalities and Chan styles: "hard" and "soft."

Autobiography and *Huatou* Chan

The earliest known Chinese spiritual autobiographies, a genre of Chinese literature, are found in the recorded-sayings (*yulu* 語錄) literature of the Chan school of Buddhism.[19] The autobiographical impulse seems concentrated in the line of Xueyan Zuqin (雪嚴祖欽; ?–1287), though autobiography may have begun even earlier with Dahui Zonggao. The Xueyan line runs: Xueyan Zuqin → Gaofeng Yuanmiao (高峯原妙; 1238–1295) → Zhongfeng Mingben. All three were hard-core *huatou* practitioners, and all three composed spiritual autobiographies—self-presentations—that were included in their recorded-sayings books. However, Zhongfeng's autobiography differs completely in both format and tone from those of his predecessors, and highlights just how idiosyncratic Zhongfeng's Chan style was. Let us first look at excerpts from the autobiographies of Xueyan and Gaofeng. Here is Xueyan giving his life story in the *Recorded Sayings of Chan Master Xueyan Zuqin*:

> I left home at the age of five and became an attendant to a superior person. I was privy to his conversations with guests. I then came to realize that there is *this matter*, came to have confidence, and trained in cross-legged Chan sitting. My whole life I have been dull-witted and experienced myriad painful sufferings. At sixteen I became a monk and at eighteen set out on pilgrimage. I had a sharp

---

[17] For a superb treatment of this text, see Heller, *Illusory Abiding*, 185–188; 199–202; 190–197; 207–215.
[18] "Way companions in close conditions need not frequently employ the stick and the shout." [家風：道伴交肩不用頻施棒喝。] (CBETA 2019.Q3, X63, no. 1248, pp. 580c24–581a1).
[19] Pei-Yi Wu, *The Confucian's Progress: Autobiographical Writings in Traditional China* (Princeton, NJ: Princeton University Press, 1990), 74–92 claims that the earliest examples of autobiography in the Chinese tradition are a *General Sermon* in the *yulu* of Xueyan Zuqin (雪嚴祖欽;?–1287) and an *Instructions to the Assembly* of Mengshan Deyi (蒙山德異; 1231–?) found as an extract in Yunqi Zhuhong's *Chan Whip* (*Changuan cejin* 禪關策進). See Broughton with Watanabe, *Chan Whip*, 15–16.

resolve to go out and clarify *this matter*. I was in the assembly of Preceptor Yuan of Shuanglin Monastery [d.u.]. . . . The honored elder Dongxia [unknown] taught us to keep an eye on the **wu** 無 *huatou* of the dog's buddha-nature: "When troublesome thoughts arise, merely at the tip of your nose lightly raise to awareness the **wu** 無—you will see that your thoughts calm down." . . . At nineteen I registered at Lingyin Monastery [in Hangzhou]. . . . I was in the office of the Guest Master. I met the Recorder of Incoming Letters, who was from Chuzhou [in southern Zhejiang], and he said: "Brother Qin, this practice-work of yours is dead water—it's useless! You haven't avoided making the two marks of movement/stillness into a pair of extremes." . . . What [the Recorder] said was correct, and I immediately changed my *huatou* to **dried turd** [**ganshijue** 乾屎橛]. All became of a single taste—in the east *uncertainty* and in the west *uncertainty*, length-wise keeping an eye on [*dried turd*] and breadth-wise keeping an eye on [*dried turd*]. . . . I passed through Zhejiang East and took up residence at the two peaks of Mt. Tianmu. One day I was walking in front of the Buddha Hall. I was relaxed, "thinking about the east and surmising about the west." Suddenly I raised my eyes and saw an ancient cypress tree. Sense-fields that I had hitherto apprehended all-at-once flew off, and things that were obstructions in my breast were tossed away and scattered. It was like coming out of a dark room into the bright sunlight, like doing a running "flip." From this point onward I had no *uncertainty* about birth, no *uncertainty* about death, no *uncertainty* about the buddhas, no *uncertainty* about the Chan patriarchs. For the first time, I was able to envision the Old Man of Jingshan [i.e., Wuzhun Shifan; Xueyan was a successor of Wuzhun] standing on the monastery grounds [and uttering his characteristic words:] "Just so happens I'm going to give you thirty whacks with my stick!"[20]

And here is the autobiography of his student Gaofeng in the *Recorded Sayings of Chan Master Gaofeng Yuanmiao*:

I left home at fifteen, at sixteen became a monk, at eighteen studied the Tiantai teachings, and at twenty changed into Chan garb and entered Jingci Monastery [near Hangzhou]. I vowed to die at the end of three years of Chan training [if I did not attain awakening]. At that point I requested instruction from Preceptor Duanqiao [Miaolun, a successor of Wuzhun Shifan], who ordered me to practice the *huatou*: **at birth where from and at death where to?** At this my thoughts remained bifurcated, and my mind failed to home in on oneness. I was not able

---

[20] CBETA 2019.Q3, X70, no. 1397, pp. 606b3–607c24.

to achieve discernment on the basis of Preceptor Duanqiao's teachings on doing practice-work. . . . Suddenly I met Brother Jing of Taizhou [in eastern Zhejiang], who spoke of Preceptor Xueyan Zuqin. [Jing] constantly asked me: "You're doing practice-work—why don't you go and give Xueyan a try?" Thereupon I was delighted, burning incense in my heart ahead of time and visiting Beijian Stupa to request instruction [from Xueyan]. . . . [Xueyan] ordered me to keep an eye on the *wu* 無. From the very start I began to do practice-work [on *wu* 無]: it was like obtaining a lamp in the darkness or being saved while dangling [over a cliff]. . . . Every time I entered [Xueyan's] door he would immediately ask: "Who is dragging in this corpse for you?" Before his voice had died down, he would drive me out with a painful whack of the stick. Every day it was just the same old question and the same old whack. Truly I was pressed to the limits of my life. . . . I could not avoid taking up my pack and ascending Jingshan. In the early part of the second month, I returned to the Sangha Hall [of Jingshan]. Suddenly, during the night of the sixteenth of the next month, in a dream I suddenly remembered a *huatou* Preceptor Duanqiao had raised for me in his room: *the ten-thousand dharmas return to the one—to where does the one return*? From this point the *sensation of uncertainty* all-at-once arose in me. I was knocked into a single slice, unable to distinguish east from west, forgetting both sleeping and eating. . . . Five years passed, and one day, while lodging in a hermitage, I was right inside [a sensation of] *uncertainty* about *this matter*. Instantly, I smashed the *ball of uncertainty*—it was like [a fish or bird] leaping out of the net![21]

These two autobiographies are records of spiritual journeys on the demanding road of *huatou* practice, and we can even speculate that there is something in *huatou* practice itself that leads in the direction of psychological depth and probing self-narration/autobiography. Certain themes rise to prominence: periodic changes of the *huatou* (certain *huatou* do not seem effective for a given practitioner at a given time); an emphasis upon the *sensation of uncertainty*; and a final smashing of *uncertainty*, which is tantamount to awakening and usually presented in stereotyped phrasing. In other words, both pieces are psychological portraits of *huatou* practice, including the frustrations encountered along the tortuous way and the eventual success at the end. The narrative focus is on perseverance through setbacks and final breakthroughs. From a literary standpoint, they are examples of *autobiography as Chan sermon* (even though Gaofeng's piece was originally in the form of a letter).

---

[21] CBETA 2019.Q3, X70, no. 1400, p. 690a10–c13.

The Format and Underlying Theme of Zhongfeng's Autobiography

The autobiography of Zhongfeng, the main successor of Gaofeng, is poles apart from those of his predecessors Xueyan and Gaofeng. Zhongfeng conspicuously *avoids any mention of huatou practice, the sensation of uncertainty, and eventual realization or awakening.* Zhongfeng's autobiography is not the record of an inner spiritual journey—it is merely the record of the travels of a solitary Chan pilgrim from place to place in the mountainous and watery worlds of the coastal provinces of Zhejiang and Jiangsu. In the stripped-down, bare-bones format of a chronology or ledger, Zhongfeng gives us little more than a staccato recital of his strings of stays in mountain hermitages and on boats (with dates). Everything else, virtually all social contact (and, from other sources, we know there was substantial social contact), is passed over in silence:

> Mr. Phantasm's [i.e., my] ancestors lived for generations in Xincheng[22] in the Hangzhou area. My family name is Sun. My grandfather moved to Qiantang.[23] [In Qiantang] my father and mother had seven boys and girls, and I, Dweller-in-the-Phantasmal, was the last. Just after I got out of infant's clothes, the only child's play I engaged in was chanting hymns and doing Buddhist rituals, and neighbors considered this strange. At seven I attended the local school, where I read the *Analects* and the *Mencius*. Before I had finished the curriculum, when I was nine, my mother died, and I stopped going to school. From early on, I had borne the ambition to leave home and become a Buddhist monk. Day after day constrained by mundane characteristics, I came up with hundreds of plans but was unable to escape. At twenty-four, without any mental effort on my part, the mundane characteristics that had bound me abruptly came untied of their own accord. This happened in 1286. In the fifth month of that year, alone I climbed [West Tianmu] Mountain[24] and did obeisance to the master [Gaofeng Yuanmiao], now deceased. Later I chanted the *Diamond Sutra*. When I came to the passage about "bearing the awakening of the Tathāgata," I suddenly attained some understanding. From this time onward I was quite steeped in the flavor of the words of the sutra texts, but *this was not awakening*. In the second month of 1287 [when I was twenty-five], a believer laywoman of the Yang family [unknown] gave me monetary support. I followed *Old Man of the*

---

[22] Zhejiang province, Jiaxing (嘉興) prefecture; about fifty kilometers southwest of Hangzhou.
[23] Zhejiang province, Hang (杭) prefecture.
[24] About sixty kilometers west of Hangzhou city in Hangzhou superior prefecture. West Tianmu is twenty plus kilometers north of Yuqian (於潛) prefecture; East Tianmu is twenty-five kilometers west of Lin'an (臨安) prefecture.

Mountains and Seas [perhaps an unknown layman] in climbing up [West Tianmu] Mountain and had my head shaved. In 1289 [at the age of twenty-seven] I filled the position of Sangha Hall Rector.[25] In 1290 [at the age of twenty-eight] I wanted to go off and conceal myself. I secretly let [a layman by the name of] Mr. Song [unknown] know of this wish, and he helped me with a donation of three *mou* of fertile fields. I was again ordered [by my teacher Gaofeng] to attend to the Sangha Hall [as Sangha Hall Rector]: before long I had nosebleeds. My master Gaofeng ordered me to serve as his personal Inner-Chamber Attendant.[26] In the spring of 1291 [when I was twenty-nine], Mr. Qu donated a landed estate.[27] [My master Gaofeng] would not accept the donation, and speedily dispatched a letter returning Qu's land. In 1292 [at age thirty] I held the position of Assistant to the Prior.[28] In 1293 and 1294 [at age thirty-one to thirty-two] all I did was dash about going to the gates of donors soliciting donations. In 1295 [when I was thirty-three] my master Gaofeng lay down from an illness and never got up again. When his burial ceremonies were finished, I left [West Tianmu] Mountain to answer my long-cherished ambition [to hide away]. In 1296 [at age thirty-four] I roamed back and forth in Wumen.[29] In the spring of 1297 [at age thirty-five], I clutched my cloth-wrapped bundle and travelled to Mt. Tianzhu in Shuzhou.[30] In the autumn I went to Mt. Lu.[31] In the winter I returned to Jiankang [i.e., Nanjing], where I hid away in a thatched hut for ten months. In the winter of 1298 [at age thirty-six], I built a Dwelling-in-the-Phantasmal Hermitage at Mt. Bian.[32] In the winter of 1299 [at age thirty-seven], I built a Dwelling-in-the-Phantasmal Hermitage at Wumen[33] and lived there during the period 1300–1301 [age thirty-eight to thirty-nine]. In 1302 [at age forty] the Dajue Monastery [on West Tianmu Mountain] requested that I take up the position of abbot, but I escaped to Nanxu.[34] In 1303 [at age forty-one] I sent Buna[35] back to Dajue Monastery [on West Tianmu Mountain]. In 1304 [at age forty-two] I returned [to West Tianmu Mountain] to maintain the stupa of my late master [Gaofeng]. In the winter of 1305 [at age forty-three], I was put in charge of the affairs of Shizi Temple [on West Tianmu Mountain].[36] In 1306–1307 [at age forty-four to forty-five] and the winter of 1308 [at age forty-six], I was doing begging rounds in the Wusong River area [of Jiangsu], and I did not return [to Shizi Temple]. In 1309 [at age forty-seven] I bought a boat

---

[25] *tangsi* (堂司) = *weina* (維那).
[26] *jishi* (給侍) = *yinshi* (隱侍).
[27] Qu Tingfa (瞿霆發; 1252–1312).
[28] *kuwu* (庫務) = *fusi* (副司) = *fusi* (副寺).
[29] The eastern shore of Lake Tai (太湖), i.e., Jiangsu province, Wu (吳) prefecture.
[30] Shuzhou (舒州) in Anhui. Tianzhu is the highest peak of Mt. Wan (皖山).
[31] Northwest of Xingzi (星子) prefecture in Jiangxi.
[32] Huzhou 湖州 in Zhejiang, on the southern shore of Lake Tai (太湖).
[33] Suzhou (蘇州) in Jiangsu, on the eastern shore of Lake Tai.
[34] Dantu (丹徒) prefecture in Jiangsu.
[35] Buna Zuyong (布衲祖雍;?–1317), at the time abbot of Dajue Monastery.
[36] Gaofeng was the founder of both Dajue Monastery and Shizi Temple, which started as a cliff cave.

in Yizhen,[37] and that summer I tied it up at Zhacheng.[38] In 1310 [at age forty-eight] I returned to Mt. Tianmu and dwelled at [Gaofeng's stupa called] "Mountain Boat." In 1311 [at age forty-nine], I once again lived on a boat in the Bian River.[39] In the spring of 1312 [at age fifty], I built a hermitage on Mt. Liu'an.[40] In autumn I went by boat to Donghai prefecture.[41] In the spring of 1313 [at age fifty-one], I went by boat to Kaisha.[42] In the summer I sent [my disciple Head Seat] Dingsou[43] to serve as abbot of Dajue Monastery [on West Tianmu Mountain] and myself lodged at a hermitage on Mt. Huan [unknown]. In the spring of 1314 [at age fifty-two], I once again took on the role of abbot at Shizi Temple. In 1315 [at age fifty-three] I built a hermitage at Dawo.[44] In the spring of 1316 [at age fifty-four], my diabetes became acute.[45] In the summer I moored my boat at Nanxun.[46] In 1317 [at age fifty-five] I dwelled at the Datong Hermitage in Danyang.[47] In 1318 [at age fifty-six] I returned once again to Mt. Tianmu. The years 1319 to 1322 [age fifty-seven to sixty] have gone by, and I am now sixty. In the summer of this year, I built a hermitage on Mt. Zhongjia.[48] From 1286 [when I first climbed Mt. Tianmu] to [the present of] 1322 is a whole thirty-seven years. Thus, I have undertaken to hide away my phantasmal traces: a plan for escaping karmic conditions. At the very start I set my heart on leaving home. My ambition was to wear rough clothes, have a dirty face, and engage in ascetic practices. Because I falsely assumed the guise of a patched-robe Chan monk, I have carried a sense of shame for my whole life. Moreover, as for literary matters, I have not undergone a proper course of learning, and *my practice has lacked awakening*. What are usually praised as good things about me are nothing more than accidents of the working out of karma! All along I have *only yearned to retire and take a rest*, not set the world right and cut off the commonplace. When

---

[37] Jiangsu province, Yangzhou superior prefecture, Yizhen prefecture; on the northern bank of the Yangze River. A zhou (舟) is a small boat or skiff for inland use. The fisherman-hermit in his small boat often appears in the literati paintings of the Yuan dynasty. For an example of the type of boat Zhongfeng may have bought, see the painting *Fisherman* (*Lutan diaoting* 蘆灘釣艇 [*Fisherman's Skiff at a Shore of Reeds*]; handscroll, ink on paper; The Metropolitan Museum of Art. 1989.363.33) by the Yuan painter Wu Zhen (吳鎮; 1280–1354) in Maxwell K. Hearn, *How to Read Chinese Paintings* (New York: The Metropolitan Museum of Art, 2008), 94–97. Also, it would be interesting to know something about the funds used to buy the boat.

[38] Another name for Huzhou (湖州) in Zhejiang.

[39] In the Kaifeng area of Henan.

[40] Luzhou (廬州) in Anhui.

[41] Haizhou (海州) in Jiangsu.

[42] Jiangsu, Changzhou (常州) superior prefecture, Jingjiang (靖江) prefecture.

[43] Dingshou Yongtai (定叟永泰; ?–1316).

[44] Jiangxi, Qingjiang (清江) prefecture.

[45] The term is *thirst illness* (keji 渴疾). According to Tatsumi Nami, ed., *Chū'i yōgo jiten* (Tokyo: Gensōsha, 2020), 113 *shōkatsu* (消渴) = *shōtan* (消癉) = diabetes. According to Paul W. Kroll, *A Student's Dictionary of Classical and Medieval Chinese* (Leiden: Brill, 2017), 500–501, *xiao* 消 is used for or graphically interchangeable with (medieval) *xiao* 痟 (*diabetes*).

[46] East of Wuxing (吳興) prefecture in Zhejiang, southeast of Lake Tai.

[47] South of Zhenjiang (鎮江).

[48] Fifteen kilometers north of West Tianmu Mountain.

[in my early days under Gaofeng] I sat [in donor's homes] and accepted donations from believers, my lack of ease reached a sky-high level. An ancient said: "When one gets to fifty, one comes to know the mistakes of the first forty-nine years."[49] Now I am sixty and reflecting on past events. Without exception, these events are veiled by delusive thought: how could any of it match up to principle? The drifting light-rays and phantasmal shadows have been changing every instant. Therefore, I have written this as a warning to myself.[50]

The above autobiography, written in the last year of his life, is not an objective and unbiased portrayal by any means, although Zhongfeng is certainly honest about his shortcomings. Unlike his predecessors, he has not sublimated the entirety of his story arc into a standard Chan dharma talk concerning Buddhist cultivation. By candidly highlighting the "dropout" aspects of his life, Zhongfeng's almost confessional self-portrait gains an unusual, and powerfully personal, immediacy. While there is no way to pinpoint where personality ends and Chan style begins, surely Zhongfeng's basic stance of honesty and humility was inseparable from what gave his Chan style such efficacy and renown.

For an inquiry into his Chan style, this autobiography is probably more relevant than any exhaustive biography based on an elaborate synthesis of all available sources.[51] Such a biography would have to include such details and dates of conventional significance as the high number of students, both

---

[49] *Huainan Zi*, 1.
[50] This autobiography is found at the end of the miscellany *Things Said East, Discussed West* ("chitchat"; *Dongyu xihua* 東語西話) in the *Zhongfeng Extensive Record*: 幻人世居杭之新城。族孫氏。祖遷錢塘。父母生子女七人。幻居其最後。方離襁褓。惟以歌唄佛事爲兒戲。鄰人異之。七歲從市學。讀論語孟子。未終。九歲喪母而輟學。蚤負出家志。以世相日拘。百計莫脫。至廿四。其所縛之世相。不待作意。而劃然自解。寔至元丙戌歲也。是年五月。獨登山禮先師。已而誦金剛經。至荷擔如來處。恍然開解。自爾經書語言頗沾其味。非悟也。丁亥二月。信女人楊氏。授以資具。從山海翁。登山薙染。己丑充堂司。庚寅欲潛去。密爲松公所知。助腴田三畝。復令參堂。未幾刃疾。先師令給侍。辛卯春。瞿公施田莊。不受俾馳書歸瞿田。壬辰充庫務。癸巳甲午惟奔走施門。元貞乙未。先師臥疾不起。奉葬畢。即去山以酬宿志。丙申往來吳門。大德丁酉春。挾袱舒之天柱山。秋之廬阜。冬還建康。匿影草廬者。十閱月。戊戌冬。結幻住菴於弁山。己亥冬。結幻住菴於吳門。庚子辛丑咸居焉。壬寅大覺請住持。而避走南徐。癸卯送布衲。歸大覺。甲辰歸寺先師塔。乙巳冬。領師子院事。丙午丁未至大戊申冬。因分衛吳松不返。己酉。買舟儀真。夏繫纜於雪城。庚戌。歸天目居山舟。辛亥復爲船居住汴水。皇慶壬子春。結菴六安山。秋舟往東寧。秋。舟次開沙。夏送定叟。住大覺。就寓環山菴。延祐甲寅春。復領師子院事。乙卯結菴大窩。丙辰春渴疾作楚。夏舟泊南潯。丁巳居丹陽大同菴。戊午。復還天目。己未庚申至治辛酉壬戌。六十歲矣。是年之夏結菴于中佳山。自丙戌至壬戌。整三十七白。而幻跡方將遠引爲避緣計。余初心出家。志在草衣垢面習頭陀行。以冒服田衣。乃抱終身之愧。且文字失於學問。參究缺於悟明。尋常爲好事者所稱。蓋報緣之偶然耳。平昔惟慕退休。非矯世絕俗。使坐隱信施。乃岌岌不自安也。古人有五十而知四十九之非。今余六十。返思往事。大率情妄所蔽。何有當於理哉。浮光幻影。變在須臾。故書此以自警云。(Gozanban 9, 386b–387b; CBETA 2019.Q3, B25, no. 145, p. 901a5–b16).
[51] For two first-rate synthetic biographies that utilize a wide variety of sources and thoroughly cover Zhongfeng's relations with students, scholar-officials, the imperial court, etc., see Heller, *Illusory Abiding*, 25–86, and Noguchi, *Gendai Zen*, 89–136.

monks and laypeople, both Hans and foreigners, that Zhongfeng attracted; his close friendship with the famous calligrapher and painter Zhao Mengfu; the titles and robe bestowed by Emperor Renzong in 1308 and 1318; and a visit by a Korean king. All these typically important events he chose to *erase* in favor of a chronology of mountain hermitages and boat living, *which was nevertheless a Chan dharma talk in disguise*. At the end Zhongfeng closes by labeling the piece a *warning* to himself. *Warning whip* is a Chan literary genre intended for the encouragement of students who are not yet awakened, as in *Guishan's Warning Whip* (*Guishan jingce* 溈山警策). By equating the events of his life with delusive thought, Zhongfeng seems to be cautioning himself that even the tranquil mountain sojourns and boat trips he favored over the years are no more than phantasms, like everything else he chose not to mention of his life. He is in effect saying: "I must be careful not to delude myself!"

The Confining Bureaucratic Chan Style of Mt. Tianmu Versus the Unencumbered Chan Style of a Vagabond Budai (布袋)

Most of the extant portraits and calligraphies of Zhongfeng are found in the collections of Japanese monasteries and private collections. After spending various lengths of time with Zhongfeng, Japanese Zen monks brought back to Japan examples of his calligraphy, portraits of him, inscriptions by Zhongfeng for portraits of him at the request of followers, elements of his personal paraphernalia, and so forth. Virtually none of his calligraphy survives in China (it was thought of as crude and unsophisticated, so it was not collected).[52] The art historian Uta Lauer quotes the Ming author Liu Zhang's (劉璋; act. 1457–1521) *Imperial Ming History of Calligraphy and Painting* (*Huang Ming shuhua shi* 皇明書畫史) on Zhongfeng's calligraphic style: "Mingben's calligraphy is classified as *willow-leaf*.[53] It is not part of any [calligraphic] conceptual

---

[52] Lauer, *Calligraphy of Mingben*, 130.
[53] The cover art of this book, a painting of the White-Robed Avalokiteśvara by Jueji Yongzhong (絕際永中; probably a Zhongfeng disciple since he calls himself "Dwelling-in-the Phantasmal Yongzhong"), carries an inscription by Zhongfeng in his willow-leaf style:

正思惟処那/伽定中不存/一法妙契圓通/塵刹播慈風
幻住明本拜手
幻住永中

Correct thought: In the cobra *samādhi* not a single dharma remains—a wondrous tallying with perfect penetration!
Throughout the worlds as numberless as dust motes Avalokiteśvara disseminates the breeze of compassion.
Dwelling-in-the Phantasmal Mingben does obeisance.
Dwelling-in-the Phantasmal Yongzhong [in seal script/*zhuanwen* 篆文]

framework—so it constitutes a single house."[54] However, Japanese monks and collectors were enamored of this unusual calligraphy and carefully preserved examples.

Two Zhongfeng portraits in Japanese collections raise the interesting possibility that Zhongfeng did not object to being portrayed with attributes that alluded to the roaming vagabond Budai of local folklore,[55] as both portraits bear autograph inscriptions by Zhongfeng in his idiosyncratic "willow-leaf style." In both portraits, he sports a full head of hair (possibly in imitation of his master Gaofeng's portraits) and is seated on a Chan master's curved-back chair with his shoes upon a footstool before him; in one portrait he holds a fly whisk, a formal attribute of a Chan master. However, an allusion to Budai might be read in the atypically plain robe and the way it is worn: open all the way down to expose the big belly. As Natasha Heller has remarked, "the loosened robe revealing Zhongfeng's belly became a primary element in his iconography."[56]

The legend of Budai seems to have grown from the story of Qici, a monk of the late ninth and early tenth centuries from Mingzhou in Zhejiang

---

(*White-Robed Guanyin*, late 1200s–early 1300s. Jueji Yongzhong [active around 1300], inscribed by Zhongfeng Mingben [1263–1323]. Hanging scroll; ink on paper; painting: 78.7 × 31.7 cm (31 × 12 1/2 in.); overall with knobs: 164 × 38 cm [64 9/16 × 14 15/16 in.]. The Cleveland Museum of Art, Purchase from the J. H. Wade Fund 1978.47.1.) The art historian Wai-kam Ho has said of this painting: "There must be no more direct and effective pictorial means of expression than the *pai-miao* technique [白描 = *plain drawing/line drawing without shading*] that can better convey the idea and feeling underlying the inscription by Chung-feng Ming-pen. By reducing these pictorial means to the barest minimum, retaining only what is absolutely essential, 'a perfect harmony is wonderfully achieved' [= the inscription line 'a wondrous tallying with perfect penetration'] between the contour lines and the interior void of the figure, which complete and illuminate each other. At the same time, a most delicate and assured control was exercised over the delineation, which moves deliberately in a studied pace with an even thickness to create one of the most elegant images ever conceived for the White-Robed Kuan-yin—simple, serene, and completely self-contained." (Sherman E. Lee, et al., *Eight Dynasties of Chinese Painting: The Collection of the Nelson Gallery-Atkins Museum, Kansas City, and the Cleveland Museum of Art* (Bloomington: The Cleveland Museum of Art and Indiana University Press, 1980), 123. Quoted in Shane McCausland, *Zhao Mengfu: Calligraphy and Painting for Khubilai's China* (Hong Kong: Hong Kong University Press, 2011), 164. The background image is *Cloth of Gold with Medallions*, 14th century. Mongol Yuan China. Silk and metallic thread lampas. H. 22 in. (56 cm); W. 31 in. (79 cm). The Metropolitan Museum of Art, Purchase, Joseph Pulitzer Bequest and Dodge Fund, 2001 (2001.595).

[54] 明本書類柳葉。雖未入格。亦自是一家。Lauer, *Calligraphy of Mingben*, 89.
[55] One is in the possession of Kogen-ji (高源寺) in Tamba (Hyogo); the second is part of the private Yabumoto (藪本) Collection in Kobe. For a discussion of these two portraits, including the calligraphy of the inscriptions, see Lauer, *Calligraphy of Mingben*, 93–105. Lauer (61) suggests the possibility of a connection between portraits of Zhongfeng and Budai. Heller, *Illusory Abiding*, 375, suggests a connection to Bodhidharma. Ide Seinosuke, "Chūhō Myōhon jisan zō o megutte," *Bijutsu kenkyū* 343 (1989), 110 suggests a connection to both Bodhidharma and Budai, as well as folk deities of good fortune: "Also, [the relationship need] not be limited to Bodhidharma portraits. Likewise, it is probably also necessary to consider a relationship to portraits of Budai, who has a corpulent frame, as well as to the folk deities who are expressions of good fortune."
[56] Heller, *Illusory Abiding*, 375.

(contiguous with the region of Zhongfeng's later stomping grounds). The earliest extant textual reference to Budai is found in the *Biographies of Eminent Monks Compiled During the Song Dynasty* (*Song gaoseng zhuan* 宋高僧傳; 988) by Zanning (贊寧; 919–1001) in a "biography of Qici of Fenghua prefecture in Mingzhou."[57] He was corpulent with a paunch, wandered about shouldering a stick with a cloth sack attached, and was known for his appetite and lack of concern for conventions. People regarded him affectionately and called him "Master Budai [Cloth Bag]," and in the Jiangsu-Zhejiang region there were many Budai portraits in Zhongfeng's time. During the Yuan, Budai was a widely accepted subject for ink paintings, and these works of art circulated among monks and scholar-officials.

Zhongfeng was no doubt aware of the image of the "free" Budai. Given Zhongfeng's self-admitted discontent with the constraints of large-scale monastic administration and his periodic escapes from them, he might well have recognized in Budai a kindred spirit, and consented to be depicted with some Budai-like characteristics (particularly if we take the calligraphic inscriptions in his own hand as a kind of approval). It is notable that these two portraits depict him neither as an orthodox Chan master in formal regalia nor as a genial ungroomed vagabond. They combine the visual signage of both, resulting in what first appears to be a curious juxtaposition: symbols of the restrictive norms of monastic Chan (the formality of

---

[57] Śākya Qici: Nothing is known of his family. Some say he was a man of Siming. *His shape was corpulent and plump, with a contracted brow and a paunch.* His speech was inconsistent; he went to sleep wherever he happened to be. He usually shouldered a stick with a cloth sack attached when he went into the town market. He begged from people he encountered. As soon as he came upon salted fish or preserved vegetables, he entered the place. He always put a little bit of it into his bag. He was called "Master Budai [Cloth Bag]" or "Changtingzi." He would lie down in the snow, but there would be no snow on his body. Because of this, people considered him extraordinary. There are verses with lines like: "Maitreya, the real Maitreya, none of the people of that time will know him!" Some say that [Budai] is a manifestation of Maitreya. Once he was standing on a great bridge. Someone asked him: "Preceptor, what are you doing here?" He said: "I'm here looking for people." He was always approaching people to beg something to eat. If a shop appeared, he would purchase items. He had all sorts of things amassed in his sack, and he could tell the fortunes of people and read omens. He had excessive *yang* energy, and his upper teeth were like wooden clogs. At the marketplace bridge he slept upright on his knees. In heavy rain his straw sandals got soaked. By this sort of thing people knew him. Heaven brought about his end at the Feng River, and people of a rural village buried him. Later in other prefectures people encountered this gentleman, also walking about carrying his sack on his shoulder. *In the Jiangsu-Zhejiang region there are many paintings of his image.* [唐明州奉化縣契此傳：釋契此者。不詳氏族。或云四明人也。形裁膖脝蹙頞皤腹。言語無恆寢臥隨處。常以杖荷布囊入鄽肆。見物則乞至于醯醬魚菹纔接入口。分少許入囊。號為長汀子布袋師也。曾於雪中臥而身上無雪。人以此奇之。有偈云。彌勒真彌勒時人皆不識等句。人言。慈氏垂迹也。又於大橋上立。或問和尚在此何為。曰我在此覓人。常就人乞啜。其店則物售。袋囊中皆百一供身具也。示人吉凶必現相表兆。亢陽即曳高齒木屐。市橋上豎膝而眠。水潦則係濕草屨。人以此驗知。以天復中終于奉川。鄉邑共埋之。後有他州見此公。亦荷布袋行。江浙之間多圖畫其像焉。] (T 2061.50.848b23–c8).

the chair, the fly whisk, the shoes, and so forth) are arrayed in tandem with those of a more informal life in rustic mountain hermitages and on boats in the wide-open spaces of Jiangnan (the Budai-like utter simplicity of the robe, the partial beard, and, most of all, the protruding belly). Intentionally or not, these portraits form a strikingly accurate visual representation of the juxtaposition that is found in Zhongfeng's autobiography. In his verbal self-portrait, it is apparent that Zhongfeng was continually pulled in two directions. Having started out his career as an administrative functionary at Gaofeng's monastic establishment Tianmu, Zhongfeng subsequently did escape from Tianmu's responsibilities to roam as freely as Budai: but at the end of his life he was to make the final reversion to Tianmu, as Gaofeng's filial son and successor.

Two Chan Records for Zhongfeng Mingben: *Zhongfeng Extensive Record* and *Zhongfeng Record B*

We have two collections of Zhongfeng's talks and writings. The fundamental collection is the thirty-fascicle *Extensive Record of Preceptor Tianmu Zhongfeng* (*Tianmu Zhongfeng heshang guanglu* 天目中峯和尚廣錄; abbreviated as *Zhongfeng Extensive Record*). There is also a Gozan edition of an ancillary collection of Zhongfeng materials, which is much smaller and consists of two texts bound together in one volume: *Dharma Talks of Preceptor Tianmu Zhongfeng National Teacher Puying* (*Tianmu Zhongfeng heshang Puying guoshi fayu* 天目中峯和尚普應國師法語; abbreviated as *Zhongfeng Dharma Talks*) and *Talks of Chan Master Tianmu Zhongfeng Guanghui* (*Tianmu Zhongfeng Guanghui chanshi yu* 天目中峯廣慧禪師語; abbreviated as *Zhongfeng Talks*). I will refer to this ancillary collection as *Zhongfeng Record B*.[58]

In Yuantong 2/1334 (about eleven years after Zhongfeng's death), Emperor Shunzong (順宗) had the *Zhongfeng Extensive Record* in thirty fascicles included in the Buddhist canon. Its compiler is listed as Zhaotang Ciji (照堂慈寂), who is none other than the Shan-da-mi-di-li (a Chinese transliteration of an unknown—perhaps Uighur?—name: 善達密的理; d. 1337) mentioned

---

[58] The Japanese Gozan edition of *Zhongfeng Record B* is found in CBETA (with some differences in content and order) under the title *Miscellaneous Record of Chan Master Tianmu Mingben* (*Tianmu Mingben chanshi zalu* 天目明本禪師雜錄; CBETA 2019.Q3, X70, no. 1402, p. 713b7).

as the writer of the two memorials to the throne concerning inclusion of the *Zhongfeng Extensive Record* in the Buddhist canon (found at the beginning and end of that record).[59] According to a preface by Zhongfeng's important disciple Tianru Weize (天如惟則; 1286–1354), Zhaotang Ciji (Shan-da-mi-di-li) was a student of Zhongfeng, hailing from a famous family of Gaochang (near present-day Turfan prefecture in the Uighur Autonomous Region of Xinjiang).[60] After Zhongfeng's death, he served as the caretaker of Zhongfeng's stupa and died at Nengren Hermitage in Wumen (Suzhou). Given that Shan-da-mi-di-li compiled Zhongfeng's main record, successfully worked to get that record into the Buddhist canon, and eventually became caretaker of Zhongfeng's stupa, he surely must have been one of Zhongfeng's most loyal and devoted students.

The earliest Chinese edition we know of is the Qisha edition of Yuantong 3/1335.[61] Japanese pilgrims, who trained under Zhongfeng and brought the Yuan edition back to Japan, had printing blocks re-carved in Japan. Four copies of the *Zhongfeng Extensive Record* found in four Japanese collections are all later impressions of a single edition printed in the Nanbokuchō (1331–1391).[62] I have used a photographic reproduction of the copy in the Seikadō Bunko in Tokyo for the following translations. This Gozan edition in the Seikadō Collection seems to be a reprint of the edition entered into the Buddhist canon toward the end of the Yuan dynasty. Its contents are as follows:

1334 First Month *Memorial to the Throne* by Shan-da-mi-di-li (善達密的理 = Ciji)

1334 Fifth Month *Statement of Insertion of the Text into the Buddhist Canon Preface* by Jie Xisi (揭傒斯)

1335 Sixth Month *Announcement of Printing* by Mingrui of Da Puning Monastery (大普寧寺明瑞)

---

[59] Shiina Kōyū, ed., *Gozanban Chūgoku zenseki sōkan 9: Goroku* 4 (Kyoto: Rinsen shoten, 2013), 654 makes the identification Zhaotang Ciji = Shan-da-mi-di-li. Shan-da-mi-di-li's two memorials are found at *Gozanban* 9, 99d–101d; CBETA 2019.Q3, B25, no. 145, pp. 687a1–688a14 and *Gozanban* 9, 496c–497c; CBETA 2019.Q3, B25, no. 145, pp. 981a16–982a1.

[60] *Preface to the [Poetry] Collection of Elder Yigan of Zhaotang* (*Zhaotang changlao Yigan ji xu* (照堂長老義感集序) contained in the *Tianru Weize chanshi yulu* (天如惟則禪師語錄): CBETA 2019.Q3, X70, no. 1403, p. 802b6–c6.

[61] Only fourteen fascicles of the Qisha (磧砂) edition are extant; these reside at the Wolung Monastery (臥龍寺) of Xi'an. For reproductions of this edition (supplying the missing fascicles from another edition), see Heller, *Illusory Abiding*, 22.

[62] *Gozanban* 9, 652.

Table of Contents for fascicles one to thirty

Extensive Record of Preceptor Tianmu Zhongfeng (*Tianmu Zhongfeng heshang guanglu*天目中峯和尚廣錄)

Practicing Disciple Servant Monk Ciji [i.e., Shan-da-mi-di-li] of the Northern Courtyard Advances Upward
(籴學門人北庭臣僧慈寂 上進)

- 1a. Seven *Instructions to the Assembly* (*shizhong* 示衆); these "instructions" to groups of followers have a less formal style than Dharma Hall talks (*shangtang* 上堂), which are highly performative and poetic; *Instructions to the Assembly* usually mark some occasion, such as New Year's Eve, the end of the New Year celebration, the beginning of a retreat, a snowfall, and so forth.
- 1b. Twenty *Instructions to the Assembly*
- 2. Two *Small Convenings* (*xiaocan*小叅); these are "small convocations to face the spirit of the deceased" (*duiling xiaocan* 對靈小叅); on the night before a funeral ceremony, at the urging of the funeral director, a Chan dialogue is carried out at the relic depository of the deceased; the theme is usually the problem of samsara.
- 3. *Prose and Verse on the Ancients* (*niangu songgu*拈古頌古); prose comments on such Chan stories as Emperor Wu and Bodhidharma, an exchange between Mazu and Baizhang, and so forth; seven-character four-line verses on Śākyamuni's birth, Zhaozhou's *wu* 無, Linji's four shouts, and so forth.
- 4a. Ten *Dharma Talks* (*fayu* 法語), all to Chan monks, many from distant lands (Yunnan, Korea, Japan, and Yiwu/Hami in Xinjiang); these are *written talks* requested by individual followers and often mark some personal occasion for the recipient, such as the follower's setting off on pilgrimage or enduring a bout of illness.
- 4b. Twelve *Dharma Talks* to Chan monks plus one *Bequeathed Admonitions to Followers*
- 5a. Five *Dharma Talks*, all to laymen
- 5b. Three *Dharma Talks*, all to laymen
- 6. Four *Letters* (*shuwen* 書問); to an exiled Korean king, with question letter attached; to a Korean official; to a layman; and to a monk
- 7. *Buddha Matters* (*foshi*佛事); Buddhist services, prayers, and worship
- 8. *Encomia on the Buddhas and Chan Patriarchs* (*fozu zan*佛祖讚); verses on Vairocana Buddha, Śākyamuni, the six Chan patriarchs, Budai, Linji, Gaofeng, and so forth

9. *Self-Inscriptions* (*zi zan* 自讚); inscriptions by Zhongfeng for portraits of him (at the request of followers).
10. *Critiques and Colophons* (*tiba* 題跋)
11a–c. Miscellany *Night Conversations in a Mountain Hermitage* (*Shanfang yehua* 山房夜話); third of the so-called *Five Leaves* or literary pieces of Zhongfeng
12a–c. *Commentary Opening Up the Meanings of the* Confidence-in-Mind Inscription (*Xinxin ming piyi jie* 信心銘闢義解); second of the *Five Leaves*
13. Commentary *Some Questions on Realizing Mind in the* Śūraṃgama (*Lengyan zhengxin bianjian huo wen* 楞嚴徵心辯見或問); first of the *Five Leaves*)
14. *Awakening to Mind in the Chan Separate Transmission* (*biechuan juexin* 別傳覺心); a discussion with interspersed eight-line poems
15. Commentary *Summary of Meanings in the* Diamond Sutra (*Jingang bore lüeyi* 金剛般若略義)
16. *House Instructions of Dwelling-in-the-Phantasmal Hermitage* (*Huanzhu jiaxun* 幻住家訓); fourth of the *Five Leaves*)
17. *In Imitation of Hanshan's Poems* (*Ni Hanshan shi* 擬寒山詩); fifth of the *Five Leaves*: words of admonition on practicing Chan in the prescriptive style of the pentasyllabic octets of Hanshan (Cold Mountain)
18a–b. Miscellany *Things Said East, Discussed West* (*Dongyu xihua* 東語西話; includes Zhongfeng's autobiography at the end)
19–20. Miscellany *Continued Things Said East, Discussed West* (*Dongyu xihua xuji* 東語西話續集; material that did not make it into *Talks in the East and Conversations in the West*)
21. One *Prose-Poem* (*fu* 賦) on "Encouraging Study"
22. Nine *Accounts* (*ji* 記; of various hermitages, including two Dwelling-in-the-Phantasmal Hermitages)
23. *Admonitions* and *Inscriptions* (*zhen ming* 箴銘); six admonitions on greed/anger/stupidity, on morality/concentration/wisdom, on joy, and forth; four inscriptions for hermitages, rooms, and a well spring
24. Nine *Prefaces* (*xu* 序) for poetry, the *Five Leaves of One Flower*, and so forth
25. Nine *Remarks* on bestowing soubriquets at the request of students (*shuo* 說)
26. Four *Prose Pieces* (of oblation to certain people); Five *Expatiations* (upon certain texts, places, and so forth); and Six *Miscellaneous Writings* (*wen shu zazhu* 文疏雜著)

27a–b and 28–30. *Poetry* (*jisong* 偈頌; songs and seven-syllable long poems; five-syllable long and short poems; seven-syllable eight lines and seven-syllable quatrains)

1324 *Conduct Record* by Niliu Zushun (逆流祖順)

Stupa Inscription by Yu Ji (虞集); stone erected in 1329

Way-Practice Stele by Song Ben (宋本)

1334 Sixth Month *Memorial Thanking Throne for Inclusion of the Text into the Buddhist Canon* by Shan-da-mi-di-li (善達密的理, i.e., Ciji)

This content shows significant differences from the usual Song-dynasty *yulu* collections, such as the *Recorded Sayings of Chan Master Dahui Pujue* (*Dahui Pujue chanshi yulu* 大慧普覺禪師語錄). For instance, the *Zhongfeng Extensive Record* lacks both "abbacy *yulus*" (discrete records for each monastery or hermitage at which the master in question served as abbot—always found at the beginning of a *yulu* collection) and the formal discourses entitled *Ascending-the-Hall* (*shang-tang* 上堂). Dahui's *yulu* contains seven abbacy records and numerous *Ascending-the-Hall* talks. Another difference is that the *Zhongfeng Extensive Record* contains commentaries on two sutras (*Śūraṃgama* and *Diamond*) and one Chan text (*Xinxin ming*). Overall, it can be said that there is a pronounced "literary" cast to the *Zhongfeng Extensive Record*: we find therein a collection of one hundred poems of admonition loosely in the style of Hanshan; three lengthy "miscellanies" or collections of "brush notes"[63]; and a large body of heptasyllabic long poems, pentasyllabic long and short poems, heptasyllabic eight-line poems, and heptasyllabic quatrains.[64] In contrast, Dahui's contains no miscellanies and a relatively small body of classical poetry. Dahui's miscellanies, *Precious Instructions of the Chan Forest* (*Chanlin bao xun* 禪林寶訓) and *Arsenal of the Chan School* (*Zongmen wuku* 宗門武庫), stand as independent works.

---

[63] On Chan miscellanies, see Chao Zhang, "Chan Miscellanea and the Shaping of the Religious Lineage of Chinese Buddhism Under the Song," *Kokusai Bukkyōgaku daigakuin daigaku kenkyū kiyō* 21 (2017): 242–282/95–135.

[64] Jason Protass, *The Poetry Demon: Song-Dynasty Monks on Verse and the Way*, Studies in East Asian Buddhism 29 (Honolulu: University of Hawai'i Press, 2021), 280 n.11: "For example, the 'expanded records' 廣錄 of Zhongfeng Mingben in thirty fascicles, *Tianmu Zhongfeng heshang guanglu* 天目中峯和尚廣錄, contains poetry and prose. The 1334 petition appended to the beginning of the Qisha canon edition indicates that the *guanglu* was compiled from several separate texts, one of which was a ten-fascicle *yulu* that did not include a section entitled *shi* [poetry]. Nonetheless, the comprehensive collection [containing *shi* poetry] anticipates the inclusive editorial practices of the late Ming."

On the question of why the *Zhongfeng Extensive Record* lacks *Ascending-the-Hall* talks, the bibliographer of Chan books Shiina Kōyū says:

> Concerning the [lack of] *Ascending-the-Hall* talks, this is because Zhongfeng did not dwell in any big and famous monasteries. On the other hand, the abundance of dharma talks [addressed to many students], letters, house instructions [implying communal living in his small hermitages], and miscellanies such as *Night Conversations in a Mountain Hermitage*, despite residence in informal mountain hermitages, show a Chan style characterized by lively interaction with monks and lay people.[65]

From the Gozan edition of the *Zhongfeng Extensive Record* I have selected for translation: four *Instructions to the Assembly* (out of a total of twenty-seven); seven *Dharma Talks* (out a total of thirty); the complete miscellany *Night Conversations in a Mountain Hermitage*; the complete *House Instructions for Dwelling-in-the-Phantasmal Hermitage*; the complete *In Imitation of Hanshan's Poems*; from the *Poetry* section: *Song of Dwelling-in-the-Phantasmal Hermitage* and *Cross-Legged Sitting Chan Admonitions*; and the two sets *Ten Poems on Living on a Boat* and *Ten Poems on Living in Town* (half of four ten-poem sets in the *Poetry* section, the other two being on mountain living and living on the water). This broad selection should be sufficient to give the reader an overall view of the Chan style expressed in the *Zhongfeng Extensive Record*.

I have worked from a photographic reproduction of the *Zhongfeng Record B* (bound as a single volume) in the National Diet Library Collection in Tokyo.[66] No Yuan or later edition is extant in China, and we know nothing of the identity of the compiler of this small collection, the date of compilation, the date of printing, and so forth. For this reason, it is sometimes deemed to be a Japanese compilation. However, a bibliographic catalogue of the Ming imperial house, *Catalogue of the Gallery of the Literary Vortex* (*Wenyuan ge shumu* 文淵閣書目), lists two Zhongfeng texts: a *Zhongfeng Extensive Record* (*Zhongfeng guanglu* 中峯廣錄 in one section; six volumes) and a *Tianmu Recorded Sayings* (*Tianmu yulu* 天目語錄 in one section; one volume). Although the Chinese *Tianmu Recorded Sayings* is not extant and we have no knowledge of its contents, given its brevity, we could speculate that it may have served as the predecessor to the similarly brief Gozan volume *Zhongfeng Record B* that is usually taken as wholly compiled in Japan. If this is the case, once this Chinese

---

[65] *Gozanban* 9, 654.
[66] *Gozanban* 9, 658–660.

work was brought back to Japan, Japanese editors appended further material, including notes recording the monasteries associated with some Zen monks after their return to Japan.

The first portion of the Gozan *Zhongfeng Record B*, which is entitled *Zhongfeng Dharma Talks*, consists of eighty-one dharma talks, thirteen dharma talks to eight Japanese Zen monks and one Japanese layman. The second portion of the Gozan *Zhongfeng Record B*, which is entitled *Zhongfeng Talks*, is a collection of 157 small pieces: dharma talks, instructions to the assembly, admonitions, buddha events, songs, accounts, ten Pure Land poems, verses, and so forth. From the *Zhongfeng Dharma Talks* portion of the Gozan *Zhongfeng Record B*, I have selected seventeen dharma talks for translation; from the *Zhongfeng Talks* portion of the Gozan *Zhongfeng Record B*, I have selected for translation one instructions-to-the-assembly piece.

Understanding the Phantasmal (*zhi huan* 知幻)

Zushun's *Conduct Record* in the *Zhongfeng Extensive Record* explains that Zhongfeng's sobriquet *Dwelling-in-the-Phantasmal* (*huanzhu* 幻住) comes from the name he gave to his ad hoc hermitages in the mountains of Zhejiang and Jiangsu: "Wherever he came to reside, he built a rustic hermitage hut, which were all called *Dwelling-in-the-Phantasmal*, and from this he took his sobriquet."[67] In Chinese Buddhist texts the word *huan* is often a rendering of Sanskrit *māyā*[68]: "art, wisdom, extraordinary or supernatural power (only in the earlier [Vedic] language); illusion, unreality, deception, fraud, trick...."[69] I have chosen *phantasm/phantasmal* (*something that is imagined but is not real*) to render Zhongfeng's use of *huan*. (*Phantasm*, perhaps, is close to the meaning of the Yogācāra term *parikalpita-svabhāva*: the *imagined nature*.) In his *House Instructions of Dwelling-in-the Phantasmal Hermitage*, Zhongfeng states unequivocally that everything is an unreal and deceptive phantasm:

> If you really want to realize this dharma-gate of great phantasm, ask that your *whole body* directly enter therein, and immediately there will not be the slightest

---

[67] 隨所寓。草創菴廬。皆曰幻住。又因以自號焉。(*Gozanban* 9, 489d; CBETA 2019.Q3, B25, no. 145, p. 976a14–15).

[68] Akira Hirakawa, *Buddhist Chinese-Sanskrit Dictionary* (Tokyo: The Reiyukai, 1997), #1040/425–426 gives *huan* 幻 = *māyā* (phantasm/illusion); *nirmāṇa* (magical creation); *nirmita* (magically created); *pratibhāsa* (apparition); *māyā-kṛta* (made of phantasm/illusion); *māyā-nirmita* (phantasmal/illusory magical creation); *māyopama* (like a phantasm/illusion).

[69] Monier Monier-Williams, *A Sanskrit-English Dictionary* (1899; repr., Oxford: The Clarendon Press, 1974), 811.

obstruction. If sometimes your feet dither and your mind-ground dilly-dallies, you absolutely must not follow the way of verbalization-produced understanding. *Everything is a phantasm*—from the outset *ready-made*. I am just a blind one who negates everything: what other practice-work could be carried out? What other road is there to seek out? That is for sure![70]

This blanket assertion concerning the phantasmal is supported by the observations of key students who knew him firsthand. For instance, his disciple Tianru Weize wrote: "This Old Fellow Zhongfeng drew on no model—he advocated the dharma approach of *great phantasm* and put an end to the *ready-made gong'an*."[71]

Since everything without exception is a phantasm, the entire Buddhist tradition, including Chan, is also phantasmal—a magician's sleight of hand. Another passage of *House Instructions of Dwelling-in-the Phantasmal Hermitage* states:

Though [Śākyamuni] used worthless yellow stuff to increase the amount of gold, unfortunately, he added another layer to the phantasm mask. At that time, for forty-nine years, through more than 300 assemblies, to phantasmal questions he gave phantasmal answers. Beautiful literary style has flourished [in the Buddhist community], and voices have boiled over. This phantasmal *sudden*, phantasmal *gradual*, phantasmal *partial*, phantasmal *perfect*—let us just put them aside without discussion! At the very end of his career, he used his phantasmal hand to hold up a phantasmal flower, saying: "I have the correct dharma-eye depository, the wonderful mind of nirvana!" The result was that Old Kāśyapa cracked a phantasmal smile and on both his shoulders bore the burden [of the Chan transmission]. From that time onward, one person's [i.e., Śākyamuni's] transmission of a falsehood became ten thousand persons' transmission of fact. Phantasm caused more phantasm in a series: a transmission and reception-of-transmission without end. Then we arrive at: Bodhidharma's facing a phantasmal wall at Shaolin Monastery; pacifying phantasmal mind; repenting phantasmal transgressions; release from phantasmal bondage; [Hongren's] asking [Huineng] his phantasmal name; [Shenxiu and Huineng's] composing phantasmal verses; polishing phantasmal tiles; dangling phantasmal feet; [Baizhang's] hanging his phantasmal fly whisk; deafening phantasmal ears; [Linji's] slapping with the phantasmal palm of his hand. From this, we extract the demented fellow [Linji] who gave a phantasmal shout like angry thunder from the blue sky. Down to: [Linji's] phantasmal

---

[70] *House Instructions for Dwelling-in-the-Phantasmal Hermitage* in *Zhongfeng Extensive Record* (Translation 4, section #5).
[71] From a *Praises for Preceptor Zhongfeng* contained in Tianru's recorded sayings: 這老漢。無榜樣。主張大幻法門。滅却現成公案。(CBETA 2019.Q3, X70, no. 1403, p. 797a8–9).

illumination and phantasmal *function*, phantasmal *guest* and phantasmal *host*, across and athwart interlocking: giving/snatching away, killing/giving life, a thousand forms and ten thousand shapes. There is no one who can get a peep at Linji's limit! Right down to the present, faceless old Chan monks of the various regions come out of Linji's gate and inherit his Chan personal realization. They receive the falsehoods and echo them. They put the single phantasm into their mouths; store various phantasms in the measureless; put their sayings into refined literary language and make their Chan encounters sound skillful; make their style elevated and their tone free and unconventional; make their commands lofty and their lineage houses great. Not one of them has been capable of going outside this phantasm![72]

Two sutras were of particular importance to Zhongfeng, the *Perfect Awakening* and the *Śūraṃgama*. These are long-popular canonical picks in the Chan tradition, from at least Guifeng Zongmi in the Tang through Dahui Zonggao in the Southern Song. Zhongfeng wrote a commentary on the *Śūraṃgama* that is included in the *Zhongfeng Extensive Record*,[73] and it is probably from the teachings of the *Perfect Awakening* that he drew his key teaching of *phantasm/phantasmal* (*huan* 幻). In a dharma talk for a lecture master from Yunnan, Zhongfeng quotes a passage of the *Perfect Awakening*:

This matter does not lie in the principles found in sutra books, nor does it lie in any sort of cultivation and realization. The approaches to realization of the three kinds of meditation taught in the *Perfect Awakening*, the twenty-five wheels [of the *vajra*-realm mandala], the twenty-five kinds of perfect comprehension taught in the *Śūraṃgama*, down to the all-at-once and step-by-step stages spoken of in the canonical teachings and everything you experience through seeing and hearing: none of this is akin to the Chan pointed to by Bodhidharma. The Chan spoken of in the teachings: none of that is free of cultivation and realization. Only Bodhidharma pointed to *one mind is Chan*. This is utterly different from what is spoken of in the sutra books. You should ponder this! The *Perfect Awakening Sutra* says: "Understand the phantasmal and detach from it, without creating any *upāyas*. Detach from the phantasmal and awaken, without any sort of graduated sequence." Debater types say: "[This sutra line] comes very close to Bodhidharma's purport, without any wading through the graduated sequence of *upāyas*." In the end they don't understand this single line *understand the phantasmal/detach from*

---

[72] *House Instructions for Dwelling-in-the-Phantasmal Hermitage* in *Zhongfeng Extensive Record* (Translation 4, sections #2–3).
[73] *Lengyan zhengxin bianjian huowen* (楞嚴徵心辯見或問; *Gozanban* 9, 323d; CBETA 2019.Q3, B25, no. 145, p. 854a3).

the phantasmal. They have already crossed over into the graduated sequences of *upāyas*! The Bodhidharma school has nothing of this sort of thing. When one is finished, all is finished, but the word finished is uncognizable.[74]

The *Perfect Awakening* passage from which Zhongfeng is quoting in this dharma talk runs as follows:

> Good Sons! All bodhisattvas and sentient-beings of this later age should detach from all phantasmal, unreal realms. Through firmly grasping a mind of detachment, they should even detach from the mind that is *like a phantasm*. Detachment is itself phantasmal—they should even detach from that. Detaching from detachment is itself phantasmal—they should even detach from that! When they obtain the state wherein there is nothing to detach from, then they have eliminated all phantasms. It is like starting a fire by rubbing together two pieces of wood. Fire emerges; the pieces of wood are used up; the ashes fly off; and the smoke dissipates. *Using the phantasmal to practice cultivation [within] the phantasmal* is just like this. Although all phantasms become used up, you do not enter annihilationism. Good Sons! Understand the phantasmal and detach from it, without creating any *upāyas*. Detach from the phantasmal and awaken, without any sort of graduated sequence. All bodhisattvas and sentient-beings of the later age who rely on this sort of practice will achieve constant detachment from all phantasms.[75]

For an explication of this ignition metaphor, a good guide is Guifeng Zongmi (780–841), who wrote numerous commentaries on the *Perfect Awakening* and influenced all later commentators. Zongmi explains that the original piece of wood is a metaphor for the phantasmal world that the practitioner works on through practice or cultivation. The second piece of wood, a tool used to rub against the original piece, is the phantasmal practice-wisdom of the practitioner. The crucial point is that *the kindled fire burns up both pieces*

---

[74] *Instructions to Lecture Master Fuyuan Tongsan of Yunnan* (Shi Yunnan Fuyuan Tongsan jiangzhu 示雲南福元通三講主): 此事不在經書義理中。不在一切脩證裏。至於圓覺之三觀。二十五輪。楞嚴之二十五圓通之所證門。乃至教中所說。頓漸階級次第等。一涉見聞皆墮情識。總不與達磨所指之禪相似。教中所言之禪。皆不離脩證。惟達磨獨指一心爲禪。與經書文字所說者迥別。宜思之。圓覺經云。知幻即離。不作方便。離幻即覺。亦無漸次。議者謂。逼近達磨之旨。亦不涉方便漸次。殊不知只箇知幻離幻。早涉方便漸次了也。達磨門下。總無是事。一了一切了。只箇了字。亦不可得。(*Gozanban* 9, 156d–157a; CBETA 2019.Q3, B25, no. 145, p. 730b8–17).

[75] 大方廣圓覺修多羅了義經: 善男子。一切菩薩及末世眾生。應當遠離一切幻化虛妄境界。由堅執持遠離心故。心如幻者亦復遠離。遠離為幻亦復遠離。離遠離幻亦復遠離。得無所離即除諸幻。譬如鑽火兩木相因。火出木盡灰飛煙滅。以幻修幻亦復如是。諸幻雖盡不入斷滅。善男子。知幻即離。不作方便。離幻即覺。亦無漸次。一切菩薩及末世眾生依此修行。如是乃能永離諸幻。(T842.17.914a15–23).

of wood.[76] Zhongfeng's *detaching from the phantasmal* is practice, and practice for Zhongfeng is, in general, *huatou* practice (plus, of course, cross-legged sitting). In the *Perfect Awakening*'s metaphor of kindling a fire, both sticks, the phantasmal mundane-and-supramundane worlds and the phantasmal *huatou*, are consumed in the resultant blaze, leaving behind only ashes that fly off and smoke that dissipates.

Detaching from the Phantasmal (*li huan* 離幻): The *Huatou*

Zhongfeng was a *huatou* master, one who advocated the *huatou* to both the monk disciples under him and to the laypeople he encountered along the way. He sprang from a lineage of *huatou* practitioners: his teacher Gaofeng used as his main *huatou* **to where does the One return?** (*yi gui he chu* 一歸何處) and Gaofeng's teacher Xueyan finally settled on the *huatou* **wu** (無). Usually, Zhongfeng referred to the *huatou* as the *huatou that has no meaning or taste* (*wu yiwei huatou* 無義味話頭), the *huatou you are practicing* (*suocan de huatou* 所參底話頭), and slight variants of these two. There was little or nothing new in Zhongfeng's *huatou* paradigm, but then none of the prominent *huatou* masters of East Asia—Zhongfeng's Chan ancestors Xueyan and Gaofeng, Mengshan Deyi (蒙山德異; 1231–?), numerous Ming Chan masters such as Dufeng Benshan (毒峯本善; 1419–1482) and Chushan Shaoqi (楚山紹琦; 1403–1473); the Koreans Pojo Chinul (普照知訥; 1158–1210) and his disciple Chin'gak Hyesim (真覺慧諶; 1178–1234), the Japanese Bassui Tokushō (拔隊得勝; 1327–1387), and so forth—show "originality" in their practice of the *huatou*. In fact, nothing in the *huatou* approach of Zhongfeng and all these masters (and many others) deviates in any significant way from the following *huatou* framework definitively laid out by the Southern Song master Dahui Zonggao in his *Letters* and *Dharma Talks*[77]:

---

[76] *Yuanjue jing da shu* (圓覺經大疏): "Explanation: Suppose there is a segment of dried wood and you use another piece of wood to rub it, creating friction and kindling a fire. Fire emerges and burns up both pieces of wood. Once the pieces of wood are used up by the fire, the smoke naturally dissipates. Once they have turned to ashes, the ashes spontaneously fly off. The form and substance of the two pieces of wood no longer constitute any sort of resistant impediment. The next four phrases match up with the dharma teaching. The original segment [of dried wood] is a metaphor for the *phantasmal falsity that the cultivator applies himself to in cultivation*. The piece of wood that rubs [the original piece of dried wood] is a metaphor for the *phantasmal wisdom of the cultivator*. The smoke is a metaphor for detaching [from the phantasmal], the ashes a metaphor for sending off [the phantasmal]." [解曰。如有一段乾本。以一木燧鑽之。火出。還將却燒二木。木火既盡。煙自然滅。既成灰燼。任運飛散。不同二木形質為礙。如次四節。以配於法。本段喻所修幻妄。木燧喻能修幻智。煙喻離。灰喻遣。] (CBETA 2019.Q3, X09, no. 243, p. 355b20–23).

[77] See Broughton with Watanabe, *Letters of Dahui*, 23–35.

1. The *huatou* practitioner must generate a singular *sensation of uncertainty*. The term *uncertainty* (*yi* 疑) refers to the sensations of hesitation, vacillation, wavering, misgiving, having qualms about something, apprehension—even dread and angst—that develop in the round of daily activities. The practitioner is to merge, to amalgamate, all these myriad instances of uncertainty and apprehension into one big sensation of uncertainty and apprehension about the *huatou*, and only about the *huatou*. Once this featureless "*huatou*-uncertainty" mass is smashed to smithereens, one is liberated.
2. The *huatou* practitioner must be neither tensed nor slack (*ji* 急/*huan* 緩 or *jin* 緊/*huan* 緩).
3. For the *huatou* practitioner saving on the expenditure of energy is none other than gaining energy (*shengli bian shi deli chu ye* 省力便是得力處也).
4. The *huatou* should become tasteless (*mei ziwei* 沒滋味). Getting taste from anything—the ancients, sutra quotations, Chan cases, Chan dialogues, the silence of sitting, the multiplicity of actions of daily life, and so forth—indicates that one has made it into a stereotyped formula or conventional usage (*kejiu* 窠臼) and taken up a comfortable residence therein. Not sitting inside any such "nest" is "no taste."
5. The *huatou* practitioner must keep on pressing hard (*ya jiangqu* 崖將去/*si ya* 廝崖) with the *huatou* no matter what.
6. The *huatou* practitioner must *pass through* (*touqu* 透取/*toude* 透得) the *huatou*.
7. The mind of samsara will collapse (*shengsi xin po* 生死心破), which is sometimes phrased as the *sensation of uncertainty* about the *huatou* will collapse (*yiqing po* 疑情破).
8. Excessive intellectual sharpness and knowledge work against *huatou* practice.

Typical of Zhongfeng's exhortations to *huatou* practice is the following from his *House Instructions of Dwelling-in-the-Phantasmal Hermitage*:

On the practiced *huatou that has no meaning or taste*, stand perfectly still like a blind one, T-shape from head to toe. Be indignant in mind as you keep pressing hard with [with the *huatou*]! At the very moment you are pressing hard, there is absolutely no need for you to seek any sort of understanding of the Chan Way or the *buddhadharma*. It is just like crashing into a silver mountain or iron wall. Aside from chewing on the indestructible *huatou that has no meaning or taste*, do no crouch down and sit on any other thought! Later there will be nothing to pull along. Just in that way make the *huatou* fixed and stable. Just go on like this diligently and steadfastly.[78]

What specific *huatous* did Zhongfeng favor? In his talks and writings, he mentions such common *huatous* as **original face** (*benlai mianmu* 本來面目) and ***wu*** (無), although often in his exhortations he does not designate any specific *huatou*. However, in his *Account of Dwelling-in-the-Phantasmal Hermitage of Mt. Bian* (*Bianshan Huanzhu an ji* 弁山幻住菴記) Zhongfeng explicitly speaks of *phantasm* as a *huatou*:

> "The buddhas of the three times—phantasms. The Chan patriarchs through the generations—phantasms. Awakening and the defilements, samsara and nirvana—all phantasms." If you have not yet awakened to this meaningless, tasteless *huatou* **phantasm**, make your spine firmly upright and tightly clasp your bare hands. Take care not to lightly let go. Outside go on your begging rounds, inside manage affairs, in the middle practice quiet sitting: do not see any characteristics such as leisurely/busy or movement/stillness. With a fierce whip, a painful whip, take awakening as your standard.[79]

Here the word *phantasm* (*huan* 幻) itself has become a phantasmal *huatou* (all *huatous* are phantasmal)! One highly metaphorical passage in Zhongfeng's *House Instructions of Dwelling-in-the-Phantasmal Hermitage* envisions this *huatou phantasm* as a majestic calligraphic image superimposed on the panorama of the Buddhist cosmos of four "continents" and the central Mt. Sumeru. This visualization of *phantasm* (*huan* 幻) evokes one mode of *huatou* practice, emphasizing the visual aspect (rather than the sound) of the *huatou*:

> Dip a writing-brush the size of five Mt. Sumerus into the water of the four great seas, and, on the continent of Pūrva-Videha in the East make a *direct-drop* stroke [i.e., the first stroke of the character for *phantasm*: 幻 *huan*]. Then, on the continent Jambudvīpa in the South make a *crooked-angle* stroke [i.e., the second stroke of the character for *phantasm*]. Slowly, on the continent Uttarakuru in the North, make a *single-dot* stroke [i.e., the third stroke of the character for *phantasm*]. Then, turn to the continent Avaragodānīya in the West to make a *half-knife* stroke [the final stroke of the character for *phantasm*]. These strokes combine to form the

---

[78] *House Instructions for Dwelling-in-the-Phantasmal Hermitage* in *Zhongfeng Extensive Record* (Translation 4, section #8).
[79] 三世佛幻也。歷代祖幻也。菩提與煩惱生死及涅槃俱幻也。爾其未證幻無義味話。堅豎脊梁。緊握空拳。慎勿輕放。外而行乞。內而執事。中而宴坐。不見有閒忙動靜之相。猛策痛鞭。以悟爲則。(*Gozanban* 9, 420b–c; CBETA 2019.Q3, B25, no. 145, p. 926a2–6).

character **phantasm**, which hangs at the summit of all-pervading space: making those of the great earth who have eyes see, those with ears hear; those with a body feel contact; those with cognition understand. You should know that the buddhas of the past a long time ago realized nirvana *in this* [i.e., **phantasm**]. The buddhas of the present right now are each completing correct awakening *in this*. The buddhas of the future will open the correct dharma-eye *in this*. Even the bodhisattvas as numerous as fine dust particles one by one are never separated from *this very locus* [of **phantasm**] as they cultivate the six perfections and produce the four minds, cross over sentient-beings to nirvana and sever the bondage of suffering.[80]

Zhongfeng's *Great Matter of Samsara* (*shengsi dashi* 生死大事)

The psychological demands Zhongfeng placed upon his charges were indeed daunting: that they should shoulder the great matter of samsara as their *own personal heavy responsibility* (*ji zhong ren* 己重任); that is, an existential question for oneself alone, a responsibility that cannot be shifted onto anyone or anything else. Zhongfeng describes this coming to terms with one's own samsaric predicament as "painful" (*tong* 痛) or "urgent" (*qieqie* 切切):

> If merely there is one who *painfully* takes the *great matter of samsara* as his *own personal heavy responsibility* and, on all occasions, stands tall and raises *this matter*, collecting it in his mind and submerging under the three rafters [of the Chan Hall] for twenty or thirty years [i.e., doing cross-legged sitting practice for two or three decades], for him it will be just like a single day. Beyond the great earth he will stride three thousand or five thousand miles, without the slightest gap. He will discard sleeping and eating, forget heat and cold.[81]

***

> But students do not take the *great matter of samsara* as their *own personal heavy responsibility*. All they want is quickly to "understand Chan." Thereupon, they crouch down to sit under that *upāya*, bore right through a whole string of ancient and modern *gong'ans*, and call that "passing through the barrier." Little do they

---

[80] *House Instructions for Dwelling-in-the-Phantasmal Hermitage* in *Zhongfeng Extensive Record* (Translation 4, section #6).
[81] *Zhongfeng Extensive Record, Instructions to the Assembly*: 惟有痛以生死大事爲己重任者。一切時中卓卓地。單提此事。蘊之方寸。向三根椽下。淹沒三十年二十年。宛同一日。於大方之外。闊跨三千里五千里。不閒絲毫。廢寢食忘寒暑。 (*Gozanban* 9, 121b, CDETA 2019.Q3, B25, no. 145, p. 704b1–4).

imagine: the single samsara barrier right under their feet is exactly the one they haven't been able to pass through! What is to be "passed through" *is none other than* the barrier of verbalization.[82]

***

When you have sufficient confidence and *urgently* take the great matter of samsara as your *own personal heavy responsibility*, do not be daunted by twenty or thirty years [of practice]. Plant your feet on solid ground, be assiduous and alert: under the three rafters [of the Chan hall] vividly practice! When you are really practicing, there are no *upāyas*, and there is no fixed rate of progress. If torpor/distraction appears before you, you must take no notice. If you can practice, practice like this! If you *can't* practice, practice like this! Never retrogress. One day deluded consciousness will be gone, and all your tactics and stratagems will be exhausted. Unaware and unknowing, you will suddenly attain awakening.[83]

Once a student has this deep sense of the inescapable personal burden, he must then "tread onward" in his *huatou* practice. Zhongfeng's *Purity Rules of Dwelling-in-the-Phantasmal Hermitage*, the charter for his own mountain hermitages by that name, has a section on this very theme：

Although you may have cut off realization-cultivation, you must still rely on *treading onward*. *Treading onward* is like an infant's need to suckle; like the fact that plants and trees must be cultivated. Brothers [of Dwelling-in-the-Phantasmal Hermitage] in front of the seven-foot section of the Chan sitting platform beneath the three rafters will externally cut off all objective-supports and internally make the mind immobile: the six organs of perception stilled and the myriad thoughts natural and detached. Upon encountering hate and attachment, they will be like an iron bull seeing the majesty of the lion; upon facing good and bad, like a wooden woman looking at the countenance of a jade person. The habit-energies of numerous past lives will be swept clean like trifling dust motes: the single speck of body-and-mind as cold as ice and snow. A worn-out skirt or dirty padding for clothing wards off the cold. Subsisting on bean leaves or dining on the goosefoot vegetable—all you must know is when you have eaten your fill. Forget about the customs of the times and go back to the style of the ancients. Look at the buddhas and the Chan patriarchs

---

[82] *Night Conversations in a Mountain Hermitage* in *Zhongfeng Extensive Record* (Translation 3, section #13).
[83] *Zhongfeng Dharma Talks* of *Zhongfeng Record B, Instructions to Chan Person Wei* (示偉禪人): 惟有信得及。切切以死生大事爲己重任。不憚三十年二十年。脚踏實地。孜孜地。向三根椽下的的地參取。政於參時都無方便。亦無程限。但有昏沈散亂現前。亦不要顧它。參得也如此參。參不得也如此參。久遠不退轉。一旦情識泯伎倆都盡。不覺不知。忽然開悟。(*Gozanban* 9, 529b–c; CBETA 2019.Q3, X70, no. 1402, p. 741b9–14).

as if you have spawned a grudge against them. Observe the self as like bubbles or a flickering flame. Investigate a single *huatou* while both walking and sitting. Your entire lifetime's phantasmal shadows—put them to rest in the morning and put them to rest at nightfall. This is not just a matter of not producing a worldly mind—you also must not produce any thought of divorcing from the worldly. Be like the tracks of the clouds in the mountains; like the marks left on water by the moon. When your locus is empty and still, do not think of it as "relaxed." When things are chaotic and troublesome, do not view it as "confused." Be diligent and resolute. By means of this you will *tread onward* into the Way.[84]

Zhongfeng: "I Am Not Awakened"

One of Zhongfeng's most striking declarations in his Chan records is his explicit denial that he has ever attained awakening. He claims that all he possesses is a level of understanding that comes from words, from books. Generally, this sort of level of understanding is tossed into the "kudzu" (useless verbal entanglement) bin in Chan texts. Let us examine two relevant passages from his miscellany *Night Conversations at a Mountain Hermitage*:

> *In the matter of the Way of the buddhas and patriarchs, I am lacking in awakening. I have no more than a confident understanding that comes from ordinary language and books.* I ponder: after the ancients obtained the purport, they no longer feared imminent danger. For twenty or thirty years they placed themselves alongside the forge at which the blacksmith forges metal [i.e., practiced for two or three decades], removing traces of *awakening* and cleansing away the principle that they had realized. Only afterwards did they enter the real and the conventional: then they didn't experience a single dharma or ordinary feeling. Their whole body was like a sharp sword, like an ancient mirror, never ceasing its functioning, never employing superfluous words. While sternly confronting a crowd of thousands [of Chan practitioners], they were unaware of being treated as "honored," unaware of being treated as "glorious." Since they possessed this sort of attitude, even if they encountered a situation in which humans and gods recommended them [for the abbotship of an illustrious monastery], they weren't embarrassed. Those still

---

[84] 幻住庵清規： 雖絕證修仍憑踐履。謂踐履者。猶嬰孩之必加乳哺。猶草木之寧免栽培。兄弟家三條椽下七尺單前。外絕諸緣內心不動。六窓虛靜萬慮儼然。遇憎愛如鐵牛見獅子之威。對善惡如木女看玉人之貌。多生習氣蕩若輕埃。一點身心冷如水雪。弊襠塵絮隨分禦寒。藿茹藜飧但知取飽。遠忽時習追復古風。視佛祖如生冤。觀自己如泡戲。一箇話頭行究坐究。百年幻影朝休暮休。不惟不起世間心。而亦不曾起離世想。如山中雲迹。似水底月痕。處空寂不知為閒。混塵勞不見其亂。孜孜爾兀元爾。是以入道之踐履也。(CBETA 2019.Q3, X63, no. 1248, p. 583c8–17).

immersed in deluded views [like me] cannot imitate this. To start with, if the traces of awakening are not yet completely washed away, then the view of doer/done arises in confusion at every turn. Doer and done are both deluded views. The traces of awakening: they must not be allowed to linger in mind! How much more so is this case with a confident understanding of the teachings, which is simply a deluded view! When you get to the substance of the ultimate Way, the closer you get, the more estranged you are from it; the nearer you become, the farther away you are. *Moreover, I have not yet been able to understand the Way, so how could I make others understand the principle of the Way? Because I have been unable to chase away this blockage in myself, I dare not falsely take charge of a big monastery and call myself a master who spreads the Way!*[85]

***

Therefore, the ancient said: "Practice must be real practice; awakening must be real awakening. Great King Yama isn't afraid of a lot of talk." These words exhaust the matter. *I am certainly not someone who has had a real awakening.* I dare not tread in the tracks of Ye Gong's [painting of unreal dragons] and Zhao Chang's [painting of unreal flowers]! I chitchat daily with people, haggling over *this matter*, but all that is just the dharma-gate that I believe is correct. It has never been about showing off my personal dazzling experience to elicit praise from others.[86]

In the first excerpt, he is making an argument for his declining abbotships of major monasteries by claiming that one who lacks understanding of the Way could not possibly lead others via the abbotship of a large and prominent monastery. His disavowal of awakening does seem to be linked in some way to his preference for a reclusive lifestyle in the mountains and on boats, as well as to his bedrock modesty. His close disciple Tianru makes much of the master's disavowal of any experience of awakening:

I reached Mt. Tianmu and attached myself to Old Preceptor Dwelling-in-the-Phantasmal. Every time I encountered him, he said: "*I have practiced Chan all my life, but I haven't attained awakening.*" In my heart I secretly entertained doubts. After this, I came to know that Old Preceptor possessed the marks of a great person: not cramped, not eccentric, not aloof, not boastful. *All his life he was unwilling to speak of his awakening.* And he also bound his followers to a strict promise to "walk underwater" and function in secrecy. His intention lay

---

[85] *Night Conversations in a Mountain Hermitage* in *Zhongfeng Extensive Record* (Translation 3, section #30).

[86] *Night Conversations in a Mountain Hermitage* in *Zhongfeng Extensive Record* (Translation 3, section #12).

in making present-day followers—those without attainment, yet professing attainment; those not yet realized, yet claiming realization; those falsely claiming wisdom; those acting like off-kilter bumpkins—come to know shame and fear. This truly is saving people of the present who are falling into perverse illnesses: it will serve as a warning to students in the future who try to appropriate an undeserved reputation. The master worked [compassionately] for people. The situation is constantly becoming something new: when I arrived here, the Old Man was [for me] a sort of "changed situation." How could anyone of ordinary perception fathom him![87]

Tianru didn't swallow the master's claim to have never awakened during an entire lifetime of Chan practice: Tianru thought Zhongfeng had indeed achieved awakening and was deliberately operating in stealth mode. The adjectives Tianru uses to describe Zhongfeng are probably the best encapsulation of the master's personality available to us: "not cramped, not eccentric, not aloof, not boastful." If we convert these four negative formulations into positives, we might then say Zhongfeng was "easygoing, within conventionality in speech and action, friendly and open, and modest." We can probably rest assured that students did not dread coming into his presence, as many students surely did with the fearsome Yuansou, Zhongfeng's contemporary who held many important Five-Mountains abbotships. Tianru clearly thought of Zhongfeng's stance on awakening as part of an *upāya* or stratagem to guide others: the master was "working [compassionately] for people."

Converging with Tianru's assessment, the Japanese scholar Noguchi Yoshitaka has called Zhongfeng's Chan "not-awakened Zen" (*migo Zen* 未悟禪), and he refers to Zhongfeng's claim to lack awakening as an *upāya*. Noguchi, in fact, argues that Zhongfeng's "not-awakened Zen" is more than just an *upāya*: "The thing that best shows the special characteristic of Zhongfeng's Zen is the slogan *not awakened*.... I called Zhongfeng's Zen *not-awakened Zen*, but this was because I was thinking Zhongfeng's *not-awakened* slogan doesn't simply stop at serving as an *upāya*—it symbolizes the very nature of his Zen."[88]

---

[87] An *Informal Talk* in *Recorded Sayings of Chan Master Tianru Weize* (天如惟則禪師語錄): 及到天目依附幻住老和尚。每每見他道。老幻一生參禪不得開悟。我心中竊有所疑。後來方知老和尚具大人相。不險不怪不矜不誇。他平生不肯自說悟由得處。而又嚴約參徒潛行密用者。意在使令時未得謂得未證謂證妄稱知識誑謼聞之徒。知所羞媿。知所畏懼。此政是切救今時墮邪之病。以為後學掠虛之戒者也。宗師為人處。局面時時新。至此老又是一番變局。豈常情所能測哉。(CBETA 2019.Q3, X70, no. 1403, pp. 763c17–764a1).
[88] Noguchi, *Gendai Zen*, 148 and 167. On *migo Zen*, see also Noguchi and Matsubara, *Sanbō yawa*, 332–334; and Noguchi Yoshitaka, "Migo Zen: Tenmoku Chūhō kenkyū," *Kyūshū Chūgoku gakkai hō* 22 (1979): 14–25.

Entanglement of *Huatou* Chan and Pure Land *Nianfo* (*Nembutsu*): Zhongfeng and Tianru

For Zhongfeng, Chan practice (*canchan* 參禪) and Pure Land *nianfo* (念佛) have the same objective: ending samsara, the beginningless cycle of rebirth. From Zhongfeng's Chan records we can say that he understood "Chan practice" to center on *huatou* practice, cross-legged sitting, constant contemplation of the *great matter of samsara*, avoidance of any search for *quick awakening*, and so forth. *Nianfo* is a Chinese translation of *buddhānusmṛti* (*recollection of the qualities of a buddha*), "one of the common practices designed to help develop meditative absorption (*dhyāna*) in the mainstream traditions."[89] In China *nianfo* came to mean recitation (out loud or silently) of the name of a buddha: *Homage to Amitābha Buddha* (*nanwu Amituofo* 南無阿彌陀佛). Thus, both *Chan* (= *dhyāna*) and the *nian* (= *smṛti*) of *nianfo* are traceable to a common Buddhist-meditation concept: *samādhi* (*meditative concentration*), the attainment of one-pointedness of mind without distraction. Indeed, *huatou* and *nianfo* have much in common as methods for attaining one-pointedness of mind.

In *Night Conversations in a Mountain Hermitage*, Zhongfeng insists that to put an end to samsara one should *enter deeply* into one or the other, not both concurrently:

> Moreover, Chan practice is for ending samsara. Doing the *nianfo* and cultivating the Pure Land is also for ending samsara. Even though the teachings established by the sages involve a thousand roads and ten thousand ruts, every one of them takes as the ultimate putting a definitive end to samsara. *However, for the purposes of destroying sense-fields, exalt only one of these gates* [either Chan or *nianfo*] *and enter deeply therein*. Therefore, an ancient said: "The slightest amount of fixity of thought becomes a cause of rebirth into the three bad rebirth paths; if suddenly deluded feelings arise, it will lead to shackles for ten thousand eons." A "combined practice [of Chan and Pure Land]?" If you are not free of this sort of chat about "Chan" and "Pure Land," you will endure a boiling over of the waves of consciousness, an agitation of feelings and sense objects. There will never be an end to it! That's why there is no way I can stop trying to explain these matters![90]

---

[89] Robert E. Buswell Jr. and Donald S. Lopez Jr., *The Princeton Dictionary of Buddhism* (Princeton, NJ: Princeton University Press, 2014), 580.
[90] *Night Conversations in a Mountain Hermitage* in *Zhongfeng Extensive Record* (Translation 3, section #8).

Zhongfeng's successor Tianru Weize remained faithful to Zhongfeng's assertion that one must take up either deep immersion in Chan or deep immersion in Pure Land *nianfo*, excluding concurrent practice of the two. Interestingly, Tianru described his own Chan as a "fluid" style resistant to pigeonholing or typecasting.[91] In a *General Sermon* Tianru echoes his master's attitude toward Chan and *nianfo*: they arrive at the same place, but people should pick one and specialize in it. Tianru says that concurrent practice of Chan and *nianfo* is like trying to stand with a foot in each of two boats—you are quite unstable and risk falling into the water:

> Upon reflecting on the matter of samsara, even an iron fellow loses heart. For this reason, the buddhas and Chan patriarchs wield great compassion and give rise to great sympathy, widely setting up oral teachings. Sometimes they teach you to raise the *huatou* to awareness, and sometimes they teach you to do the *nianfo* and cultivate the Pure Land, making you sweep away false thought and the mind of craziness, making you recognize your *Old Man Master* and come to know **my original face**.... A *huatou* is like an iron broom, sweeping away [the two extremes of] *is* and *is not*. The more you sweep, the more remains; the more remains, the more you sweep. If you are unable to sweep, forfeit your life in the name of sweeping. Suddenly, you will have swept clean the entire sky! A single road will open through the myriad distinctions. Chan worthies! Make effort in the present life—you must finish *the matter*. Do not make yourself subject to a surplus of ill-fortune for everlasting eons. This is essential. Also, among both lay and monk disciples of the Buddha, there are those who practice the *nianfo* and cultivate the Pure Land. Among them some are uncertain: "Nianfo and Chan practice are not the same—are they?" They don't know: "Are Chan practice and *nianfo* not the same and yet the same?" Chan practice is for ending samsara, and *nianfo* is also for ending samsara. Chan practice is *direct pointing to the human mind, seeing the Nature and becoming a buddha*. Nianfo is *comprehending the Mind-Only Pure Land and seeing the Innate-Nature Amitābha Buddha*. Having said "Innate-Nature Amitābha Buddha" and "Mind-Only Pure Land," how could there be non-sameness? The [*Perfect Awakening*] *Sutra* says: "It is like the four gates to a great walled-city. People from all over are not limited to using one gate." Thus, although the gates by which they

---

[91] An *Instructions to the Assembly* in *Recorded Sayings of Chan Master Tianru Weize* (天如惟則禪師語錄): "Throughout the regions there are various kinds of Chan: *sea-dipper Chan* [a calabash split in two as a scooper]; *sea-clam Chan* [when it opens its mouth, one can see all the way to the internal organs]; *iron-plane Chan* [a metal tool that scrapes off excrescences]. My Chan, on the other hand, is *bottle-gourd-floating-on-the-water Chan*. At the slightest touch, it immediately moves; press down, and it immediately flips over. It's so lively there is no way for you people to pin it down!" [諸方有海蠡禪。海蚌禪。鐁鎁禪。老僧底却是水上胡蘆禪，觸著便動。捺著便轉。活鱍鱍地無你奈何處。] (CBETA 2019.Q3, X70, no. 1403, p. 755a17–18).

enter are different, their arrival in the city is the same. Chan practice or *nianfo* accord with what is appropriate for varying capacities. How could there be any difference between them? However, within *nianfo* there is the efficacious and the non-efficacious. How is this? If someone is only mindful in mouth but not mindful in mind, it is non-efficacious. If, in recitation after recitation of the *nianfo*, mouth and mind tally, and mind and buddha step after step are not apart from each other, then it is efficacious.... Preceptor Dwelling-in-the-Phantasmal [Zhongfeng] had a saying: "Chan practice is only for completely clarifying [the *great matter* of] samsara; *nianfo* only plans to end samsara." *Just stick to one side and gain entrance to it*. The two gateways [of Chan and *nianfo*] are almost without difference. Although these gateways are almost without difference, nevertheless it is impermissible to use them concurrently. Chan practice is simply Chan practice; *nianfo* is simply *nianfo*. If you talk about them as if they were two heads [on one body], neither head will show results. An ancient had a simile for this: "It is like trying to stand astride two boats—you are not firmly secured to this side or that side. When you are not firmly secured on the two sides, you may even get away with it, but beware of falling into the water! Remember! Remember! Strive! Strive!"... *Nianfo* is just reliance on the four-syllable *huatou* **A-mi-tā-bha**—there is no explaining such a thing to anyone else. In the case of a neophyte Chan practitioner who perhaps has not yet set about [Chan practice] or does not yet have the inclination to do so, this also is not something that can be explained to anyone else. It is just the ***original face*** of each of all you people! Even if you have not been able to recognize this ***original face*** and immediately fuse with the body of the buddhas, twenty-four hours a day—during speaking and silence, movement and stillness, walking, standing, sitting, and lying down—don't rely on favors from anybody else! Just have a secret *personal* realization concerning this! *This is* "setting about doing," and *this is* "having the inclination." You must immediately understand and own the matter.[92]

---

[92] *Recorded Sayings of Chan Master Tianru Weize* (天如惟則禪師語錄): 思量生死事。鐵漢也灰心。由是佛祖運大慈悲。興大哀憫。廣立言教。教你參禪學道。或教你提箇話頭。或教你念佛修淨土。令汝掃除妄想狂心。認取主人翁。識取本來面目....一箇話頭如鐵掃帚。是也掃非也掃。轉掃轉多轉多轉掃。掃不得拚命掃。忽然掃破太虛空。萬別千差一路通。諸禪德。努力今生須了卻。莫教永劫受餘殃。這箇是要緊話也。又有出家在家諸佛子念佛修淨土者。自疑念佛與參禪不同。蓋不知參禪念佛不同而同也。參禪為了生死。念佛亦為了生死。參禪者直指人心見性成佛。念佛者達惟心淨土見本性彌陀。既曰本性彌陀惟心淨土。豈有不同者哉。經云。譬如大城外有四門。隨方來者非止一路。蓋以入門雖異到城則同。參禪念佛者亦各隨其根器所宜而已。豈有異哉。然而念佛之中亦有靈驗不靈驗者。何以故。但以口念而心不念者。不靈驗也。口與心聲聲相應。心與佛步步不離者。有靈驗也....幻住和尚有云。參禪只為明生死。念佛惟圖了死生。但向一邊挨得入。兩條門路不多爭。門路不多爭。卻不許互相兼帶。參禪者單單只是參禪。念佛者單單只是念佛。若是話分兩頭。彼此都無成就。古人有箇喻子云。譬如腳踏兩邊船。這邊那邊都不著。兩邊不著尚無妨。照顧和身都陷卻。記取記取。勉之勉之....念佛者只是靠取阿彌陀佛四字話頭。別無他說。若是初心參禪者恐未有下手處。未有趣向處。然此亦無他說。只是汝諸人各各有箇本來面目。不曾認得這箇本來面目。直下與諸佛同體。你十二時中語默動靜行住坐臥莫不承他恩力。但於此密密體認。即此便是下手處。即此便是趣向處也。便須直下承當。(CBETA 2019.Q3, X70, no. 1403, pp. 766c13–767c5).

Tianru wrote a dialogue on this topic of Chan/Pure Land, *Some Questions on Pure Land* (*Jingtu huowen* 淨土或問). This text, in twenty-six sections, shows some similarities to Zhongfeng's miscellany *Night Conversations in a Mountain Hermitage*. Tianru's *Some Questions on Pure Land* begins with the arrival of a "superior person of Chan" as a guest at "Old Man Tianru's "Lying-in-the-Clouds Room" and closes with the Chan guest's doing full prostrations to Old Man Tianru and exclaiming how fortunate he has been to hear these answers. Zhongfeng's *Night Conversations in a Mountain Hermitage* opens with a hermit arriving at night at Mr. Phantasm's mountain hermitage and their doing night sitting on the sitting platform. In the morning at the cock's crow the hermit cannot quite remember what was said during the night. *Some Questions on Pure Land* argues that, given that *there are no dharmas outside mind*, if one grasps the meaning of either Chan or Pure Land, one grasps the meaning of both.[93]

Zhongfeng and the "Nanzhao" (Yunnan) Pilgrim Xuanjian (玄鑒; d.u.)

Students who came to South-of-the-Yangze to train under Zhongfeng hailed from all over: Chinese, Mongol officials, monks from Turfan in the northwest and Yunnan in the southwest, Koreans, Japanese, and so forth. The diversity of ethnic origins found among Zhongfeng's followers may be due to the immense and diversified empire created by the Mongol conquests.[94]

---

[93] *Some Questions on Pure Land* closes with the following: "Old Man Tianru said: 'Having seen the buddha [Amitābha] of the Joyful Country [i.e., Sukhāvatī], you will see all the buddhas of the ten directions. Having seen all the buddhas of the ten directions, you will see the *Innate Heavenly Real Buddha*. Having seen the *Innate Heavenly Real Buddha*, you will obtain the *Great Functioning right in front of you*. Only afterwards will you extend this to the vow of great compassion to broadly transform all sentient-beings. This is called *Pure Land Chan* and also called *Chan Pure Land*. Thus, Yongming Yanshou's *having Chan and having Pure Land* is like a tiger that has grown horns on its head. In the present lifetime you will be a teacher of humans. In future births you will become a buddha or Chan patriarch. How could you not confirm this? Strive! Strive!' Thereupon the Superior Chan Person was delighted but startled. He panicked for a long time, as if he had lost something. Old Man Tianru then again announced to him: 'If you grasp the meaning of Chan or Pure Land, then you grasp the meaning of both: there are no dharmas outside mind—don't misunderstand!' The Superior Man then bowed twice, touching his forehead to the floor: 'I am most fortunate! Today I have come to know something to be depended upon.' He then retired." [既見樂邦之佛。即見十方諸佛。既見十方諸佛。即見自性天真之佛。既見自性天真之佛。即得大用現前。然後推其悲願。廣化一切眾生。此名淨土禪。亦名禪淨土也。然則永明所謂有禪有淨土。猶如帶角虎。現世為人師。來生作佛祖。豈不驗於此哉。勉之勉之。於是禪上人者既喜且驚。蹙然久之如有所失。天如老人乃復告之曰。禪與淨土了即俱了。心外無法莫錯會好。上人乃稽顙再拜曰。吾多幸矣。今吾知所歸矣。謝而退。] (T 1972.47.302b28–c9).

[94] Shane McCausland, *The Mongol Century: Visual Cultures of Yuan China, 1271–1368* (Honolulu: University of Hawai'i Press, 2015), 9: "The Mongol government imposed a hierarchy upon Yuan society whereby Mongols occupied the top rank, followed by the so-called *semu* (or *semuren* 色目人, literally, 'people with coloured eyes') referring mainly to the Central and Inner Asian peoples whose loyalty to the

Of Zhongfeng's Chinese disciples, among the most important were the monks Tianru Weize and Qianyan Yuanzhang (千巖元長; 1284–1357);[95] the calligrapher and painter (and close friend) Zhao Mengfu (趙孟頫; 1254–1322);[96] and the layman Feng Zizhen (馮子振; d. 1348).[97] An example of a Mongol lay disciple is Layman "Sameness Hermitage" (Tong'an 同菴居士), a Mongol official whose name in Chinese transliteration is given as Ban-la-tuo-yin (般剌脫因).[98] As mentioned earlier, the compiler of the *Zhongfeng Extensive Record* was Shan-da-mi-di-li (善達密的理; d. 1337; = Zhaotang Ciji 照堂慈寂), who hailed from a famous family of Gaochang (Turfan). Zhongfeng also gave dharma talks to various Korean monks, including a Head Librarian

---

Mongols had been long proven. The residents of China proper were divided into the Han—people who had lived in the north China region under the former Jin, who were not necessarily ethnic Chinese and had come under Mongol rule during the mid-thirteenth century—and, lowest in status, 'southerners' (*nanren* or *nanman* or *manzi*), subjects of the former Southern Song dynasty whom the Mongols regarded with some suspicion as a different race from the Han."

[95] *Continued Five Lamps Meet at the Source* (*Wu deng huiyuan xulüe* 五燈會元續略; 1648 addition to the *Wu deng huiyuan* of 1252): "Chan Master Qianyan Yuanzhang of Mt. Fulong in Wuzhou: He was from Xiaoshan of Yue, family name Dong. His family for generations had been scholars. At nine he was reading various unofficial books. He could repeat from memory whatever passed before his eyes. At nineteen he had his head shaved at Lingzhi Monastery in Wulin. The Master met monks who were being given food in Chengxiang superior-prefecture, and he followed them to receive the offerings. As it happened, Zhongfeng was on the dharma seat and called out: 'What is your daily activity?' The Master said: 'Recitation of the buddha-name [*nianfo*].' Zhongfeng said: 'Where is that buddha right now?' The Master dithered. Zhongfeng scolded him in a sharp tone. The Master thereupon knelt and requested a dharma summary. Zhongfeng conferred upon him Zhaozhou's *wu* 無 *huatou* and ordered him to practice it. Thereupon, in a thatched hut on Mt. Lingyin, he soon again took up other duties. He was compliant with mundane conditions, and ten years swiftly passed. He then returned to Mt. Lingyin, and for ten years his ribs did not touch the mat [on the sitting platform]. One day he went to a look-out pavilion, and, upon hearing the cry of magpies, had an awakening. He hastily went to see Mingben and described in detail his awakening. Mingben reproved him again. The Master was exasperated and returned. In the stillness of the night suddenly a mouse was eating the cat's food and fell into his bowl, making a sound. Dazed, he had an awakening. He again went to confront Zhongfeng. Zhongfeng asked: 'Why did Zhaozhou say *wu* 無?' The Master said: 'The mouse ate the cat's food!' Zhongfeng said: 'Still not there!' The Master said: 'The food bowl is smashed!' Zhongfeng said: 'What about *after it has been smashed*?' 'Pound it to smithereens and you have tiles.' Zhongfeng then gave a smile [of approval]." [婺州伏龍山千巖元長禪師: 越之蕭山董氏子。家世宗儒。九歲即就外傳諸書。經目成誦。十九薙髮於武林靈芝寺。會行丞相府飯僧。師隨眾受供。適中峯在座。即呼曰汝日用何如。師曰念佛。峯曰佛今何在。師擬議。峯厲聲叱之。師遂跪求法要。峯授以趙州無字話令參。於是縛茅靈隱山中。未幾復以他務移動。隨順世緣倏忽十載。復還靈隱。脇不沾席者三年。因往望亭聞鵲聲有省。亟見峯具陳悟因。峯又斥之。師憤然來歸。夜將寂忽鼠食猫飯墮其器有聲。恍然開悟。復往質於峯。峯問曰趙州何故言無。師曰鼠食猫飯。峯曰未在。師曰飯器破矣。峯曰破後如何。師曰築碎方甓。峯乃微笑。] (CBETA 2019.Q3, X80, no. 1566, p. 511c6–17). His dharma talks in *Recorded Sayings of Preceptor Qianyan* (千巖和尚語錄) show that he taught *huatou* practice. See, for instance, CBETA 2019.Q3, J32, no. B273, p. 215b2–c4.

[96] Heller, *Illusory Abiding* has information on Zhao and his relationship with Zhongfeng. See her *Index*, p. 470. See also Natasha Heller, "Between Zhongfeng Mingben and Zhao Mengfu: Chan Letters in Their Manuscript Context," in *Buddhist Manuscript Cultures: Knowledge, Rituals, and Art*, ed. Stephen C. Berkwitz, Juliane Schober, and Claudia Brown (New York: Routledge, 2009), 109–123. For Zhao's calligraphy and painting oeuvre, see McCausland, *Zhao Mengfu: Calligraphy and Painting for Khubilai's China*.

[97] See Heller, *Illusory Abiding, Index*, p. 457.

[98] He is the recipient of a talk involving *huatou* practice in Selected *Dharma Talks* in *Zhongfeng Extensive Record* (Translation 2, section #6).

Ung (雄藏主) and a Head Seat Yŏn (淵首座), both of which contain standard *huatou* discourse.[99]

A small group of pilgrims came to Zhongfeng from Yunnan in the southwest. The leader of this group is referred to as "the Nanzhao monk Xuanjian" (南詔僧玄鑑), though the Nanzhao kingdom had disappeared centuries before and been replaced by the Dali state (大理國),[100] which in turn was extinguished by Khubilai khan in 1253. Sometime during the first two decades of the fourteenth century, Xuanjian and his compatriots arrived at one of Zhongfeng's hermitages. Zhongfeng's *Way-Practice Stele* states:

> The Nanzhao monk Xuanjian had a pure understanding of a contemplation system of the canonical teachings, possessing eloquence and nobility. He always said: "I have heard that Great China has the Chan school. Such is the case—is it not? I will follow these Chan people, and, if they are not on point, I shall make them change their Chan personal realization, bringing them over to my contemplation system of the canonical teachings. That is the reason I have come to this country [i.e., China]." Upon hearing a single utterance of the Master [Zhongfeng], he immediately awakened to his former error and penetrated the dharma-source. He had a plan to return [to his native Yunnan] and expound the Way, but died in the Middle Wu area [i.e., the lower reaches of the Yangzi River]. The followers of Xuanjian painted a portrait of the Master [Zhongfeng] and took it back to their country. The image emitted a divine light that lit up the heavens. Nanzhao subsequently changed from a canonical-teachings orientation to Chan and accepted the Master as the founder of their [Yunnan] Chan school.[101]

We have no dates for this Xuanjian, so we cannot pin down his arrival date. He was a scholar of the canonical teachings (possibly Tiantai teachings) who was antagonistic to Chan claims and intended to challenge Chan on its own turf. The encounter with Zhongfeng led to Xuanjian's coming over to Chan. The relationship between Xuanjian and Zhongfeng did not get off to a

---

[99] Selections from *Zhongfeng Dharma Talks* in *Zhongfeng Record B* (Translation 10, sections #2 and #4).

[100] According to Wilkinson, *Chinese History: A New Manual*, 5th ed., 382 and 840, *Nanzhao* (南詔) means *Heavenly* or *Great Kingdom* in Tibeto-Burman. The *nan* element does not mean *south*. For a history of the Nanzhao kingdom based on Chinese sources, see Charles Backus, *The Nan-chao Kingdom and T'ang China's Southwestern Frontier* (Cambridge: Cambridge University Press, 1981).

[101] *Way-Practice Stele* in *Zhongfeng Extensive Record*: 南詔僧玄鑑。素明教觀。辯博英發。每曰。吾聞大唐有禪宗。使審是耶。吾將從其學。使或未當。吾將易其宗旨。而俾趣教觀。由其國來。一聞師言。便悟昔非。洞法源底。方圖歸以唱道。而殁于中吳。鑑之徒畫師像歸國。像出神光燭天。南詔遂易教為禪。奉師為禪宗第一祖。(*Gozanban* 9, 494c–495a; CBETA 2019.Q3, B25, no. 145, p. 980a5–10).

good start: in a night conversation, according to Zhongfeng, Xuanjian laced his words with "stale and rotten kudzu" (*chenlan geteng* 陳爛葛藤) from Chan books, spouting highfaluting talk filled with Chan cliches. Zhongfeng was disappointed by this poor performance but refrained from delivering any sort of criticism, probably another example of his soft style. The Master wrote two poems for Xuanjian, which included criticism of Xuanjian, with a preface:

> Two Poems as Instruction for Lecturer Xuanjian
>
> Lecturer Xuanjian of Yunnan, you know of the purport of the Chan *separate transmission outside the teachings*. You crossed over thousands of miles to come to western Zhejiang. From the time we met to the time we parted was exactly three years. One time you sought me out in the Guest Quarters, and we had a night conversation with the lakes and mountains as a backdrop. On that occasion you raised several items of stale and rotten kudzu from Chan texts, unconsciously biting on your thumb. We were on the verge of parting, and things were rushed: I had no wish to refer to your transgression and was about to let pass this one thing. At a future date, you will pass Kuanglu [i.e., Mt. Lu in Jiangxi] while on your way to your native place of Yunnan. It would be impermissible for you to demonstrate such ugliness [i.e., a propensity for kudzu-talk]: you would be criticized by others, and the criticism would accrue to me as well. Thus, today I present you with these two poems:
>
> When the crazy mind is not yet stopped, that is *hectic Chan*.
> You journeyed across thousands and thousands of miles.
> You died before my eyes—thirty whacks of the stick.
> After cracking open your brain—a single ray of light.
> Old pages from long ago—totally useless!
> New paragraphs of today—forget them at once!
> I have heard that your land of Yunnan is beautiful.
> Sometime in the future, return also to the Chan sitting platform!
>
> ***
>
> A monk's disposition should break out from nets and cages—
> To cram your whole body into one: this won't get you anywhere!
> You crush a single dust mote as if it possessed some meaning—
> You pop open ten thousand images, but there are no tracks to be found!
> Deshan burned his [*Diamond Sutra*] commentary, but his delusions had died before that—

Later he knocked at [Longtan's] gate, but he had reached the end of the road before that.[102]

[Deshan's] defilements that had piled up over eons were suddenly blown away:

In the darkness of night at Longtan's place, the wind stirred during the fifth watch.[103]

The second of Zhongfeng's poems for Xuanjian reveals much about the Yunnanese Xuanjian's relationship to Chan and Zhongfeng. Both Deshan and Xuanjian were lecture masters, specialists in the canonical teachings, who harbored resentments against the Chan school. Both set off on missions to

---

[102] The Korean compendium *Record of the Treasure Store of the Sŏn Approach* (*Sŏnmun pojang nok* 禪門寶藏錄; preface 1293) gives a convenient summary of the story of Deshan and Longtan: "When Chan Master Deshan Xuanjian [德山宣鑑; 780–865] was a seat master [i.e., lecture master], he lived in western Sichuan and lectured on the *Diamond Sutra*. He said: 'The teachings state that, within the wisdom attained after the *vajrasamādhi*, for a thousand eons one trains in [the self-benefit] conduct of the buddhas; and for ten-thousand eons in [the benefitting-others] conversion work of the buddhas; only after that does one become a buddha. But the Chan monks of the South speak of [a quick path of] *mind is buddha*.' He became indignant, so he loaded up his commentaries as baggage and made a pilgrimage to the South to destroy these Māra people. When he first arrived in Lizhou in Hunan, at the side of the road saw an old woman selling deep-fried rice-cakes. He set down his commentaries to buy some *dim sum* [lit., *dot/perk up the mind*, i.e., a snack] to eat. The old woman said: 'The baggage you're carrying—what is it?' Deshan said: 'Commentaries on the *Diamond Sutra*.' The old woman said: 'I have a question. If you can answer it, I'll give you a deep-fried rice-cake *dim sum* free of charge. If you can't answer it, go someplace else and buy one!' Deshan said: 'Just ask!' The old woman said: 'The *Diamond* says that past mind is unascertainable; present mind is unascertainable; future mind is unascertainable. Advanced Seat—just which *sum* [*mind*] do you intend to *dim* [*dot/perk up*]?' Deshan was silent. The old woman then instructed him to go practice Chan with Longtan [lit., *Dragon Pool*]. Just as he was striding through Longtan's gate, he asked: 'For long I've been heading toward Longtan, but now that I've arrived here, I see neither *pool* nor *dragon*.' Longtan said: 'You've *arrived in person* at Longtan!' Deshan paid his respects and withdrew. He thereupon took his commentaries and, in front of the Dharma Hall, raised a torch, saying: 'No matter how much abstruse discourse is in these commentaries, they're like one fine hair placed into the great sky. No matter how many vital points are in these commentaries, they're like a single drop tossed into an immense river.' He then burned them." [德山宣鑑禪師。為座主時。在西蜀。講金剛經。因教中道。金剛喻定後得智中。千劫學佛威儀。萬劫學佛化行。然後成佛。他南方便說。即心是佛。遂發憤擔疏鈔行脚。直往南方。破這魔子輩。初到澧州。路上見一婆賣油糍。遂放下疏鈔。買作點心喫。婆云。所載者是什麼物。山云。金剛經疏鈔。婆云。我有一問。你若答得。布施油糍作點心。若答不得。別處買去。山云但問。婆云。金剛經云。過去心不可得。現在心不可得。未來心不可得。上座欲點那箇心。山無語。婆遂指令參龍潭。才跨門便問。久嚮龍潭。及乎到來。潭又不見。龍又不現。潭云。子親到龍潭。山乃設禮而退。遂取疏鈔。於法堂前。將火炬舉起云。窮諸玄辯。若一毫置於大虛。竭世樞機。似一滴投於巨壑。遂燒之。 碧巖錄] (CBETA 2019.Q3, X64, no. 1276, p. 812a22–b10). The *Sŏnmun pojang nok*'s source is the *Blue Cliff Record* (碧巖錄; T 2003.48.143b23–c20). See Jeffrey L. Broughton with Elise Yoko Watanabe, *Core Texts of the Sŏn Approach: A Compendium of Korean Sŏn (Chan) Buddhism* (New York: Oxford University Press, 2021), 123–205.

[103] Poetry section in *Zhongfeng Extensive Record*: 示玄鑑講主二首(并引): 雲南鑑講主知有教外別傳之旨。越一萬八千里。而來西淛。自相見至相別恰三載。一日尋我客中。夜話湖山間。因舉宗門下數段陳爛葛藤。不覺咬斷拇指。臨別忽忽不欲。徵其罪犯。且放過一著。異日抵匡廬。而之故鄉。却不得出露醜惡。被人叫罵。而累及我也。就以二偈贈之。

狂心未歇為禪忙　萬八千程過遠方　喪盡目前三頓棒　揮開腦後一尋光
陳年故紙渾無用　今日新條亦頓忘　見說雲南田地好　異時歸去坐繩牀
衲僧用處絕羅籠　拶著渾身是脫空　輥破一塵如有旨　撥開萬象竟無蹤
德山夢寐情牛死　良遂敲門路已窮　積劫塵勞忽吹盡　黑龍潭下五更風

(*Gozanban* 9, 469b–c; CBETA 2019.Q3, B25, no. 145, p. 962a5–17).

challenge Chan people and perhaps convert them to the teachings approach. And, finally, both came to an understanding of the error of their ways and achieved awakening under the tutelage of a Chan master, Longtan in the case of Deshan and Zhongfeng in the case of Xuanjian.

The *Zhongfeng Conduct Record* repeats the story that, due to the efforts of the Yunnan group of monks after their return home (without Xuanjian as he had died on the way), Zhongfeng was designated "the founder of a [Yunnan] Chan school":

> As external protectors of Master Zhongfeng, those who arrived from such distant places as the Western Region, the northern [Mongol] court, and the eastern barbarians [i.e., Koreans and Japanese] came on the heels of one another to visit him. The Nanzhao monk [Xuanjian] possessed a pure understanding of the teachings and discernment. His coming eastward was truly for the sake of inquiring about the dharma. Xuanjian led off the group, and, beneath the Master's words, he had an awakening. He was succeeded by five monks, including Pufu. They had a portrait of Master Zhongfeng painted and took it back to [Yunnan in] the South. When they arrived at the city of Zhongqing, the four classes of believers there welcomed the image as it entered the city. An unusual light from the image lit up the heavens, and ten thousand eyes looked up in reverence at the portrait. They were zealous in their confidence in the dharma. Due to this, a Chan school was established [in Yunnan], and Master Zhongfeng was accepted as the founder of a [Yunnan] Chan school.[104]

Zhongfeng and Japanese Zen

Zhongfeng's contact with Japanese Zen pilgrims from around 1306 until his death in 1323 was very extensive—a veritable stream of Japanese visitors found their way to the master's gate. The *Great Dictionary of Zen Studies* lists sixteen dharma successors for Zhongfeng, including Qianyan Yuanzhang, Tianru Weize, and Nanzhao Xuanjian.[105] Seven of these sixteen are marked as Japanese; four of these seven have dharma talks recorded in *Zhongfeng Dharma Talks* of *Zhongfeng Record B*.[106] These seven Japanese monks who

---

[104] *Conduct Record* in *Zhongfeng Extensive Record*: 為師外護。遠至西域北庭東夷南詔。接踵來見。南詔沙門素閑教觀。東來問法寔。自玄鑑始。鑑嘗於師言下有省。繼而普福等五比丘。畫師像南歸。至中慶城。四眾迎像入城。異光從像燭天。萬目仰觀。翹勤傾信。由是興立禪宗。奉師為南詔第一祖。(*Gozanban* 9, 489a–b; CBETA 2019.Q3, B25, no. 145, pp. 975b18–976a3).

[105] Komazawa daigaku nai Zengaku daijiten hensanjo, *Shinpan Zengaku daijiten* (Tokyo: Taishūkan shoten, 1985), 17 (lineage charts).

[106] The seven are as follows:

are considered to be Zhongfeng's dharma successors crossed over to Yuan China between the years of 1306 and 1318. We can speculate that there was in Japanese circles an informal word-of-mouth network concerning pilgrimage information about Chan teachers and sites in Yuan China.

Out of these seven, Gōkai Honjō (業海本淨; ?–1352) is the purest example of utter fidelity to Zhongfeng's Chan style. In 1318, together with comrades, he crossed to Yuan China and trained under Zhongfeng at Mt. Tianmu, eventually inheriting Zhongfeng's dharma. After Honjō returned to Japan, he revered the mountains and waters in the Zhongfeng manner, going on pilgrimage to various natural locations and never "emerging into the world" to teach. Finally, in 1348, he came into possession of land in Kai (present-day Yamanashi prefecture) and opened a Tenmokusan Seiun Monastery ("Mt. Tianmu Perching-in-the-Clouds Monastery"; 天目山棲雲寺), where he propagated *Dwelling-in-the-Phantasmal* Zen.[107] Even the waterfall, cliffs, and well of this mountain in Kai resembled the topographical layout of Zhongfeng's Mt. Tianmu in China.

Other Japanese Zen pilgrims who visited Zhongfeng (or his successor Qianyan Yuanzhang) for instruction include Kohō Kakumyō; Jakushitsu Genkō; Kaō Sōnen; Betsugen Enshi; and Daisetsu Sono.[108] (Kaō Sōnen may

1. Kosen Ingen (古先印元; 1295–1374): crossed to Yuan China in 1318; obtained the dharma of Zhongfeng and later went on pilgrimage visiting many teachers.
2. Enkei Soyū (遠溪祖雄; 1286–1344): crossed to Yuan China in 1306; trained seven years with Zhongfeng and obtained sanction from him; in 1316 he returned home.
3. Muin Genkai (無隱元晦; ?–1358): during the Enkei era (1308–1311) crossed to Yuan China with his comrade Fukuan Sōki; trained with Zhongfeng and received his sanction; in 1326 returned home in the company of Myōsō Saitetsu and Kosen Ingen (has two dharma talks in *Zhongfeng Dharma Talks* of *Zhongfeng Record B: Gozanban* 9, 531a–532a).
4. Fukuan Sōki (復庵宗己; 1280–1358): two theories: in 1310 with Muin Genkai or in 1318 together with Kosen Ingen and Myōsō Saitetsu crossed to Yuan China; trained with Zhongfeng and received his sanction; Zhongfeng died in 1323, and Sōki stayed at Zhongfeng's stupa for three years; in 1326/1321/1325 returned home (has a dharma talk in *Zhongfeng Dharma Talks* of *Zhongfeng Record B: Gozanban* 9, 515a–b).
5. Gōkai Honjō (業海本淨; ?–1352): (has a dharma talk at *Zhongfeng Dharma Talks* of *Zhongfeng Record B, Gozanban* 9, 504b–c).
6. Myōsō Saitetsu (明叟齊哲; ?–1347): in 1318 crossed to Yuan China in the company of Gōkai Honjō and Kosen Ingen; trained under Zhongfeng and received his dharma; in 1326 with Muin Genkai and Kosen Ingen returned home (has a dharma talk in *Zhongfeng Dharma Talks* of *Zhongfeng Record B: Gozanban* 9, 517b–c).
7. Kansai Ginan (關西義南; d.u.): crossed to Yuan China and trained under Zhongfeng; in 1350 returned home.

[107] On the Genjū ha, see Harada Kōdō, "Chūsei ni okeru genjū ha no keisei to igi," *Komazawa daigaku bukkyō gakubu kenkyū kiyō* 53 (1995): 21–36. On Sōtō school Zen monks who had relations with the Genjū ha, see pp. 28–29.

[108] Here are brief descriptions:

1. Kohō Kakumyō (孤峰覺明; 1271–1361): in 1311 crossed to Yuan China and visited Zhongfeng; after visiting numerous other teachers, returned home.
2. Jakushitsu Genkō (寂室元光; 1290–1367): in 1320 together with Kaō Sōnen and others crossed to Yuan China; visited Zhongfeng at Mt. Tianmu and subsequently visited numerous other teachers; returned home in 1326.

well be the illustrious ink painter "Kaō," known for such works as the *Preceptor Clam Man* in the Tokyo National Museum.[109]) Let us look closely at Jakushitsu Genkō (寂室元光; 1290–1367), generally regarded as one the greatest of the medieval Zen poets.[110] In 1320 he became one of the last Japanese pilgrims to study with Zhongfeng, who died in 1323; Jakushitsu could not have studied with him for very long.[111] By contrast, Enkei Soyū (遠溪祖雄) had left for Yuan China in 1306, fourteen years before Jakushitsu left, studied with Zhongfeng for seven years, and remained in China for three more years, returning home in 1316, four years before Jakushitsu even left for China. Five other Japanese monks who are said to have received Zhongfeng's seal reached Zhongfeng between about 1308 and 1318, anywhere from a decade or so to two years before Jakushitsu arrived at Zhongfeng's place. The upshot is, when Jakushitsu arrived at West Tianmu Mountain, Zhongfeng was nearing the end of his life.

There is no mention of Jakushitsu in either the *Zhongfeng Extensive Record* or the *Zhongfeng Record B*. There is, however, a relevant passage in a dharma talk in *Recorded Sayings of Preceptor Eigen Jakushitsu* (*Eigen Jakushitsu oshō goroku* 永源寂室和尚語録):

Instructions to Zen Person Chin: In the winter of Yanyou 7/1320 of the Great Yuan dynasty I, together with Kaō Sōnen [?–1345] and Don'an Shun [?–1357], climbed Mt.

---

3. Kaō Sōnen (可翁宗然;?–1345): in 1320 together with Jakushitsu Genkō and others crossed to Yuan China; visited Zhongfeng and many other teachers; returned home in 1326 (has two dharma talks in *Zhongfeng Dharma Talks* of *Zhongfeng Record B*: *Gozanban* 9, 509b–510d).
4. Betsugen Enshi (別源圓旨; 1294–1364): was of the Sōtō lineage; in 1320 crossed to Yuan China and visited Zhongfeng and other teachers; in 1330 returned home.
5. Daisetsu Sonō (大拙祖能; 1313–1377): in spring 1344 together with comrades crossed to Yuan China; after visiting several teachers, trained with Zhongfeng's disciple Qianyan Yuanzhang and achieved awakening under him; after Qianyan died, together with comrades returned home.

[109] This hanging scroll, ink on paper (86.8 × 34.5), is an Important Cultural Property in the Tokyo National Museum (A-10931). See emuseum.nich.go.jp/detail?langId = ja&webView=&content_base_id = 100309&content_part_id = 0&content_pict_id = 0.
It has two seals at the lower right: the upper one is a red relief engraving of "Kaō" (可翁), and the smaller seal below it bears the characters "Ninga" (仁賀). There are two theories: (1) the painter is one Kaō Ninga, the *ga* element indicating affiliation with the Takuma (詫磨派) school of Buddhist painting; and (2) it is by the Zen monk Kaō Sōnen. Other ink paintings, such as *Bamboo and Sparrows* and *Plum and Sparrows*, have the same two seals. See Gregory Levine and Yukio Lippit, *Awakenings: Zen Figure Painting in Medieval Japan* (New York: Japan Society, 2007), 116–119. "Kaō" is sometimes associated in art history with the ink painter Mokuan Reien (黙庵靈淵), who crossed to Yuan China sometime between 1326 and 1329 and studied both Chan and ink painting. Mokuan is sometimes dubbed the second coming of the Chinese monk-painter Muqi Fachang (牧谿法常; Jap. Mokkei Hōjō), the most famous Chinese painter in Japan during the Muromachi period.
[110] Iriya Yoshitaka, *Nihon no Zen goroku* 10: *Jakushitsu* (Tokyo: Kōdansha, 1979), 290 gives an overall evaluation of Jakushitsu's poetry: "Such splendidly crystalline poetry is unmatched in other Zen monks of the time" [これほど見事に結晶した詩偈は、当時の禅僧には他に類がない。]. For a treatment of some of Jakushitsu's poems, see Harada Ryūmon, *Jakushitsu Genkō* (Tokyo: Shunjūsha, 1979). For a biography, see Kodama Osamu, *Jakushitsu Genkō no shōgai* (Kyoto: Shibunkaku shuppan, 2014).
[111] Noguchi Yoshitaka, "Jakushitsu Genkō to Chūhō Myōhon," *Zen bunka* 242 (2016), 30.

Tianmu to visit the Old Man Dwelling-in-the-Phantasmal. At the time snow filled the thousands of cliffs, and [Zhongfeng's] solitary [Dwelling-in-the-Phantasmal] Hermitage was completely silent. We three stood in a row in front of Zhengfeng and bowed. Each of us thought that we were having a personal meeting with the founder Bodhidharma at Shaoshi Peak [like Huike's interview in the snow at Bodhidharma's cave]. We inquired about the essential truth of Zen, but much to our regret, because of our ill-advised ignorance, we could not understand the fine points of the teaching he handed down.[112]

We might infer from the last line that Jakushitsu and the other Japanese Zen monks in his party were not sufficiently proficient in spoken Chinese: when Zhongfeng spoke, it was difficult for them to follow. This must have been a major hurdle for all Japanese monks on pilgrimage to Chan sites in China. The renowned poet Chūgan Engetsu (中巖圓月; 1300–1375), who was in Yuan China from 1325 to 1332, on his return to Japan, said in a letter to a fellow Japanese monk:

I was in Jiangnan [i.e., the area south of the Yangze River] . . . . There were a lot of Japanese monks wandering among the rivers and lakes of Wuyue [i.e., Jiangsu and Zhejiang]. However, because the customs and language were so different [from Japan], none were able to practice as they thought they would, and they returned home without bringing to fruition their great ambition to seek the dharma.[113]

The above account of the initial snowy encounter with Zhongfeng is from Jakushitsu himself in one of his dharma talks, but we have another more detailed version of these events from a slightly later source compiled by a successor of Jakushitsu at Eigen-ji, the *Jakushitsu Chronological Record*:

Master Jakushitsu heard of Preceptor Tianmu Zhongfeng's reputation for inciting people to the Way in both China and foreign countries. He got on a boat

---

[112] 示珍禪者：太元延祐庚申冬。與然可翁俊鈍菴。同登天目山。謁于幻住老人。時雪滿千岩一菴闃爾。吾儕三輩。前立列拜。各做親見鼻祖於少室峯前之想。因扣以宗門要訣。第恨疎鈍之跡。弗克領會委曲垂示之旨。(*Eigen Jakushitsu oshō goroku*, vol. 2, 430–431; T 2564.81.133b27–c3).

[113] Quoted in Iriya Yoshitaka, *Gozan bungaku shū*, Shin Nihon koten bungaku taikei 48 (Tokyo: Iwanami shoten, 2016), 334–335. Iriya remarks concerning both the Jakushitsu comment above about not comprehending Zhongfeng's words and Chūgan's generalization about Japanese Zen monks in China: "Mention of such candid confessions is extremely rare—these are really important examples. However, the great majority of Japanese monks with experience studying in China all shut their mouths and never spoke of internal [personal] matters." [このような率直な告白に接することは、非常に珍しい。まことに貴重な例である。しかし他の大部分の留学経験僧は、みな口をつぐんで内実を語らない。].

and went south [to Yuan China]. When he ascended Mt. Tianmu, the sun had reached the point of late afternoon. Snow was piled up in the courtyard. He, together with his compatriots Kaō Sōnen and Don'an Shun, were lined up before Zhongfeng. Zhongfeng only wrote on the forearm of Master Jakushitsu four characters: "Come tomorrow [and I will teach you]." Master Jakushitsu hastily went straight to the face-washing shelf and cupped water in his hands to wash off [the writing].[114]

By washing the words off his arm, Jakushitsu expressed his earnestness by implying *please give me instruction right now*! *Conduct Account of Preceptor Jakushitsu* adds a few more interesting details:

In the winter of Yanyou 7/1320, together with his compatriots Kaō Sōnen and Don'an Shun, Master Jakushitsu ascended Mt. Tianmu to visit the Old Man of Dwelling-in-the Phantasmal Hermitage. When the Old Man saw that his [i.e., Jakushitsu's] inquiries were scrupulous, he patted Jakushitsu on the head three times [as the Buddha did in welcoming disciples] and wrote out for him a dharma talk, bestowing the name Jakushitsu [*Silent Room*].[115]

The formal details here—the pat on the head three times, the dharma talk, and the bestowal of the name Jakushitsu—appear to reinforce the assertion that Jakushitsu is a formal heir of Zhongfeng.

Jakushitsu studied under several other Chinese masters before returning to Japan in 1326. Once back in Japan, he remained faithful to Zhongfeng's reclusive style of Zen, residing in complete obscurity in mountain hermitages for many years. At the thirtieth anniversary of Zhongfeng's death in 1353, Jakushitsu composed an encomium for his teacher Zhongfeng, which is included in the "Praises of the Buddhas and Chan Patriarchs" section of the *Recorded Sayings of Preceptor Eigen Jakushitsu*:

Preceptor Zhongfeng: If we were to discuss the worldview of this old preceptor, it is as follows: "Even the mountains and rivers of the great earth are phantasmal.

---

[114] *Eigen kaisan Enō zenji kinen roku* (永源開山円応禅師記年録) for the year 1320 when Jakushitsu was thirty-one: 師聞天目中峰和尚道振華夷。附船便南邁。登天目山。日方逮晡。積雪満庭。同行可翁俊鈍庵。與俱侍立不退。 峰於師臂端。獨書明日來也四字。師徑趨后架。掬水洗之。(*Eigen Jakushitsu oshō goroku, bekkan*, 14). The compiler Wafu Sainin (和甫斉忍; d.u.) became abbot of Eigen-ji in 1428. The line "come tomorrow and I will teach you" (明日來向汝道) appears several times in the *Jingde chuandeng lu* (景徳傳燈錄; T 2076.51.325b8–9 and 421a26).

[115] *Jakushitsu oshō gyōjō* (寂室和尚行状): 延祐庚申冬。與然可翁俊鈍庵。同登天目山。謁于幻住老人。幻住老人見其問話諦。當把手摩頂者三。仍寫法語一篇。賜號寂室。(*Eigen Jakushitsu oshō goroku, bekkan*, 92). The compiler was Jakushitsu's successor Miten Eishaku (弥天永釈; 1337–1406).

Even form/emptiness and light/darkness are phantasmal. Even the buddhas of the three times are phantasmal. Even the Chan patriarchal masters through the generations are phantasmal. Down to: Awakening, nirvana, *tathatā*, *tattva*, and so forth—every one of them is a phantasm." Thirty years after he covered his light, the thing that remains [i.e., a portrait] is not a phantasm. [In the painting] he holds a fly whisk made of deer-tail and sits on a curved chair: swirling flames glittering and gleaming, imposing and lofty! His grandeur vies with West Tianmu Mountain itself in eminent coldness: he compels all the people of the great earth to look up in reverence!

A body filled with the adornments of ten thousand merits.
With a tongue that covers space in the ten directions, how he speaks of things!
At present I cannot avoid trying to force [his portrait] to speak.
Right on down from the Buddha himself, he is one of a kind![116]

Jakushitsu's true legacy from his teacher Zhongfeng was a profound preference for a secluded life in the mountains, far away from the great monasteries and capital cities, as we see in the following set of poems that he composed for a fellow recluse by the name of Superior Person Kō:

In the winter of Kan'ō 1/1350 I climbed Kanayama in Bizen [i.e., the southeastern portion of Okayama prefecture] to visit the secluded hermitage of Superior Person Kō. I took up my writing brush and composed verses upon the four postures in the mountains, posting them on a wall.

Walking in the Mountains:
Mists far and near—lost my way.
At the side of a mountain stream, I stumble and injure a toe.
The sound of the flowing water is in harmony with the sound of my bearing the pain.

Standing in the Mountains:
Straw clothes and a diet of goosefoot, I pass my mornings and evenings.
All day long a thousand peaks enter my two eyes.
Can't remember how many times spring green has turned to autumn yellow.

---

[116] 中峯和尚。若論這老和尚面前。則山河大地也是幻。色空明暗也是幻。三世諸佛也是幻。歷代祖師 也是幻。乃至菩提涅槃眞如實相等。一一靡有非幻者也。掩光之後三十年。留得個非幻底。握塵尾拂。踞曲彔床。煒煒煌煌堂堂巍巍。勢與西天目山爭其高寒。逼使盡大地人瞻仰肅恭而已矣。
萬德莊嚴圓滿身 虛空爲舌若何申 我今不免強道取 自佛已來唯一人
(*Eigen Jakushitsu oshō goroku*, vol. 1, 388–391; T 2564.81.113b8–17).

Sitting in the Mountains:
Sitting cross-legged on a boulder sitting-platform—a single figure.
Neither enjoying stillness nor despising clamor.
A solitary, floating cloud—we're in sync with each other.
Lying Down in the Mountains:
A high pillow and ivied window—relaxing in idleness.
The wind's blowing breaks off an old pine branch,
Cannot help but startle me, rousing from deep sleep.[117]

The quiet of the mountains in Okayama that Jakushitsu describes in these four short poems has much in common with the atmosphere of Zhongfeng's *Ten Poems on Living in the Mountains* (composed in 1312 when he was living on Mt. Liu'an in Anhui). The first and sixth of Zhongfeng's mountain-living poems run:

In my heart what desire and what hatred!
Before others ashamed of my many shortcomings.
Circling about reclaiming pieces of clouds—mending for a tattered robe.
Climbing up perilous stone paths—wooden walkway on the cliff made of withered vines.
Thousand peaks surround the perimeter—a narrow hut.
Ten thousand sense-objects empty and idle—a single monk.
Beyond this *ready-made gong'an* [i.e., beyond this mountain scene],
There is no *buddhadharma* to keep on transmitting.

***

A single person dwelling in the empty mountains is appropriate,
Forgetting both clamor/stillness and idleness/busyness.
I have only heard that the bright sun melts the golden three-legged cauldron [used to prepare the elixir of immortality],
But have never seen the blue-green moss burn up a boulder sitting-platform.

---

[117] 庚寅冬登備前金山訪功上人幽居。援毫賦山中四威儀書壁上云。
山中行
煙霞遠近失歸程 溪邊跌脚指頭破 流水聲和忍痛聲
山中住。
草衣藜食閙[=閑]朝暮 千峯盡日入雙眸 不記青黃能幾度
山中坐。
石榻跏趺惟一箇 全非樂寂兼嫌喧 獨有閑雲相許可
山中臥。
高枕羅窓縱怠惰 天風吹折老松枝 叵耐驚吾濃睡破
(*Eigen Jakushitsu oshō goroku*, vol. 1, 49–52; T 2564.81.102b15–24).

Stamping its seal on the sky—the moon over a barrier of mountains.
Washing clean heaven and earth—the frost of an entire forest.
I have no need of guests' coming—incessant superfluous talk.
This matter is perfectly clear, cutting off all concealments.[118]

In the final phase of his career, Jakushitsu reluctantly accepted the abbotship of a monastery erected specifically for him, the Eigen-ji in Ōmi (Shiga prefecture). Even this parallels the pattern of Zhongfeng, who in the end returned to take over Gaofeng's Mt. Tianmu monastery. Both Japanese and English scholarly works on Jakushitsu focus overwhelmingly on his poetry (he was, after all, one of the best of the medieval poets in Chinese), with scant attention given to his Zen teachings, found in the Zen-sermon portions of his recorded sayings. Jakushitsu absorbed not only Zhongfeng's aversion to taking up abbacies at major monasteries and his poetry of reclusion; Jakushitsu also absorbed Zhongfeng's emphasis on rigorous *huatou* practice, including even Zhongfeng's signature designation for the *huatou*: "the *watō* that has no meaning or taste" (*mu gimi watō* 無義味話頭)." Here is a Jakushitsu dharma talk:

If you want to transcend samsara and arrive directly at the rank of the buddhas and Zen patriarchs, just twenty-four hours a day in all four postures, never letting go for an instant, with no break at all: investigate the *watō that has no meaning or taste*! Now, what is this *watō that has no meaning or taste*? It is: "What was **my original face** before my father and mother conceived me?" Just raise the **ball of great uncertainty** concerning this *watō*. Forget eating and sleeping; cast off heat and cold. Stretching far into the distance and tightly meshed—continuously keep on practicing [this *watō*]. It is just like chewing on an iron bar or swallowing a prickly burr. There is no way to get your craw on it! If suddenly you chew it up and swallow, you are said to be a person of "great penetration and great awakening." Just go on engaging in this sort of practice. Even if in this lifetime you are not able to achieve penetration, this sort of resolve is solid and will entail no retrogression. When you arrive at the end of your life, you will not lose human form. You will not fall into a bad rebirth path. When you are reborn, it will be sure to be "one

---

[118] 山居十首(六安山中作)

胷中何愛復何憎 自愧人前百不能 旋拾斷雲脩破衲 高攀危磴閣枯藤
千峯環繞半間屋 萬境空閒一箇僧 除此現成公案外 且無佛法繼傳燈
一住空山便厭當 兩忘喧寂與閒忙 但聞白日銷金鼎 不見青苔爛石床
印破虛空千嶂月 洗清天地一林霜 客來不用頻饒舌 此事明明絕覆藏
(*Gozanban* 9, 472b and d; CBETA 2019.Q3, B25, no. 145, p. 964a4–b14).

Introduction 51

hearing and a thousand awakenings." That is the efficacy of *prajñā*. Make effort! Make effort![119]

In another of his dharma talks, Jakushitsu laid down a program of *Ten Necessities for Zen*,[120] which in places echoes his teacher Zhongfeng's words (given in parentheses):

> *First Necessity*: Samsara is the *great matter*, and impermanence is swift. You must not, even for a split-second, forget contemplation of this! (Zhongfeng: "Samsara is the *great matter*, and impermanence is swift: this is the correct contemplation of the student."[121])
>
> *Second Necessity*: Walking, standing, sitting, and lying down, restrain your body-mind and never violate the rules and ceremonies.
>
> *Third Necessity*: Do not grasp an extremist version of emptiness nor boast of your zeal; do not fall into the wrong views of the two vehicles [i.e., hearer and independent buddha].
>
> *Fourth Necessity*: Make your mind collected and be heedful in your words: day and night do quiet cross-legged sitting and stay far away from useless false thought.
>
> *Fifth Necessity*: Do not mistakenly recognize *numinous luminosity* [as your own *Mr. Man-in-charge*] and then proceed [contentedly] to sit inside the ghost cave of Black Mountain. (Zhongfeng: "Via mind [i.e., the storehouse consciousness], afflicted mind, the six sense consciousnesses, and linguistic conventions, you falsely act in concert with the floating light-rays and phantasmal shadows of *numinous luminosity* right in front of you—mistakenly recognizing [this *numinous luminosity*] as your own *Mr. Man-in-charge*!"[122] Also, Zhongfeng: "There is a class of people who

---

[119] Found in a dharma talk to Great Worthy Zenkyō (善教大德) in Jakushitsu's Zen record: 示善教大德: 若欲超脫生死直至佛祖之位。只十二時 中四威儀內不棄寸陰。無有間斷。參究無義味話頭。且喚甚麼爲無義味話頭。父母未生以前。那個是我本來面目。只將此話頭起大疑團。忘寢食廢寒暑。綿綿密密參去參來。恰如咬鐵橛子吞栗棘蓬相似。直得無下觜處。忽然蹉口咬得破吞得下。謂之大徹大悟底之人。唯如此修行去。直饒今生打未徹。此志堅固永不退失。逗到臨命終時。人身不失。惡趣不墮。重出頭來。必是一聞千悟。豈非般若靈驗何哉。記取記取勉旃。(*Eigen Jakushitsu oshō goroku*, vol. 2, 374–377; T 2564.81.130c20–131a2).

[120] Found in a dharma talk to Zen Person Shingen (真源禪者) in Jakushitsu's Zen record: 一者要須生死事大無常迅速。須臾不忘念。/二者要須行住坐臥檢束身心。不毀犯律儀。/三者要須不執偏空不誇精進。勿墮二乘見。/四者要須攝意慎語。日夜靜坐遠離閒妄想。/五者要須莫認昭昭靈靈。坐黑山下鬼窟裏。/六者要須廢寢忘餐。壁立萬仞堅起鐵脊梁。/七者要須看父母未生前。那箇我本來面目。/八者要須雖參話頭工夫綿密。勿急求悟明。/九者要須寧不發明。經百千劫不生第二念。/十者要須大心不退。大法洞明紹續佛慧命。(*Eigen Jakushitsu oshō goroku*, vol. 2, 321–322; T 2564.81.128b27–c14).

[121] *Dharma Talks* in *Zhongfeng Extensive Record*: 生死事大無常迅速。乃學者之正思惟也。(*Gozanban* 9, 163b; CBETA 2019.Q3, B25, no. 145, p. 735b8–9).

[122] *Night Conversations in a Mountain Hermitage* in *Zhongfeng Extensive Record*: 以心意識。向相似語言上。妄自和會箇目前昭昭靈靈底浮光幻影。認爲主人公。(*Gozanban* 9, 245b; CBETA 2019.Q3, B25, no. 145, p. 796a5–7; Translation 3, section #7).

falsely recognize the shadows of the six sense-objects as their very own *Mr. Man-in-charge*."[123])

Sixth Necessity: Forego excessive sleeping and eating: make your iron spine erect before a towering ten-thousand-foot cliff. (Zhongfeng: "Make your iron spine erect and wield the long sword that touches heaven."[124])

Seventh Necessity: Keep your eye on the *watō* [*huatou*]: *before my father and mother conceived me, what was my original face*? (Zhongfeng sometimes recommended the common *huatou what was my original face* to Japanese students.[125])

Note that in two other dharma talks in Jakushitsu's Zen record, we find the following variations on the *original face watō*:

JAKUSHITSU: "You must, twenty-four hours a day, continuously and without interruption, investigate the *watō*: *after I'm dead and cremated, what will be my original nature*? This is overlooking the banks of birth-and-death: the *true state* wherein you gain great energy!"[126] (Zhongfeng: "You should give a fierce stab to this single *huatou* taught by Preceptor Tieshan: *after I'm dead and cremated, what will be my original nature*?[127])

JAKUSHITSU: "If you seek to see clearly your *original face* and the *scenery of your original ground*, just, twenty-four hours a day without a moment's interruption, keep on investigating the *watō*: *when you die, at what locus will you calm your mind down*?"[128] (Zhongfeng: "Just take the *huatou when you die, at what locus will you calm your mind down* and place it on your desk of official documents: silently probe!"[129])

---

[123] *Night Conversations in a Mountain Hermitage* in *Zhongfeng Extensive Record*: 有一等妄認六塵緣影爲自己主人公。(*Gozanban* 9, 253b; CBETA 2019.Q3, B25, no. 145, p. 802b3-4; Translation 3, section #13).

[124] *Commentary Opening Up the Meanings of the* Confidence-in-Mind Inscription (*Xinxin ming piyi jie* 信心銘闢義解) in *Zhongfeng Extensive Record*: 竪起生鐵脊梁。横按倚天長劒。(*Gozanban* 9, 288a; CBETA 2019.Q3, B25, no. 145, p. 828b12).

[125] See, for instance, Translation 10, sections #14 and #15.

[126] Dharma talk to Great Teacher Ki'un (希運大師) in Jakushitsu's Zen record: 須將死了燒了那個是我性之話。二六時中綿綿密密無有間斷參究去也。是乃臨生死岸頭。大得力底消息。(*Eigen Jakushitsu oshō goroku*, vol. 2, 334-335; T 2564.81.128c17-19).

[127] *Dharma Talks* in *Zhongfeng Extensive Record*: 宜將鐵山和尚所示。死了燒了那箇是我性遮一句。猛與一拶。(*Gozanban* 9, 165d; CBETA 2019.Q3, B25, no. 145, p. 737b5-7). Tieshan was a successor of Xueyan Zuqin and thus of the same line as Zhongfeng.

[128] Dharma talk to Great Teacher Myō (明大師) in Jakushitsu's Zen record: 若要明見本來面目本地風光。只將四大分散時。向甚麽處安身立命話。二六時中無斯須少間。究來究去。(*Eigen Jakushitsu oshō goroku*, vol. 2, 335; T 2564.81.128c22-25).

[129] *Dharma Talks* in *Zhongfeng Extensive Record*: 但將四大分散時。向何處安身立命話。置之案牘几席之上。默默參究。(*Gozanban* 9, 196a; CBETA 2019.Q3, B25, no. 145, p. 760a5-6). This dharma talk is for a lay official, Layman Zhuyi (主一居士).

Eighth Necessity: Though your practice-work on your *watō* may be scrupulous, do not *in haste seek awakening*. (Zhongfeng: "You must never through all eternity produce a single thought that seeks for a mind of *quick awakening*. If such a mind should arise, it is false thought—never yoked to the Way."[130])

Ninth Necessity: Even if you go through hundreds of thousands of eons without attaining enlightenment, do not engender any "backup" thought [i.e., any thought apart from the *huatou*]. (Zhongfeng: "To do practice-work all you need is that your confidence be sufficient. If, from the very first thought, your confidence is sufficient for this, then in this way for as long as thirty years you won't produce any 'backup' thought."[131])

Tenth Necessity: Ensure that your mind of the *great matter* never retrogresses, that the great dharma is bright, and that you continue the buddha wisdom life. (Zhongfeng: "In studying the Way you must merely make sure the great mind that painfully contemplates the impermanence of samsara does not retrogress. If this mind does not retrogress, there will be no one who fails to clarify the *great matter*. This is non-retrogression for the sake of the *great matter*. This is the number-one *upāya*. There is no *upāya* that surpasses this."[132])

When we add to this list Jakushitsu's strong preference for wandering and mountain living, the result is a quite direct inheritance of Zhongfeng's Chan style.

Jakushitsu's friend the Zen monk Bassui Tokushō (拔隊得勝; 1327–1387) indirectly inherited some of Zhongfeng's Chan style, although Bassui never went to China and so never had personal contact with Zhongfeng.[133] Bassui's

---

[130] *Zhongfeng Dharma Talks* (first portion of *Zhongfeng Record B*): 永不要起一念要求速悟之心。此心才生即是妄念。永不與道相應也。(*Gozanban* 9, 520c; CBETA 2019.Q3, X70, no. 1402, p. 736a7–8; Translation 10, section #10).

[131] *Zhongfeng Dharma Talks* (first portion of *Zhongfeng Record B*): 做工夫只要信得及。從最初一念信教及之。如是三十年永不生第二念。(*Gozanban* 9, 518a; CBETA 2019.Q3, X70, no. 1402, p. 734c12–13).

[132] *Zhongfeng Talks* (second portion of *Zhongfeng Record B*): 學道惟要痛念生死無常之大心不退。此心若不退。更無不明大事之人。此箇為死生大事不退。即此便是第一方便。更無方便過於此者。(*Gozanban* 9, 540a; CBETA 2019.Q3, X70, no. 1402, p. 715b23–c1).

[133] For a modern Japanese translation of Bassui's *Mixture of Mud and Water Collection of Enzan* (*Enzan wadei gassui shū* 塩山和泥合水集; published 1386), see Furuta Shōkin, *Nihon no Zen goroku* 11: *Bassui* (Tokyo: Kodansha, 1979), 149–412. (The term *mixture of mud and water* refers to compassionate *upāyas*.) The *Mixture of Mud and Water Collection of Enzan* is contained in Yamada Kōdō, ed., *Zenmon hōgo shū*, vol. 1 (1921; repr., Tokyo: Shigensha, 1996), 75–170. Arthur Braverman, trans., *Mud & Water: The Collected Teachings of Zen Master Bassui* (Somerville, MA: Wisdom Publications, 2002), 25–179 contains a complete English rendering. Practice of the *watō* (*huatou*) is an important element in this Bassui work.

Zhongfeng inheritance came via his teacher Kohō Kakumyō (孤峰覺明; 1271–1361), who in 1311 crossed to Yuan China and visited Zhongfeng, and later through contact with Jakushitsu at Eigen-ji. Bassui spent seventeen years in wandering and staying in small hermitages, never more than three years in any one place. As a translator of Bassui has remarked, "Many of the Rinzai teachers Bassui visited, including Kohō, had some connection with the Chinese Zen master Chūhō Myōhon [Zhongfeng Mingben] who lived at a hermitage, the Genjūan [Dwelling-in-the-Phantasmal Hermitage], in Tenmokuzan [Mt. Tianmu]."[134]

Zhongfeng's influence on medieval Japanese Zen was not limited to reclusive and provincial monks like Gōkai Honjō, Jakushitsu, and Bassui; some of the most illustrious monks of the elite metropolitan Gozan (Five-Mountains) Zen establishments in Kyoto and Kamakura, *ones that never went to Yuan China*, looked to Zhongfeng as a model.[135] For example, Musō Soseki (1275–1351) in the early phase of his career admired Zhongfeng; Gidō Shūshin (1325–1388) gave lectures on the *Zhongfeng Extensive Record* to monks and to the shogun; and Kiyō Hōshū (1361–1424) compiled *Non-Duality's Extracts from the Zhongfeng Extensive Record* (*Chūhō kōroku funi shō* 中峰廣錄不二鈔[136]). This single Chinese Chan teacher Zhongfeng Mingben had an astounding influence across a wide spectrum of Japanese Zen, perhaps something like the influence Mengshan Deyi (蒙山德異; 1231–?) had on Korean Sŏn—Mengshan in his lifetime became a magnet for Korean Sŏn pilgrims, and later his sayings circulated widely in Korea.[137]

---

[134] Braverman, *Mud & Water*, 11.
[135] Joseph D. Parker, *Zen Buddhist Landscape Arts of Early Muromachi Japan (1336–1573)* (Albany: State University of New York Press, 1999), 167–174 states: "Chung-feng's [i.e., Zhongfeng's] reputation also spread quickly in the Five Mountains temples in the first decades of the Nambokuchō or Northern and Southern courts period (1336–92), and this was also when the first Five Mountains Zen printings of his collected sayings and other writings were completed in Japan. His influence is also seen in the writings and activities of a number of the most important Five Mountains monks, including those of the influential Chinese monk Chu-hsien Fan-hsien, the well-known poet Betsugen Enshi, and a painter and close friend of Gidō [Shūshin], Tesshū Tokusai (d. 1366). Perhaps most importantly for the Kitayama monks was the extremely high respect given Chung-feng by the individual monk that historians generally regard as the most important single monk for the establishment of the Japanese Five Mountains system, Musō Soseki. Musō, who was Gidō's teacher in Zen, modeled himself very closely on Chung-feng in early life until he took the abbacy of Nanzen-ji in 1325, through such activities as avoiding calls to head large Five Mountains temples despite requests from his teacher Kohō Kennichi (1241–1316), the *bakufu* warrior government in Kamakura, and the emperor. We can see the continuing interest in Chung-feng's writings up through the Kitayama period. For example, Gidō gave extensive lectures to his fellow monks and also to the shogun on Chung-feng's writings, while as we have seen Kiyō Hōshū wrote out the text of Chung-feng's collected sayings."
[136] A manuscript of this text (author's colophon dated 1420) is found at Tōfuku-ji in Kyoto.
[137] After the invention of what is now called "Han'gŭl" orthography in the 1440s, a vernacular Korean translation-explication (*ŏnhae* 諺解) of Mengshan's sayings was carried out. This alone highlights the extent of his influence in Korea. See Broughton with Watanabe, *Core Texts of the Sŏn Approach*, 41–43.

Zhongfeng, Tianru, and Ming-Dynasty Linji Chan

The Chan style of Zhongfeng Mingben and his major disciple Tianru Weize was influential throughout the subsequent Ming period (1368–1644) and into the Qing dynasty. As the Chan historian Ibuki Atsushi says, "In the Ming period, the *nianfo gong'an* [念佛公案, i.e., using *nianfo* as a *huatou*] that had emerged in the Yuan dynasty [with Zhongfeng and Tianru] spread widely throughout the Buddhist world [of China]."[138] The following attempts a brief sketch of Linji Chan during the Ming. It is important in any examination of Ming-dynasty Chan to avoid seeing the *nianfo* elements of many Ming-dynasty Chan masters through a "Japanese Rinzai Zen lens." Such a lens conditions us to view any sort of *nianfo* (*nembutsu*) as an *excrescence* on the body of *pure Zen*. This we must disregard. To make a preliminary foray into Ming Chan, for the sake of convenience, I rely for source texts upon *yulu*-type material in two Chan anthologies compiled by the late-Ming figure Yunqi Zhuhong (雲棲袾宏; 1535–1615)[139]: the *Chan Whip* (*Changuan cejin* 禪關策進; 1600) and *Ming Chan Masters* (*Huangming mingseng jilüe* 皇明名僧輯略; undated).[140] This is admittedly a small sample, but it should give us some sense of Ming Chan.

The *Chan Whip* consists of two collections: *Front Collection* (divided into *First Gate* and *Second Gate*) and *Back Collection* (*Single Gate*), with a total of forty comments by Zhuhong scattered throughout. The *First Gate* is subtitled *Extracts from the Dharma Sayings of the Chan Patriarchs* and consists of thirty-nine sections of sayings. These Chan sayings constitute about seventy percent of the entire book. The Chan masters featured in these thirty-nine sections chronologically run from the late Tang (800s) through the Five

---

[138] Ibuki Atsushi, *Chūgoku Zen shisō shi* (Kyoto: Zen bunka kenkyūjo, 2021), 640.
[139] For a book-length treatment of Zhuhong, see Chün-fang Yü, *The Renewal of Buddhism in China: Zhuhong and the Late Ming Synthesis* (New York: Columbia University Press, 2020).
[140] Translations of the full titles are *Whip for Spurring Students Onward Through the Chan Barriers* (T 2024.48.1097c10–1109a16) and *Abbreviated Collection of Famous Monks of the Imperial Ming* (CBETA, X84, no. 1581, p. 358, c6). For an annotated translation of the former, see Broughton with Watanabe, *Chan Whip*. Zhuhong's sources for the *Chan Whip* include the following: some version of *Outline of the Buddhas and Patriarchs* (*Fozu gangmu* 佛祖綱目; 1633), a general record of Buddhism in chronological format from Śākyamuni down to the early Ming; the five transmission-of-the-flame records of the Song (all thirty fascicles); various recorded sayings (*yulu*); and miscellaneous biographies (*za zhuan* 雜傳), i.e., such Song works as *Precious Lessons of the Chan Grove* (*Chanlin baoxun* 禪林寶訓) and *Precious Mirror of Men and Gods* (*Rentian baojian* 人天寶鑑). Zhuhong describes his sources for *Ming Chan Masters* as follows: "Those who were born in the Yuan and died in our Ming dynasty are recorded. If they died in the Yuan, they are not recorded. Each of the ten masters from Chushi [i.e., the first of the ten masters] on down has a *yulu*. I am not able to copy out the complete contents of these *yulu* books. I have recorded a small portion of their formal talks in the Dharma Hall, instructions to the assembly, general sermons, prose and verse comments on the ancients, poetry, and so forth." [皇明名僧輯略: 生於元。示寂於本朝者錄。示寂於元者不錄。楚石以下十家。各有語錄。不能悉具全書。其上堂示眾普說拈頌題咏諸雜著等。皆錄少分。] (CBETA 2019.Q3, X84, no. 1581, p. 358b5–7).

Dynasties, Song, Yuan, and Ming periods. Almost all are Linji masters, many in the Yangqi wing of Linji. The entries for Xueyan Zuqin (?–1287), Xueyan's disciple Gaofeng Yuanmiao (1238–1295), Gaofeng's disciple Zhongfeng, and Zhongfeng's disciple Tianru Weize form the core of the *First Gate*. The final saying belongs to Xiaoyan Debao (1512–1581), Zhuhong's teacher in the Gaofeng line.[141] Here we are only concerned with the Ming-dynasty entries in the *First Gate*.

Ming Chan Masters, Zhuhong's Chan compilation focusing exclusively on Ming-dynasty figures, presents the sayings of ten Chan masters from the Ming (there is also an appendix of eight minor Ming Chan figures and a second appendix for a Korean Sŏn master[142]). The following is a mélange of snippets from the sayings of these ten masters of *Ming Chan Masters*, eight of whom are also featured in the *Chan Whip*.[143] Some quotations below derive from the sayings of the same master in the *Chan Whip*:

1. Chan Master Chushi Fanqi (楚石梵琦禪師; 1296–1370)
   Chushi was in the line of Yuansou Xingduan (元叟行端; 1255–1341), a contemporary of Zhongfeng.
   Ming Chan Masters includes ten examples from his 110 *Poems of Longing for the Pure Land* (*Huai jingtu shi* 懷淨土詩), which include such lines as the following: "There is an Amitābha in your own mind"; "The mind-only Pure Land is neither high nor low"; and "the self-nature Amitābha neither comes nor goes."[144] Such Pure Land poetry is traceable to the Pure Land poetry of Zhongfeng and Tianru.[145]

---

[141] The *Second Gate* is entitled *Extracts from the Painful Practice of the Chan Patriarchs*: its twenty-four sections are mainly miniature vignettes, consisting of a few lines describing the arduous practice undertaken by Chan exemplars. The *Back Collection* is entitled *Extracts from the Sutras to Authenticate* and consists of forty-seven short excerpts from Mahayana sutras/treatises, Mainstream sutras/treatises (as well as a few other types of pieces).

[142] This is the Korean Venerable Poje (Poje sonja 普濟尊者 = Naong Hyegŭn 懶翁慧勤; 1320–1376). After Naong's saying in the *Chan Whip* (section #34), Zhuhong comments: "As for this recorded-sayings book, in Wanli 25/1597 Xu Yuanzhen of Fujian was part of an expeditionary force [to repel the second Japanese invasion of] Korea [Chosŏn] and obtained it there. It had never been seen in China. Therefore, I have recorded the gist to make it known." [評曰。此語錄萬曆丁酉。福建許元真東征。得之朝鮮者。中國未有也。因錄其要。而識之。] (T 2024.48.1104a23–25; Broughton with Watanabe, *Chan Whip*, 123–124).

[143] *Ming Chan Masters* #1 = *Chan Whip* section #33; #2 = #36; #3 = #37; #4 = #38; #6 = #35; #8 = #26; #9 = #39; and #10 = #41.

[144] 淨土詩 (略舉十首): 有箇彌陀在自心。....惟心淨土無高下。自性彌陀不去來。(CBETA 2019. Q3, X84, no. 1581, p. 361a8–b18).

[145] Jason Protass, *The Poetry Demon*, 67: "Pure Land poetry was reinvigorated in the Yuan with works by Zhongfeng Mingben and [his disciple] Tianru Weize 天如惟則 (1286–1354), and flourished in the early Ming with 110 "Poems of Longing for the Pure Land" 懷淨土詩 by the Chan master Chushi Fanqi 楚石梵琦 (1296–1370)." For Fanqi's collection of 110 Pure Land poems, see Yu Delong, ed., *Chushi Fanqi quanji* (Beijing: Jiuzhou chubanshe, 2017), 361–385. Ten of Zhongfeng's Pure Land poems are included in *Zhongfeng Talks* in *Zhongfeng Record B* (*Gozanban 9*, 546c–547a; CBETA 2019.Q3, X70, no. 1402, pp. 718c17–719a13). For Zhongfeng's collection of 108 Pure Land poems, see CBETA's No.

2. Chan Master Dufeng Benshan (毒峯本善禪師; 1419–1482)
   Ming Chan Masters: "Make your body-mind free and easy, in fusion and calmed. Urgently take the great matter of samsara as your very own responsibility [a Zhongfeng saying]. Rouse your spirit to keep an eye on [the *huatou*]: *who is this one doing nianfo*? You must focus on this word *who*. Produce a deep *sensation of uncertainty*: uncertainty about *who is this one doing nianfo*? Therefore, it is said: 'Great uncertainty and great awakening. Small uncertainty and small awakening. No uncertainty and no awakening.' Indeed, a good saying. As soon as you have a mind of urgency, your *sensation of uncertainty* will be massive. The *huatou* [*who*] will spontaneously appear."[146]

3. Chan Master Konggu Jinglong (空谷景隆禪師; 1392–?)
   Konggu was in the line of Gaofeng Yuanmiao.
   Chan Whip: "Preceptor Youtan had students lift to awareness [the *huatou*] *who is doing the nianfo*? At present, you don't have to use this type of method: just go ahead and use ordinary *nianfo*. If you just use [ordinary] *nianfo*, never losing track of it, suddenly, in your encounters with sense-objects, you will knock out a line [of verse as a token of your] transformation-of-the-basis [i.e., awakening]. For the first time, you will come to know that the *Pure Land of calm and light is not apart from here*, that Amitābha Buddha is not anything beyond the confines of *your own mind*."[147]

   Also, in a dialogue in *Ming Chan Masters* Konggu says: "As for concurrent practice [of Chan and *nianfo*], an ancient [quoted by Tianru Weize] called it trying to stand astride two boats—you are sure to fall into the middle!"[148]

1402-A 天目中峯和尚懷淨土詩 一百八首 (CBETA 2019.Q3, X70, no. 1402, p. 744c3–4). No. 1402-A is appended to *Miscellaneous Record of Chan Master Tianmu Mingben* (*Tianmu Mingben chanshi zalu* 天目明本禪師雜錄). This collection is also contained in Yu Delong, ed., *Zhongfeng Mingben quanji* (Beijing: Jiuzhou chubanshe, 2018), 581–593. See also Heller, *Illusory Abiding*, 315–320 and Natasha Heller, "Pure Land Devotional Poetry by a Chan Monk," in *Pure Lands in Asian Texts and Contexts: An Anthology*, ed. Georgios T. Halkias and Richard K. Payne (Honolulu: University of Hawai'i Press, 2019), 540–548.

[146] 使身心灑落。虛融淡泊。切切以了生死大事為己重任。抖擻精神。看這念佛底是誰。要在這誰字上著到。深下疑情。疑這念佛底是誰。故謂大疑大悟。小疑小悟。不疑不悟。良哉言也。你若纔有切切之心。疑情重也。話頭自然現前。(CBETA 2019.Q3, X84, no. 1581, pp. 361c24–362a4).

[147] 優曇和尚。令念佛的是誰。汝今不必用此等法。只平常念去。但念不忘。忽然觸境。遇緣。打著轉身一句。始知寂光淨土不離此處。阿彌陀佛不越自心。(T2024.48.1104c2–5; Broughton with Watanabe, *Chan Whip*, 127–129).

[148] 兼行。則古人謂之脚踏兩邊船。必陷中間也。(CBETA 2019.Q3, X84, no. 1581, p. 365a2–3).

At the end of *Ming Chan Master*'s Konggu Jinglong section, Zhuhong comments:

"Various Chan masters have students probe [the *huatou*] **who is doing the nianfo**? Only this master [Konggu Jinglong] says that it is not necessary to use this sort of [*huatou*] method. It is a matter of devising a medicine appropriate to the illness, implementing a teaching adapted to the student's capacity. Each of the two methods [the *huatou who is doing the nianfo* and ordinary *nianfo*] has a purport. You should not affirm one of them and negate the other."[149]

4. Chan Master Tianqi Benduan (天琦本瑞禪師; active late 1400s)

Tianqi Benduan was in the line of Gaofeng Yuanmiao.

Chan Whip: "All day long [you're doing ordinary] *nianfo*, but you are unaware that it's all a case of [mind] is *nianfo*. Given that you're unaware of this, you must keep your eye on [the *huatou*]: ***who is doing the nianfo***? With your eyes fixed on this *huatou* and your mind fixedly raising this *huatou* to awareness, you must seek to settle *this*!"[150]

5. Chan Master Jiefeng Ying (傑峯英禪師; d.u.)

Ming Chan Masters: "Lecture Master Dadu An came for an audience. Master Jiefeng Ying asked what sutra the Lecture Master lectured on. Answer: 'The *Diamond Sutra*. At the line *there is nothing coming from anywhere and nothing going anywhere* I attained an awakening.' The Master: 'Since there is no coming and going, how did you manage to get here.' Answer: 'Precisely a matter of *no coming and no going*!' Master: 'Where are you right now?' The scholar answered with a single shout. Master: 'A powerful shout stops everything. When your four great elements disperse [at death], where will you find peace and stability?' Answer: 'Throughout the great world, where is there anything that is not self?' Master: 'What about when you suddenly encounter the raging fire at the end of an eon and everything in the great thousands of worlds is destroyed?' Answer: 'I've arrived here but I *don't understand*!' Master: 'The sixth patriarch *didn't understand* while chopping firewood and treading the pestle. Bodhidharma *didn't know* while facing a wall for nine years. You *don't understand*. What

---

[149] 袾宏曰。諸師多教人參念佛是誰。惟師云不必用此等法。隨病製方。逗機施教。二各有旨。不可是此非彼。(CBETA 2019.Q3, X84, no. 1581, p. 366a11–13).

[150] 終日念佛。不知全是佛念。如不知。須看箇念佛的是誰。眼就看定。心就舉定。務要討箇下落。(T 2024.48.1104c16–18; Broughton with Watanabe, *Chan Whip*, 129–130).

do you *see*?' Answer: 'I'm just a *non-understander*!' Master: 'Blind fellow! Please sit down and have a cup of tea!'"[151]

6. Chan Master Chushan Shaoqi (楚山紹琦禪師; 1403–1473)

   Ming Chan Masters: "Just raise to awareness the single phrase **Amitābha Buddha** and install it in your heart. Silently probe [this *huatou*] and constantly with a whip give rise to the *sensation of uncertainty* about: *who ultimately is this one doing nianfo*? Probe again and again. You must not calculate existence/non-existence. And you should not have your mind wait for awakening."[152]

7. Chan Master Xingyuan Huiming (性原慧明禪師; died 1386)

   Ming Chan Masters:

   For miles the level lake: the single mirror [of mind] opens.
   The six bridges [of the sense fields] are narrow and steep: slippery like moss.
   Even if you're not stagnating on the journey,
   Reaching *here*, you stumble as usual![153]

8. Chan Master Xueting (雪庭禪師; born 1450–1456)

   Ming Chan Masters: "Resolutely, on the *huatou what was my original face before my father and mother conceived me*, take no heed of whether you are gaining energy or not gaining energy, no heed of whether you are experiencing torpor/distraction or not experiencing torpor/distraction. Secretly, continue to raise to awareness [the *huatou my original face*]. Keep an eye on the *sensation of uncertainty* that suddenly arises—it will be like a stalk of grass or a snowflake abruptly thrown into a blazing flame."[154]

9. Chan Master Guyin Jingqin (古音淨琴禪師; active early 1500s)

   Chan Whip: "While walking, standing, sitting, or lying down, do not allow the single phrase **Amitābha** to be interrupted. You must have confidence in: *if the cause is deep, the result is deep*. This brings about a situation in which you are doing *nianfo* without putting in any effort.

---

[151] 勘辯： 大都安講主來參。師問講主講甚麼經。答云。金剛經。曾於無所從來亦無所去處得箇省處。師曰。既是無來無去。因甚得到這裏。答云。便是無來無去底。師云。即今在甚麼處。答一喝。師云。下喝行拳都且止。四大分散時向何處安身立命。答云。盡大地那裏不是自己。師云。忽遇劫火洞然。大千俱壞時如何。答云。我到這裏却不會。師云。六祖不會破柴踏碓。達摩不識九年面壁。你不會。見箇甚麼。答云。我只是不會。師云。瞎漢。請坐喫茶。(CBETA 2019.Q3, X84, no. 1581, p. 369a4–13).

[152] 單單提起一句阿彌陀佛。置之懷抱。默然體究。常時鞭起疑情。這箇念佛的畢竟是誰。返復參究。不可作有卜無度。又不得將心待悟。(CBETA 2019.Q3, X84, no. 1581, p. 370a8–11).

[153] 淨慈次韻： 十里平湖一鏡開。六橋險峻滑如苔。直饒不滯程途者。到此依然喫跌迴。(CBETA 2019.Q3, X84, no. 1581, p. 372b16–18).

[154] 決定向這父母未生已前那箇是我本來面目話頭上。不管得力不得力。昏散不昏散。密密提撕去。看他疑情頓發。如烈燄光中忽擲莖茅片雪。(CBETA 2019.Q3, X84, no. 1581, p. 372c21–23).

If you can do this from moment to moment with no gaps, it is guaranteed that the *nianfo* will become a oneness. If, at that very moment, you can know *the person doing the nianfo*, then [for you] Amitābha and 'I' will manifest as one."[155]

10. Chan Master Xiaoyan Debao (笑巖德寶禪師; aka Yuexin 月心 [1512–1581]; in the Gaofeng line; one of the two teachers Zhuhong trained under in the capital Yanjing during his early career)

   Chan Whip: "With fury produce a fresh burst of determination and lift the *huatou* to awareness. With respect to the *final wrap-up word* [i.e., the *huatou*] you must make the *sensation of uncertainty* lasting—deep and intense. Either silently probe [the *huatou*] with a closed mouth or look into [the *huatou*] while saying it out loud: as if you have lost an item important to you. You must find it yourself personally, and you must get it back yourself personally. In the context of your daily activities, always and everywhere, have no duality of thought."[156]

The picture of Linji Chan during the Ming presented by these two Chan anthologies is as follows:

1. The *huatou*-practice Chan of Dahui Zonggao is pervasive in the 1400s and 1500s. Dahui's terminology for *huatou* practice is sprinkled throughout the sayings of many of these ten Ming Chan masters.
2. Some Ming Chan masters discourage concurrent practice (*jianxing* 兼行) of Chan and *nianfo* (a Zhongfeng position).
3. The most popular *huatous* are probably the **who** of **who is doing the nianfo** and **my original face** of **what was my original face before my father and mother conceived me.**
4. There are two types of *nianfo*: 1. *nianfo* as a *huatou* (*nianfo gong'an* 念佛公案 = *canjiu nianfo* 參究念佛 ["probing" or "practicing" *nianfo*]) and 2. "ordinary *nianfo*" (*pingchang nianfo* 平常念佛) or "straightforward *nianfo*" (*zhi nian* 直念), that is, ordinary chanting of the name of Amitābha Buddha (either out loud [*chusheng nianfo* 出聲念佛] or silently [*monian Amituo* 默念彌陀]).

---

[155] 行住坐臥之中。一句彌陀莫斷。須信因深果深。直教不念自念。若能念念不空。管取念成一片。當念認得。念人彌陀與我同現。(T 2024.48.1104c29–1105a2; Broughton with Watanabe, *Chan Whip*, 130–131).

[156] 憤起新鮮志氣。舉箇話頭。要於結末字上。疑情永長。沈沈痛切。或杜口默參。或出聲追審。如失重物。務要親逢親得。日用中一切時一切處。更無二念。(T 2024.48.1105a12–15; Broughton with Watanabe, *Chan Whip*, 132–133).

5. Some Ming Chan masters hold that, if using the *nianfo* as a *huatou* is "inappropriate" or "inconvenient" (*bu bian* 不便), it is permissible to use "ordinary *nianfo*."
6. There is little mention of "going to be reborn" (*wangsheng* 往生) in Amitābha's Pure Land Sukhāvatī.

Ming Chan was deeply entangled with various ideas of Pure Land *nianfo* (念佛), a development that expands on the Chan/Pure Land orientation of Zhongfeng and Tianru during the Yuan dynasty. Zhuhong in the late Ming also compiled a Pure Land work that shows the influence of Zhongfeng in this area, *Distinguishing Doubts about Pure Land* (*Jingtu yi bian* 淨土疑辨):

> Someone asked: "The discourse of Pure Land is nothing more than *surface dharma*. One who is in the know should directly awaken to the Chan realization, but, at present, people just give praises to Pure Land. I am afraid that this has led them to attachment to phenomenal characteristics and a failure to clarify the principle-nature [in the Chan manner]."
>
> [Zhuhong] answers: "In the *Śūraṃgama Sūtra* it says: 'Returning to the original-nature [i.e., principle-nature] is non-dual. *Upāyas* are multifarious.' If you comprehend this point, then Chan realization and Pure Land are different routes back to the same place: your doubts will immediately dissolve. The ancients, in this matter, expounded and propagated both sides: it was not a case of *one is enough*. As Great Master Zhongfeng said: 'Chan is the Chan of Pure Land; Pure Land is the Pure Land of Chan.' But those who cultivate this must revere [Zhongfeng's slogan] *enter deeply into one gate*. These words are a remarkable fixed axiom that will remain unchanged for ten thousand generations."[157]

In fact, Zhongfeng's Chan style reaches all the way to the Qing dynasty: Chan Master Jineng's (濟能禪師) *Horned Tiger Collection* (*Jiaohu ji* 角虎集; 1770), in a manner comparable to *Ming Chan Masters*, draws material from fifty-seven *yulu* on Chan/Pure Land. The title comes from the fourfold Chan-and-Pure-Land schema attributed to Yongming Yanshou: the third alternative, *having Chan and having Pure Land*, is described as a "tiger with horns."[158] This schema was well-known to Zhongfeng—in *Night Conversations in a Mountain Hermitage* he says that Yongming Yanshou's sorting of Chan and Pure Land

---

[157] 淨土疑辨: 或問。淨土之說。蓋表法耳。智人宜直悟禪宗。而今只管讚說淨土。將無執著事相。不明理性。答。歸元性無二。方便有多門。曉得此意。禪宗淨土。殊途同歸。子之所疑。當下冰釋。昔人於此。遞互闡揚。不一而足。如中峰大師道。禪者淨土之禪。淨土者禪之淨土。而修之者必貴一門深入。此數語。尤萬世不易之定論也。(T 1977.47.420a9–18).
[158] See Translation 2, n.27.

into *four phrases* was intended as an *upāya* that teachers employ to suppress or encourage students as the situation requires.[159] The *Horned Tiger Collection* says of Jineng: "He was ordered to keep his eye on the **dried turd** *huatou*. . . . one day, while eating, he lifted his head to look at the window shutter and suddenly had an awakening. . . . The Master in his late years *deeply entered the one gate of Pure Land*." The term *deeply entering one gate*, of course, echoes Zhongfeng's insistence upon specialization in either Chan or *nianfo*.

Perhaps it is appropriate to end with Zhuhong's evaluation of the Zhongfeng sayings in the *Chan Whip*:

> [Zhongfeng:] In doing practice-work during illness it is not necessary for you to exhibit zeal and be brave and ferocious, nor is it necessary for you to raise your eyebrows and dart fierce looks. All you must do is make your mind like wood or stone and your thought like dead ashes. Cast this four-elements [i.e., earth, water, fire, and wind] phantasm-body beyond the worlds of the ten directions. It's all up to you: if you're ill, okay; if you're brought back to life, okay; if you die, okay; if someone gives you nursing care, okay; if there's no one to give you nursing care, okay; if the smell is fresh, okay; if it's a putrid smell, okay; if you're cured, restored to health, and live for 120 years, okay; if you die, and, dragged by past karma, are put into a cauldron of boiling water or a charcoal furnace in one of the hells, okay. In this way, while immersed in the sense-fields, you won't be shaken a bit. Just urgently take up a *tasteless huatou*, and, at the pillow [of your sickbed] next to your stove for preparing medicines, silently inquire [into the *huatou*] on your own. You must never let go [of the *huatou*]!
>
> Zhuhong's comment: The thousands upon thousands of words of this old man [Zhongfeng] only teach people to keep an eye on the *huatou*—to do real practice-work in the hope of true awakening. He was earnest and straightforward. For a thousand years onward, Zhongfeng will provide an earful of advice. A detailed account of his teachings is to be found in his complete book [i.e., the *Extensive Record of Preceptor Tianmu Zhongfeng*]. You should look the whole thing over on your own![160]

---

[159] Translation 3, section #8.
[160] 病中做工夫。也不要爾精進勇猛。也不要爾撐眉努目。但要爾心如木石。意若死灰。將四大幻身。撇向他方世界之外。由他病也得。活也得。死也得。有人看也得。無人看也得。香鮮也得。臭爛也得。醫得健來。活到一百二十歲也得。如或便死。被宿業牽。入鑊湯爐炭裏也得。如是境界中。都不動搖。但切切將箇沒滋味話頭。向藥爐邊枕頭上。默默咨參。不得放捨。評曰。此老千言萬語。只教人看話頭。做真實工夫。以期正悟。諄切透快。千載而下。如耳提面命。具存全書。自應遍覽。(T 2024.48.1102a11–22; Broughton with Watanabe, *Chan Whip*, 103 105). Most of this Zhongfeng saying is found in a dharma talk to an ill Chan monk in *Zhongfeng Extensive Record* (Gozanban 9, 178c; CBETA 2019.Q3, B25, no. 145, p. 747b5–11).

Translation 1
Selections from *Instructions to the Assembly* in *Zhongfeng Extensive Record*

Instructions to the Assembly

[1] On New Year's Eve, the Master instructed the assembly: "'If you want to know the meaning of *buddha-nature*, you should contemplate [the passage of] *time* and *origination-by-dependence*.'[1] So right now—what time is it? It is the twenty-ninth day of the twelfth month. Since this is not a big month [of thirty days but a small month of twenty-nine days], this is the time when the year ends. An ancient said: 'When you are embroiled in samsara, the metaphor is 'the thirtieth day of the twelfth month.'"[2] The year is over; the months are over; and the days are over. Within the 360 days of [the coming] year, what things will you succeed in accomplishing? If you cannot succeed in doing them, you will end up wasting that entire year. How could you just go and waste an entire year? From limitless eons down to today, the whole thing will have been a waste! If you are unsuccessful today in putting your foot down and making a stand, in raising your *huatou* and turning over a new leaf, in fiercely making progress, then, even before the coming year is over, you are guaranteed that it, too, will have been a waste! It will not be only the coming year when you fail to be fierce in zeal—a hundred thousand years will also just be wasted. You, sirs, are wasting *time* and *origination-by-dependence*! You pay no heed to the fact that, because of this waste, the more karma you accumulate, the smaller your Way-power becomes: how could this possibly benefit the principle behind your leaving home and studying the Way? I exhort you people: with a single blow of the iron rod hack off your remaining years' considerable amount of laziness, self-indulgence, torpor, and restlessness! Tomorrow is the beginning of the New Year. Rouse your zeal and make your

---

[1] Mujaku Dōchū, *Daie Fukaku Zenji sho kōrōju* (Kyoto: Zen bunka kenkyūjo, 1997), 238 says this is "a saying for final day of the twelfth month" [忠曰因臘月三十日語]. *Pearl in the Wicker-Basket* (*Kōrōju* 栲栳珠; 1723) is Mujaku's commentary on *Letters of Dahui*. The line is usually attributed to Baizhang Huaihai (白丈懷海; 749–814). See, for instance, *Guiding Principle of the Linked Lamp-Flames* (*Liandeng hui yao* 聯燈會要; 1183; CBETA 2019.Q3, X79, no. 1557, p. 64a16–17).

[2] Untraced.

supranormal energy fierce. Put in one day's work and you're sure to accrue one day's results. Don't delay—get with the program! May you not fail in living up to your ambition to leave home and go on pilgrimage. As with people who go up a mountain, each makes effort on his own. Again, I say: 'Tonight is the twenty-ninth of the twelfth month.' Everywhere people are welcoming in the new and sending off the old. If you patched-robed Chan monks are only motivated by what's right in front of your face, you'll end up "[sitting in] a *nest*" [i.e., you will find yourself sitting in a *nest* or *lair* of stereotyped formulas].[3] You'd be better off reciting the single *mantra* [of the *Heart Sutra*], which at least would cancel out any possibility of your not being quick-witted in your remaining years: "the great divine incantation, the great bright incantation."[4] Try listening to the tower bell as it tolls the five watches of the night [i.e., try listening to its marking of the passage of *time* and *origination-by-dependence*]: a hundred thousand phantasmal dharmas—all perfect!

[2] On the first day bound by the rules of the summer retreat,[5] the Master instructed the assembly: "The great assembly relies on the bodhisattva vehicle to cultivate tranquility, taking the great, perfect awakening as our monastic park, with our body-minds peacefully dwelling in the *wisdom of sameness*.[6] More than two thousand years ago, old Śākyamuni drew on the ground the outline of an enclosure: the ancient rules of the cloistered retreat prohibited any stepping

---

[3] Dahui Zonggao's *Correct Dharma-Eye Depository* (*Zheng fayan zang* 正法眼藏): "You people spend your entire lives in the Chan monasteries seeking for *this matter* without ever getting it. It does not lie in words! Among you there are many with white hair and yellowed teeth who sit inside a *nest* [i.e., stereotyped formulas], never able to stick your heads out for your whole life. You know nothing of your mistake. Getting *taste* from the sayings of the ancients is taking their sublime sayings as a *nest*. Getting *taste* from the chanted sounds and meanings of the sutras is taking the sutras as a *nest*. Getting *taste* from the *gong'ans* of the ancients is taking the dialogues, substitution sayings, additional sayings, pressing-down/lifting-up sayings, and praising/condemning sayings of the ancients as a *nest*. Getting *taste* from the mind-nature is taking *the three realms are mind only* and *the myriad dharma are consciousness only* as a *nest*. Getting taste from silence and wordlessness is taking closing the eyes and sitting motionless like Bhīṣma-svara Buddha in the ghost cave of Black Mountain as a *nest*. Getting *taste* from daily activities and actions is taking raising the eyebrows, blinking, and lifting the *huatou* to awareness as a *nest*." [你諸人一生在叢林參尋此事無所得者。不在言也。其間多有頭白齒黃坐在窠臼裏一生出頭不得。都不知非。向古人言句上得些滋味者。以奇言妙句為窠臼。於經教中聲名句義上得滋味者。以經教為窠臼。於古人公案上得滋味者。以古人問答代語別語抑揚語褒貶語為窠臼。於心性上得滋味者。以三界唯心萬法唯識為窠臼。於寂默無言無說處得滋味者。以閉口藏眼威音那畔坐在黑山下鬼窟裏不動為窠臼。於日用動轉施為處得滋味者。以揚眉瞬目舉覺提撕為窠臼。] (CBETA 2019.Q3, X67, no. 1309, p. 630a7–17).

[4] *Heart Sutra*, T 253.8.849c17.

[5] The summer retreat lasts for three months, from the sixteenth day of the fourth month to the fifteenth day of the seventh month. Chan monks are required to maintain residence in one place. It derives from the three-month rainy season retreat (*vārṣika*) of Indian Buddhism.

[6] In Yogācāra theory, the sixth consciousness or *defiled mind* (*kliṣṭamanas*) observes the eighth consciousness (the *storehouse consciousness*/*ālayavijñāna*), which is the stream of karmic seeds from past lives, and mistakenly considers it to be a self. When the defiled mind flips over, it becomes the *sameness knowledge* or *impartiality wisdom* (*samatājñāna*). Asvabhāva's commentary on Asaṅga's *Mahāyānasaṃgraha* says: "The defiled mind turns over and so the impartiality wisdom is obtained." [攝大乘論釋: 轉染污末那故得平等性智] (T 1598.31.438a17–18).

outside [that enclosure] for the assembly of monks at that time. This morning, the fifteenth day of the fourth month, is the time for those appropriate rules of the Sage [i.e., the Buddha]: taking up the deep past for the sake of naturally carrying on your practice. In front of you [for the next ninety days will be] the binding cord [of the summer-retreat restrictions]—let us put that aside without further discussion. Again, why is this summer retreat about the *wisdom of sameness*? Because intrinsic wisdom is *sameness*, which pervades the worlds of the ten directions. One who lacks the wisdom of *sameness* does not look reverently at the buddhas and does not gaze [in compassion] at sentient-beings. This is called *sameness of nature and characteristics*. Before, you contemplate the past; after, you reach to the future. This is called *sameness of the three times*. Morality, concentration, wisdom—all the way to licentiousness, anger, and stupidity—are called *sameness of single thought-moments*. Delusion and then samsara, awakening and then nirvana—these are called *sameness of immovables*. Big as space, minute as a mustard seed—these are called *sameness of freedom-from-characteristics*. Down to: seeing forms, forms are all *sameness*; hearing sounds, sounds are all *sameness*. If you examine things closely like this, in the case of the binding retreat rules of the fifteenth day of the fourth month, binding is also *sameness*. In the case of the loosening of the retreat rules on the fifteenth day of the seventh month, loosening is also *sameness*. With the ninety days between these two dates, every single day is *sameness*. Every single hour is *sameness*. Every single thought-moment is *sameness*. At just such a time, what do you call *binding rules*? What do you call implementing a *loosening of the binding rules*? What do you call carrying out a summer retreat or not carrying out a summer retreat? The old fellow with the yellow face [Śākyamuni] arrived *here*, and, without realizing it, *Unreserved Functioning* was discovered. Although you may not be single-minded about the matter, if you have not truly proceeded toward the inside of the intrinsic wisdom of *sameness*, planted your feet on solid ground, and achieved a sharp awakening at least one time, even if you use the word *sameness* to stop up every dangerous place in all of space, you will not derive much benefit therefrom. With *this matter*, you just cannot win the argument in that way. You must be as staunch as something that has smashed to the ground. During these coming ninety days, chew sideways and chew up and down on your *huatou that has no meaning or taste*.[7] Press on it morning and night. Press it to the utmost limit. When your chewing is exhausted, you will be like a dumb person who has a dream [and cannot tell anyone about it]. At such a time, there will be nothing to obstruct your expounding things as you please: You'll call non-sameness sameness and sameness non-sameness! You will also obtain that described [in

---

[7] Zhongfeng's typical phrasing for the *huatou*.

the *Lotus Sutra*[8]] as 'I am the Dharma King, free to do as I will within dharma.' Remember that an ancient had a verse that goes:

> To protect beings, it is necessary to kill them.
> Once the killing is done, for the first time, *peaceful dwelling* [i.e., a retreat].
> If you can understand the idea in this,
> Your iron boat will float on water.[9]

Isn't it that killing beings and protecting beings is *sameness* of single thought-moments? Haggling in that way blinds the eyes of people. This most certainly is not a trifling matter. And listen to another verse:

> Each [Chan monk] returns to the Hall.
> Ninety days with a prohibition on anyone stepping out.
> Is the intention any different from giving life/killing?
> Difficult to grasp onto the ancient rules.[10]

When you have not yet reached the *sameness* state of body-mind, how could it be easy to clearly understand [the real meaning of] *peaceful dwelling* [i.e., a summer retreat]?"

[3] During a snowfall, the Master instructed the assembly: "A snowflake or two: flies onto people and immediately disappears. Three to five feet of snow: accumulates on the thatched eaves and presents a problem. Silver buddha images of three thousand realms emanate numinous light rays—pervade both existence and emptiness. Jade dragons with eight million broken scales—there is no place to conceal them. Regret of the plum flower [that blooms in the snow]: a solitary fisherman in his straw raincoat returning home just before twilight. Now tell me, you motionless Chan people sitting on your sitting cushion with your Chan boards [i.e., arm and back rests]—how do you relate to all this? An ancient said: 'Today snow is falling. The Chan community has three types of monks. One type of monk, at his place on the Chan sitting platform, is *clarifying self*. One type, at the sutra-reading desk, is *chanting snow poetry*. One type is around the stove *talking about the next meal in the hall*.'[11]

---

[8] T 262.9.15b6.
[9] For example: *Recorded Sayings of Layman Pang* (*Pang jushi yulu* 龐居士語錄; CBETA 2019.Q3, X69, no. 1336, p. 134b1–2).
[10] Untraced.
[11] Appears in Dahui Zonggao's miscellany *Chan Arsenal*, where it is attributed to Yuantong Faxiu (圓通法秀; 1027–1090) of the Yunmen line: "The Master Dahui said: 'Chan Master Yuantong Xiu, during a snowfall, said: "In a snowfall there are three types of Chan monks. The superior-grade monks do cross-legged sitting in the Sangha Hall. The middle-grade ones grind their ink and apply their writing brushes to composing snow poems. The inferior-grade ones hover around the stove and talk about eating." I, in

Of these three types of monks, who should receive the offerings of humans and gods? Should receive/should not receive—let's set that aside without further discussion. Chan venerables! Do you know the principle by which rain forms into snow, and water freezes into ice? Rain's forming into snow is assuredly a magical transformation of creation—it's fitting that you don't understand it. Water freezes into ice—quickly a liquid flow all-at-once becomes a solid form. Metal and stone do not compare in hardness. A simile may be useful for clarification. The buddha-nature is like water. Over innumerable eons, due to the coldness of delusion, thought-moment after thought-moment [the buddha-nature becomes] congealed, and thus the 'buddha-nature water' coagulates into ice. But, even during the time it is ice, that ice never stops being 'buddha-nature water' [even though you cannot see its flowing or pouring any longer]. There is no way it could ever lose the functions of flowing and pouring that it had before the coldness of delusion transformed it. Some of you aren't using the sun of wisdom to melt [the ice]: there is no possibility of a spontaneous transformation on its own. Given this sort of analysis, do you think that you will be able to evade this simply by having the thought that you are tending toward the Way? Some of you mistakenly say: 'When the ancients came across this-and-that and snapped their fingers, they immediately *knew the way home*—the ancients did not need to rouse supernormal energy and expend painful work [to realize the way home]!' In the end, you are unaware that, if you haven't aroused supernormal energy and done painful work in the past, and just trust to coming across this-and-that and snapping your fingers, you won't come to know how to *get home*. There has never been a single buddha or a single Chan patriarch who did not rely on the sun of wisdom to melt the cold ice of delusion and turn it back into buddha-nature water! The single *huatou* you people are practicing today: when you've reached a state of sufficient confidence and attained stability in it, how could [the *huatou*] not be the true wisdom [of the sun that melts the ice]? One dawn, your practice-work will have ripened, and the time will have arrived. Even a ten-thousand-foot ice-mountain will turn to water; even an eighty-thousand-foot snow peak will become water, both flowing smoothly back into the buddha-nature sea. Even if snow were to pile up in the sky, and ice were to be generated in a fire, still I have never heard of the freezing of that limitless sea. Chan worthies! Do not tell this Upper Seat to

Jianyan 1/1127 [of the Southern Song], was at Huqiu's place and saw for myself these types of monks. I could not help but laugh, and then I realized that these words of our senior [Yuantong] were not false.'"
[大慧普覺禪師宗門武庫: 師云。圓通秀禪師因雪下云。雪下有三種僧。上等底僧堂中坐禪。中等磨墨點筆作雪詩。下等圍爐說食。予丁未年冬在虎丘。親見此三等僧。不覺失笑。乃知前輩語不虛耳。] (T 1998B.47.956b9–12).

elaborate on this simile. It is just that the dharma-principle is like this. And listen to my verse:

Frozen clouds enclose on all four sides, and the snow is endless.
Who can right now regard this as water?
The only reason [you're unable to do so] is that you haven't yet *glimpsed the flower*.
Open the window—you can still gaze at the translucent green gem!"[12]

[4] On the night of the fifteenth in the first month [i.e., the end of the New Year celebration], the Master instructed the assembly: "[At the time of the Lantern Festival marking the end of the New Year] the Tathāgata Sumerupradīparāja and Bhaiṣajyaguruvaiḍūryanirbhāsa Buddha met at a crossroads and joined hands to look at the lights of the paper lanterns piled up in the shape of 'Sea-Turtle Mountain.'[13] Suddenly they came upon the thick-eyebrowed Old Fellow of Snowy Peak [i.e., Śākyamuni] who, facing an assembly of one hundred, was speaking a four-line verse:

Mind-only is buddha—buddha is mind-only.
This saying has been transmitted from ancient times to the present.
But you don't know for yourself that *the lantern is the light*,
And vainly go on searching amid things outside yourself.

At the time, the two Tathāgatas could not help laughing, saying in a stern voice: 'What you say is correct—it only lacks awakening! Just this [slogan] *mind is buddha—buddha is mind-only* is a saying that is completely comprehensible to a three-year old. Why wouldn't anyone awaken [if only hearing the slogan was all it takes]? But talking about a meal does not cure hunger. The

---

[12] This snow poem by Zhongfeng is included in the great collection of Song and Yuan Chan verse *Chan School Miscellany: A Sea of Poison* (*Chanzong za duhai* 禪宗雜毒海; 1714; CBETA 2019.Q3, X65, no. 1278, p. 101b1–2).

[13] Sumerupradīparāja is described in the *Vimalakīrti Sutra* (維摩詰所說經; T 475.14.546b1–4); Bhaiṣajyaguruvaiḍūryanirbhāsa is described in the *Bhaiṣajyaguruvaiḍūryanirbhāsa Tathāgata Original-Vow Merit Sutra* (藥師琉璃光如來本願功德經; T 450.14.405a1–6). This story is untraced. In Song and Yuan times, at the Lantern Festival on the first full moon of the New Year, colored paper lanterns were piled up to make a mountain, which was called "Sea-Turtle Mountain." In mythology, three of these fabulous giant sea turtles bear on their backs the paradise islands of Penglai, Yingzhou, and Fangzhang. As a foursome, they uphold the pillars of the world. There is a quatrain by Yang Wanli (楊萬里; 1127–1206) entitled "Director Chen Jianshu on the Fifteenth Day of the First Month Mild Weather" (和陳塞叔郎中乙巳上元晴和): "Ten hamlets of Shahe people are at their most boisterous. In the three thousand worlds the moon has hit its midpoint. Buy paper lanterns—don't spend it on *Dongpo* paper [i.e., written admonitions to the emperor]. This year's Sea-Turtle Mountain [of paper lanterns] won't enter the palace!" [十里沙河人最鬧。三千世界月方中。買燈莫費東坡紙。今歲鰲山不入宮。]

question to ask is: what is the *true state*[14] of being awakened?' [Śākyamuni] then said: 'I will try to clarify with a metaphor. Suppose there is someone who has lost a one-inch pearl. Even a hundred thousand coins of cash would fall short of its purchase price. If he does not get this jewel back, even if he dies ten thousand times over, he will not be able to alleviate his searching mind: engraved into his lungs and liver, carved into his mind and backbone, figuring in his dreams at night, penetrating everything he sees and hears. Thought-moment after thought-moment, he never forgets [the jewel]. He is industrious and never gives up. Every day that he does not get it back is a day in which his thoughts do not attain a stopping-to-rest. Every year that he does not get it back is a year in which his mind does not find any stopping point. The more the jewel fails to appear, the more zealous his efforts become. The more he does not get it back, the stronger and braver he becomes. Down to the point where his feelings are used up and his thoughts become exhausted. His thoughts are painful, and his spirit has reached the end of the road, forgetting both cold and heat, neglecting both sleeping and eating. Years upon years pile up—he is truly at the point where he cannot fathom much of anything. Suddenly, the jewel is in his hands: round, smooth, and gleaming. His mind that has been running around searching for thirty years all-at-once enters a state of stillness. This is *awakening*. His searching for this jewel when his mind is worn down and his physical form is haggard—what else could this be but *practice*! Suddenly, he sees this jewel, and his spirit becomes bright and clear—what else could this be but *awakening*! Without having gone through the difficulties of his *practice/searching*, how could he have come to the joys of *awakening/acquiring*? At this point, suddenly [even this *awakening/acquiring*] is dispersed by a single shout from the teacher: only then does the student *see* that *lantern is lantern* [i.e., *buddha is buddha*] and *lantern light is lantern light* [i.e., *mind is mind*]. [At the Lantern Festival] the towers are lofty, and the horses and carriages dash about, crisscrossing. Flowers are spread all over: golden lotuses. Flames in a series: jade candle upon jade candle. Bearded Zhang Third-son and dark Li Fourth-son[15] [i.e., everybody and his brother are

---

[14] Iriya Yoshitaka and Koga Hidehiko, *Zengo jiten* (Kyoto: Shibunkaku shuppan, 1991), 216 define *xiaoxi* 消息 as follows: *dōsei* 動靜 (*a state of affairs*; *the way things are*); *jyōkyō* 情況 (*the state of things*; *conditions*); *jittai* 実態 (*true condition/state*; *the realities*). Henceforth, I will use *true state* as the rendering. In fact, *xiaoxi* is close to Sanskrit *yathā-bhūta* (*as it truly is*). The modern Chinese meaning of *news* tends to complicate matters.

[15] Appears in Dahui Zonggao's miscellany *Chan Arsenal*: "Old Kaisheng Jue of Hezhou in the beginning practiced under [Ying]fu Tiejiao of Changlu Monastery. For a long time, he got nothing out of it. He heard of Dongshan Wuzu's Dharma Way and took the most direct route to arrive at Wuzu's dharma seat. One day in his room Wuzu conferred the following question: 'Śākyamuni and Maitreya are his slaves. Now, tell me: Who is he?' Jue said: 'Bearded Zhang Three and dark Li Four [i.e., everybody and his brother].' Wuzu okayed these words. At the time Preceptor Yuanwu was Chief Seat. Wuzu raised Jue's words with

there]. Ten thousand people drunk in the sea, helping each other homeward. Demon spirits as numerous as the sands of the Ganges; great officials who serve as assistants in imperial rituals; craziness without break in a hundred playhouses. At just that moment, a couplet that is free of involvement with either awakening or delusion and that shares the joy of ascending peace: what would such a couplet be like?

Lapis lazuli fills up the belly, concealing the bright moon.
Lotus flowers from head to foot, emitting a jewel-like radiance."[16]

him. Yuanwu said: 'That may be good, but I fear it's not yet complete. He shouldn't let go of it—he should investigate this line further.' On the next day Jue entered Wuzu's room, and Wuzu conferred the same question as before. Jue said: 'What I said to you yesterday.' Wuzu: 'What did you say?' Jue: 'Bearded Zhang Three and dark Li Four.' Wuzu: 'Wrong! Wrong!' Jue: 'Why did the Preceptor yesterday say it was right?' Wuzu: 'Yesterday it was right, and today it is wrong!' Jue immediately had a great awakening." [大慧普覺禪師宗門武庫： 和州開聖覺老。初參長蘆夫鐵脚。久無所得。聞東山五祖法道。徑造席下。一日室中垂問云。釋迦彌勒猶是他奴。且道。他是阿誰。覺云。胡張三黑李四。祖然其語。時圓悟和尚為座元。祖舉此語似之。悟云。好則好。恐未實。不可放過。更於語下搜看。次日入室垂問如前。覺云。昨日向和尚道了。祖云。道什麼。覺云。胡張三黑李四。祖云。不是不是。覺云。和尚為甚昨日道是。祖云。昨日是今日不是。覺於言下大悟。] (T 1998B.47.954c1–10). Also appears in *Universal Flame-of-the-Lamp Record of the Jiatai Era* (*Jiatai pudeng lu* 嘉泰普燈錄; 1204): "Bearded Zhang Three and dark Li Four one after the other singing *la la*!" [鬍張三。黑李四。箇箇解唱囉囉哩。] (CBETA 2019.Q3, X79, no. 1559, p. 389c2).

[16] Untraced.

Translation 2
Selections from *Dharma Talks* in *Zhongfeng Extensive Record*

Dharma Talks

[1] Instruction to Venerable Xianyue of Yiwu [i.e., modern Hami in Xinjiang] (Sanskrit name: Niao-bo/ba-la-shi-li[1])

The *buddhadharma* has no element of *haggling*, no element of *passable/not too bad*, no element of *logical arranging*. Just break apart everything, split open the myriad things, and cut off calculation: rely only on a single *huatou*! From today onward, guard [this *huatou*] until you arrive at the time of awakening—only then will you be allowed to *catch your breath* [i.e., resume normal breathing after exertion/*take a rest*].[2] But if you have not yet reached the self-realization found at the bottom of the bucket and are [prematurely] *desirous of catching your breath*—right there you will have already made a mistake! This single mistake will immediately cascade into a hundred mistakes, a thousand mistakes! This most certainly is not a small karmic condition [with few consequences]. In doing practice-work, most essential is the attainment of stability. Most essential is the ability to be unconstrained. Most essential is not being turned by sense-objects that go against you or go along with you. Most essential is being able to make yourself master and make your footing secure. Most essential is being able to endure *withered-and-pale*[3] [conditions] and maintain

---

[1] In the *Self-Inscription* section of the *Zhongfeng Extensive Record*, there is an inscription requested by Venerable Xianyue of Gaochang (Sanskrit name: Niao-ba-la-shi-li) [高昌顯月長老梵名鳥巴剌室利請] (*Gozanban* 9, 228a; CBETA 2019.Q3, B25, no. 145, pp. 783b19–784a3). Otherwise, unidentified. *Yiwu*, an abbreviation of *Yiwulu* (伊吾盧), is a transliteration from Uighur.

[2] *General Sermons of Chan Master Dahui Pujue* (大慧普覺禪師普說): "Preceptor Baiyun Duan had a case of belching. Whenever he ate roasted radishes [i.e., *daikon*] he made sounds of catching his breath. Later, on the verge of death he made several burping sounds." [蓋白雲端和尚有膈氣。每喫煨蘿蔔取氣作聲。後臨終時。噎氣數聲 (CBETA 2019.Q3, M059, no. 1540, p. 955b3–4).

[3] Dahui's miscellany *Chan Arsenal* (大慧普覺禪師宗門武庫): "Preceptor Yexian Sheng was *severe and cold, withered and pale* [i.e., in his monastery living conditions were strict, with deprivation as the norm]. While his Chan monks respected him, they were afraid of him. While Fushan Yuan and Tianyi Huai were wandering monks, they went on a special visit to Sheng for consultation. At that very time it was snowy and cold. Sheng cursed and evicted them—and went so far as to sprinkle water on the overnight lodging room. All the clothes became completely wet. All the other monks became angry and left. Only Yuan and

your *stillness-and-silence*. Most essential is to penetrate what is right in front of your eyes—not get deluded by all the sense-fields of the world. Most essential is not thinking about clothing when cold, not seeking food when hungry, not having your eyes follow forms, not having your ears chase after sounds. Most essential is that you be a single body-mind like an iron chisel, and not get yourself chiseled by the "Chan Way" or the "*buddhadharma*." Most essential is that, even if you fail to awaken during your whole lifetime, you never, under any circumstances, produce any "backup" thought [i.e., a thought other than the *huatou*]. And there is one more item that is most essential: even before your mouth has opened, you've already spoken; even before your writing-brush has hit the paper, you've already written it; even before your practice has achieved penetration, you've already awakened. Do you comprehend? Do you understand? Do you have confidence? Right now, the *great matter* shouldn't be your concern—bear the *small matters* one by one.

[2] Instruction to Ascetic Teiichi [*Solid-and-Immovable*] of Japan[4]

Monks are non-monks; laypeople are non-laypeople. Six times six has always been thirty-six. Laypeople are laypeople; monks are monks. Even if at high noon the temple bell tolls for the third watch of the night, both monks and laypeople are okay. In the final analysis, there is no gap between them, no room for any gap. Suddenly you understand. Laughing, you look at a "big bug" [like me, i.e., an "old tiger"[5]] that sprouts two wings. Do you understand? If you do not understand, then don't be hasty and in a rush. Why have you disregarded your father and mother and attached yourself to this great Chan assembly, casting yourself into the forests and valleys? It isn't to seek out food and clothing, is it? It isn't to seek out fame and profit, is it? Since it is not to seek out food and clothing, or seek out fame and profit, in the end, *what is*

Huai together folded up their sitting paraphernalia, put in order their clothes, and again took a sitting position in the lodging room." [葉縣省和尚嚴冷枯淡。衲子敬畏之。浮山遠天衣懷在眾時。特往參扣。正值雪寒。省訶罵驅逐。以至將水潑旦過。衣服皆濕。其他僧皆怒而去。惟遠懷併疊敷具整衣。] (T 1998B.47.944a12–15).

[4] Unidentified.
[5] Dahui's *Correct Dharma-Eye Depository* (*Zheng fayan zang* 正法眼藏): "Hermitage Head Tongfeng was asked by a monk: 'Hermitage Head is *here* and suddenly meets a *big bug* coming along. What would you do?' Hermitage Head made the roar of a *big bug*. The monk assumed a pose of dread. Hermitage Head gave out a great laugh. The monk said: 'This brigand!' Hermitage Head said: 'Where does that leave me?'" [桐峯庵主因僧問。庵主在遮裏。忽遇大蟲來。又作麼生。主便作大蟲吼。僧作怕勢。主大笑。僧云遮賊。主云爭柰我何。雪竇云。是則是。兩箇惡賊。只解掩耳偷鈴。] (CBETA 2019.Q3, X67, no. 1309, p. 615b9–11).

it for? Not to mention the fact that you have crossed over a great distance of tens of thousands of miles, going to the trouble of a sea voyage [from Japan] to come here [to China]. Truly, right under your feet you have the single causal nexus of the *great matter* of impermanence in samsara. You have passed through vast eons to reach your present birth: you have seen ever more dark delusion and have sunk further and further in the wheel-turning of samsara. Today you must cast off your life, forget your bodily form, use up your ordinary vital energy, and proceed toward the interior of that emptiness and stillness. Lift to awareness a single *tasteless huatou* of the ancients and silently keep an eye on it: continuously keep an eye on [that *huatou*]. Just free your mind of wishes: have your thoughts stop any rushing around seeking, have your consciousness not grasp objective-supports, have your thoughts free of indulgence. Pay no attention to mountains, forests, towns, and markets, quiet/noisiness, and leisure time/busy time. Today *in that way* keep an eye on [the *huatou*]. Tomorrow *in that way* keep an eye on [the *huatou*]. Suddenly your eyelids will fall off and your skull will be drilled right through—then you'll be able to say: *solid and immovable*. Things will "click," and immediately you'll be *solid and immovable*: all matters will be auspicious. When the dark Persian [i.e., Bodhidharma] comes running from the Eastern Sea, his eyebrows and nostrils three feet wide, blathering on about samsara and wheel-turning and about falseness and truth, you, in your straw sandals, with your two ears, will suddenly hear his voice. [You'll answer:] "Monks/laity? I don't know anything at all about that! Don't know anything at all!" "Who can tell them apart?"

> The spring breeze blows and scatters flowers of [the sixth patriarch's place] Lingnan.
> One by one the outflows are exhausted: the *true state*![6]

[3] Instruction to Superior Person Mingzhong[7] During His Illness

When a patched-robed Chan monk makes his *single chess move* [i.e., *that single matter* of Chan],[8] he doesn't differentiate "disturbed" and "clarified"; he is resistant to "polishing" and "dying"; he severs "past" and "present"; he does not

---

[6] Perhaps a couplet by Zhongfeng himself.
[7] Unidentified.
[8] Mujaku Dōchū, *Daie Fukaku Zenji sho kōroju* (Kyoto: Zen bunka kenkyūjo, 1997), 222: "*Single chess move* is a metaphorical expression, meaning *that single matter*." [一著子: 忠曰。託某詞。言那一事也。]. *Pearl in the Wicker-Basket* (*Kōroju* 栲栳珠; 1723) is Mujaku's commentary on *Letters of Dahui*.

preserve "common person" and "sage." That is why the ancients spoke of this [*single chess move*] as the *upward mechanism*, the *final phrase*, the *wisdom eye at the top of the head*, the *arm amulet*.[9] Linji at once gave out a shout that was like angry thunder; Deshan at once delivered a whack of his stick that was like a quick rain.[10] They didn't rely on effortful work; they didn't wade through graduated steps; they took things in hand and immediately acted; they plucked things up and immediately put them to use; they were a racing current outpacing the sword; they were a speedy flame faster than the wind. The correct eye looks on without rejoicing. *Here* does not involve anything that can be obtained through thought, intellectual understanding, arranging, and assigning. Superior Person Zhachuan Mingzhong! You are unexpectedly confined to your sickbed due to illness. I tell you Preceptor Zhenxie[11] had a saying:

> This old monk has a method for attaining repose:
> Eight sufferings simmer, but no harm at all!
> And what is the method for being in repose? The answer:
> Know that self is a dream.
> Realize illness is like an illusion.
> Merely guard the One Mind.
> Do not generate other thoughts.[12]

Of course, this is a method for attaining repose, but never mind! [Zhenxie] had another saying:

> *Repose* is non-movement.
> *Ease* is non-action.
> Transcend the mind that roosts in dualities and have nothing to rely upon.[13]

---

[9] Originally a Daoist protective amulet, used here as a metaphor for the buddha-nature. *Rentian baojian* (人天寶鑑; 1230): "If you are endowed with the [wisdom] eye at the top of the head and the arm-amulet, then Śākyamuni and Maitreya are dried turds, Mañjuśrī and Samantabhadra are common persons of the vast world, thusness and nirvana are posts for hitching donkeys, and the Buddhist canon is paper for wiping abscesses." [若是頂門具眼肘後有符。釋迦彌勒是乾屎橛。文殊普賢是博地凡夫。真如涅槃是繫驢橛。一大藏教是拭瘡疣紙。] (CBETA 2019.Q3, X87, no. 1612, p. 2a1–3).

[10] Linji's shout and Deshan's stick are ubiquitous in Chan literature. For instance, in one of Dahui's abbacy records: "At just that moment, supposing Deshan's stick was like raindrops and Linji's shout like running thunder, they were doing somersaults on a felt carpet [i.e., smooth circular movements in complete freedom] and moving toes inside one's shoes [i.e., something invisible to other people]." [大慧普覺禪師語錄。 正當恁麼時。設使德山棒如雨點。臨濟喝似雷奔。還如氈上翻筋斗。鞾裏動指頭。] (T 1998A.47.844a17–19).

[11] Zhenxie Qingliao (真歇清了; 1088–1151). Ishii Shūdō holds that a prime target of Dahui's *silence-as-illumination* (*mozhao*黙照) criticism was the Caodong teacher Zhenxie. See Ishii Shūdō, "*Daie Sōkō to sono deshitachi* (*hachi*)," *Indogaku bukkyōgaku kenkyū* 25, no. 1 (1977): 257–261.

[12] Untraced.

[13] Untraced.

Of course, this is a method for attaining repose, but Never mind! If you're lost here, Superior Person [Mingzhong], I give you this summary [of Zhenxie]:

> Whatever you can verbalize is deluded consciousness, calculation, discrimination, and selecting/rejecting—all of that is temporary and leads to divergence. How could this be the true ultimate! Do you want to know a method for attaining repose? The four elements and five aggregates are it. The organ-body and vessel-world are it. The four-hundred and four illnesses are it. The mountains, rivers, and great earth are it. Your hearing, seeing, knowing, and being aware are it—among all differentiated sense-objects, there are none that are not it.

Bah! [In the *Filial Piety Classic*, Confucius rebuts his disciple Cengzi's simplistic formulation of filial piety as simply following a father's commands, and defines filial piety as requiring a son to remonstrate with a father who engages in unrighteous conduct. In the same vein, with Confucius's words, I must remonstrate with Zhenxie's formulation:] "What words are these?"[14] The four elements, five aggregates, and the differentiated sense-objects are *all* corrupted, non-repose characteristics! If you call *all that* a method for attaining repose, it's like the [tyrannical official Zhao Gao's] calling a deer a horse [i.e., it's like intentionally stating a bald-faced lie as a test to see who goes along with it]![15] And even if you *don't* call all that a method for attaining repose, it's still like calling a deer a horse! Even if you eliminate these two alternatives and supply some other option, you will not have avoided [the problem]: that would still be calling a deer a horse. *Before Preceptor Zhenxie has even opened his mouth* [*to recite the above sayings*], you must throw off delusive calculation and keep from falling into *yes/no*. Your very own eye [at the top of your head] will all-at-once open, and you will clearly comprehend the Source. And when, for the first time, you come to understand the teachings of the entire Buddhist canon, that [too] will be calling a deer

---

[14] *Xiao jing* (孝經), *Jianzheng* (諫諍). The disciple Cengzi asks if simply following a father's commands can be called "filial piety." Confucius responds with this line (saying it twice) and proceeds to argue that, when a case of unrighteous conduct is concerned, a son must by no means keep from remonstrating with his father. See ctext.org/xiao-jing/filial-piety-in-relation-to-reproof/zh?en=on.

[15] *Shiji* 史記 (*Qin Shihuang Benji* 秦始皇本紀, 57): "[Counselor-in-chief] Zhao Gao was about to engage in rebellion. He feared that the various officials would not obey him, so he first set up a test. He presented a deer to Ershi, saying: 'It is a horse.' Ershi laughed and said: 'Isn't the Counselor-in-chief mistaken in saying that a deer is a horse?' He then asked others. Some of them were silent. Some of them said 'horse' to comply with Zhao Gao. Some said 'deer.' Zhao Gao then applied the law to all those who said 'deer.' Later all officials feared Zhao Gao." [趙高欲為亂。恐群臣不聽。乃先設驗。持鹿獻於二世曰。馬也。二世笑曰。丞相誤邪。謂鹿為馬。問左右。左右或默。或言馬以阿順趙高。或言鹿。高因陰中諸言鹿者以法。後群臣皆畏高。] (ctext.org/pre-qin-and-han?searchu=趙高&en=off&page=3).

a horse. The seventeen hundred Chan cases: calling a deer a horse. Down to: when all the old Chan preceptors of the world pick up the hammer and hold the fly whisk upright [in teachings students], that is calling a deer a horse. Such calling-[a-deer-a-horse] talk, and such understanding as comes from it, is calling a deer a horse. Do you understand? In case you don't understand, at your stove where you prepare your medicines and [while resting your head] on the pillow [of your sickbed], just silently probe your *tasteless huatou*. Never let it go. Suddenly your pillow will fall to the ground, and you will forget both your illness and your medicine! You, a patched-robed Chan monk, will make your *single chess move*, and you will come face to face with reality. Once you have arrived *here*, there will be nothing about this very body-mind of yours and your illness that will not be a method for attaining repose! Nevertheless, don't ever call a deer a horse.

[4] Instruction to Superior Person Lin[16] During His Illness

Of old, Preceptor Zhenxie[17] had a verse:

> Visiting an old friend and discussing matters of the heart really can be painful.
> Years have passed and I am now lying alone in the Nirvana Hall [i.e., infirmary].
> At the gate no passing travelers, the paper of the windows tattered.
> The stove filled with cold ashes, sitting mats with frost on them.
> After contracting an illness, one for the first time really knows that the body is suffering.
> When healthy, one is quite busy for the sake of other people.
> This old monk has a method for attaining repose:
> Eight sufferings simmer, but no harm at all![18]

An ancient composed this verse:

> Hurt by the floating fragility of self and the world,
> Realizing the arising-extinguishing of dream-illusions.

---

[16] Unidentified.
[17] See n. 9.
[18] Appears in *Admonitions of the Ebon-Robed Gate* (*Zimen jingxun* 緇門警訓; 1313; T 2023.48. 1091a27–b?).

> Pointing out the objective-supports of delusive thought,
> Giving instruction in the true quiescence of this Way.[19]

These fifty-six syllables [of Zhenxie's verse] cover just about the whole matter, constituting a model of the *true person* of the Way. People studying Buddhism should come to know [this model] from personal experience—then they will become aware that they have not yet realized the boundaries of *this mind*. The entire body is illness; every realm is illness. When you are approaching the end of life and thoughts arise in your mind, do not ask about whether you will become a buddha or a Chan patriarch. Everything is conditioned by illness. In the middle of all this, if someone points to a single dharma and says: "this is not illness," that is an utterly false point of view. Also, why would you only speak of "illness" when you are finally forced to embrace the [sickbed's] pillow and mat as you sink into sickness? The eye of the Great Doctor King of the Snow Mountains [Śākyamuni] could not endure looking upon this, and so for forty-nine years at more than three hundred assemblies he spoke of dust motes, spoke of worlds, and today [those talks] have been assembled into the teachings of the great Buddhist canon: a medicinal prescription for curing this illness. Today, the single *huatou that has no meaning or taste*[20] that you are practicing is the divine medicine secretly transmitted within these prescriptions. Once you have contracted a fatal *gaohuang* illness [i.e., an illness just below the heart and above the diaphragm, the inmost part of the body—untreatable by medicine], always take the *single thought* of the non-retrogressing, unchangeable herbal concoction [i.e., the *huatou*]. Constantly imbibe this divine medicine, medicine that certainly will cure this illness, hitting the mark a hundred times out of a hundred. In the case of those who take this medicine in the present but fail to achieve recovery, it is because they have some sort of aversion to the application of the medicine, and so it is ineffectual. If you cannot completely empty out this aversion, not only will [the medicine] be ineffective, you'll find that your grasping onto [your evaluation of] the medicine will itself turn into an illness. And it sure won't be easy to cure that! What I am calling *aversion* is any "backup" thought. What is a "backup" thought? It is when you separate from the correct thought of the *huatou* that you are practicing and move even a tiny bit onto such sense-objects as good/bad or awakening/delusion. This is what is called a "backup" thought. This is aversion to the medicine [of the *huatou*]. Truly, if you can over time

---

[19] Untraced.
[20] Zhongfeng's typical phrasing for the *huatou*.

refrain from committing this crime of aversion, then, thought-moment after thought-moment in a continuum, you will be kept safe in repose; you will be kept safe in danger; you will be kept safe in life; you will be kept safe in death. Outside and inside will meld, and, if you persevere in that way, suddenly you will be "yoked." This illness will all-at-once disappear. Both medicine and aversion [to the medicine] will simultaneously disappear. And the method for attaining repose will appear right in front of you! You should know this and make effort.

[5] Instruction to Superior Person Xiyou[21] upon Going on Pilgrimage

There is a *single phrase* [i.e., the *huatou*] along the edge of your walking stick. There is a *single phrase* on the bottom of your straw sandals. There is a *single phrase* in the outside world of your three-thousand mile [pilgrimage]. There is a *single phrase* in [the inner world of] your six sense-gates. If you come to realization within [the inner world of] your six sense-gates, then there is no need for you to separately investigate [via a pilgrimage in] the outside world of three thousand miles. If you come to realization on [the pilgrimage] in the outside world of three thousand miles, then [there is no need for you to separately investigate] the six sense-gates that lie wholly inside you. It is merely that the *single phrase* of the walking stick lies only along [the edge of] the walking stick. The *single phrase* on the bottom of your straw sandals lies only on the bottom of your straw sandals. You must never move off [the *single phrase*]! Do you comprehend? Exhaust the limitless *dharmadhātu*: *that* is your walking stick; pervade the ten directions of space: *that* is your pair of straw sandals. If you "*pick up* the walking stick," you'll lose "the sandals"; if you "*put on* the straw sandals," you'll lose "the walking stick!" You must realize that the walking stick has no walking-stick-ness for you to pick up, the straw sandals no sandals-ness for you to put on. If you are intent on *picking up* and *putting on*, then you will simultaneously lose the whole shebang! But if you are not intent on [*picking up* and *putting on*], how will you be able to bring the walking stick and straw sandals into play [on your pilgrimage]? [Answer:] Just hang the *huatou* that you are practicing between your eyebrows and silently keep an eye on it. Is [the *huatou*] the walking stick? Is it the straw sandals? Is it [the pilgrimage] in the outside world of three thousand miles? Is it [your inner world of the] six sense-gates? When keeping an eye on [the *huatou*] reaches a *not-able-to-keep-an-eye-on*

---

[21] Unidentified.

state, the *cool eye*[22] will come upon you and you'll suddenly see right through things! From the outset your seven-foot walking stick and pair of straw sandals have always been the *fields of your native village*." If you pick them up with the hand of confidence, then your take-off point is not far away. If you fail to obtain remarkable clarity on top of the *huatou*, rest assured that your being deluded by the walking stick and the straw sandals will persist beyond just one lifetime, and, in the end, you will not derive the slightest bit of benefit [from the pilgrimage]! In both ancient times and in the present, eminent scholars on pilgrimage who have been deluded by their walking stick and straw sandals—we cannot possibly know their number! Today, how could you be willing to fall to this delusion? To reiterate, a verse says:

> There is a *single phrase* [i.e., the *huatou*] that cannot be concealed.
> On your pilgrimage route of three thousand miles you search for your home village.
> If you opened your eyes before even picking up your walking stick,
> For the first time, on the long road of months and years, you would have confidence.[23]

[6] Instruction to Layman Sameness Hermitage (Commissioner Ban-la-tuo-yin[24] [a Mongol official])

Your own mind is endowed with all *buddhadharmas*. Outside of your mind there are no other *buddhadharmas* that you can seek out. Even if you could seek for them, it would be incorrect, and all of that would be false thought and deluded consciousness, not ultimate dharma. You should know that your own mind has neither the sagely nor the common. If your surmising has gotten free of sagely/common, then you are "yoked" with your own mind. Your own mind has neither hatred nor attachment. If your distinguishing has gotten free of hatred/attachment, then you are "yoked" with your own mind. Your own mind has neither seizing nor rejecting. If your feelings have gotten free of seizing/rejecting, then you are "yoked" with your own mind. Your own mind lacks any karmic action of good/bad or active/still. If you can get free of all these, then you are "yoked" with your own mind. However, talk about

---

[22] Xu Yin (徐夤) of the Tang, a scholar-official who became a recluse, has a couplet: "The *cold eye* looks on in stillness and truly loves to laugh; the slanted heart accords with talk but is resentful." [上盧三拾遺以言見黜: 冷眼靜看真好笑。傾懷與說却爲寃。].
[23] Probably a verse by Zhongfeng.
[24] Heller, *Illusory Abiding*, 113: "Ba-la-tuo-yin was in the highest ranks of government under Renzong, serving as assistant director of the Left 左丞 from 1312 until the fifth month of the next year. He was then promoted to assistant director of the Right 右丞, a position he held for a year and a half. How the two men met is not clear." Heller adds in 113 n. 66, "Bala is possibly 'Borak.'"

"getting free of sagely/common, getting free of hatred/attachment," etc., is absolutely forbidden. In your getting rid of one type of mind—specifically [and effortfully] getting free of it—your very act of getting free *is precisely* arising/extinguishing. But if you do not exert mind at all, then how can anyone speak of any principle of getting free of something? Therefore, an ancient said:

> The divine light shines alone,
> The beautiful Way of the myriad ancients.
> Having entered this gate,
> Do not preserve intellectual knowledge.[25]

Just knowing that your own mind has no gap between sage and common person—that is intellectual knowledge. Also, just knowing the standard of getting free of sagely/common—that is itself falling into intellectual knowledge. You should know that the principle of getting free of something is utterly unconnected to any exertion of mind. Merely, at a time of awakening, do not wait for getting free of anything and simply entertain a *natural non-attachment and non-grasping*. It is this very non-attachment and non-grasping thought that we call *getting free*. Right now, this mind of yours has not yet attained awakening. All you must do is place smack in the middle of your daily activities the [following] *huatou*: **when the four elements are falling apart, where is tranquility and stability?** Silently keep an eye on it. It is unnecessary to engage in any thought at all, unnecessary to have any thought of *doing* cultivation. As soon as you engender such a thought, you are immediately ensnared by the term *cultivation*. In the sagely vision, there is no place at all for the engendering of thought. Business as usual: silent practice of your *huatou*. Ripen it over a long time, and suddenly you will attain awakening. It is like suddenly remembering something you had long forgotten. At that time, deluded feelings are emptied out, and intellectual knowledge is destroyed. The singular self-mind in its entirety is alone revealed: everywhere freedom. The hundreds of thousands of cogitations simultaneously come to a rest. The hundreds of thousands of sense-objects—at that very thought-moment you have gotten free of them. The dharma-gate of peace and joy—nothing surpasses it!

[7] Instruction for Layman Wu[26]

Chan is the Chan of Pure Land; Pure Land is the Pure Land of Chan. Of old, Preceptor Yongming Yanshou separated Pure Land and Chan into four

---

[25] Untraced.
[26] Unidentified.

possible alternatives.[27] Because [some] scholars are unaware of the schema [Yanshou] set up, they give off contrary and recalcitrant vibes, saying "Chan is Chan, and Pure Land is Pure Land!" Little do they know that Chan practice is for ending samsara, and the *nianfo* [of Pure land] is also for ending samsara. Originally samsara has no root. Due to delusion about Innate Nature, it springs forth. If one discerns Innate Nature, then samsara is banished without waiting for any banishment. Once samsara is banished, is there Chan? Is there Pure Land? Of old, Mahāsthāmaprāpta Bodhisattva by means of *nianfo* gained the non-arising patience of mind.[28] The great bodhisattva Avalokiteśvara through hearing and pondering cultivated the three wisdoms to realize perfect penetration.[29] Are those Chan? Are they Pure Land? Both are the bequeathed intention of the two great bodhisattvas. Both great bodhisattvas are guide-attendants of paradise. [Layman Wu,] you have never been the least bit contrary! At present, students of the two tenets [Chan and Pure Land]—what is it in their vision that makes them so contrarian? I have repeatedly tried to find the answer to this and have finally figured out the very source of their contrariness. I will try my hand at a summary: it is merely that students of the two tenets are not rooted in the *great matter of samsara*. Some employ a Chan that does not feel pain over samsara to "till the field of empty verbosity." Some use a Pure Land that "elevates oneself, always behaving in a self-satisfied manner." And so [with both tenets] the upside-down view of *is/is not* is on display. If there is no unseen tally with the vow and practice of

---

[27] These four alternatives do not appear in the works of Yongming Yanshou (904–975) but are attributed to Yanshou in Dayou's (大佑) *Gist of the Pure Land* (*Jingtu zhigui ji* 淨土指歸集; 1393): "He [Yanshou] instructed with verses on the four alternatives of practicing Chan and the *nianfo*. #1: *Have Chan no Pure Land*. Out of ten people, nine stumble and trip. When the realm of sense-objects appears, they suddenly follow them. Means merely enlightened to the principle-nature. No wish to go to be reborn in the Pure Land.... #2: *No Chan have Pure Land*. Ten-thousand cultivation practices, and ten-thousand people discard them. They only obtain a vision of Amitābha. What anguish that they do not attain awakening! Means not yet enlightened to the principle-nature. Their only wish is to go to be reborn in the Pure Land.... #3: *Have Chan have Pure Land*. Like a tiger with horns. In the present life you become a teacher of people. In future lives you become a buddha or patriarch. Having deeply penetrated the *buddhadharma*, you are to be called a teacher of humans and gods.... #4: *No Chan no Pure Land*. An iron platform together with a copper staff. For ten-thousand eons and a thousand lifetimes. There is nothing for anyone to rely upon. Not enlightened to buddha-principle. Also, don't wish to be reborn in the Pure Land." [永明料揀：永明智覺禪師。從上韶國師。得單傳之旨。專修淨土之行。延壽三學者。會同諸說。為宗鏡錄一百卷。又慮學者執空見為進修。撰萬善同歸集言。大乘菩薩六度萬行恒沙法門。皆當稱性修之。其示參禪念佛四料揀偈。一曰。有禪無淨土。十人九蹉路。陰境若現前。瞥爾隨他去。謂單明理性。不願往生。流轉娑婆。則有退墮之患。陰境者。於禪定中。陰魔發現也。如楞嚴所明。於五陰境。起五十種魔事。其人初不覺知魔著。亦言自得無上涅槃。迷惑無知。墮無間獄者是也。二曰。無禪有淨土。萬修萬人去。但得見彌陀。何愁不開悟。謂未明理性。但願往生。乘佛力故。速登不退。三曰。有禪有淨土。猶如戴角虎。現世為人師。來生作佛祖。既深達佛法。故可為人天師。又發願往生。速登不退。腰纏十萬貫。騎鶴上揚州。四曰。無禪無淨土。鐵床并銅柱。萬劫與千生。沒個人依怙。既不明佛理。又不願往生。永劫沉淪。何由出離。欲超生死。速登不退者。當於此四種擇善行之。] (CBETA 2019.Q3, X61, no. 1154, p. 379b16–c9).

[28] Appears in Pudu's (普度) *Precious Mirror of the Lotus School of Mt. Lu* (*Lushan lianzong baojian* 廬山蓮宗寶鑑; 1305; T 1973.47.317b6–7).

[29] Appears in Chao Yong's (超永) *Complete Documents of the Five Lamp-Flames* (*Wudeng quanshu* 五燈全書; 1693; CBETA 2019.Q3, X82, no. 1571, p. 504c23–24).

the ancient buddhas, will the two tenets ever come close to being calmed? Layman, you have long been on intimate terms with the study of Pure Land, and you also esteem the Way of *direct pointing* of Shaolin [i.e., Chan]. Just take the [following] *huatou*: *what was **my original face** before my father and mother conceived me*? Place it within your mind when you are doing *nianfo*. Thought-moment after thought-moment you must not let go [of this *huatou*]. You must be diligent about never releasing it. As you practice-work ripens, your seeing-knowing will become ever clearer and your Way-power ever firmer. One day, in the state where doer/done is forgotten and your breathing has calmed, you suddenly will attain all-at-once awakening. For the first time you will come to believe that my words have not deceived you. But, if you falsely latch onto my words *before* you have attained awakening, not only will you find yourself sitting in a *nest* [of stereotyped formulas], the Way will recede further and further away from you! I warn you—I warn you!

Translation 3
Night Conversations in a Mountain Hermitage in Zhongfeng Extensive Record

Night Conversations in a Mountain Hermitage I

[1] I, Mr. Phantasm, was in retirement deep in the mountains, when out of the blue a hermit passed my gate. Together we did a session of night sitting, facing each other on the Chan platform. At that time, the mountain moon was shining through the window as bright as the daytime sun.

HERMIT: "I have heard that 'rational-concept scholars' [i.e., scholars who study the sutras and treatises, and interpret textual meanings] consider the *dhyāna* of *dhyāna-samādhi* to be equivalent to Bodhidharma's Chan of *singular transmission and direct pointing*. They hold that Bodhidharma had a so-called *Treatise on Fetal Breathing*,[1] transmitted

---

[1] Refers to a short work in the Daoist compendium *Seven Bamboo Slips of the Cloud Book-Box* (*Yunji qi qian* 雲笈七籤) entitled *Great Master Bodhidharma's Secret Formula of the Miraculous Functioning of the Internal Reality That Allows Staying in the World and Keeping Human Form* (*Damo dashi zhushi liuxing neizhen miaoyong jue* 達磨大師住世留形内真妙用訣). The opening and closing passages run as follows: "When of old I was in the western country [i.e., India], I [Bodhidharma] received a transmission of the miraculous practice fetal breathing, which allows one to stay in the world [for a long time] and keep human form [without dying]. A master named Bejeweled Crown transmitted to me a secret formula. Question: 'Now you are about to go eastward and travel to China and various other countries to transmit widely the secret dharma of the mind-ground. In these various countries a lot of people suffer from calamities of cold and heat, and the ones who are harmed all die. You intend to transmit the mind-dharma in these lands. Those who hope to keep bodily form and not be attacked by calamities and sickness—to be able to stay in the world for a long time and keep human form without dying—I am not sure that is possible, is it?' The Master [Bodhidharma] said: 'It is possible.' Another question: 'Tell me how this could be possible!' The Master said: 'The root of being born begins with fetal breathing. This is precisely the combining and mingling of spirit and the pure breath. . . . The ordinary person's inhalation-exhalation cycles are different from that of the sage. The ordinary person's breath enters and leaves at this throat; the sage's divine breath is always in the sea of breath. The sea of breath is the root of primal breath: the place to dwell. It is below the navel and in union with the stomach. It is also the uterus, the sea of breath, the joining of child and mother. The Way-person can maintain it in an unbroken continuity. This is a return to the Source, a return to the place of original birth, firmly abiding and congealed, not transforming and not scattering. This is in all cases the meaning. Invincible, the divine consciousness is mostly still: spontaneously long life. This is the true formula for the mystery of staying in the world [for a long time] and keeping human form [without dying]. If you abide in spontaneous breathing, spirit steers your breath, and there is no exhaling through the nose. This allows true fetal breathing. After the two sense-fields behold each other, sexual desire stirs. Once sexual desire has stirred, the pure breath descends into the erect stalk and spills out. All this is brought on by sexual desire, which is uncontrollable. Thereupon, there is the sorrow of drainage and the disappearance of the root.'" [達磨大師住世留形内真妙用訣: 吾昔於西國。授得住世留形胎息妙。師

The Recorded Sayings of Chan Master Zhongfeng Mingben. Jeffrey L. Broughton, Oxford University Press.
© Oxford University Press 2023. DOI: 10.1093/oso/9780197672976.003.0004

for generations, and they tendentiously quote the line: "the eighth consciousness [i.e., the storehouse consciousness] stays in the *womb*, grounded only in *unitary breathing*, and so it's called *fetal breathing*."[2] They hold that *dhyāna-samādhi* of our [Bodhidharma Chan] is grounded only in this *unitary breathing*. Today those who discuss such matters get entangled in this theory and abandon our Bodhidharma Chan to become students of two-vehicles *dhyāna-samādhi* [i.e., the two Hīnayānist vehicles: hearer and independent buddha]. What about this?"

PHANTASM: "These people are not slanderers [of Bodhidharma Chan]: they are simply unaware of the Chan indicated by Bodhidharma. They mistakenly think that there is no *dhyāna* outside the four *dhyānas* and eight *samādhis* [of the Hīnayāna]. Little do they know that, when Bodhidharma long ago followed in the succession of the twenty-seven Indian patriarchs, he called Chan the *mind-realization of the Tathāgata's ultimate*. This Chan has many names. It is also called *highest-vehicle Chan*. It is also called *supreme-truth Chan*. In fact, [this Chan,] and the four *dhyānas* and eight *samādhis* of the two vehicles and the outsider Ways, are as far apart from each other as heaven and the deep abyss. You should know that this [Bodhidharma] Chan does not rely on explanations in the sutras. Nor does it rely on the fruits of any cultivation and realization. It does not rely on what is understood through seeing and hearing. It does not rely on any method one can access. Therefore, we say it is the *separate transmission outside the teachings*. Only the sentient-being of great mind who perfumes buddha-seeds over many lifetimes, yet never wades through stages of the path, will, upon a single hearing, experience a thousand awakenings and obtain the 'great *dhāraṇī*.' After that, whether staying alone on a lonely mountain peak or entering shops in the marketplace, he will be able to 'let his hands hang free' [i.e., set aside the standard monastic clasped-hand posture, and practice *upāya* to save beings]. Lengthwise or crosswise, going against or going along with [i.e., in complete freedom], the Way this being walks will transcend ordinary

---

名寶冠。傳吾秘訣。問曰。令欲東游震旦。及諸國土。弘傳心地密法。其諸國土。人多遇寒暑為災患。所傷例皆死喪。意欲擬向此土弘傳心法。願求留形。不為災患疫疾所侵。長能住世。留形不死。不知得以否。師云。得。又問曰。雲如何即得。師云。夫所生之本。始胎息。即是神與精氣相合凝結 . . . 則凡人呼吸。與聖人殊。凡人息氣出入於咽喉。聖人息神氣常在氣海。氣海。即元氣之根本也。所居之處也。即臍下。合太倉。亦為子宮。為氣海。即子母相合。道人能守之。綿綿不絕。此是返本還源。歸本生之處。而堅住凝結。不化不散。此即皆其義也。不敗。神識多靜。即自然長生。留形住世要妙之真訣也。師曰。若住自然之息。神御氣。即鼻無出息。令為真胎息也。凡夫之人。二境相睹之後。即情慾動。情慾動即精氣悉下降於莖端。而下洩之。皆為情慾所引。制御不得。遂有眹渝之憂。衰喪其本也。]. //zh.m.wikisource.org/zh-hant/雲笈七籤/59. Also see Stephen Eskildsen, *Daoism, Meditation, and the Wonders of Serenity: From the Latter Han Dynasty (25–220) to the Tang Dynasty (618–907)* (Albany: State University of New York Press, 2015), 257.

[2] This does not appear in the above *Treatise on Fetal Breathing* and remains untraced.

delusion. Speaking or silent, expanding or contracting, he won't take up sitting in a *nest* [of stereotyped formulas]. How could [such Chan] possibly be called *dhyāna-samādhi* or *fetal breathing*? Bodhidharma's *not establishing the written word and direct pointing to the human mind* went through six generations to arrive at the Great Master Huineng. The Master [Huineng] said: 'If you speak of this Chan of *direct pointing*, you've already gone on a twisting route far away from it.'³ If you consider what Huineng said, how could Chan permit any words or texts that could possibly be transmitted? In the world an [apocryphal Bodhidharma text entitled] *Treatise on Fetal Breathing* does indeed circulate, and I don't know what liar stained the sagely master's name by authoring it. How much more so in the case of later people who wanted to exploit Bodhidharma by conspiring to concoct false teachings in his name! You must know that this was not a case of their cheating Bodhidharma: they were cheating their own minds! In the first place, the World-honored-one was saddened by sentient-beings' cheating themselves within samsara, creating their own bondage without end. Therefore, he showed them the mind-dharma, wanting them to cease engaging in self-deception. If now, on the contrary, they use this very mind-dharma for purposes of self-deception, where can they go that will not bring in its wake self-deception?"

[2] SOMEONE ASKED: "Chan invokes a *separate transmission outside the teachings*, but is there really such a thing as a *separate transmission*? I am always coming across rational-concept scholars who are quite confused about this, and disputes are inevitable."

PHANTASM: "Rational-concept scholars take as their job discriminating terms and characteristics, but in this [matter of the *separate transmission outside the teachings*] they are incapable of [the understanding that comes from] emptying out their [habitual] principle of discrimination. If they could only go all the way to the end of the *ultimate standard*,⁴ then, toward the two words *separate transmission*, they would emit the *single laugh*, gaining release [from all doubt⁵]! If you ask why, the four tenets [i.e., the

---

³ Untraced.
⁴ Broughton with Watanabe, *Letters of Dahui*, letter #35.6 (pp. 222–223): "But the present-day party of perverse teachers of silence-as-illumination just takes sinking into silence as the *ultimate standard*—they call this 'the matter prior to the appearance of Bhīṣma-garjita-svara Buddha' [i.e., the first buddha of the *alaṃkāra* eon], or they call it 'the matter of the eon of nothingness before the world begins.' Having no confidence in the existence of awakening, they consider awakening a deception; they consider awakening 'starting second' at a game of chess; they consider awakening as *upāya*-speech; they consider awakening a term to lure beings along. People like this cheat others and cheat themselves, mislead others and mislead themselves. You must be careful!" [大慧普覺禪師語錄: 而今默照邪師輩。只以無言無說為極則。喚作威音那畔事。亦喚作空劫已前事。不信有悟門。以悟為誑。以悟為第二頭。以悟為方便語。以悟為接引之辭。如此之徒。謾人自謾。誤人自誤。亦不可不知。] (T 1998A.47.933c6-11). See also letters #58.6 and #59.1 (pp. 310–311).
⁵ Supplied from *Jiatai pudeng lu* (嘉泰普燈錄): "Now the single laugh, all-at-once gaining release from all doubt." [今一笑頓釋所疑。] (CBETA 2019.Q3, X79, no. 1559, p. 432a22).

secret-teaching tenet, the Tiantai tenet, the *Vinaya* tenet, and the Chan tenet] in common transmit the purport of the single buddha: no tenet must be left out. Thus, 'the buddhas speak dharma with a single voice, [but the audiences understand in various ways].'[6] In the sutra it is said 'there is only the one buddha-vehicle, not two or three vehicles.'[7] How could there be anything separate from the four tenets? [The problem comes when] any of them arrogates to itself the exclusivity of a specialist separate from the others: none of them shows anything at all that is separate from the one buddha-vehicle. It is like the efficacy of the four seasons in constituting a full year, but the seasons of spring, summer, autumn, and winter are separate. The reason why they function as a single year is precisely because they cannot be separated out. The secret-teachings tenet is spring. The tenet of Tiantai [Zhiyi], Xianshou [Fazang], and Ci'en [Kuiji] is the summer. The South-Mountain *Vinaya* tenet is the fall. The [Chan] Shaolin *single-transmission* tenet is the winter. [The rational-concept scholars,] with their logical talk, know only that Chan is a transmission separate from the other tenets, but they don't know that the other tenets are also the separate transmission of Chan! If you bring together [all four tenets], the secret-teachings tenet proclaims the mind of the single buddha who out of great compassion saves beings. The teachings tenet expounds the mind of the single buddha's elucidation of great wisdom. The *vinaya* tenet holds to the mind of the single buddha's adornment of great practice. The Chan tenet transmits the mind of the single buddha's perfect fulfilling of great awakening. Given that you can't mistake one of the four seasons for another, how could there be an instance where they are non-separate?

SOMEONE: "We don't say that any of these three tenets are 'separate transmissions,' so why do we openly say that the Chan tenet is a 'separate transmission?'"

[PHANTASM] REPLIES: "From the point of view of principle, [what you say] is so. The other tenets all enter through a specific gate, and, by means of study, [practice] reaches completion. Only Chan *internally* does not wade through the delusions of thinking and calculating. *Externally*, it does not pile on feats of scholarship or cultivation-and-realization. [For Chan,] from the distant past to the present, nothing has ever been lacking. If you turn your mind to seizing anything, you've already crossed over to an *itinerary*. Even if you completely understand and own something, it will turn into an *ordeal*. Truly, [Chan's separate transmission] is a separateness way beyond separateness! Somebody who goes around restraining a picture [of

---

[6] *Vimalakīrti Sūtra*, T 475.14.538a2–3.
[7] *Lotus Sutra*, T 262.9.7b2–3.

a horse] to lasso a horse: how could he be up to knowing what's really going on? [When such a person] hears that our Chan has a teaching of 'separate transmission outside the teachings [i.e., engagement with the real horse rather than a picture of the horse],' it's no wonder he's shocked!"

[3] SOMEONE ASKED: "Yongjia takes *clarity and stillness* as medicine and takes *staying in darkness and confused thought* as illness.[8] What about this theory vis-à-vis the Chan transmitted by Bodhidharma?"

I [PHANTASM] SAID: "The teaching of cultivation-and-realization that is clarified in the encapsulation found in the ten chapters of the *Yongjia Collection* overall appropriates [Tiantai's] *stopping-and-discerning* method,[9] beginning with 'stopping thoughts and forgetting sense objects,' and next proceeding to 'sense objects and cognition both in dark stillness.'[10] At the point of [the *Yongjia Collection*'s] separately posited 'ten methods for contemplating mind,'[11] there is the utmost profundity and subtlety: a deep comprehension of non-arising. Nevertheless, only Bodhidharma taught how to directly clarify your own mind. Once this mind is clarified, it's like someone's arriving home: he will naturally be able to make a living as the occasion demands. This is truly why [the person who has clarified his own mind in the Bodhidharma mode] never again cites prolix quotations from the verbal teachings [of the sutras]. When he [i.e., Bodhidharma] was expediently leading Shenguang [i.e., the second patriarch Huike], Bodhidharma only said: "Externally, cut off all objective supports; internally, make the mind free of panting. With the mind like a wall, it will be possible to enter the Way."[12] I have never heard of any other verbal teaching [of Bodhidharma] beyond this. Only if you are one who has achieved a true realization within your own mind do you know for sure that advancing by stages [in the manner of the *ten methods for contemplating mind*] to pass over to the other shore is not equivalent to [Bodhidharma's] teaching of *direct pointing*. The *Yongjia Collection* is not the only text [that falls into this category]. Tiantai Zhiyi's three contemplations [of empty, provisional, and middle] and Xianshou

---

[8] *Chan School Yongjia Collection* (*Chanzong Yongjia ji* 禪宗永嘉集): "Confused thought is illness; karmic indeterminacy is also illness. Stillness is medicine; clarity is also medicine. Stillness destroys confused thought; clarity destroys karmic indeterminacy." [亂想是病。無記亦病。寂寂是藥。惺惺亦藥。寂寂破亂想。惺惺治無記。] (T 2013.48.390c4–5). Yongjia Xuanjue (永嘉玄覺; 675–713) received approval from the sixth patriarch Huineng after studying under him for only one day and night. Early in his career Yongjia had studied Tiantai.

[9] Tiantai Zhiyi's (538–597) graduated system of *śamatha* (*calmness*) and *vipaśyana* (*insight*).

[10] *Chan School Yongjia Collection* (*Chanzong Yongjia ji* 禪宗永嘉集), T 2013.48.389b23 and 388b15.

[11] *Chan School Yongjia Collection* (*Chanzong Yongjia ji* 禪宗永嘉集), T 2013.48.391b10–14.

[12] An early appearance of this Bodhidharma line is in Zongmi's *Chan Prolegomenon* (*Chanyuan zhuquanji duxu* 禪源諸詮集都序): "Bodhidharma took wall-examining to teach people how to pacify mind: 'Externally, stop all objective supports; internally, make the mind free of panting [i.e., wheezing or gasping for breath]. With the mind like a wall, it will be possible to enter the Way.'" [達摩以壁觀教人安心。外止諸緣。內心無喘。心如牆壁。可以入道。] (T 2015.48.403c27–29). See Jeffrey Lyle Broughton, *Zongmi on Chan* (New York: Columbia University Press, 2009), 129.

Fazang's contemplation of the four *dharmadhātus* intricately exhaust the ultimate principles of mind. Suppose that all the buddhas of the past were to pop up again in the world and teach about mind—we can foresee that they would not surpass this [Bodhidharma Chan]! Thus, the fact that the *Yongjia Collection* is not the same as Bodhidharma is because of this difference: one is based on verbal teachings, and one is divorced from verbal teachings. If we seriously examine the matter, it is like the *Perfect Awakening Sutra*'s distributing the three contemplations [i.e., *śamatha*, *samāpatti*, and *dhyāna*] into twenty-five wheels,[13] or the *Śūraṃgama Sūtra*'s verifying the eighteen *dhātus* and seven great elements as the twenty-five kinds of perfect penetration.[14] It cannot be that only these two sutras [formulate intricate verbal teachings]. Just wade through the cultivation-and-realization methods narrated in the sutras: none rides in the same road-ruts as the *direct-pointing* Chan transmitted by Bodhidharma. Should you ask why, if you are even minimally acquainted with the verbal teachings, you know that they cannot serve as a *separate transmission outside the teachings*."

SOMEONE: "If that is so, then does Bodhidharma's Chan differ [in some fundamental way] from the verbal teachings of all the buddhas?"

[PHANTASM] REPLIES: "I have searched in the Way of the buddhas and patriarchs for any feature that is identical [to Bodhidharma Chan] and haven't been able to find any, but how could there be any difference that is susceptible to our seeing? Haven't you heard that the sutra says: 'In *dhāraṇī* [i.e., ultimate principle] there is no written word, but the written word reveals *dhāraṇī*?'[15] As for 'in *dhāraṇī* there is no written word,' Bodhidharma tallies with this in his *direct pointing*. As for 'the written word reveals *dhāraṇī*,' the various tenets [of the verbal teachings] base themselves on this to guide people. However, [my assertion] that Bodhidharma's Way differs from the tenets [of the verbal teachings] is not a case of my fetishizing the outré via some concoction out of my own head, but simply a continuation of the Buddha's handing over the mind-dharma at Vulture Peak solely to Mahākāśyapa! The Way that he handed over solely to Mahākāśyapa isn't a private thing handed over to only one person at Vulture Peak. It is the numinous mind that is the common endowment of all sentient-beings in the *dharmadhātu*. Therefore, when the World-honored-one out of compassion established

---

[13] T 842.17.918a–919b.
[14] T 945.19.130a–131b.
[15] *Great Perfection of Wisdom Sutra* (大般若波羅蜜多經; T 220.7.957a13–15) and *Sheng tianwang bore boluomi jing* (勝天王般若波羅蜜經; T 231.8.720c4–6). *Yongjia chanzong ji zhu* (永嘉禪宗集註) provides a gloss on *dhāraṇī* as ultimate principle: "However, ultimate principle is wordless; we rely on texts and words to clarify its purport. The *Great Perfection of Wisdom Sutra* says: 'In *dhāraṇī* there is no written word, but the written word reveals *dhāraṇī*.'" [然而至理無言。假文言以明其旨。大品云。總持無文字。文字顯總持。] (CBETA 2019.Q3, X63, no. 1242, p. 316b22–23).

the teachings, he was intricately adaptable to the faculties, both sharp and dull, of sentient-beings. The *upāyas* the World-honored one expounded—great and small vehicles, partial and perfect teachings, same teaching [i.e., one vehicle] and separate teachings [i.e., three vehicles], open teaching and secret teaching—he couldn't stop [from establishing such things].

[4] SOMEONE ASKED: "In [the sutras] there are verbal teachings that are the same as the *direct pointing* of the Chan house. For example, the *Huayan Sutra* says: 'Know that all dharmas are the self-nature of mind, and do not rely on anyone else's awakening.'[16] And the *Lotus Sutra* says: 'This dharma is not something that mental reflection and discrimination can understand.'[17] The *Diamond Sutra* says: 'Whatever has characteristics is unreal' and 'this dharma is levelness, without high or low.'[18] The *Perfect Awakening Sutra* says: 'If you know that this is a flower in the sky, then there is no samsaric wheel-turning and no body-mind that undergoes samsara.'[19] The *Śūraṃgama Sūtra* says: 'The six faculties and their six sense objects have the same origin; bondage and liberation are of the same origin; and knowing-understanding makes for more knowing-understanding.'[20] All throughout the sutras and treatises you can stack up words like these [i.e., I could go on and on]. *Direct pointing* never had to wait for Bodhidharma's version of it!"

PHANTASM: "Didn't I cover this already? These sutra quotes 'reveal *dhāraṇī*.' But if one has never experienced even a single instance of true realization in one's own mind, simply speaking of medicine [as the sutras do] will not cure the illness. For people who have achieved true realization, how could it be the case that only the words of the Mahāyāna sutras and treatises are capable of tallying with the Chan of Bodhidharma? There has never been any kind of speech, coarse or subtle, including even the sound of wind or the dripping of rain, that did not tally with the Chan of Bodhidharma's *direct pointing*! If you can't achieve in your own mind a wondrous tallying with what is beyond the representation of words, and you merely memorize words from the sutras and treatises that are similar to [Bodhidharma's *direct pointing*], then it's the approach described by the ancients as 'relying on another to achieve understanding and thereby obstructing your own awakening.'[21] It is like [valuable] gold dust getting in your eyes, and [the harm of that is] very clear! You should ponder this deeply and entertain no confusion! It isn't only the words in the sutra texts that differ from the

---

[16] T 279.10.89a2–3.
[17] T 262.9.7a20.
[18] T 235.8.749a24 and 751c24.
[19] T 842.17.913c4–5.
[20] T 945.19.124c6–10.
[21] *Precious Instructions of the Chan Forest* (*Chanlin baoxun* 禪林寶訓; 1174–1189), T 2022.48.1026a16–17. Dahui Zonggao was one of the original compilers.

principle behind Bodhidharma's *direct pointing*. For example, in the Chan lineage, from the second patriarch [Huike's] pacification of mind, the third patriarch's repenting for transgressions, Nanyue's polishing the tile, Qingyuan's dangling his leg, down to [Bimo's using] a wooden spear, [Xuefeng's] turning the three balls,[22] the employment of the stick and the shout, to the various encounters in the 1700 Chan standards [of the *Record of the Transmission-of-the-Lamp-Flame of the Jingde Era*], all is plain and easy to understand, with nothing hidden—a few tricks of the trade for handing over [the Chan mind-seal]. How could there be any gap or obstacle for you? If you haven't been able to achieve a penetration of what is right under your feet and you intend to direct your deluded consciousness to examining even the smallest ink traces of the written word[23] and memorizing them in your mind, this is called 'poison entering the mind.' It will be like oil getting into flour [i.e., you'll never get it out.[24]] It is also said: 'Ghee is of an excellent flavor, a thing that the world considers a rarity. But, when ghee encounters a person of this sort, it turns into a poisonous drug.'[25] In fact, *this matter* is not something to which one applies the mind. It is not something to which one applies mental effort. It does not involve positioning oneself somewhere. It does not involve putting one's hand to some matter. You must on your own, right where you are, advance a step at a time, and then you'll be able to 'yoke' [with Bodhidharma's *direct pointing*]. [If you do so,] whatever your words and actions, every single one of them will flow from your heart. You'll be like the lion cub who seeks no companion. For the first time you will realize that the 1700 Chan standards are all lies: fox slobber[26] and poison. How could you be willing to have

---

[22] For details on these Chan stories, see Noguchi and Matsubara, *Sanbō yawa*, 38–40, nn. 8–13.

[23] Yoshizawa Katsuhiro, ed., *Shoroku zokugo kai* (Kyoto: Zen bunka kenkyūjo, 1999), 283–285: "The term *yuanzi jiao* simply means *characters/writing/written language*. . . . The variations *yuanzi, yuanzi jiao, yi zi, yi zi jiao, zi jiao* all have the same meaning. The *jiao* means *traces*." [元字脚はただ文字と云うことなり。. . . 元字、元字脚、一字、一字脚、字脚並びに同一義なり。脚は猶お跡というがごとし。]. *Explanations of Colloquial Words in Zen Records* (*Shoroku zokugo kai* 諸録俗語解) is a compilation of glossaries of difficult words and phrases in nineteen Chan texts by Kyoto Rinzai scholar-monks dating to sometime after 1804.

[24] Supplied from Broughton with Watanabe, *Letters of Dahui*, letter #13.1 (p. 118): "A prior noble one said: "Even if you might break the precepts to the magnitude of Mt. Sumeru, you must not be 'perfumed' by even a single perverse thought from these perverse teachers. If a mustard seed's amount of it is present in your consciousness, it's like oil's getting into flour— you'll never get it out." [大慧普覺禪師語錄: 先聖云。寧可破戒如須彌山。不可被邪師熏一邪念。如芥子許在情識中。如油入麪。永不可出。(T 1998A.47.922b25–27).

[25] *Jingde chuandeng lu* (景德傳燈錄), T 2076.51.444b26–27.

[26] *Fox slobber/wild-fox slobber* (*ye huxian* 野狐涎) is a disparaging term for the words of Chan talk and Chan books. The Zhongfeng records use this term several times. For instance, a dharma talk in the *Zhongfeng Extensive Record*: "Most Chan students of the present time haggle over words. None of them is willing to turn backward to engage in the practice of self-reflection. Therefore, the ancients viewed Chan talk as wild-fox slobber." [如今之禪學者流。多是商量箇語話。皆不肯回頭扣己而參。所以古人目禪語爲野狐涎唾。] (*Gozanban* 9, 157d; CBETA 2019.Q3, B25, no. 145, p. 731a14–16). Also, in one of the

anything at all to do with such things? Such a shame! Every now and then there is a clever fellow who does not seek self-awakening. Day and night he sits inside a poison pit [i.e., the pit of the word], dividing things into *upwards/downwards, showing the whole/showing only half, beginning gate/final gate, receiving students head-on/supporting students from the side, feeling out students/engaging in give-and-take between host and guest, gently snatching/clear-cut victory-defeat*, and so forth. [These clever fellows] investigate this and that, attaching commentary at the side of everything. They're outspoken and engage in skillful searching. They fix labels to everything and call this the 'gate key' to the Chan method, dazzling those who come after them. Furthermore, they select out sayings and classify them into 'Chan functions,' saying such things as 'those words of honored monks raise up completely the *upwards* and are not involved with *branches-and-leaves*.' Or they say: 'Those words of honored monks are novel and wondrously skillful, outdistancing both past and present.' [Or they say:] 'Those words of honored monks are the Chan of a Way-person, tasteless with no moisture at all.' They compare this and that and churn things around in their heads, but little do they imagine that Chan persons of previous generations who have achieved great comprehension were old and shabby, full of holes, with nothing at all to protect. [These old and shabby Chan masters], in responding to the capacities of beings, said the appropriate thing and took the appropriate action. Right from the outset they engaged in no selection process whatsoever: they were like thunder and lightning. Even if you try to find their tracks, [it is too late since] their 'sword' has gone someplace else! Also, how could they consent to being limited by seeing and surmising? They were playful in their severe karmic encounters and tailored their skillful speech, all in the desire to guide later students and make Chan exalted! Moreover, honored Chan monks of previous generations matched karmic capacities [of students] to the instructions they delivered. Their sayings were of different sorts: *coarse/subtle, open/secret, expansive/abbreviated*. But, in fact, every one of these sayings arose from *true mind*, from the beginning free of any effortful fabrication. They were like a huge bell or great drum that gives off a sound when struck. The volume and purity of the sounds of the bell or drum is rooted in the specific instrument at hand. Some instruments do not measure up: but if you want to add a minute bit of help from the outside, then you will lose [the instrument's] original truth. Chan people of the present, when they are about to take the great seat [to give a dharma talk] and brandish the fly whisk, right at the start take in hand the books of Chan recorded sayings and select passages to memorize, or they fish and hunt through the theories of the hundred classical philosophers to provide 'talking handles': this is the [gang of pseudo-]masters who *talk Chan*. Not only are they incapable of loosening people's stickiness and eliminating their bondage, but they also lose their own original truth and destroy their own Way-eye. Despite such deluded habit-energies, they praise each other to the skies. Having lost their heavy regard for the Chan ancestral courtyard [i.e., the Chan school], how could they possess the principle of 'raising the Chan community and making the dharma clan flourish'? In the first place, the World-honored-one's emergence in the world and Bodhidharma's coming from the West were because they both wanted to loosen the stickiness and eliminate the bondage of every person on earth. It's that *you*, right from the start, don't know good from bad! You have taken your one innately pure and spotless *state* and falsely polluted it with limitless sense objects such as sounds and forms. You lack any place to get footing, and arrive at abandoning relatives, severing affections, relying on a teacher, and studying the Way. Nevertheless, the pollution right in front of you is not washed away. Then you add on a lot of intellectual knowledge of the *buddhadharma*, causing a repeat of the loss of your original mind. What a shame! No wonder the teaching masters of previous generations can't help laughing out loud! They pop up and spit out a [word of splendid] functioning and confer a directive. Like a sword that can sever a hair blowing in the wind, they can with a single stroke sever multiple places at once. They want immediately to cut off the life-faculty of samsara: truly they do so because of real compassion and sympathy for the pain of others. They didn't chart out high and precipitous teaching approaches in order to pile up reverence from later students! In fact, our predecessors who achieved great comprehension at the very beginning [of their careers] were not yet definitively clear about the *matter of self* and so travelled widely over mountains and seas, seeking out people to resolve things. Suddenly they smacked right into a twisted and tricky *huatou*, one they could not break through—and it was like swallowing a chestnut in its burrs. [Such a *huatou*] is like meeting the enemy: [what is needed is] diligence in passing through cold and heat, disregard for sleeping and eating, not taking a moment's break until the end of life. They resolved not to accept anyone's instruction too easily. And they did not accept any searching that involved the written and spoken word. They just wanted to wait for a true karmic opportunity to arise spontaneously, one in

---

abbacy *yulu* of the Yuan-dynasty recorded sayings *Xiaoyin Daxin chanshi yulu* (笑隱大訢禪師語錄) we find. "Don't ask about the karmic stories of the Chan patriarchal masters—they are all wild-fox slobber." [莫問祖師機緣。總是野狐涎唾。] (CBETA 2019.Q3, X69, no. 1367, p. 703a8).

which they could smash the *ball of uncertainty*.²⁷ Ever since there has been a Chan method, all those who tallied and achieved realization have been like this. Therefore, every single one of them has been calm and attentive to detail. Even when they are casually walking about, they are like the lion cub that startles the flock. This is the rationale behind Chan's talk about *doing practice-work* [i.e., raising the *huatou* to awareness]."

[5] SOMEONE ASKED: "Preceptor Yongming [Yanshou] compiled the *Mind-Mirror Record* in one hundred fascicles, which extensively quotes Mahāyāna sutra-treatise texts and 'marries' [these canonical sources] with our Chan of Bodhidharma's *direct pointing*.²⁸ The intention [to match up canonical sources with Chan sources] is indeed a remarkable one, but it

---

²⁷ This is a major theme of Dahui's letters. According to Dahui, the practitioner must generate a singular sensation of uncertainty. The term uncertainty (*yi* 疑) refers to sensations of hesitation, vacillation, wavering, misgiving, having qualms about something, apprehension—even dread and angst—that develop within the round of daily activities. The practitioner is to merge or amalgamate all these myriad instances of uncertainty and apprehension into one big sensation of uncertainty and apprehension about the *huatou*, and only about the *huatou*: a merger of all the little uncertainties of daily life into a monolithic, massive uncertainty. Once this featureless mass of *huatou*-uncertainty is smashed, one is liberated. See Broughton with Watanabe, *Letters of Dahui*, 29–30, 33–34.

²⁸ This enormous compendium of the Five-Dynasties figure Yongming Yanshou (永明延壽; 904–976) is traditionally dated to Jianlong (建隆) 2/961 of the Song. Yanshou's own preface states: "Now, to explain the overall intention of the [Chan] patriarchs and buddhas and the correct tenet of the sutras and treatises, I will pare down the complicated texts, seek out just the essentials, set up imaginary questions and answers, and extensively quote proofs and clarifications. Raising the One-Mind as the tenet, the myriad dharmas will be illumined as if they are in a mirror. I will arrange the meanings of the ancient literary productions and scoop up an abridgement of the perfect explications of the treasure canon. Raising this in concert, I call it a record: divided into one hundred fascicles arranged in three sections." [今詳祖佛大意。經論正宗。削去繁文。唯搜要旨。假申問答。廣引證明。舉一心為宗。照萬法如鏡。編聯古製之深義。撮略寶藏之圓詮。同此顯揚。稱之曰錄。分為百卷。大約三章。] (T 2016.48.417a19–23). The opening passage states: "Now, the Chan patriarchs designate the Chan principle and transmit the correct tenet of silent alignment; the buddhas elaborate the teachings gate and set up the purport of the explications.... I widely quote the sincere words of the Chan patriarchs and buddhas, which tightly mesh with the great Way of perfect constancy. I will pluck the essential purport of the sutras and treatises, which perfectly complete the true mind of resolution. Joining these three sections together into a single panorama, they gather everything in an exhaustive treatment right here." [詳夫。祖標禪理。傳默契之正宗。佛演教門。立詮下之大旨。... 廣引祖佛之誠言。密契圓常之大道。遍採經論之要旨。圓成決定之真心。後陳引證章。以此三章。通為一觀。搜羅該括。備盡於茲矣。] (T 2016.48.417b5–17). The idea is that the canonical teachings of the sutras and treatises coincide with Chan: Chan and the teachings constitute a single panorama. Yanshou may have inherited this stance from Zongmi's *Chan Prolegomenon*. The first section of the *Mind-Mirror Record* is the "Designating the Tenet" section (標宗章; first half of fascicle one); the second is the "Question-Answer" section (問答章; from midpoint in fascicle one through fascicle ninety-three); and the third is the "Quotations to Authenticate" section (引證章; from fascicle ninety-four through fascicle one hundred). The three sections contain a staggering number of quotations from Buddhist literature. Fascicles ninety-seven and ninety-eight contain seventy-four sets of sayings and stories of Chan teachers. This jumbled cache of Chan material presents Bodhidharma Chan as a whole, not a particular sectarian lineage of Bodhidharma Chan. In the ninety-seventh fascicle, overlap with early material in the *Bodhidharma Anthology* is considerable; for a list, see Jeffrey L. Broughton, *The Bodhidharma Anthology: The Earliest Records of Zen* (Berkeley: University of California Press, 1999), 146. In the ninety-eighth fascicle we find sayings of Layman Pang, Hanshan's poems, Wolun, Nanquan, Fenzhou Wuye, Shenxiu, Guishan, Linji, Shitou, Huangbo, Yangshan, Caotang (i.e., Guifeng Zongmi), Baizhang Huihai, Banshan, Damei, Yantou, Mt. Niutou Zhong, Longya, Deshan, Dazhu, and many others. Perhaps Yanshou inherited some of this stock from Zongmi's lost *Chan Canon*. See Albert Welter, *Yongming Yanshou's Conception of Chan in the Zongjing lu: A Special Transmission Within the Scriptures* (Oxford: Oxford University Press, 2011).

doesn't seem to avoid taking out the drill to investigate texts and explain the meanings therein. [What about this?]"

PHANTASM: "Not at all. After Bodhidharma came from India to this land, his Way of *direct pointing* was transmitted through six generations, arriving at Caoxi [Huineng, the sixth patriarch]. Caoxi then transmitted through nine generations, arriving at 'Chan Master Great Fayan.'[29] Fayan then transmitted [his dharma] through two generations, arriving at Yongming Yanshou [i.e., Yanshou has Chan credentials]. During this interval, wise and excellent Chan people left behind extraordinary footprints, appearing in an evolution that illuminated past and present; but textual scholars of the *tripiṭaka* [i.e., the Buddhist canon] could not stop from arguing against our Chan Way. Hence, Preceptor Yongming, who across many lifetimes had expanded his powers of wisdom and eloquence, made a great collection of the sutra teachings, transmitting and articulating them. [His *Mind-Mirror Record*], in a free and unbridled style, right and left meets up with the Source, and so this book is called the '*dhāraṇī* gate of the written word.' He caused the *tripiṭaka* textual scholars to no longer dare to relegate our Chan to a niche outside the precincts of the buddha-sea.[30] [His *Mind-Mirror Record*,] and Preceptor Mingjiao's [i.e., Fori Qisong's] *Buttressing the Teachings Compilation*,[31] embody detailed inquiries into the hundred classical philosophers and provide an encyclopedic penetration into all sorts of books. They extend the true compassion of the Buddhist school and block off grave jealousy from the Confucian school. These two books constitute a buddhas-and-patriarchs 'seawall' [that protects Chan]. There should be no talk about [Yongming and Mingjiao's works being liable to the charge of] 'taking out the drill to investigate texts and explain the meanings therein.' If we did not have these two masters' true sincerity and profound understanding, we would never be able to follow their example [in legitimizing Chan]!"

---

[29] This is the posthumous title given to Fayan Wenyi (法眼文益; 885–958) by the Southern Tang king Lijing. Fayan is the putative founder of the Fayan school of Chan, one of the "five houses." He compiled the *Ten Rules of the Chan Approach* (宗門十規論; CBETA 2019.Q3, X63, no. 1226, pp. 36b2–39a24). His disciple Tiantai Deshao (天臺德韶; 891–972) was the teacher of Yongming Yanshou. For a *kakikudashi* treatment with notes of the *Fayan Record* in the *Wu jia yulu* (五家語錄), see Tsuchiya Taisuke and Yanagi Mikiyasu, trans., *Hōgenroku Mumonkan*, Shin kokuyaku daizōkyō, Chūgoku senjutsu bu 1–6, Zenshū bu (Tokyo: Daizōshuppan, 2019), 9–116.

[30] He showed that Chan is not "outside" the teachings, that the teachings and Chan constitute a single panorama. This was the position of Zongmi's *Chan Prolegomenon*.

[31] Fori Qisong (佛日契嵩; 1007–1072) of the Yunmen line compiled *Buttressing the Teachings Compilation* (*Fujiao bian* 輔教編), which consists of five essays. The book shows how Buddhism and Confucianism (*ru fo* 儒佛) coincide and complement each other. The last essay is "Praise of the *Platform Sutra*." For a Japanese translation, see Araki Kengo, *Hogyō hen*, Zen no goroku 14 (Tokyo: Chikuma shobō, 1981). Also see Elizabeth Morrison, *The Power of Patriarchs: Qisong and Lineage in Chinese Buddhism*, Sinica Leidensia 9 (Leiden: Brill, 2010).

SOMEONE SAID: "Preceptor Yongming also produced the *Common Goal of the Myriad Good Deeds Collection*,³² which is not the same teaching as that of the *Mind-Mirror*. Why do these two compositions run counter to each other?"

I [PHANTASM] SAID: "Mind is the root of the myriad good actions. The *Mind-Mirror* rolls the myriad good actions back into the One-Mind. The [*Common Goal of the Myriad Good Deeds*] *Collection* disperses the One-Mind into the myriad good actions [such as the six perfections]. This contraction and expansion, closing and opening, are always in a state of interpenetration. In fact, [these two books serve to] prevent Chan people who have not yet awakened from marginalizing the myriad good practices, and stops *tripiṭaka* scholars from complaining that our Chan does not embrace the myriad good practices. [These two books] clarify matters, and they are not slipshod about it! Of teachers throughout all-under-heaven, from ancient times to the present, if we forsake Yongming, there's no one left!"

SOMEONE: "So the Chan house must not fail to cultivate the myriad good practices [such as the six perfections]?"

I [PHANTASM] SAID: "The Bodhidharma line only values awakening to your own mind. Once this mind is clarified, there is no error whether you cultivate the six perfections and myriad good practices or don't cultivate them. If you cultivate them, there is to be no grasping at cultivator/cultivated. If you do not cultivate them, there are to be no such errors as *trusting to the feelings*³³ and *losing mindfulness*. If you have not understood your own mind, then both cultivation and non-cultivation will be empty falsehoods. Chan people ought to take *enlightened mind* as the real essential: the *myriad good practices* should be taken as second in the sequence."³⁴

---

³² This three-fascicle work in question-answer format by Yanshou holds that all the various types of Buddhist cultivation are rooted in the One-Mind, and that Chan and the various good actions of the bodhisattva's six perfections complement each other. It favors Zongmi's preferred formula of "all-at-once awakening and step-by-step practice" (T 2017.48.987c5). "Good deeds" includes such traditional Buddhist practices as chanting sutras, recitation of a buddha's name, repentance, and so forth. See Albert Welter, *The Meaning of Myriad Good Deeds: A Study of Yung-ming Yen-shou and the* Wan-shan t'ung-kuei chi (New York: Peter Lang, 1993).

³³ Zhongfeng's miscellany *Continued Talks in the East and Conversations in the West* shows the term *loose/uninhibited* (*fangyi* 放逸) as a synonym for *giving free rein to feelings* (*renqing* 任情), that is, trusting the whims of one's own mind. See Zhongfeng *Extensive Record* (任情放逸而罔其進乎不可乎; CBETA 2019.Q3, B25, no. 145, p. 916b8–9). Zongmi in his *Chan Letter* (sometimes called the *Chan Chart*) uses *giving free rein to innate feelings* to describe the practice of the Hongzhou house, of which he is critical: "The above three houses show differences in their levels of understanding: for the first [i.e., the Northern house], everything is unreal; for the second [i.e., the Hongzhou house], everything is real; and for the last [i.e., the Oxhead house], everything is nonexistent [i.e., empty]. If we discuss them in terms of their conceptions of practice, the first subdues mind to extinguish the unreal; the second believes in giving free rein to innate feelings; and the last has the mind take a rest so that it no longer arises." [中華傳心地禪門師資承襲圖: 又上三家見解異者。初一切皆妄。次一切皆真。後一切皆無。若就行說者。初伏心滅妄。次信任情性。後休心不起。(CBETA 2019.Q3, X63, no. 1225, p. 33c9–11). See Broughton, *Zongmi on Chan*, 87.

³⁴ This is a formulation of all-at-once awakening and step-by-step practice (頓悟漸修).

[6] SOMEONE ASKED: "What is the relationship between the ten [bodhisattva] stages[35] and Chan?"

PHANTASM: "I have heard that the tenth-stage [bodhisattva] is endowed with the [six] supranormal powers, but the Sage [i.e., the Buddha] erected those [ten stages] in conformity with the [inexpressible] principle he came to comprehend, and so an ancient said: 'The ten stages are like bird-tracks in the sky [i.e., impossible to speak of and impossible to show].'[36] All Mahāyāna bodhisattvas make use of [the ten stages], but you should not grasp the ten stages as really existent. Bodhidharma's discourse was only about *seeing the Nature and becoming a buddha*. All the rest—buddha-bodies and buddha-lands, stages and ranks, cause-and-effect, and so forth—those he omitted, never speaking of them. And so Bodhidharma Chan is the personal realization of the mind of the buddhas. It is set up solely for those with the capacity for the perfect-and-sudden superior vehicle. Speaking of this *becoming a buddha*, Bodhidharma Chan turns its back on expounding "the *Real*." If you ask why—it is that Bodhidharma Chan shows the *correct dharma-eye depository* to limitless sentient-beings. Every one of these beings [including you] is originally a buddha. So why would you think that you had to wait for someone to point to this *seeing the Nature* before you could *become a buddha*? It is impossible for a buddha to *become* a buddha! So why even make the ten stages a subject of discussion?"

[7] SOMEONE ASKED: "An ancient said: 'If you eliminate the weeds [i.e., defilements] and admire the [original] breeze, then you're just intending to *see the Nature*. [But, right now, the *Nature* of the superior person—where is it?]'[37] Great Master Fu said: '[If you want to know where the Buddha went to,] it's this very voice!'[38] Beyond these, is there any other principle for *seeing the Nature*? If not, then what is a student to do in bearing the burden [of practice]?"

---

[35] For details on the ten stages (*daśabhūmi*) and the six supranormal powers (*abhijñā*) below, see Robert E. Buswell Jr. and Donald S. Lopez Jr., *The Princeton Dictionary of Buddhism* (Princeton, NJ: Princeton University Press, 2014), 218–220 and 8–9.

[36] *Huayan Sutra*, T 279.10.180c24–27.

[37] The first of the "three sayings used in the private quarters" of Doushuai Congyue (兜率從悅; 1044–1091). *Five Lamp-Flames Meet at the Source* (*Wu deng huiyuan* 五燈會元; 1252): "In his room [Doushuai] set up the three sayings to test students. The first: 'If you eliminate the weeds [i.e., defilements] and admire the [original] breeze, you're just intending to see the Nature. But, right now, the Nature of the superior person—where is it?' The second: 'If you can come to know the Self-Nature, then you will escape samsara. When the glint in your eye drops to the ground, how will you escape?' The third: 'If you can escape samsara, then you know where you are going to. When the four elements disintegrate, where will you go to?'" [室中設三語以驗學者。一曰撥草瞻風。祇圖見性。即今上人性在甚麼處。二曰識得自性。方脫生死。眼光落地時作麼生脫。三曰脫得生死。便知去處。四大分離。向甚麼處去。] (CBETA 2019.Q3, X80, no. 1565, p. 365b18–21).

[38] A couplet by Shanhui Dashi (善慧大士; 497–569), *Five Lamp-Flames Meet at the Source* (*Wu deng huiyuan* 五燈會元; 1252): "If you want to know where the Buddha went to, it's this very voice." [欲識佛去處。祇這語聲是。] (CBETA 2019.Q3, X80, no. 1565, p. 67b3–4).

PHANTASM: "If you anticipate exclusively talking about the Nature, you might as well memorize all of the discussions of the ancients about ultimate principle! But, if you do that, the more you talk about the Nature, the farther away you will be. In fact, the principle of *seeing the Nature* is divorced from characteristics of verbalization, divorced from characteristics of thinking, divorced from characteristics of discrimination, divorced from characteristics of seizing/abandoning. [One who sees the Nature] makes the *Great Functioning* flourish, and his actions will certainly partake of the completely real. If you try to preserve even the least bit of intellectual understanding, then you'll be turning your back on coming fact-to-face with Substance. [Of the Chan discourse] that one encounters at present, all and sundry are talking about this *seeing the Nature*. When questioned by other people about this Nature, they immediately spout: 'There is nothing that is not [the Nature]!' Then, from the sutra teachings they quote as proof that 'all dharmas that arise are only manifestations of mind.'[39] It would be good if I could make you understand [just one thing]: even if you can explain [the Nature], and even if you can prove [the Nature] to the point of clear understanding, if you want to yoke up with it moment after moment, [the Nature] will still be very far away! Should you ask why this is so, it is because you haven't come face-to-face with Substance and awakened at the very locus wherein the life-force is severed and doer/done are exhausted: all [you've got] is just five-aggregates consciousness, or the employment of externalities [such as medicine or mantras] to manifest supranormal powers. Whenever you are talking, this Nature exists. Even though this Nature exists whenever you are talking, at the very moment that you are talking, you're in a state of delusion. Further, don't say that your ignorance covertly arises, and your perversion happens unexpectedly. When you're solemnly talking [about the Nature, you and the Nature] seem to be two different things. Hoping to yoke [yourself up to the Nature] moment after moment: how is this even possible? You must realize that, right in front of the *true person*, it's impermissible to even talk about this principle of yoking! How much more so is this the case with non-yoking! You should know that people with these sorts of mistaken views fall into two types of error. First: when on their own they arouse the mind [of awakening] and study the Way—they only want to talk about interpenetration with the Way. At the beginning they do not have the absolute determination to discern the correct thought: *samsara is the great matter*. Second: a class of teachers with wrong views who pay only marginal heed to whether a student's *causal stage* [i.e., when practice is not yet completed] is correct or incorrect. Seeing only that the student has a little natural talent,

---

[39] *Śūraṃgama Sūtra*, T 945.19.109a2–3.

these teachers think about the skillful application of *upāya*. They don't require that the student do practice-work to maintain correct thought. They just blindly take a *huatou* on the order of **mind is buddha** or **discern mind in forms** and dabble in vague and absurd talk about it. They just want to pull the student into an access [to awakening]: they just wait for him to open his mouth and immediately everything's finished! In today's Chan community, such practices are becoming a [dismal] trend. Truly, I don't know what they plan to accomplish from this! The *Perfect Awakening Sutra* and the *Śūraṃgama Sūtra* have been censuring this sort of mistaken viewpoint for more than two thousand years. The Sage knew ahead of time that sentient-beings of a latter age would have this deluded habit-energy, and so he created the sorts of intricate dialogues [found in these sutras]. He certainly knew the mistakes they would make and was trying to make them undergo change. Why do [students today] not take on *samsara is the great matter* as their own heavy responsibility? They only apply themselves to the power of verbalization, thinking they will attain realization through this. Suddenly they hit upon a person with the true eye, who waves his hand horizontally to show disapproval and says: 'Three things are incorrect!' Quickly there is confusion in their minds. If they meet with censure from that person, their anger is immeasurable. If even once one really wants to yoke up with *this matter*, the first thing to do is painstakingly sweep away all the extraordinary verbal formulations and marvelous sayings that one reads and hears. If even the slightest thing remains stagnating in one's mind, it's called 'bad poison's entering the mind.' Even a buddha will find it difficult to save such a person! In general, students are temporarily drawn into a grass *nest* [of stereotyped formulas] by those teachers. This is because [the teachers] themselves place a high value on intellectual understanding. If you positively want to serve as master on the shores of samsara—and even if Śākyamuni and Maitreya pour the Chan Way and the *buddhadharma* right into your heart—just keep an eye on the *single phrase* [i.e., the *huatou*]: *for which you can get nothing from another*. Spontaneously, you will vomit up bad thoughts. How could you have affirmed and accepted such evil poisons? Because you don't have a correct level of understanding, even when your eyes are open, you're *buried by other people*. If you indeed just want to understand Chan, you need not, even for a moment, aimlessly explain this or that metaphor/simile. [Bad] teachers make you bore right through the kudzu-verbiage of the 1700 Chan standards—no difficulty at all!—but this brings no benefit. It would be better to be a tender-hearted one who has understood nothing throughout his entire life. If I could hand over *this matter* to you [i.e., explain *this matter* to you], then, in the case of Xiangyan, when of old he was a student of Guishan, there would have been no need for his entering Nanyang and dwelling in a hut [where he awakened upon hearing the sound of tiles' striking bamboo].[40] And, in the case of Ānanda, at the dharma assembly of the *Śūraṃgama Sūtra*, it would have been all right if Śākyamuni hadn't been troubled and moved to tears [over Ānanda's being nearly seduced by the harlot Mātaṅgī].[41] Don't say: 'Once I harmonize [with awakening], it'll be correct!' Even a truly awakened person, if he feels any need to emphasize this awakening, is already *out of correspondence*! How much more is this the case when, via mind [i.e., the storehouse consciousness], afflicted mind, the six sense consciousnesses, and linguistic conventions, you falsely act in concert with the floating light-rays and phantasmal shadows of *numinous luminosity* in front of you—mistakenly recognizing [this *numinous luminosity*] as your *Mr. Man-in-charge*! If you treasure this sort of thing in your heart, you will be the type who piles delusion upon delusion. If you go on over a long time without fixing this, in the distant future you'll invite the karmic retribution of 'false-talk-about-*prajñā*.' In a century when your shadow-body dies, what will such gnawing on your navel amount to? According to the old story of National Teacher Nanyang Huizhong:

> [HUIZHONG'S GUEST SAID:] 'Recently, the *buddhadharma* in the South, for the most part, has changed. The [southern teachers] all say that, in the four-elements body there is a Spirit-Nature, which neither arises nor extinguishes, and, when the four-elements body is destroyed, this Nature remains indestructible.' [Huizhong responded:] 'This level of understanding is equal to the non-Buddhist outside Ways of India!'[42]

Also, there is the saying of Preceptor Changsha: 'There are students of the Way who don't know 'the *Real*'—all along they have mistakenly recognized Spirit-[Nature as 'the *Real*'].'[43] These words put a finger on the present-day tendency to mistakenly recognize [phantasmal] shadows conditioned by the six sense-objects as the [real] characteristic of one's own mind. As the *Śūraṃgama Sūtra* says: 'Reject the boundless great sea and recognize a single bubble of foam as the entire tidal flow.'[44] And then there is a type who says vaguely about *tathatā*: 'All the worlds of the ten directions are the Self. This Nature bundles up the sky and circulates throughout

---

[40] *Jingde chuandeng lu* (景德傳燈錄): "Thereupon with a tearful farewell [Xiangyan Zhixian 香嚴智閑;?-898] left Guishan. He arrived at Nanyang and witnessed the bequeathed traces of National Teacher Nanyang Huizhong. He then took repose there. One day when he was in the mountains clearing weeds and brush, there was the sound of tiles' striking against bamboo. Suddenly he burst out in laughter and attained a vast awakening. He hastily returned to bathe and burn incense in obeisance to Guishan." [遂泣辭溈山而去。抵南陽覩忠國師遺迹。遂臨止焉。一日因山中芟除草木。以瓦礫擊竹作聲。俄失笑間廓然惺悟。遽歸沐浴焚香遙禮溈山。(T 2076.51.284a8-11).
[41] *Śūraṃgama Sūtra*, T 945.19.106c9-20.
[42] Probably based on National Teacher Nanyang Huizhong (?-775) section in *Jingde chuandeng lu* (景德傳燈錄), T 2076.51.437c17-26.
[43] A verse by Changsha Jingcen (長沙景岑; d.u.), a successor of Nanquan Puyuan (748-835), in *Jingde chuandeng lu* (景德傳燈錄; T 2076.51.274b17-18).
[44] T 945.19.110c29-111a1.

the *dharmadhātu*. It merges past and present and fuses sage and ordinary person. There is no gap between it and the myriad forms.'[45] They then quote as proof sayings of ancients: 'If you pick up a blade of grass, it becomes the sixteen-foot golden body'[46] or 'on the tip of a hair the world of the Jewel King appears.'[47] Regrettably, talking about food does not cure hunger and talking about clothes does not cure the cold! Why? You must have *in that way* personally awakened at least once. Even if you have personally awakened *in that way*, you must also encounter a guide who is the real thing: he will sweep away the traces of that very awakening from you. If you don't, we call it 'experiencing a thorn in the heart and grasping at medicine till it becomes a disease': so how could *this* [*matter*] be totally concluded by mere intellectual or verbal comprehension? It is a fact that your samsaric sense-fields inherited through immeasurable eons down to today must be completely overturned: then you must at once *forget* the effort involved in powering that overturning! How could a person of small faculties and shallow aptitude possibly aim for such a goal? This kind of talk really is not overblown: it is urgent for those suffering in samsara to consider things this way. When the others, who only engage in *talking about Chan*, turn their back and spit, why should I refrain from commenting [on their ridiculous drivel]?"

[8] A Master by the name "Return-to-the-West" passed by my gate, saying: "I practice recollection of Amitābha Buddha's [name], seeking to be reborn in his Pure Land. This way of escaping samsara seems easier than practicing Chan. And, therefore, I have accepted the protection of Amitābha Buddha's vow-power. There is no way for me to get a grasp on the practice of Chan: it lacks the protection that comes from a Sage's power [i.e., Amitābha's power]. If one is not a person of great faculties and sharp aptitude, it is difficult to enter [Chan's] 'hearing but once and having a thousand awakenings.' Therefore, Chan Master Yongming Yanshou said: '[If one has Chan but no Pure Land, one is susceptible to] the criticism that, out of ten people, nine stumble and trip.'"[48]

[PHANTASM SAID:] "Bah! What are you saying? If that were so, then there would be a separate Chan outside Pure Land! If that were truly so, then the two words *buddha* and *dharma* would be contradictory! Then there would be no entrance into the principle of perfect fusion. You fail to comprehend this

---

[45] See the Changsha Jingcen section of the *Jingde chuandeng lu*, T 2076.51.274a12–15.
[46] Zhaozhou Congshen (趙州從諗; 778–897) section of the *Jingde chuandeng lu*, T 2076.51.277a10–11.
[47] *Śūraṃgama Sūtra*, T 945,19.121a6–7.
[48] See Translation 2, n. 27.

skillful *upāya*. You are limited to your own [narrow] level of understanding and are slandering the wise ones who have preceded you. Now, Yongming Yanshou's sorting of Chan and Pure Land into *four phrases* was intended to follow the twists and turns of the karmic capacities of beings: they are no more than a special *upāya* [that teachers employ] to suppress or encourage students [as the situation requires].[49] This is the idea spoken of in the teachings: 'The one-vehicle Way is explained as threefold.'[50] For example, the masters Changlu, Beijian, Zhenxie, and Tianmu compiled literary works on the Pure Land, but they all based their discourses on the Chan position of *mind is one's own nature*.[51] From the very outset they all arrived at the same place. During that time there were [the following sorts of] guides who pointed the way. Dharma Master Xi of the eastern capital [Luoyang] in a state of *samādhi* saw the name "Chan Master Yuanzhao Ben" emblazoned in a lotus flower, and, coming to doubt that Ben was a master of the *single transmission* [of Chan], thought: "How could his name be emblazoned here?" So he went to interrogate Ben about this. Yuanzhao Ben said: 'Although I am in the Chan gate, I adhere to the combined practice of Pure Land [and Chan].'[52] At the time, Yuanzhao Ben was deceiving people by rolling out this splendid *upāya*. [Dharma Master Xi] was not the only one who came asking questions. How could [Yuanzhao Ben] have truly been [practicing both Pure Land and Chan] like this? Dim people don't comprehend the varieties of *upāya*. Being

---

[49] See Translation 2, n. 27.

[50] *Lotus Sutra*, T 262.9.13c17–18.

[51] Changlu Zongze (長蘆宗賾; d.u.), a Song-dynasty Linji master of the Yunmen school, is known as the compiler of the *Pure Rules of the Chan Garden* (*Chanyuan qinggui* 禪苑清規). He is listed as a Pure Land patriarch in the *Paradise Anthology* (*Lebang wenlei* 樂邦文類; T 1969A.47.193c13–24). Beijian Jujian (北磵居簡; 1164–1246) was in the Dahui wing of the Linji school. His Pure Land tendency is mentioned in Tianru Weize's *Some Questions on the Pure Land* (*Jingtu huo wen* 淨土或問; T 1972.47.293c20–22). Zhenxie Qingliao (真歇清了; 1088–1151) was in the Hongzhi Zhengjue line of the Caodong school. For his Pure Land tendency, see *Precious Mirror of the Lotus School of Mt. Lu* (*Lushan lianzong baojian* 廬山蓮宗寶鑑: 真歇了禪師淨土宗要; T 1973.47.318c20–319a1). Tianmu is Mieweng Wenli (滅翁文禮; 1167–1250), who was in the Songyuan wing of the Linji school. His Pure Land tendency is also mentioned in Tianru Weize's *Some Questions on the Pure Land* (*Jingtu huo wen* 淨土或問; T 1972.47.293c20–22).

[52] Dayou's (大佑) *Gist of the Pure Land* (*Jingtu zhigui ji* 淨土指歸集; 1393): "Chan Master Yuanzhao Ben secretly cultivated Pure Land karma.... Dharma Master Xi of Zifu Monastery in the [eastern] capital shut his gate to nourish the Way. He had no contact with the world and often went on divine wanderings in the Pure [Land] region. He did not engage in baseless talk with others. One day he walked to Huilin Monastery to pay his polite respects. People asked him why, and he answered: 'While in *samādhi*, I saw an exceedingly great golden lotus in the Pure Land, which had the caption Monk Zongben of Yongming Monastery. Other small lotuses were attached—they were uncountable. These were all people who had been transformed by the Chan Master [Zongben]. For this reason, I made a special excursion to pay my respects.' Someone asked Chan Master [Zongben] about this: 'You, Master, are of the Chan special transmission. Why is your name marked in the Pure Land?' The Master said: 'Because, although my footprints lie in the Chan approach, my heart stays with Pure Land karma.'" [密修淨業: 圓照本禪師。密修淨業。…京資福寺曦法師者。杜門養道。不與世接。往往神遊淨域。不妄與人言。一日步至惠林。殷勤致敬。人問其故。答曰。吾於定中。見淨土金蓮極大。題云永明寺比丘宗本。其他附麗小華。不可勝數。皆禪師所化人也。為此特往修敬。或問禪師云。師乃別傳之宗。何得標名淨土。師曰。雖迹在禪門。而留心淨業故也。] (CBETA 2019.Q3, X61, no. 1154, p. 392a8–17). Dharma Master Xi is otherwise unknown; Chan Master Yuanzhao Ben is Huilin Zongben (慧林宗本; 1020–1099) of the Yunmen school.

inflexible, such people say that outside Chan there is a separate Pure Land that you should commit to. They quote as a pretext Yongming Yanshou's *four phrases* of Chan and Pure Land. Isn't that quite a mistake!"

THE GUEST STOOD UP FROM HIS SEAT, SAYING: "Please try to explain this further."

PHANTASM SAID: "Pure Land is mind, and Chan is also mind. In substance they are one but in name dual. The deluded ones grasp onto the names [*Chan* and *Pure Land*] and, because of this, are in the dark about their substance. The awakened ones comprehend the substance and, because of this, understand the names. Why make a special case out of Pure Land? As is said in the teachings: 'Know that all dharmas are the self-nature of mind.'[53] Also: 'The many things and the myriad forms are all sealed by the *one dharma*.'[54] If you merely awaken to the Chan of your own mind, then the myriad dharmas of the three realms will merge into the numinous Source. All activities will be of the *wholly real*, with no selecting whatsoever. There has never been any difference between the two lands, east [i.e., the world we inhabit] and west [i.e., Amitābha's Pure Land]. How could there be two different countries—pure and defiled? Contract the infinity of worlds [between this world and the Pure Land] in a single step: the jewel ponds and golden grounds [of the Pure Land] fill up the whole world, stretching a single moment into eternity. The blue-green bamboo and yellow flowers both revert to *correct entrance* [i.e., meditative concentration]. The moon reflecting on the four great seas illuminates every dust mote. The Buddha's spiral tuft of hair between the eyebrows, five Mt. Sumerus in size, shines on every location. Old Bodhidharma suddenly forgets the bright-moon jewel in his hand, and Amitābha Buddha loses the yellow-gold seal. The Chan gate is all superfluous words; Pure Land is just a nominal term. The wrong view of *names/substance* melts away; deluded feelings of *is/is not* are exhausted. The sixteen-foot body of a buddha and a blade of grass: which is inferior and which superior? The three thousand worlds and half a dust mote: which is many and which few? This is called the 'the dharma gate of sameness of a single taste.' If you're not completely awakened, how will you attain the principle of liberation? Moreover, Chan practice is for ending samsara. Doing *nianfo* and cultivating the Pure Land is also for ending samsara. Even though the teachings established by the sages involve a thousand roads and ten thousand ruts, every one of them takes as the ultimate putting a definitive end to samsara. However, for the purposes of destroying sense-fields, exalt only one of these gates [either Chan or *nianfo*]

---

[53] T 279.10.89a2–3.
[54] This line of the *Dharma Lines Sutra* (*Faju jing* 法句經) is quoted in Yanshou's *Zongjinglu* (宗鏡錄), T 2016.48.928c5–6.

and enter deeply therein. Therefore, an ancient said: 'The slightest amount of fixity of thought becomes a cause of rebirth into the three bad rebirth paths; if suddenly deluded feelings arise, it will lead to shackles for ten thousand eons.'[55] A 'combined practice [of Chan and Pure Land]?' If you are not free of this sort of thing and [fruitlessly] chat about Chan and talk of Pure Land, you will endure a boiling over of the waves of consciousness, an agitation of feelings and sense objects. There will never be an end to it! That's why there is no way I can stop trying to explain these matters!"

[9] SOMEONE ASKED: "Bodhidharma at the beginning handed down the Way of the *single transmission* and *direct pointing*. After more than ten generations of transmission, this Way divided into the five houses [of Linji, Caodong, Guiyang, Yunmen, and Fayan]. Why? It can't be that Bodhidharma's one-house teaching split up into five different things, can it? If [the one-house Bodhidharma teaching harbors] no differentiations, how could a five-house teaching come out of it?"

PHANTASM SAID: "The so-called five houses have *five-housed* that personage [i.e., Bodhidharma], not *five-housed* his Way. Haven't you heard: 'The purport that the buddhas and patriarchs handed down is regarded as the *transmission of the flame-of-the-lamp*.'[56] If you comprehend the meaning of *transmission of the flame-of-the-lamp*, then you harbor no uncertainty about [the flame] becoming fivefold. Let me explain this in terms of a mundane lamp flame. There are lantern lamps. There are shallow-cup lamps. There are lapis-lazuli lamps. There are candle lamps. There are twisted-paper lamps. In terms of flame, they are one; in terms of the vessel from which the flame emerges, they are not the same. Although we say that the vessels are different, they are all perfectly capable of destroying the darkness of samsara's long night. How could this hold only for the five houses of today? Of old, the single lamp flame of Bodhidharma altogether went through four generations to arrive at the Great Doctor [i.e., the fourth patriarch Daoxin], from whom sprang the [collateral] line of the Oxhead school.[57] In five generations it arrived at Great Fulfillment [i.e., the fifth patriarch Hongren], from which sprang the line of Shenxiu's Northern school. In six generations it arrived at Caoxi [i.e., the sixth patriarch Huineng], from which sprang Qingyuan, Nanyue, and Shenhui. These three people shouldn't be mixed up. The momentum of the situation made it so: downward from each line, branches split off and factions spread. People of ability proliferated: even without their dividing, there was dividing. What

---

[55] *Jingde chuandeng lu* (景德傳燈錄), T 2076.51.317c12–13. The ancient is Deshan Xuanjian (德山宣鑒; 780–865).
[56] Untraced.
[57] On the schools of early Chan such as Oxhead and Northern, see Zongmi's *Chan Letter* (*Chan Chart*) in Broughton, Zongmi on Chan, 69–100.

is today called the 'five houses' sprang from the two factions of Nanyue and Qingyuan, flowing down to these five people [i.e., Linji, Dongshan, Guishan, Yunmen, and Fayan]. You're not aware that each is like the water of a whirlpool, overflowing until it becomes a great flood. Waves ahead and waves behind, without waiting for each other, they press near to the sky, drenching the sun: a vastness without limit. How could you just take in the panorama of these [five flows/schools] at a single glance! That's why there was no choice but to divide [the great flood into five schools]!"

SOMEONE SAID: "As for the dividing up of these five houses, there's more to it than just an abundance of people [i.e., these five teachers]: among [the five houses] their Chan personal realizations are not the same!"

PHANTASM SAID: "It's not that they are different. It's just that there is a great sameness amid small differences, and that's all. As for *great sameness*, the sameness is in the single lamp flame of Bodhidharma's Mt. Shaoshi. As for *small differences*, they show differences in how teachers speak *upāyas* [to students]. Examples: Guiyang's *reticent adornment*; Caodong's *meticulous precision*; Linji's *painful acuteness*; Yunmen's *lofty antiquity*; and Fayan's *terse clarity*.[58] Each [method] emerges out of his own innate disposition, but, in their interactions between father and son [i.e., teacher and student], they have not the lost the old [Bodhidharma] "step." In terms of [how these teachers] speak and use *upāyas*, they are alike in the way they step along. They weren't setting out to do it deliberately but that's how it came out! If eminent monks of the present want to exalt the differences [of their own school] and make themselves into a *one-house transmission*, that's an intolerable mistake! If they do that, how could it be adequate for transmitting the life-lamp by which the buddhas and patriarchs illuminate the world? Today's streams of Chan are mired in their own Chan personal realizations, giving rise to false levels of understanding that cut empty space into two. They mutually [bicker over] weak points and strong points. I know that all the [real] masters of the five lineages are covering their noses [so as not to smell the stink of today's Chan].

[10] SOMEONE ASKED: "The world calls stories of the karmic encounters of the buddhas and patriarchs *gong'an*. Why?"

PHANTASM SAID[59]: "*Gong'an* is a [Chan] metaphor derived from the use of this term for the *official documents of a government office*. They are the repository

---

[58] *Eye of Humans and Gods* (*Rentian yanmu* 人天眼目; 1188) gives such summaries of the Chan tenets of the five houses. For instance: "As for the Caodong tenet, its house style is yoked to meticulous precision in words and actions." [曹洞宗者。家風細密言行相應。] (T 2006.48.320c6).

[59] Zhongfeng's definition of *gong'an* has attained considerable circulation within scholarship on Chan. Mujaku Dōchū's (無著道忠; 1653–1744) Zen encyclopedia *Notes on Images and Implements of the Zen Forest* (*Zenrin shōki sen* 禪林象器箋; completed 1741) begins its *gong'an* entry with this Zhongfeng definition (down to "three times and ten directions"): Yanagida Seizan, ed., *Zenrin shōki sen*, Zengaku sōsho 9, vol. 1 (Kyoto: Chūbun shuppansha, 1979), 606; CBETA 2019.Q3, B19, no. 103, pp. 599b12–600a5. The terms

of the norms through which the Kingly Way [i.e., the state] brings order to disorder. This is the real relationship: the element *gong* [of the word *gong'an*, which means *public/impartial*] refers to the single cart-rut [i.e., a single norm or law] of the sages and worthies, and the people of all-under-heaven treat this ultimate principle as the path to be followed. The element *an* [of the word *gong'an*, which means *document*] refers to the correct text of the principles carried out by the sages and worthies. Government offices are found everywhere throughout all-under-heaven, and, wherever there are government offices, one finds official documents. This is because of the intention [on the part of the government] to use [these official documents] as norms for cutting off all that is incorrect in all-under-heaven. When the *gong'ans* are carried out, principles and norms function as they should. When the principles and norms are being applied, then all-under-heaven is in a state of correctness. If all-under-heaven is in a state of correctness, then the Kingly Way is governing well. Now, calling stories of the karmic encounters of the buddhas and patriarchs *gong'an* is the same thing, because these [karmic encounters] do not embody the personal viewpoint of any single individual: they embody an understanding of the numinous Source, tally with the marvelous purport, smash samsara, and transcend deluded calculation. They are the ultimate principle received from the enlightened ones of the three times and ten directions. Moreover, [the stories of the karmic encounters of the buddhas and patriarchs] cannot be understood in terms of meaning, cannot be verbally transmitted, cannot be explicated via texts, cannot be measured by means of consciousness. They are like a drum smeared with poison[60]: whoever hears it dies! They are like a great ball of fire: whoever encounters it is incinerated! Therefore, Śākyamuni's speaking of *separate transmission* at Vulture Peak transmitted *this*; Bodhidharma's speaking of *direct pointing* at Shaoshi pointed to *this*. Since the split into the Northern and Southern lineages and the offshoots called the five houses of Chan, all Chan good friends have seized that *transmission* and sustained that

---

gong'an (= *official government document*) and *huatou* (= *phrase*) are often blurred in modern Chan scholarship (and even within the Chan records themselves), and this lack of precision has engendered some confusion. Yunqi Zhuhong's (雲棲袾宏; 1535–1615) *Correcting-Errors Collection* (*Zheng e ji* 正訛集) provides helpful clarification: "*Gong'an* is an official document of a government office, that by which judgment is rendered on right/wrong, and the dialogic karmic encounters of the Chan patriarchs render judgments on birth/death. Therefore, [Chan] calls them [*gong'an*]. In every one of these dialogic encounters there is a crucial single phrase, and that is the *huatou*." [公案者。公府之案牘也。所以剖斷是非。而諸祖問答機緣。亦只爲剖斷生死。故以名之。總其問答中緊要一句。則話頭。] (CBETA 2019.Q3, J33, no. B277, p. 78c26–28). In other words, *gong'an* is the dialogic "story," and *huatou* is the vital single phrase within that "story." Example (with *huatou* in bold): "Yunmen was asked by a monk: 'What is a buddha?' Yunmen replied: '**Dried turd.**'" [*Wumen guan* 無門關: 雲門因僧問。如何是佛。門云乾屎橛。] (T 2005.48.295c6).

[60] *Nirvana Sutra*, T 374.12.420a8–10.

pointing. In an encounter in which the student inquires and the master responds, it is a matter of getting an ox from [from the student] and returning to him a horse. Whether rough words or fine words, there is an instantaneous exchange of whatever words come to mind: like a sudden thunderclap that does not permit covering one's ears [to block out the noise]. Examples are **cypress tree in the front of the garden, three catties of linen thread**, and **dried turd**: these constitute *the road of no meaning* that bores right through people. They are as impenetrable as a silver mountain or iron wall. Only the person who possesses the clear eye can confront and snatch up what is beyond the spoken and written word [i.e., *the road of no meaning*]. [In Chan encounters] 'one speaks first and the other is [instantly] in harmony,' like bird tracks in the sky or scratches on the water left by the moon's reflection. The thousand roads and ten thousand cart-ruts represent unbridled freedom: you must never hesitate! From the remote time in the past when Śākyamuni at Vulture Peak held up a flower until the present day, [there have been innumerable *gong'ans*]. How could they possibly stop at the 1,700 standards [of the *Jingde Era Transmission of the Flame-of-the-Lamp*]? There is nothing more to it: people waiting for awakening must take up [these *gong'ans*] as testimony [on awakening]. We most certainly do not want people to increase their memorization [of *gong'ans*] and rely on that memory corpus for topics of conversation! What the world calls 'venerable monks' are the high officials of the 'Chan government.' Their compiling flame-of-the-lamp books and collecting recorded-sayings books are the *official* [*government*] *documents* that record Chan discourses and expositions. In the intervals between helping students, or in the leisure moments when they closed the door [to their private room], from time to time the ancients did raise [*gong'ans* for consideration], passing judgments on them, composing verses on them, differentiating them. But they weren't doing that in order to flaunt their knowledge or to contend with the ancient worthies! In fact, they were motivated by the painful thought that the great dharma was in a state of ruin. Therefore, in a roundabout fashion they implemented *upāyas*, making an opening for the wisdom-eyes of posterity. All they wanted was to enable later people to achieve realization. The *gong-* [= *impartial/public* in the word *gong'an*] refers to blocking out any sort of self or private understanding. The *an*-element [= *document*] refers to tallying with the [idea or intention of the] buddhas and patriarchs. Thus, once the [student] has passed through the *gong'an*, his deluded consciousness is exhausted. If his deluded consciousness is exhausted, samsara is voided. If samsara is voided, the Buddha Way 'rules.' 'Tallying' means that the buddhas and patriarchs had great pity for sentient beings who had bound themselves to samsaric delusion and who, for accumulated eons down to today, could not attain release on their own. Therefore, [the buddhas and patriarchs] deployed words within wordlessness, conferred analogues within no-analogues, desiring that people be released from the ropes of delusion. How could words and analogues once again become subjects of discussion and argument [i.e., how could *gong'ans* themselves become the subject of discussion and argument]? Moreover, for people in the world, when an incident arises that they are unable to normalize, they must seek rationality from a government office: the *official functionary raises as a standard a government document* that calms or settles it. This is like a student who cannot decide on his own whether his awakening [is correct or not]. He questions his teacher, and *the teacher raises as a standard a gong'an* to decide [whether the student's awakening is correct or not]. A *gong'an* is a wisdom-torch to illuminate the darkness of deluded consciousness, a *golden rod*[61] that lifts off the blindness-membrane in seeing and hearing, a sharp axe that severs the life-faculty of samsara, a divine mirror that reflects the faces of the sage and the ordinary person. The Chan patriarchal mind employs [the *gong'an*] to illuminate; buddha mind employs [the *gong'an*] to reveal. Nothing surpasses [the *gong'an*] as the crucial element for complete transcendence, far-ranging release, great comprehension, and realization that is identical [to that of the buddhas and patriarchs]! The phrase *gong'an* is awe-inducing only to the person who knows dharma. If you are not such a person, how can you possibly steal a peek into [a *gong'an* that] *looks like something, but you can't say for sure*? Oh no! The deluded ones in the world, without examining the Source, always employ their natural gift of cleverness to engage in wide investigation and extensive memorization. They get exoteric and esoteric transmissions and only apply themselves to comprehension through verbalization. They don't seek for awakening in [their own] mind, and this causes confusion even in the cases of the superior rules of the 'stick and shout.' They fall into the dense forest of deluded thought. Even stampeding dragons and elephants [i.e., superior practitioners][62] get ensnared in the deep trap of *is/is not*. Love and hate flow from their eyes, seizing and rejecting fill their breasts. An ancient's metaphorical teaching about ghee's becoming a poisonous concoction is proof of this.[63] As for the decline in the Chan community, this is the root cause. Aah! It is like government officials who enrich themselves in the world through bribery. If the selfish and private mind gains a single

---

[61] A golden rod (*jinbi* 金篦) was originally a medical instrument used by doctors in ancient India to remove eye membranes from blind people. In the secret teachings it is used by the *ācārya* (*teacher*) in the *abhiṣeka* (*anointment*) to remove the "membrane of ignorance" from the eyes of the student.
[62] *Vimalakīrti Sūtra*, T 475.14.547a25–26.
[63] *Jingde chuandeng lu* (景德傳燈錄; T 2076.51.444b26–27): "Now, the superior flavor of ghee is a rarity in the world, but when it meets this class of person, it flips over into a poisonous concoction." [且醍醐上味為世珍奇。遇斯等人翻成毒藥。]. The speaker is Fenzhou Wuye (汾州無也; 760–820).

victory, we can only hope that the impartial Way remains effective in maintaining public stability. Can this be achieved?

[11] SOMEONE ASKED: "The *gong'ans* of the patriarchal masters are based on students' asking questions due to their uncertainties; and the ancients, who were of great, quiescent mind, responded to those questions much like the striking of a great drum [and its echoes] in an empty valley. This was no more than destroying the *sensation of uncertainty* for people and ripping open the 'nests' [they 'sit in,' i.e., the stereotyped formulas or conventional usages they are mired in]. Therefore, it is said: 'Our Chan personal realization is without verbalization and has not a single teaching to give to people.'[64] In fact, our predecessors have been teachers of people, and could not hold back from the give-and-take of questions and answers—single sayings and half-lines spread all through the Chan community. Those of later generations who received these *contentless* [*words*] and echoed them over and over called them *gong'ans*. [*Gong'ans*] are rooted in this single principle [of 'nonverbal and without a single teaching to give to people']. But the 'haggling' in our present-day Chan community is not in accord with this at all! [In present-day Chan we find the format of] question and answer: What is a buddha? What was Bodhidharma's intention in coming from the West? Examples [of answers] include [such *gong'ans* as]: **three catties of linen thread, dried turd, Mt. Sumeru**, and **don't engage in false thought**.[65] [Present-day Chan followers] call these *plain and simple* and consider [*gong'ans* such as] **examining the old woman, falling into words, begging bowl, up in a tree**, etc.,[66] as *upwards* or *showing the whole thing* [i.e., fully exposing the ultimate]. Sometimes [present-day Chan followers] take all the karmic exchanges and arrange them in terms of Linji's *three mysteries*; sometimes they take these various sayings and divide them into Fenyang's *four phrases*.[67] In the middle of all that they engage in convoluted talk and clever discussions, fully covering all the 1,700 *gong'ans*, giving each a different name, and judging the worth of each as 'high' or 'low.' I'm not at all sure that this was what the ancients intended!"

PHANTASM SAID: "The sayings of the patriarchal masters emerge from an unconditioned mind of great quiescence. [In responding to the capacities of beings] they say the appropriate thing and take the appropriate action. Right from the outset they engage in no selection process whatsoever. Sometimes

---

[64] *Jingde chuandeng lu* (景德傳燈錄; T 2076.51.318a2–3): "Xuefeng asked: 'From of old what dharma has the Chan style taught people?' The Master [Deshan Xuanjian 德山宣鑒; 780–865] said: 'Our Chan personal realization is without verbalization and has not a single teaching to give to people.' [雪峯問。從上宗風以何法示人。師曰。我宗無語句。實無一法與人。]."

[65] For details, see Noguchi and Matsubara, *Sanbō yawa*, 99, n. 2.

[66] For details, see Noguchi and Matsubara, *Sanbō yawa*, 99, n. 3.

[67] For details, see Noguchi and Matsubara, *Sanbō yawa*, 99, nn. 4–5.

they pick up and sometimes they let go: everything is rooted in the purport of Bodhidharma's *direct transmission*. As soon as they start to speak, their audacity is apparent, and absolutely nothing is concealed. [The patriarchal masters] are like the moon in the sky.[68] When a person who goes to the east sees the moon, it goes east with him. A person who goes to the west thinks that the moon goes west with him. A person who stays at the midpoint without moving thinks that the moon is remaining unmoving along with him. Each grasps his own viewpoint. There are different points from which to view the moon—moving to the east, moving to the west, and unmoving—but the full moon remains *as is* overhead in the sky. In fact, the moon has never followed along with this person's moving to the east, moving to the west, or remaining stationary. These wide-ranging explanations, which are all different, are due to a failure [on the part of the observer of the moon] to penetrate to the dharma-source. This is like how the emptiness inside a vessel is determined by the shape of the vessel [i.e., though there are differences in the squareness or roundness of vessel shapes, there is no fixed reality to the emptiness inside].[69] When the clear-eyed Chan masters who preceded us raised [sayings for the consideration of students], sometimes they were repressing [the student] and sometimes they were lifting [the student]. And we should not take this 'tongueless speaking'[70] [of Chan masters] as some sort of realization-awakening: such sayings are to be understood as one-off Chan encounters [i.e., the Chan master's skillful manipulation of words in dealing with a specific student]. As soon as [the student] wades into [a master's] *letting loose/snatching up* and *going against/going along with*, he will be at a loss—simply because his awakening to principle is not yet exhaustive. Thus, even though *gongans* constitute a single principle, the differences among them are like a person's entering the sea: the further he goes in, the deeper the water becomes. Eventually, he arrives at the very bottom of the great abyss. Suddenly he looks backwards and realizes that [all the way through it has been the very same sea]; there has never been some other sea. If he does not personally at least once reach [the bottom of the sea of awakening], a heart of uncertainty will spontaneously arise without his compliance. This is like a monk's question to Mazu: 'What is a buddha?' Mazu said:

---

[68] For a similar simile, see *Śūraṃgama Sūtra*, T 945.19.120c25–28.
[69] This simile appears in the dharma talks section of the *Zhongfeng Extensive Record*: "You should know that this matter is like the emptiness inside a vessel that follows the shape of the vessel, like how water accords with the direction of its flow. Though there are differences of squareness/roundness [in vessels] or movement/stillness [in the course of the water], there is no reality to the squareness/roundness or movement/stillness." [須知此事如空之循器。如水之隨流。雖有方圓動靜之殊。而無方圓動靜之實。] (CBETA 2019.Q3, B25, no. 145, p. 740b6–7).
[70] *Wumen guan* (無門關), T 2005.48.295b25–c4.

'Mind itself *is* buddha!'[71] In the case of this *gong'an*, even people who haven't practiced Chan at all will all comprehend completely. But, when they try to inquire into the *ultimate purport* [of this *gong'an*], even many of those who have practiced for a long time and accumulated much learning will misunderstand. How is this so? When you ask them 'what is it that is called mind,' they will already have started down the road [of verbalization and intellectual understanding]. *Here* there must be appropriate guidance: they absolutely must *on their own* hurdle over [intellectual understanding] and take hold of the matter! If they start over and take another look, their looking [at the *gong'ans*] will be perfectly clear—like bumping into one's own father at a crossroads. Spontaneously, when amid activities, they will tally with the *cart-rut*. There is a type who hasn't done practice-work, hasn't discerned the mind-ground, hasn't been able to sever the life-faculty of samsaric great uncertainty that is right under his feet. With his only asset being cleverness, he takes the most appropriate quotations from ancient and modern texts to haggle and conjecture over an understanding of the ancient and modern *gong'ans*. Little does he imagine that, not having comprehended samsara, he is not the equal of the *true person* who understands nothing at all! Though [the *true person* who understands nothing at all] doesn't understand, suddenly one day he will give rise to a mind of confidence and engage in true practice and real investigation. Despite everything, for him there will come a time of awakening. The one who comes to understand through cleverness alone certainly will not produce correct confidence and achieve awakening. [However,] recently in the Chan community, there has been a desire to rush to get people [i.e., disciples], never mind any expectation that these students be clever. Teachers pick up a book and creep along phrase after phrase [i.e., spelling everything out], as if instructing children how to read their first characters. [These teachers] are hoping that the disciples will come to understand their teachings and cooperate in helping to spread them. This is no different from trying to blow air into a fishing net to inflate it! Practitioners who are the *real thing* will be unwilling to eat this sort of evil poison. But, if [such *real* practitioners] encounter ancient and modern Chan stories, they will not want to comprehend them using mind. They will simply raise one [Chan story], put it right up front, and produce the resolve necessary for coming to an understanding of samsara. Standing before a ten-thousand-foot wall, they will eternally go on practicing with it. If they gallop onward and manage to smash the *ball of uncertainty*, then a zillion *gong'ans*—including deep/shallow, difficult/easy, same/different—they'll bore right through the whole string of them!

---

[71] *Mazu Daoyi chanshi guanglu* (*Sijia yulu* 1) 馬祖道一禪師廣錄 (四家語錄卷一), CBETA 2019.Q3, X69, no. 1321, p. 4a19–20. The questioner is Damei Fachang (大梅法常; 752–839).

Spontaneously, they won't ask anybody about anything. If, in some cases, their mind-eye is not yet opened, they are unwilling to investigate self and practice, and they feel the need to seek instruction from others, then, even if Śākyamuni and Bodhidharma were to open their livers and give up the last drops from their gall bladders to provide them instruction, all it would do is block up their mind-eye even more! Think about it! Think about it!

Night Conversations in a Mountain Hermitage II

[12] SOMEONE ASKED: "Bodhidharma came from the west. His house style was steep and perilous: before anything was even said, [students] 'hit the jackpot' [i.e., achieved realization]. Having already waded through the stages of the [Chan] journey, what would be the need for [such students] to engage in so-called *practice-work*? How much more so would it be the case with *withered cross-legged sitting* on the sitting cushion, which is like guarding the ghost of a corpse! In the case of Chan, how could one possibly gain attainment through cross-legged sitting? Wouldn't such a thing be heaping shame on the former Chan patriarchs?"

I [PHANTASM] SAID: "No, there is no shame upon them. The fact is, you see only one side of things and fail to see the other. For example, Longtan asked a question of Tianhuang:

> I, your student, have followed you, Preceptor, for a long time, but I've never received your instruction on the mind-essence.' Tianhuang said: 'If you bring tea, I'll raise my hand; if you come with an inquiry, I'll lower my head. Where am I not giving you instruction on the mind-essence?' Longtan understood Tianhuang's purport.[72]

If we speak of this *gong'an* from the student standpoint, it is extremely expedient. If we speak of it from the Chan-approach standpoint, it fails to put a halt to 'wading through the stages of the [Chan] journey.' Another example:

> Xiangyan was asked by Guishan about [*my original face*] *before my father and mother conceived me*. Xiangyan could not come up with a reply and so sought Guishan to speak one for him. Guishan did not give his assent. Subsequently, [Xiangyan] completely gave up his practice, entered Nanyang [in Henan], and dwelled in a hermitage. Quite a bit later, he heard the sound from a tile's striking a piece of bamboo and suddenly [awakened].[73]

---

[72] *Jingde chuandeng lu* 景德傳燈錄, T 2076.51.313b18–22. Longtan Chongxin (龍潭崇信; d.u.) was a successor of Tianhuang Daowu (天皇道悟; 748–807).

[73] See Dahui Zonggao's *Zheng fayan zang* (正法眼藏; CBETA 2019.Q3, X67, no. 1309, p. 591c3–14).

During Xiangyan's time [at that hermitage], although he never employed the term 'doing practice-work,' he was diligent in maintaining his practice. 'Thinking of this [Guishan matter], he rested in this [i.e., Guishan's question about *my original face*].'[74] What was he planning to accomplish from this? Although he was not capable of immediately achieving understanding [i.e., coming to understanding when he was with his master Guishan], he passed months and years before eventually awakening. The purport that he awakened to—how could we possibly say that it was not the purport transmitted by Bodhidharma? In the case of those at present who do practice-work but do not get numinous effects:

(1) They lack the ancients' true determination.
(2) They do not take samsaric impermanence as the *one great matter*.
(3) They are unable to discard the habit-energies they have accumulated over innumerable eons.

All day long, following one teacher or another's instruction, they raise a *huatou* to awareness. They get up on their sitting cushion, and, even before their seat is warm, torpor or distraction envelops them on all sides. They lack the eternally non-retrogressing body-mind. What a difficulty: 'How then could there be a Maitreya who descends from the Tuṣita Heaven [or a spontaneous Śākyamuni]?'[75] These words exhaust the matter. Frequently, when we see someone [whose practice-work] falls short of success, we don't call to account our own failure to measure up and instead consider that the *buddhadharma* is in decline and the Chan community in its autumn twilight, making the excuse:

> Nowhere are there [real] masters of forged metal, and besides, there are no friends to whip students forward—not to mention the fact that hot water and cooking fire are not conveniently at hand, and so the morning porridge and noon meal [of the monastery] can't be prepared. When [monastic] customs and manners are left uncultivated, the environment falls into an absurd confusion. This is why my practice-work has gone all bad!

If this explanation were to gain widespread circulation, everybody training in the Way would take it as a pretext [to slack off in their practice-work]! It

---

[74] Playing on *Book of Documents* (*Shang shu* 尚書), "Counsels of the Great Yu" (*Da Yu mo* 大禹謨 9). See ctext.org/shang-shu/counsels-of-the-great-yu.
[75] *Huangbo Duanji Wanlinglu* (黃蘗斷際禪師宛陵錄): 那得天生彌勒自然釋迦。(T 2012B.48. 387a14–15).

would be like a farmer who blames the fact that wet and dry weather are not on time and so stops plowing his fields. How can he hope to have an autumn harvest? It is just that [today's] practitioners of the Way, faced with sense objects that go along with them and go against them, in the blink of an eye produce a single thought and want to differentiate [into good/bad]: I know that the fault for their being in bondage to the samsaric wheel for numberless eons is based in this! Haven't you heard? The old monk of the Snow Peaks [i.e., Śākyamuni] discarded the honor and glory of his ten-thousand-chariot state, and for six years lay down on ice [to sleep] and chewed on cork-trees [for sustenance]. He forgot his own body while freezing and undergoing hunger. And then there came the night of his seeing the bright star and awakening. From the Buddha on down, the twenty-eight patriarchs of India all roosted on crags and dwelled in caves. Or they mixed their traces in with the differentiated mundane world. Their *true mind* was not extinguished; their real practice did not deviate. They were all capable of realizing self and transmitting the seal of the buddha-mind. Bodhidharma went to the east, and, before Baizhang appeared,[76] the Oxhead school of Chan [descended from the fourth patriarch Daoxin] emerged as a collateral branch [of the Bodhidharma line]. The Southern and Northern lineages split off into two factions. They all, with a sickle at the waist and a spade on the shoulder, burned and seeded their fields, tended to their farm work, watched over their stove, shouldered the task of the mortar and pestle, in shabby clothes begged for food, made their body-and-mind as hard as iron and stone, made their feelings like ice and frost—carrying on one shoulder the objective of the buddhas and patriarchs: the *one great matter of causation*. They feared nothing at all. Since they had a good foothold in practice, wherever they arrived was necessarily the target. At that time [i.e., before Baizhang], how could there have been such things as the spacious living accommodations of the [state-sponsored] Five Mountains and Ten Monasteries;[77] remarkable formulas such as Linji's *three mysteries* and the Caodong school's *five ranks*; non-pareil formulations such as *letting loose/taking in* and *killing/giving life*; and the incomparable language of prose and verse comments on Chan standards, critiques of the sayings of others, and substitutions for answers in Chan dialogues? [Before Baizhang,] there was no adding on of carving and polishing: the jade from the outset was flawless. How could they have needed any regulatory standards? Their eyes from the outset were naturally correct. Once Baizhang established the Chan community, broad fields

---

[76] Baizhang (749–814) is traditionally known as the first formulator of the "pure rules" of the Chan community.
[77] For the Five-Mountains system, see Introduction, n. 1.

and big buildings in an instant popped into existence according to wish. However, *true causes* [i.e., practice] daily declined, errors daily increased; institutions and rules daily became more complicated; rituals and righteousness were daily pared away. Several hundred years on, teaching masters such as Linji, Deshan, Yunmen, and Zhenjing, their spirits indignant, gave angry scoldings in all directions, looking down upon [some monks] as if they were promiscuous women or soldier-menials. Therefore, these teachers upbraided monks for not embodying the fundamentals of the Way: for only applying themselves to verbal comprehension and to deceiving one another. Later, there were masters who watched the fleeting movements of [students'] eye pupils [for signs of their level of understanding]. Such masters explicated Chan in all the regions, but their explications were very much like Ye Gong's [paintings of] dragons and Zhao Chang's [of] flowers[78] [i.e., artistic images and not the real thing]. [The artists] Ye Gong and Zhao Chang were already themselves unreal [i.e., devoid of essence/*svabhāva*]—how much more is this the case for the imitations [i.e., the paintings] that came from Ye Gong and Zhao Chang! Ah! Regrettably, the graphs for *crow* and *how* are often mistaken for [the similar graph for] *horse*. Truly, this is not something that goes on only today! From this it may be seen that those who have truly practiced and really awakened are rare not only today—in the past they were also hardly ever seen. It all boils down to samsaric delusion and the defiled habit-energy of ignorance shift along in a flow, moment after moment without a hair's breadth of a gap. [Even] if you did none of the following: "enter your bones and marrow to painfully produce the *correct thought* [of resolving the *great matter*] *of samsara*"; "lift the *huatou* to awareness as if meeting a bitter enemy"; "throw away one or two lifetimes to ram against [this *huatou*]"; and "wait for a vast awakening," there is no case in which you wouldn't become one of the deceptions ones of Ye Gong and Zhao Chang! Perhaps we could quote the third patriarch [Sengcan's] line, 'if there were no hate and attachment, [the *ultimate Way*] would be perfectly clear,'[79] and Yongjia's line, 'don't

---

[78] The *New Preface* (*Xin xu* 新序) by Liu Xiang (劉向) of the Han period: "Ye Gong Zihao liked dragons. With a drawing compass he drew dragons, and with a chisel he copied dragons. In his home he had carvings of dragons. A man heard about this and regarded it as inferior. He made the head of a dragon peep in at the window, with the tail stretching into the hall. When Ye Gong saw this, he dropped everything and ran away. He lost his spirit, but the five colors [of that dragon] were [like his own paintings] not real. This is a case of Ye Gong's not liking dragons: he liked seeming dragons but not [real] dragons." [葉公子高好龍。鉤以寫龍。鑿以寫龍。屋室雕文以寫龍。於是夫龍聞而下之。窺頭於牖。拖尾於堂。葉公見之。棄而還走。失其魂魄。五色無主。是葉公非好龍也。好夫似龍而非龍者也。] (ctext.org/xin-xu/za-shi-wu/zh?searchu=葉公). Juefan Huihong's (覺範慧洪; 1071–1128) literary collection *Shimen wenzi chan* (石門文字禪): "It is just like Zhao Chang's painting flowers: he draws the life in them and presses against the real. They are transmitted in the world as a treasure, but, in the end, they are not real flowers." [正如趙昌畫花。寫生逼真。世傳為實。然終非真花耳。] (CBETA 2019.Q3, J23, no. B135, p. 689b29–30).

[79] *Xinxin ming* (信心銘; T 2010.48.376b20–21).

eliminate false thought and don't search for the *real*[80] to prove it: '*Just this* is awakening to principle—how could you, in a single lifetime or two of making hardships for your body and suffering for your mind, turn it into the attainment [of awakening]?' The circulation of this theory would shake the minds of Ye Gong and Zhao Chang to no end! Haven't you thought about the saying of Yongjia: 'If there is reduction of dharma assets and extinction of karmic merit, there are no cases in which it hasn't arisen from mind [i.e., storehouse consciousness], afflicted mind, and [the six sense] consciousnesses.'[81] These words painfully point at those who are not searching for correct awakening. They falsely employ mind [i.e., the storehouse consciousness], the afflicted mind, and [the six sense] consciousnesses to act in concert with the language of similitudes. One person transmits a lie, and ten thousand people transmit the lie as truth! This is nothing more than the graphs *crow* and *how* being mistaken for the graph for *horse*. Therefore, the ancient said: 'Practice must be real practice; awakening must be real awakening. Great King Yama isn't afraid of a lot of talk.'[82] These words exhaust the matter. *I am certainly not someone who has had a real awakening*. I dare not tread in the tracks of Ye Gong's [painting of unreal dragons] and Zhao Chang's [painting of unreal flowers]! I talk daily with people about this and that, haggling over *this matter*, but all that is the dharma-gate that I believe is correct. It has never been about showing off my dazzling knowledge to elicit praise from others. Even if I did have the confidence of others, that would not add to my joy! Even if I did not enjoy the confidence of others, how could I dare to become angry? Thus, confidence or no confidence is very much a matter of the mind of the person in question. How can one be joyful or angry about these things? Such things are only understandable to one who is walking the same Way. Even if I am ridiculed as nonsensical, how could I shun [my obligation]?"

[13] SOMEONE ASKED: "In the case of a Chan practitioner who cannot achieve awakening, are there *upāyas* that can enable him to achieve awakening? If this practitioner goes round and round without awakening, concerning the *great matter* of samsaric impermanence: in a later lifetime, or even lifetimes after that, will there still be some principle of awakening for him?"

PHANTASM SAID: "Sharp question! *This matter* is a matter right under the feet of the person in question. It has never involved anyone else, and it cannot be shoved off onto someone else. Therefore, it is said: 'Delusion is your own

---

[80] *Yongjia Zhengdao ge* (永嘉證道歌; T 2014.48.395c9–10).
[81] *Yongjia Zhengdao ge* (永嘉證道歌; T 2014.48.396b1–2).
[82] *Wu deng huiyuan* (五燈會元; CBETA 2019.Q3, X80, no. 1565, p. 235c16–17). The ancient is the Song-dynasty Linji figure Shending Hongyin (神鼎洪諲; d.u.).

delusion; awakening must be your own awakening.'[83] If you don't awaken on your own, then even Śākyamuni or Bodhidharma can do nothing for you! Most teaching masters of the present can do nothing at all in the case of a student who has not awakened, and so they lead students by setting up ingenious karmic encounters and administering twisted *upāyas*. However, students don't take the *great matter of samsara* as their own heavy responsibility! All they want is to quickly 'understand Chan.' Thereupon, they crouch down to sit under those *upāyas*, bore right through a whole string of ancient and modern *gong'ans*, and call that 'passing through the [awakening-] barrier.' They are totally unaware that the *samsara-barrier* right beneath their feet is exactly the one they have been unable to pass through, and the thing they passed through was no more than the *verbalization-barrier*! How could it be only a matter of having no benefit? On the contrary, there is harm done to your *great matter of self*. If someone is a splendid person who truly is practicing for the sake of the *great matter of samsara*, even if Great Teacher Bodhidharma pops up in the world and fully inserts the profound principle of the buddhas and patriarchs into his eight-consciousnesses-field, he will surely from the root spit out [that profound principle]. Why is this so? Because awakening must be awakening on one's own. How could it have even a half-penny's connection to anyone else! Even if you come to the end of your life without having awakened, if you just firmly maintain correct thought—when alive, alive with [this correct thought], and, when dead, dead with [this correct thought]—there will be no need at all to seek for even one fine hair's worth of intellectual understanding. If you can in this way guard with fidelity [this correct thought], it will be just one or two lifetimes [until awakening]: do not worry about not achieving awakening. [But say,] sitting in *stillness-and-silence*, your defilements temporarily calm down; suddenly inside the five-aggregates consciousnesses you realize a principle just like [the true principle]: you come to rely on it and are convinced it is correct. You quote words from the sutra teachings as proof and hold them in your mind. You do not realize that this disease is a *dependent comprehension* of the five-aggregates consciousnesses—truly the root of samsara, not *seeing the Nature*! Firmly grasp [your practice] until it comes to completion, and be unwilling to seek out decisions and choices from other people. All over the place you just want people to stamp you with the 'winter-melon seal.'[84] What do you plan to accomplish with this? Also, there is a class of people who falsely

---

[83] A similar saying by Zhenjing Kewen (真淨克文; 1025–1102) appears in *Gu zunsu yulu* (古尊宿語錄; CBETA 2019.Q3, X68, no. 1315, p. 288a12–13).

[84] It seems like a real seal, but it is a fake. See *Foguo Yuanwu chanshi Biyanlu* (佛果圜悟禪師碧巖錄; T 2003.48.221c2–4).

recognize the shadows of the six sense-fields as their very own *Mr. Man-in-charge*. And they quote as proof the words of the ancient: 'You who are not yet awakened, listen to a single saying: *who is moving your mouth right now?*'[85] Generally, practitioners who have not obtained correct awakening are not only useless on the samsaric shore: in broad daylight and clear skies, with both eyes wide-open, upon encountering sounds and forms, at the slightest provocation they produce deluded feelings and thoughts: they fail to attain freedom! When others criticize them, they produce fundamental ignorance and engage in fighting with these others. This is what a crazy person does! Also, there are some who study the Way for a lifetime, without attaining any sort of awakening. They then come to have no confidence [in the very existence of awakening]. Soon they sweep the correct thought of studying the Way into the [tiny, hidden-away] closet of *nothing-to-do*[86] and never again produce the thought of seeking out awakening. People such as this are said to 'lose correct thought.' Having lost correct thought, they must not say that in a later lifetime, or even lifetimes after that, they will still be unable to attain realization: [in that case,] even if they pass through innumerable [lifetimes], way into the future, [without practice] a time of realization will not come for them. This is like not tilling the soil of good fields, and hoping for the five grains to sprout spontaneously. It's unreasonable."

[14] SOMEONE ASKED: "If one practices Chan for his whole life without awakening, what is the karmic result?"

PHANTASM: "Bean seeds don't produce hemp or wheat; grass roots don't give birth to pine or camellia trees. Now, even though practicing Chan is said to be an effortless dharma method,[87] I am just afraid that this is not true practice. As Preceptor Yongming said:

> Suppose one has practiced but has not yet attained a penetrating realization, has trained in the Way but not yet gotten results—[the teachings have] passed through his ear faculty and will forever constitute seeds for the Way. Birth after

---

[85] *Baozhi heshang shi'eshi song* 寶誌和尚十二時頌 in *Jingde chuandeng lu* 景德傳燈錄 (T 2076.51.450c1–2).

[86] Yoshizawa Katsuhiro, ed., *Shoroku zokugo kai*, 9.30 glosses *wushi jia* 無事甲 thus: "The *jia* 甲 can also be *ge* 閣 or *jia* 夾. In an old commentary on the *Kuya man lu* [枯崖漫錄; a brush-notes collection of Chan anecdotes dated 1263] we find: 'The *ge* 閣 can be *jia* 甲 or *jia* 夾. All are colloquial language.' In colloquial language, there are many cases of usage for sound only without being restricted by the meanings of the characters. A *ge* 閣 is a tiny hidden-away room or closet [奥の小ざしき或いは物おき]. The phrase *wushi jia* 無事甲 should be translated as *useless place* [無用の處]." This exegesis is confirmed by *Jiatai pudeng lu* (嘉泰普燈錄; 1204): 有宗坐在無事閣裏。 (CBETA, X79, no. 1559, p. 441, b24). This phrase appears in Dahui Zonggao's prohibitions concerning *huatou* practice—what the practitioner is not supposed to do. See Broughton with Watanabe, *Letters of Dahui*, letters #10.5 and #32.1 (pp. 109 and 205).

[87] See, for example, Dahui Zonggao's *Zheng fayan zang* (正法眼藏; CBETA 2019.Q3, X67, no. 1309, p. 630c15–16).

birth he will not fall into the three evil rebirth paths, lifetime after lifetime he will not lose human form. Right at the very moment he pops up in another rebirth, he will attain a thousand awakenings upon hearing only once.[88]

These words are the truth. Even if people in the world simply cultivate a little bit of good karma for a short time, they will still acquire superior benefit. In the teachings it is said: 'The merit from hearing the five names [of this sutra] surpasses the merit derived from filling up the [three thousand] worlds with [the seven] treasures and giving them all away.'[89] How could this be a lie? From the first production of the aspiration for awakening, the original purpose is to settle the *great matter of samsara*. Perhaps you have gone twenty or thirty years without having attained awakening—still you must not seek out some other *upāya* [i.e., other than the *huatou*]. Just have your mind entertain no other objective-supports, cut off all delusive thoughts in your mind, and work diligently at never abandoning [the *huatou*]. Just stand your ground against the *huatou* you are practicing. Just stake your life on it—in life live together with [the *huatou*] and in death die together with [the *huatou*]. Who cares whether it is three lifetimes or five lifetimes, ten lifetimes or a hundred lifetimes! If you haven't attained a penetrating awakening, whatever you do, don't take time off! If you possess this *correct cause*, don't worry about 'I haven't yet clarified the *great matter*.' Therefore, it is said in the teachings: 'Even in sentient-beings of the latter age, if they can for a single thought-moment produce the non-retrogressing mind, it is identical to correct awakening.'[90] These words exhaust the matter, but today's students do things in the opposite way. As soon as they first produce the aspiration for awakening, their footing becomes unstable. I fear that [in that case] their sense-objects will change in a flash; a plethora of thoughts will arise; they will lose their secure grip on being *Mr. Master-in-charge*, and they will flow into mistaken paths. Because of this, from thought-moment to moment they chase after this and that, urgently anticipating transcendence [i.e., awakening]. Little do they know: these thoughts of chasing after this and that become a blockage, mistakenly obstructing the desire to realize the correct cause of the *great matter of samsara*. For quite some time things remain unresolved. There are three types who [lack firmness and therefore are prone to] suddenly shift:

---

[88] *Wan shan tonggui (Fu Yongming chanshi chuijie)* 萬善同歸集 (附永明壽禪師垂誡); T 2017.48.993b12–14.

[89] *Da fangguang yuanjue xiuduoluo liaoyi jing* (大方廣圓覺修多羅了義經; T 842.17.921c18–20 and 921c26–28).

[90] Untraced. There is a similar line in *Da fangguang fo huayan jing* 大方廣佛華嚴經 (T 278.9.430c21–22).

1. Some are unable to abandon their 'mind of victory' [i.e., the mind that seeks awakening] and shoulder a lot of cleverness, to say nothing of the fact that their teacherly friends catch them in the net of 'awakening to principle.' They come to prize only verbal comprehension, lack any self-awareness, and wade through [the traps of] intellectual knowledge. They paste *semblance prajñā*[91] onto their consciousness-field. They call themselves 'realized' or 'enlightened.' They are unaware that this is a lie, and so the habit-energy that exits from their mouths and enters their ears is all a muddled mess. Transformative *upāyas* are obsolete [in dealing with them]. Few people escape falling into this rut. This is the first [of the three types].

2. Some have inferior determination and are narrow in their knowledge and experience. Whatever stage of practice-work they find themselves in, their grounding is unsteady. They mistakenly think that this 'effortless' dharma method has no numinous efficacy whatsoever. They do [practice-work] for a limit of ten or twenty years, and, when they do not yoke up [with awakening], hastily change their *prior cause* [i.e., change the style of practice-work they have engaged in up until that point], in some cases taking recitation of a buddha-name as their [new] *direct-track* practice. Morning to evening they finger their string of beads, seeking pure karma. Perhaps, using the teachings of the Buddha's whole career—the pronouncements from the Buddha's mouth—they declare: 'I'm practicing Chan, but it has no numinous effects.' They cannot help following lines of text and counting the number of characters, thinking that they are planting good causes. They say: 'I'm not wasting my time!' They hate doing proper practice but fear the karmic retribution [that surely comes from discarding practice]. They sink into obscurity, with a dirty face and in coarse straw-clothes [engaging in such activities as] as grinding grain in a mortar and tending to a stove fire. They bring ascetic pain to their physical bodies to aid their practice. Sometimes they secretly chant mantras, in a hidden way repenting for offenses, mistakes, and so forth. All of this goes against correct confidence. They wade through heterodox teachings that are far from Buddhism. This is the second [of the three types].

3. Some from the outset have lacked the seeds of confidence. When they encounter sense-objects, they produce [deluded] thoughts. Beneath the rafters of the three roots [i.e., greed, anger, and stupidity]—before their seats on the sitting platform are even warm [from doing cross-legged sitting]—in their eight-consciousnesses-field they unceasingly grab onto

---

[91] *Mohe bore boluomi jing* (摩訶般若波羅蜜經): "The Buddha said: 'If there are good sons and daughters who say that there is a perfection of wisdom to be apprehended, this is semblance perfection of wisdom.'" [佛言。有善男子善女人說有所得般若波羅蜜。是為相似般若波羅蜜。] (T 223.8.295b14–15).

objective-supports. They have not been capable of chewing to pieces a single *huatou*. They are susceptible to the rising/falling of hundreds of delusions. Before they've even been practicing for three to five years, they say: 'I've been practicing Chan but I haven't awakened!' They then cast the matter into the [tiny, hidden-away] closet of *nothing-to-do*[92]—thought-moment after thought-moment they follow along with sense-objects, each thought flowing on like a successive wave. They willingly proceed right to death's door. These are people who have never done a *reverse examination* [upon themselves]. This is the third [of the three types].

We are now in the last years of the *semblance dharma* [i.e., the second of the three periods of the dharma] in this Chan community. The patriarchal Way is run down and has grown cold. If Way-practitioners do not sustain a determined, non-retrogressing, iron-and-stone body-and-mind, then they will end up on one or another of these roads [i.e., the above three types]! Having lost great resolution in their own mind, [these three types] increase the deep sorrow of the buddhas and patriarchs. The dharma clan's decline has never been rooted in anything other than this. Little do people imagine: the correct confidence for practicing Chan is met once in a thousand lifetimes, once in a hundred generations. If you are emerging from a daze and unable to press directly forward in the hope of achieving true liberation, in just the interval it takes to produce a thought, you'll be ten thousand miles up in the white clouds. If you want the seed-wisdom of *prajñā* to again enter your mind, rotten grain seeds are not going to sprout a second time!

[15] SOMEONE ASKED: "Are there differences between the way that the ancients exerted themselves in the practice of Chan, and the way present-day people do?"

PHANTASM: "In their study of the Way, the ancients never asked whether the Way had been attained or not. Before their feet had even stepped past the gatekeeper [of the monastery], they first chopped the *furtive mind*[93] in two, so that it could never be resuscitated. But present-day people are completely dominated by *furtive mind*. This is the real difference between those of the present and the ancients—they have nothing in common. What is samsara?

---

[92] See n. 86.
[93] Yoshizawa Katsuhiro, ed., *Shoroku zokugo kai*, 125.565 glosses *furtive mind* (*touxin* 偷心) as *incorrect thought* (*bu zheng nian* 不正念). In Translation 11 (an Instruction to the Assembly in *Zhongfeng Talks of Zhongfeng Record B*) Zhongfeng glosses *furtive mind* as follows: "What do I mean by *furtive mind*? If you merely separate from the *huatou* you are practicing and see the separate existence of a 'self,' that's *furtive mind*." [何謂偷心。但離却箇所參底話外。別見有箇自己。是偷心。] (*Gozanban* 9, 542c; CBETA 2019.Q3, X70, no. 1402, p. 716c16–17). The term *touxin* 偷心 could also be translated as *negligent mind, nonchalant mind, stealthy mind, underhanded mind, cunning mind, compromised mind, acquiescent mind*, etc.

Samsara is the existence of *furtive mind*! What is nirvana? Nirvana is annihilation of *furtive mind*. Let me try to put this into a metaphor. Samsara is the great illness, and the oral teachings of the buddhas and patriarchs are the good medicine. *Furtive mind* is what the medicine wards off. The oral teachings of the buddhas and patriarchs cure the great illness of samsara: this is where ancient times and the present are identical. How could there be a principle [of the Way] that lacks curative powers? Medicine is just for warding off [illness]. The ancients simply ingested the medicine, and almost all of them obtained its divine efficacy. As for present-day people, those prescriptions and medicaments are still around: they continue to provide for warding off [illness]. But not only do [present-day people] fail to cure the illness, they even undergo an increase in heterodox misunderstandings, making even the great physicians pull the lapels of their garments together in respectful salute and withdraw! What is *furtive mind*? It is another name for deluded consciousness, capable of snatching away one's very own supreme dharma assets. Therefore, Yongjia said: 'If there is reduction of dharma assets and extinction of karmic merit, there are no cases in which it hasn't arisen from mind [i.e., storehouse consciousness], afflicted mind, and [six sense] consciousnesses.'[94] Moreover, I will briefly raise for consideration several stories of our predecessors [the ancients]—they could be said to be models for the present.[95] For instance, the sixth patriarch [Huineng] arrived at Huangmei, and was simply ordered to work the pestle in the pestle room. When Guishan was in Baizhang's assembly, he filled the position of head cook. Yangqi for more than ten years was simply in charge of all temple affairs. Wuzu Fayan at Haihui Monastery filled the position of mill-master. Yunfeng was responsible for donations from fund-raising. Xuedou was responsible for maintaining toilet facilities. Ciming practiced under Fenyang, sometimes laughing, and sometimes scolding. Huanglong questioned Ciming and only met with abuse. During those times all kinds of stories emerged. [For these ancients,] sense-objects that went against them and went along with them proliferated; but, as *people on duty*, their *correct cause* was bright, and they completely killed off *furtive mind*. They took on the mixed-up confusion of these different sense-objects and one after the other made them dissolve back into principle. The fact is, wherever they went, they met up with the Way. But present-day people are unwilling to kill off *furtive mind* quickly—that's all there is to it! Indeed, they are not yet genuinely earnest about the *matter of self*! Although they lodge in the arena of emptiness,

---

[94] See n. 81
[95] For the details of the following stories, see Noguchi and Matsubara, *Sanbō yawa*, 140–142, nn. 3–10.

they let their thoughts gallop off to the region of seizing/rejecting. A certain type erects a new Chan monastery. If we compare this type [to the ancients] to determine which is superior and which inferior, they are as dissimilar as a heavenly crown and dirty sandals. If you ask why, when present-day people harbor a little bit of superior natural endowment, they invariably want to go for a famous name and high position. One should be ashamed of such contemptible matters to the end of one's life! How could [such seekers of fame and fortune] assent to serving in such monastic positions as mill-master or head cook? Generally, even when their monastic abode is tranquil, and they can take leisurely meals, they haven't gotten what they really want: how could they possibly be willing to take on a position in the pestle room or serve as fundraiser [who dutifully visits donors]?[96] When [this type, at the time of a dharma talk,] holds the handle of the fly whisk and takes his seat on the lion-chair, the *correct cause* becomes ever more faint, *furtive mind* ever more ascendant. Even though this type wants to confer [correct] thought on later descendants and serve as a tree providing cool shade [to disciples], how can they possibly do it? We can use this to divine the vicissitudes of the teachings, and the strong and weak points of the present and ancient times. None of this is unconnected to the existence or non-existence of *furtive mind*. On this point I allow no debate!

[16] SOMEONE ASKED: "As for *furtive mind* in sages and ordinary people, is there a gap between them in this or not?"

I [PHANTASM] SAID: "What sort of thing is *furtive mind*? It is simply none other than the ultimate essence of the Tathāgata's *wondrously bright original-mind*.[97] If one's determination to seek the Way is not genuine and not earnest, and covered up by various false thoughts, there occurs a 'flip' [from the *wondrously bright original-mind*] to *furtive mind*. As with grubs that infest a grain store, what harms the grain is the grubs. As in the case of a fire that breaks out in a store of wood, what burns up the wood is the fire. When one's thought of seeking the Way is genuinely earnest, even though people ordinarily cannot go for a single day without sleeping and eating, this [genuinely earnest] person will be able to forget about [sleeping and eating]. But what about when one's *furtive mind* has not been done away with? For example, take someone who, for his own profit, willingly takes a lowly job under another person. Even though all day long he works hard to the point of exhaustion,

---

[96] Note that the young Zhongfeng himself performed such duties. His autobiography (translated in the Introduction) states: "In 1293 and 1294 [at age thirty-one to thirty-two] all I did was dash about going to the gates of donors [soliciting donations]." [癸巳甲午惟奔走施門。] (*Gozanban* 9, 386c-d; CBETA 2019. Q3, B25, no. 145, p. 901a15–16). His cherished ambition, however, was to escape such confining monastic roles and hide away in the mountains and on the lakes.

[97] *Śūraṃgama Sūtra*: "All the things in all the worlds are the wondrously bright original-mind of bodhi." [一切世間。諸所有物。皆即菩提妙明元心。] (T 945.19.119b5–6).

[because he's pursuing his own profit] he never gets weary and fatigued. If he fails in some small aspect of his job and is subject to whipping and harsh verbal abuse, as is appropriate, he still won't shrink from the work at hand. How is he able to set aside his sense of shame and disgust [about doing such degrading work] in this way? The reason is simple: his *seeking-profit mind* is genuinely earnest, and so kicks in in this situation. [But] say he were to shrink from the exhausting work, and fear such punishment and shame—*he would then lose his profit*: but he is so fixated on reaping his phantasmal profit that he is quite capable of burying his extremely heavy sense of shame and disgust at himself. By comparison, our Chan group is pursuing the sagely Way, but is unwilling to kill off the unreal *furtive mind*: what about this state of affairs? How does the ordinary person differ from the sage, and how does the sage differ from the ordinary person? The only difference is *furtive mind*. People of the Way must be vigilant about this!"

[17] SOMEONE ASKED: "In doing practice-work, a lot of people are obstructed by *torpor* and *distraction*.[98] Even if they exert supranormal powers to the utmost, they are unable to ward off these [illnesses]. Doesn't this come about because the power of their faculties is subnormal?"

PHANTASM SAID: "Not so. You should know that torpor and distraction, just as they are, are *the scenery of your native land* [i.e., *your original face*].[99] In terms of ultimate principle, [torpor and distraction] are not two opposing things. You simply don't believe that torpor and distraction have always lacked any self-nature, any real substance! They come trespassing when your very own *single correct thought* [i.e., the *huatou*] of Chan practice is not genuine and not earnest. You should know that, if your first thought is not genuine and

---

[98] *hunshen* 昏沈 = *styāna* = torpor; *sanluan* 散亂 = *vikṣepa* = distraction. Sometimes *diaoju* 掉舉 (= *auddhatya* = restlessness) is substituted for *sanluan* 散亂. *Abhidharma saṃgītiparyāya pādaśāstra* (*Apidamo jiyimen zulun* 阿毘達磨集異門足論): "What is *torpor*? Answer: 'The whole body is heaviness; the mind is heaviness; the body lacks pliancy, the mind lacks pliancy.... What is *restlessness*? Answer: 'The various existents make the mind lack stillness and repose." [云何惛沈。答。所有身重性。心重性。身不調柔性。心不調柔性。... 云何掉舉。答。諸有令心不寂不靜。] (T 1536.26.416b12–24). Dahui in one of his general sermons (*pushuo* 普說) refers to *torpor* and *restlessness* as two types of illness experienced by Chan monks and lay Chan practitioners: "At the present time, not only Chan monks, but members of the scholar-official class who are clever and bright and erudite and learned in books, collectively have two types of illness. If they are not given to concentrating mind, they are given to quelling delusive thought. By [expending effort to] quell delusive thought, they fall into the ghost-cave of Black Mountain. In the canonical teachings, this is called *torpor*. [By expending effort to] concentrate mind, thoughts flutter upward in confusion. One thought follows another in a continuum, and, before the earlier thought has even ceased, a later thought has continued the series. In the canonical teachings, this is called *restlessness*." [大慧普覺禪師語錄: 今時不但禪和子。便是士大夫聰明靈利博極群書底人。箇箇有兩般病。若不著意。便是忘懷。忘懷則墮在黑山下鬼窟裏。教中謂之昏沈。著意則心識紛飛。一念續一念。前念未止後念相續。教中謂之掉舉。] (T 1998A.47.884c17–21).

[99] In a Dahui dharma talk: "The ancients had no alternative when they saw a student who had lost his head and mistakenly recognized the image in the mirror as his own head [like Yajñadatta in the *Śūraṃgama Sūtra*]. Therefore, the ancients established *upāyas* to guide such a student, making him come to recognize the scenery of his native land and clearly see his original face." [大慧普覺禪師語錄: 古人不得已。見學者迷頭認影。故設方便誘引之。令其自識本地風光明見本來面目而已。] (T 1998A.47.910a27–29).

earnest, then [torpor and distraction] will enter from your first thought; and, if your second thought is not genuine and earnest, then [torpor and distraction] will enter from your second thought! But, if your hundredth thought or thousandth thought *is* genuine and earnest, then, finally, there will be no place at all for [torpor and distraction] to enter. However, if your final thought-moment [at death] shows a slight lack of the genuine and earnest, then from that final thought-moment [*torpor* and *distraction*] will have gained entrance. If, from the very outset, your single thought is genuine and earnest [and remains so] directly down to the time at which the mind-flower manifests enlightenment, and this genuine and earnest mind is never interrupted, then what you call *torpor* and *distraction* will recede into the distance, until you become unaware of any traces [of their existence]. The person who never criticizes himself for the fact that his thoughts for the Way are not genuine and earnest, and considers *torpor* and *distraction* to be obstacles, is like a person sitting inside a dark room and criticizing his own eyes for not seeing things clearly! There is no difference. If a person who is doing real practice-work sees *torpor* and *distraction* before his eyes, he is already mistaken. If he goes beyond this to produce a thought that he must ward off this *torpor* and *distraction*, he has taken the mistake even further. However, if he is incapable of warding off [this *torpor* and *distraction*] and hence becomes worried and fearful, he is even more mistaken. Suppose he could ward off this *torpor* and *distraction*, and *things nakedly as they are* lay right before his eyes: this would be piling mistake upon mistake! Even if this careless person hears it said that *torpor* and *distraction* from the outset are *the scenery of one's native land*, and he goes on to mistakenly recognize [*torpor* and *distraction*] as 'correct,' rolling them up into a single ball free of all discriminations—this would not overcome the mistake!"

SOMEONE, UPON NOTICING THAT I [PHANTASM] HAVE USED THE WORD *mistake* QUITE A LOT, ASKED: "How does one exert mind so that one cannot make a mistake in regard to *torpor* and *distraction*?"

THEREUPON I [PHANTASM] SAID TO HIM: "If there is any application of mind to produce exertion, then there will be a sequence of mistakes. As soon as you see *torpor* and *distraction*, whether you exert mind or do not exert mind, it will all be a topsy-turvy bundle of mistakes!"

SOMEONE SAID: "This *upward* sort of talk—I'm a beginning student, and I can't get ahold of how to enter [awakening]."

PHANTASM: "Those training in the Way must only awaken to their very own true mind-ground. Having hit awakening on the head, buddhas and sentient-beings are in the same rut of the same road, and there has never from the outset been any *upward* or *downward*. Just because you don't know [the nature of] *torpor* and *distraction*, when you are deluded by an encounter with them, I am forced to explain things through words and language. At present, I have no recourse except to expose the basis for this *torpor* and *distraction*. From incalculable eons, you have been very heavily contaminated by adventitious defilements, and this is the basis of your *torpor* and *distraction*. Right now, when you see forms and hear sounds, thought-moment after thought-moment you pair up with these sense-objects. Feelings of attraction/repulsion and seizing/abandoning rise and fall, and there is no putting a stop to the disturbance: this is the basis of *torpor* and *distraction*. Your very first single thought that you want to transcend birth and go beyond death is the basis of *torpor* and *distraction*. Your need to practice Chan and study the way is the basis of *torpor* and *distraction*. Your need to become a buddha or patriarch is the basis of *torpor* and *distraction*. Your wanting to strive for unexcelled, perfect awakening, to proceed toward nirvana, is the basis of *torpor* and *distraction*. All the way down to: within the various mundane and supramundane dharmas, if you preserve even the slightest amount of thought, all of it will be the basis of *torpor* and *distraction*! Once that basis is severed—inside, outside, and in the middle of the three thousand great-thousand worlds—even if you were to seek out an iota of *torpor/distraction*, you wouldn't be able to apprehend any at all. Right where you cannot apprehend, not only would you have no *torpor* or *distraction*, but you would also not be able to apprehend *tathatā* and the reality-limit! Moreover, the traces of sage/ordinary person and delusion/awakening—they would be nowhere to be found! Stop employing useless intellectual understanding to 'bury' the mind of the Chan patriarchal masters!"

[18] Someone asked a question about why so many practitioners turn their backs on *beginner's mind*.

PHANTASM: "In the case of those who carry the burden of a *lack*, their hearts are [unfulfilled and] *vacant*. When they fulfill what they have been waiting for, their feelings become *lazy*. This is an eternal principle of people [of the world] and is the same throughout all-under-heaven, whether in ancient times or the present. Making your mind vacant is okay, but feeling lazy is not okay. If you ask why, the limitless Way of the sages has always been received via a vacant mind, but the inexhaustible karma of the afflictions has always increased due to feelings of laziness. Indeed, if your thoughts lack a master, defilement and purity will accord with conditions, and, in a single moment, there will be ten thousand unreal transformations. If you do not go to the Way, then you will go to karma; if you do not go to awakening, then you will go to delusion. There will never be an end to it!"

When by chance the discussion turned to this topic, suddenly there was an old monk who stood up and said: "I remember that in old times when I was in lay life, I could chant from memory four [of the seven] fascicles of the *Lotus Sutra*. I thought to myself: 'After I shave my head and put on monk's robes [to leave home], I will certainly be able to go back and memorize the remaining three fascicles.' How could I have known in advance [that it would not work out this way]? Twenty years after leaving home, not only had I neglected the three fascicles I hadn't yet memorized, even the four fascicles I had been able to chant were completely forgotten!"

At the time I [Phantasm], the listener, could not help but hold my nose [so as not to smell the bad odor]. Thereupon I said to the assembly: "Compared to life after you've left home, when in lay life you bear the burden that, there is something lacking, and you're always [engaging in practice to] vacate that thought: Therefore, day and night you entertain thoughts [about how you should be practicing]. However, once you have fulfilled your hope of leaving home and you are suddenly released from mundane entanglements, your *mind of quiet* day-by-day turns to laziness. Even though you were not expecting to forget [your practice], you do forget it. When you try to seek out the source of this failure, you find that there is no difference from the case of other present-day practitioners. Within the four seas there is no home [where one should dwell]; there is only *one person* in the ten-thousand-mile [world]. *The* lack *that you are bearing is only your desire to understand Chan*: One day you meet a teacher with a bad teaching method, and that teacher skillfully sets up questions that lead you into the weeds! Perhaps through cleverness he acts in concert with your deluded consciousness, and, via the spoken and written word, presses down a seal on you [i.e., 'sanctions' your level of understanding]. You say to yourself: 'I've fulfilled what I was waiting for!' Little do you imagine: your *mind of quiet* day-by-day turns lazy; false thoughts lying hidden away rise to the surface. Even if, when speaking, you seem to be awakened, when you come face to face with mundane sense-objects, you revert to delusion. Not only have you not reached the stage of great liberation of the ancients, your search for that mind—which in previous days bore the burden of a *lack* and was diligent in wanting to understand—rapidly ceases to exist. Aah! The learning of the sages and worthies—how could it stop here? Indeed, your sense of a *lack* isn't deep enough, and the time-frame behind your hope of fulfilling that *lack* doesn't go the distance! Students must be diligent about this!"

[19] SOMEONE ASKED: "After one has an awakened mind, is there practice?"

PHANTASM: "This question is difficult to explain in words. In the *awakened mind* you just spoke of, *mind* is not *your* own mind. Where would such *awakening* come from? Because *awakening* is not a truly existent dharma, *mind* is also *no-mind* [i.e., is not a truly existent dharma]. If in your mind there is no such thing as *this mind*, even if you take a panoramic view of space, the ten thousand images, sentient-beings, non-sentient things, and so forth, everything is blended together. If you are desirous of seeking out even the slightest characteristics of self/other or this/that, you will be unable to apprehend such characteristics. In the state where you cannot apprehend them, there is neither bondage nor liberation, neither seizing nor abandoning, neither false nor real, neither delusion nor awakening. In a single thought-moment there is sameness, and the myriad dharmas are all *tathatā*. How could there possibly be something called *carrying out practice*?"

SOMEONE SAID: "Due to ignorance over accumulated eons, subtle contaminated habit-energies still linger in my seeing and hearing. Because I have not been able to disperse them quickly, surely it is not okay for me to forego *carrying out practice*?"

PHANTASM: "'Outside mind there are no dharmas; outside dharmas there is no mind.' If you see that there is even the slightest bit of deluded habit-energy that is not yet exhausted, it is so because your mind of awakening is still imperfect. You must sweep away the traces of imperfection. It is okay to postulate another way of living in which you hope to [*carry out practice*] and attain great penetration [i.e., awakening]. But if you say that your mind of awakening is unfinished and you are *carrying out practice* to finish things, this is like holding an armful of firewood to put out a fire: it will only increase the blaze. An ancient said: 'You should use buddha knowing-seeing to cure it.'[100] I don't know what sort of thing buddha knowing-seeing is, but if you really yoke up with buddha knowing-seeing, then the phrase *cure it* is superfluous."

[SOMEONE] SAID: "If that is so, then is there no [need to] speak of *carrying out practice*?"

[PHANTASM] ANSWERS: "Concerning this, you need not delude your own mind with any question of whether *carrying out practice* exists or does not exist. Please just zealously apply the horsewhip! If you reach the bottom of the pail and even one time the bottom drops out, then, concerning any question of whether *carrying out practice* exists or not, you will have a silent tallying at your core [i.e., within your breast].

[20] SOMEONE ASKED: "Chan people speak of 'not cutting off bad, not cultivating good; not abandoning greed, hostility, and stupidity; not practicing precepts, concentration, and wisdom.' They call this the teaching of *the single nature is sameness*. Does such a thing exist?"

PHANTASM: "Ordinarily I would really want to discuss this, but I don't have the leisure time for it. However, since you have now asked the question, I will try to address it in a succinct manner. Now, Bodhidharma awakened to

---

[100] Li Tongxuan's (李通玄; 635–730/646–740) *Xin Huayan jing lun* 新華嚴經論, T 1739.36.727a9–10.

the mind-realization of the buddhas. He did not follow along in the same ruts as the two vehicles and the outsider [non-Buddhist] Ways. It is merely that, in the *one-mind dharmadhātu*, there are neither buddhas nor sentient-beings; and, when it comes to samsara and nirvana, these are both 'superfluous words.' Also, what bad is there that should be cut off? What good is there that should be cultivated? And how could [there be a need to] abandon greed, etc., and practice precepts, morality, etc.? Present-day Chan students, though not yet awakened to the essential purport of one-mind, stealthily make this sort of *ultimate-principle talk* into their very own viewpoint. They mistakenly produce a 'crazy' intellectual understanding: they indulge in chasing after ordinary-person delusions, violate the rules of correct behavior of the disciplinary code, and end up casting themselves into a prison. This is called 'wanting to paint a tiger but the thing comes out looking like a dog.'[101] If you really want to know the inside story of cutting off bad and cultivating good, you don't have to investigate meanings found in textual sources: all you must do is vigorously investigate your own mind. When your investigation reaches the place that cannot be investigated, your mind-eye will open, and, for the first time, you will understand that [all such formulations as] 'you should cut off bad, you should not cut off bad, you should cultivate good, you should not cultivate good,' and so forth, are like the dream of a mute person. Therefore, any talk of ultimate principle refers to the fact that bad, greed, and so forth are all one's own mind. And so, in one's own mind, there is no principle concerning anything to be cut off or anything to be abandoned. Therefore, it is said: 'There is no need to cut off, no need to abandon.'

SOMEONE SAID: "Since you have said 'there is no need to cut off, no need to abandon,' would carrying out [bad] actions be okay—involve no problem?"

PHANTASM: "Given what you have just said, the buddhas and patriarchs have unending pity for you! I said that bad, greed, and so forth are all your own mind—I *did not assent* to producing thought and cutting it off. How could I possible assent to the production of thought and the carrying out of [badness, greediness, and so forth]?"

SOMEONE SAID: "Now, I have awakened to the understanding that bad, greed, and so forth are my own mind. Since I am not allowed to cut them off, and I am not allowed to carry them out, just where must I put this bad, greed, and so forth?"

PHANTASM: "You're one deluded person! You should know that all bad karma, greed, hostility, and stupidity, ignorance, defilements, all the various troublesome defilements, and so forth lack any self-nature. They all arise from

---

[101] See *Wu deng huiyuan* (五燈會元; CBETA 2019.Q3, X80, no. 1565, p. 334a10–11).

the delusions of your own mind. Therefore, they exist in dependence on your false [thought]. This is like the fact that water depends on coldness to freeze into ice. Once this mind is awakened, then the false thoughts ride the awakening and dissipate. This is like the fact that ice, due to being shone upon by the wisdom-sun, reverts to the state of water. Once it has transformed into water, you now say: 'Where did the ice go to?' Such a person is truly piling delusion upon delusion!"

SOMEONE SAID: "A certain person has already had an awakening, but when his evil and greed come face to face with sense-objects, they are just as they were originally. What about this?"

PHANTASM: "This involves two sorts of cases. In one case the mind of awakening is not yet total, and various false thoughts linger on. If this type does not advance in cultivation, in the end he will revert to perverted thought. In the second sort, the mind of awakening is already perfected, and he clearly sees all dharmas, but his understanding is like the dream he had last night. This type then manifests [a form] in the world, where he practices cooperation with others [i.e., one of the four means of conversion] and *seems to have* badness, greediness, and so forth. Little do others imagine: this type's *true mind* is transcendent. As for practicing [cooperation with others and seeming to have evil greed, and so forth], when a person of inadequate capacity forces his efforts in this even a tiny bit, he is sure to commit a mistake. You should be aware of this!

[21] SOMEONE SAID: "There are people daily engaged in performing myriad good actions. Are they near to or distant from the substance of the ultimate Way?"

PHANTASM: "The substance of the Way is rooted in the unconditioned, which cannot be increased or decreased by good actions or bad actions. Now, the creation of bad is rooted in delusion. The Sage [i.e., the Buddha] saw the destruction of delusion as a step-by-step process. Therefore, he had people carry out good actions. As good actions gain ascendancy, delusion dissipates; when delusion has dissipated, bad actions are spontaneously dispelled. Once bad actions have been dispelled, the myriad good actions are also forgotten. An ancient [the sixth patriarch Huineng] had a teaching: 'Don't reflect at all on good/bad, and you will naturally enter the mind-substance.'[102] *Mind-substance* is another term for the ultimate Way. If you expel bad and preserve good in the hope of attaining the substance of the ultimate Way of our [Chan school], the Way will be far off! Let me try to clarify this with a metaphor. There are people who consider the stinky

---

[102] *Liu zu dashi fabao tan jing* (六祖大師法寶壇經; T 2008.48.360a13–14).

smell of the latrine to be 'bad' and burn incense to perfume away the smell. This is not as good as putting oneself in a *state of no-feces-and-urine*. Thus, *latrine* is a metaphor for bad actions; *perfuming with incense* is a metaphor for good actions; and the *state of no-feces* is the substance of the Way. People are afraid of the darkness of a dark room, so they hold up a lamp to illuminate it. This is not as good as putting oneself in a state of great brightness. *Dark room* is a metaphor for bad actions; *holding up a lamp* is a metaphor for good actions; and *state of great brightness* is a metaphor for the substance of the Way. Furthermore, there are those who fear the cold of ice and snow, and they find it necessary to burn firewood to dispel the cold. This is not as good as putting oneself in a state of a balmy room. *Icy cold* is a metaphor for bad actions; *burning firewood* is a metaphor for good actions; and *state of a balmy room* is the substance of the Way. Thus, when you burn incense, the perfuming smell only comes and goes. When you hold a lamp, the flame ignites or blows out. When you burn firewood, you will sometimes be near the heat and sometimes far off. Only the substance of the Way is unchanging through the eons, constantly existing down through the generations. How could [the substance of the Way] have any connection to *coming or going, igniting or blowing out, near or far off*? As for [your question about] cultivating good actions and its connection with being in union with the Way, the principle of being *near to or far from* [the substance of the Way] is just as I have explained! I would be remiss if I did not explain this matter."

[22] SOMEONE ASKED: "I have already heard the [meanings of the] two words *good/bad*. As for the principle of *good/bad*, perhaps the world has not yet been able to elucidate the matter. [The world] considers flogging with a whip and heaping angry abuse to be *bad*, and those who can endure this *bad* with forbearance and without looking for payback to be *good*. [The world] considers holding a sword and killing others to be *bad*, and those who accept such harm without forming [an angry] thought[103] to be *good*. [The world] considers using lasciviousness and violence to get the things you are greedy for to be *bad*, and employing serenity and quiet to observe the precepts and recite and memorize texts to be *good*."

PHANTASM: "This sort of talk is all [mere] footprints of *good/bad*. I think the principle of *good/bad* is not as you state. If I were to speak exhaustively of the principle of *good/bad*, it would be none other than: in the production of all your thoughts and the things you anticipate, no matter whether big or small, superior or inferior, if you want nothing more than to benefit others, it's all *good*. If you merely want to benefit self, it is all *bad*. If these are things

---

[103] See *Diamond Sutra*, T 235.8.750b13–18.

that can give benefit to others, even if they involve angry abuse and rejection, it is all *good*. But if they are things that benefit self, even if serene and accommodating, it is all *bad*. Therefore, the sages and worthies set up teachings because they were eager to save people, and they had no time for food or rest because of their mind of ultimate goodness; but most of the crowd does the very opposite. Even if [a person wears the same] clothes and hats as the sages and worthies, and adds literary embellishment to their words and actions, if he lacks a mind that benefits others, it is already extremely *bad*. How much more so is this the case with someone whose feelings of violent anger leave him shaking uncontrollably? If you take actions like this and yet hope for the one word *good*, you'll be as far from *good* as heaven is from earth! How could that be called the *ultimate Way*?"

[23] SOMEONE ASKED: "The books of Confucius and Mencius speak about the Kingly Way and consider the zenith to be [virtuous rule by] benevolence and righteousness. The books of Laozi and Zhuangzi speak of the Emperor's Way and consider the zenith to be [rule by] non-action. The books of the Hundred Schools speak about miscellaneous aspects of the Hegemon's Way [i.e., rule by tactics and military force] and consider the zenith to be merit and profit. The books of our Buddhist school only clarify the Original-Nature: they say that 'the place where all dharmas arise is none other than the place where mind manifests' and consider the zenith to be the *single thought of non-arising*. It seems that each stakes a claim to a single approach and is incapable of fusing with the realm of Great Sameness. In the end, is there any principle [by which to unify them]?"

PHANTASM: "If you say there is no [unifying principle], you are being too limited; if you say there is [a unifying principle], you are being too unrestrained. The Sagely Way does not seize [on such extremes]. What it does seize on is *deep entrance into one approach*, making the person awaken on his own. After awakening, once the fences [between the three approaches] have been breached, you will clearly see that the sages of the three teachings clasp hands at a place outside of words and forms, and that there is no gap between the supramundane and the mundane. If you are not yet awakened, even if you take the four repositories of books [i.e., the traditional schema of classics, histories, philosophers, and literary collections] to hunt for your inner mind, and you imbibe and spit out [those texts at will], you still will not be able to escape the reproach of [being sullied by] 'wide-learning and self-view.' This is precisely what in India was called 'clever outside [non-Buddhist] Ways.' Therefore, if a trainee does not seek out correct awakening but applies himself to the trivialities found in texts, what is he, if not an idiot? Present-day people who shoulder even a smidgen of cleverness in many cases are unwilling to deaden their minds and forget delusive discrimination to seek out correct awakening. They are always seizing on *proof* in texts and [Chan] sayings. Not only does this not supplement [true] principle, it increases delusive cognition and discrimination, going against the Sagely Way. What are we to do to make sure teaching expedients do not decay and the Chan community does not decline?

[24] SOMEONE ASKED: "In the Chan school there is a book called *Blue Cliff Collection*. When Yuanwu [Keqin] was dwelling on Mt. Jia, he took up *Xuedou's Verses on Ancient Standards*, arranged the essential points thereof, and evaluated the words and phrasing, [ultimately producing the multilayered *Blue Cliff Record*]. He raised matters in a detailed and meticulous fashion; his explanations were minute and clear. If one were to talk about the elegance [of Yuanwu's final product], it is like opening the cover of a jewel collection: bright pearls and great conches are piled up all about. If you talk about its plenitude, it is like cutting off [the fast flow of the river at] Yumen—the waves in reverse [make the river's level] rise and fall. Extraordinary! If you are not someone who has apprehended the dharma and is in freedom, you can't reach up to [this book]. How does it come about that people who on their own are trying to open the doors and windows [to awakening] very often use this [i.e., the *Blue Cliff Collection*] as a set of steps [to awakening]? Miaoxi [i.e., Dahui Zonggao] investigated and came to understand this situation. He feared that students were being caught up in the flow [of elegant words in this text] and thereby forgetting to return [to their *original face*]; and so, when [Miaoxi] entered Min [Fujian], he smashed the printing blocks [for the *Blue Cliff Record*.][104] Today, temple publishers are once again

---

[104] The story of Dahui's destroying the printing blocks of the *Blue Cliff Collection* is endlessly repeated, without much inquiry into its origins. Perhaps one of the formative sources is the *Chanlin baoxun* (禪林寶訓), a Song miscellanea or "brush notes." Dahui and Zhu'an Shigui (竹庵士珪; 1083–1146) collected about one hundred excerpts from *yulu* and biographies. Later the Eastern Wu monk Jingshan (浄善; d.u.) augmented this collection, increasing the total entries to about 300. In an entry added by Jingshan we find quotation from a (presumably lost) letter: "Xinwen's [letter to Zhang Zishao] says: 'The Way of the separate transmission outside the teachings is the uncomplicated ultimate core: there has never been any other teaching. Our predecessors implemented this core without ever entertaining any doubts, maintaining it without change. During the Tianxi era [1017–1021; Northern Song] Xuedou Chongxian [980–1052], using his talents of eloquence and broad learning, playing with beautiful thoughts and seeking novelty in polished artfulness, continued Fenyang Shanzhao's [947–1024] verses on the ancients. This 'caged in' the students of the time, and from this point Chan style underwent a drastic change. During the Xuanhe era [1119–1125; Northern Song], Yuanjue Keqin [1062–1135; teacher of Dahui] put forth his own ideas, apart from those [of *Xuedou's Verses on Ancient Standards*,] and created the *Blue Cliff Collection*. At that time, of pure scholars who transcended the age of the ancients—like such venerables as Way-Person Ning, Sixin, Lingyuan, and Fojian—none could change course from Yuanjue's theories. Thereupon students of later generations treated his words as rare and valuable, chanting them in the morning, studying them in the evening, and referring to them as the 'ultimate learning.' None of them realized this was a mistake. How painful! The mind arts of students deteriorated. At the beginning of the Shaoxing era [1131–1162; Southern Song], Fori [i.e., Dahui Zonggao] went to Min [Fujian]: he tried to pull and guide the students he encountered, but they would not budge. They were rushing about endlessly, becoming so immersed [in the

publishing it. In this last period [of the dharma] won't an increasing number of students bore into this text [and be dragged along in its elegance]?"

PHANTASM: "No. Every one of the limitless sentient-beings has right underfoot the single *ready-made gong'an*.[105] During the forty-nine years [Śākyamuni spoke dharma, until he transmitted to Kāśyapa] at Vulture Peak, he never produced any elucidations. Bodhidharma came thousands of miles from the West and never gave any instruction. Deshan and Linji groped around but were never able to hit upon it. How could Xuedou have been able to write verses on this [*ready-made gong'an*], and Yuanwu have been able to render judgments on it? Even if the *Blue Cliff Collection* consisted of thousands upon thousands of fascicles, how could it add or subtract a single thing from that *ready-made gong'an*? Of old, Miaoxi [Dahui] failed to pursue this principle to the limit and so smashed the printing blocks, an action very much like prohibiting a stone woman from giving birth to a child! At present, the gentlemen who are carving new blocks for a reprint [of the *Blue Cliff Collection*]—aren't they trying to entice the stone woman into bearing a child? This is even more laughable [than Dahui's attempt]!"

Blue Cliff Collection] that they were coming to ruin. Dahui then smashed its printing blocks to clear away its theories. This dispersed delusions, rescued those drowning, gouged out complications, negated problems, crushed perversity, and revealed the correct. He shook them up on purpose: Chan monks came to some realization of their mistake and no longer so esteemed that book. So, if not for the fact that Dahui's enlightened state and foresight mounted the vow power of compassion to save beings from the ruins of the latter dharma, the Chan community would be in a frightening state! (*Letter to Zhang Zishao*)." [心聞曰。教外別傳之道。至簡至要。初無他說。前輩行之不疑。守之不易。天禧間雪竇以辯博之才。美意變弄求新琢巧。繼汾陽為頌古。籠絡當世學者。宗風由此一變矣。逮宣政[和]間。圓悟又出己意離之為碧巖集。彼時邁古淳全之士。如寧道者死心靈源佛鑒諸老。皆莫能迴其說。於是新進後生珍重其語。朝誦暮習謂之至學。莫有悟其非者。痛哉。學者之心術壞矣。紹興初。佛日入閩見學者牽之不返。日馳月騖浸漬成弊。即碎其板闢其說。以至祛迷援溺剔繁撥劇摧邪顯正。特然而振之。衲子稍知其非而不復慕。然非佛日高明遠見乘悲願力救末法之弊。則叢林大有可畏者矣。(與張子韶書。). (T 2022.48.1036b19–c3). Xinwen Tanfen (心聞曇賁; Song period; d.u.) was in the Huanglong wing of the Linji school. His letter to the powerful scholar-official Vice Minister Zhang Zishao (i.e., Zhang Jiucheng 張九成) may be an early source for the story of Dahui's destroying the printing blocks. Broughton with Watanabe, *Letters of Dahui*, letter #48 (pp. 265–270) is a Dahui letter to Vice Minister Zhang, known as "Old Vimalakīrti." Araki Kengo, *Daie sho*, Zen no goroku 17 (Tokyo: Chikuma shobō, 1969), 193: "Zhang was one of the laymen in whom Dahui placed the most fervent trust. When Zhang fell afoul of the clique of Qin Hui 秦檜 [1090–1155; execrated Song capitulationist] and was exiled, Dahui was also implicated and exiled to Hengzhou. The role that the intellectual tie connecting these two played in the development of the history of Song thought was extremely important."

[105] See section 10 above. Zhongfeng's metaphor runs: *gong'an* = official documents of a government office → norms or standards that cut off the incorrect → stories of the karmic encounters of the buddhas and patriarchs found in the flame-of-the-lamp records and *yulu*. The phrase *xiancheng gong'an* (現成公案/見成公案) is an "old chestnut" in Chan/Zen studies. Perhaps a modern Chinese definition of *xiancheng* is helpful: *yijing zhunbei hao bu yong linshi zuo huo zhao de* (已經準備好，不用臨時做或找的 = *ready-made*—no need at the time to make it or seek it out). See Dictionary Department, Institute of Linguistics, Chinese Academy of Social Sciences, *The Contemporary Chinese Dictionary (Chinese-English Edition)* (Beijing: Foreign Language Teaching and Research Press, 2002), 2080. The definition of *xianchengfan* (現成飯) is *yijing zuocheng de fan* (已經做成的飯 = *food ready for the table*), convenience food that is already prepared. The term *xianchengfan* is also slang for unearned gain (*bu lao er huo de liyi* 不勞而獲的利益), benefit or profit that you get without being put to any trouble.

[SOMEONE ASKED]: "If that is so, then the *ready-made gong'an* right under the feet of the practitioner on duty has no relationship to the oral teachings of the buddhas and patriarchs. In that case, how could the practitioner on duty put [the *ready-made gong'an*] to the test and realize it?"

I [PHANTASM] SAID: "There is no putting to the test! And there is nothing to be realized! The only important thing is for the practitioner on duty to *turn the light backwards and take a step back*. If, with one step, the things in front of him that he sees and hears and is aware of completely *flip over*, then he will know that the sound of the waterfall in the wind and the sound of the stream after the rain—every sound—is a verse [from Xuedou's verses]; the rolling thunder in the empty mountains and the whistling of the wind on a clear day—every sound—is a judgment [from Yuanwu's judgments and comments]. Furthermore, heaven is high and earth substantial, night dark and day bright—the myriad forms are always furiously speaking [dharma]. *This* is called 'the *Blue Cliff Collection* of the *ready-made gong'an*.' Even a hundred thousand Xuedous and Yuanwus, looking upward at the bluff [that cannot be climbed], would have to pull the lapels of their garments together [out of respect, and retreat in the face of] what lies beyond words and forms. How could one put even a single unit of verbalization upon it? You do not yet fully know this purport [beyond words] from your own experience! Within this *upāya* approach, one success or one failure, one disparaging of the student and one lifting-up of the student, is no more than business as usual. You say: 'The *Blue Cliff Collection* invariably makes trainees bore into intellectual knowledge, blocking their own awakening.'" On the contrary, if we infer the minds of the two teachers [Xuedou and Yuanwu], I think that is not so. The World-honored-one with his correct dharma-eye observed the sentient-beings of the *dharmadhātu*, saying: 'Every one of them is endowed with the merits of *tathāgata* wisdom. Merely because of false thought and grasping, they are unable to realize it. I will teach them the sagely Way to free them of all attachments.'[106] Thus, how could the Buddha not have known that the sagely Way was already in the lot of sentient-beings, that every one of them was endowed with it, and that he could not teach it to them via verbalization? When it comes to responding to the distinctive levels of karmic abilities present at more than three hundred assemblies, [Sakyamuni's] voicing of [sutra content types such as] *great/small, partial/all-embracing*, and *half/complete*—there was not a day that such teachings did not emerge from his mouth. But trainees of both the past and present have failed to comprehend that these phrases are *upāyas*. They have pointed to them as

---

[106] *Huayan Sutra*, T 279.10.272c25–273a1.

real dharma, and each of them has grasped his own understanding of them, producing a confusion of heterodox views. They have beaten the drum and danced in the [mistaken] arena of *is/is not* and galloped in the [mistaken] rut of *doer/done*. Even if you were to engineer the removal of the *Blue Cliff Record* from the Buddhist canon, nothing would change! Moreover, this is so with the sagely teachings [of Buddhism]: how much more so is this the case with other books? Nevertheless, if you investigate the hits and misses of the oral teachings [of the Chan patriarchs], the only crucial thing is whether the practitioner on duty is *genuinely earnest* or *not genuinely earnest* about the *matter of self*. If he is genuinely earnest about the *matter of self*, then he will know that even a short remark or single word can be effective in transcending samsara. It is said in the teachings that the goose, lord of birds, can select out the milk [from a mixture of milk and water].[107] If, in the teacher–student relationship, there is a sincere aspiration [on the part of the student] to clarify the *matter of self* and to bear the burden of the Chan vehicle, he will resolve not to assent to reliance on exegesis of the texts. He will be able on his own to *take hold of self and practice*. The existence or nonexistence of the *Blue Cliff Record* is irrelevant! Not worth discussing!"

[25] SOMEONE ASKED: "All of the Chan monks of the various regions consider Preceptor Gaofeng's[108] ordering people to burn a finger[109] upon receiving the precepts to be *strange*. Isn't that so?"

PHANTASM: "I also have personally heard of this strangeness. I asked my former master [Gaofeng] about this talk concerning his strange [order]. My former master said:

> Nothing strange about it! Because people are unaware it is an *upāya*, they say such things. How could it be that I don't know about Great Teacher Bodhidharma's

---

[107] *Saddharmasmṛtyupastānasūtra*, T 721.17.379c8–9.
[108] For excerpts from the autobiography of Gaofeng Yuanmiao (高峯原妙; 1238–1295) found in *Recorded Sayings of Gaofeng Yuanmiao*), see the Introduction. Zhongfeng's teacher Gaofeng used as his main *huatou* **to where does the One return?** (*yi gui he chu* 一歸何處). Zhongfeng's autobiography in the Introduction treats his relationship with Gaofeng.
[109] Lingfeng Ou'yi's (= Zhixu 智旭; 1599–1655) *Lingfeng Ou'yi dashi zonglun* (靈峰蕅益大師宗論) says: "Great Master Gaofeng encouraged ascetic practices. His strength shored up the Chan patriarchal Way when it was in decline. When there were Chan students, he ordered them that they must first burn a finger and receive the precepts, and then he would transmit to them the mind-core." [高峰大師，勵頭陀行，力扶祖道之衰。有參學者，必先令然指受戒，方乃授以心要。] (CBETA 2019.Q3, J36, no. B348, p. 404a25–26). *Lotus Sutra*, T 262.9.54a1–9 speaks of burning the forearm (*bi* 臂), and *Śūraṃgama Sūtra*, T 945.19.132b1–21 speaks of burning a finger (*zhi* 指). Heller, Illusory Abiding, 377, in describing the portrait of Zhongfeng Mingben in the Yabumoto (藪本) Collection, says: "But while the fly whisk is prominent, Mingben's left hand is more significant. On closer examination we see that the hand is shown in a way that displays the stump of his little finger. His biography mentions that he burned his arm as a youth before he had taken the precepts. While it is possible that this was the point at which he burned off his finger, and that 'arm' (*bi* 臂) in the biography is a mistake for (or an exaggeration of) 'finger' (*zhi* 指), it seems more likely that Mingben initially burned incense on his arm and later burned off his finger, perhaps as an act

purport of *single transmission*, *direct pointing*, and *seeing the Nature*? For him even words were not established—so how could there be precepts to be received? However, two reasons exist for Bodhidharma's not speaking of the precepts. The first is he was displaying the Chan personal realization; the second is he [always] examined [the abilities of] people. As for his displaying the Chan personal realization, Bodhidharma focused on taking the transmission of the buddha-mind seal as the Chan personal realization—his sole priority was this *single transmission*. He made students at one jump directly enter the *tathāgata* stage, without wading through the steps of the great and small vehicles. The purport of his Chan personal realization was of this sort. Had he spoken of the precepts, he would have been turning his back on [this Chan personal realization]. As for his examining [the abilities of] people, in general, in the Bodhidharma line, all are sharp receptacles of superior faculties. Anyone who from past lives has not been impregnated with the seed-wisdom of *prajñā*, and does not possess the faculties for the highest vehicle, cannot enter therein. People of this kind are deeply impregnated with and well-forged in the three trainings of precepts, concentration, and wisdom. There is no need whatsoever to have them receive the precepts a second time. Therefore, in Bodhidharma's time, it was fitting that he did not speak of the precepts. Though he did not speak of the precepts, I have never heard that he made people break them. From Bodhidharma on down, those who possessed the faculties for the great vehicle from all directions rose like clouds and welled up like the sea. From ancient times till the present [Bodhidharma's teaching] has continued, and all [his inheritors] have left out any talk of the precepts, which is natural in the case of the purport of the Chan personal realization. Right from the start I have never heard of any transmitter of the buddha-mind personal realization who did not guard the precepts/discipline. Of old, Preceptor Cishou[110] was an outsize worthy of the Chan approach. Every time he hoisted up [the dharma] he praised in the extreme people who received the full precepts. Preceptor Zhenxie[111] established meetings for encouraging the raising of the aspiration for awakening, at which he promulgated [the precepts] for the four groups [of lay people and home-leavers]. These two teachers employed the step-by-step approach of transformation by *upāya*. Of old, Preceptor Zhantang Zhun[112] practiced

---

of devotion upon full ordination." Also see Ide Seinosuke, "Chūhō Myōhon jisan zō o megutte," *Bijutsu kenkyū* 343 (1989): 106–107.

[110] Huilin Huaishen (慧林懷深; 1077–1132), a Yunmen school master. For his Pure Land tendency, see *Jingtu ziliang quanji* (淨土資糧全集; CBETA 2019.Q3, X61, no. 1162, p. 538c1–2).

[111] Zhenxie Qingliao (真歇清了; 1088–1151) was in the Hongzhi Zhengjue line of the Caodong school. For his Pure Land tendency, see *Precious Mirror of the Lotus School of Mt. Lu* (*Lushan lianzong baojian* 盧山蓮宗寶鑑: 真歇了禪師淨土宗要; T 1973.47.318c20 319a1).

[112] Zhantang Wenzhun (湛堂文準; 1061–1115) was in the Huanglong wing of the Linji school.

under Chan Master Liangshan Sheng,[113] and Sheng said: 'Scarecrow novice! You have not yet received the precepts. How dare you say you want to study the buddha-vehicle!' Zhantang lifted his hands, saying: 'Is the *maṇḍala* platform the precepts? Are the three-times ceremony, pure conduct, or *ācārya* [i.e., the title of one who teaches proper conduct] the precepts?' Sheng was astonished. Zhantang said: 'Notwithstanding that, how could I presume to fail to receive the teaching [of the precepts]?' He then visited Vinaya Master Kang'an[114] and received the full precepts from him. From ancient times, within the Chan approach, there have been a lot of instances of discussion of the precepts: I do not need to enumerate the many instances. Given this, how could one say [receiving the precepts] goes against the Shaolin [Chan] personal realization and is *strange*? *Upāyas* are something adapted to the time and the situation. Because we know [*upāyas*] are an aid to true principle, we can have no doubts about them. I remember that I first entered the monastic assembly during the Kaiqing and Jingding eras [of the Southern Song; 1256–1264]. Jingci Monastery [in Hangzhou superior prefecture in Zhejiang] and Shuangjing Monastery [i.e., Wanshou Monastery on Mt. Jing in Hangzhou] both had no less than four to five hundred monks in their assemblies. Their abbots and chief monks assuredly are not relevant [to this discussion], but in the common quarters there were in fact one or two monks who drank spirits [and thereby violated the precepts]. Although they did not drink constantly, village people and those monks on adjacent seats of the Chan platform never failed to reproach them for this. Except for the drinking [of spirits], I rarely heard stories of other matters [that contravened the precepts]. At present, from top to bottom, there is no shirking [of the precepts] leading to dissipation and failure to revert [to correct form]. Of old, the Buddha enunciated the five precepts for the sake of the 'white-clad' lay people. For monks there were such disciplinary codes as the *Four-Part Vinaya* and the *Mahāsāṃghika Vinaya*,[115] and the great precepts called the 'three sets of pure precepts' and the 'complete set of precepts.'[116] [Some of today's monks] even evade the precepts [that should be maintained by lay people]—how much more so the deportment mandated by the full *Vinaya*! Guishan said: 'The prohibitory stipulations and offenses bind even the beginner.'[117] However, the *beginner's mind* is but a single step—those who transmit the Chan buddha-mind personal realization are on a journey of a thousand miles! There has never been a person who could not walk a single step and yet was able to reach the end of a thousand-mile journey. An ancient said: 'Observing the precepts in studying the Way is grasping the fundamental practice.'[118] Sometimes, even if the person's

---

[113] Otherwise unknown.
[114] Otherwise unknown.
[115] T 1428.22 and 1425.22.
[116] The Mahāyāna precepts spoken of in the *Fanwang jing* (梵網經; T1484.24) and the *Yingluo jing* (瓔珞經; T 1485.24).
[117] *Guishan jingce zhu* (溈山警策註; CBETA 2019.Q3, X65, no. 1294, p. 470b4–5).
[118] Untraced.

faculties are sluggish, and for a whole lifetime his Way-eye is not bright, he is still able to get the protection of precepts-power. If he does not lose the thought [of obtaining] the Way, then in a future life the Way will be easy for him to achieve. Among the sutras, the two sutras *Śūraṃgama* and *Perfect Awakening* are essential discourses on the Mahāyāna *perfect-and-sudden*. Please try to read them over. *They always hold the precepts to be an essential endeavor*. Therefore, an ancient said: 'The precepts are the foundation, and the Way is the house. If these two did not exist, where would this body lodge?'[119] This is the reason why I comply with the establishment of the *upāya* [of receiving the precepts]. And how could that possibly be *strange*? If you consider having people observe the precepts as *strange*, [you should note that] Baizhang established quite a few protocols and rules of propriety, embracing all aspects of walking, standing, sitting, and lying down.[120] If you compare this to Bodhidharma's purport of *direct pointing to the human mind*, could it be anything other than *strange*? Someone said: 'After monks take up the quiet life [in Chan sites], there is no way they can pass even a single day without [observing the precepts].'[121] Little do you imagine: *the precepts and* vinaya *are the root of the Chan community*. There has never been a case of the continued existence of the branches and leaves after the root has been severed. Aah! When the Way-substance dies off, precepts-power is extinguished. When precepts-power is extinguished, then the rules of propriety are lost. How could the minds of the people of all-under-heaven stay on the Way? My showing the precepts to people today—how could there be anything *strange* about that?

All this is the truthful words of my former teacher [Gaofeng]. When he happened to be asked a question, unconsciously he opened his cloth bag [i.e., the cloth bag of Budai] and fluently chatted. Those of you who are in the know—don't take me as a blabbermouth!"

[26] SOMEONE ASKED: "Buddhas and bodhisattvas all possess supranormal powers.[122] Are these supranormal powers dependent upon cultivation-and-realization?"

PHANTASM: "Supranormal powers are both dependent upon cultivation-and-realization and not dependent upon cultivation-and-realization. Supranormal powers are something that buddhas and bodhisattvas, across innumerable eons, bring into being by wholeheartedly practicing the four immeasurable minds,[123] six perfections, and all sorts of good actions. As for my saying

---

[119] Untraced.
[120] See n. 76.
[121] Untraced.
[122] See n. 35.
[123] Immeasurable minds = *apramāṇa* (*the unlimited*): loving-kindness; compassion; empathetic joy; and equanimity.

dependent upon cultivation-and-realization, if not for the perfuming spoken of above, [the buddhas and bodhisattvas] would not possess [these powers]. As for my saying *not dependent upon cultivation-and-realization*, you should know that the six perfections and merit derived from many good actions by the buddhas and bodhisattvas is not for the sake of coming into possession of the supranormal powers: it is none other than great compassion perfuming the roots of their minds, a natural outcome of their vow and practice. If the buddhas and bodhisattvas entertained even a single thought of desiring to seek out supranormal powers, then they would be head-on obstructed by that single thought. Even if they cultivated all the good practices, and so forth, the whole thing would become a contaminated causal factor. [In that case,] how could they come to possess these supranormal powers of freedom, liberation, and magical transformations? When there has not been any realization of the mind-realization of the buddhas and the various unconditioned vows and practices, as in the case of those who have attained the small fruits of the other two vehicles [i.e., hearer and private buddha] and those following outsider [non-Buddhist] Ways, [such hearers, private buddhas, and outsiders] may possess the magical transformations that come from supranormal powers, but these are not [real] supranormal powers. They appear through the power of [unreal] illusion: all accomplished by conditioned thought. In fact, that they can manifest strange phenomena that delude people is nothing more than arising-and-extinguishing causal factors. Now, the supranormal powers manifested by minds perfumed by great compassion and the unconditioned vow and powers of the buddhas and bodhisattvas is especially excellent and participates in the sameness of the dharma-nature. Even if [the buddhas and bodhisattvas] at their pleasure cause a single one of their pores to reveal a hundred thousand rays of light and a hundred thousand ornaments that fill up the *dharmadhātu*, and all of them obtain fulfillment: in the liberated minds of the buddhas and bodhisattvas, there is no perception of possessing these supranormal powers; there is no perception of manifesting these supranormal powers; and there is no perception of relying on these supranormal powers to obtain enjoyment and fulfillment. How can we know this? Because supranormal powers participate in the sameness of the dharma-nature. Because in the dharma-nature there is no sameness/difference, self/other, doer/done, and various discriminations. We know that supranormal powers are also so."

SOMEONE SAID: "We must not say that the supranormal powers of the buddhas and bodhisattvas are not dependent at all on cultivation-and-realization. If they are not dependent on cultivation-and-realization, then why do ordinary persons [who have not engaged in cultivation and attained realization] not possess them?"

PHANTASM: "Concerning the supranormal powers of the dharma-nature, ordinary persons have always possessed them. However, ordinary persons and other species [beyond humans] are all simply in a darkened state and haven't noticed. Ordinary persons simply lack the uncreated vow and practice, the six perfections, realized power, and the supranormal powers of adornment. Didn't I say this before? Because the buddhas and bodhisattvas have minds perfumed with great compassion, they have supranormal powers: they do not carry out practice in order to seek out supranormal powers! Allow me to clarify this with a metaphor. In this world there are sentient-beings who commit the ten great bad actions[124] without ever thinking of repentance. These people, at the end of life, because of the power of karma, directly enter a hell, undergoing various sufferings. When these people were in the midst of creating this [bad] karma, it was merely because delusion entered their minds, and they gave license to their feelings to do those things. They certainly did not entertain the thought: 'Now that my karma has *ripened*, I will certainly enter a hell!' Presumably, hell has no self-nature—it isn't a real dharma. It is no more than a result of one's own deluded karma. You should know that the liberation and supranormal powers of the buddhas and bodhisattvas *likewise* have no self-nature and are not real dharmas. They are really the result of the *ripening* of precepts/concentration/wisdom, the six perfections, and so forth. How could you have any further doubt about this?"

[27] SOMEONE ASKED: "The twenty-seven patriarchs of India all had supranormal powers. When we get to Bodhidharma, he also had supranormal powers. From Bodhidharma onward, why is it that [Chan patriarchs] have not possessed supranormal powers? In the interval [down to today] I have perhaps heard of only a few people [who possessed such powers], but I haven't seen many."

PHANTASM: "From what I have heard, the followers of the outside Ways in India all possessed 'effortful *dhyāna*' and supranormal powers of magical transformation. When the buddha-lamp was first being transmitted and illuminating the world, without the possession of supranormal powers, Buddhism would not have been able to embrace those followers of outside Ways. In India, [to cross over to nirvana] all sentient-beings, buddhas and bodhisattvas engaged in magical transformations. As response-bodies they became patriarchs, so they could transmit the torch. That is why Bodhidharma is said to be a response-body of Avalokiteśvara Bodhisattva.[125] From Bodhidharma onward, in the interval [down to

---

[124] For lists of the ten bad actions, see Noguchi and Matsubara, *Sanbō yawa*, 210–211, n. 3.
[125] Juefan Huihong's ((覺範慧洪; 1071–1128) miscellany or "brush notes" *Linjianlu* (林間錄): "In old discourse it is often said that Bodhidharma is a response body of Avalokiteśvara." [舊說多言達磨乃觀音應身。] (CBETA 2019.Q3, X87, no. 1624, p. 256a21).

today], perhaps only a few people have possessed supranormal powers. These were sages and worthies, separated by generations, who arose to aid in the hoisting up of the teaching of the Chan personal realization. Those who did not possess [supranormal powers] simply took awakening to the [Chan] buddha-mind personal realization as their root. In fact, the buddha-mind personal realization is the *correct cause* of hundreds of thousands of *samādhis* and the supranormal powers. How could there be karmic results that do not come into being from causal factors? Generally speaking, if by chance truly awakened people show miraculous powers, they immediately dispel them. They certainly do not assent to getting mired in them as something extraordinary. If such people were to consider them extraordinary, then they would lose sight of their *original mind*. Moreover, if this is the case even with the awakened, how much more so should it be with those who have not yet awakened? Students today do not seek correct awakening, and falsely generate a single moment's mind of ['splendid'] supranormal powers and *samādhis*. They are identical to adherents of outside Ways: they have eternally turned their back on the correct cause [of supranormal powers]. Sometimes there are people who say: 'Supranormal powers did reach China with the transmission [of Buddhism], but some feared slander of this tendency to manifest strange phenomena, and so they just aren't playing up [this aspect of the tradition]!' This theory not only causes confusion of self—it confuses others. How could it be the ultimate principle?"

Night Conversations in a Mountain Hermitage III

[28] Someone made an inquiry concerning what he had come to know [through learning] "I've been accumulating learning for half a lifetime. As for the oral teachings of the buddhas and patriarchs, I am on the verge of exhausting my fishing and hunting. Whenever I have the texts in hand, there has never been an instance in which I didn't understand [their contents]. However, from the very beginning of my learning, I have been unable to shear off delusive bondage and dry up the waves of consciousness on the surface of attraction/repulsion. What about this?"

PHANTASM: "While for the most part you speak of what you have come to *know* [through learning], you're unable to pick out what [level of *knowing*] you have reached. There is *numinous knowing*; there is *true knowing*; and there is *false knowing*. Now, *numinous knowing* is called the 'Way.' *True knowing* is called 'awakening.' *False knowing* is called 'intellectual understanding.' They are all the same in having the word *knowing*: but with [the adjectives] *numinous*, *true*, and *false*, they differ from each other twice as much as a day differs from an eon! Students fail to surmise the existence of this principle [of levels of knowing], and just drift about on *knowing*, falsely producing grasping and engendering *is/is not*. This leads not only to ruin of the Way Source, but also buries the student himself. As Minister Pei Xiu said: 'Where there is blood and breath there must be *knowing*. Whatever has *knowing* must necessarily be identical to Substance.'[126] This is talking about the *knowing* of *numinous knowing*.[127] In the case of this *knowing*, there is no gap between sages and ordinary persons or between delusion and awakening. The substance of mind has possessed [this kind of *numinous knowing*] right from the outset. It neither increases nor decreases. As [for *true knowing*,] the *Huayan Sutra* says: "Know that all dharmas are the self-nature of mind, complete the wisdom-body, and do not rely on anyone else's awakening.'[128] As the *Perfect Awakening Sutra* says: 'If you know that [all dharmas] are like a flower in the sky, then there is no wheel-turning samsara.'[129] [The *Perfect Awakening Sutra*] also says: 'If you know the phantasmal, then you are already detached [from the phantasmal], and there is no need to create *upāyas* [for detaching from the phantasmal].'[130] These quotations are talking about *true knowing*, which issues from awakening. If the clouds of delusion have not parted, and perception has not been cut off; if spirit is not unmoving, and you don't suddenly remember what was long-forgotten; if you don't attain liberation in this very thought-moment, and [realize that] wherever you stand is *the real*: then everything else [is subject to origination by dependence and] certainly cannot be by chance. [As for *false knowing*,] the *Perfect Awakening Sutra* also says: 'Sentient-beings are obstructed by intellectual understanding; the bodhisattva has not yet detached from awakening.'[131] [The *Perfect Awakening Sutra*] also says: 'As for sentient-beings of the latter

---

[126] Pei Xiu's (裴休; 797– 870) preface to Guifeng Zongmi's (圭峰宗密; 780–841) commentary *Da fangguang yuanjue xiuduoluo liaoyi jing lueshu* (大方廣圓覺修多羅了義經略疏; T 1795.39.523b10). The *Yuanjue jing* was Zongmi's favorite sutra. The eminent Tang statesman Pei Xiu was a fervent Buddhist practitioner and illustrious calligrapher. Pei and his teacher Zongmi were exceptionally close, with Pei writing prefaces to many of Zongmi's works as well as his funerary inscription.

[127] *Numinous knowing* (*lingzhi* 靈知) is the core of Zongmi's Chan. He considered numinous knowing to be the basis of the highest of the three canonical teachings as well as the basis of the Heze school of Chan. *Chan Prolegomenon* (*Chanyuan zhuquanji duxu* 禪源諸詮集都序): "The mind of empty stillness is numinous knowing that never darkens. This knowing of empty stillness is your True Nature. Whether deluded or awakened, mind from the outset is spontaneously knowing. [Knowing] is not produced by conditions, nor does it arise in dependence on sense-objects. The one word knowing is the gate of marvels." [空寂之心靈知不昧。即此空寂之知。是汝真性。任迷任悟心本自知。不藉緣生不因境起。知之一字眾妙之門。] (T 2015.48.402c28–403a2). See Broughton, *Zongmi on Chan*, 88; 90; 92–93; 95; 97; 123; 137; 140.

[128] T 279.10.89a2–3.
[129] T 842.17.913c4.
[130] T 842.17.914a20–21.
[131] T 842.17.917b20–21.

age who hope to complete the Way, there must be no making them seek awakening. This only increases their stock of learning and reinforces their self-view."[132] These are all words that painfully point to a *false knowing*, a dependent comprehension. With *false knowing*, even if you deeply investigate ultimate principle, penetrate to the Nature-source, engage in a flowing torrent of discussion all day long—even before you've finished discussing you are already deluded! Therefore, Śākyamuni in the Snow Mountains showed traces of his awakening; but only at the very end [of his teaching career], in front of an assembly of thousands, did he hold up a flower to reveal the [true] principle of his awakening. Later, the thousands of different expedients and devices of the Chan patriarchs were close to this in being like a ball of fire. Touching [any of the Chan expedients] is like being cut by the sharpness of the *Tai'e Sword*.[133] Hearing them is like the sound of a thunderclap. Drinking them is like drinking insect venom! When it comes down to the speech/silence and activity/stillness [of everyday life, the Chan patriarchs] flawlessly created for others a narrow path [to awakening]—a most important thing. Thus, the Chan approach does not permit standing immobile at the locus of awakening, condemning this [sort of awakening] as 'dharma dust' and rejecting it as a level of understanding with a thorn in it. *One must want to forget both delusion and awakening*, not stopping until they have been combined into the one numinous Source. If you have not yet arrived at this point, then by your *knowing* you will give form to various delusions: you'll be like a blind one holding a torch for a daytime walk! Not only is it of no benefit in the sunlight—if you hang onto the torch for a long time, the fire will burn the hand holding the torch! I also am in the dark about *true knowing* and unable to escape the fault of *false knowing*. I was asked about this, and so I give this explanation as a self-admonition.

[29] SOMEONE ASKED: "The compound *dust-travail* [= Sanskrit *kleśa*, i.e., the *afflictions* or *defilements* of greed, hostility, stupidity, etc.] is a term used by the world. I do not know what to take as the cause and the meaning of *dust-travail*."

PHANTASM: "*Delusion* is the cause [of the *dust-travails*]; *defilement* is the meaning [of *dust-travail*]. *Delusion* is the deluding of your own mind: you do not comprehend that all dharmas lack self-nature. *Lacking self-nature* refers to the fact that the Nature from the outset is empty—because there is no [subject that] knows. You do not comprehend that [all dharmas] lack self-nature, and engender false feelings, recognizing all dharmas as 'really'

---

[132] T 842.17.920a8–9.
[133] One of the ten precious swords of ancient China. During the Spring-and-Autumn period (777 to 476 BCE) it was forged by Blacksmith Ou (Ou Yezi 歐冶子) at the request of the King of Chu.

existent. Once you've fallen into this 'sea of existence,' then thoughts of *seizing/abandoning* or *going along with/going against* arise from 'me myself.' If things go along with [your own mind], then you feel attraction; if they go against [your own mind], then you feel repulsion. If attraction, then you seize the thing; if hatred, then you discard it, going round and round in a shifting current. If it goes along with what you love, you produce happiness; if it goes against what you love, you produce anger. [These delusions] very subtly lie latent in the field of your consciousness: springing up unpredictably; rising and disappearing at any time. You crookedly follow feelings into torment; and chase after your thoughts as they flutter about. *Defiled* becomes the six realms of rebirth [i.e., hell-beings, hungry ghosts, animals, asuras, humans, and gods]; *purified* becomes the four noble ones [i.e., hearer, private buddha, bodhisattva, and buddha]. Although awakening and delusion are different, looked at from the point of view of the *dust-travails*, they are the same. If one asks why, it's because the True Nature that is innately pure from the past to the present has never allowed for any increase or decrease, gain or loss, of even a single dharma. [This True Nature] is filled to the brim; contains everything completely; its numinous light reaching everywhere; with no fixed characteristic anywhere. Because sentient-beings are not yet awakened, they come to chase after sense-objects. This is merely wading through "supports" or "things," and all of it is characterized by the *dust-travails*. Both sages and ordinary persons encounter defilement. Now, the *dust-travails* can harm the essence of the precepts, can pollute the fount of *samādhi*, can darken the mirror of wisdom, can moisten the roots of greed, can aid the flames of anger, can enlarge the clouds of stupidity, can open the way to the bad, can close the gate to the good, can assist the workings of karma, can dissolve the power of the Way. If I were to speak of all the mistakes involving the *dust-travails*, there would be no end of it! In general, for today's students, *all* actions and activities are the *dust-travails*: and they just want to place their *self* in an [impregnable] region where not a single thing can encroach. If the least matter [threatens to] 'conscript' their mind, or even the most minute job impinges upon their thoughts, they say it will dissolve their Way-power—they always flail their arms about and leave, resolving that they will never so much as look back; their willpower is strained. They are people who repeatedly fall into delusion: you cannot discuss the Way with them. If you ask why, it is because they are incapable of reflecting on the fact that the origin of the *dust-travails* is rooted in delusion, not something that emerges out of [everyday] affairs! If [the *dust-travails*] did emerge from [everyday] affairs, well then, you'd better not eat when you're hungry [because the *dust-travails* would contaminate you]; you'd better not dress warmly when it's cold; you'd better not have a house to live in; you'd better not use a road to walk on. Assuredly, if things were like this, you would quickly die! Because this [i.e., the fact that *dust-travails* do not arise from everyday affairs] is unmistakably a natural thing, we take no notice that the grains we eat emerge from [the everyday affair of] tilling the soil; that the clothes we hang on ourselves emerge from [the everyday affair of] the shuttle of a loom; that the houses we live in emerge from [the everyday affair of] construction; that the roads we tread on emerge from [the everyday affair of] roadwork. If all sorts of people did not apply themselves to such tasks, then how would we get all the things we need to stay alive? Again, we take no notice that the people who are practicing the Way right now from the outset have lacked [any essence], and arose from the *dust-travails* of the nourishing of their fathers and mothers. They grew up from the *dust-travails* of their parents' embrace. Also, we take no notice that the buddhas and patriarchs from the past, even people equipped with great virtue, never failed to eat meals and wear clothes, never failed to dwell in houses, and never failed to trek along [on roads]. Because these [buddhas and patriarchs] were awakened to the perfectly pure self-mind that fills the *dharmadhātu*, allowing room for nothing else, in a single moment they overturned the 80,000 *dust-travails*, making them into 80,000 buddha-events. Therefore, Yongjia said: 'If you don't see even a single dharma, that is the *tathāgata* and can be called *Avalokiteśvara*.'[134] How could anyone, outside their awakening to their own mind, see a separate dharma designated *dust-travail*? Therefore, in the assemblies of the *Huayan Sutra* various good teachers all temporarily make use of these *dust-travails* for the sake of practicing the bodhisattva path and cultivating the bodhisattva practice, taking them as an essential gate for adorning the pure lands of the buddhas. You should know that, apart from the *dust-travails*, there are no six perfections; abandon the *dust-travails*, and there are no four immeasurable minds;[135] empty out the *dust-travails*, and there are no sages and worthies; exhaust the *dust-travails*, and there is no liberation [from samsara]. In fact, the *dust-travails* are the womb of the buddhas and patriarchs of the three times, the bodhisattvas of the ten directions, the limitless good teachers, all morality-concentration-wisdom, and all virtuous merits as numberless as the grains of sand of the Ganges. If there were no *dust-travails*, then the activities of the sages and worthies would lack any principle from which to sprout. Aah! Students do not comprehend this meaning, falsely producing *pleasure/disgust* [at the *dust-travails*]. If you try to use the *dust-travails* to

---

[134] *Yongjia Zhengdao ge* (永嘉證道歌; T 2014.48.396c11–12).
[135] See n. 123.

eliminate *dust-travails*, it will increase your delusion even more! The sages take pity on this sort of thing. Therefore, the *Śūraṃgama Sūtra* says: 'At the tap of a finger, the *ocean-seal* [i.e., the meditative *samādhi* that is like the smooth ocean surface] will reflect all light [i.e., phenomena], but if you instigate even a moment of thought, the *dust-travails* will quickly arise.'[136] How could these words deceive anybody? How can everyone here tally with the mind of the Sage [i.e., the Buddha]: *the* dust-travails *are marvelous functioning*! Even if you are thinking you want to wash away the *dust-travails* with thousands of efficacious [Buddhist] practices, the Sage [i.e., the Buddha] would still censure that as a delusionary construction. Even washing away the *dust-travails* meets with censure! How much more is this the case when, your mind clogged up by *dust-travails*, you don't bother to search for correct awakening, hastily concocting the excuse, 'but I'm obstructed by nothing!'— you're doing nothing but cheating your own mind!"

[30] SOMEONE ASKED: "The praise heaped upon you for your pursuit of the Way is received enthusiastically by people. Why do you not follow the conditions of our times and take a seat [i.e., take up residence as abbot] in a single monastery, spreading the teachings according to your abilities and extending the mind set up by the buddhas and patriarchs? Moreover, your withdrawal into quietude is a small matter of personal integrity. If you hold firmly to this [i.e., your state of reclusion] and do not return [to a life of active monastic leadership], will you be able to avoid becoming a criminal in dharma?"

PHANTASM: "After undergoing unanticipated praise in the past, every day now I am hearing this sort of talk. Even so, the reason I am not ashamed in this heart of mine is that there is an explanation for it. If one really is possessed of the Way of [working for the benefit of] others but decides to preserve his high integrity [hidden away as a recluse], firmly maintaining [that status] and not working for others, then he *is* a criminal in the dharma. That much is inescapable. But, if one really is not possessed of the Way of [working for the benefit of] others but only wants to seize the opportunity to reel in a reputation, turning his back on principle and forcibly [creating a scenario of] working for others, I do not know whether he can or cannot avoid being named a criminal. If he cannot avoid it, then, compared to the crime of one who firmly maintains [the status of a recluse] and does not work for others, the crime [of the one trying to reel in a reputation] is double! Knowing this principle very well, I dare not venture to serve [as an abbot]. I have silently reflected on this matter, and there are three energies essential to serving as an abbot. [With these three in hand,] there is almost no chance of failure as an abbot: 1. Way-energy; 2. conditioning-factor energy;

---

[136] T 945.19.121b1–2.

and 3. wisdom-energy. Way-energy is the substance; conditioning-factor energy and wisdom-energy are the function. If you are possessed of the substance, even if you lack the function, you can still become an abbot. However, you will be unable to embrace teaching expedients and will not be equipped with [appropriate responses to various student] deportments. But if the Way-substance is missing, even if you have thousands of miraculous powers, if you try to use them, there will be no corresponding benefit. Even if you have conditioning-factor energy and wisdom-energy, you will be able to accomplish nothing. If substance and function are both lacking, how could one venture to serve [as an abbot]? If he has no [bad] karmic fruits, there is no need to discuss it; if he does have [bad] karmic fruits, how could he not have dissatisfaction in his heart? *In the matter of the Way of the buddhas and patriarchs, I am lacking in awakening. I have no more than a confident understanding that comes from ordinary language and books.* I ponder: after the ancients obtained the purport, they no longer feared imminent danger. For twenty or thirty years they placed themselves alongside the forge with which the blacksmith forges metal, still removing traces of *awakening*, cleansing away the principle that they had realized. Only afterwards did they enter the real and the conventional: they didn't experience a single dharma or ordinary feeling. Their whole body was like a sharp sword, like an ancient mirror, never ceasing its functioning, never employing superfluous words. While sternly confronting a crowd of thousands [of Chan practitioners], they were unaware of being treated as 'honored,' unaware of being treated as 'glorious.' Since they possessed this sort of attitude, even if they encountered a situation in which humans and gods recommended them [for the abbotship of an illustrious monastery], they weren't embarrassed. Those still immersed in deluded views cannot imitate this. To start with, if the traces of *awakening* are not yet completely washed away, then the view of *doer/done* arises in confusion at every turn. *Doer* and *done* are both deluded views. The traces of awakening: they must not be allowed to linger in mind! How much more so is this case with a confident understanding of the teachings, which is simply a deluded view! When you get to the substance of the ultimate Way, the closer you get, the more estranged you are from it; the nearer you become, the farther away you are. *Moreover, I have not yet been able to understand the Way, so how could I make others understand the principle of the Way?* Because I have been unable to chase away this blockage in myself, I dare not falsely take charge of a big monastery and call myself a master who spreads the Way!"

THE GUEST SAID: "Indeed, as is said, in both past and present, grand monasteries have lined up in clusters. Generation after generation there has been no lack of people to hold the fly whisk [i.e., function as abbots of those monasteries]. Wouldn't you say that all of them have lost both substance and function?"

PHANTASM: "Your question is well-informed, but you haven't heard the saying: '[The successors of the Buddha] one after another entered *samādhi*, but one after another each [successor] *did not know* [the *samādhi* of his predecessor].'[137] In spite of *not knowing* [the *samādhis* of these abbots], you secretly want to discuss their propriety with me. Wouldn't that compound my shortcoming?"

At that the guest and I looked at each other and gave a laugh.

[31] SOMEONE ASKED: "While for half a lifetime I have sojourned in the arena of [Buddhist] voidness-tranquility, my mind has been running around in the region of fame and profit. I blame the creator of things for not coming to my aid. Unexpectedly, I took on the *name* 'abbot' [of a monastery]—I was pleased to undertake that role. Since I have been carrying this *name* upon my shoulders, I am not as serene as I was before taking it on. If you ask why, it is because my heart is beset by success or failure in hundreds of tasks, and by the joy and anger issuing from a host of people. If my attention lapses and misses even some tiny item, then, before I even turn around, calamity and shame have gathered about me. Could the buddhas and patriarchs of the past possibly been like this?"

PHANTASM: "When you first accepted the *name* ['abbot'], you didn't think about the fact that it was the start of your taking on the demands [of 'abbot']. *Name* in the world has never arisen in isolation, springing to life suddenly. In fact, a *name* [or reputation] is brought about through actualities. The relationship between *name* and the actualities [behind it] is like a shadow's following after a form, like a piece of apparel's deriving from silk threads, like food's deriving from rice and grains. *Demands* means seeking for actualities [i.e., the hard accomplishments that earn one a *name*]. If you invoke *name*, which is the shadow, you must seek for the actualities that constitute the form creating it. If you talk about the *name* 'clothing and food,' you must seek the actualities of silk and grains. When at the very beginning you took upon your shoulders the *name* of 'abbot,' you should have first taken on responsibility for ensuring the correct condition: making sure the *dharma is long abiding*. Without such an actuality, it

---

[137] *Shishuang Chuyuan chanshi yulu* (石霜楚圓禪師語錄): "The Master ascended the seat and said: 'The World-honored-one's *samādhi*—[his successor] Mahākāśyapa did not know it. Mahākāśyapa's *samādhi*—Ānanda [the second successor to the Buddha] did not know it. Ānanda's *samādhi*—Śāṇakavāsin [the third successor to the Buddha] did not know it. The sages of the past did not know each other's *samādhis*.'" [上堂云。世尊三昧迦葉不知。迦葉三昧阿難不知。阿難三昧商那和修不知。從上諸聖三昧互相不知。] (CBETA 2019.Q3, X69, no. 1338, p. 190a3–4).

is no different from discussing a shadow separate from its form or conversing about food/clothing while abandoning grain/silk. The more talk there is, the more distant actual efficacy becomes. The more closed-in the workings of the mind, the more the *Great Functioning* [of the *buddhadharma*] is perverted. The more aflame your grasping of objective-supports, the more the correct condition [for being abbot] dies off. If you can quickly discard these [i.e., talk, mind workings, and the grasping objective-supports], you will still have a method for managing things. If you flow onward [the way you are going] and forget to return, you will surely end up in a hell! Moreover, what is *name* [worth], that we so wrangle over and esteem it? In my opinion, it is not our esteeming *name*—it is because we grasp at the existence of the self. And because of the existence of that self, attachment-views are produced. As for attachment-views, none is more extreme than [attachment to] *name*, and therefore *name* is unique among the five desires. Desire lurks in the mind: hidden and difficult to discern. [Desire,] upon encountering objective-supports, is propelled into motion. No person can oppose it. No sage can suppress it. Even if [such instruments of punishment as] axes and saws are to the front of you, and kettles and cauldrons to your rear, you won't even have time to notice: [when you are being flung about by the desires,] how could you [find the leeway] to fear the karmic effects [of these fearful instruments]? However, the most beautiful example of *name* is 'sages and worthies,' and 'Way-virtue.' Second place is 'accomplishment and benefit,' and third place is 'technique and ability.' Therefore, some pretend to be a sage or worthy to catch it [i.e., *name*] with a net; some ride Way-virtue to seek it; some specialize in technique and ability to snatch it up; some steal accomplishment and benefit to gain possession of it. [The idea of a] 'beautiful *name*' is rooted in your mind, and your deluded consciousness races about after it. When it comes to what you say and what you do, the only thing you're striving for is *name*. When it comes to the question of the actualities behind that *name*, you're turning your head away and paying no attention. Even if you fuss about this matter all day long, no matter what you do, it is obvious you'll fail. Occasionally you do get the karmic result that you seek [i.e., *name*]. Suppose you get a 'beautiful *name*' that endures for a hundred generations without waning—one day the conditions for this karmic recompense will stop, and yesterday's *name* will become today's shame. The higher the *name*, the more extreme the shame! Therefore, we know that *name*, which is not real, is but a tool for latching onto defeat and shame. In the first place, sages see through to the bottom of principle, and preserve the actuality on the inside. They only fear forgetting this [actuality] for a moment. Therefore, for uncountable eons they only seek the ultimate Way: this is smashing the Māra of samsara and returning to the actuality of the numinous Source. They cultivate the six perfections and everywhere implement the four immeasurable minds[138]: this is the actuality of raising great kindness and opening great compassion. [Śākyamuni,] at more than three hundred dharma assemblies, spoke the partial and complete teachings: this was the actuality of observing the faculties of beings and responding to their illnesses, bringing benefit to sentient-beings and saving them. At the very end, he held up a flower and handed over his robe to Mahākāśyapa: this was the actuality of sealing mind with mind, and transmitting from vessel to vessel. When it comes to the hundred thousand superior practices, and merits as numerous as grains of sand in the Ganges, there is not one of them that does not flow from the realm of the Reality-limit. This is called 'Pure Reality.' Internally, there is no [perception of] doing anything; externally, there is nothing hankered after. There is no boasting to oneself; there is no waiting for anything from others. There is only power that is unceasing. That correct mindfulness—of treading on Reality—is a necessity. Because [the Buddha] sincerely carried out the actualities [behind the *name*] completely and perfectly, his various epithets and beautiful *names*, such as 'supreme teacher,' 'honored among men and gods,' '*udumbara* flower,' and 'storehouse of light,' came to him with no expectation on his part. Suppose a sage for an instant were to entertain even the slightest thought of hankering for *name* in the external world: even if this sage were to spend millions of eons as uncountable as the grains of sand in the Ganges in firmly cultivating a host of good actions, not only would he not acquire a beautiful *name*, he wouldn't be able to escape slander for chasing after falsity! The ancients were only distressed when the actuality did not exist—they were not distressed when *name* failed to arrive. We know that it is the actualities that beckon *name*. Therefore, throughout all-under-heaven, both past and present, there has never been one who had *name* without having the actualities behind it. What's called 'the actualities of an abbot'—what sort of actualities are those? From afar, [abbots] receive the teaching-substance of the former buddhas; nearby, they adhere to the teaching expedients of the Chan patriarchs. Internally, they preserve authenticity of self; externally, they produce confidence in humans and gods. They do not make the wise run ahead; they do not make the stupid fall behind. They do not love what goes along with [their own minds]; they do not hate what goes against [their own minds]. They give a

---

[138] See n. 123.

level kindness to all beings without interruption. These are all the actualities of standing in for a buddha to hoist the teachings and occupying the rank called 'teacher.' If there are places where your energy is not up to it, you should 'retreat and nourish,' 'conserve and store up.' You certainly should not be careless! If you are thinking of borrowing the least *upāya* to help these actualities along, that would be like using the light of a firefly to assist the blazing sun. A sage only knows that one must practice actualities. How could you think there is any other way of gaining *name* beyond practicing actualities? It is analogous to piling up grains and silk—then you will have the *names* 'food' and 'clothing.' There is no need to seek them out, for they arrive spontaneously. Ever since there has been a Chan community, this beautiful *name* 'abbot' has been like dangling a bull's-eye [for monks to aim at]. Those who embrace wisdom and show ability can shoot the arrow of written and spoken eloquence. But, if they do not attend to actualities, they will be struck by their own arrow. How could they possibly hit that bull's-eye? Thus, in the case of the contraction or extension of the teachings-gate and the rise or fall of the Way of dharma—is [the key] *name* or actualities? We cannot disregard these two!

[32] There was someone who asked about *advancing* and *retiring* [i.e., taking up an abbotship in the world, or going into reclusion in the mountains as Mr. Phantasm has].

PHANTASM: "We rely on the lifebuoy of our four-elements [physical body] floating in the sea of the three realms—infinitesimal like a single grain of millet in a gigantic storehouse. Bolting forward in an *advance* or deigning to *retire*, even if a thousand or ten thousand miles in a day, what gain/loss is there to speak of? Precisely because the likes and dislikes of human feelings vary, when we *advance*, we say it is good or bad; and, when we *retreat*, we say it is good or bad. People are unable to examine ultimate principle from a distance, and they are prone to being deluded by 'good' or 'bad.' Faced with a single *advance* or a single *retreat*, they merely trust to their false delusions and, in the end, lack the ability to serve as host [rather than guest]. Only sages and worthies are not this way. When [sages and worthies] *advance*, they invariably follow the Way and think of how to save people; when they *retire*, they invariably follow the Way and think of how to mend their own shortcomings. When carrying out an *advance* or a *retirement*, even if faced with hundreds of setbacks, they are relaxed and free of sorrow. How about this in comparison to: *in the end, lack the ability to serve as host [rather than guest]*? If you only work toward your own plan for attaining honor and favor, when you *advance*, you will meet karma, and, when you *retire*, you will be overturned by your delusions. The residual traces 'good' and 'bad' will suddenly be all confused. When you have called forth karmic recompense, gallantly do not hide! Practitioners of the Way— why aren't you properly selective concerning *advancing* and *retiring*?"

[33] SOMEONE ASKED: "As for *impartiality* and *self-interest*, I have received instruction on *self-interest*, but what does *impartiality* mean?"

PHANTASM: "What kind of person would I be, were I to dare arbitrarily to engage in a rash discussion of this? I have heard in the past that an ancient said: 'The word *impartiality* is the original mind of the buddhas and patriarchs, the sages and worthies. [*Impartiality* is] the largest and brightest— standing forbiddingly alone. Even heaven-and-earth cannot overwhelm it; even ghosts and spirits can't sneak a peek at it.' But if you choose to make discriminations concerning it, there is extreme *impartiality*, big *impartiality*, and small *impartiality*. Extreme *impartiality* is the Way. Big *impartiality* is the [Buddhist] teachings. Small *impartiality* is temple property and monastic duties. In olden times, the old man Śākyamuni, on the night he beheld the bright star, uttered: 'Inconceivable! Sentient-beings are endowed with the merit-characteristics of *tathāgata* wisdom!'[139] Here [Śākyamuni] clarifies that both sages and ordinary persons are endowed with this numinous [wisdom], causing it to be transmitted without limit. The Way, which is extreme *impartiality*, finds its deep source right here. Later, at more than three hundred dharma assemblies, he adapted to the faculties of beings and established different paths of teachings, using written and spoken words as vast as the mountains and seas. The teachings, which are the big *impartiality*, take this as their ground plan. These teachings covered the five regions of India, and their light spread to China. Monasteries and their equipment spread to every realm. This is the reason for the arising of the small *impartiality* of temple property and monastic duties. If not for the Way, there would have been no way to reveal these teachings. If not for the teachings, there would have been no way [for monks] to take responsibility for the temple property and monastic duties. If not for temple property and monastic duties, there would be no way to unfold this Way. These three complete and assist each other. In fact, they equally emerge from the *impartiality* of the original mind of the buddhas and patriarchs, and sages and worthies. Moreover, that heaven covers everywhere, that earth supports everywhere, that seas immerse everywhere, and that the season of spring nourishes everywhere: these are indeed extreme [*impartiality*]. My *impartiality* does not yet extend everywhere, but nor is it yet extreme [*impartiality*]. Should you

---

[139] See n. 106. The above saying of an ancient is untraced.

ask why: if you are talking about the *Way*, it completely includes the three realms [of desire, form, and non-form], penetrating the ten directions of space. There is not a single sentient-being that does not take part in the same realization [as the buddhas]. If you are talking about the *teachings*, then the three vehicles and steps of the ten [bodhisattva] stages, the grades in rank of the myriad practices and six perfections, are established in vast numbers. There is not a single sentient-being who cannot enter through one of those gates. If you are talking about *temple property and monastic duties*, lofty gates and great compounds have been opened; spacious halls and private rooms are there to be occupied [by practitioners]. For every single meal, the bell is struck and the drum beaten, [as a signal to] warn both those in the nether world and those in this world, making them arrive at the same time so they can all receive their meal. The reason why people do not reach the region of the buddhas and patriarchs, and sages and worthies, is that they do not exist in *impartiality*. If they do not exist in *impartiality*, then, when they are in stillness, they store up anxious thoughts, and, when they are in action, they wade through calamites and shame. If they investigate, they get stuck in stupidities; if they accomplish something, they increase their transgressions. Afterwards, they fall into one of the three [unhappy] rebirths of the six destinies: bondage for ten thousand lifetimes! In the end, there is no principle by which they can loosen their own bonds. Truly, this is because their minds do not exist in *impartiality*. For example, take Li Lou.[140] He stumbled and fell to the floor of a dark room: even though his eyesight had the 'divine light' that could see for a thousand miles, he could not even perceive the tiniest little thing [right in front of him]! Therefore, the teachings of the sages could not but enlighten his darkness. From the outset people proceed toward peace of mind, but they lack awareness that what brings about peace of mind is *impartiality*. People proceed toward merit and wisdom, but they lack awareness that what assists merit and wisdom is *impartiality*. People look up to sages and worthies, but they are not aware that reaching the rank of a sage or worthy involves *impartiality*. People have affection for the buddhas and patriarchs, but they do not know that tallying with the buddhas and patriarchs involves *impartiality*. There is not the slightest gap between *impartiality* and original mind. Therefore, the sages point to the Way of extreme *impartiality* to make this mind bright. They establish the teachings of big *impartiality* to illuminate this mind. They take on the temple property and

---

[140] See *Mencius*, Li Lou shang. Li Lou was a contemporary of the Yellow Emperor (Huangdi 黃帝). His eyesight was so sharp that he could see the tip of an autumn hair at more than one hundred paces.

monastic duties of small *impartiality* to rectify this mind. Mind and *impartiality* are different names for the same substance. Thus, as for the principle of *impartiality*, you must not be negligent, you must not be rigid. It is not a created thing. It is free of delusions and artificialities: the single straight Way. Only the mind of extreme truth and extreme reality can tally with it. The slightest foray into thinking is non-*impartiality*. Therefore, the sages and worthies seize [*impartiality*] and practice it. They hasten toward it, never deviating from it by even a fine silken thread. Whenever they let mind produce thoughts, they do not allow for deliberation. They do not have to wait for extreme *impartiality* to shine forth. As for people in the world who ignore this *impartiality*, it is not that they are ignoring this *impartiality*; it is just that they are deceiving their own minds. If they knew that you cannot deceive your own mind, then, spontaneously, at times of action, *impartiality* and its brightness would unite. At times of stillness, *impartiality* and its illumination would unite. They pass through the teachings and the Way and hold to temple property and monastic duties: they never lose this *impartiality*. As for *impartiality*, if people throughout their whole lives do not know it and are in the dark about it, nothing can be done about that. Every now and then there is someone who knows [*impartiality*] but turns his back on it and instead makes a display of extreme *impartiality* to capture fame with a net; or borrows the teachings of big *impartiality* to gain a higher rank; or steals the temple property and monastic duties of small *impartiality* to accomplish his desires. Sinking deeply [into his desires] and drowning in grave [defilements], he fails to think about what the effects will be. And he does not stop at self-deception. In a country of old, a certain monastery was about to be converted into a warehouse, but a single monk forcefully refused and would not go along.[141] When this was brought to the king's attention, the king conferred a sword upon his messenger, saying: 'If he refuses for a second time, behead him! If he shows no fear of death, exempt him!' Thereupon the messenger explained the king's instruction to the monk. The monk laughed and craned his neck [offering to be beheaded], saying: 'To die for the sake of the *buddhadharma*—in fact, I willingly tempt it!' At the point when he [i.e., the monk] was about to crane his neck, right to the end, he showed no fear. Why did he for a transient moment put [such unreasonable] strong effort into this? I suppose it came out of his true sincerity. When we try to deduce his mind, how could it possibly have been simply for the sake of the small *impartiality* of monastic property and duties? He had a deep intention

---

[141] Story untraced.

concerning the teachings and the Way. Yao Junsu,[142] Governor during the Sui dynasty, sent down an order having all monks come to the city. Those who firmly stood their ground and remonstrated with him were beheaded. At the time there was a monk, Daoxun. He mounted the stairs [of Yao Junsu's compound] and revealed his thoughts, resisting Yao's order. Junsu looked right at Daoxun and said: 'This monk has guts—to be so manly and brave!' Subsequently, Yao exempted him. For the sake of [protecting] the teachings of great *impartiality*, [Daoxun] touched the sharp point of the sword and welcomed the blade—without any fear of dying. Again, why did he for a transient moment put [such unreasonable] strong effort into this? The letters of Wuzu Fayan of East Mountain roughly state: 'The fact that this summer all the manors are ruined by drought doesn't worry me at all. But, in my room, when I raise the *huatou* of *dog has no buddha-nature* and not a single person understands—this truly worries me!'[143] When we try to get to the source of [Wuzu's] intention, he was conscientiously assisting and supporting the Way of extreme *impartiality*. He dared not forget it for a moment. Thus, his saying 'all the manors are ruined by drought doesn't worry me' is not a case of his not worrying. If you compare the smallness of temple property and monastic duties to the extreme Way, then, in the case of temple property and monastic duties, it is okay to omit worrying about them. As for the monastic property and duties, they are established with the root goal of making the teachings prosper and transmitting the Way. If the teachings are not invigorated and the Way is not transmitted, even though there are soaring towers and overflowing halls, as well as money and grains in such surplus that they fill up the three thousand worlds, not only does this not mend *impartiality*, it's enough to be a trouble for the teachings and the Way! The preservation or extinction of *impartiality* is connected to the rise or fall of the dharma Way. Be careful! Be careful!"

[34] There was someone who asked about [awe-inspiring] authority.

PHANTASM: "In all-under-heaven there are two types of authority. To wit, the two are the authority that comes from Way-virtue and the authority that comes from expedient force. The authority of Way-virtue emerges from heaven; the authority of expedient force emerges from people. What emerges from heaven makes people comply with mind; what emerges from people makes people comply only with outward forms. Thus, the [heavenly] authority that makes them comply with mind is not just authority in a single state—the blowing of the wind makes such authority reach far beyond ten

---

[142] *Sui shu* 71, Biographies (*liezhuan* 列傳), 36.
[143] *Precious Instructions of the Chan Forest* (*Chanlin baoxun* 禪林寶訓; 1174–1189), T 2022.48. 1023a25–b2.

thousand miles. Also, authority is not only for today: the voice of authority is transmitted for a hundred generations. How do I know this is so? Ancients whose Way-virtue was pure and complete: people of the present draw from the style [i.e., "wind"] they bequeathed and look up to the residue of their fervency, enabling [people of the present] to extinguish drunkenness of mind. How much more so would this be the case if they were to meet and have a talk [with the ancients] in the present day: could there be anyone who would not be in awe? Their authority that makes people comply with mind derives completely from their extreme sincerity. In fact, they possess the principle of naturalness, which does not allow the addition of even the slightest bit of deliberative thought. Now, as for the authority coming from Way-virtue, there is certainly no doubt that people are moved to comply with mind. If sages and worthies were frivolously to usurp this Way-virtue to make people comply, how could people go along with that? Moreover, as for the beauty of Way-virtue, even sages and worthies cannot monopolize use of it to make people comply. But, when the ignorant of the world abandon Way-virtue and stick to expedient force, they fail to recognize the danger they put themselves in. All day long they noisily criticize people for not *complying with me*. What is the mistake here? Thus, the authority that comes from expedient force, even if capable of making people comply with outward forms, lasts only for a short time. Turn your face away, and there is *no authority*. How can there be authority after death? It is not only that they cannot retain authority after death. People, carrying resentment in their hearts, when they remember past instances of this authority's making them comply, engage in payback, and the resulting calamities are uncountable. Therefore, we know: the authority of past days rarely fails to become the calamity of later days. Fortunately, we have received the great instruction of the four immeasurable minds[144] in the wake of the Great Sage [i.e., the Buddha] of the western region. The influence of authoritative power: it is fitting that it should not be anticipated after death."

SOMEONE SAID: "I have heard that for rectifying the minds of people of all-under-heaven, there is nothing better than rewards and punishments: beneficial acts are rewarded, and authoritative power doles out punishments. [As a Buddhist monk] I am certainly at a distance from the worldly Way. As for the necessities of [running] a monastic establishment, if the assigned person is not doing his job, is it all right if I don't want to impose my authority [in the worldly Way] on him?"

PHANTASM: "Clearly, karmic retribution will take care of it. The sages and worthies have demonstrated the proper standards: who would dare to change

---

[144] See n. 123.

them? If you use your authority on them [i.e., monks under you] and they don't reform, what can you do about it? You should make them revert to their own Way-virtue. I have never seen a case in which people possessed of Way-virtue—their extreme sincerity spread throughout inner self and outer world—failed to believe and obey. How should one employ authority? Despite the reality that there has never been a day in this world when authority did not exist, those who commit violence and do evil deeds have not the least fear of this authority. How is it that this authority, in the end, does not affect them? Not the least concerned that their Way-virtue is not whole and complete, it never occurs to them to go into retreat to nourish it. For those who strive to *select talent* solely through holding the handle of authority, even if they face no calamities in the present, they will certainly incur calamities after their death! Those who hear this should be afraid!"

[35] SOMEONE ASKED: "Our dharma must have external protectors—only then can it be carried out. Consequently, there is the statement that 'the *buddhadharma* is handed over to kings and great ministers.'"[145]

PHANTASM: "As a phenomenological statement, this passes muster, but as a theoretical statement, I have reservations. Should you ask why, the pearl of the Marquis of Sui [i.e., an aristocrat of the Spring-and-Autumn period] was free of imperfection, and people disregarded the dangers of the deep sea to seek it.[146] The jade piece of Bian He [i.e., a Chu man of the Spring-and-Autumn period] was flawless, and the world considered even the price of many walled cities to be too slight to exchange for it.[147] The principle here is solid: if *you yourself* are not in possession of the pearl [sewn into] your garment,[148] and the jade in your bosom is not there, then, even if you speak the language of an inferior and grovel when you approach people [i.e., kings/potential powerful external protectors], such people will distance themselves from you. Why on earth should [potential protectors] be interested in 'disregarding the dangers of the deep sea to seek [the treasure] or considering even the price of many walled cities to be too slight to exchange for [the treasure]?' That is the reason the buddhas and patriarchs take Way-virtue as their very own responsibility, making a unity of the level and hazardous places, forgetting both self and world. What point would there have been in their seeking out external protectors: they couldn't possibly have hidden their Way-virtue from view, so kings and ministers

---

[145] See *Nirvana Sutra*, T 374.12.381a28–b1 and T 375.12.621a10–11.
[146] *Huaninanzi* (淮南子), Lanming xun (覽冥訓): "It is like the pearl of the Marquis of Sui or the jade of He. The one who gets it is fortunate, and the one who loses it is impoverished." [譬如隋侯之珠。和氏之璧。得之者富。失之者貧。] ctext.org/huainanzi/lan-ming-xun/zh.
[147] For the story of Bian He (卞和), see *Hanfeizi* (韓非子), He shi (和氏). ctext.org/hanfeizi/he-shi.
[148] *Lotus Sutra*, T 262.9.29a5–16.

esteemed their sincerity and sidled up to them! The ignorant of the world pay no heed to the state of their own Way-virtue. They invariably want honor and favor, rushing through the gates of the powerful and praising them as external protectors. If they do not get what they want, sighs of resentment form in their speech, and a tone of massive anger floats over their appearance, not stopping until reaching calamity and shame. How could a receptable who embraces the Way be like this?"

[36] SOMEONE ASKED: "If something is deficient in the monastic property or monastic duties [i.e., problems in infrastructure such as the Monks Hall, kitchen, latrines, etc.; farming fields; posts held by monks], is it okay to dash ahead vigorously to repair the problem?"

PHANTASM: "Good medicines are invariably gathered at the residence of a good physician. Money is always tossed into the shop of a great merchant. If the trees are flourishing, birds congregate. If the pond is full, the moon comes [to show its reflection]. Of old, the Great Recluse of the Snow Mountains [Śākyamuni] cast aside the honor and dignity of being king of a ten-thousand-chariot state to undergo six years of hunger and cold. He did not view the great-thousand worlds as any heavier than a single bubble: why would he have had worldly concerns? Upon reaching the day when his myriad merits were perfectly accomplished, at a tower of many jewels, possessed of many ornaments, people circumambulated him. Although he crossed over to extinction two thousand years ago, the remnants of the style he bequeathed still fill up the world. As [the *Mencius*] says: 'What proceeds from you will return to you.'[149] I have heard: when the bodhisattva brings to completion [his practice in] the world, even if he is not possessed of [the accoutrements of monastic property], he does not criticize 'those who do not aid me.' He just intensively practices the six perfections and broadly spreads the four [immeasurable] minds.[150] Those he transforms become perfectly ripened, and various donors bring offerings [to assist in keeping the monastic establishment going]. If [these donations] are accepted, [the donors] leap up and dance in joy. Benefitting self and benefitting others are equally called liberation. This is called 'the merit-field of the completion of monastic parks.' Present-day monks, in doing [their daily practice], turn their backs on ultimate principle and only make effort toward attaining their evil wishes. If they don't have a piece of land, they sometimes squeeze those who have much; or they bring brute power down upon others; or they sue to make them fearful; or they use the arts of intimidation to gain a victory

---

[149] *Mencius*, Liang Hui wang xia
[150] See n. 123.

over them. Though they may temporarily achieve [their goal], it is nothing but the karmic roots of defilement! How could this be beneficial to [the production of] a merit-field? They argue, taking the saying *monastic structures are for a millennium, but monks are for but a morning*[151] as their ground plan. Little do they think: how can you get *monastic structures that last for a millennium* if you're not suffused with concentration and wisdom, and benefit both self and others? If there is no foundation, it is like discarding the pond but still beckoning the bright moon [to shine on the pond and give off reflections], or throwing away the tree and still expecting a flock of birds to gather [in the tree]! It is illogical! It is illogical!

[37] SOMEONE ASKED: "As for the protocols of *speaking dharma*, one must use the Mt. Sumeru Seat in the Raining-Flowers Hall [i.e., an extension of the Dharma Hall where the abbot can ascend the high seat and deliver talks].[152] Isn't this correct?"

PHANTASM: "If you are talking about protocol, that is so. If you are talking about *speaking dharma*, how could it possibly be the case? *Dharma* has no fixed characteristics; *speaking* also has no fixed characteristics. To swing about the fly whisk of white deer hair [i.e., the symbol of authority] and flap one's lips is *speaking* in terms of the characteristics of phenomena. Thus, our Buddha, without rising from the *bodhi* seat, without emerging from his *serpent concentration*, without moving his broad and long tongue, without showing a single dharma characteristic, was always *speaking* fervently—why would there be any need to wait for the forty-nine years [of his teaching career] and his more than three hundred dharma assemblies for his *speaking*? Thus, the bodhisattvas are capable of relinquishing what is difficult to relinquish: they consider giving to be *speaking dharma*. They are capable of maintaining what is difficult to maintain: they consider holding to the rules of discipline to be *speaking dharma*. They are capable of enduring what is difficult to endure: they consider patience to be *speaking dharma*. For them, cultivating the six perfections and four immeasurable minds[153] is all *speaking dharma*. Thus, Avalokiteśvara's manifesting thirty-two magical transformations in response to gods, snake spirits, ghosts, celestial musicians, and so forth—these are all instances of *speaking*

---

[151] This is a common saying in Chan literature. See, for instance, Dahui's *Zheng fayan zang* (正法眼藏; CBETA 2019.Q3, X67, no. 1309, p. 570c2 and CBETA 2019.Q3, X67, no. 1309, p. 609b3).

[152] A Raining-Flowers Hall appears to have been a building separate from the Dharma Hall where dharma talks could be delivered. For instance, Juefan Huihong's (覺範慧洪; 1071–1128) literary collection *Shimen wenzi chan* (石門文字禪) mentions such a structure: "Also, next year at Miyin Chan Monastery [密印禪寺] an extension was added behind the Dharma Hall and made into a Raining-Flowers Hall." [又明年。增廣善法堂之後。為雨花堂。] (CBETA 2019.Q3, J23, no. B135, p. 677a18).

[153] See n. 123.

dharma.[154] Surely there is no need for further explanation! Thus, from the [stories of the] Chan patriarchs of ancient times we have[155]: [Bimo's using] a wooden spear; [Xuefeng's] turning the three balls; [Touzi's] dangling oil; [Daowu's] dancing with a bamboo tablet; [Gao Liangjian's] being separated by the river and invited by [Deshan's] waving a fan in his hand; Huike's standing in the snow and having his mind pacified [by Bodhidharma]; holding erect an empty fist in a thatched hut; sitting cross-legged in a mountain cave; swinging a wooden gong in the middle of the dusty streets; casting a fishing line into a riverbank of white water-grass and yellow reeds; striking the ground; knocking on the ship's side; drawing the bow; [doing cross-legged sitting] facing the wall; dwelling on a solitary peak; meeting someone unexpectedly on a narrow road; getting an ox [from a student] and returning to him a horse: these are the Way that is beyond the ordinary! These are instances of calling an earthenware jar a temple bell: having your mind reside outside of verbalization. A thousand roads and ten thousand ruts, the sound of the golden bell [that proclaims the commencement] and the jade chimes [that proclaim the close][156]—how could they all be found only in a [formal] Raining-Flowers Hall! Same for a Mt. Sumeru Seat! If your mind is identical to the Way, though there may be *only your form and shadow to console each other* in [remote] mountain caves and desolate wastelands, there will never be a time when you are not sternly approaching the great assembly [in the Raining-Flowers Hall] and spreading the teachings. If [your mind] is not identical to the Way, though you may wear luxuriant apparel, occupy the great seat of the honored one, with questions [coming to you] like the massing of clouds, your answers pouring out as if from a jar of water, your persuasive words overcoming the audience: all of it will only increase your conceit, play up to your mundane feelings, and you'll get hooked into worldly customs! To call this '*speaking dharma* to benefit beings' or 'spreading the teachings on behalf of the buddhas' is certainly not something that I know anything about!"

[38] SOMEONE ASKED: "In the case of the ancients, after getting the purport [i.e., awakening], some dwelled on a solitary peak, others let their hands hang at their sides [in civilian fashion] as they entered the marketplace [to work for the sake of beings];[157] some propagated various [Buddhist]

---

[154] *Śūraṃgama Sūtra*, T 945.19.128b26–28.

[155] For the following stories of Chan lore, see Noguchi and Matsubara, *Sanbō yawa*, 280–282, nn. 5–17.

[156] *Mencius*, Wan zhang xia: "Confucius is called the great completion. The great completion is when the sound of the golden bell proclaims the commencement of the sequence, and the jade chimes proclaim the close of the sequence." [孔子之謂集大成。集大成也者。金聲而玉振之也。金聲也者。始條理也。玉振之也者。終條理也。] ctext.org/mengzi/wan-zhang-ii?searchu=金聲.

[157] They set aside the normal *chashou* (叉手) hand-gesture of monks and worked for the sake of beings. In *chashou* hand-gesture the left hand makes a fist around the thumb and is held against the body at the solar plexus. The right hand gently covers the left.

teachings, others solely lifted up the correct directive [of Chan]; some had many 'sticks' [i.e., a counter for disciples] overflowing the room, others did not encounter a single student; some became extinct and nothing more was heard of them, others had a reputation that echoed throughout the universe; some personally suffered the difficulties of the world, others were submerged in sickness. Although they all hastened to the gate of [Bodhidharma's] Mt. Shaoshi [i.e., Mt. Song near Luoyang], each of them walked the roads of the world. How is this so?"

PHANTASM: "If we speak of in terms of sameness, they were the same in being awakened to the true self-mind of Bodhidharma's *direct pointing*. If we speak in terms of difference, they were different in their respective illusionary karmic endowments from the three times [of past, present, and future]. If we observe them from the viewpoint of karmic conditions, it was not a matter of their taking pleasure in stillness and dwelling on a solitary peak, nor was it their loving noisiness and entering the marketplace with their hands hanging at their sides. They propagated various [Buddhist] teachings but never waded into heterodox teachings. They lifted the correct directive [of Chan] but for them it was not an exclusive approach. Although disciples filled their gates, they didn't cater to disciples. Though [they subscribed to the slogan] *I have only my form and shadow to console each other*, they didn't cut themselves off from beings. Even if they finished their lives without anyone hearing of them, they didn't esteem reclusion. Even if they had a reputation that echoed throughout the world, they didn't [esteem] open prominence. When it came to flourishing or withering, calamity or good fortune, everything was rooted in their individual karmic conditions. If you see things with the correct eye that is like a thunderbolt, [all karmic conditions] are no more than flying dust passing before your eyes. How could [karmic conditions] stir thoughts of attraction/revulsion or seizing/abandoning? Therefore, Longmen said: 'Karmic conditions are illusory. Why would you forcibly act against them?'[158] Wuzu Fayan said: 'The myriad things exist in this Way. [They are of] *a single taste*: just trust to the karmic conditions in front of you.'[159] If you do not have ultimate principle to see [karmic conditions] as reflections in a mirror, then you will not be able to remain undeluded by the floating/sinking of mundane characteristics."

[39] SOMEONE ASKED: "As for the person who occupies the rank of teacher, his substituting for the buddhas in hoisting the teaching is grounded in obtaining [splendid] disciples to continue the life-power of wisdom.

---

[158] *Gu zunsu yulu* (古尊宿語錄; CBETA 2019.Q3, X68, no. 1315, p. 227b10). Longmen (龍門) is Foyan Qingyuan (佛眼清遠; 1067–1120), a successor of Wuzu Fayan.
[159] *Fayan chanshi yulu* (法演禪師語錄; T 1995.47.667c5–8).

At the present time, of inheritors of the five Chan schools, only the Linji school has an intact bloodline: the other schools [i.e., Caodong; Guiyang; Yunmen; and Fayan] are all heirless. How can they hand over and receive [the flame-of-the-lamp] now that they have lost their continuity of transmission? Well, is it that karmic conditions make this so?"

PHANTASM: "The Way of the Sage, although hidden or manifest according to the occasion, is dependent upon its fixed allotment [of fate]. One cannot add or subtract even a tiny bit in such matters as lengthening or shortening in endurance over time, the flourishing or decline of the people involved, and the rise or fall of the teachings. Of old, our patriarch [Bodhidharma], before he had left India, had already received the prediction of Prajñātara [i.e., teacher of Bodhidharma and twenty-seventh patriarch]. This can be verified. Before Qingyuan Xingsi [d. 740] and Nanyue Huairang [677–744] had even appeared in the world, the five Chan schools already had their fixed allotment [of fate]. At the time that the five schools were flourishing, they already had their fixed allotment of how long they would last. It's just that they were in the dark concerning these matters—there was no way they could know. Some say:

> The Linji Way goes beyond the usual common sentiments, and its methods for leading people are acute. Its functioning is perfect, its words vibrant. Its forging of people [in the furnace of Chan] proceeds as fast as your turning over your hand. Therefore, the Linji house's reputation has escaped decline for a long time. The other schools were quite the opposite, and it is fitting that they did not continue forever in the world.[160]

This theory [about the superiority of the Linji school] not only slanders the wise ones of old and renders purely subjective decisions on right and wrong: it is utterly ignorant of heavenly principle. Thus, in recent times, those who occupy the rank of teacher fail to think about equalizing mind, propagating the teachings, and making sure the dharma is long-lasting. Instead, they are constantly anxious about securing successors, imitating the actions of common villagers! They use power and wealth to force their will on others; use fame and rank to entice others; use avarice to win out over others; and use duplicity to cheat others. Given this, even if they transmit for thousands upon thousands of generations without decline, how could they possibly be of benefit to [true] principle? They are not just of no

---

[160] Appears in the Qing-period text *Shending Yunwai Ze chanshi yulu* (神鼎雲外澤禪師語錄; CBETA 2019.Q3, J33, no. B280, p. 324c13–15). It is unclear what source Zhongfeng is quoting.

benefit: they are, in fact, harmful in the extreme! Therefore, Yuetang used the metaphor of over-watering melons at noon [on a hot summer day and causing them to rot].[161] There is the criticism of Shishi that he bored holes in the armpits [of his disciples] and inserted wings [so they could fly like a bird].[162] Both stories are foundational: I don't know what you are planning to accomplish if you don't pay attention to them! When we get to Yunmen of old, he obtained the dharma from Chen Zunsu [i.e., Muzhou Daoming], but Chen Zunsu made Xuefeng his final successor.[163] The Chan community down to the present has honored this action. Also, for example, Cishou visited Fojian on Mt. Jiang, and in the room there transpired a strange encounter.[164] [Cishou became Fojian's disciple, but then] wanted to change his lineage. Fojian, in the end, rejected this. The Chan community even ended up praising this! They feared that our [Chan] Way would not spread to others. What is there to resent in differences in Chan lineages? It is like dividing up the lamp-flame of the eastern room to illuminate the western room: just a matter of latching onto this smashing of darkness and illumination [of both rooms] as the splendid thing! Why would you go around whining about: *where does that darkness and my lamplight come from?*"

---

[161] *Precious Instructions of the Chan Forest* (*Chanlin baoxun* 禪林寶訓; 1174–1189): "Yuetang was the longest-serving abbot at Jingci Monastery. Someone said to him: 'Preceptor, you have been practicing the Way for years, but I have heard of no disciples among your followers. Isn't that unworthy of your teacher Miaozhan [Sihui; 1071–1145]?' Yuetang did not reply. On another day he asked this again, and Yuetang said: 'Have you not heard of the ancient one who planted melons because he loved them so much? At midday in high summer, he watered them. The melons in a short time turned rotten. Why? It is not that he was not diligent in his love for them: his watering them was not timely, and he thereby ruined them. Venerable masters from all over exhort their patched-robed Chan monks, but fail to observe the state of their followers' Way karma or the depth of their capabilities, being fixated on wanting to speed up the production of disciples. However, when one examines [the disciples'] Way-virtue, it is stained; when one investigates their words and actions, they are discordant. [The teachers] say that [their disciples] are impartial and correct, but they are perverse and glib. Is this not loving disciples to the point of watering them beyond what they deserve? This is just like watering melons at noon. I am profoundly worried that those in the know will laugh, so I do not do it.'" (*North Mountain Record*). [月堂住淨慈最久。或謂。和尚行道經年。門下未聞有弟子。得不辜妙湛乎。月堂不對。他日再言之。月堂曰。子不聞。昔人種瓜而愛甚者。盛夏之日方中而灌之。瓜不旋踵而湊敗。何也。其愛之非不勤。然灌之不以時。適所以敗之也。諸方老宿提挈衲子。不觀其道業內充才器宏遠。止欲速其為人。逮審其道德則淫污。察其言行則乖戾。謂其公正則邪佞。得非愛之過其分乎。是正猶日中之灌瓜也。予深恐識者笑。故不為也。(北山記聞)。] (T 2022.48.1035c20–29).

[162] Zhe'an Huibin's (者菴惠彬) miscellany *Impartial Discussions of the Chan Community* (叢林公論; 1189): "Today's Chan masters do not ask whether [their disciples] are up to snuff or not. Take, for instance, Fuyang Shouxu, who bored holes in the armpits [of his disciples] and inserted wings [so they could fly like birds]. His idea was: 'our Chan lineage is magnificent and should have a lot of disciples who are dharma successors!' [A disciple] said: 'I have been in your assembly for years. After seeing you, Master, it is as if I've unloaded a heavy load, as if I've taken off my dirty clothes! I rejoice and will be happy for the rest of my life! I have completely obtained your Way!' The motive here lies only in picking up assistance, assuming another's fame, and coveting inappropriate benefit. Aah!" [今之為師者不問可否。例以撫養收恤。鑽腋出羽。意謂我宗盛大。多有法嗣弟子。曰某入眾有年。見師之後如卸重擔。如脫穢裝。慶快生平。盡得師道。意在提援冒名苟利而已矣。嗚呼哀哉。] (CBETA 2019.Q3, X64, no. 1268, p. 772b15–18).

[163] See *Wu deng huiyuan* (五燈會元; CBETA 2019.Q3, X80, no. 1565, p. 303b1–8).

[164] See *Wu deng huiyuan* (五燈會元; CBETA 2019.Q3, X80, no. 1565, p. 347c23–24). Cishou (慈受) is Huilin Huaishen (慧林懷深; 1077–1132).

[40] SOMEONE ASKED: "The *Śūraṃgama Sūtra* says:

> After my extinction, bodhisattvas and arhats will manifest various forms in [the time of] the latter dharma. Though they will act in accordance with their teachings, until the very end they will never say: 'I am a true bodhisattva' or 'I am a true arhat,' or let it leak out that they enjoy a secret karmic cause [for awakening] or denigrate students of this later time. The only exception will be, at the very end, of their lives when they bequeath a saying.[165]

When I look at those who today occupy the rank of teacher, they declare their own awakening before humans and gods. If practitioners do not believe them, they lay out for those practitioners their vow [to save all sentient-beings]. This seems to go against the sincere words of the ancient buddhas, increasing the deluded habit-energy of posterity. Is this permissible or not?"

PHANTASM: "This sort of talk has been around from way back. For example, the five flame-of-the-lamp records[166] compile the basic lore about the Chan patriarchs, and the first matter of importance is to narrate stories of awakening. At the very moment of a patriarch's awakening, it was like his suddenly remembering things long forgotten, like a mute person seeing his dream [and being unable to tell others about it]: he alone knows it. It is not within the sense perception of anyone else. This is called the 'self-realization *samādhi*.' But, if [the Chan patriarchs] were to *shut down their mouths* and decline to speak, how could we have such Chan stories as [Mazu Daoyi's] asking where the wild duck is flying to, [Niaoke Daolin's] blowing on a fine hair, [Lingyun Zhiqin's] seeing the peach blossoms, and Upper Seat Fu's hearing the sound of the bugle?[167] In fact, there are reasons for the disclosure of these stories: sometimes they are due to inquiries by the teacher; sometimes it is a matter of encountering a situation and expounding things; sometimes it is a matter of expressing one's realization without any bias; sometimes it is matter of responding to the occasion and concealing the truth in order to avoid [the greater mistake of] circulating evil speech—it was probably unavoidable. Throughout, there have also been a lot of people who did not give outward form to the content of their awakening. Because they had already been entrusted with the patriarchal flame-of-the-lamp, how could there fail to be proof

---

[165] T 945.19.132c8–14.
[166] Refers to the Song-period texts *Jingde chuandeng lu* (景德傳燈錄; 1004); *Tiansheng guang denglu* (天聖廣燈錄; 1036); *Jianzhong jingguo xu denglu* (建中靖國續燈錄; 1101); *Liandeng hui yao* (聯燈會要; 1183); and *Jiatai pu denglu* (嘉泰普燈錄; 1204). Each is thirty fascicles.
[167] For these Chan stories, see Noguchi and Matsubara, *Sanbō yawa*, 298, nn. 2–5.

[of their awakening]? When there is no textual proof, it is probably because they concealed the deep secret [of their awakening], lacking any desire to reveal it. As for people who have really attained awakening, even though they never allow the word *awakening* to dangle from their lips and teeth, they are like mountains that contain jade and trees with flowers blooming all over, like the sea's abyss that holds pearls and great waves that are clear and transparent: they evince the principle of naturalness. Chan craftsmen—the *real thing*—only rely on what they themselves have gotten, leaving it to others to decide [whether they are the *real thing* or not]. Truly, it is unnecessary for them to quote the story of their awakening to solicit the belief of others. And there is also no need for them to set their minds to skillfully devising a story of their awakening to convert other people. They break down the distress of the students who come to them. They only, case by case, according to the students' powers, relate [their stories of awakening]. If students fail to believe these stories, the teachers merely trust to things—that's it! If [merely trusting to things] allows for arising-disappearing dharmas [in the minds of their students], then those students will lose correct concentration. In that case, would it be better for teachers to keep the principle of their awakening a secret, or better to let it leak out?"

[41] SOMEONE ASKED: "Chan people at the end of life die in cross-legged sitting posture. There are some people who cannot do it. I do not know what [practice method one should] habitually *maintain* to be able to do so."

PHANTASM: "There is nothing for you to *maintain*! This [i.e., dying in cross-legged sitting] is mostly connected to one's karmic background, so you shouldn't be careless. Now, in the case of the person of awakened mind, his delusions have disappeared; his sense-objects have been stilled; his views have been renounced; his grasping has been forgotten—and so right from the beginning [such awakened people] never pay any mind to this [dying in cross-legged sitting posture]. If a person at the end of his life is not suffering from illness or disabilities, then [the principle here] is perfectly clear. One makes a transcendent escape alone: one just gets up and leaves! How could there be any more to it? Moreover, in the world, even among those people who never studied the Way nor engaged in practice, there are some who die in cross-legged sitting posture and win respect from people, developing a great glow at the point of death. If this is not karmic recompense [for actions in past lives], just what is it? In most cases, people who study the Way do not exert effort at investigating to the limit the *mind-essence*. Beforehand, they think that, at the point of death, it won't be possible for them to die solo [in cross-legged sitting posture], and this makes them dread the ridicule of others. Those who get worked up obsessing over this [i.e., dying in cross-legged sitting posture] as *important* have a sort of external Māra that rides on this *importance* and gains entrance, letting you people know beforehand the time [of your death] and creating all sorts of queer phenomena. Little do you know that Māra is at work, and so you fall into the three bad rebirth destinies [of animals, hungry ghosts, and hell-beings]. Of what benefit to principle is this? Every now and then there is a person of truly awakened mind who, at the point of death—either poisoned, or having an encounter with calamity, or for a long time enwrapped in some strange sickness—has limbs that can't support him and lacks the ability to say even a word. Nevertheless, he is one whose everyday Way-power cannot be snatched away. He just holds onto correct thought and awaits the end of his life, never failing to tally with ultimate principle. At the point of death, if he has not on his own seen through the [empty] mundane world, or if his mind has been rendered chaotic by the words of living people, or if he forces the production of the thought *what I am to do*, then the devastation will not be small. In the Chan school there are honored monks who have indicated the set time when they will die in cross-legged sitting posture. The fragrance of incense blankets people; birds fly over and wild beasts run past, making mournful cries; grasses and trees wither; the flames [from the cremation] disperse into colors; śarīra [i.e., relics, often crystalline substances in the cremated remains] glow to the point where various supernatural phenomena and unfathomable things startle the four classes of the Buddhist community [i.e., monks, nuns, laymen, and laywomen]. But all this is because, for lifetime after lifetime, birth after birth, [these honored Chan monks] have resided within the ranks of good teachers and have been perfumed by concentration and wisdom. Their superior karmic causes could not be obscured, and so as a result they obtained this rare karmic recompense. It is not that these honored [Chan] monks *made exertion* to bring this about: a bodhisattva, in one of the [ten bodhisattva] stages, came to this world and propagated the teachings, manifesting these superior characteristics. It is not something one [mere] lifetime's worth of practice and study could achieve. This explanation that it is connected to karmic recompense exhausts the matter!"

[42] SOMEONE ASKED: "Dharma expositions everywhere involve giving people a [*huatou*] of the *road of no meaning*[168] to investigate—that's the *live word*! Your dharma expositions [in this *Night Conversations in a Mountain*

---

[168] Refers to the *huatou* that has no meaning or taste (*wu yiwei huatou* 無義味話頭). Zhongfeng often uses this phrasing.

Hermitage] all have tethered people to the assumption that everything is 'real.' Are you not trafficking in the *dead word*?"

I [PHANTASM] SAY: "You're trying to live within the *live word* [found in these dharma expositions] that you've come across everywhere, but you won't countenance dying within the *dead word* [that is also found in these dharma expositions]. This is genius! However, if you were able to completely die [even] beneath that *dead word*, after a long time, from within that dead state, you would suddenly spring back to life—*then* you'll know an unsurpassed sort of *live*!"

When our night conversation arrived at this point, mountain fowl suddenly cried out, and in the east the sun was gradually growing bright. I was getting sleepy. The guest forgot what he was going to say. After a while, he woke up from dozing. He tried to recall what we had talked about all night long, but, in the end, couldn't remember a single word. By chance, a postulant had gathered writing-brush and paper and brought [a transcript of this conversation] to show me. At that I became angry and signaled to him: 'For me, these words never existed! This is what's called the 'smell of the morning porridge and the pre-noon meal' [i.e., the evanescent smell of the two meals per day in Chan monasteries]. You should bury that!'"

Translation 4
House Instructions for Dwelling-in-the-Phantasmal Hermitage in *Zhongfeng Extensive Record*

House Instructions for Dwelling-in-the-Phantasmal Hermitage

[1] One day when Mr. Phantasm[1] was occupying his phantasmal room, sitting on his phantasmal seat, and holding his phantasmal fly whisk, his phantasmal disciples all gathered round like clouds with questions: "Why are pine trees straight? Why are brambles tangled? Why is the snow-goose white? Why is the crow black?" Mr. Phantasm stood his fly whisk upright and stated to the assembly: "In the case of this phantasmal fly whisk, when standing upright, it is not standing upright of itself: it is standing upright in dependence on phantasm. When horizontal, it is not horizontal of itself: it is horizontal in dependence on phantasm. When handled, it is not handled of itself: it is handled in dependence on phantasm. When released, it is not released of itself: it is released in dependence on phantasm. When you clearly observe such phantasms, you see they stretch throughout the ten directions and fill up all the three times. When standing upright, no upright-ness. When horizontal, no horizontal-ness. When handled, no handled-ness. When released, no released-ness. Complete knowing *in that way* penetrates free of any obstruction. You will immediately see that the pine tree depends on phantasm to be straight; that the brambles depend on phantasm to be tangled; that the snow-goose depends on phantasm to be white; that the crow depends on phantasm to be black. If we were to see free of this phantasm, the pine tree from the outset would be non-straight; the brambles from the outset would be non-tangled; the snow-goose would be non-white: how then could the crow be black? You should know that this 'screen' of phantasm arises from the sense-organ of the

---

[1] On Zhongfeng and phantasm/illusion, see "Understanding the Phantasmal (*zhi huan* 知幻)" in the Introduction. Another translation of this short piece is William Dufficy, trans., *The Illusory Man by Zhongfeng Mingben* (Las Vegas, NV: Independently Published, 2022).

eye. Phantasmal seeing lies latent in your mind-ground, producing the discrimination of phantasms: you see straight as non-crooked and point to white as non-black. This *completely imagined nature* arises from every side.[2] [Due to this nature,] from the distant past to the present you have been bound to the wheel of samsara.

[2] Hence, this involves the great renunciant of the Snow Mountains [Śākyamuni]. His eyes could not endure seeing [suffering in the world]. As soon as he emerged from his mother's womb, he walked a circle in seven steps, looked in the four directions, and pointed at heaven and earth. Such a huge fuss over something that's not very unusual: he brought ultimate truth—which he'd realized millions of eons ago—to the purity-level of humans, making a total mess out of it! If you investigate this sort of amazing foundation [laid by Śākyamuni], it did not increase or decrease phantasmal dharmas one whit! Old Yunmen said: 'If at that time I had seen [Śākyamuni], I would have struck him dead with one blow of my stick—that is my excellent plan for peace in all-under-heaven.'[3] Although [Śākyamuni] 'increased the gold by doctoring it with yellow [paint],' unfortunately, in the process he added one more layer to the 'screen' of phantasm. At that time, for forty-nine years, through more than three hundred assemblies, to phantasmal questions he gave phantasmal answers. Beautiful literary style flourished [in the Buddhist community], and voices boiled up all over the place. [These voices babbled about] 'phantasmal *sudden*,' 'phantasmal *gradual*,' 'phantasmal *partial teaching*,' 'phantasmal *perfect teaching*.' Let's just put this stuff aside without discussion! At the very end of his career, he used his phantasmal hand to hold up a phantasmal flower, saying: 'I have the *the correct dharma-eye depository, the wonderful mind of nirvana*!' The result was that his disciple old Kāśyapa cracked a phantasmal smile, and henceforth on his shoulders bore the burden [of the

---

[2] The three natures (*trisvabhāva*) are a trademark of the Yogācāra school. Xuanzang's *Demonstration of Consciousness-Only* (*Cheng weishi lun* 成唯識論): "Because it everywhere calculates, it is called the *completely imagined*. There are a multitude of types of things, spoken of as 'this and that': the subject who completely imagines discriminates these unreal things. From this discrimination of this and that unreal thing, all sorts of things are completely imagined: falsely grasped aggregates, sense fields, and psycho-physical elements become essence-like differentiations of self/dharmas. These falsely grasped essence-like differentiations in their totality are called the *completely imagined nature* [*parikalpita-svabhāva*]. . . . The foundational ground of the two [i.e., grasper and grasped] in reality arises in dependence on karmic conditions. This nature is not non-existent and is called the *arising-dependent-on-something-else* [*paratantra-svabhāva*]. . . . The completely accomplished real nature of all dharmas, which is revealed by dual voidness, is called the *completely perfected* [*pariniṣpanna-svabhāva*]." [周遍計度故名遍計。品類眾多。說為彼彼。謂能遍計虛妄分別。即由彼彼虛妄分別。遍計種種所遍計物。謂所妄執蘊處界等法若我自性差別。此所妄執自性差別。總名遍計所執自性。... 二所依實託緣生。此性非無。名依他起。... 二空所顯圓滿成就諸法實性。名圓成實。] (T 1585.31.45c14–18; 46a18–19; 46b10). The *arising-dependent-on-something-else* minus the *completely imagined* equals the *completely perfected*.
[3] *Yunmen Kuangzhen chanshi guanglu* (雲門匡真禪師廣錄; T 1988.47.560b17–19).

Chan transmission]. From that time onward, one person's [i.e., Śākyamuni's] transmission of a falsehood became ten thousand persons' transmission of fact. Phantasm was in turn the cause of phantasm, in an infinite series: a transmission and reception-of-transmission without end.

[3] Then we arrive at Bodhidharma's facing a phantasmal wall at Shaolin Monastery; [Huike asking for Bodhidharma to] pacify phantasmal mind and administer confession for phantasmal transgressions; [Huike's gaining] release from phantasmal bondage; [the fifth patriarch Hongren's] asking Huineng's phantasmal name; [Shenxiu and Huineng's] composing phantasmal verses [in response to Hongren's request for each person in the assembly to write a verse]; [Huairang's] polishing a phantasmal tile [to make a mirror]; [teaching by such non-verbal methods as] dangling phantasmal feet and drooping a phantasmal fly whisk; [Baizhang's shout that] deafened Mazu's phantasmal ears [for three days]; [Linji's] slapping [Huangbo] with his phantasmal palm. From all this, we extract the demented fellow [Linji], who gave a phantasmal shout like an angry crack of thunder from the blue sky. Down to [Linji's] phantasmal *illumination* and phantasmal *function*, phantasmal *guest* and phantasmal *host*, across and athwart: *giving/snatching away, killing/giving life*, a thousand forms and ten thousand shapes.[4] There is no one who can catch even a peep of Linji's limit! Right down to the present, faceless old Chan monks of the various regions emerge from Linji's gate as successors in his line, inheriting his falsehoods and echoing them. They put the *single phantasm* into their mouths; store various phantasms in the measureless; put their sayings into refined literary language to make their Chan encounters sound skillful; make their style elevated and their tone free and unconventional; make their commands lofty and their lineage houses great. But not even one of them has been capable of going outside this phantasm!

[4] Phantasm! Its purport is perfect; its meaning full; its substance great; its function all-embracing. It has been part and parcel of the buddhas and patriarchs from beginning to end, over eons as numberless as the grains of sand of the Ganges: unfathomable! Every now and then, there are people who are incapable of understanding this *great phantasm* that lies outside of the indications left behind by words. Some [of these who lack understanding of the *great phantasm*] take a certain teacher's exposition of Chan as 'simple' and

---

[4] This is vocabulary from the *Record of Linji*. See Jeffrey L. Broughton with Elise Yoko Watanabe, *The Record of Linji: A New Translation of the* Linjilu *in the Light of Ten Japanese Zen Commentaries* (New York: Oxford University Press, 2013).

'clear.' Some take a certain teacher's exposition of Chan as 'perfect' and 'lively.' Some take this [or that Chan master] as 'eminent' or 'antique.' Some take this one as 'severe,' this one as 'meticulous,' this one as 'having literary polish,' this one as 'crude,' this one as 'lacking artistry.' They exalt [these Chan masters'] superiority and try to do imitations of them, or they despise their inferiority and discard them. They muddle up the *true pivot* [and bring it down] to the level of [mere] artifice; they reduce the *core-purport* to the level of a [mere] musical instrument. Their learning daily piles up; their assertions of *yes* or *no* daily increase more and more. The *great meaning* is daily rendered ever more perverse; the true Chan style daily declines. Little do they realize: when their predecessors, scholars who deeply comprehended this *great phantasm*, spit out a phrase or delivered a command, their simplicity and clarity was a phantasm, their perfection and lively style also a phantasm, their eminence and antique quality also a phantasm, their meticulousness also a phantasm. When we get to their nimbleness and literary polish, or their crudity and lack of artistry, all of it flows forth from the wheel of *great phantasm*. One turn of this phantasm-wheel is like a river's bursting through, or the wind's coursing through the atmosphere: totally cutting off *logical arranging* and utterly free of any selection process. It accords with the karmic propensities of the [sentient-being] vessels. At the times the ancients were killing and at the times they were giving life, if they had preserved even a speck of the affect of discriminating and seizing/rejecting—hiding such affect in their striking of students or acceptance of them—then the ancients would have been no different from poison. How could they in that case be called *nectar* or *ghee*?

[5] There are people who read widely in Chan books and memorize a lot. They desire to tally with the Patriarchal Master [Bodhidharma's] intention in coming from the West to disseminate dharma. How could the [Chan] Way of *not establishing the written word and directly pointing to the human mind* result in such a tortuous detour? If you really want to realize this dharma-gate of *great phantasm*, ask that your *whole being* directly enter therein, and immediately all obstruction, even the slightest, will disappear. If on occasion your feet dither and your mind-ground falters, you must not follow the sort of understanding that issues from verbalization: ' "Everything is a phantasm, from the outset *ready-made*!" I'll just cover my eyes with my hands and negate everything: what other practice-work could there be to carry out, what other road could there be to seek out? That's for sure!' Why do you rely on deluded feelings and consciousness, falling into a grass 'nest' [of stereotyped formulas]? The moment you want to compete with those ancients who achieved solo liberation and awakening, the distance between you and them exceeds that between

heaven and earth! Examples [of such ancients include]: Xiangyan's hearing the sound of tiles's striking against bamboo and awakening; Lingyun's seeing the peach blossoms and awakening; Taiyuan's hearing the horn and awakening; and Dongshan's crossing the river and awakening. All these figures had extinguished *furtive mind*.[5] They had escaped intellectual understanding, exhausted doer/done, forgotten gain/loss: like space fusing with space, like throwing water into water. They never tried to force things, so how could they have allowed such a thing as covering the eyes with the hands [and negating everything]? In a state of non-knowing and non-awareness, they sloughed off sense-fields: spontaneously, in both speech and silence, and movement and stillness, they were not engirded by secondary matters. Theirs was the gate of great liberation. Only those of dead mind, forgotten perception, extinguished affect, and dispelled views can enter here. If the tiniest bit of mind, thought, and cognition fails to be exhausted, even though you pass through past and present, all the while transcending verbal semblances—wishing to hold hands with the ancients in the sea of great quiescence—how would that be different from adding the light of a firefly to the sun's illumination? [The two things] are not the same type! If today you are already holding hands with the ancients and responding to *this time*, you shouldn't just talk that way and then immediately take a rest!

[6] Dip a writing-brush the size of five Mt. Sumerus into the water of the four great seas, and, on the continent of Pūrva-Videha in the East make a *direct-drop* stroke [i.e., the first stroke of the character for *phantasm*, from the left side downward: 幻 *huan*].[6] Then, on the continent Jambudvīpa in the South [where human beings reside] make a *crooked-angle* stroke [i.e., the second stroke of the character for *phantasm*, beneath the first stroke]. Slowly, on the continent Uttarakuru in the North, make a *single-dot* stroke [i.e., the third stroke of the character for *phantasm*, attached to the second stroke]. Then, turn to the continent Avaragodānīya in the West to make a *half-knife* stroke [the final stroke of the character for *phantasm*, on the right side]. *These strokes combine to form the character* **phantasm**, *which hangs at the summit of all-pervading space*: making those of the great earth who have eyes see, those with

---

[5] See Translation 3, n. 93.

[6] Robert E. Buswell Jr. and Donald S. Lopez Jr., *The Princeton Dictionary of Buddhism* (Princeton, NJ: Princeton University Press, 2014), 869: "Mt. Sumeru [= Meru] stands in the middle of the world as its axis and is eight leagues (*yogjana*) high. It is surrounded by seven mountain ranges of gold, each separated from the other by an ocean. At the foot of the seventh range, there is a great ocean, contained at the perimeter of the world by a circle of iron mountains (*cakravāda*). In this vast ocean, there are four island continents in the four cardinal directions, each flanked by two island subcontinents. The northern continent is square, the eastern semicircular, the southern triangular, and the western round."

ears hear; those with a body feel contact; those with cognition understand. You should know that the buddhas of the past a long time ago realized nirvana *in this* [i.e., *phantasm*]. The buddhas of the present right now are each completing correct awakening *in this*. The buddhas of the future will open the correct dharma-eye *in this*. Even the bodhisattvas as numerous as fine dust particles one by one are never separated from *this very locus* [of *phantasm*] as they cultivate the six perfections and produce the four minds,[7] cross over sentient-beings to nirvana and sever the bondage of suffering. Down to: among the limitless sages and worthies there is not a single one who does not rely on *this phantasm* to possess supernormal transformations and attain freedom. Why do people all day long—bending, turning, looking up, looking down, moving, being still, speaking, being silent—make visual contact with everything incessantly, *but fail to awaken on their own*? They mistakenly think that they are separated from those sages, worthies, buddhas, and patriarchs by the limitless *dharmadhātu*. They willingly sink on dry land and vainly undergo the wheel-turning of samsara. Today, just for you, I have produced the drawing of a model [i.e., the incredibly big character *phantasm*] that puts everything out there, including the 'kitchen sink!' As I said above: 'Ask that your *whole being* directly enter therein.' I have made all the calligraphic strokes and dots quite clear. Enjoyment everywhere is *ready-made*. Along with the buddhas of the three times and the patriarchs down through the ages, you will tally with both principle and phenomena, emerging from sameness and disappearing into sameness. What else could constitute a hindrance or an obstacle? Yet you still preserve observing and hearing, and you still stagnate in your accomplishments!

[7] From ancient times to the present there has never been a case of a buddha or patriarch who did not rely on the dharma-gate of *great phantasm* to obtain awakening and liberation. In addition, I would have you know: within the entirety of the *dharmadhātu*, there is neither past nor present: only sentient-beings and non-sentient things. There has never been a case of a single being who did not rely on the dharma-gate of *great phantasm* for its endowment of arising-abiding-changing-ceasing. You should know: *phantasm* has no sages or common persons; *phantasm* has no *this* and *that*. If you comprehend this phantasm, *in that* you do not see awakening and nirvana; *in this* you do not see arising-abiding-changing-ceasing. All of this phantasm-after-phantasm is perfectly filled: no duality, no dichotomy. Because there are no distinctions

---

[7] *Immeasurable minds* = *apramāṇa* (*the unlimited*): loving-kindness; compassion; empathetic joy; and equanimity.

and no interruptions, it is not a matter of stubbornly insisting on anything. The thusness of dharmas is just so. If *in this* [arising-abiding-changing-ceasing] you have not yet been able to shed the purity of white dew [of the ninth month] and leap into complete [miraculous] functioning, it is not necessary to be carelessly in a rush—just manage an iron-and-stone body-mind and display [such an attitude] for a lifetime or two!

[8] Upon the practiced *huatou that has no meaning or taste*,[8] stand perfectly still like a blind person, a block from head to foot. Be indignant in mind[9] as you keep pressing hard with [with your *huatou*]! At the very moment you are pressing hard, there is absolutely no need for you to seek any sort of understanding of the Chan Way or the *buddhadharma*. It is just like crashing into a silver mountain or iron wall. Aside from chewing on the indestructible *huatou that has no meaning or taste*, do not hunker down over any 'backup' thought! This mind of being anxious is like taking up a position at the top of a hundred-foot pole. Or, you are trying to get your footing on the face of an eighty-thousand-foot cliff: in front of you there is nothing to grab onto, behind you there is nothing to help you. Just *in that way* make [the *huatou*] fixed and stable.[10] Just *in that way* go on diligently and steadfastly.

[9] You should know: the dharma-gate of *great phantasm* lies right under your feet: having never shifted in the slightest, waiting only for your deluded feelings to be cancelled, your views extinguished, your false steps trampled into ruin. Then you will know that the occasions of Taiyuan's hearing the horn and awakening, and Dongshan's crossing the river and awakening, are not separate from *me*. When you reach this point, you must further *give a swift kick to this dharma-gate of great phantasm* that you have entered, overturning it, without leaving behind even a trace of any linkage to it. Then, for the first time, you will be a great man, quickly entering the gate of shedding [the purity

---

[8] Zhongfeng's typical phrasing for the *huatou*.

[9] This is one of the Three Essentials of Zhongfeng's teacher Gaofeng Yuanmiao. *Gaofeng Yuanmiao chanshi yulu* (高峰原妙禪師語錄): "If you are thinking of engaging in genuine Chan practice, you absolutely must possess the Three Essentials. The first essential is having the faculty of *great confidence*. You know perfectly well there is *this matter*: as if you are leaning against an unshakeable Mt. Sumeru. The second essential is the determination of *being greatly indignant*: as if you have encountered the scoundrel who killed your father, and you immediately want to cut him in two with one thrust of your sword. The third essential is having the *sensation of great uncertainty*: as if you have in secret committed an atrocious act, and this is the very moment when you are about to be exposed, but you are not yet exposed." [若謂著實參禪。決須具足三要。第一要有大信根。明知此事。如靠一座須彌山。第二要有大憤志。如遇殺父冤讐。直欲便與一刀兩段。第三要有大疑情。如暗他做了一件極事。正在欲露未露之時。] (CBETA 2019.Q3, X70, no. 1400, p. 687b5–8).

[10] It is clear this line refers to the *huatou* from a similar line in a dharma talk in the *Zhongfeng Extensive Record*: [但只靠教箇話頭穩密] (CBETA 2019.Q3, B25, no. 115, p. 745b18–19).

of autumn dew and leaping into complete miraculous functioning]. If you keep even a single joyful thought, yesterday's delusion—as it used to be—will continue. *This matter* is not something that you speak about and then immediately take a rest, nor something that you see and then take a rest. You absolutely must, from beginning to end, be the great one who is not susceptible to being caged in by a single dharma: only then will you be equal to serving as true member of the clan that bears the burden of the great dharma. The Way of the dharma is *not* something ancient. Peoples' minds are lazy, whether teachers or followers: they just go around seeking intellectual understanding about this and that. Day and night they are seduced, building up a belly-full of 'the Chan Way and the *buddhadharma*.' The [tenacious] life-faculty of samsara is what has kept them from releasing their grip as they hang from the cliff, and thereby from coming back to life from death. Once more they fall into the sea of venomous poison, never realizing their mistake. What a shame! What kind of guideline is this for the practice of Chan and study of the Way?

[10] However, I, the Head Seat, certainly am not this sort of person [who seeks intellectual understanding about this and that]. It's just that I myself am unwilling to obscure the correct karmic causes for Chan practice, all the more so for the sake of people who fortunately have not experienced this perverse error. Every one of them is an upright personage who is unwilling to fall into someone else's 'nest' [of stereotyped formulas]. [Such upright personages] have come here as followers [to my Dwelling-in-the-Phantasmal Hermitage], but here I am not a teacher who guides others—I'm not establishing my own school in a state of co-dependence with students. *In a half-bay grass-roofed room, I merely map out truth/reality to manage ordinary life.* On this point I say: 'As for the dharma-gate of *great phantasm*, if it's not marvelous awakening [that you are after], you definitely should not rush to enter this gate.' It is like my exposition of this character *phantasm* [*huan* 幻]. In both the present and the past, it is acknowledged that, if you want to search out your *single person* [i.e., *true person*] therein, then, right in the middle of this phantasm, jump up and enter; straighten your back and sit; extend your feet and walk; trust to your mind in your actions; 'let go and bring things to closure.' [This sort of] freedom in everything is extremely difficult for people. What is the reason for that? It is because their minds continue to preserve knowables, and they have never awakened to shedding [those knowables]. At every locus [they find themselves in], before they even turn around, they are bound by phantasms. The knowables they entertain, and the state of non-knowing: there is no difference at all between them! As the [Tiantai] scholars of the teachings say: 'One is provisional, and all is provisional; there is no middle or empty that

is not provisional.'[11] Under this theory, in the end, there are no dharmas left out. It is only that [the people bound by phantasms] are not awakened, and turn all this into something disseminated by written and spoken word. How could the *buddhadharma*, in the end, encompass a duality of teachings [i.e., the sutra literature] and Chan? With miraculous awakening, the teachings *are* Chan; with the preservation of knowables, Chan is [just] the teachings. Therefore, the *Perfect Awakening Sutra* says: 'Sentient-beings of the latter age hope to complete the Way. Do not order them to seek awakening—they will only increase their intellectual learning and reinforce their self-view.'[12] This saying is in peril of extinction!

[11] For example, when Preceptor Huitong [as Attendant to Niaoke] saw Niaoke blow on a hair, he at that time attained awakening;[13] when Deshan saw Longtan blow out the candle, he immediately understood the Chan personal realization.[14] Present-day people merely see the *easiness* in the awakening of such predecessors, failing to realize the *difficulties* [these predecessors] encountered prior to attaining awakening. If [present-day people] did realize the *difficulties* [these predecessors encountered prior to attaining awakening], then the *easiness* of these ancients would also be the *easiness* of present-day people. If they do not realize the *difficulties* [these predecessors encountered prior to attaining awakening] and want to imitate that sort of *easiness* [i.e., that of Huitong and Deshan above], they will not avoid deluded consciousness and will be drawn into a mere semblance of *prajñā*, piling up samsaric sense-fields and thus deepening their entrapment in samsaric wheel-turning. The *easiness* of the awakening of the ancients—let's set that aside without further discussion! But what of the *difficulties* of the time when they were not yet awakened? For example, when the second patriarch [Huike] was not yet awakened, he stood waist-deep in the snow but did not perceive the cold. He cut off the arm he was born with but did not perceive pain. His *singular manner* constitutes not only a *difficulty* for present-day people: [attaining this *singular manner*] was also a *difficulty* for the second patriarch himself! Because of the truth of his search for dharma, he forgot this *difficulty*. From the second patriarch on down, they approached teachers for the sake of the Way, and suffered pain because of the impermanence of samsara. All realized personages without

---

[11] Emended according to the underlined portion in Zhiyi's *Mohe zhiguan* (摩訶止觀): 一空一切空無假中而不空。總空觀也。一假一切假無空中而不假。總假觀也。一中一切中無空假而不中。總中觀也。即中論所說不可思議一心三觀。歷一切法亦如是。(T 1911.46.55b15–19).
[12] T 842.17.920a8–9.
[13] *Gu zunsu yulu* (古尊宿語錄): "Niaoke blew on a hair, and his Attendant [Huitong] immediately attained the purport." [鳥窠吹起布毛。侍者當下得旨。] (CBETA 2019.Q3, X68, no. 1315, p. 185c10–11).
[14] *Jingde chuandeng lu* (景德傳燈錄; T 2076.51.317b13–22).

exception endured such *difficulties* prior to their awakening. You should know: the samsara of the ancients is identical to the samsara of present-day people! The work present-day people put in to tread the Way is identical to the work the ancients put in to tread the Way! The ancients sustained true sincerity and forgot about *difficulties*: this was how they brought about their *easiness*. Present-day people chase after the false and discard *difficulty*: they invariably want to imitate just the *easiness* [of the ancients]. Therefore, within this one *buddhadharma*, though [present-day people] are the same [as the ancients] in realizing that all is phantasm, they are different [from the ancients] in terms of benefit/harm and superiority/inferiority. This is the argument of the ancients: *no easiness*!

[12] When an old granny [i.e., a kind Chan teacher] draws someone to *this* [*matter*] on a particular occasion, Way-followers who are *the real thing* call it an 'insult,' but they also call it 'the real dharma's being stitched onto someone.' They also call it 'teaching an evildoer.' They also call it 'blinding the correct-eye of the student.' Today, [chatter about] this and that is never-ending. Still, these numerous [Chan] 'public announcements' on doing practice-work are geared to the practitioner on duty who is sincere for the dharma and spontaneously treading forward step by step. But how could [such 'public announcements'] constitute a model or principle for teaching people? Such minds that 'work for dharma' are neither true nor sincere. They've neither suffered nor experienced *urgency*. Even thousands upon thousands of *upāyas* can bind them, making them grave and solemn like corpses. This is no different from blowing into a fishnet in the hope of inflating it!

[13] Other examples include Guishan's filling the post of Head Cook; Xuefeng's serving as Head of Foodstuffs; Baoshou serving as Street Fundraiser; and Yanzu's serving as Mill Master. These trifling jobs—how could true dragons and elephants [i.e., such great Chan teachers] have occupied them? In fact, it was because they were true to the Way, and forgot the polarity of base/inferior. [In comparison to] such [dragons and elephants], present-day people bear only slight wisdom. Sometimes they fill these types of jobs in the Chan community but are incompetent: they then make the mistake of waving their arms about and blaming those in charge. When we observe this sort of thing, the truth of the ancients and falsity of present-day people are crystal clear. Phantasmal people in phantasmal dharmas: they have never really awakened! Present-day [people] merely see some injustice on the road [but do not go on to draw their sword to help the party suffering the injustice]. Quite the case, I think!

[14] Having reached this point, I might just as well take the dharma-gate of *great phantasm* as explained in the past and go on piling up more disclosures [of *great phantasm*]. Past is phantasm that has already gone by. Present is phantasm that is right before your eyes. Future is phantasm that is to come. The entire Buddhist canon speaks in dependence upon phantasm. The 1,700 Chan standards, stale kudzu-verbiage, arise from phantasm. Awakening and nirvana come into being rooted in phantasm. *Tathatā* and *prajñā* rely on phantasm to appear. Kindness, compassion, joy, and equanimity are generated by phantasm. The six perfections and myriad practices are established in reliance on phantasm. The three vehicles and ten bodhisattva stages are sequences in reliance on phantasm. Morality, concentration, wisdom, greed, anger, stupidity, defilements, impermanence, samsara, and so forth emerge from phantasm; as well as light, darkness, forms, emptiness, hearing, seeing, awareness, knowing. None of them would exist without being endowed by *my phantasm*! How could *pine trees straight/brambles tangled/snow-goose white/crow black* be the only phantasm? Down to: heaven covers by phantasm; earth holds up by phantasm. The sea drenches by phantasm; spring nourishes by phantasm. Peaches are red by phantasm; plum blossoms are white by phantasm. Delusion is *difficulty* by phantasm; awakening is *easiness* by phantasm. I speak by delusion; you hear by delusion. The myriad forms are sealed by the single delusion. Within this seal of great delusion there are no surplus dharmas left over. It is just like the fly whisk in Mr. Phantasm's hand [i.e., in my hand]. Right now, put your eyebrows together with the King of Mt. Sumeru [and have a discussion]. Now, tell me: Is this phantasm? Is this not phantasm? If you say 'is phantasm,' you annoy Mr. Phantasm and fall into the net of phantasm, unable to extricate yourself for ten thousand eons! If you say 'is not phantasm,' please get rid of all polarities such as speech/silence and movement/stillness: Come right out and lay bare your *true state*!"

Translation 5
In Imitation of Hanshan's Poems in *Zhongfeng Extensive Record*

In Imitation of Hanshan's Poems

There was a guest who sought me out and asked: "*Practicing Chan* is said to be the doorway to monastic life. Chan surely cannot be known through conjecture. I simply do not know what this single word *practice* [*can* 參] means. Please explain."

I said: "The word *practice* refers to the pathways that the ancients had to use to resolve doubts in students' minds to clarify the matter of *self*. Some examples are [Huike's] pacifying mind and the repenting of transgressions; [a monk's] washing his bowl and hearing the sound of the water, and so forth. When one's uncertainty about samsara is not yet resolved, the situation is much like falling into a net and wanting to escape, or bathing in black lacquer and trying to remove the stain. [Such a person] has the countenance of looking from afar at knowledge without yet 'removing the wrapping' or 'taking off the shoes.' In his breast he feels a dangerous unease. He speaks out without thinking to ask questions, failing to tally with a single word [of the teacher]. Furthermore, he goes on to make more inquiries, only increasing the problem. At some point, he stops eating and drinking, disregards sleep, and forgets his weariness: he becomes immovable in the face of wind and rain, cold and hot, impervious to fortune/misfortune and security/danger. His thoughts of practicing fail to bring him clear discernment—endlessly! This is called *true practice*. All the rest is merely a *semblance* [of practice], not practice itself. What is a *semblance* [of practice]? It is like [a low-ranking] Stove Master[1] [carrying out his duties] at the edge of the Chan platform [in the Sangha Hall]: he absorbs a word or two of *semblance talk* [about

---

[1] Yifa, *The Origins of Buddhist Monastic Codes in China: An Annotated Translation and Study of the* Chanyuan Qinggui (Honolulu: University of Hawai'i Press, 2002), 170–171: "Although the stove master is officially appointed by the rector, he is chosen by the monks in charge of coal. On the first day of the tenth month, he lights the heating stove, and on the first day of the second month he extinguishes it. He prepares the stove before the break from the abbot's sermon and adds coal each morning before breakfast. Gauging the room temperature at all times, he adds or removes coal to maintain the desired heat."

practice], storing it away in his deluded consciousness without noticing what he is doing. In the course of time, he encounters sense-objects, and suddenly [this *semblance talk* about practice] finds its way into action. This is called 'a dependent power of intellectual knowledge.' *This is not practice.* Sometimes, from within the square booklets of Indian scriptures, he uses his clever talents to accumulate broad learning and extensive memorization. At the points where he understands, he acts in concert with various devices of the patriarchs, boring into these anecdotes and kneading them into shape. *This is not practice.* Sometimes, he follows the rules and patterns [of the Chan monastery], without violating any regulations. In stillness, silence, and serenity he does cross-legged sitting all day long, gathering in sense-objects. *This is not practice.* Sometimes, he looks for questions to propose [to the teacher], memorizing past Chan encounters [from Chan books]. In the halls and in the abbot's room, he painstakingly attacks debate opponents, employing the crazy customs of the time. *This is not practice.* Speaking generally, it is merely that, if you in your heart really lack the *correct thought* of the great matter of samsara, whether it's *only my form and shadow consoling each other* in a mountain cave [i.e., dwelling solo in a remote place] or whether it's *shoulder-to-shoulder and heel-to-heel in a vast crowd* [i.e., circulating in the marketplace], everything is simply biases in the direction of some tendency or other—and consequent attachment. *That is not what I call practice!*"

The guest also said: "In recent times honored Chan monks have taught people to produce the *sensation of great uncertainty*[2] and keep an eye on one of the *no-meaning-or-taste words* [i.e., *huatous*][3] of the ancients. Could this be called *practice*?"

I said: "Each of the patriarchs who transmitted the flame-of-the-lamp had a realization. At the beginning [of the Chan tradition, no one] had yet heard of the existence of awakening via keeping an eye on the *huatou* and producing the *sensation of uncertainty*.[4] Precisely because Chan encounters burgeoned, growing to the point of overflowing—not to mention the fact that students in their samsaric hearts were not truly *urgent in their suffering* and were not committed to crossing through the Chan gate—all these students were plagued by deceptive delusions. Because of this, those

---

[2] This is a major theme of Dahui's letters. See Translation 3, n. 27.
[3] Zhongfeng's typical phrasing for the *huatou*.
[4] The following is one of Zhongfeng's interesting generalizations about the *huatou*: the *huatou* is not found at the early stages of the Chan tradition, but, once the number of students ballooned and became impossible for teachers to handle ("spreading to the point of overflowing"), teachers could not properly attend to them and came to rely on the simple device of the *huatou*.

occupying the rank of teacher had no alternative but to take this *huatou that has no meaning or taste* and shoot it into students' consciousness-fields, putting the students in a bind where they could neither swallow [the *huatou*] nor spit it out. [Students] would gnaw on it but were unable to grind it up. They were [told to be] diligent and steadfast [with the *huatou*] right in front of their faces, like a silver mountain or iron wall. They were not allowed to forget the thought [of the *huatou*] for even a moment. After many days and months, their sense-faculties and sense-objects would suddenly become exhausted, mind and sense-fields both forgotten, unaware and unknowing: through [this method] they entered awakening. Although [the *huatou*] is not something separate from [the employment of] a skillful *upāya*, it is *near to the very meaning of practice*. Sometimes, if students do not really take the great matter of samsara as their own personal responsibility, teachers and disciples both become wheel ruts on the road, brambles in the Chan patriarchal garden, polluted dregs in the buddha sea. How could that be called *practice*? Having participated in the back-and-forth of question-and-answer sessions [with students], I subsequently drew quotations from the content of those sessions. Perchance this material became the one hundred poems of *In Imitation of Hanshan's Poems*.[5] Here

---

[5] *Hanshan's Poems* (*Hanshan shi*) has usually been treated as a Tang poetry collection by shadowy recluses, and the focus has been on questions of dating, authorship, use of colloquial (old *baihua*) language, 1960s countercultural themes, and so forth. The poems are overwhelmingly pentasyllabic octets. The standard editions are Xiang Chu, ed., *Hanshan shi zhu* (Beijing: Zhonghua shuju, 2000) and Iritani Sensuke and Matsumura Takashi, eds., *Kanzan shi*, Zen no goroku 13 (Tokyo: Chikuma shobō, 2019). There is a commentary by Hakuin Ekaku (白隠慧鶴; 1685–1768) entitled *Report of What an Icchantika [i.e., Hakuin] Has Heard About* Hanshan's Poems (*Kanzanshi sendai kimon* 寒山詩闡提記聞; published 1746). See Gōtō Kōson, ed., *Hakuin oshō zenshū* (1934–1935; repr., Tokyo: Ryūginsha, 1967), 4.27–364. Available at archive.org/details/hakuinoshozenshu04hakuuoft/page/42/mode/2up. Robert G. Henricks, trans., *The Poetry of Hanshan: A Complete, Annotated Translation of Cold Mountain* (Albany: State University of New York Press, 1990) is a reliable translation. Henricks (pp. 433–437) summarizes the themes: against greed and snobbery of the rich; against eating fish and meat; exhortative/didactic; karma; attacks on corrupt/insincere Buddhists; *carpe diem*; aristocratic ladies; wine poems; critics of Hanshan's poetry; Hanshan the mountain; joys of simple life (farming); the place where I live; the poor scholar; Daoist themes; effects of time on beauty and youth; graveyards and the netherworld; the vanity of wealth and rank; the man of worth overlooked, and so forth. For a close reading of *Cold Mountain* from a Buddhist perspective, see Paul Rouzer, *On Cold Mountain: A Buddhist Reading of the Hanshan Poems* (Seattle: University of Washington Press, 2016). Rouzer discusses the Hanshan of the Beats on pp. 3–5. A partial translation is Burton Watson, trans., *Cold Mountain: 100 Poems by the T'ang Poet Han-shan* (New York: Columbia University Press, 1970). Iriya Yoshitaka, *Gūdō to etsuraku: Chūgoku no zen to shi* (Tokyo: Iwanami shoten, 1983), 33 emphasizes that Hanshan is not a Chan monk: "However, even in the sort of poems [that use a lot of Chan terminology], he does not present himself as a propagator of Chan. He only presents himself as *this is the way I live*." Zhongfeng's *In Imitation of Hanshan's Poems* could hardly be further from a presentation of *this is the way I live*. Zhongfeng's collection is a consistent warning to Chan practitioners about what is required and what must be avoided in *practicing Chan* (*canchan* 參禪). In fact, each poem begins with the phrase *practicing Chan*. The patterns are: In practicing Chan, do not (*mo* 莫). . . .; In practicing Chan, such-and-such is proper (*yi* 宜); In practicing Chan, it is necessary to (*yao* 要). . . .; Practicing Chan is for the sake of (*wei* 為). . . .; In practicing Chan, there is no (*wu* 無). . . .; Practicing Chan is not (*fei* 非). . . .; Practicing Chan cuts off (*jue* 絕). . . .; Practicing Chan is supreme in (*zui* 最). . . .; Practicing Chan is not about (*bu* 不). . . . Zhongfeng's "imitations" are not rooted in the themes of *Hanshan's Poems*. The genre of imitation of *Hanshan's Poems* is relatively common in the *yulu* collections of Song and Yuan Chan masters.

I am not daring to engage in self-promotion. The fact is, I am pained that the Way of the *separate transmission outside the teachings* is falling into oblivion. Truly, all I want is to whip onward those with a beginner's mind."

Someone said: "The Chan approach has the principles of *live word* and *dead word*; complete raising and half-raising; capturing and releasing without bias; giving and snatching away in freedom. How could you fail to make this clear? Isn't it a little late to be wanting to bind people with 'real' dharmas [that are actually unreal]?"

I said: "In the world there are some people who are capable of striding in thousand-mile steps but to the end of their lives cannot even cross over their own threshold. I don't believe it. Those teachers who give and snatch away freedom are errorless in their practice, boundless in their awakening, profound in their power to nourish, like thousand-mile colts. They are rash and unbridled in their legs, and they have the attitude of chasing after the wind and the sun, which are unreachable: they themselves don't know this. If those teachers maintain in their hearts the [mistaken] *view* of giving and snatching away freedom, then persons and dharma would not be empty, doer and done would be in a state of association. That would be no different from Māra and followers of outsider Ways! You should know that, in the substance of true stillness, there is no basis to rely upon. The traces of this giving and snatching away freedom: they cannot possibly be explicated or studied! The slander that accrues to those who awaken but are unable to repeat the transmission: knowers of dharma fear this! Way-persons see it in the mirror!"

[1]
The single phrase *practice Chan*:
The moment you say it, you're already too late!
Just as you are about to investigate that subject heading [i.e., *practice Chan*],
Suddenly you fall into water and mud.
Propagating the *buddhadharma* has not even half a word,
Upāyas have multitudinous forks in the road.
As a little twist to lay upon my compatriots who *practice* [*Chan*],
I will chant one hundred poems.

A CBETA search turned up eighteen examples of collections that contain poems in imitation of Hanshan. One is *In Imitation of Master Hanshan's Poems: Forty-One Poems* (擬寒山子詩。四十一首) found in *Yuansou Xingduan chanshi yulu* (元叟行端禪師語錄; CBETA 2019.Q3, X71, no. 1419, pp. 537b16–538c9). Yuansou Xingduan was a contemporary of Zhongfeng (see Introduction, n. 10).

[2]

In practicing Chan, *do not become attached to cross-legged sitting*:
When sitting-in-forgetfulness, time easily passes.
With folded legs, you try to seize lightness and tranquility;
With sagging head, you go on searching in a state of indolence.
If you're not up to the task, you'll sink into emptiness,
Certainly following the unreal creations of your thoughts.
The day will never come when your mind-flower blooms:
In vain you'll wear out your sitting cushion!

[3]

In practicing Chan, *do not use intellectual knowledge*:
When intellectual knowledge is plentiful, it's "adoring the odd and playing with the strange."
Gong'ans are just your spreading your lips and teeth,
Sutra books are just your blocking up your own leather-sack body.
Raising things for discussion exhausts your innards;
Talk won't mend any fissures.
Strike the Māra of samsara!
The "black-lacquer bucket" is still unresolved.

[4]

In practicing Chan, *do not dink with playthings*:
Their flowing rays of light are fast as a drill.
How could you be willing to wade through mental pondering?
How could you allow any sort of delay?
Don't shift even for a moment—
Don't allow even the slightest gap.
Let go of your grip as you hang from a steep cliff,
Companionless in both heaven and earth!

[5]

In practicing Chan, *do not wade through objective-supports*:
Objective-supports are heavy, and you'll be dragged down by them.
The mundane Way ripens as occasion demands,
Mundane feelings day by day increase.
The circumstances for practice-work—you haven't even caught a glimpse;
The power to respond spontaneously—you have difficulty focusing.
Since early on you failed to seek out *stopping-to-rest*,
Don't be resentful toward heaven for your wheel-turning plight in samsara!

[6]

In practicing Chan, *do not allow habitual laziness*:
Laziness and the Way are mutually contradictory.
All day long be at ease,
Year after year at leisure.
Be afraid when you hear the striking of the wooden fish[6] in the corridor.
Be anxious when you hear the striking of the board in front of the Chan Hall.
In that way you'll arrive at the "[non-existent] year of the donkey":
He [i.e., you, the *true person*] opens the eye of the Way.

[7]

In practicing Chan, *do not activate thoughts*:
To activate thoughts is to lose the *upāya* [i.e., the *huatou*].
Seizing/rejecting accords with the shiftings of deluded feelings,
Attraction/repulsion follows the turnings of sense-objects.
Mustang horses try to chase after strong winds;
Wild monkeys try to grab onto lightning bolts.
Spit clings to the dirt on the ground,
The mind of stupidity will turn you into a tiny flake.

[8]

In practicing Chan, *do not violate the precepts*:
Movement and stillness alike become error and vexation.
Doing, and stopping from doing—truly you should keep them separate.
Permitted actions, and prohibited actions—how could you allow excesses here?
You should cut off all *arranging* inside and outside.
You should comprehend both self and other.
Scurry out to the *maṇi* jewel of the mind!
Its rays of light illuminate the heavenly shore.

[9]

In practicing Chan, *do not engage in choosing*:
In the whole world everything is "norms."
There is no interval between leisure and being busy.

---

[6] Yifa, *The Origins of Buddhist Monastic Codes in China*, 296.n. 21: "Various extant sources provide us with interesting explanations for the fishlike shape of this [signaling] instrument.... As it was thought that a fish never closes its eyes, it was adopted as a symbol of unrelenting vigilance and rigor."

Why have you divided up speech and silence?
If you divorce from attraction/repulsion for a single thought-moment,
The three realms [of desire, form, and non-form] will be spontaneously clear.
You're again about to ask "Why?"
In the future Maitreya will come!

[10]
In practicing Chan, *do not go along with self*:
In your actions, you must align with ultimate principle.
In your practice-work, you must take it to the limit;
In your aspiration, you must go all the way to the bottom.
In the blink of an eye, delusive thoughts are generated;
In a swarming confusion, sense-objects are aroused.
In broad daylight you're about to "plug your ears and steal a bell" [i.e., deceive
yourself]:
But it will be impossible to block the ears of the sky!

[11]
In practicing Chan, *self-assent is proper*:
In your heart you're always outspoken and taking a stand against something.
You have no intention of producing zeal—
You're spontaneously fierce.
Every single thought-moment—like a scorching fire;
Your square-inch mind—cold as ice.
When both cold and heat are forgotten,
Your gold won't revert back to unrefined ore!

[12]
In practicing Chan, *stepping backwards is proper*:
Don't trudge down the roads of other people.
You're carrying on your shoulders a board,
Dragging along a three-foot announcement.
Gain and loss—how could they be relevant?
Yes and no—disregard them both.
Instantly, you'll arrive back home:
The ten thousand forms will open the door for you!

[13]
In practicing Chan, *having the eye is proper*:
The mediocre and vulgar: take a rest from looking at them.
From a thousand miles away discern baseless critiques—
How can you push and pull a carriage with only two wheels?
See the mind of the buddhas and patriarchs:
Melt the courage of the ogres and spirits.
Be a ray of light that shimmers across the world—
Don't let your eyebrows cover up your eyes!

[14]
In practicing Chan, *simple-and-plain is proper*:
Simple-and-plain never misses in ten thousand tries.
Be a minute particle wafting through space,
Yield before the three thousand worlds.
Be ever more estranged from "talky" topics,
Be ever more compact in body-mind.
At one go you directly reach the end:
You'll be capable of squeezing juice from the woody fruits [drupes] of the jacktree!

[15]
In practicing Chan, *exerting energy is proper*:
True-Mind blood drips drop-by-drop.
Like climbing a cliff thousands of feet high,
Like engaging an enemy of ten thousand men.
At the point of death, you'll have no leisure-time for mulling things over!
When you're no longer around, there will be no regrets to bear!
If you were to suddenly raise up your head from the cold earth,
There will be nothing other than *śūnyatā*.

[16]
In practicing Chan, *the simple-and-direct pathway is proper*:
Intend only to clarify the *Self-Nature*.
Perfectly clear: neither sage nor common person;
Perfectly distinct: nothing missing or extra.
Being about to go toward [any place] is Māra!
Being about to leave [any place] turns into illness.
The Great Man who *sheds-and-deletes*
Spontaneously yokes up with every sense-object.

[17]
In practicing Chan, *as-soon-as-possible is proper*:
Should you hesitate, you'll fall into a grassy wasteland.
The cracks and shadows are constantly shifting:
How will you possibly guard your phantasmal body?
Right *here*: you don't understand!
Turn around: there's no place to look!
Send word to the people of esoteric "dark-learning"—
Don't wait for your abacus to be turned upside-down!

[18]
In practicing Chan, *impartiality-and-fairness is proper*:
Never seek the "strange and odd."
True *functioning* severs all concealments,
Ultimate principle lacks formation/disintegration.
Pull down the gate of the Chan patriarchal teachers!
Smash the stockade of Māra's army!
With your bare hands protect your household,
Banish any obstacles—every single sense-object!

[19]
In practicing Chan, *resolve is proper*:
Don't let Chan become just a "talky" topic.
In the blink of an eye: you fall into "following the old routine";
The obvious: that is not the ultimate!
Just have the desire to end samsara,
And don't be stingy with your life.
In a single step you'll connect with *śūnyatā*—
Buddhas and Māras hear the order!

[20]
In practicing Chan, *discarding-and-carving-off is proper*:
The life-faculty must be uprooted.
Livelihood: sweep it away a second time;
Life work: scrub it off again.
If for ten thought-moments you have an emptiness that is boundless,
For ten thousand ages, you'll sigh with excitement.
When you let go of a single tip of a hair,
Its radiance will swallow up the six directions.

[21]
In practicing Chan, *it is necessary to clarify principle*:
Principle is the mind-king's substance.
Principle is always practiced in association with phenomena,
And found only in the company of wisdom.
The *dharmadhātu* is its source;
The Chan River takes it as its riverbed.
The withered tree in the rear garden—
Don't try to revive it!

[22]
In practicing Chan, *it is necessary to take the direct-and-quick*:
There is nothing to fear.
In your daily rounds, cut off alienation/closeness;
In your activities, have no discrimination.
The dharma-nature has always been sameness,
Ultimate principle unbent.
The seven *tathāgatas* of the past[7]
Rode the same rut as "right now."

[23]
In practicing Chan, *it is necessary to arrive home*:
No need to be loquacious about it.
Treading on the path is free of *unripe/ripened*;
Being on the road is not a matter of *near/far*.
The square-inch of your mind is always immobile—
A step or half-step [closer to arriving home]—what's the difference?
Treading onward will wear out your straw sandals;
At the gate of your home: not yet the slanting sunlight of early evening.

[24]
In practicing Chan, *it is necessary to shed-and-delete*:
Why must you suffer *pouring too much wine* or *pouring not enough*?
You must immediately implement the principle of the Way:
As for things, follow the teachings to eradicate them!
This is not training to be insentient—

---

[7] The seven buddhas of the past are Vipaśyin, Śikhin, Viśvabhū, Krakucchanda, Kanakamuni, Kāśyapa, and Śākyamuni. The first three are the last three of the thousand buddhas of the preceding *vyūhakalpa*, and the last four are the first four of the thousand buddhas of the present *bhadrakalpa*.

Spontaneously, you'll stick to nothing!
You'll just produce another [karmic] thread
By going on pilgrimage to distant places.

[25]
In practicing Chan, *it is necessary to have zeal*:
Don't sink in stagnant water.
Move like you're walking on smooth ice,
Walk like you've come upon a great battle array.
Day and night, be "formidable" without rest:
Beginning to end, be "up" without limit.
Stick it out until your skull is dried up,
And a radiance will arise at the very end of your life!

[26]
In practicing Chan, *it is necessary to be of high elegance and antique simplicity*:
Completely taste all sorts of hardships.
Self and world are equally illusory flowers in the sky;
Fame and profit are like excrement.
Deeply pursue the Snowy Peak tracks [of Śākyamuni].
Distantly tread in the Shaolin footsteps [of Bodhidharma].
A practitioner of the Way should be like this—
No flaunting of *doer/done*!

[27]
In practicing Chan, *it is necessary that the eight consciousnesses be smashed*:
All the ten thousand things are self-created.
Glory/disgrace and *security/danger*,
Survival/annihilation and *fortune/woe*:
From the outset they are *manifest actions* [emerging from the *storehouse consciousness*],
Results caused by past karma.
Once this is perfectly clear to you,
There are no transgressions in the world.

[28]
In practicing Chan, *it is necessary to be a person of the original allotment*:
Just maintain a state of being dull-witted.
How can you go on about *cold/warm*?

How can you involve yourself in discussions?
Be steadfast like a withered wooden post,
Be just like a pile of rice in a granary.
As a *single slice* you'll love the heavenly *real*:
The heavenly *real* is never apart from your square-inch mind.

[29]
In practicing Chan, *it is necessary to be solitary and obstinate*:
The person of *plainness* does not quarrel with anyone.
In broad daylight facing the wall of *śūnyatā*,
Pure dust piles up on the antique cauldron.
When you encounter sense-objects, be unconcerned:
According with karmic conditions is no painful ascetic practice.
Last night [the antique cauldron] was heating up the sky,
And the sugar jar cracked due to the heat!

[30]
In practicing Chan, *it is necessary to have deep confidence*:
You can't follow the shallow and the near.
You intend to hang from a precipice,
Unyielding as the naked sword approaches.
Put on the robe of the ancient buddhas,
And hang from your waist the seal of the Māra King.
The source of the Way traces back to Karmic-Merit Mountain,
Everything is inherited from the pregnant mother of compassion [i.e., the good teacher].[8]

[31]
Practicing Chan is for the sake of samsara:
That's no ordinary matter!
From beginning to end,
Expel *this* and finish off *that*.
Going as far back as ten thousand eons,
Samsara has never come to a stop.
But today you're in doubt and hesitating—
Just start over again from the top!

---

[8] *Huayan Sutra*: "Good sons! The *kalyāṇamitra* [good friend/guide] is like a compassionate mother because she gives birth to Buddha offspring." [善男子。善知識者。如慈母。出生佛種故。] (T 279.10.421b25–26).

[32]

Practicing Chan is *for the sake of completing the Way*:
The Great Man should be on guard.
Xuefeng's star was about to sink,
But at Sea-Turtle Mountain Yantou swept away all Xuefeng's useless talk.[9]
Quickly do a *body-flip*:[10]
Don't get yourself into another encirclement.
Change your alignment to go on the journey:
Once you get outside the gate, all is wild grasslands!

[33]

Practicing Chan is *for the sake of jumping over*:
Get free of any wheel-ruts on the great earth.
Your square-inch mind is a pit thousands of feet deep,
Ten thousand miles of unbroken iron!
Leap to the time before Bhīṣmagarjitasvararāja Buddha—[11]
Negate those limitless eons!

---

[9] Dahui's *Zheng fayan zang* (正法眼藏): "The two [Yantou and Xuefeng] were stuck in a snowstorm at Sea-Turtle Mountain. Each day, Yantou just slept, and Xuefeng intensely applied himself to cross-legged sitting. Xuefeng called out: 'Elder brother! Elder brother! Get up! You're just concerned with sleeping.' Yantou gave a shout: 'Eat and get some sleep! Every day sitting on the Chan platform you're just like the dirt of seven villages. In the future you'll freak out the men and women of the village families.' Xuefeng touched his chest and said: 'I'm not yet secure here! I dare not deceive myself!' Yantou said: 'I mistakenly thought that on a future day you would raise the great teaching at a thatched hut on some lonely peak. Yet you still engage in this sort of talk! If things are really like this, then try to explain to me, one by one, your level of understanding.' Xuefeng said: 'When I first arrived in Zhejiang to visit Preceptor Yanguan, he raised the meaning of form and *śūnyatā*. I was able to gain an entrance [to awakening].' Yantou said: 'For the next thirty years don't raise this again!' Xuefeng said: 'And then I saw Preceptor Dongshan's verse on crossing the river and awakening to the Way. I had an awakening.' Yantou said: 'With that sort of thing, you'll never save yourself!' Xuefeng said: 'And then I asked Deshan if a student should make discriminations among the tenet-vehicles that have come down to us.' Deshan whacked Xuefeng with his stick, saying: 'What are you saying?' At this moment I suddenly experienced the falling out of the bottom of the bucket. Yantou gave a shout and said: 'Haven't you heard it said that what comes through the front gate is not the house treasure.' Xuefeng said: 'What should I do?' Yantou said: 'If in the future you want to raise the great teaching, one by one it should flow from your very own breast. Then you will cover both heaven and earth.' Xuefeng all at once had a great awakening. He did a full prostration, got up, and said several times in a row: 'Elder brother! Today for the first time at Sea-Turtle Mountain I have completed the Way! Today for the first time at Sea-Turtle Mountain I have completed the Way!'" [二人到鼇山阻雪。巖頭每日祇是打睡。雪峰一向坐禪。峯喚云。師兄師兄且起。只管打睡。頭便喝曰。噇眠去。每日牀上恰似箇七村裏土地。佗時後日魔魅人家男女去在。峯自點胷云。某甲遮裏未穩在。不敢自謾。頭曰。我將謂汝異日向孤峯頂上盤結草菴播揚大教。猶作遮箇語話。若實如此。據汝見處一一說來看。峯云。初到浙中見鹽官和尚舉色空義。得箇入處。頭曰。此去三十年切忌舉著。峯云。又因見洞山和尚過水悟道頌。有箇省處。頭曰。若恁麼。自救也未徹在。峰云。又問德山從上宗乘中事學人還有分也無。德山打一棒云。道甚麼。我此時豁然如桶底脫。頭喝曰。汝不聞道從門入者不是家珍。峰云。如何即是。頭曰。佗後若欲播揚大教。一一從自己胷襟流出將來。與我葢天葢地去。峯於言下大悟。跳下禮拜起來連聲云。師兄。今日始是鼇山成道。今日始是鼇山成道。] (CBETA 2019.Q3, X67, no. 1309, p. 603a1–20).

[10] The term *fanshen* (翻身) refers to the *transformation of the basis* (*āśraya-parāvṛtti* = *zhuanyi* 轉依) of the Yogācāra school.

[11] *Lotus Sutra*: "Formerly, immeasurable and limitless eons ago, there was a Buddha named Bhīṣmagarjitasvararāja." [乃往古昔。過無量無邊不可思議阿僧祇劫。有佛名威音王如來。] (CBETA 2019.Q3, T09, no. 262, p. 50b28–29).

Turn your head to illumine the "caltrop-adorned" bronze mirror.
An exuberant energy will enliven your appearance!

[34]
Practicing Chan is *for the sake of cutting off learning*:
Intending to do anything is a big mistake!
Wholly shed the Chan of literary writing,
Once more discard fetters of idleness.
Eliminate the snake [that is mistakenly thought to be] dead,
Smash the [divination] shell of the numinous tortoise.
With not a half-penny to dangle from your waist,
You'll [have 100,000 strings of cash and mount] a crane to fly over to [be prefect in] Yangzhou![12]

[35]
Practicing Chan is *for the sake of the ultimate*:
Enter directly into the *thunderbolt samādhi*.
Empty out the two extremes of awakening and delusion—
Combine common person and sage into the single Way.
The nocturnal moon sinks into the settled pool,
The antique mirror hangs in the great sky.
You intend to look with your eyes:
That's falling into a lapis-lazuli pit-trap![13]

[36]
Practicing Chan is the *direct pointing* [taught by Bodhidharma].
Before raising [a thought], the mind first is *let go*.
When you move your feet, there are a thousand roads to walk;
When you lift your eyes to the sky, there are thousands of miles of clouds.
Bodhidharma's *pacifying mind* is an alloy like brass,
Repenting transgressions is like adding water to milk.
The whack of the stick and the shout are as swift as the wind—
They're just for warming up the Chan courtyard!

---

[12] From the *Stories of Yin Yun* (*Yin Yun xiaoshuo* 殷芸小說) by Yin Yun 殷芸 of the Liang dynasty.
[13] *Wu deng quanshu* (五燈全書): "With feet of faith, you tumble into a lapis-lazuli pit-trap; for no reason, you smash to bits a coral branch." [信腳踏翻琉璃穽。等閒擊碎珊瑚枝] (CBETA 2019.Q3, X82, no. 1571, p. 240a18).

[37]
Practicing Chan is *for the sake of the matter of self*:
You must clarify taking hold of the self.
Don't turn your head over *gain/loss*,
Take a rest from talking about *yes/no*.
Be unwilling to stroll through little alleys and byways—
Just put your desire into seeking the Source.
When all flows from your very own heart:
Excellence beyond compare!

[38]
Practicing Chan is *for the sake of perfect-and-sudden*:
How can you possibly divide the faculties of beings into *sharp/dull*?
The grasses and trees harbor no biases—
All sentient-beings have their various allotments.
The One Dharma "seals" all situations;
The Buddhist canon is what cuts off verbal arguments.
If you are still intent on searching for "reasons,"
Then you as a Way-person have got problems!

[39]
Practicing Chan is *for the sake of seeking awakening*:
In your heart cut off all pondering.
Your only desire [in *huatou* practice] should be to smash the *sensation of uncertainty*:
Resolutely decline to go down the road of verbalization.
Forget about both eating and sleeping,
Completely disregard body-mind.
Losing your footing and stumbling as you're getting into bed,
Your bondage is severed: *as you were when born from your mother*!

[40]
Practicing Chan is *for the sake of clarifying the Chan personal realization*:
The Way does not value the attainment of "dependent" supernormal powers.[14]
The flower [Sakyamuni held up] on Vulture Peak still exists;
[Bodhidharma was buried] at Xiong Peak, but his marrow has not been exhausted.

---

[14] Supernormal powers dependent upon alchemical recipes, charms, mantras, and so forth.

When your mind is empty, the ten thousand ages of the past combine;
When your biased views disappear, the five Chan houses are all the same.
When you entertain deluded consciousness, discriminations still exist—
The Chan courtyard: so many tiers!

[41]
In practicing Chan, *there is no sharp/dull*:
Chan does not value study and learning.
Wondrous awakening lies in the sensation of *true uncertainty* [of *huatou* practice]:
Ultimate accomplishment merely produces exasperation.
You allow yourself to say: "He lacks the karmic conditions [for awakening],"
And point-blank state: "I have the allotment [for awakening]."
With a single step, the bottom of the bucket is punctured—
A tiny brow-mite[15] has swallowed primordial chaos!

[42]
In practicing Chan, *there is no past/present*:
Just don't seek extremes.
At your seat on the sitting platform, you're a solitary shadow;
In front of the window, a square-inch of hiddenness.
Keep both your aspiration and your practice secret,
Make both your achievement and your awakening deep.
Throw open the inexhaustible storehouse!
Then, every bit of dirt you pinch up will be yellow gold!

[43]
In practicing Chan, *there is no noble/base*:
No one is deficient in the least.
Secretly keeping watch over things involves true sincerity:
Tenaciously maintain only *correct thought*.
You're bored with climbing the ladder at the imperial court,
You've become disgusted with its palanquins and towers.
When awakening comes, your mind-eye will empty out—
Obviously, you won't have any view of the duality [of *noble/base*]!

---

[15] Brow-mites are said to nest in the eyelashes of mosquitoes.

[44]
In practicing Chan, *there is no rare-and-special*:
The only thing to value is a mind free of delusion.
As you encounter sense-fields, extinguish both buddhas and Māras:
Right in front of your eyes, destroy both *śūnyatā* and forms [*rūpa*].
Questions have causes—
Leave no footprints when you engage in action.
When you're never apart from the everyday and ordinary,
Your whole body will be spontaneously luminous!

[45]
In practicing Chan, *there is no such thing as skillfulness*:
Chan is not a matter of being awakened or illumined.
What you're taking as a ray of light,
From what crevice is it coming?
Buddhas and Chan patriarchs are balls of clay to play with,
Elephants and dragons [i.e., great Chan masters] are fodder to eat.
At the very bottom of the sea, the black-bearded Persian Bodhidharma
Laughs at everyone he meets!

[46]
In practicing Chan, *there are no limits*:
From ancient times to the present Chan has been called "the highest attainment."
Leap down and smash the rope-bottomed chair [you use for cross-legged sitting]!
Pick up your Chan stick and break it in two!
You must carry out the patriarchal mandate on your very own,
For it's difficult to be in the vicinity of the buddhas.
When you examine it closely,
You'll find that everything is merely *appearances*.

[47]
In practicing Chan, *there are no secret instructions* [just for initiates]:
All that is necessary is to *slice off* samsara.
Drool is constantly coming down from your mind—
Blood is constantly dripping from your eyes!
Take no break from exhausting your thoughts;
Do a thorough penetration of the teachings in your head.
Supposing you have not yet yoked with principle:
How long will it take for samsaric wheel-turning to stop?

[48]
In practicing Chan, *there are neither monks nor laypersons*:
The four fundamental qualities of the physical world all function as one axle.
For a single thought-moment, you became subject to fundamental delusion:
For ten thousand deaths, you've been constantly chasing after things.
Push open the gate of samsara—
Smash the defiled hells!
Let us go hand in hand down to the "smoky vines" [i.e., the dark place of cultivation],
Together singing the tune *Returning to My Home Village*.

[49]
In practicing Chan, *there are neither stupid persons nor wise ones*:
But you consider yourself a "lofty one."
The wise fall into false knowledge,
The stupid drop into moral indeterminacy.
Attack and destroy the two extremes—
Flip over and return to the middle path.
Pluck up the branch of brushwood
Covering up the meaning of Bodhidharma's coming from the West!

[50]
In practicing Chan, *there is neither stillness nor noisiness*:
Stop being caged in by sense-objects.
Hearing and seeing have the duality [of stillness/noisiness];
But, when you blend [stillness and noisiness], there's no pit to fall into.
"The moon has sunk to the bottom of the pond;
The wind is blowing hard at the tops of the trees!"
If you're intending to look for your home village,
The road will be long—on what day will you arrive?

[51]
Practicing Chan *is not a matter of rational study of meanings*:
How could you allow frivolous rational conjecturing?
Pull up the roots of kudzu verbiage,
Untie your bondage to verbal terminology.
The *single phrase* [i.e., the *huatou*] is the primal chaos of iron—
A thousand sages couldn't bore through it!
Miss an opportunity with your mouth, and suddenly you've bitten open
The sky, which emits an angry roar!

[52]

Practicing Chan *is not step-by-step trivialities*:
Ultimate Substance cuts off extremes.
It's impossible to employ a mind with limits
To study the unconditioned Way.
One realization is all realizations:
One understanding is all understandings.
Behold from a distance the rabbit [i.e., the Hīnayāna hearer] crossing the river:[16]
Now that's a real affliction!

[53]

Practicing Chan *is not a matter of things that can be seen*:
The visible falls into the category of *upāya*.
You're still putting up with chasing bird tracks in the sky,
You're still experiencing lightning flashes.
When the numinous mirror of mind copies all forms,
Substance-and-function will become a *single slice*.
But, if you intend to gouge out your two eyes,
The floating clouds will block out the sun's face.

[54]

Practicing Chan *is not a matter of things that can be heard*:
The questions and answers [of Chan dialogues] are futile differentiations.
In *speech/silence*, unreal shadow rolls unreal shadow into a ball;
In *letting go/gathering in*, cloud combines with cloud.
The drum of stone sounds on a clear day,
The temple-bell sends someone off in the misty evening.
If you are unable to forget both the mouth that speaks and the ear that hears,
A multitude of unreal echoes and silences will come into play.

---

[16] The simile of three animals crossing the river comes from Tiantai texts. *Daming sanzang fashu* (大明三藏法數): "The three animals crossing the river comes from the *Tiantai si jiaoyi* and the *Fahua xuanyi*.... The elephant crossing the river is like the bodhisattva.... The horse crossing the river is like the independent buddha.... The rabbit crossing the river is like the *śrāvaka*." [三獸渡河 (出天台四教儀并法華玄義)。...象渡河者喻菩薩之人也。...馬渡河者喻緣覺之人也。...兔渡河者喻聲聞之人也。] (CBETA 2019.Q3, P181, no. 1615, pp. 640b1–641a8).

[55]
Practicing Chan *is not a matter of exhortations and guidance*:
Enticing students: how could that last very long?
Transcendence must come from one's own mind;
Monastic meals are far from what the Buddha talked about.
Stride forward in one step!
Don't lag behind ten thousand other people!
If you go at it with this sort of plan,
Every step you take will be free of any "nest" [of stereotyped formulas].

[56]
Practicing Chan *is not a matter of strategy-and-tactics*:
Just lift to awareness the *first phrase* [i.e., the *huatou*].
The buddhas and patriarchs cannot steal a peek at that!
How could ogres and spirits dare to try and spy that out!
Be as still as Mt. Sumeru,
And as active as a fireball.
Everywhere cut off things that are concealed:
Right before you there is nothing to seek!

[57]
Practicing Chan *is not a matter of stopping thoughts*:
You must plan to see the Miraculous Nature for yourself.
In the blink of an eye, you fall into the orbit of sense-objects;
Disconnected, you drop into biased extremes.
Arising-and-extinguishing is the cause of unreal *tracks*—
Primal chaos has neither a back nor a front.
Right here, awaken to *non-arising*!
In sense-objects, have no truck with *upāyas*!

[58]
Practicing Chan *is not a matter of having a high opinion of oneself*:
Ultimate principle pervades both past and present.
In your searching, don't follow *them*:
Your attainment must tally with that of the Chan patriarchs.
Every phrase you utter—in tune with the song;
Every gate you enter—on the lookout for teachers.
Should you make the slightest mistake here,
Your state of wakefulness will become salt-land weeds.

[59]
Practicing Chan *is not a matter of hogwash-talk*[17]:
It is necessary to be finished with the old *gong'ans*.
Trust to your inner mind in investigating dharma—
Be like hot embers on ice in acting for others [like a bodhisattva].
The Way has always cut off the dichotomy *distant/nearby*:
How could principle allow blurriness?
If your deluded perception stalls on even the tiniest thing,
How will you be able to manage *self/them*?

[60]
Practicing Chan *is not a matter of outside-the-teachings*:
It's not *inside-the-teachings* either!
Those two are capable of blending into each other—
The one Way has neither forward nor backward.
Every single dharma coincides with the true Chan personal realization,
Every single place involves an auspicious meeting.
But, if you preserve even the least discriminative thought,
You'll run straight into Māra's army.

[61]
Practicing Chan *cuts off knowables*:
Cognitive knowing, in all cases, is self-deception.
Though you may have the numinous light of a candle in a cave,
The *thing-in-itself* belongs to the unconditioned.
The Chan stick that "whomps" blind students
Sweeps away the doubts you entertain on the sitting platform.
If you keep on preserving such *traces*,
The nodes on your branches will produce more branches.

[62]
Practicing Chan *cuts off doer/done*:
Walk alone with no companions.
You've never followed extremes,
And never set up a gate for visitors.

---

[17] Dahui favored this term *duzhuan* 杜撰. Broughton with Watanabe, *Letters of Dahui*, letter #18.3 (p. 138): "At the present time, there is a type of fellow [i.e., teachers of perverse Chan] who *talks hogwash*. They themselves don't have a stable footing, yet they just teach people to 'unify mind in stillness- sitting.' While sitting, students are taught not to voice even a sound. This faction can only be called 'truly pathetic.'" [今時有一種杜撰漢。自己腳跟下不實。只管教人攝心靜坐。坐教絕氣息。此輩名為真可憐愍。] (T 1998A.47.924c13–15).

With an empty stick, whip the iron ox—
With a phantasmal rope, pull the stone tiger along.
The Chan *mechanism* brings people to life:
But doubt kills off the Chan patriarch of Shaolin [i.e., Bodhidharma].

[63]
Practicing Chan *cuts off sage/ordinary person*:
The three realms [of desire, form, and non-form] are submerged inside this pen for livestock.
Contamination/purity: you encounter the confusions of others;
Awakening/delusion: you return to the blindness of self.
You do a handstand, your eyes like those of a high-ranking official;
You're a "red meatball" scurrying about.[18]
You want fame: it's not to be had—
Past and present: who even deigns to look at you?

[64]
Practicing Chan *cuts off stages*:
Be broad and level, straight and even.
You intend to act and are on your toes,
But you fall directly into the storehouse consciousness, mind, and the sense consciousnesses.
Throughout the three realms, you drum on the "crazy flower" [that blooms out of season]—
Over thousands and thousands of miles, you plant thorn patches.
Go on ahead and make inquiries of all the Old Teacher Wangs![19]
Oh no! What a shame!

---

[18] *Zhenzhou Linji Huizhao chanshi yulu* (鎮州臨濟慧照禪師語錄): "Spoken at a dharma-hall convocation: 'Beyond the red-meatball [mind] there is the one true person [i.e., true mind] who can't be ranked. That [true person/true mind] is constantly exiting and entering from the face-gates of all of you [like the dazzling rays of light emitted from the face-gate of a buddha]. Those of you who have not seen this with your very own eyes: Look! Look!'" [上堂云。赤肉團上有一無位真人。常從汝等諸人面門出入。未證據者看看。] (T 1985.47.496c10–11). The "red meatball" (*chi routuan* 赤肉團) is traceable to the first of the four types of mind in Guifeng Zongmi's *Chan Prolegomenon* (*Chanyuan zhuquanji duxu* 禪源諸詮集都序): "The first mind is *hṛdaya*. This means meatball mind. This is the five-viscera mind within the body. (Details in the five-viscera theory of the *Yellow Courtyard Classic*.)" [一紇利陀耶。此云肉團心。此是身中五藏心也 (具如黃庭經五藏論說也)] (T 2015.48.401c18–19).

[19] Broughton with Watanabe, *Letters of Dahui*, letter #3.6 (p. 76): "If your confidence is insufficient, then do as you please: make inquiries of the Old Master Wangs in the North and in the South. But for every *fox doubt* that any teacher resolves for you, there will always be another *fox doubt*." [若信不及。一任江北江南問王老。一狐疑了一狐疑。] (T 1998A.47.918c5–6). Mujaku Dōchū, Daie Fukaku zenji sho *kōroju* (Kyoto: Zenbunka kenkyūjo, 1997), 106 (a superb commentary on *Letters of Dahui*) glosses *fox doubt* (*hu yi* 狐疑) thus: "You ask that teacher and do not understand, and a *fox doubt* is unresolved. You ask this teacher and again don't understand, and so another *fox doubt* is unresolved. There's no end to it" [忠曰。言問彼師而未了。故狐疑未決。問此師而復未了。故狐疑未決。終無了期而已。].

[65]

Practicing Chan *cuts off any instructional materials*:
Right from the get-go don't be at a loss!
Give a shout and retreat to Zhaozhou's *wu* 無!
Go out and meet Yunmen's glare!
You're dwelling in bondage like a pearl scooting around on a tray,
You're blocked from passing through the heavenly road.
There's no need to pick up a single speck of dust,
And hand it down reverently with both hands.

[66]

Practicing Chan *cuts off the two extremes existence and non-existence*:
The Way-person isn't planning anything at all.
You're writing out Sanskrit *siddham* letters in space!
You're drawing Daoist talismans inside a dream!
Does not exist: what need is there to chase that away?
Is not non-existent: what need is there to remove that?
If you don't endorse *huatou* practice,
You'll waste your time in dead practice-work!

[67]

Practicing Chan *cuts off both true and false*:
It is impossible to find an analogy for this.
Phantasmal names and designations are merely the two extremes;
The unreal flowers in the sky are of every shade and description.[20]
The wise ones want to sweep them away—
The stupid ones are always trying to get closer to them!
In your behavior you seem to be toiling away,
But it all constitutes slander of the dharma.

[68]

Practicing Chan *cuts off cultivation-and-realization*:
The *cobra samādhi* of the Buddha amid samsara,

---

[20] *Hanshan's Poems* (寒山子詩集): "To consign oneself to being a clerk is troubling. *Worldly matters are of every shade and description.* I haven't yet been able to throw off mundane fashions. And so, they track me down for visits. Yesterday there was a memorial service for Xu Wu. Today we send off Liu San to his grave. Day after day I cannot relax. Because of this, I am disconsolate and dejected." [出身既擾擾。世事非一狀。未能捨流俗。所以相追訪。昨弔徐五死。今送劉三葬。日日不得閑。為此心悽愴。] (CBETA 2019.Q3, J20, no. B103, p. 662a9–11). See Xiang Chu, ed., *Hanshan shi zhu*, 365–366; Iritani and Matsumura, eds., *Kanzan shi*, 206–207.

The *thunderbolt cage* within the three existences [of desire, form, and non-form],
The great perfect mirror-wisdom throughout the ten directions,
Everywhere the pure dharma-body,
Tathatā as far as the eyes can see!
If you disturb even a single hair,
You'll end up yoked with the *donkey year* [i.e., an impossible year that will never come].

[69]
Practicing Chan *cuts off illumination-and-awakening*:
The Way-person *takes a rest* from conjecturing.
Smash to bits the pearl of the luminous moon!
Slice off the binding lasso of yellow gold!
Pick up the red-spotted snake!
Release the crane into the blue sky!
In going or staying, don't hesitate:
As always, you're not yet free of blunders.

[70]
Practicing Chan *cuts off unreal reflected images*:
Don't allow yourself to concoct *appearances*.
Elephants and dragons [i.e., great Chan masters] simply tread onward;
Buddhas and Chan patriarchs despise turmoil.
You search through every realm but find no *tracks*—
Who of you dares to face directly into the sun?
Should you be one of those who are praised as *awakened*,
Come here quickly and eat my Chan stick!

[71]
Practicing Chan *is the easiest thing to do*:
All that is necessary is to utterly use up *now*.
Don't concoct a dream of before you were born—
Why would you produce more branches on the nodes of branches?
When the sun shifts, flowers appear to grow higher than the stones;
When there is a break in the clouds, the moon appears on the pond.
How could there be any differences among the ten thousand dharmas?
In a life of hardship, bring into focus the *sensation of uncertainty* [of *huatou* practice].

[72]
Practicing Chan *is the most simple-and-quick*:
In your thoughts, forget arising-and-extinguishing.
Don't get caught in the birdcage of hearing and seeing—
Leap completely over verbalization.
Last night you were a "foolish and ignorant person":
This morning you've become "one of outstanding talent."
You adore this gate of liberation,
What a shame that you're not fierce and ardent!

[73]
Practicing Chan *is the most ready-made*:
Right from the outset you're not separated from it by even a thread!
A *tathāgata*'s light fills your eyes,
A bodhisattva's face fills your body.
"Perfect hearing is hearing without hearing";
"Wondrous seeing is seeing without seeing."
If you fall prey to these two heavy barriers,
You'll be like an arrow shooting into a hell!

[74]
Practicing Chan *is most efficient in saving energy*[21]:
There's no need to seek anything from others.
The strongman's shoulders flex—
The master-king's shadow flips.
When you have even the slightest doubt that is not yet dissolved,
Take care that you discern the bull's eye.
When you turn your head to look back at your native village,
It's surrounded by iron wall after iron wall!

[75]
Practicing Chan *is the broadest*:
There are no obstructions at all.
It spans across the ten directions of space—
Reaches throughout the three realms of existence.
You haven't waded through *transcendence and subtlety*—
How could you have with *hatred/attraction*?

---

[21] *Gaining energy* (*de li* 得力) and *saving energy* (*sheng li* 省力) are Dahui terms. See Broughton with Watanabe, *Letters of Dahui*, 31–32.

Momentarily you are not *in correspondence*—
Just as [countless times] before, you've been reborn in a skin bag!

[76]
Practicing Chan *is the most illumined*:
The *Great Functioning* has no norms.
You've revealed the snake of three poisons [greed, hostility, and stupidity],
You've released the robbers of the six senses.
You've created karmic causes everywhere,
And they have all become karmic merit.
Don't let the people on the streets know about this,
Lest they give rise to slander.

[77]
Practicing Chan *is the quickest liberation*:
Don't be scrawled upon by other people!
Coming and going—holding nothing back,
Outside and inside—empty and open.
When you're happy, these pairs are given—
When you're angry, these pairs are snatched away.
Don't be captivated by any place you touch:
That is called "true liberation."

[78]
Practicing Chan *is most pleasureful*:
You're not bound by the six sense-fields.
True illumination: how could there be *pondering*?
Numinous functioning: that's not karmic action [with karmic results]!
At a single place realize the unconditioned:
Finish with your training in the thousand Chan approaches.
For eons you've been falling into samsaric wheel-turning—
It's because you've been putting things off!

[79]
Practicing Chan *is the most withered-and-pale*:[22]
Forget censure and praise!
Steadfastly maintain your practice-work,

---

[22] The term *kudan* (枯淡) is associated with strict and severe living conditions in a Chan monastery, sometimes with deprivation as the norm. For instance, Dahui's *Chan Arsenal* (*Dahui Pujue chanshi zongmen wuku* 大慧普覺禪師宗門武庫): "Preceptor Yexian Sheng's Chan style was *severe-and-cold*,

Be diligent in carrying things out.
It'll be like *drinking a soup of wood-shavings*,
Or *eating a meal of iron nails*.
This mind of yours must be direct and bright:
Don't fear being burned through by emptiness!

[80]
Practicing Chan *is the most quiescent*:
Empty your square-inch mind of any rustling sounds.
Your four-elements body lodges on the Chan sitting platform,
Your two eyes hang on the corner of the wall.
The *ball of uncertainty* [of huatou practice] hasn't cracked open,
And you're vainly drilling more holes beyond the holes of your feelings.
Just make your will firm and stable:
And don't be anxious that the sun in the sky is wan.

withered-and-pale. While his Chan monks respected him, they were afraid of him. While Fushan Yuan and Tianyi Huai were wandering monks, they went on a special visit to Sheng for consultation. At that very time it was snowy and cold. Sheng cursed and evicted them—and went so far as to sprinkle water on the overnight lodging room. All the clothes became completely wet. All the other monks became angry and left. Only Yuan and Huai together folded up their sitting paraphernalia, put in order their clothes, and again took a sitting position in the lodging room. Sheng arrived and bellowed at them: "You two! Now that things have come to this pass, if you don't leave, I'll give you a whack with the stick!" Yuan stepped forward and said: "We two have come several thousand miles just to practice your Chan. How could we immediately depart because of a ladle of water sprinkled on us? Even if you beat us to death with your stick, we won't go!" Sheng laughed and said: "If you two want to practice Chan, then hang up [your things in the Monks Hall]. He went on to request Yuan to fill the position of Head Cook. The assembly had suffered from Sheng's *withered-and-pale* [style in running his monastery]. When Sheng perchance went out to the manor, Yuan stole the key, took barley flour, and made "five-flavor congee" [i.e., "congee for the eighth day of the twelfth month," the morning of the Buddha's awakening and the end of the most intense week of sitting in the Chan calendar]. Just as the congee was cooking, Sheng suddenly came back and hurried over to the Monks Hall. When the congee meal was over, sitting outside the Monks Hall, he summoned Head Cook Yuan. Yuan arrived and confessed: "In fact, I took the barley flour to boil congee. From my heart I implore the Preceptor to punish me." Sheng had Yuan calculate the cost of the barley flour, estimate the value of his robe and bowl, and return the cost. Sheng gave Yuan thirty blows of the stick and expelled him from the monastery. Yuan stayed over in the town, committing himself to the care of a Way-friend to escape, but Sheng was not satisfied. Yuan said: "If you won't countenance my returning, I only implore you to let me enter your room for consultation along with the members of the assembly." Sheng still wasn't satisfied. One day, when Sheng went out into the street, he saw Yuan standing alone in front of an inn and immediately said: "This is a room rented out by the monastery! How long have you been staying here? Have you paid your room bill?" Sheng had him calculate the rent owed and dunned him for it. Yuan, giving no appearance of objecting, got the money by doing begging rounds in town, and made repayment. Sheng again one day went into the street and saw him on his way back from doing his begging rounds. Sheng said to the assembly: "Yuan truly has the aspiration to practice Chan!" He subsequently called for his return." [葉縣省和尚嚴冷枯淡。衲子敬畏之。浮山遠天衣懷在眾時。特往參扣。正值雪寒。省訶罵驅逐。以至將水潑旦過。衣服皆濕。其他僧皆怒而去。惟懷併疊敷具整衣。復坐於旦過中。省到訶曰。爾更不去我打爾。遠近前云。某二人數千里。特來參和尚禪。豈以一杓水潑之便去。若打殺也不去。省笑曰。爾兩箇要參禪。却去挂搭。續請遠充典座。眾苦其枯淡。省偶出莊。遠竊鑰匙取油麵作五味粥。粥熟省忽歸赴堂。粥罷坐堂外令請典座。遠至首云。實取油麵煮粥。情願乞和尚責罰。省令算所直估衣鉢還訖。打三十拄杖出院。遠舍於市中。託道友解免。省不允。又曰。若不容歸。祇乞隨眾入室。亦不允。一日出街次。見遠獨於旅邸前立。乃云。此是院門房廊。爾在此住許多時。曾還租錢否。令計所欠追取。遠無難色。持鉢於市化錢還之。省又一日出街見之。持鉢歸為眾曰。遠真有意參禪。遂呼其歸。] (T 1998B.47.944a12-29). Also, *kudan* is used as an aesthetic term for a style or mode of poetry.

[81]
In practicing Chan, there is *no observing the precepts*:
Why would you go on preserving such intellectual understanding?
Your lack of introspection is your own blindness,
Your desires increase your *adoring the odd and playing with the strange*.
Samsara is a solid stockade;
The wheel of samsara has no cracks.
You sit and wait for the melting away of karmic recompense.
But what will come is your repayment of unpaid debts!

[82]
In practicing Chan, one *does not guard self*:
You insistently demand to speak about the principle of the Way.
A Mt. Sumeru of conjectures!
[The *huatou*] ***cypress tree in the courtyard***: that's it!
You are merely beating the drum of your lips and teeth—
You're unwilling to worry about samsara.
When Chan arrives on the scene, the glint in your eye sinks:
You try to bite your navel but can't reach it!

[83]
In practicing Chan, one *should not measure*:
That is following along the verbal road in a state of confusion.
As the *gong'an* ripens, keep in mind:
Master-and-disciple is a secret transmission.
The mundane Way is grabbing onto things more and more:
Aren't you concerned about *self*?
Ten volumes of the old *Transmission of the Flame-of-the-Lamp Record*,
And you turn it into a prosaic notebook listing monastic fixtures!

[84]
In practicing Chan, one *does not try to understand concepts*:
As soon as you hear something, you memorize it:
The Tuṣita heaven has *three barrier-gates*;
The Caodong house of Chan lists *five ranks*;
The *Śūraṃgama Sūtra* selects *perfect penetration*;
The *Huayan Sutras* explain the *ten stages* of the bodhisattva.
But when you get to the *huatou*, you get to the *self*:
That's the one arena where rational understanding doesn't hold!

[85]
In practicing Chan, one *does not stick to things*:
You must at once become a buddha!
Be willing to take the mind of samsara,
And bury *yes/no* in some cave.
In the past, you've fallen into following your old routine;
In the present, you're not taking much notice.
Cast your teeth out of pig iron:
With a single bite, the bone is immediately visible!

[86]
In practicing Chan, one *does not take the body into account*:
At once you should become a neighbor of death!
Empty the three times [of past, present, and future] from your square-inch of mind,
Cut off the six kinds of blood relations from your pair of eyes.
Outside your gate are all the regions beyond your native village;
There's no house-treasure sewn into your clothes.
Who gathers at the bottom of the blue sea,
Repeatedly washing away dharma dust?

[87]
In practicing Chan, one *should not be slack*:[23]
In your own mind, you must pass judgment on yourself.
Delusion and awakening are two separate roads:
Beginning and end are a single continuum.
Pick up the eight ranges of metallic mountains [that encircle the desire realm]!
Reveal your *vajra*-drill!
"Unreal magical transformations are non-stop":
Exchange this for what your eyeballs see!

[88]
Practicing Chan—*an unyielding self*:
Humans and gods all praise its beauty.
A martial-and-heroic spirit is an annoyance to the Chan community;
A true Chan style shakes up the screens and arm-rests [in the Chan Hall].
A thousand "sages" [in the Chan Hall] raise their eyes to look,

---

[23] This is a theme of Dahui's letters.

And ten thousand "numinous beings" tilt their ears to listen.
The *single phrase* [i.e., the *huatou*] cuts off all understanding,
And strikes at the marrow of Bodhidharma!

[89]
In practicing Chan, one *does not seek to be superior*:
Being superior is an illness of Chan people.
Being superior is the attitude of an *asura* [i.e., beings who wage warfare against the gods],
Being superior is Māra's military order.
Being superior is not the arena of liberation;
Being superior is the trap of wheel-turning samsara!
Only the buddhas are free of the mind of being superior;
That's why they are called "passed beyond superior."

[90]
In practicing Chan, one *does not seek fame*:
Practicing Chan is not for the sake of profit.
Practicing Chan does not wade through thinking;
Practicing Chan doesn't involve understanding meanings.
Practicing Chan is just practicing Chan!
Practicing Chan is not identical to anything.
When "practice" arrives, there is nothing that can be practiced:
You should know that Chan is indeed "a joke"!

[91]
Practicing Chan *is the highest meaning*:
Completely leaping over the ultimate and conventional truths.
[When Emperor Wu asked, "Who are you?"] Bodhidharma replied: "I don't know."
The sixth patriarch Huineng said: "I can't read."
The ancient moon illumines the forest tops,
The high wind blows beyond the peaks.
A group of children are expounding
What they call "the meaning of Bodhidharma's coming from the West."

[92]
Practicing Chan *is wanting to awaken to your mind*:
[Such awakening] embraces both the past and the present.
You look up at the vastness of the heavens,

And the end you reach is like the depths of the sea.
Reputation is severed in the three times [of past, present, and future]:
The *real* is laid bare throughout the ten directions.
Perfect limpidity contains both *śūnyatā* and forms—
A rare flower blooms in the evening forest!

[93]
Practicing Chan *is not joke discourse* [*prapañca*]:
Just desire to tally with numinous knowing.
Learning is not something you acquire from others;
Formulating is self-deception.
Refined gold has passed beyond the stage of heating;
An ancient mirror has passed beyond the stage of polishing.
If you have not yet forgotten seeing and hearing,
How could you possibly escape the conditioned realm?

[94]
In practicing Chan, *Chan has an aim*:
Once you've awakened to that aim, there's no longer any Chan!
Bodhidharma's Mt. Shaoshi is deserted: only the moon is left over.
Śākyamuni's Vulture Peak is solitary: only the sky is left.
Recognize Bodhidharma's voice that speaks of *direct pointing*.
Face Bodhidharma's shadow that talks of *single transmission*.
Seeking for the profound in the past or right now
Is a trivial pursuit to be pitied!

[95]
Practicing Chan *is a matter of karmic conditions*:
You've gone on hunts and have wandered throughout the regions.
Just awaken: daybreak on a thousand mountains.
What do you know: the hair on your temples has turned autumn white!
Practice-work just increases grasping and bondage,
Textual learning just prolongs frivolity.
You'll end up at the curtain in front of a buddha shrine,
The shrine lamp illuminating your ancient anguish!

[96]
In practicing Chan, *why the big hurry*?
You go eastward and then gallop westward.
You're running after the heavenly-*real* Buddha,

But chasing down a servant boy.
In *śūnyatā* you bestow the stick and shout upon students;
In your sandals you apply the pincers and hammer to prod them onward.
Even if you had the esoteric teachings of the immortals,
That wouldn't get you out of the impure muddied water!

[97]
In practicing Chan, *who is performing the song-and-dance?*
Bodhidharma's Mt. Shaoshi had Shenguang [i.e., the second patriarch Huike].
The snowfall was heavy and piled up to his waist;
His knife was light and with it he cut off an arm.
A "true wind" offends the great dharma,
A "heroic spirit" ruins the Chan personal realization.
Some say that, after a thousand years,
Robbers will make offerings of stolen goods in front of the Chan gate!

[98]
Practicing Chan *has no state or condition*:
State or condition lies in the Chan practitioner on duty.
Intrinsically pure: body-pervading whiteness;
Intrinsically non-existent: bone-penetrating poverty.
His mind a hanging ancient mirror,
His heart an accumulation of spring warmth.
Don't wait for your eyes to reopen—
There has never even been a single dust-mote in them!

[99]
In practicing Chan, *how does one practice?*
You absolutely must avoid prattle and chatter.
Wag your tail and submerge yourself in a jar of pickled vegetables—
Lower your head and enter a thatched hut.
Verbalization is not the *upwards*.
The non-verbal is like using a compass.
If you don't yet "get" this sort of purport,
In the front, three; and in the rear, three [i.e., this purport cannot be calculated in numbers].

[100]
In practicing Chan, *practice the inexhaustible*:
"Practicing the exhaustible"—it's not even worth discussing!
You should release cranes at Green Pine Rampart,
And look for the ox at Jade-Green River village.
Heavy rain: a road of moss;
Cloud cover: a front-gate of creeping vines.
If you are searching for a Chan practitioner,
Go home and ask the World-honored-one!

Translation 6
Song of Dwelling-in-the-Phantasmal Hermitage in *Zhongfeng Extensive Record*

Song of Dwelling-in-the-Phantasmal Hermitage

The genuine state of phantasm is stored in Dwelling-in-the-Phantasmal Hermitage. All phantasmal karmic causes enter [this hermitage] by phantasm. Phantasmal clothing and phantasmal food provide here for a phantasmal life. Phantasmal awakening and phantasmal Chan cancel phantasmal [deluded] consciousness. The six windows [of sense perception] contain the phantasmal *dharmadhātu*. Phantasmal existence and phantasmal *śūnyata* are established in dependence upon phantasm. The Master of Dwelling-in-the-Phantasmal Hermitage walks and then sits again. In stillness he keeps an eye on the phantasmal flower to produce a phantasmal result, letting go and then gathering in [students]. With a phantasmal rope, he reins in the phantasmal ox [i.e., the unchecked mind] the student is riding. At some point, the ox will come to a stop: eighty thousand phantasmal sense-objects have been squeezed into a mass. At some point, [the ox] will go to sleep: upon a single awakening to this phantasmal dream, [the student] will come to reside in the four *dhyānas*. At some points, [the ox of the student] will become active: phantasmal sea-waves will turn over and over, and the mountains will soar. At some point, [the ox] will become still: in the light of phantasmal magical-transformations, the phantasmal shadows will die down. If at some point, there is a phantasmal bodhisattva, he will come and grab phantasmal people and consult about phantasmal dharmas, [saying]: "I am phantasmal; you are phantasmal; phantasm is bottomless; phantasmal birth; phantasmal death; phantasmal nirvana." [Phantasmal things are like] holding a tortoise-hair fly whisk in Vimalakīrti's room or the Serpent King's daughter's holding a mud-ball in the palm of her hand [deep under the sea].[1] Then we have the phantasmal

---

[1] *Jingde chuandeng lu* (景德傳燈錄): "A lecture monk asked: 'I have no doubts about the three vehicles and twelve divisions of the teachings. But what is the *meaning* of Bodhidharma's coming from the West [i.e., the *meaning* of Chan]?' The Master [Sanping Yizhong 三平義忠; 781–872] said: 'A tortoise-hair fly

gong'ans[2] of Chan: with them one must *manage* phantasmal realization and phantasmal cultivation. But one must not say that such *managing* is itself phantasmal, spouting: "[*Managing*] does not exist." This very *does not exist* is nameless and phantasmal! If a student has not yet comprehended the wheel of true phantasm, then, whether this student acts or does not act, his body-mind will be going against things. Phantasmal mind will suddenly produce phantasmal Māras. Phantasmal blindness will suddenly impede the phantasmal eyes. A mirage, an empty flower in the sky, a city of the *gandharvas*, heavenly halls, hells, the term *awakening*: you ask where these phantasms arise from! Leave it to the clouds, the moon, the streams, and the mountains! You want to see the phantasmal master in his hermitage? Just come to grips with: *as usual* is incorrect!

---

whisk; a rabbit-horn staff." [講僧問。三乘十二分教某甲不疑。如何是祖師西來意。師曰。龜毛拂子兔角拄杖。] (T 51.2076.316c7-9). A couplet in *Hanshan's Poems* (寒山子詩集): "When a ball made of mud is submerged in water, then, for the first time, you will know the wisdom of *there is no meaning*." [水浸泥彈丸。方知無意智。] (CBETA 2019.Q3, J20, no. B103, p. 666b8-12). See Xiang Chu, *Hanshan shi zhu*, Vol. 1 (Beijing: Zhonghua shuju, 2000), 232-234; Iritani Sensuke and Matsumura Takashi, *Kanzan shi* (Tokyo: Chikuma shobō, 2019), 123-124.

[2] Zhongfeng is probably referring to *huatous*.

Translation 7
Cross-Legged Sitting Chan Admonitions (with Preface) in *Zhongfeng Extensive Record*

Cross-Legged Sitting Chan Admonitions (with Preface)

No Chan, no sitting; no sitting, no Chan. Nothing but Chan, nothing but sitting; and yet Chan, and yet sitting. Chan is a different name for sitting; sitting is another term for Chan. Immovable for one single thought-moment is sitting; the return of the ten thousand dharmas to the Source is Chan. Some say: "Moral discipline and concentration are the meaning of sitting, and wisdom is the meaning of Chan. It is not something that those of deluded feelings can elucidate." How could there be any gap between movement and stillness? Therefore, you should be aware that [Chan] is not separate from the four postures [of walking, standing, sitting, and lying down], and yet is not identical to the four postures.

Thus, I have composed this *Admonitions*, which says:

> The practice of Chan places value on becoming enlightened to samsara. If you don't understand samsara, everything is useless hustling and bustling about. Ultimate principle doesn't preserve even *the smallest ink traces of the written word*.[1] So, just what are [these Chan genres] called *admonitions* and *inscriptions*? Some say that in practicing Chan one *must do cross-legged sitting*. [They assert:] "Alone, firm up your backbone as if made of iron and be like a lone individual facing an enemy of ten thousand. Distraction and torpor: give them a rest, let them go!" [On the other hand,] some say that in practicing Chan one *must not do cross-legged sitting*. [They assert]: "Movement and stillness have never been two things!" Yangqi[2] for ten years beat on the defilements, passing through both dangerous defiles and the Chan patriarchal barrier-gates. Sitting and yet not sitting, his mind ran around concerning

---

[1] See Translation 3, n. 23.
[2] For a biography of Yangqi Fanghui (楊岐方會, 992–1049), see *Chanlin sengbao chuan* (禪林僧寶傳; CBETA 2019.Q3, X79, no. 1560, pp. 547c19–548b7).

external matters. He scoured his loincloth and trousers, emptying out defilements; he expended his time driving in stakes and rowing the stern-oar. His mind empty, he passed the imperial examination and knew it was time to return home. Not sitting and yet sitting, his mind returned to a state of urgency, as if a fishbone were stuck in the square-inch of his mind: hard to dislodge. When the topic became impermanence and samsara, unconsciously fresh blood would flow from his eyes. *In that way* cross-legged sitting and *in that way* Chan. Don't trouble yourself over [Chan's slogans] *direct pointing* and the *single transmission*. Loosen your bellyskin and simply *maintain*. Who bothers about such a thing as practicing for thirty years in the world of dust? *In that way* Chan and *in that way* cross-legged sitting. Even if you wear out seven sitting cushions, have the unswerving determination of a blind one. But you are willing to let your body-mind sink into laziness. Chan is precisely cross-legged sitting, and sitting is Chan. "It's one, it's two": abandon both extremes! Make your single *huatou* fixed. Cease boring into deluded consciousness and relying on deluded feelings. In sitting-Chan all that is necessary is to attain the "death" of thoughts. Today and tomorrow: *only like this*. If you are really a Great One, in just one step you will make yourself reach right to the bottom. In sitting-Chan, don't worry about whether your sitting gains a lot. A hundred years of time or a single thought-moment, the Old Man drinks the milk as if it were the great sea. It is necessary to sweep away the samsaric Māras. How could sitting-Chan possibly be easy? Don't block wisdom with cleverness. The 1700 Chan standards are decomposed kudzu vines. Why would you use mind to seek out intellectual understanding? In sitting, reach the forgetting of sitting: Chan is empty. Spit out words until they cease: the personal realization of Shaolin Chan. Just get rid of the whole mass! You'll understand before you even open your mouth. If you possess the will to do sitting-Chan, you must be *in that way*. If you are not like this, you should be ashamed. Discard essence and life; detest being tardy! The karmic causes behind the *great matter*: not something where a little will do. If you intend to use this to compose your own *Cross-Legged Sitting Chan Admonitions*, not only will you be cheating yourself, but you will also be slandering me!

Translation 8
Ten Poems on Living on a Boat in *Zhongfeng Extensive Record*

Ten Poems on Living on a Boat (1309: Composed on a Boat)

[1]
How does one restrain human emotions from day to day?
Live on a boat and trust to wherever it goes!
How have I come to be solitary—a *discard* from human society?
Due to karmic causes, a rough awkwardness is my true allotment.
My leaky boat unimpeded, in the sky [my sail] billows—
No harm in rowing with a short oar; the nearby shore shifts.
The *buddhadharma* knows something about effortlessness:
Even if the sun is broiling hot, the boat catches an assist from a puff of wind.

[2]
The light sinks into the blue-green of the water as I steer the boat:
Seems as if an ascent to the heavens would require no ladder.
The shadows of the fish follow the movement of the boat,
The distant cries of the wild geese are in time with the sound of the oar.
How many times have I waited for the moon while stopping over at North-of-the-Plums?
Or been in tune with the mists while tied up at West-of-the-Willows?
For thousands of miles, I have taken up the *teaching post* of the broad lakes:
Freely traveling there and staying over here, never losing my way!

[3]
The person is in the boat, the boat is on the water;
Water is everywhere, letting the boat proceed.
In a narrow spot of the water-lily embankment, I employ the bamboo pole;

In the deep reeds near shore, I use the oar to push off sideways.
Thousands of miles of streams and mountains, I can touch them with my
    fingers—
A single river's breeze and the moon, I welcome them.
I'm beyond the usual age for riding a reed across the river [like
    Bodhidharma].
I've never known this feeling before!

[4]
A great mansion—who knows how many "bays" wide—
Not equal to the quarters of a single small boat!
Whenever I feel like it, I tie up the boat's rope and invite the bright moon;
When it seizes me, I move my small boat to look at distant mountains.
The four seas are my home: receptive to the genuine state of phantasm;
The five lakes are my mirror: reflective of my aging face.
The *compliance/confrontation* of teaching students always involves *upāyas*:
Who has the time to open widely the barrier-gates of the buddhas and
    patriarchs?

[5]
Home is in the boat: the boat *is* home—
On the boat, *anything* is life.
The boat has a mast of rabbit horn, not wood;
The boat has a hawser of tortoise hair, not hemp.
The froth floating on the water would fill tens of thousands of gallons,
The *empty whiteness*[1] in the room [where I sit] would fill a thousand
    cartloads.
The mountain clouds and the moon's reflection on the stream
    encircle me—
My livelihood is heavenly-made: how could I possibly boast about it?

[6]
With my water pot [*kuṇḍikā*] and begging bowl, I lodge on a tiny skiff;[2]
North or south of the rivulet: I spontaneously linger or depart.
I've often chased a single cloud or hidden myself away in a wild gorge,
Or under a luminous moon passed by a gray-blue island.

---

[1] A couplet in the *Hongzhi chanshi guanglu* (宏智禪師廣錄): "Doing cross-legged sitting in the center of a ring: the locus of empty whiteness. Even though you have gone through innumerable eons, it is impossible for this to shift." [端坐環中虛白處。縱經塵劫箇難移。] (T 2001.48.84a18–19).
[2] Translations of this poem and poem #9 are found in Heller, *Illusory Abiding*, 160–162.

The mundane waves churn: it's impossible to be in the same rut with them;
The human sea surges up: who would share in that flow?
At dusk, the water and the sky are of the same color—
I shall moor at that ancient sandbank!

[7]
"A floating house that moves has no blueprints"—
Idly setting out to travel, I make this joking comment.
Wearing a straw raincoat in the drizzle: the boat accordingly gets heavy;
This itinerant Chan monk passes through the winter cold: the boat seems light as paper.
The sail is full: I know that the wind has power;
The rudder is receptive; I'm aware that the water has no feelings.
An ascetic is not accustomed to the art of handling a boat:
How many times have I lost the pair of eyes I was born with?

[8]
Upon being questioned about why I live on a boat:
"I am a single indolent Chan monk with no worldly function at all."
Throwing out a fishing line to angle for fish: not for me!
Brandishing a boat-pole to maneuver: not within my capabilities!
I pole the boat and it overturns: a thousand feet of snow;
I let go of the rudder and lose control: a gourd-full of ice.
Even if a hawser existed, it would be up in a withered cedar tree—
I lose myself in the sky and crank out kudzu verbiage!

[9]
I am too lazy to discuss the [root wisdom] of the front three or back three [i.e., the Monks Hall]:
Indeed, living on a boat beats dwelling in a hermitage.
Indeterminate locus: the *real* ten-foot square abbot's room!
Unfixed characteristic: the *live* sangha park!
At a misty village, in the country of waters, I make a dawn offering;
At a bank under the moon, flowers at the water's edge, I do evening practice.
Sometimes guests come and knock on the boat to inquire about the Way:
This ascetic has no need to mutter on about such things!

[10]
This boat's *no-mind* is like my *no-mind*:
I and the boat are friends in cutting off past and present.
Before sea foam has arisen, I take the rudder in hand;
As the boat approaches shore, I don't try to steer it.
I give the stage to wind and moon: the boat is the three karmas [of body, speech, and mind];
I strum and fret the rivers and lakes: the oar is my one arm [of Huike].
I wander all over the place on the unrelenting flow of the Chan River—
The *huatou*: *from all this* it trickled down to the Chan community!

Translation 9
Ten Poems on Living in Town in *Zhongfeng Extensive Record*

Ten Poems on Living in Town (Composed in Bianliang/Kaifeng)

[1]
The ancients praised the Great Recluse [the Buddha] for living in town,[1]
With lanes of willows and flowered thoroughfares, flutes and string instruments.
After all, the visual forms [of the town] before you: there is no dharma separate from them;
Therefore, beyond the sounds [of the town]: there is the [soundless] Chan *single transmission*.
On brocaded lanes, at the breaking of dawn, golden stirrups sound out;
On embroidered roads, at springtime, people sport hairpins with kingfisher feathers.

---

[1] There is no mention in the biographical sources of Zhongfeng's going to the city of Bianliang (i.e., Kaifeng). Cishou Huaishen (慈受懷深; 1077–1132), before the destruction of the capital Kaifeng in the Song-Jin conflict, describes the city as follows: "a noisy city of red dust, a cave of tigers or palace of Māra." [紅塵鬧市。虎穴魔宮]. (慈受懷深禪師廣錄; CBETA 2019.Q3, X73, no. 1451, p. 93a13). Quoted in Jason Protass, *The Poetry Demon: Song-Dynasty Monks on Verse and the Way* (Honolulu: University of Hawai'i Press, 2021), 217. Heller, *Illusory Abiding*, 159, n. 59 says of the Bianliang connection: "This is problematic, as Mingben stayed largely in the Zhejiang area and a trip to Kaifeng is not noted elsewhere." Though some Japanese students of Zhongfeng, such as Gōkai Honjō (業海本淨;?–1352) and Jakushitsu Genkō (寂室元光; 1290–1367), after returning to Japan remained utterly faithful to Zhongfeng's reclusive mountain style and shunned the big Zen establishments (at least until the final stage of their careers), the theme of these ten poems, "recluse in town" or "hermit in the town/marketplace," had substantial influence on some of the Zen monks of the elite metropolitan Gozan monasteries of Kyoto and Kamakura. Joseph D. Parker, *Zen Buddhist Landscape Arts of Early Muromachi Japan (1336–1573)* (Albany: State University of New York Press, 1999), 138: "The Kitayama monks [in Kyoto] applied the landscape to their lives in a variety of ways, but one of the most important in landscape-painting inscriptions was the theme of 'the hermit at court' or the 'hermit in the marketplace.' Through developing this theme in terms meaningful for their lives inside and outside the walls of the Five Mountains monastic complexes, the Kitayama monks were integrating images of nature with those of culture, of the natural world and recluse poets with life at court and textual study." Some of these Kitayama Zen monks were behind the printing of the Chan records of Zhongfeng, including the four sets of poems on boat living, mountain living, living on the water, and town living. For translations of this poem and poems #5, #8, #9, and #10, see Heller, *Illusory Abiding*, 167–172.

Who is right before your eyes—do you know clearly?
Vacantly chasing after this sort of thing is truly pitiful!

[2]
The green rivers and blue mountains are visual sense-objects:
When your mind is empty, how could you possibly get near to them?
Since you have no worldly pursuits, you can bear adapting to the unrefined—
Living in town is the closest thing "to the *real*!"
The streets with shops sealed by moonlight connect to back lanes,
The teahouse on the east connects to the western neighborhood.
The patrons who come have no need for discourses on Linji's formula of guest/host—
Fine ancient "seal-script" calligraphy fills the residences in spring.

[3]
Footprints without limit are everywhere at the seashore—
Ready-made mountains and rivers won't put up with boasting.
The market-town: it's okay for me to store my monk's tin staff there;
The city: there's no harm in its serving as my home.
The four walls are transparent, connecting the roof to the moonlight;
The numerous pillars are red and white, surpassing the hedges of flowers.
A seeing and hearing that doesn't rely on keeping up *upāyas*:
I just follow karmic conditions to banish the passing of time.

[4]
How does living in the mountains resemble living in town?
I am in a state of no-mind toward the sense-objects of both: composed.
Calling card in hand, I advance: a drinking establishment;
I ring the doorbell: a tavern's sign in front.
Drowning in great dreams: I'm quite adept at that!
Confused by empty terms: I've not quite gotten rid of that!
In broad daylight a mendicant without any plan—
Outside my gate the grass is deep, but I'm too lazy to weed it!

[5]
Samsaric arising-and-disappearing goes round and round: what's it like?
Ten-thousand kinds of cosmetics: the *sahā* world [i.e., this world system].
Flourishing at the imperial court: a dream during the third watch of the night;

A lifespan of one-hundred years: a single moment.
The pavilions are so high they play with the moon, and the streets go on forever;
The sounds of the flower sellers are right at hand, the markets and bridges plentiful.
This ascetic practitioner is satisfied with the town-living mode—
I laugh at those [mountain recluses] who hide away midst the vines and creepers.

[6]
A Chan summer rainy season retreat in the town marketplace is one of complete freedom:
A hundred *ready-made* Chan *gong'ans* that cut off rushing about seeking!
Sellers of green cabbages and purple mustard seeds clog up the streets,
Stocks of white rice and blue-gray firewood are stacked against the doors.
For the twenty-four hours of the day, people have enough to make a living;
For thousands of years, conditions for the Way have been universal.
If you preserve mistaken views about things outside your mind,
You are guaranteeing you'll pin the tail on the "year of the donkey" [i.e., a non-existent year]!

[7]
The mountains and the rivers: I've been there and done that;
I've moved around a lot, and I got tired of the noisiness of traveling sedan-chairs.
The jumble of human shadows: a babbling bedlam—
The confusion of marketplace sounds: in full swing!
The lantern lights of a thousand pavilions mark the way:
The songs of thousands of woodwind instruments serve as a guide.
I take delight in *dhūta* [austerities] and disregard *engirding mind*:[2]
The limitless *dharmadhātu* is sameness-practice!

---

[2] *General Sermons of Chan Master Dahui Pujue* (大慧普覺禪師普說): "Members of the scholar-official class, in studying the Way, don't get beyond two wrong branches in the road. One is [effortfully] *quelling delusive thought*; the other is [effortfully] *concentrating mind*. *Concentrating mind* is what the perverse hogwash teachers call *engirding mind*. *Quelling delusive thought* is what the perverse hogwash teachers call *silence-as-illumination*. If these two illnesses, *engirding mind* and *silence-as-illumination* are not eliminated, you'll never be capable of escaping samsara!" [士大夫學道。不出二種歧路。一曰忘懷。一曰著意。所謂著意者。杜撰長老喚作管帶是也。忘懷者。杜撰長老喚作默照是也。管帶默照二種病不除。則不能出生死。] (CBETA 2019.Q3, M059, no. 1540, p. 961b17–19). Thus, the term *guandai* (管帶) = *to keep the mind secured, as with a girdle*. See Broughton with Watanabe, *Letters of Dahui*, 17–19.

[8]
Living in the mountains eliminates suffering—there are no human relationships.
I'm not living in the mountains: I'm training to be a *recluse in town.*
A new bondage: my sitting cushion invades the visual forms of the marketplace—
A shift in routine: my Chan backrest is near the smoke of kitchen chimneys.
The sun is warm among the flowers in the courtyard, embracing the birds of spring;
The wind is strong in the eaves and trees, agitating the evening cicadas.
The begging bowl is common to all monks: [as a monk in town] I'm like snow out of season—
[In town] who will have in common with me the watering of the mind-field?

[9]
Living in town, I don't need to spend money to buy mountain land—
The scenery here is more than the eye can take in, and my mind is at ease.
A roan horse with a black mane and tail: the trample of its hoof beats;
A butterfly playing in the cloudless sky: the effortless glide of its wings.
I experience the forgetting of sense-objects: there is no need to effortfully banish them;
Grasping is fading away, and my mind is always fused with the *natural.*
For how many eons have I been going back and forth in samsara this way?
It's certainly hard to transmit the *true state* to others!

[10]
The town marketplace, at a site selected by divination, is near to the Way!
Every single aspect tallies with Original Reality.
If you have the slightest thought of "getting something," you're pulled in by Māra:
If you intend to preserve any "fixed thought," demons are in your neighborhood!
In the monastery, a prohibition against nocturnal walks: the temple bell's ringing is nearby;

In the alleys of town, a hastening of the coming year: the drum rolls are urgent.
The discourses on dharma characteristics of the *tathāgatas* of the three times
Are at one time new, and then new all over again!

Translation 10
Selections from *Zhongfeng Dharma Talks* in *Zhongfeng Record B*

[1] Instruction to a Chan Person

Superior person! If you want to leap over samsara, in your daily activities directly execute *that chess move!*[1] Do not ask whether you are gaining energy or not gaining energy.[2] For ten thousand eons, a thousand lifetimes, just be *like this*. When you can't raise [the *huatou*] to awareness, fiercely rally [the *huatou*]! When you can't lift [the *huatou*] to awareness, you simply must lift it up! Whatever you do, don't remain in a state of ease: ease is not the purport for which Bodhidharma came from the West. Don't even care about losing your life! As soon as you care about losing your life, you've lost the correct principle. You must not sit inside such dichotomies as *stillness/noisiness* or *idleness/busyness*. When you are hearing, seeing, and being aware, just constantly make a *single thought* [i.e., the *huatou*] sever every support you have. It's not only a matter of forgetting any anger: you must also forget any delight. But being ordinarily in tune with this forgetting is itself to be forgotten! With feet of confidence tread over the waters of the Eastern Sea! Denial does not deny; affirmation does not affirm. If you are off by even a tiny bit here, you'll be missing by a thousand miles!

***

---

[1] Broughton with Watanabe, *Letters of Dahui*, letter #16.5 (p. 134): "I imagine that you are meeting the Participant in Determining Governmental Matters [Li Hanlao] on a day-to-day basis. Other than the board game of chess, have you been discussing these sorts of things with him? If you're merely playing chess and haven't talked about these sorts of things—right when the black and white stones are not yet divided up, overturn the board, and scatter the stones! Then question him. Seek out *that single chess move!*" [參政公想日日相會。除圍棋外。還曾與說著這般事否。若只圍棋。不曾說著這般事。只就黑白未分處。掀了盤。撒了子。却問他。索取那一著。(T 1998A.47.924b1–5). Mujaku Dōchū, Daie Fukaku zenji sho *kōrōju* (Kyoto: Zenbunka kenkyūjo, 1997), 209 (a commentary on *Letters of Dahui*) glosses *that single chess move* (*na yi zhuo* 那一著) thus: "That single chess move of *Aah!*" [忠曰。囚下一著子也]. *Aah!* is the sound one emits upon awakening.

[2] *Gaining energy* (*de li* 得力) is another Dahui term. See Broughton with Watanabe, *Letters of Dahui*, 31–32.

[2] Instruction to a Sŏn Person ([Korean] Head Librarian Ung)

Doing practice-work only involves a mind of confidence: knowing with confidence that there is this *great matter*.[3] Raise to awareness the *huatou* that you are practicing, and day and night just go on practicing in that way! At the very moment you are practicing, there are no such principles as *pure oneness/no pure oneness* or *gaining energy/not gaining energy*. *Pure oneness* and *gaining energy* are both forms of false awareness. It is not the case that *this matter* "really" exists somewhere within the borders of your practice-work. When you are raising the *huatou* in your practice, it's just a single *there's-no-alternative*! There should be no "backup" object of sense perception. If today you're not able to practice, today *there's-no-alternative*. If tomorrow you're not able to practice, tomorrow *there's-no-alternative*. Down to: if for thirty years you're not able to practice, it's just one big *there's-no-alternative*. Perhaps you've not yet reached the point of awakening: if you have even a half of a speck of a thought of, *how do I do it*, the whole shebang falls into delusive calculation—this isn't true practice-work! *This matter* must face off against the *great matter of samsara*. [Chan's *this matter*] is not a mundane thing that can be studied, or sought after, or to which you can apply mental effort. Practicing Chan is like chewing on an iron spike: At the very moment you are chewing, where is there any *how-do-I-do-it*? If you can endure quite a bit of *there's-no-alternative*, then you will immediately possess the tenacity of a Way-person of strength and application. Head Librarian Ung of Korea asked for a few words of a "warning whip," and so I impart to him these words with my writing brush.

***

[3] Instruction to a Chan Person

Practicing Chan involves no karmic effort whatsoever! All you need is a single correct thought for the *great matter of samsara*. With genuine earnestness raise to awareness the *huatou* you are practicing. There's no need for *zeal*, or *torpor/distraction*, or *comparing*. Get rid of mental evaluations, which transform into distraction. Just seek out stability and abide therein. Don't ask about the passing of the years or months. If you have just one day's worth of spirit,

---

[3] Ung is unidentified.

then practice for one day: Over a long time, don't change, don't alter. When unconsciously you naturally come upon awakening, it will be like *before you attained awakening*! You absolutely must not employ the storehouse consciousness, defiled mind, and sense consciousnesses to conjecture about any principles of the *buddhadharma*. Don't be worried about your not establishing karma in line with [advancing in] the Way. Strive! Old Man Phantasm delivers this teaching.

***

[4] Instructions to Head Seat Yŏn of Korea

In practice-work[4] we speak of giving rise to the *sensation of uncertainty*.[5] You should know that the sensation of uncertainty, right from the start, involves no guidance, no specific posture, no specific awareness, no "handle," no personal inclination, no *upāya*, no effortful doing or arranging things: it involves no separate rationale. If you can get rid of [all these approaches], it will enable you to produce *[the sensation of] uncertainty*. What is called *uncertainty* is nothing other than the single *great matter of samsara* that you have never clarified for yourself: just uncertainty about this *great matter of samsara*. Why [does samsara] come from innumerable eons in the distant past, flowing down to the present? What is the clue? From today it will flow into the future. Does it have any definite end? *Just this* is the locus of uncertainty. From of old, the buddhas and patriarchs all conformed to this uncertainty: their uncertainty about [samsara] was neverending. When spontaneously your mind-road is severed, delusion melts away, intellectual knowledge is exhausted, *doer/done* is forgotten, and without being aware of it, you undergo a sudden yoking-up: this is the time when the *sensation of uncertainty* is smashed. The ancients of olden times never discarded the pattern of keeping an eye on the *huatou*, practicing the *gong'an*, and getting up on the sitting cushion [for cross-legged sitting]. This is of the utmost urgency! Just bring your uncertainty to bear upon the *great matter of samsara*! After going three thousand or five thousand miles [on pilgrimage], you encounter someone. Before you've even taken off your straw sandals, you instantly ask him: "I [am on pilgrimage] for the sake of *samsara is the great matter, and impermanence is swift.*"

---

[4] Yŏn is unidentified.
[5] This is a major theme of Dahui's letters. See Translation 3, n. 25.

Thousands upon thousands of people have left home like this, walking on pilgrimage like this. They have sought out people [as guides] like this. They have studied the Way like this. They never acted for the sake of any sort of "backup" matter. Even if there had been [such a "backup" matter], they would not have acted for the sake of such a thing. Later generations of the Chan school should not have a lot of announcement bulletins [i.e., clear-cut, obvious statements] or kudzu vines [i.e., entangling verbiage]. Often, before a Chan monk's feet have stepped through the gate [of a Chan monastery], he is seduced by some type of verbalization and has fallen into the stereotyped formulas of kudzu, calling it the "*buddhadharma*" or the "Chan Way." He washes into the net of intellectual knowledge and is unable to extricate himself. He learns more and more, and this becomes a hindrance to *knowing*. He has never really had any true relationship to the Way! The eyes of honored Chan monks of recent times cannot bear to look at this sort of corrupt practice in the Chan community. Before you have even opened your mouth, just use the *huatou that has no meaning or taste*[6] to sweep away what is right in front of your face! All that is needed is for you to throw away all your mundane objective supports and miscellaneous thoughts, including "Chan Way," *buddhadharma*, "spoken and written words," and so forth. Just make yourself produce the *sensation of great uncertainty* about this *huatou* and go on practicing! At the very moment you are practicing, there's no need for you to practice by clarifying the *buddhadharma*. There's no need for you to practice by coming to understanding the Chan Way. There's no need for you to practice by seeking for an all-encompassing intellectual knowledge. As for the application of your mind to practice, there's no alternative: you yourself have the *great matter of the impermanence of samsara*. Therefore, when your practice reaches the point at which the *huatou* is smashed, then the *great matter of samsara* will be smashed right along with it. [When your practice reaches] the point at which you are enlightened about the *great matter of samsara*, then you'll be enlightened about all examples the written and spoken word right along with it. Beyond samsara no separate *huatou*; beyond the *huatou* no separate samsara. *Though the ancients of the past awakened to the Way by having the [sensation of] uncertainty about samsara, today's [Chan] people awaken to the Way by having the [sensation of] uncertainty about the* huatou.[7] The things about which they entertain the [sensation of] uncertainty are both similar and different. But in the case of the Way they awaken to, there is no ancient or present: no real difference whatsoever. At the very moment you are having [the sensation of]

---

[6] Zhongfeng's typical phrasing for the *huatou*.
[7] This italicized line is one of Zhongfeng's insightful generalizations about the *huatou*.

uncertainty about the *huatou*, don't seek for any *upāya*. You must believe that practicing Chan involves no *upāyas*. And don't seek for something to which you have a personal inclination. You must realize that practicing Chan doesn't involve personal inclination. And don't seek for any "handle." You must realize that practicing Chan involves no "handles." What we refer to as *upāya* is precisely the *huatou*. *Upāya is* the *huatou*. Personal inclination [*is* the *huatou*]. "Handle" [*is* the *huatou*]. All you need is to have enough confidence to rest in stability. In this lifetime practice of the *huatou*: decide that you need to hammer home penetration of this *huatou*! If you've not yet hammered it home, there's never been any obstacle to your doing so. It's just that you yourself lack a sort of fierceness, lack a sort of firmness, lack an attitude of non-retrogression, lack enough confidence. Grab [the *huatou*] tightly! If you can just grab tightly this correct thought of practicing the *huatou*, pay no heed to any *torpor/distraction*. Pay no heed to [such dichotomies as] *movement/stillness* and *talk/silence*. Pay no heed to *birth–old age–illness–death*. Pay no heed to *pain/pleasure* and *what goes along with you/what goes against you*. Pay no heed to *achievement/no achievement*, and so forth. Down to: eliminate anything beyond this correct thought of practicing the *huatou*. Even if the buddhas of the three times and the Chan patriarchs down through the generations simultaneously appear right in front of you, even if the truth of the highest meaning and the essence of the unexcelled dharma pour down into you mind, you must at that very moment vomit them out. Pay no heed to them: *this matter* does not lie with the buddhas and patriarchs, does not lie with sense-objects, does not lie with the written word, does not lie with intellectual knowledge. It lies only in your having sufficient confidence in the ultimate locus of the *great matter of samsaric impermanence*. Therefore, there is no alternative to this samsara. Practice the *huatou* of the ancients: get rid of anything beyond the single thought of practicing the *huatou* of the ancients. And if you intend to investigate any "backup" thought [i.e., thought other than the *huatou*], this will be like trying to sweep away the waves to get to the water. An ancient said: "[If you understand,] the secret is at your side."[8] Also: "There is not a single dharma to give others."[9] As for [any sort of] learning and maintaining [what you have learned], all I am teaching you today is to keep an eye on this *huatou*! You must not stop! If you detach from this *huatou* and

---

[8] A saying found in many Chan texts. For instance, *Foguo Keqin chanshi xinyao* (佛果克勤禪師心要): "If you understand, then the secret is at your side." [汝若會即密在汝邊矣。] (CBETA 2019.Q3, X69, no. 1357, p. 471c8).

[9] A common saying in Chan texts. For instance, *Yuansou Xingduan chanshi yulu* (元叟行端禪師語錄): "Our Chan school has no verbalization. And it does not have a single dharma to give others." [我宗無語句。亦無一法與人。] (CBETA 2019.Q3, X71, no. 1419, p. 531a14).

produce some other thought or calculation, you'll roll right into a situation where you have no relationship [to awakening]. After some time, when your practice-work [on the *huatou*] has ripened and the appropriate time has arrived, the *sensation of uncertainty* will be smashed. You must realize that uncertainty and practice, in combination with this *huatou*, enact a return to *self*. Further, there is not a single dharma that confronts your deluded feelings; there is not a single dharma for you to understand or not understand. Therefore, it is said in the teachings: "The myriad forms are sealed by the single dharma."[10] *But there is no way to inquire into this single dharma: this is the reason why the* huatou *exists.*[11] Just possess a mind willing [to plant buddha-seeds], and you certainly won't be deceived.[12] Sŏn person Yŏn of Korea daily resided in the Monks Hall. Because he has not yet penetrated to keeping an eye on the *huatou* [i.e., has not yet attained proficiency in *huatou* practice], he produced writing paper for an instruction by me. I directly took my writing-brush to provide this answer for him.

***

[5] Instruction to Head Fu

According to what you have said, twenty-four hours a day you are unable to function as *Head*.[13] [This is because] you do not know how to eliminate everything beyond the *huatou* that you are practicing. And, for that matter, what are you referring to with your phrase *functioning as Head*? You should know that this *huatou* is [*functioning as Head*]! Just constantly make this *huatou* that you are practicing inseparable from your thoughts: then you'll immediately be able to *function as Head*. And you shouldn't produce any notion of *being able to function as Head*. In the great aspiration of the ancients there was never any discourse about *functioning as Head*. As Guishan said: "Forcibly function as *controller*; don't fall in with human feelings."[14] Recycling other people's talk about zeal is not the Way!

---

[10] Yanshou's *Zongjinglu* (宗鏡錄): "As the verse in the *Dharma Lines Sutra* says: 'The myriad forms are sealed by the single dharma.'" [如法句經頌云。森羅及萬像。一法之所印。] (T 2016.48.584a25–26).

[11] This is another of Zhongfeng's generalizations about the *huatou*.

[12] A saying favored by Dahui. See Broughton with Watanabe, *Letters of Dahui*, letter #16.2 (p. 131): "Just possess a mind willing [to plant buddha-seeds], and you certainly won't be deceived." [但辦肯心。必不相賺。] (T 1998A.47. 924a6–7).

[13] Fu is unidentified.

[14] *Guishan jingce zhu* (溈山警策註; CBETA 2019.Q3, X63, no. 1239, p. 229c20).

Also: The discourse of keeping an eye on the *huatou* in the midst of *torpor/distraction, yes/no, things that go against you/things that go along with you*: this discourse has never involved any difficult-to-fathom principle. It's natural that you can't understand it since you forcibly try to produce *knowing*. For instance, at the very moment you are keeping an eye on the *huatou*, you should rouse your spirit and, in the middle of *torpor/distraction* and *things that go against you/things that go along with you*, keep an eye [on the *huatou*]. Over time, *torpor/distraction, things that go against you/ things that go along with you*, and deluded feelings will melt away. There are people who, when they see appear before their eyes these situations of *torpor/distraction* and *things that go against one/things that go along with one*, quickly give rise to false doubt, saying: "After all, is there any other *upāya*, by which I might remove these habit-energies of *torpor/distraction* and so forth?" [This reaction] puts the blame on the capacity of faculties, karma inherited from the past, and all sorts of sense-objects. As soon as they produce such a thought, they've immediately added another layer of *torpor/distraction* to the *torpor/distraction* already present. In the middle of the *things that go against one/things that go along with one*, they've increased the *things that go against/things that go along*! Therefore, I teach you the following: at the very moment you experience *torpor/distraction*, right on top of that very *torpor/distraction*, just keep an eye on [your *huatou*]. But there's no *something* that you can keep your eye on. It's also not the case that you keep your eye on *torpor/distraction* as if it were a *something*. I also don't teach you to try to find some handhold in the *torpor/distraction* and *things that go against you/things that go along with you*. I only teach you: on top of the *torpor/distraction* and so forth, simply raise to awareness the *huatou* and keep an eye on it. Never let it go! Also, don't falsely produce any "backup" discriminations: "This is *torpor/distraction, things that go against me/things that go along with me*, and so forth; this is not *torpor/distraction, things that go against me/things that go along with me*, and so forth." In general, all that is necessary for doing practice-work is to awaken to the *huatou*. There is no need for you to push away *torpor/distraction* and so forth. You should merely painfully remember the *great matter of samsaric impermanence* and simply raise the *huatou* to awareness. Produce the *sensation of great uncertainty*[15] to seek for correct awakening. Merely be earnest in thinking about samsara: spontaneously your *huatou* practice will be meticulous! When your keeping an eye on the *huatou* is meticulous, *torpor/distraction* and so forth will spontaneously fail to appear. Whenever you are doing practice-work

---

[15] This is a major theme of Dahui's letters. See Translation 3, n. 27.

and you see the existence of *torpor/distraction* and so forth, it is precisely because your thought of samsara is not urgent enough, and you are not intimate enough with keeping an eye on the *huatou*!

Also: When on top of the *huatou* you produce *[the sensation of] uncertainty*, I fear you may fall into a discourse of mental reflection. That would be an error! When the ancients had not yet resolved this *great matter of samsara*, for twenty or thirty years, for thousands and thousands of miles [on pilgrimage], they would immediately say to whomever they met: "I am acting for the sake of the *great matter of samsara*!" What about keeping an eye on the *huatou* and producing *[the sensation of] uncertainty*? Though [the ancients] didn't keep an eye on the *huatou* nor produce *[the sensation of] uncertainty*, their single thought *I've not yet resolved the great matter of samsara* was *their very own locus of uncertainty*! In recent times, people training [in Chan], sad to say, don't consider samsara to be *the matter*. The situation is exacerbated by the fact that this Chan school of ours is flourishing and its sayings multiplying. When [a Chan monk's] feet have just walked through the gate [of a Chan monastery], the first thing he does is to assign himself the job of memorizing Chan sayings. There is a yawning gap between him and grasping the correct thought of acting for the sake of [the *great matter*] *of samsara*. Honored Chan monks of recent times have not been able to do stop doing this. Take this *huatou that has no meaning or taste*[16] and in the blink of an eye put it into the field of your eight consciousnesses: this will make you remove all your intellectual knowledge. *Simply focus your uncertainty upon the fact that you do not understand this* huatou! The uncertainty you experience will be like colliding with a silver mountain or iron wall. You won't be able to advance even one inch. As soon as you produce any "backup" thought, you've fallen into mental reflection. Not producing any "backup" thought: that alone *is* the sensation of uncertainty. In the middle of this sensation of uncertainty, spontaneously sever all the illnesses of knowing and intellectual understanding. Suddenly, at the very locus where you experience this uncertainty, you'll do a *flip*, and then you'll *know* what these sayings and phrases of the ancients were talking about. Truly, you'll have [at your disposal] a great ball of fire or a sword than severs a falling feather. You mustn't commit an infraction. Just muster a mind of confidence. You'll understand everything!

***

---

[16] Zhongfeng's typical phrasing for the *huatou*.

[6] Instruction to Zen Person Gen (Dwells at Shinnyo Monastery in the Capital. Name Kosen. Dharma Successor of the Master)

This mind in delusion becomes samsara, and in awakening becomes nirvana.[17] However, the delusion of samsara is assuredly difficult to banish. Little do you imagine: the nirvana of awakening is like gold dust in the eyes. You should know that *prajñā* is like a great ball of fire, allowing nothing to approach! The mind with which you are doing practice-work is unwilling to be truly urgent. From your very first thought-moment, you are incapable of the complete *chopping off* shown by a palm-tapping blind one. Twenty-four hours a day he firmly goes "tap-tap" like someone who has undergone the *great death*. Rely on the *huatou* that you are practicing, and everything will be *chopped off*. But you are always in a *non-chopping-off* state, so you produce strange calculations, or the notions *difficult/easy*. You are inducing distinctions, delusive feelings, and confused interactions to enter your heart. Unable to *cut off* wherever you are, you immediately set up ten heavy boulders, hoping to rely on this boulder-power to *cut off* floating thoughts and illusory notions. This is like using stones to press down grass. You set up a thousand heavy boulders, but they still cannot press down the grass. When you turn around, you notice the grass is burgeoning wildly!

You never think about the fact that the impermanence of samsara is beginningless, you want to yoke up with the most efficacious karmic causes [i.e., practice]—but there is no special *upāya*. There's only a single *huatou* to practice. Just immediately acquire it! It is a single definitive *correct thought* that does not retrogress, does not change, does not shift: in life same as life and in death same as death. Suppose that, at a time when you are not yet awakened, thousands of Śākyamuni Buddhas and Maitreya Bodhisattvas were to pour the *buddhadharma* equal to the four great seas into your ear-faculty, it would all be delusion and defilement! None of it would be ultimate. If your reliance on a single *correct thought* [i.e., the *huatou*] is unsteady, then this perversity and falsity will [relegate you to] thousands of ruts in the road, and there will never come a time when you'll be able to *stop-to-rest*. Be careful! Be careful! Zen Person Gen: Strive!

---

[17] Kosen is Kosen Ingen (古先印元; 1295–1374, a Rinzai Zen monk. Ingen crossed to Yuan China in 1318 in the company of Myōsō Saitetsu (明叟齊哲;?–1347) and Gōkai Honjō (業海本淨;?–1352); obtained the dharma of Zhongfeng and later went on pilgrimage visiting many teachers. Returned home in 1326 in the company of Muin Genkai (無隱元晦;?–1358) and Myōsō Saitetsu.

[7] Instruction to Zen Person Tetsu (Resides in Shinnyo Monastery in the Capital. Later Called Myōsō. Dharma Successor to the Master)

Of old, a monk asked Mazu: "What is a buddha like?"[18] Mazu said: "Mind *is* buddha."[19] This single phrase is truly *soothing on the outside and sly on the inside*. Every single person can understand this teaching. But when one comes to ask this person: "Which one is your mind?"—he'll point to the east and point to the west, approve of forms and approve of *śūnyatā*, talk about the Way and talk about principle, going round and round with no relationship to much of anything. Moreover, since mind is already something than cannot be zeroed in on, what *is* it that is called 'buddha?' There simply are no clues by which to investigate this. You simply must come to know *this matter*! Only then can you decisively awaken. If you haven't awakened, even if you exhaust the world in trying to discern the significance of this saying *mind is buddha*—and do so right up until the point at which the glint in your eyes drops to the ground [and you die]—your search for *this mind* will never lead to your perceiving it! You will be voluntarily undergoing samsaric wheel-turning. Remorse will surely befall you. If you call this being a Chan practitioner, you are a village bumpkin, and you'll always be one. You won't be capable of taking up *why Zhaozhou spoke the huatou wu* 無, standing still upon it, and, at one go, getting on with your practice like a palm-tapping blind one. If you don't personally reach the stage of great penetration and great awakening, undoubtedly, you'll never be able to *take a rest*. If you can make this sort of firm determination to investigate and, in the course of time, all-at-once awaken, then you'll come to understand the saying *mind is buddha*. With this word *wu* 無, everything else becomes superfluous talk. Zen Person Tetsu of Shengmen Monastery sought a warning whip—Old Phantasm wrote one out.

[8] Instruction to Superior Person Dinglin Liaoyi

If you are [named] Liaoyi [*Understands-Oneness*], then you are finished with the myriad affairs.[20] Now then, how do you understand oneness? If you

---

[18] Myōsō is Myōsō aitetsu (明叟齊哲;?–1347). The Rinzai monk Saitetsu crossed to Yuan China in 1318 in the company of Gōkai Honjō and Kosen Ingen; trained under Zhongfeng and received his dharma; returned home in 1326 with Muin Genkai and Kosen Ingen.

[19] *Mazu Daoyi chanshi guanglu* (馬祖道一禪師廣錄) *Si jia yulu* 1 (四家語錄卷一): (CBETA 2019.Q3, X69, no. 1321, p. 4a19–20)

[20] Liaoyi is unidentified.

want to seek out this sort of understanding, all your effortful applications of mind are 'rough seas on level ground' [i.e., will get you sudden unforeseen troubles], and you'll end up with no understanding at all! Just all-at-once put *why Zhaozhou spoke the word wu* 無 into your breast and silently press on it for a whole lifetime, fastening it firmly to your body-mind. Keep on pressing hard with [this *huatou wu* 無]! At the very moment you are pressing hard, it won't be possible for you to understand and won't be possible for you to not understand. *Understanding/not understanding* are both false views. If you take up residence inside these false views, you'll go round and round, without your attaining any understanding. Just spread this *huatou* you are practicing throughout your breast. Today: just practice *in that way*; tomorrow: just practice *in that way*. Right at the locus of your practicing, all sorts of extraordinary, rare sense-objects will appear in front of you: all of them 'weirdnesses' of Māra [to be ignored]. You must not acknowledge any "backup" thought or the removal [of any "backup" thought], down to: you must not take discrimination or *seizing/abandoning* as your standard. All these thoughts fall into the stage of conceptual consciousness. You must jettison those sense-fields of samsara: [they bring] great calamities. If, for twenty or thirty years, you do not attain awakening, merely add more firmness to your pressing on [the *huatou*]: in life same as life and in death same as death. Resting in a *single thought* of the *huatou* you are practicing, bring forth a calm stability: no moving, no shaking. In the course of time, delusive feelings will cease to arise, false thoughts will smooth out and sink. When you are aware of nothing at all, suddenly there will occur a fierce awakening. You'll then come to know the Way's ultimate *Oneness* [i.e., the *Oneness* of your own name]. Before you even embarked on pilgrimage [at the beginning of your Chan career], you already *understood* completely [i.e., the *Understands* of your own name]. Truly, you did not have to wait until there was some other thing you understood in order to understand: that's why you are called Dinglin [*Settled-Forest*]! If you have not really awakened *in that way* at least once, then you cannot *in that way* be called by the name *Understands*, and you cannot be called by the name *Oneness* [i.e., your name Liaoyi]. And you want to be called Dinglin. But that is far off! I am not speaking empty words here. Chan Person Yi: your thoughts of the Way are scrupulous, your years filled up. You are fully endowed with the form to transcend the patriarchal Way. Just possess a mind willing [to plant buddha-seeds], and you certainly won't be deceived!

[9] Instruction to Chan Person Yin

Just have confidence in yourself and raise to awareness the *huatou* that you are practicing.[21] Stretch out your journey: go on with your practice of pressing on [the *huatou*] for eternity, and spontaneously there will come a time of awakening. You must not, as you are practicing, produce any stirrings of doubt. And you must not produce any thoughts of seeking a quick awakening. All this is like walking on a road: if your energy is at maximum, you'll spontaneously arrive [home]!

While you are practicing the *huatou*, that is, doing practice-work, all the rare and extraordinary things you see or hear or become aware of: they are all Māra sense-objects. Merely refrain from any thought of chasing after them, and, after a long while, they will spontaneously loosen their hold. If you, even for the blink of an eye, produce a thought-moment of attachment, from that point onward you'll have fallen into Māra's realm. You may dub it "enlightenment," but it will actually be a kind of insane confusion!

Awakening to the Way is like arriving home. All the sense-objects right in front of you are *your old home*: every single one of them is natural, reliable, and obvious. You won't have even the tiniest thought of doubt. If you do preserve even a half-dot's worth of doubt, then it certainly isn't *your old home*! You must go on with your practice of pressing on [the *huatou*]. Otherwise, you'll be hoodwinked into a heterodox view.

In practicing the *wu* 無 *huatou*, all you must do is raise the sensation of uncertainty[22] upon the *wu* 無. Practice: *why did Zhaozhou say wu* 無? Twenty-four hours a day, just practice *in that way*. While you are practicing, do not inquire about whether you have mental reflection and discrimination or do not have mental reflection and discrimination. [The dichotomy] *mental reflection/not having mental reflection* belongs to false thought. Right now, you must only raise the sensation of uncertainty upon the *huatou* that you are practicing, down to: you must not produce discriminative thought concerning sense-objects. Merely divorce from everything beyond the *huatou* you are practicing. If you raise any thought other [than the *huatou*]—even a buddha-thought or a dharma-thought—all of them are incorrect thoughts, seeds of samsara.

The person who is doing real practice-work, twenty-four hours a day, thought-moment after thought moment, is like someone trying to put out a fire on his head. He is like a lone individual facing an enemy of ten thousand.

---

[21] Yin is unidentified.
[22] This is a major theme of Dahui's letters. See Translation 3, n. 27.

Why would he explore any leisurely sort of practice-work? Upon encountering mundane conditions where your life is at stake, what sort of [leisurely] practice-work could there be? If you want to enlighten others, what sort of leisurely practice-work could there be? If you want to question a student who is searching for Chan sayings and understanding, even if that student were a first-class person, in three days you couldn't bring him to enlightenment—his mind would be at a loss, and you would have no skillful expedients to employ. All this is pursuing false samsaric turnings. This isn't doing practice-work! For the most part, a person doing practice-work is like a thief who wants to filch the gold and silk of others. When walking, he walks to filch things; when sitting, he sits to filch things; when at leisure, he's at leisure to filch things. When busy, he's busy at filching things. How could he be willing to reveal his intention to filch things? The person of distinction sees that, the more urgent the desire to filch things, the more secretive the mechanism of concealment. Thought after thought he's like this; moment after moment he's like this. Over time, he does not retrogress, and he is guaranteed to reach the rank of the ancients. During the twenty-four hours of the day, how could his making himself *master* prove to be anything less than fixed? You just want to follow someone else's false-thought-turnings in samsara. Force yourself to be a director of things! Run to the sitting cushion and serve as a model! But if from moment to moment you run around seeking and are unwilling to *stop-for-a-rest*, you'll never come to a *time of yoking up*. Remember! Remember! Time is like a flow: quickly engage in self-reflection!

[10] Instruction to Chan Person Ran

In practicing Chan just have confidence in your single *huatou* and only practice this single one.[23] Only this is *correct practice*. Suppose you're using the *huatou why Zhaozhou said wu* 無; and another *huatou* like **to where does the One return** comes up, you must not adopt it! Before long, it will spontaneously go away. Right now, your only job is to throw off your single long-term body-mind. Go practice! And absolutely do not seek for quick success. If you maintain any thought of quick success, for a long time you'll be stuck inside the net of intellectual understanding. Practicing Chan involves just maintaining a single correct thought of resolving the painful *great matter of samsara*. Guard the *huatou* you are practicing for twenty or thirty years, down to the point where, for a whole lifetime, you just keep on doing things *in that way*. You must never

---

[23] Ran is unidentified.

through all eternity produce a single thought that seeks for quick awakening. If such a mind should arise, it is false thought: never yoked up with the Way.

You must not seek quick awakening. Your practice-work will ripen, and the time will arrive. It is like walking on a road: *without any expectation of arrival*, you just keep on making steps without stopping, without break. Spontaneously, you will arrive. Chan Person Ran! Just keep on having confidence *in that way*. You must not study somebody else's quick awakening: that would be going down a perverse road. You should confirm what I have said by talking to a lot of people in your "hometown."

[11] Instructions to Chan Person Ying

In the Chan line there is a type of sharp person who, at the very first time he hears the words of the teacher, seems to be able to comprehend: immediately understanding and "owning" the words.[24] At the time, the teacher doesn't study the question of whether this student has awakened or not: the teacher just waves the student through in an instant. Thereupon, the student pivots and proceeds to teach others based on what he has perceived for himself. He feels no need to produce uncertainty concerning the *huatou*, valuing only his own *ready-made comprehension*. He's become entangled and has entered the net of [useless] knowing. Every time he speaks it sounds the same; his actions are unrelated [to awakening].

There is a type of dull-witted novice. He hears it reported that "in the practice of Chan one must keep an eye on the *huatou* and arouse a *great sensation of uncertainty*,[25] and only then will one attain all-at-once awakening." Thereupon, [this sort of dull-witted novice] firmly pecks away for twenty or thirty straight years on the *huatou* that he is practicing. Consistent from beginning to end, he is unwilling to let go [of his *huatou*]. After a long while, his false delusions do dissipate. However, after he has awakened [to some degree], whenever he encounters students requesting instruction, he invariably wants to make them do the practice-work of keeping an eye on the *huatou* and rousing the *sensation of uncertainty*. Seemingly, this sort of master is acting for the sake of others. However, though he speaks of the "difficulty of advancing into [the sagely realm]," he always fails to embrace empathetically the varying innate characters of students.

---

[24] Ying is unidentified.
[25] This is a major theme of Dahui's letters. See Translation 3, n. 27.

Though the Chan school has always spoken of *direct pointing to the human mind*, the approaches it has offered for accessing awakening have involved innumerable wheel tracks: every one of them has been different. Chan teachers have relied on the single principle of *direct pointing*. They have followed people's innate characters. Since everyone's own way of awakening is different, ways of enticing them [employed by teachers] are different. Once you plumb to the source of this ultimate principle, it is to be expected that all [methods will lead to] escaping from the *great matter of samsara*. How could it be otherwise? The consciousness-natures [i.e., personalities] found in sentient-beings show many differences: [Teachers] cannot just do a single piss and leave it at that! Also, some people have the theory that, after awakening, one necessarily *sees*; there's also the theory that, having attained access to awakening, one necessarily *puts it into practice*. All this has to do with the state of awakening. But it's impossible to reach the bottom [of awakening] in one stride! One will still be engirded by mistaken views and attachments. No teacher can give others the way to dissolve glue and remove bondage. They've got to put it into practice. *A single awakening is awakening for all time*: cut off any such talk! Though the ancients did not have the practice of keeping an eye on the *gong'an* [i.e., *huatou*] and rousing the *sensation of uncertainty*, merely before awakening they would assiduously apply mental effort. This is utterly different from people at present. If you teach people of the present *not* to do practice-work, every single one of them will sit down inside the net of perverted thinking!

An ancient had a saying: "If you rely on someone else to create your understanding, you will block your own approach to awakening."[26] The *Perfect Awakening Sutra* says: "Sentient-beings of the latter age hope to complete the Way. Do not order them to seek awakening. That will only increase their intellectual learning and reinforce their self-view."[27]

[12] Instructions to Librarian Rong

You talk of *no-taste* at the time of rallying the *huatou* to awareness, but what do you intend to call *taste*?[28] But let's set aside this talk about *taste* for a moment. Just where are you progressing to, step by step? Your wanting to look for *taste* and your wanting to progress by steps are both fundamentally false-thought. You intend to maintain this mind that wants to do practice-work

---

[26] *Chanlin baoxun* (禪林寶訓; T 2022.48.1026a16–22). The speaker is Fayan Qingyuan (佛眼清遠; 1067–1120).
[27] T 842.17.920a8–9.
[28] Rong is unidentified.

to clarify samsara, but this mind of yours goes around and around with no relationship [to awakening]. You want to know *taste* right this very moment? Just go on being continuous and unbroken on the *huatou* you are practicing! There is no need to look for some other *upāya*. *Able to do [practice-work]/not able to do [practice-work]*: just keep on practicing [your *huatou*] to the very end. This is precisely the principle behind *taste*; this is precisely the principle behind making progress. Wanting to seek out some other *taste* or progress beyond this is utterly perverted thinking. You'll never finish in ten thousand eons! The ancients, in their study of the Way, acted only for the *samsara is the great matter and impermanence is swift*. Though they did not have the *huatou* by which to practice, they instead asked *how* and instead looked for *how*. To slash at the backs of their students, they hit with the stick; to pen up the jaws of their students, they slapped with the palm of the hand. That already was the mind of [excessively kind] *old-woman Chan*. What further measuring could they possibly have employed? What further could they possibly have said? The self-confidence of the people of today is inadequate. There's no alternative! I bestow upon you for your practice this *huatou that has no meaning or taste*. Disliking *no-taste* and trying to seek to make progress are like talking about your dreams after you have opened your eyes [in the morning]. Superior Rong is part of the assembly at Mt. Shuangjing. His attitude to the Way is firm and dedicated. He brought writing paper to ask for warning-whip words from me. I directly took my writing-brush and instructed him as above.

[13] Instructions to Chan Person Su

In practicing Chan, from the outset there are no *upāyas*.[29] All you must do is press on the correct thought [i.e., the *huatou*]: a single slice of reality that serves as *the great matter of samsara*. Lift to awareness the *huatou* you are practicing. Pay no attention to whether it takes twenty or thirty years. Do it *at one go*, without ever changing direction. At the locus where you are unable [to generate the sensation of] uncertainty, go on with generating uncertainty! At the locus where you are unable to press hard [with the *huatou*], go on pressing hard! In both cases—where you cannot [generate the sensation of] uncertainty and where you cannot press hard—there is no need to produce some "backup" thought. It's necessary for you to ask: How do I go about [generating the sensation of] uncertainty? How do I go about pressing hard [with the *huatou*]? Uncertainty is just uncertainty concerning the *huatou* you

---

[29] Su is unidentified.

are practicing; pressing hard is just the necessity to press hard on the *huatou* you are practicing. Except for the *huatou* you are practicing, don't make some other *ease* or *stillness*, *rarity* or *extraordinariness*, *numinous efficacy*, and so forth into a "nest" [i.e., stereotyped formula or conventional usage] for yourself. As soon as you become aware that the *huatou* you are practicing is failing to appear right in front of you, then immediately and meticulously raise it to awareness. Go on practicing it unceasingly thought-moment after thought-moment. Just possess a mind willing [to plant buddha-seeds], and you certainly won't be deceived!

[14] Instructions to Layman Nakaura of Japan

What is your *original face* before your father and mother conceived you?[30] Nakaura [中浦], have you once and for all yoked up with the principle of the ultimate *middle* [*naka* = 中]? If you have not yet been able to do so, *this matter* is not something you talk about and then take a rest. You must merely lift to awareness the above *huatou* [*original face*]. Press on this *huatou* for an entire lifetime: be a solitary, quiet body-and-mind with a vacant kind of determination. Be silent, like someone who has undergone the *great death*. Even if you fail to bring about awakening, most definitely do not take a rest! If you just manage a mind of firm understanding, then, with both body-mind and sense objects, you'll hit the target without even trying. What further doubts could you have? What further doubts could you have?

[15] Instructions to Layman Chichoku, Buddhist Name *Straightness Hut*, Imperial Bodyguard Taira of Japan

Of old, Layman Pang asked Mazu: "The one who is not a companion of the myriad dharmas—what person is that?"[31] Mazu said: "When you suck up all the water of West River, then I'll tell you!"[32] These words are as *straight* as the strings of a musical instrument. But, if you intend to wade on through mental pondering, you'll be unable to bear the *crookedness* of the place you are right now. Also, Layman Pang said: "Difficult! Difficult! I've spread

---

[30] Nakaura is unidentified.
[31] Chichoku is unidentified.
[32] *Pang jushi yulu* (龐居士語錄; CBETA 2019.Q3, X69, no. 1336, p. 131a19–21).

uncountable amounts of linseed oil on the wood of this door-screen!" His wife said: "Easy! Easy! As easy as taking a nap without taking off your clothes." His daughter Lingzhao said: "Neither difficult nor easy: the intention of the patriarchs is on every blade of grass!"[33] Although these three people spoke of *difficult/easy*, they didn't realize that, at that very moment, their *straightness* was like the strings of a musical instrument. You are intending to look for the extremes of *difficult/easy*, and so are unable to overcome *crookedness*. The Old Man of Vaiśālī [Vimalakīrti] said: "Straight mind is the site of the awakening."[34] Because he was divorced from all winding *crookedness*, it was as if he resided in this principle of ultimate *straightness*. If you are unable to open your mind and understand, there's no need at all to come up with any "backup" thought. Just install in your mind the *huatou* **what was my original face before my father and mother conceived me**? Silently practice! Diligently investigate! Assiduously bring a sense of uncertainty to bear [upon the *huatou*]! Perform courageously! Perform until you reach the state of *deluded feelings forgotten and consciousnesses exhausted*. Suddenly you will have a fierce awakening. Then, for the first time, you will enjoy confidence that the time of delusion is *straight*, the time of awakening is *straight*, the time of attainment is *straight*, the time of loss is *straight*. You will ascend to the halls of the heavens, descend to the hells, sit on the lotus pedestal, enter the sword-pit. And there won't be a single moment when you are not an integral whole with the principle of ultimate *straightness*. When you arrive *here*, there is no buddha to seek out, no sentient-being to discard. You'll be a person of *straightness and more straightness*. Imperial Bodyguard Layman Taira, Buddhist name *Straightness Hut*, brought paper to ask me for *warning-whip* words about entering the Way. I directly took my writing-brush and answered him as above. I here append an explanation in verse:

Speech *straight*, action *straight*, and mind *straight*.
If you intend to preserve intellectual knowledge, you'll immediately hit perversity.
The *huatou* is to be practiced in daily activities until penetration is reached.
When you can say [the *huatou*] is [*straight*] as an instrument's strings, you'll have "experienced the road."

---

[33] *Pang jushi yulu* (龐居士語錄; CBETA 2019.Q3, X69, no. 1336, p. 134a18–20).
[34] *Vimalakīrti Sūtra*, T 475.14.542c10–15.

[16] Instructions to Chan Person Jia of Understanding Hermitage

The *great matter* of samsara is not something that you talk about and then take a rest, nor is it something that you understand and then take a rest.[35] What you can speak of, and what you can understand, all of it is karma-consciousness of beginningless wheel-turning. You must promptly spit out such things! Only raise to awareness the *huatou* you are practicing and press on it with your true body-mind for an entire lifetime. Sit beneath the three rafters [of the Chan monastery Monks Hall] and be like a person who has undergone the *great death*. In your chest cut off breathing! Forget seeing and hearing and extinguish intellectual knowledge. There will be only a single *huatou* that you are practicing: stand still on it and go on practicing. Even if you don't awaken in one lifetime, this *correct thought* [i.e., the *huatou*] that you are practicing will remain immutable and unchanging. When you pop up in a future birth, you are guaranteed to reach "upon one hearing, a thousand awakenings." This is a settled matter. As the ancient said: "Just possess a mind willing [to plant buddha-seeds], and you certainly won't be deceived!"[36] Chan Person Jia of Understanding Hermitage asked for a warning-whip talk, and so I instructed him like this.

[17] Instructions to Lecture Master Jian of Yuxi

The *buddhadharma is your own mind*.[37] This mind is the teachings of the entire Buddhist canon. Explanations and annotations do not confute [this mind]. Guidance given by the buddhas of the three times does not bring forth this mind. Looking up at the 1700 Chan patriarchs does not bring this mind into view. People in every place on earth chase after it but never catch up with it. From ancient times until the present there have been hundreds of thousands of interpretations, but they are all nothing more than doing the *chashou mudrā* "behind the back of" this mind.[38] Hence Caoxi [Huineng] said: "If you speak of this Chan *direct pointing*, you've already gone on a twisting route far away from it."[39] This is like the type of *sumō* bout where the fighter feels that,

---

[35] Jia is unidentified
[36] See n. 12.
[37] Jian is unidentified.
[38] A mindfulness hand gesture. The right hand is formed into a circle, and the left thumb is tucked into the circle. The knuckle of the right hand rests against the sternum. The fingers of the left hand wrap around the right.
[39] Untraced.

if he doesn't force a fast resolution, he's in danger: with the blink of an eye, his life will be in the opponent's hands. How could you allow a stoppage of your *true functioning* while sunk in thought: only comprehending afterward? If, while pissing, you're unable to make the piss come out, you shouldn't try to hurry up and rush the matter. Before any phrase is voiced or after it is voiced, comprehend them in order: there is no harm in producing a mind of truly resolute confidence.[40] Within your own body, guard the *huatou that has no meaning or taste* and rouse a fierce attitude in your ordinary life. Be diligent and steadfast, like a blind one making his way forward! Do not ask whether it will take twenty or thirty years: all you have is the time of a single day. Do it for that one day! If, for a long time, your mind of confidence remains firm, your ambition secret—and you're unaware of all this—suddenly you will attain awakening. Then you will realize that this Way is not something you get from other people. You will be like a mute who has had a dream [but cannot tell anyone of it]! From olden times, whether the teachings or whether Chan, how many people with extinguished mind and wisdom have *here* attained instant liberation? Right when you are doing [practice-work], if you preserve even a single thought of an external objective-support, a single thought of *seizing/rejecting*, a single thought of *attraction/revulsion*, a single thought [of any kind], you'll have yielded to discriminative thoughts that falsely follow things in the samsaric flow. And if you preserve a deluded consciousness consisting of even one thought of memorizing, retaining, studying, understanding, and so forth, you'll be unable to respond with a thought of *cutting off*. Wishing for "Jian destroyed, and the light lost" is no different from eliminating steps while trying to go forward. You'll never manage to come into a *yoked-up* state. Lecture Master Jianof Yuxi, asked for a warning-whip, and, despite being ill, I directly took my writing-brush to respond to him.

---

[40] Translation more than tentative—simply a placeholder for a better rendering of this line.

Translation 11
Instructions to the Assembly from *Zhongfeng Talks* in *Zhongfeng Record B*

Instructions to the Assembly

On the evening of the day before yesterday, the Head Seat and the Rector arrived at this hermitage and announced [to me]:

> The beginning of the [ninety-day] summer retreat is near. We request that you speak to your general assembly of monks about this, perhaps going as far as allowing them two or three days of free time. You should request that they pass through the hermitage and have a cup of tea with you, so you can talk together for a short time and provide a *warning whip* for them. Unexpectedly, we've continuously encountered dark skies and rain, making the roads slippery and inconvenient. This has made for the loss of twelve days: human affairs have intersected with our two monasteries. It will not be possible to achieve Mr. Phantasm's wish to keep far away from the world.

Now that I think of it, everybody in this great assembly has "eaten practice to their fill." Ordinarily, when they arrive at this hermitage, every one of them has knocked against the experience of the sitting cushion. How could [the time between] *knotting up the summer retreat* [i.e., the beginning of the retreat] and *dismissing the summer retreat* [i.e., the end of the retreat] constitute [some sort of special and separate] practice-of-the-Way period? If you speak of this matter in terms of ultimate principle, the summer retreat begins as soon as one for the very first time arouses the aspiration for awakening. Twenty-four hours a day keep an eye on the *huatou that has no meaning or taste*.[1] Before you've broken through, it will be the summer retreat! For twenty or thirty years push toward a state in which your spirit is extinguished and consciousness exhausted. When, in a still place, you suddenly attain a fierce realization, that is the *time of the ending of the summer retreat*. Days of self-indulgence: how can you consider a trifling ninety days [of summer retreat]

---

[1] Zhongfeng's typical phrasing for the *huatou*.

to be some sort of restriction or limit? As a rule, in the case of those who do practice-work without obtaining any numinous efficacy, the real problem is that their *furtive mind* is not yet dead. Therefore, they extend their months and years in vain. There is no other illness at work here. If your *furtive mind* dies today, then today you're immediately *yoked up*! If it dies tomorrow, then tomorrow you are immediately *yoked up*! What do I mean by *furtive mind*? If you separate from the *huatou* that you are practicing and see the separate existence of a *self*: that's *furtive mind*. If, beyond the *self* that you see, you also see the existence *self* and *others*: that's *furtive mind*. If, when your practice-work is pure and ripening, you come to know that the Way is pure and ripening: that's *furtive mind*. If, when your practice-work is not pure and ripening, you come to know that the Way is not pure and ripening: that's *furtive mind*. When torpor and restlessness appear right in front of you: that's *furtive mind*. When torpor and restlessness do not appear, and there is only the *huatou* that you are practicing, intertwined with the *sensation of uncertainty*[2] in a continuum: that's *furtive mind*. However, if, at the locus of your keeping an eye on the *huatou*, you even momentarily produce a single thought, regardless of whether it is common thought or a sagely thought, a true thought or a false thought: put it down as *furtive mind*. If suddenly there is a clever person, who provides a road that is not connected at all to what I have said—a Way, a principle, a seeing, a hearing—this is *furtive mind* inside *furtive mind*. The buddhas cannot save you with medicine: you will merely attain a lot of *furtive mind*! Just *in that way* rely on your *original allotment* and rest in the *huatou* you are practicing. Be like a breathing dead one of modeled clay or carved wood. Externally, do not see the existence of the great assembly; internally, do not see the existence of a self. In a manner as cold as ice, cut off seeing and hearing. *In that way* go on *maintaining*. You can rest assured that you will certainly be a successful candidate [in the exam] of mind-emptiness. This disrespectful piece of writing will stand in for the tea conversation with members of the assembly [that the Head Seat and the Rector recommended]. I, this Upper Seat, have spent many days ensconced in the mountains to avoid human affairs. It is not necessary to inquire about the whereabouts of Phantasm's traces. Even if you were to see me, we would not talk together. Fortunately, the Head Seat and the Rector understand this!

---

[2] This is a major theme of Dahui's letters. See Translation 3, n. 27.

Chinese Text for Translation 1: Selections from *Instructions to the Assembly* in *Zhongfeng Extensive Record*

(Four excerpts in *Gozanban* 9: 127a–c; 128d–129c; 136a–d; 136d–137c. CBETA 2019.Q3, B25, no. 145, pp. 715b10–718a13.)

示眾

[1]　除夜示眾。欲識佛性義。當觀時節因緣。且只今是甚麼時節。臘月二十九。既非大盡乃是年窮歲極之時也。古人謂。生死交接之際是臘月三十喻。年盡月盡日時俱盡也。且一年三百六十日內。還辦得甚麼事來。若辦不得。未免虛喪此一年。豈但虛喪此一年。自無量刧來至于今日。摠是虛喪過了。或不便從今日脚跟下做箇立地。提起所糸話。別立生涯。猛利做向前去。來年雖未過。敢保又是虛喪。豈但來年或不猛利精勤。便百千年亦只是虛喪。諸仁者。虛喪時緣也。不管儞以虛喪故。積業愈多。道力愈微。何有補於出家學道之理哉。奉勸諸人。以鐵拄杖把殘年許多懶墮自恣昏沉掉舉。一劃劃斷。向明日大年初一為始。奮起精進。勇猛神力。做一日。便要見一日功程。及早討箇倒斷。庶不孤出家行脚之志願也。如人上山各自努力。復云。今夜臘月廿九。處處迎新送舊。惟有衲僧面前動著。便成窠臼。不如念一道真言。消遣殘年不唧嚠。是大神呪。是大明呪。試聽五更樓上鍾。百千幻法皆成就。

***

[2]　結夏示眾。大眾踞菩薩乘修寂滅行。以大圓覺為我伽藍。身心安居平等性智。此是二千年外老釋迦畫地為牢。與當時眾比丘。禁足安居之古制也。今朝四月十五。適當聖制之辰。拈出陳年曆日頭為諸人因行掉臂去也。前面一絡索。且置之不論。復如何是安居平等性智。然性智平等故。盡十方剎土。更無有不平等者仰觀諸佛。俯視眾生。是謂性相平等。前觀過去。後及未來。是謂三際平等。諸戒定慧及[婬-壬+(工/山)]怒癡。是謂一念平等。迷而生死。悟而涅槃。是謂不動平等。大而虛空。細而纖芥。是謂離相平等。乃至見色色平等聞聲聲平等。審如是則四月十五結。結亦平等。七月十五解。解亦平等。於中

九十日。日日平等。時時平等。念念平等。政與麼時。喚甚麼作結。喚甚麼作解。喚甚麼作安居不安居。黃面老漢到這裏。不覺全機敗露。雖然事無一向。儞若不曾真正向平等性智中。脚踏實地穎悟一回。直饒將平等二字。盡虛空充塞殆徧。無乃益其高下耳。此事只恁麼說不過。須是硬曝曝地。向此九十日。於無義味話上。橫蹴竪蹴。朝挨暮挨。挨到極處。蹴到盡時。如啞子得夢。恁時不妨任意指陳。喚平等作不平等。亦得喚不平等作平等。亦得所謂我爲法王。於法自在。記得古人有偈謂。護生須是殺。殺盡始安居。會得箇中意。鐵船水上浮。莫是殺生與護生一念平等麼。恁麼商量。瞎人眼目。甚非細事。更聽說偈。各自歸堂。九旬禁足。意何殊生殺。難將古制拘。未到身心平等處。豈應容易白安居。

***

[3]　遇雪示衆。一片兩片飛入人間。尋不見。三尺五尺積向茅簷。難辨的。銀象三千界靈瑞身光。有空皆徧。玉龍八百萬敗殘鱗甲。無地可埋。梅華之恨獨深漁蓑之歸未晚。且道與蒲團禪板邊坐堆堆底人。有何交涉。古者道。今日雪下。藂林有三種。僧一種向被位頭究明自己。一種向經案上吟詠雪詩。一種向火爐角說喫堂供。此三種僧。那箇合受人天供養。合受不合受。置之勿論。諸禪德。儞還知結雨爲雪。凝水爲冰底道理麼。然結雨爲雪。固是造物變化。宜乎不知。如凝水爲冰。遽以流注之質。頓成堅礙之形。雖金石。不可與較其固。請以喻明之。佛性猶水也。以無量刦中。迷妄之寒氣。念念凝合。由是結佛性之水爲冰也。且政當冰時。未嘗不具佛性之水。奈何迷妄之寒交結未化。雖全體是水。而不得爲流注灌漑之用耳。或不以智慧之日融之。安有自化之理。如是觀察。向道之念可得而免諸。或謂古人相逢彈指便解知歸。豈必待奮神力下苦工而後然哉。儞殊不知。或不曾奮神力下苦工於曩昔。任儞相逢彈破指頭。也無儞知歸之理。未有一佛一祖。不因智慧之日。融化迷妄之寒冰。而能復其佛性之水也。今日一箇所糸話。信得及處。靠得穩時。豈非真智慧耶。一旦工夫熟。時節至。千丈冰山也是水。萬尋雪嶺也是水。滔滔然流歸佛性之海。任儞空中積雪。火裏生冰。未聞凍合。無邊之海。諸禪德。莫道本上座長於譬喻。蓋法理如是也。更聽一偈。凍雲四合雪漫漫。孰解當機作水看。只爲眼中花未瞥。啟窓猶看玉琅玕。

***

[4]　元宵示衆。須彌燈王如來。與藥師琉璃光佛。昨夜在十字街頭相遇。乃攜手看鰲山燈火。忽撞見箇厖眉雪頂老漢。向百衆人前。說四句偈謂。惟心即佛佛惟心。此話相傳古到今。對面不知燈是火。區區徒向外邊尋。時二如來忍俊不禁。乃厲聲曰。儞說也是。惟欠悟在。只箇即心是佛。即佛惟心。說與三歲小兒悉皆領會。奈何不悟。說食

不療飢也。請問悟時消息。乃曰。試以喻明。有人失去徑寸之珠。雖百千兩金。不足與較其價之輕重。使此珠不獲。雖萬死莫酬其尋求之心。鏤之肺肝。刻之心膂。形之夢寐。貫之見聞。念念不忘。孜孜不捨。一日不獲。則一日之念不休。一年不獲。則一年之心不廢。愈不見愈精勤。益不獲益勇銳。乃至情消想竭。思苦神窮。寒暑兩忘。寢食俱廢。積年累歲。正於無可捉摸處。驀忽入手。圓陀陀光漾漾。其三十年馳求之心。一時頓息。是謂悟也。其尋覓此珠於心勤形瘵之際。豈非參乎。忽頓見此珠於神明意朗之頃。豈非悟乎。苟不因參尋之難。安有此悟獲之喜也。與論至此。忽被簡傍不甘底一喝喝散。惟見燈自是燈。火自是火。樓臺突兀車馬交馳。華敷井井金蓮。燄續條條玉燭。胡張三。黑李四。萬人海裏醉扶歸。查沙鬼。大齋郎。百戲場中狂未歇。正恁麼時。且不涉悟迷共樂昇平底句。如何舉似。琉璃滿腹藏明月。菡萏渾身放寶光。

Chinese Text for Translation 2: Selections from *Dharma Talks in Zhongfeng Extensive Record*

(Seven excerpts in *Gozanban* 9: 162d–163b; 170b–171a; 177b–178a; 179a–d; 181c–182b; 195a–c; 206d–207c. CBETA 2019.Q3, B25, no. 145, p. 735a12–768a20.)

法語

[1] 示伊吾顯月長老(梵名烏鉢剌室利)
佛法無商量分。無湊泊分。無安排分。但是拌得一切。打開萬般。絕計較。單單只是靠取一箇話頭。自今日守到箇悟底時分。方許儞取氣。儞若未到桶底子自脫之時。便欲取氣。直下蹉過了也。只此一蹉過。便是百蹉千蹉。甚非小緣。做工夫最要緊。是把得住。最要緊。是放得下。最要緊。是不隨逆順境轉。最要緊。是做得主定立得脚牢。最要緊。是耐得枯淡守得寂寞。最要緊。是識得眼前破。不被世間一切境界惑。最要緊。是寒不思衣。飢不求食。眼不隨色。耳不逐聲。最要緊。是一箇身心。如鐵橛子。不受一切禪道佛法穿鑿。最要緊。是盡生不悟明。決不起第二念。更有一件是最要緊處。口未開時已說了也。筆未動時已寫了也。糸未透時已悟了也。儞還知麼。儞還會麼。儞還信麼。如今大事爲儞不得。小事各自支當。

***

[2] 示日本丁一頭陀
　僧非僧俗非俗。六六從來三十六。俗是俗僧是僧。從教日午打三更。僧亦得。俗亦得。畢竟本來無間隔無間隔處。忽承當。笑看大蟲生兩翼。會麼。若也不會。且莫忽忽草草。儞因甚不顧父母之養而依附大僧。投身林谷。莫是爲求衣食麼。莫是爲求名利麼。既是不求衣食不求名利。畢竟爲箇甚麼事。況是遠逾數萬里。航海得得而來。實爲自家脚跟下。有一種生死無常大事因。遠經曠刼而及今生。愈見昏迷。轉加沉墜。今日須是捨命忘形盡平生氣力。向他空閑寂寞中。提起古人一則無滋味話。默默自看。看來看去。但心無希望。意絕馳求。識不攀。念不流逸。不問山林城市。靜閙閑忙。今日也與麼看。

明日也與麼看。忽爾眼皮破。髑髏穿。便解道丁一卓二。築著便是卓二丁一。百事大吉。海東走出黑波斯。眉毛鼻孔長三尺。說甚麼生死與輪迴。說甚麼虛頭與真實。草鞋兩耳忽聞聲。僧俗由來都不識。都不識。誰辨的。春風吹破嶺南花。一一漏盡真消息。

***

[3] 示明忠上人病中

衲衣下一著子。攪澄不異。磨涅不痕。坐斷古今。不存凡聖。所以古人謂之向上機。末後句。頂門眼。肘後符。臨濟即之而喝。如怒雷。德山據之而棒。如疾雨。不依工用。匪涉階梯。提得便行。拈得便用。奔流度刃。疾燄過風。正眼看來未爲慶快。這裏豈容心思意解。安排擺布而爲得哉。雪川忠上人。偶因臥病。余謂之曰。真歇和尚有云。老僧自有安閑法。八苦交煎總不妨。且如何是安閑法。對曰。知身是夢。了病如幻。惟守一心。不生異念。豈非安閑法乎。余因不顧。又曰。安即不動。閑即無爲。超出二途栖心。無寄。此豈非安閑法乎。余亦不顧。上人茫然若有所失。余遂示其畧曰。汝所說者乃情識計度分別取捨。皆暫時岐路。豈真究竟耶。要識安閑法麼。四大五陰是。根身器界是。四百四病是。山河大地是。見聞知覺是。以至一切差別塵緣。無有不是者。咄。是何言歟。且四大五陰及差別塵緣等。皆是敗壞不安之相。若喚作安閑法。大似指鹿爲馬。若不喚作安閑法。亦是指鹿爲馬。直饒去此二途。別資一路。未免。亦是指鹿爲馬。要得不指鹿爲馬。須是向他真歇和尚未啟口已前。掀翻情量。不墮是非。己眼頓開。洞見源底。始知一大藏教。是指鹿爲馬。千七百則公案。是指鹿爲馬。以至天下老和尚。拈槌竪拂。是指鹿爲馬。如是指說如是悟解。亦是指鹿爲馬。會麼。脫或不會。但切切將箇沒滋味話頭。向藥爐邊枕頭上。默默咨叅。不得放捨。忽然枕子落地。病藥兩忘。衲衣下那一著子。覿體現前。到此即其身心及與諸病。無有不是安閑法者也。雖然。切忌指鹿爲馬。

***

[4] 示琳上人病中

昔真歇和尚有偈謂。訪舊論懷實可傷。經年獨臥涅槃堂。門無過客窗無紙。爐有寒灰席有霜。病後始知身是苦。健時多爲別人忙。老僧自有安閑法。八苦交煎總不妨。古人作此偈。傷身世之浮脆。了夢幻之起滅。指情妄之所緣。示斯道之真寂。五十六言網羅殆盡。真道人之龜鑑也。學佛之士。當向這裏體取。則知未了此心之際。通身是病徧界是病。盡形畢命起心動念。更不問儻成佛作祖。皆是病緣。於中或有人指出一法不是病者。悉是妄見。又豈待形拘枕席。跡涉沉痾。而謂病耶。由是雪山大醫王眼不耐見。四十九年三百餘會塵說剎說。今結集爲一大藏教。是治此病之藥方。今日所叅底一箇無義味話頭。

是方中所秘傳之神藥。要起此膏肓必死之病。常以一念不退轉不變易之湯。使向一切時中送此神藥。然此藥之治此病。百發百中。今之服藥而病不瘳者。蓋與藥忌並進。所以不取効也。苟不能盡其所忌。不惟不効。將見執藥成病。又未易療之也。所謂忌者。即第二念是也。何謂第二念。便是儞離却箇所叅話頭正念之外。更於善惡悟迷境上。微動一毫。是謂第二念也。此則藥之忌也。誠能久不犯其所忌。則念念相續。安亦守。危亦守。生亦守。死亦守。表裏混融。如是持守。忽爾相應。其病頓如失去。若藥若忌。同時俱失。便是安閑法現前也。宜知之以自勉。

***

[5] 示希有上人行脚
　有一句子。在拄杖頭邊。有一句子。在草鞋根底。有一句子。在三千里外。有一句子。在六根門頭。向六根門頭薦得。則三千里外底。不用別尋。三千里外薦得。則六根門頭底。總在裏許。惟是拄杖頭一句子。只在拄杖頭。草鞋根底一句子。只在草鞋根底。不得動著。還知麼。盡無邊法界。是條拄杖。遍十方虛空。是緉草鞋。拈得拄杖。則失却草鞋。著得草鞋。則失却拄杖。須知拄杖無儞拈處。草鞋無儞著處。儞若擬心拈著。則一齊都打失了也。且不擬心。又爭得拄杖草鞋入手。但將箇所叅底話頭。掛在眉毛眼睫間。默默自看。是拄杖耶。是草鞋耶。是三千里外耶。是六根門頭耶。看到無可看處。冷眼被儞驀忽看破。元來七尺主丈[=拄杖]。一緉草鞋總是故鄉田地。信手拈來。則去地不遠矣。儞若不於話頭上儞儻分明。管取被箇主丈[=拄杖]草鞋惑。過一生。到頭殊無毫氂所益。古今行脚高士。被主丈[=拄杖]草鞋惑者。莫知其數。儞於今日。豈肯復爲其惑耶。重說偈曰。有一句子藏不得。三千里路覓家鄉。未拈主丈[=拄杖]先開眼。始信途中歲月長。

***

[6] 示同菴居士 (般剌脫因院使)
　一切佛法。是自心具足。心外別無佛法可求。縱使求得。亦非諦當。皆是妄想情識。非究竟法也。當知自心無聖凡。離聖凡之量。則與自心相應。自心無憎愛。離憎愛之分。則與自心相應。自心無取舍。離取舍之情。則與自心相應。自心乃至無一切善惡動靜造作等。能一切俱離。則與自心相應。然而說箇離聖凡憎愛等。最是不許。將一種心去。特地離佗。只箇離處。宛然生滅。或不用心。又如何說箇離底道理。所以古人云。神光獨耀。萬古徹猷。入此門來。莫存知解。但知道自心無聖凡之間也。是知解。又知道離聖凡之量也。落知解。當知此箇離之之理。亦不屬用心。但是悟明時。不待離。而自然不著不執矣。只箇不執不著之念。是名曰離。如今此心未曾悟明。只

消將箇四大分散時。向何處安身立命話。置之日用中。默默自看。都不要作一切想。亦不要作修行想。纔作此想。便被箇修行名字籠絡。在聖見中。於都不作想處。依舊默默參取所參話頭。久之純熟。忽然開悟。如久忘忽記。那時情妄空。知解泯。一箇自心。全體獨露。隨處自在。百千念慮。同時休息。百千緣境。當念俱離。安樂法門。無越此也。

***

[7] 示吳居士

　禪即淨土之禪。淨土乃禪之淨土。昔永明和尚離淨土與禪爲四料揀。由是學者不識建立之旨。反相矛盾。謂禪自禪。淨土自淨土也。殊不知參禪要了生死而念佛亦要了生死。原夫生死無根。由迷本性而生焉。若洞見本性。則生死不待蕩而遣矣。生死既遣。則禪云乎哉。淨土云乎哉。昔大勢至菩薩以念佛。心得無生忍。觀世音大士從聞思。修三慧取證圓通。今之禪乎。淨土乎。皆二大士之遺意也。二大士常侍安養導師。左右未嘗少悖。今二宗之學者。何所見而獨悖之耶。予返復求之。遂得其悖之之源。試略言之。蓋二宗之學者不本乎生死大事耳。以不痛心於生死禪。則耕空言。以自高淨土。則常作爲而自足。由是是非倒見。雜然前陳。若非古佛願行冥符。則二宗或幾乎息矣。居士久親淨土之學。復慕少林直指之道。直以父母未生前那箇是我本來面目話。置之念佛心中。念念不得放舍。孜孜不可棄離。工夫純熟。識見愈精明。道力益堅密。一旦於忘能所。絕氣息處。豁然頓悟。始信予言之不爾欺矣。脫或於未悟之頃。妄執予言爲己見。不惟坐在窠臼中。則亦去道愈遠矣。誠之誠之。

Chinese Text for Translation 3: *Night Conversations in a Mountain Hermitage* in *Zhongfeng Extensive Record*

(*Gozanban* 9, 238d–279a. CBETA 2019.Q3, B25, no. 145, pp. 791a1–821b7. Noguchi and Matsubara, *Sanbō yawa*, 1–305)

山房夜話上

[1] 幻人僻居窮山。忽隱者過門。與對牀夜坐。時山月吐輝窓白如晝。隱者曰。聞義學以禪定之禪。配吾達磨單傳直指之禪。以達磨曾有所謂胎息論。遞相傳受。而曲引第八識住胞胎時。惟依一息而住。故云胎息者。以方吾禪定亦依止一息而住。今議者遂枝蔓其說。離吾達磨爲二乘禪定之學。何如。
　幻曰。彼非謗也。是不識達磨所指之禪也。將謂離四禪八定之外。別無所謂禪。殊不知。達磨遠繼西天二十七祖。以如來圓極心宗之謂禪也。此禪含多名。又名最上乘禪。亦名第一義禪。與二乘外道四禪八定之禪。實天淵之間也。當知是禪不依一切經法所詮。不依一切修證所得。不依一切見聞所解。不依一切門路所入。所以云教外別傳者也。惟大心衆生。夙熏佛種。不涉階梯。一聞千悟。得大總持。自此或獨宿孤峯。或入鄽垂手。縱橫逆順。道出常情。語默卷舒。不存窠臼。安有所謂禪定胎息之謂乎。蓋達磨不立文字直指人心。凡六傳至能大師。師云說箇直指。早是曲了也。此說之下。豈容別有所謂語言文字而可傳受者邪。世有胎息論。不知何等謬妄之人。誣罔聖師而作。況是後之欲欺達磨者。乃跡其說。互相作妄。要知。非欺達磨也。乃所以欺自心也。原夫世尊四十九年說法。寔哀憫衆生之自欺於生死中。妄自纏縛。卒莫之已。所以示其心法。欲其不自欺。今反以其心法而自欺。則何所往而不自欺也。

[2] 或問。禪稱教外別傳。果有別傳之理否。每見義學紛紛於此。不能無議。
　幻曰。義學以分別名相爲務。而於此不能盡分別之理。使盡究其極則。於別傳二字。當一笑而釋矣。何則夫四宗。共傳一佛之旨。不可闕一也。然佛以一音演說法。教中謂。惟一佛乘。無二無三。安容有

四宗之別耶。謂各擅專門之別。非別一佛乘也。譬如四序成一歲之功。而春夏秋冬之令。不容不別也。其所不能別者。一歲之功也。密宗。春也。天台。賢首。慈恩等宗。夏也。南山律宗。秋也。少林單傳之宗。冬也。就理言之。但知禪爲諸宗之別傳。而不知諸宗亦禪之別傳也。會而歸之。密宗乃宣一佛大悲拔濟之心也。教宗乃闡一佛大智開示之心也。律宗乃持一佛大行莊嚴之心也。禪宗乃傳一佛大覺圓滿之心也。猶四序之不可混。既不可混。非別而何。

或者謂。彼三宗皆不言別傳。惟禪宗顯言別傳者。何耶。

對曰。理使然也。諸宗皆從門而後入。由學而後成。惟禪。內不涉思惟計度之情。外不加學問修證之功。窮刻迫今。不曾欠少。擬心領荷。早涉途程。脫體承當。翻成鈍置。誠別中之別也。彼按圖索馬者。烏足以知之。聞吾禪有教外別傳之說。無怪其驚且駭矣。

[3] 或問。永嘉以惺惺寂寂爲藥。昏住亂想爲病。此說與達磨所傳之禪如何。

余曰。永嘉集中。十篇大指。所明修證之說。大約取止觀法門。首則息念忘塵。次則境智冥寂。至於別立觀心十門。至玄至妙。深達無生。惟達磨只教人直下明取自心。此心既明。如人到家。自能隨時作活。更不廣引言教者。良有以也。其曲引神光處。惟言。外絕諸緣。內心無喘。心如牆壁。乃可入道。此外不聞別有言說。但真實於自心中有所契證者。則知循階級。歷涯岸。與直指之說。大不侔矣。豈惟永嘉然。至若天台之三觀。賢首之四法界觀。皆曲盡此心之至理。使過去諸佛。再現世間。演說心法。逆知其無有過於此者。然不與達磨同者。蓋即言教。離言教之別耳。盡理言之。如圓覺以三觀互分爲二十五輪。及楞嚴以十八界七大性證爲二十五圓通。豈止此二經。但涉經教中所陳修證法門。亦皆不與達磨所傳直指之禪。同途共轍也。何則使苟涉言教。則不得爲教外別傳也。

或謂。若然則達磨之禪與諸佛言教。異耶。

對曰。我於佛祖之道。覓同相尚不可得。而何異之可見耶。爾不聞教中謂總持無文字。文字顯總持之說乎。然總持無文字。則達磨契之而直指也。文字顯總持。則諸宗即之而引導也。且達磨之道。異於諸宗者。非其尚異而私出乎自己之智臆也。乃遠繼靈山最後獨付大迦葉之心法也。其獨付大迦葉之道。亦非靈山一人之私有者。即盡法界衆生共稟之靈心也。故世尊興慈。運悲。垂教。設化之際。曲徇衆生利鈍等差之根器。其所謂大小偏圓。同異顯密之方便。不容自已也。

[4] 或問。間有言教與禪家直指之說同者。如華嚴謂。知一切法。即心自性。成就慧身。不由佗悟。如法華謂。是法非思量分別之所能解。如金剛般若謂。凡所有相。皆是虛妄。及是法平等。無有高下。如圓覺謂。知是空花。即無輪轉。亦無身心。受彼生死。如楞嚴謂。根塵

同源。縛脫無二。及知見立知等。以至諸經諸論中。其相似之語。層見疊出。亦豈待達磨直指而後然耶。

　幻曰。余不云乎。此文字顯總持者也。苟不曾向自心中真實契證一回。徒說藥不療病也。若是真實有所契證之人。豈惟大乘經論之語。能契達磨之禪。但是鹿言細語。至若風聲雨滴。未有不與達磨所指之禪相契者。苟不能妙契自心於言象之外。但將大乘經論相似之語。記憶在心。古所謂依佗作解障自悟門。又以金屑入眼為喻。甚明。宜深思之。勿自惑也。豈惟經教文字不同達磨所指之理。且如禪宗門下。自二祖安心。三祖懺罪。南嶽磨磚。青原垂足。至若擎叉。輥毬。用棒使喝。及一千七百則機緣。莫不皆是八字打開。兩手分付。直下更有何物為閒為礙。儞若不曾向己躬下透脫得過。擬將情意識。領覽一箇元字脚。記憶在心。是謂雜毒入心。如油入麪。又云。醍醐上味。為世所珍。遇斯等人。翻成毒藥。蓋知。此事無人用心處。無人著意處。無人指[1]足處。無人下手處。直須親向自己躬下。蹉步一踏到底。始解相應。凡欬唾掉臂。一一從目[2]己胷中流出。如師子兒不求伴侶。始知前面一千七百則。皆脫空妄語。狐涎雜毒。焉肯涉佗毫髮。惜乎。聞有一等聰明之士。不求自悟。日夕坐在雜毒坑中。分向上向下。全提半提。最初末後。正按旁敲。照用主賓。縱奪死活等。曲搜旁注。強立巧求。安箇名字。喚作宗門關鍵。眩惑後人。更或揀辨言語。區分機要。謂那箇尊宿語。全提向上。不帶枝葉。謂那箇尊宿語。新奇巧妙。凌爍古今。那箇尊宿語。是道者禪。乾曝曝地。百般比況。萬種搏量。殊不知。前輩大達之士。胷中七穿八穴。無一物可守。臨機應物。信手拈來。初無揀擇。直下如迅雷掣電。擬覓蹤由。則劍去久矣。又安肯局於見量。弄峻機。裁巧語。思欲鼓誘後昆。俾其宗尚者哉。且前輩尊宿。應機垂示。其語言有鹿細。顯密。廣略之不同途者。蓋各各發自真心。初無造作。如洪鐘巨鼓。隨扣而聲。其聲之大小清濁。本乎一定之器。或器之不逮。苟欲微加外助。則失其本真矣。今之禪流。將欲據大牀揮塵尾。首取諸家語要。揀擇記持。及漁獵百氏之雜說以資談柄者。是說禪之師也。不惟不能與人解粘去縛。而亦自失本真。喪壞道眼。如此妄習。互相趣尚。既失祖庭之重望。又安有所謂起叢林。興法社之理哉。原夫。世尊出世。達磨西來。咸欲與盡大地人。解黏去縛。是儞最初不識好惡。把自家一片本來清淨潔白田地。妄以無邊聲色污染得。無措足處。及乎捨親割愛依師學道。且前面之污染。莫之洗滌。而又添入如許多佛法知解。使伊重失本心。深可憐憫。所以前輩唱導之師。忍俊不禁。出來吐一機。垂一令。如吹毛劒。向伊重處一截。直欲斷其生死命根。誠以真慈痛憫而然。豈圖門高戶峻。以重後學之仰望邪。蓋前輩大達之士。

[1] Correction in margin = 措
[2] Correction in margin = 自.

最初皆是的的以己事未明。跨山越海。求人決擇。忽撞著箇聱訛話頭。透脫不去。如吞栗棘蓬相似。又如遇怨敵相似。孜孜于懷。經寒涉暑。廢寢忘餐。至於終身。無斯須間斷。決不肯容易覓人開示。亦不肯向文字語言上尋討。直欲待其真機自發。打破疑團。而後已。自有宗門以來。凡有契有證者。莫不皆然。所以一箇箇腳跟穩密。等閑動步。如師子兒驚群動衆。故宗門以此相因。而有做工夫之說焉。

[5] 或問。永明和尚作宗鏡錄百卷。廣引大乘經論之文。配吾達磨直指之禪。其志亦奇矣。似亦不免開鑿尋文解義之端乎。

幻曰。不然。達磨自至此土。其直指之道。六傳至曹溪。溪又九傳至大法眼。眼又二傳而至永明。其間哲人偉士。奇蹤異行。雖後先錯出。照映今古。而三藏學者。不能無議於吾道。由是永明和尚。弘多生智慧辯才之力。該羅經教。述而辨之。其縱橫放肆。左右逢原。是謂即文字之總持門也。俾三藏學者。不敢置吾徒於佛海之外。與明教和尚之輔教編。精搜百氏博達群書。伸釋氏之真慈。杜儒門之重嫉。此二書乃佛祖之墻岸。謂開鑿尋文解義之端。不可也。苟無二師之真誠玄解。甚不可彷效而作也。

或謂。永明和尚。復出萬善同歸集。與宗鏡之說不同。何著述之自反也。

余曰。心乃萬善之本也。宗鏡則卷萬善歸一心。此集則散一心入萬善。其卷舒開合。未嘗不相通也。蓋防禪者之未悟而畧萬行也。亦止三藏學者。議吾禪之不該萬行也。故申而明之。非苟然也。古今天下之師。捨永明其誰歟。

或謂。禪家於萬行。不可不脩邪。

余曰。達磨門下只貴悟明自心。此心既明。於六度萬行。無修與不修之過。或修之則無能修所修之執。或不修則無任情失念之差。苟此心未了。則修與不修俱名虛妄。禪者宜以明心為要。萬行可以次之也。

[6] 或問。十地階級。與禪如何。

幻曰。聞十地乃具神通。聖人約其所至之理而建立。故古人謂。十地如空中鳥跡。凡大乘菩薩等。靡不由之。而不可以定執也。達磨只論見性成佛。自餘身土地位因果等。俱畧而不言者。蓋達磨之禪。乃諸佛心宗。獨為圓頓上乘之機而設。說箇成佛。已背真詮。何則以正法眼藏。觀無邊眾生。各各本來成佛。又何待指其見性而後成邪。佛尚無可成。何十地之復論哉。

[7] 或問。古者謂撥草瞻風只圖見性。傅大士謂。只遮語聲是。莫離此外。別有見性之理否。或無則學人便與麼負荷時如何。

幻曰。若使一期說性。則不妨徧將古人極理之談。從頭記一遍過。其如轉說轉遠何。蓋見性之理。離言說相。離思惟相。離分別相。離取捨相。繁興大用。舉必全真。儞擬存一毫知見。則覿體相背矣。今之眼見耳聞。孰不說箇見性。被人問著箇性。便道無有不是者。乃引教中謂諸法所生惟心所現之說爲證。好教儞知。說也說得是。證也證得分曉。只是要與之念念相應。不勝其遠矣。何則蓋不曾從命根斷處。能所盡時。覿體契悟得來。皆陰識依通爾。凡說時有箇性。雖說得有箇性。於正說時亦未嘗不迷。更莫說。儞無明暗起。邪妄橫生。儼然與說時似有兩箇。欲望其念念相應。其可得哉。須知真正人前。尚不許說箇相應底道理。矧乎不相應者哉。當知此等異見之人。有二種過差。一則自家發心學道時。只要說得與道相通。初無決定要洞明生死大事之正念。第二是一等謬見之師。畧不顧學者因地正不正。惟見其稍負天資。必欲巧施方便。不待其做工夫守正念。惟一味將箇即心是佛。即色明心底相似話頭。互相熱瞞。只要控他箇入處。只待其口開便了。今之禪林。相習成風。正不知何所圖邪。如圓覺楞嚴訶斥此等謬見於二千年外。蓋聖人預知末世衆生有此妄習。故作如是曲申問答。必使其知非而自改也。奈何其不以生死大事爲己重任者。惟務言通自以爲了。忽然撞著箇真正眼目人。搖手向伊道三箇不是。早是心中七上八下。便若遭其訶斥。則怒氣不勝其高矣。儞若真實要與此事相應一回。最先痛以眼見耳聞奇言妙語。盡情掃去。苟使其有絲髮凝滯于心中。是謂惡毒入心。佛亦難救。大抵學人固是被他師家一時引入草窠裏。亦是自家有所重於解會而然。儞若必欲要向生死岸頭做得主宰。設使釋迦彌勒。將禪道佛法傾入儞肺肝。只把箇不從佗得底一句子照看。自然惡心嘔吐也。儞豈肯受此惡毒。以其無此正見。所以開眼受人埋沒。儞若果然只要會禪。不消頃刻間等閑說箇喻子。便教儞將千七百則葛藤。一時穿過。有甚麼難。以其無益。不如固[3]盡生不會底最親切。此事若可以與你過付得。則香嚴昔在溈山門下。不用入南陽住菴。阿難於楞嚴會中。不勞悲泣也。儞莫說道和會便是。箇真正悟明底人。必欲要將箇悟處來主張。早是不相稱矣。而況以心意識。向相似語言上。妄自和會箇目前昭昭靈靈底浮光幻影。認爲主人公。寶之於懷抱。實迷中之倍人也。久之不悛。遠招妄談般若之報。百年影謝。噬臍何及哉。昔忠國師謂。近來南方佛法。大槩變了。盡謂四大身中有箇神性。不生不滅。四大壞時。此性不壞。此等見解。與西天外道等。又如長沙和尚。有學道之人不識真。只爲從前認識神之語。皆指今日妄認六塵緣影爲自心相者。即楞嚴所謂棄却百千大海。認一漚爲全潮者也。更有一等儱侗真如底。便道。盡十方

---

[3] Translation follows Noguchi and Matsubara, *Sanbō yawa*, 58 固 = 箇.

世界是箇自己。此性包虛空徧法界。混古今融聖凡。與森羅萬象無所間然。遂引古人拈一莖草是丈六金身。一毛端上現寶王剎等語爲證。爭奈說食不療飢。說衣不治寒。何也。須是親曾與麼悟一回始得。直饒儞親曾與麼悟了。又要遇本色宗匠。與你掃其所悟之跡。不然則謂之見刺入心。執藥成病。此豈以言通意達而爲了哉。蓋無量刼來生死根塵。今日要與和盤翻轉。又要儞與所翻之力頓忘功用。豈小根淺器者。所能擬哉。此說實非鼓惑。惟切於痛爲生死者以爲然。自餘惟務說禪之士。將反面而見唾。則吾亦何敢辭。

[8] 或有號西歸子者。過門曰。某念阿彌陀佛。求生淨土。其透脫生死。似易於參禪。蓋遠承阿彌陀佛願力冥資故也。爾參禪無把捉。無聖力冥資。苟非大根利器。一聞千悟者。難於趣入。以故永明壽禪師有十人九蹉路之譏。

咄。是何言歟。審如是。則淨土外別有禪耶。使果有之。則佛法二字。自相矛盾。安有會入圓融之理哉。爾不達善權方便。局於己見。誣謗先哲。夫永明揀禪淨土爲四句。乃曲徇機宜。特方便抑揚耳。蓋教中所謂於一乘道。分別說三之意也。如長蘆北磵眞歇天目諸師。作淨土章句。皆寄談即心自性之禪。初無異致。間有指。東都曦法師。於定中。見蓮華標圓照本禪師之名。疑其單傳之師。安得標名於此。故往質之。照曰。雖在禪門。亦以淨土兼修耳。當時圓照。謾展善權。不孤來問。豈眞然耶。昧者。不達權變。剛謂禪外別有淨土可歸。及引永明禪淨土四句爲口實。不亦謬乎。

客避席曰。試請辨之。

幻曰。淨土心也。禪亦心也。體一而名二也。迷者執其名。以昧其體。悟者達其體。以會其名。豈特淨土然。如教中謂。知一切法。即心自性。又云。森羅及萬象。一法之所印。但悟自心之禪。即其三界萬法。混入靈源。舉必全眞。初無揀擇。既無東西兩土之殊。安有淨穢二邦之異。促十萬億土於跬步。寶池金地充塞寰區。延一剎那頃於永年。翠竹黃花同歸正受。四大海月塵塵獨朗。五須彌毫處處分輝。老達磨頓忘明月珠。阿彌陀失卻黃金印。禪門皆剩語。淨土亦虛名。名體見銷。是非情盡。丈六身一莖草。何劣何優。三千界半點塵。孰多孰少。是謂一味平等法門。苟非眞正全身悟入。安有解脫之理哉。且參禪要了生死。念佛修淨土亦要了生死。聖人設教。雖千塗萬轍。一皆以决了生死爲究竟。然破生死根塵。惟尚一門深入。古人謂。毫釐繫念。三途業因。瞥爾情生。萬刼覊鎖。兼修云乎哉。或不如此。談禪說淨土。沸騰識浪。鼓扇情塵。卒未有已也。余所以不能無辯。

[9] 或問。達磨始以單傳直指之道。至十餘傳而分爲五家宗派者。何也。不可破裂達磨一家之說。異而爲五耶。儻不異則安有五家之說乎。

幻曰。所云五家者。乃五家其人。非五家其道也。爾不聞。佛祖授受之旨。目爲傳燈。苟知傳燈之義。則不疑其爲五也。請以世燈言之。有籠燈焉。有蓋燈焉。有瑠璃燈焉。有蠟燭燈焉。有紙撚燈焉。謂燈則一也。而所附之器不同爾。雖曰不同。未有不能破生死長夜之幽暗者。豈惟今之五家爲然。昔達磨一燈。凡四傳至大醫。則有牛頭一宗。五傳至大滿。則有北秀一宗。六傳至曹溪而下。則青原南嶽荷澤。此三人者。便自不可得而混矣。此勢使然也。蓋各宗之下。枝分派衍。人物蕃昌。乃不分而分矣。今之謂五家者。乃出自南嶽青原兩派之下。沿流至此五人。不覺。其各各如奔匯之水。溢爲巨浸。前波後浪。各不相待而粘天沃日。浩無邊涯。是可以一目觀之哉。乃不得不分焉。

或謂。五家之分。不止於人之盛。就中各有宗旨不同。

幻曰。非不同也。特大同而小異爾。云大同者。同乎少室之一燈也。云小異者。乃語言機境之偶異爾。如溈仰之謹嚴。曹洞之細密。臨濟之痛快。雲門之高古。法眼之簡明。各出其天性。而父子之間。不失故步。語言機境。似相蹈習。要皆不期然而然也。使當時宗師。苟欲尚異而自爲一家之傳。則不勝其謬矣。以若所爲。豈堪傳佛祖照世之命燈乎。今之禪流泥乎宗旨。而起夾截虐空之妄見。互相短長。余知。五宗之師。於大寂定中。莫不掩鼻矣。

[10] 或問。佛祖機緣。世稱公案者。何耶。

幻曰。公案乃喻乎公府之案牘也。法之所在。而王道之治亂。實係焉。公者乃聖賢一其轍。天下同其途之至理也。案者乃記聖賢爲理之正文也。凡有天下者。未嘗無公府。有公府者。未嘗無案牘。蓋欲取以爲法而斷天下之不正者也。公案行則理法用。理法用則天下正。天下正則王道治矣。夫佛祖機緣。目之曰公案亦爾。蓋非一人之臆見。乃會靈源契妙旨。破生死越情量。與三世十方百千開士同稟之至理也。且不可以義解。不可以言傳。不可以文詮。不可以識度。如塗毒鼓。聞者皆喪。如大火聚。嬰之則燎。故靈山謂之別傳者傳此也。少林謂之直指者指此也。自南北分宗。五家列派以來。諸善知識。操其所傳。負其所指。於賓扣主應。得牛還馬之頃。龜言細語信口捷出。如迅雷不容掩耳。如庭前栢樹子麻三斤乾屎橛之類。畧無義路與人穿鑿。即之如銀山鐵壁之不可透。惟明眼者能逆奪於語言文字之表。一唱一和。如空中鳥跡。水底月痕。雖千途萬轍。放肆縱橫。皆不可得而擬議焉。遠自鷲嶺拈花。迨于今日。又豈止乎一千七百則而已哉。無佗。必待悟心之士。取以爲證據耳。實不欲人益記持而資談柄也。世稱長老者。即叢林公府之長吏也。其編燈集錄者。即記其激揚提唱之案牘也。古人或匡徒之隙。或掩關之暇。時取以拈之判之。頌之別之。豈爲炫燿見聞。抗衡古德而然。蓋痛思大法之將弊。故曲施方便。開鑿後昆之智眼。欲俾其共證之爾。言公者防其己解。案者必期與佛祖契同也。然公案通則情識盡。情識盡則生死空。生死空則佛道洽矣。所云契同者。乃佛祖大哀眾生自縛於生死情妄之域。積刼迨今莫之自釋。故於無言中顯言。無象中垂象。待其迷繩既釋。安有言象之可復議乎。且世之人。有事不得其平者。必求理於公府。而吏曹則舉案牘以平之。猶學者有所悟解不能自決。乃質之於師。則舉公案以決之。夫公案。即燭情識昏暗之慧炬也。揭見聞瞖膜之金篦也。斷生死命根之利斧也。鑑聖凡面目之神鏡也。祖意以之廓明。佛心以之開顯。其全超迥脫大達同證之要。莫越於此。所謂公案者。惟識法者懼。苟非其人。詎可窺其彷彿也。嗟。世之迷妄者。不考其源。每以聰明之資。廣尋博記。顯授密傳。惟務言通。匪求心悟。致使棒喝交馳之勝軌。墮情想之稠林。龍象蹴踏之靈蹤。陷是非之深穽。愛憎溢目。取捨盈懷。古人醍醐毒藥之喻。驗於斯矣。叢林之替。莫有不本於此者。嗚呼。猶吏曹竊法以貨天下之賄賂。巳[4]私一勝。欲望公道有治平之効。其可得乎。

[11] 或問。祖師公案。本於學者因疑致問。而古人大寂滅心中。如虛谷巨鼓隨扣而應。持不過與人破疑情。裂窠臼而已。所以云。我宗無語句。亦無一法與人。蓋前輩既爲人所師。不得已而酬酢。一言半句流落叢林。後之承虛接響者。目之爲公案。乃本於此一箇道理。今之叢林商量。大不如此。乃以問佛問西來意之一問一答。如麻三斤乾屎橛須彌山莫妄想之類。喚作單提淺近者。以勘婆話墮托鉢上樹等爲向上全提者。或以眾機緣列歸三玄。或以諸語言判入四句。中間。曲談巧辯。網羅千七百則公案。各立異名。互存高下。不識。古人之意果爾否。

幻曰。祖師語言。蓋出於大空寂無爲心中。信手拈來。初無揀擇。凡一拈一放。本於達磨單傳之旨。口開見膽。絕無覆藏。譬如月之在天。其東行者視之則月與之俱東。西行者謂月與之俱西。中間不動者謂月與之不動。各執所見。互有東西不動之殊。而滿月當空。實未曾循其東西。而依其不動者也。其泛說不同者。蓋由未徹法源底耳。所以有循器定空之喻。前輩明眼宗師舉似之頃。或抑或揚。又不可以此開口不在舌頭上之語爲證。其有於一機一境上會得。纔涉著縱奪逆順處。罔知所措。無佗。特悟理之未盡。然公案雖是一箇道理。其差別處。如人入海。轉入轉深。久之直到九淵之底。驀忽回首一看。則知未嘗別有海也。苟不親到一回。則胷中之疑。不約而自至矣。只如僧問馬祖。如何是佛。祖云。即心是佛。此箇公案雖不曾參禪者。亦皆領會得過。及乎扣其極致。則久条宿學亦少有不錯會者。何則殆問伊喚甚麼作心。早是路頭生也。遮裏要指點得的當。直須親曾逴得在手。反覆看一遍。看教明明白白。如十字街頭撞著親爺相似。自然舉

[4] Note: in the *Gozanban* 9 text of the *Zhongfeng Extensive Record* 巳 sometimes = 己 or 已. Here 巳 = 己. Other instances have not been marked, but they have been taken into consideration in the translation.

起便合轍也。或有一等不曾做工夫。不曾洞明心地。不曾截得腳跟下生死大疑命根子斷。惟以聰明之資。向古今文字上。將相似語言。較量卜度會盡古今公案。殊不知。既不了生死。返不如箇不會底最真。雖曰不會。忽然一日。發起信心真參實究。却有箇悟明之時。惟聰利而領會者。不復生正信而穎悟也。近來叢林。欲速於得人。亦不待學者聰利。師家把著本子逐一句。如教童蒙。讀上大人相似。欲其領會共資玄化。此無異吹網欲滿者。本色道流。既不肯食此惡毒。但遇著古今因緣。都不要將心解會。只消舉起一箇。頓在面前。發起決要了生死之正志。壁立萬仞。與之久遠參去。驀爾撞破疑團。則百千萬則公案。深與淺。難與易。同與別。一串穿過。自然不著問人也。如或心眼未開。不肯扣已而參。必欲求人開示。縱使釋迦達磨。披肝瀝膽以示之。益障其心眼耳。思之思之。

山房夜話中

[12] 或問。達磨西來。門風險絕。言前薦得。已涉途程。安有所謂做工夫。況枯坐蒲團。如守屍鬼。且禪豈可以坐而得邪。無乃辱累先宗者乎。

余曰。不辱累也。爾蓋知此而不知彼也。如龍潭問天皇。學人久依和尚。不蒙開示心要。皇曰。儞擎茶來。我則舉手。儞來問訊。我則低頭。那裏不是與儞開示心要處。潭遂領旨。此箇公案。以學者言之。不勝快便。以宗門言之。又不止涉途程而已。又如香嚴被溈山問父母未生已前事。不能加對。乃求溈山爲說。山不允。遂盡棄所習。入南陽住菴。久之忽以瓦礫擊竹有聲。始能瞥地。彼時雖不形做工夫之名。其孜孜退守。念茲在茲。爲何所圖邪。雖不能直下領畧。而歷涉歲月方乃省悟。其悟之之旨。謂非達磨所傳之旨乎。今之做工夫不靈驗者。第一無古人真實志氣。第二不把生死無常做一件大事。第三拌捨積刼已來所習所重不下。十二時中。雖隨人舉箇話頭。方上蒲團坐席未溫。其昏沉散亂左右圍繞。又不具久遠不退轉身心。難矣哉。安有天生彌勒。斯言盡之矣。往往見無所成者。不責己之不逮。而返以佛法下衰叢林秋晚。爲辭而言。在處上無煅煉之師。旁無策進之友。況是湯火不便。粥飯不齊。規矩荒蕪。境緣謬亂。致使工夫由之而廢墜。此說之行。更無有學道之人。不以此爲口實。譬如農夫責水旱不時而廢耕耘。則安有秋成之望哉。但是學道人對違順境。瞥生一念欲與之分別。予知其纏縛萬刼生死之咎。必基於此矣。爾不聞。雪嶺老沙門。棄萬乘尊榮。六年之間。臥氷囓蘖。忘形於凍餒之中。乃有夜覩明星之悟。自佛以降。西天二十八祖。皆嚴棲穴處。或混跡於差別門頭。以真心不泯實行無差。皆克證己躬傳佛心印。及達磨東邁。百丈未生。牛頭橫出一枝。南北宗分兩派。皆腰鎌荷鍤。火種刀耕。執爨負舂。鶉衣丐食。鐵石身心。冰霜懷抱。以佛祖大事因緣。一肩負荷。了無畏怯。蓋行處既親。所到必的矣。彼時安有五山十刹之廣居。三玄五位之奇唱。放收殺活之異作。拈頌判別之殊音。不加雕琢而玉本無瑕。安用規模。而眼元自正。自百丈建叢林已來。廣由大宅指顧如意。其奈正因日墜。謬妄日滋。紀綱日繁。禮義日削。數百載前提唱之師。如臨濟德山雲門真淨。氣憤憤地。怒罵諸方。如婬女兵奴視之。蓋責其不體道本。惟務言通。互相欺誑者也。已而聞有眼自定動之師。喻諸方說禪。如葉公之龍。趙昌之花。然葉公趙昌已自不真。矧乎復有效葉公趙昌者出。烏焉成馬之歎。正不在今日也。由是觀之。其真參實悟之士。不惟鮮遇於今日。在往昔亦未嘗多見也。無佗。蓋生死情妄。無明結習。念念遷流。間不容髮。苟不有入骨入髓。痛為生死之正念。提起話頭。如遇怨敵。便拌一生兩生。與之抵睚。待其廓然開悟。靡有不為葉公趙昌之所惑者。或有引三祖謂但莫憎愛洞然明白。與永嘉不除妄想不求真之語相證云。只遮箇便是悟理。何假一生兩生勞形苦志。以為得邪。此說之行。搖動葉公趙昌之心。卒莫之已也。殊不思。永嘉有損法財滅功德。莫不由斯心意識之語。痛指其不求正悟者。妄將心意識。和會相似語言。一人傳虛。萬人傳實。又不翅烏焉成馬也。所以古人道。參須實參。悟須實悟。閻羅大王不怕多語。斯言盡之矣。予固非實悟者。惟不敢輕蹈葉公趙昌之轍耳。尋常與人東語西話。較量此事。皆是自信法門。初非炫耀見聞要譽於人也。人或見信。余不加喜。或不見信。亦何敢怒。然信不信。皆當人之自心。庸何喜怒為哉。惟同道乃知。或若以妄誕見譏。則吾亦何敢諱。

[13] 或問。參禪不克開悟。還有方便可使其開悟否。如或展轉不悟。其生死無常大事。向後之又後世。還有自了之理否。

幻曰。快哉問。此事是當人己躬下事。初不干第二人連累。亦不屬第二人排遣。所以云。迷是自迷。悟須自悟。苟不自悟。縱是釋迦達磨。亦為儞不得。今時師家。多是不奈學者之不悟何。所以巧設機緣。曲施方便。以啟迪之。而學者又不以生死大事。為己重任。惟欲速於會禪。於是便向佗方便中蹲坐。盡將古今公案一串穿却。謂之透關。殊不知。腳跟下一座生死牢關。政好不曾透得。其所透者乃言說之關耳。豈惟無益。返有害於己事也。若是箇真實為生死大事底好人。縱是達磨大師出現世間。把諸佛祖玄要道理。盡情放在伊八識田中。也須和根吐却。何以如此。蓋悟須自悟。豈干佗人半錢事。若也終身不悟。但只堅持正念。生與同生。死與同死。不必妄求一毫知解。苟能如是操守。只隔得一生兩生。不患其不悟明也。或有坐在靜默中。於塵勞暫息之頃。忽於陰識中。邐省得箇相似底道理。便乃依約為是。勾引經教中語言證過。含於心中。不知。此病是陰識依通。真生死本。非見性也。堅執為了。不肯求人決擇。到處只要人把冬瓜印子與之印過。此何所圖哉。又有一等妄認六塵緣影爲自己主人公。及引古人謂未了之人聽一言。只遮如今誰動口之語爲證。大率參學不獲正悟者。不惟生死岸頭用不得。即今白日青天。大開兩眼。遇聲遇色。動輒生情起念。不得自由。人或非之。則發起根本無明。與之爭執。此蓋狂人之所爲也。又或有盡生學道。無所悟入。便乃不信。尋而把箇學道之正念。擎在無事甲中。更不復起求開悟之心。如此等人。謂之失正念。既失正念。莫說後之又後世不能自了。縱使徧歷塵沙。盡未來際。亦無自了之時。譬之良田不加耕耨。而望其五穀自生。無是理也。

[14] 或問。盡世參禪。不獲開悟。有何果報。

幻曰。豆種不生麻麥。草根不產松樁。蓋參禪雖曰是無功用法門。但恐其不真參耳。如永明和尚謂。假使參而未徹。學而未成。歷在耳根。永爲道種。世世不落惡趣。生生不失人身。纔出頭來。一聞千悟。皆誠言也。世之暫修片善。尚獲勝利。教中有聞五種名。超刹寶施福。豈事虛語哉。最初發心。本期決了生死大事。或三十年二十年。未即開悟。不須別求方便。但心不異緣。意絕諸妄。孜孜不捨。只向所叅話上。立定脚頭。只拚取生與同生死與同死。誰管三生五生。十世百世。如不徹悟。決定不休。有此正因。不患大事之不我明也。故教中謂。末世衆生。能發一念不退轉心。即同正覺。斯言盡之矣。今之學者反是。於最初發心。便自立脚不穩。惟恐境緣倏變。念慮俄興。做主不牢。流入異路。以之念念馳求。速期超越。殊不知。返爲此馳求之念所障。把箇要了生死大事底正因。妄自遮障。久之不決。忽爾遷變者有三。或者勝心不捨。頗負聰明。矧乎師友之罔其悟理。惟尚言通。不自覺知。涉入知解。以相似般若。粘綴識田。自謂了明。莫知虛妄。則其口出耳入之習。紛紛皆是。化權衰替。鮮有不墮其轍者。此其一也。或者志氣狹劣。識見淺陋。每向工夫邊。倚靠不穩。將謂此無功用法門。絕無靈驗。惟限以十年二十年。或不相應。遽變前因。或以念佛爲徑路修行。朝暮掐數珠。求淨業。或以一代時教。佛口所宣。我既參禪不靈。未免循行數墨。旋種善因。自謂不爲虛度。或厭煩受用。畏懼報緣。自甘陸沈。垢面草衣。負舂執爨。苦其形體。以資事行。或密持呪語。或潛懺罪愆等。皆是自違正信。遠涉異端。此其二也。或元無信種。遇境興心。三根椽下。坐席未溫。八識田中。攀緣不斷。一箇話頭。咬嚼未破。百般情妄。起滅無時。不至三年五載。遽謂參禪不悟。擎向無事甲中。念念循塵。心心流浪。甘赴死門。未嘗返省者。此其三也。當此叢林像季。祖道荒涼。參學道流。苟不負決定不退轉鐵石身心。則於此三途。不之此則之彼。既失自心之大志。益增佛祖之深哀。法社凋零。未有不本於此者。殊不思。叅禪正信。是千生一遇。百世一。出儻不能一往直前以期真脫。轉念之間。白雲萬里。欲望般若種智復入于心。猶敗穀之芽無復萌矣。

[15] 或問。古人今人參學用心有以異乎。無以異乎。

幻曰。古人學道。未問道之得與不得。脚未跨門首。先將箇偷心。一斬兩段。更不復生。今人純以偷心爲主。此正今古之同異。判然不相涉矣。何謂生死。有偷心是。何謂涅槃。盡偷心是。請以喻言之。生死是大病。佛祖言教是良藥。偷心是藥之所忌。以佛祖言教。治生死之大病。此古今之同然者。安有不治之理。惟是藥有所忌。古人純服藥。鮮有不獲其神效者。今人方藥之未已而繼投之以忌。不惟不治其病。將見增益異證。使大醫主亦斂袵而退矣。何謂偷心。乃識情之異名也。能刼奪自家無上法財。故永嘉謂。損法財滅功德。莫不由斯心意識。且畧舉前輩數段因緣。可爲今時龜鑑者。只如六祖到黄梅。但令槽廠去。潙山在百丈會中充典座。楊岐十餘年惟總院事。演祖於海會充磨主。雲峯之化緣。雪竇之持淨。慈明參汾陽。惟戲笑譏訶。黄龍扣慈明。惟遭詬罵。中間差別之緣錯出。違順之境橫生。但是當人。正因炳煥。死盡偷心。任其異境紛如。一一消歸至理。又何所往而不與道相遇哉。今之人偷心不肯遽死者無佗。蓋己事之不真切耳。雖寄身於空寂之場。而馳念於取捨之域。一種是作興保社。較其優劣。則天冠地履之不相侔矣。何則如今人稍負天資。必欲遠附清名。高攀勝軌。凡猥屑等事。終身不齒。安肯作磨主充典座乎。凡住處雖安居暇食。尚不遂其所欲。安肯入槽廠而爲化士乎。至若手橫麈柄身坐猊牀。正因益微。偷心愈熾。欲其垂念後昆作清涼樹。其可得哉。用是卜化權之盛衰。今古之得失。未有不係乎偷心之有無也。予於此不容不辯。

[16] 或問。偷心於聖凡。有間邪。無間邪。

予曰。偷心何物。即如來妙明元心之至體耳。以其求道之志不真不切。爲諸妄所蔽。轉爲偷心也。猶蟊生於禾。害禾者蟊也。亦猶火生於木。燒木者火也。但求道之念真切。雖寢食於人不可一日無之之事。尚能廢忘。何偷心之不泯哉。譬如人之爲利養甘執賤役於人。雖竟日奉勞苦。而不生疲厭。方一毫不盡其役。則鞭笞罵辱。應時交接。皆所不憚。何其忘羞惡之若是邪。無佗蓋求利養之心真切而致然也。使其憚勞苦畏楚辱。則失利養矣。彼區區爲浮幻之利養。而能忘極重之羞惡。較吾儕之希求聖道而不肯死虛妄之偷心者。何如哉。然凡何異聖。聖何異凡。惟偷心而成異耳。道人可不慎諸。

[17] 或問。做工夫多爲昏沉散亂所障。用盡神力。屏打不去。無乃根力有所不逮而使之然乎。

幻曰。非也。當知昏沉散亂。全體是本地風光。其實際理地中。無二法也。爾其不委。且昏沉散亂初無自性。亦無實體。皆是自家一箇參禪底正念不真不切上入來。當知第一念不真切。即從第一念入。第二念不真切。即從第二念入。乃至百千念真切。竟無所入。或最後一念稍不真切。則便從最後入矣。若使自最初一念真切。直至心花發明之際。其真切之心。了不間斷。則所謂昏沉散亂。杳不知其蹤矣。往往不責爲道之念不真切。而以昏沉散亂爲礙者。是猶自處暗室而責己眼之不能洞視物象者。無以異也。且真實做工夫之人。面前見有昏沉散亂。錯了也。更起念要屏打箇昏沉散亂。又錯了也。然而屏打不去而生憂懼者。更是錯了也。設使屏打得箇昏沉散亂去。面前淨倮倮地。錯之又錯者也。更有箇鹵莽之人。見說昏沉散亂元是本地風光。認以爲是。終日與之輥作一團。而不生分別者。此又不勝其錯也。

或者見余連說許多錯字乃問。如何用心。即得於昏沉散亂上不錯去。

乃謂之曰。苟有心可用。則展轉成錯矣。纔見有昏沉散亂。凡用心不用心。都是顛倒錯謬。

或謂。遮箇向上話。我初機學人。不能得入。

幻曰。學道只要悟明自己真實心地。既悟得諦當。佛與衆生。同途共轍。初無向上向下。只爲你不識昏沉散亂。動遭其惑。於是語言露布。強爲指陳。今則事不獲已。索性將箇昏沉散亂根本。盡情揭露去也。儞無量刼來。爲客塵煩惱染習太重。是昏沉散亂之根本。儞即今見色聞聲。念念與諸緣作對。其愛憎取捨之情。起滅無定。是昏沉散亂之根本。儞最初一念。要超生越死。是昏沉散亂之根本。要參禪學道。是昏沉散亂之根本。要成佛作祖。是昏沉散亂之根本。要希求無上大菩提。趣向涅槃。是昏沉散亂之根本。乃至於世間出世間種種法中。苟存毫髮念慮。莫不皆是昏沉散亂之根本。若根本既斷。於三千大千世界內外中間。欲覓一毫昏沉散亂。了不可得。於不可得處。不惟無昏沉散亂。至若真如實際。俱不可得而有也。且聖凡迷悟之跡。向甚處安著。休將閑學解埋沒祖師心。

[18] 或以學人鮮有不背其初心者爲問。

幻曰。負所欠者其懷虗。滿所期者其情逸。此人之常理。天下古今共之。然懷可使之虗。情不可使之逸也。何則無邊聖道。未有不由虗懷以納受之。無窮結業。未有不因逸情以滋聚之。蓋心念無主。染淨隨緣。一刹那間。變化萬狀。不之道則之業。不之悟則之迷。曷有已也。

偶論及此。忽有老比丘作而言曰。憶昔在俗時。能皆誦法華經四卷。自謂。童齓方服之後。必可通背其所未記之三卷。豈期。出家二十年。不惟廢其未記之三卷。其已誦之四卷亦皆忘失。時聞者莫不掩鼻。

因謂衆曰。當在家也。以負出塵之所欠。每虗其懷抱。故能朝思暮想而受之已。而既滿出家之所期。頓脫塵累。閑情日逸。曾不期忘而忘之矣。原其所失。與今之叅學者無以異焉。且四海無家。一身萬里。其所負之欠。惟欲會禪而後已。一旦遇教壞之師。巧設問端。控其入草。或將聰明之資和會情識。於語言文字上。一印印住。自謂滿所期矣。殊不知。閑情日逸。妄見潛生。則說時似悟。對境還迷。不惟不到古人大解脫之地。求如前日負所欠而孜孜欲會之心。亦茫然無有矣。嗚呼。聖賢之學。豈止是哉。蓋負所欠之懷不深。而希所滿之期不遠也。學者可不慎諸。

[19] 或問。悟心之後。有履踐否。

幻曰。此說難於措言也。所云悟心者。心不自心。悟從何得。悟既不立。心亦無心。心無其心。縱觀虛空萬象。有無情等。覿體混融。欲覓一毫自佗彼此之相。了不可得。於不可得處。無縛無脫。不取不捨。離妄離真。非迷非悟。一念平等。萬法皆如。復有何事可言履踐哉。

或謂。積刼無明。微細染習。尚留觀聽。未即頓消。不可無履踐也。

幻曰。心外無法。法外無心。若見有纖毫情習未盡。即是悟心不圓而然也。或心悟不圓。須是掃其未圓之跡。別立生涯以期大徹可也。其或謂悟心未盡。以履踐盡之。如抱薪救焚。益其熾矣。古人謂。當以佛知見治之。余不識佛知見為何事。或果與佛知見相應。則治之之說亦贅且剩矣。

曰。若然則無履踐之說乎。

答曰。茲不必預以有無履踐自惑于心。請勤加鞭策。到桶底子一回脫落。其履踐之有無。當有以默契于中矣。

[20] 或問。禪者有不斷惡。不修善。不捨貪嗔癡。不習戒定慧。是謂一性平等之說。有諸。

幻曰。此余平生深欲辯而未暇也。今既有所問。當罄而言之。夫達磨悟諸佛心宗。不與外道二乘同轍。惟一心法界中無佛。無眾生。至於生死涅槃。皆名剩語。又何惡可斷。何善可修。及捨貪等而習戒定耶。今之學禪者。於一心之要旨。曾未悟入。遽以此極理之談。竊為己見。妄興狂解。恣逐凡情。破壞律儀。自投籠檻。是謂畫虎不成反類狗也。若必欲要知斷惡修善之底蘊。不必廣尋文義。但只勤究自心。究到無可究處。心眼洞開。始知惡之可斷。不可斷。善之可修。不可修等。當如啞子得夢。所以極理之談者。謂惡與貪等皆是自心。則自心無可斷可捨之理。所以云。不必斷不必捨也。

或謂。既曰不必斷與捨。則行之可無礙乎。

幻曰。爾作是說。誠佛祖之所哀矜而不已者。謂惡等皆是自心。尚不許起心斷。又焉得許伊起心行之也。

或曰。今雖悟知惡貪等是自心。既不許斷。又不許行。其惡貪等。必向何處安著。

幻曰。爾甚惑也。當知一切惡業。及貪嗔癡。與無明煩惱。種種塵勞等。俱無自性。皆由迷自心。故依妄而有。如水因寒結而為冰。此心既悟。則諸妄乘其所悟而消。如冰因慧日所照。復化為水。既化水已。今云。冰復向何處安著。此寔迷中倍人也。

或謂。某人者。已嘗有所悟入。而惡貪等對境遇緣。亦猶自若。此又何如。

幻曰。此有二種。一者悟心未盡。諸妄尚存。苟不進修。則終歸顛倒。一者悟心已圓。洞視諸法。了如昨夢。因示現世間。行同事攝法。似有惡貪等。殊不知。其真心了然超越。當知此行或力量不及者。少加勉強。俱不免過失矣。

[21] 或曰。人有日營萬善者。與至道之體親乎。疎耶。

幻曰。道體本乎無爲。善惡不可加損也。原夫造惡根於迷妄。聖人觀破迷妄之漸。故使之爲善也。善業勝而迷妄消。迷妄消則惡自遣矣。諸惡既遣。萬善亦忘。古人有善惡俱莫思量。自然得入心體之說。謂心體者即至道之異名也。苟遣惡而存善。欲望吾至道之體。不勝其邈矣。試以喻明之。人有惡廁屋之臭以香熏之。莫若置身於無糞穢之地可也。然廁屋喻惡也。香熏喻善也。無糞穢之地。乃至道之體也。人有畏幽室之暗。則執炬以燭之。莫若處於大明之地可也。暗室喻惡也。執炬喻善也。大明之地即至道之體也。復有懼冰雪之寒者。必爟薪以解之。莫若措躬於陽和之室可也。冰寒喻惡也。爟薪喻善也。陽和之室。乃至道之體也。然焚香有斷續。執炬有起滅。爟薪有離在。惟至道之體窮刼不變。積世常存。安有斷續起滅離在之謂哉。修善之於合道也。其親疎之理若是。豈容不辯哉。

[22] 或問。善惡二言。已嘗聞矣。謂善惡之理。世或未能辨。有以鞭笞怒罵爲惡。能忍是惡而不加報者爲善。有以持刃殺人爲惡。以順受其害而不形諸念慮者爲善。有以淫蕩暴亂貪多務得爲惡。以安舒靜默齋戒誦持爲善。

幻曰。斯說皆善惡之跡也。謂理則未然也。使盡言善惡之理。無佗。凡起念動心。所期之事。無大小無優劣。但欲利人皆善也。惟欲利己皆惡也。事或可以利人。雖怒罵擯斥。皆善也。事或可以利己。雖安徐承順。皆惡也。以故。聖賢垂教立化。汲汲於濟世。而無食息之暇者。皆至善之心也。惟衆人反是。雖聖賢其衣冠。文藻其言行。苟不有利人之心。已不勝其惡矣。況暴怒之氣搖動而不息者乎。以若所爲而望善之一言。猶隔霄壤。豈至道云乎哉。

[23] 或問。孔孟之書。言王道。極於仁義而已矣。老莊之書。言皇道。極於無爲而已矣。百氏之書。雜入覇道。極於功利而已矣。吾佛之書。單明性理。謂諸法所生。惟心所現。極於一念不生而已矣。似各擅一門。而不能融會於大同之域。果別無理乎。或別有理乎。

幻曰。謂無則局。謂有則放。聖道俱不取也。其所取者。貴在一門深入。使之自悟。悟後藩籬既決。洞見三教聖人。握手於言象之表。而不有出世世間之間。脫或未悟。縱以四庫書。漁獵于肺肝。含吐於齒頰。特不能脫多聞我見之誚。如西天所謂聰明外道者是也。故學者不求正悟而尚區區於文字之間者。非愚而何。今之稍負聰明者。多不肯死心忘情。以求正悟。每取證於文字語言。不惟無補於理。而增長識情分別。動違聖道。如之何。化權之不衰。叢林之不替也。

[24] 或問。宗門中。有碧巖集者。乃圓悟住夾山時。取雪竇頌古。分綱列要。言批句判。舉揚細密。開發詳明。語其富麗。則如揭開寶聚。而明珠大貝委積橫陳。語其充溢。則如掣斷禹門。而逆浪回瀾掀昂起伏。偉矣哉。非得法自在者。不可及矣。奈何。自開戶牖之士。每資此爲階級。尋而妙喜知之。恐學者流而忘返。嘗入閩碎其板。今書坊仍復刊行。丁茲季運。無乃益學者之穿鑿乎。

幻曰。非也。無邊眾生。各各脚跟下。有一則現成公案。靈山四十九年。詮註不出。達磨萬里西來。指點不破。至若德山臨濟。摸索不著。此又豈雪竇能頌。而圓悟能判者哉。縱使碧巖集有百千萬卷。於佗現成公案上。一何加損焉。昔妙喜不窮此理。而碎其板。大似禁石女之勿生兒也。今復刊此板之士。將有意於攛掇石女之生兒乎。益可笑也。

曰。然則當人脚跟下見成公案。了不與佛祖言教有交涉。則當人何所考而證之乎。

予曰。無所考也。亦無所證也。惟貴當人瞥爾回光退步。一踏與目前見聞覺知。一翻翻轉。則知風前瀑韻。雨後溪聲。無一字非頌也。雷震空山。籟鳴清晝。無一音非判也。至若天高地厚。夜暗晝明。萬象森羅。熾然常說。是謂見成公案之碧巖集者也。雖百千雪竇圓悟。亦當望崖歛衽於言象之表。又安能置一元字脚於其間哉。爾其未諳此旨。彼之建化門中。一成一壞。一抑一揚。特世相之常分耳。爾謂。碧巖集必使學人穿鑿知解。障自悟門。逆推二師之心。恐不爾也。如世尊以正法眼。洞觀法界眾生。各各具有如來智慧德相。但以妄想執著。不能證得。我當教以聖道。令離諸著。然佛豈不知聖道。亦在眾生分上。各各具足。非可以語言教之者。及乎應酬三百餘會差別之機。則大小偏圓頓漸半滿之聲。無日不出乎口。而今古學者不達其語言方便。指以爲實法。各執所解。異見紛然。鼓舞於是非之場。交馳於能所之轍。俾一大藏教去碧巖集。亦不相遠。且聖教尚爾。況佗文字乎。雖然。逮極究言教之得失。實在當人爲己事之真切不真切耳。或爲己事真切。則知片言隻字。果有超越生死之驗。如教中謂鵝主擇乳也。或師資之間。誠有志於克明己事。荷負宗乘。決不肯依文解義。自能扣己而叅。政不在碧巖集之有無也。何足議哉。

[25] 或問。諸方莫不以高峯和尚令人然指受戒爲異者。然乎否耶。

幻曰。亦嘗親聞其異矣。因以異之之說。扣之先師。先師曰。不異也。彼不識權變而然。我寧不知。達磨大師單傳直指見性之旨。文字尚不立。何戒可受乎。然達磨不言戒者。有二理存焉。一觀宗。二驗人。觀宗者。達磨專以傳佛心印爲宗。惟務單傳。俾之一超直入如來地。不涉大小二乘階級。其宗旨如是。言戒則背矣。驗人者。凡達磨門下。皆上根利器之士。非夙熏般若種智具最上乘根性者。不可涉入。如此等人其於戒定慧之學。深熏熟煉。政不待復令其受戒也。故達磨之時。宜乎不言戒。彼雖不言。而亦未聞令人故毀之也。自達磨而下。其具大乘根性者。四方八面。雲興海湧。古今沿襲而來。亦皆畧而不言戒者。乃宗旨之當然也。初未聞有不守戒律而傳佛心宗者。昔慈受和尚。乃宗門碩德。每於舉揚之次。極讚人具受戒法。眞歇和尚。建勸發菩提心會。與四眾敷宣。此二師。乃權變之漸也。昔湛堂準和尚。㕝梁山乘禪師。乘曰。驅烏未受戒。敢學佛乘乎。堂捧手曰。壇場是戒耶。三羯磨梵行阿闍黎是戒耶。乘乃驚異。堂曰。雖然。敢不受教。遂詣康安律師。受具足戒。從上宗門中言戒之事。尤多。不及繁舉。由此言之。則受戒。豈可謂之背少林宗旨而爲異也。所云權變者。隨時適宜。知有補於理。故不疑也。思。我初入眾時。乃開慶景定間。如淨慈雙徑。皆不下四五百眾。其住持頭首。固不在言。眾寮中間。有一人半人飲酒。雖不常飲。而鄉人鄰單。未嘗不以此誚之。除飲之外。佗事鮮有所聞。今則自上至下。蕩而忘返。無所避忌。昔佛說五戒。爲白衣設。比丘自有四分僧祇等律。及三聚具足大戒。且白衣之戒尚逸。而況律儀乎。溈山亦云。止持作犯。束斂初心。然初心一步也。傳佛心宗千里也。未有一步不能行而能到千里者。古人謂。持戒學道。是把本修行。或根性遲鈍。一生道眼不明。亦得戒力擁護。道念令不忘失。則來生易於成辦也。如言教中。以楞嚴圓覺二經。是大乘圓頓之要詮。請試撿閱。其中未嘗不以戒爲要務。故古者謂。戒爲基址。道爲屋廬。二者若無。一身安寄。此余所以從權設變也。復何異哉。若以教人持戒爲異。如百丈建立許多威儀禮法。凡行住坐臥。靡不周該而悉備。較之達磨直指人心之旨。得非異乎。或謂。自安眾以來。其叢林禮法。不可使一日無也。殊不知。戒律乃叢林禮法之根本。未有絕其根本而枝葉自能存者。嗟乎。道體喪而戒力消。戒力消則叢林之禮法失矣。安得天下人心復存乎道。我於今日。而以戒示人者。何異之有。此皆先師誠諦之語。偶因所問。不覺打開布袋。譊譊若此。識者。毋以我爲好辯云。

[26] 或問。佛菩薩皆具神通。此神通還屬修證否。

　幻曰。神通亦屬修證。亦不屬修證也。夫神通者。是諸佛菩薩。於久遠刼中。純以四無量心六波羅蜜。及種種善行之所熏習而然也。言屬修證者。苟不因如上種種熏習。則不具也。言不屬修證者。當知佛菩薩所行諸波羅蜜。及眾善功德等。非爲求具神通而然。乃其大悲熏心本已。願行之當然者。使佛菩薩苟有一念欲求神通。則當頭被此一念障住。縱盡修諸善行等。皆成有漏之因。安得具此自在解脫變化之神通耶。或未曾契證諸佛心宗。及種種無作願行。而至自餘二乘小果及外道等。亦各有神通變化。非神通也。乃幻力變現。皆有作思惟成就。實顯異惑衆之生滅因也。夫佛菩薩大悲熏心。無作願力。所現之神通。殊勝與法性平等。雖於一毛孔。現出百千光明。百千莊嚴具。充塞法界。隨其欲樂。皆獲滿足。而佛菩薩解脫心中。不見有具是神通者。亦不見有現是神通者。亦不見有依是神通而獲受用滿足者。何以知之。蓋神通與法性平等。然法性無一異自佗能所分別之差。則知神通亦爾也。

或謂。佛菩薩神通。不可謂之全不屬修證。若果不屬修證。則凡夫緣何不有耶。

幻曰。凡夫於法性之神通。亦未嘗不具。而凡夫及異類。皆昧畧而不自知也。但凡夫闕於無作願行。諸波羅蜜。所證之威德。莊嚴之神通耳。前不云乎。佛菩薩。以大悲熏心而然。非爲求神通設也。請以喻明之。世有造十大惡業。不思懺悔之衆生。此人命終。由業力故。直入地獄。受種種苦。此人政當造業時。但爲迷妄入心。恣情而作。決不曾有一念謂我業熟時。決入地獄也。蓋地獄無自性。亦無實法。乃由自己妄業之所致爾。當知佛菩薩解脫神通。亦無自性。亦無實法。寔由戒定慧。諸波羅蜜等。成熟之所致爾。復何疑哉。

[27]　或問。西天二十七祖。皆有神通。洎達磨亦有神通。自達磨已降。何以不具神通。中間或聞一人半人。亦不多見。

幻曰。聞。西天外道。皆具有作思惟。變化神力。佛燈初傳。將照明世間。非具神通者。不能攝彼外道。蓋西天皆化佛。化菩薩。應身爲祖。以傳命燈。故達磨謂是觀音應身。自達磨已降。中間或有一人半人。亦具神通者。乃聖賢間世而起。助揚宗教耳。其不具者。惟以悟佛心宗爲本。蓋佛心宗。乃百千三昧神通之正因也。安有果報不自因而著者。凡真實悟心之士。或偶生神異。則當念遣除。決不肯滯此爲奇也。苟以爲奇。則失本心矣。且悟者尚爾。況未悟耶。今之學者。不求正悟。而妄興一念神通三昧之心。乃外道眷屬。永背正因必矣。或有人謂。神通亦有傳受至東土。恐致顯異之譏。故不傳。此說不惟自惑。又且惑人。豈至理也。

山房夜話下

[28]　或者以所知爲問曰。僕嘗積學半生。凡佛祖言教。漁獵殆盡。每臨文對卷。未嘗無所知。獨不能剪情縛於見聞之初。乾識浪於愛憎之表者。何也。

幻曰。子槩言所知。而不能擇其至者。有靈知焉。有真知焉。有妄知焉。夫靈知之謂道。真知之謂悟。妄知之謂解。言所知則一也。謂靈。謂眞。謂妄。則日刦相倍矣。學者不揣其理。泛於所知。妄生執著。引起是非。不惟汩喪道源。而亦沉埋自己。如裴公謂。血氣之屬。必有知。凡有知者。必同體。此言靈知之知。此知於聖凡迷悟。無所間然。心體本具。了無加損者也。如華嚴謂。知一切法。即心自性。成就慧身。不由他悟。如圓覺謂。知是空華。即無輪轉。又云。知幻即離。不作方便等。此言眞知。端從悟入。苟非迷雲豁開。斬絕見量。不動神情。如久忘忽記。當念解脫。立處皆眞。自餘決不可偶然也。又圓覺謂。衆生爲解礙。菩薩未離覺。又云。末世衆生。希望成道。無令求悟。惟益多聞。增長我見等。此皆痛指依通妄知之謂也。其妄知者。雖深窮至理。洞徹性源。使終日肆懸河之辯。即其所辯而與之俱迷。政不待辯後而迷也。故迦文於雪山。示其悟跡。末後於百萬衆前。拈一枝華。顯其悟理。已而諸祖門庭。其設施。雖萬不同。皆近之如火聚。觸之如太阿。聞之如雷霆。飲之如蠱毒。至若語默動靜。了無縫罅與人作蹊徑者。良有以也。然宗門中。尚不許向悟處垜跟。乃非之爲法塵。斥之爲見刺。必欲其兩忘迷悟。混入靈源而後已。或未至此。則以其所知。動形諸妄。如瞽者執炬而復晝行。不惟無益於明。使久不擲去。將見火其所執之手矣。予亦昧眞知者。而不能逃妄知之責。因其致問故。說此以自警。

[29] 或問。塵勞二字。世所共稱。不識塵勞以何爲因。以何爲義。

幻曰。以迷妄爲因。以染污爲義。謂迷妄者。以迷自心故。不達一切法無自性。謂無自性者。性本空寂。無知見故。以不達無自性而引起妄情。認一切法爲實有。既墮有海。則其取舍順逆之念。皆自我起。順之則愛。逆之則憎。愛則取受。憎則捨離。展轉遷流。順愛生喜。逆愛生怒。微細微細。潛伏識田。騰躍不定。起滅無時。徇情膠擾。逐念紛飛。染而六凡。淨而四聖。雖悟迷有間。謂塵勞則等也。何則本來清淨。眞實性中。亙古迨今。不容別有一法爲增爲減。爲得爲失。彌滿充塞。周徧含攝。廓徹靈明。了無住相。衆生未悟。動逐境緣。但涉所依。皆塵勞相。無問聖凡。咸遭污染矣。夫塵勞者。能傷戒體。能濁定源。能昏慧鏡。能潤貪根。能資恚燄。能長癡雲。能開惡道。能閉善門。能助業緣。能消道力。使盡說塵勞之過。無有窮已。今之學人。槩言動作施爲皆是塵勞。直欲置身於一物不侵之域。或少事役其情。微務干其慮。謂消道力。必欲掉臂。徑去不肯回顧。其志亦苦矣。而返墮迷中之倍人。不可與之論道也。何則蓋不能返照塵勞所起。乃根於迷妄。非出於事務也。若出於事務。則飢不當食。寒不當衣。居不當屋廬。行不當道路。審如是。則死無日矣。其必當然。則不思所食之穀出於耕鋤。所掛之衣出於機杼。所居之屋廬出於營繕。所履之道路出於開闢。使各各俱不涉事而歷務。則資身之具。何所從而得耶。復不思即今行道之身。本來無有。皆自父母養育之塵勞而生。撫抱之塵勞而長。又不思從上佛祖。道大德備之人。未有不食不衣。不居不履者。以其廓悟圓滿清淨之自心。充塞法界中不容佗。一刹那間。轉八萬塵勞。爲八萬佛事。故永嘉云。不見一法即如來。方得名爲觀自在。安有了悟自心之外。別見有一法爲塵勞耶。是故華嚴會上諸善知識。皆借此塵勞。爲行菩薩道修菩薩行。以至莊嚴佛淨土之一種要門。當知離塵勞無六度。捨塵勞無四心。虐塵勞無聖賢。盡塵勞無解脫。蓋塵勞是三世佛祖。十方開士。無邊善知識。一切戒定慧。恒沙善功德之胎孕。苟不有塵勞。則聖賢事業。無出生之理。嗟乎。學者不了此義。妄生忻厭。無乃將塵勞去塵勞。轉增迷悶而已。聖人哀之。故楞嚴有如我按指。海印發光。汝暫舉心。塵勞先起。斯言豈欺人哉。安得人人於此遠契聖心。即塵勞爲妙用者哉。使以百千功行欲洗滌塵勞。聖人尚訶之爲妄作。然洗滌塵勞。尚遭訶斥。矧乎。心塵壅塞。不求正悟。遽以一切無礙而爲口實者。非欺罔自心而何。

[30] 或問。子之道譽。頗爲人所喜。胡不徇時緣坐一刹。隨力闡化。以張佛祖建立之心。且靜退小節。苟執之不返。其能免爲法中之罪人耶。
　幻曰。自嬰不虞之譽。日聞斯言。然所以無愧於此心者。有解焉。使其果有爲人之道。擬全高節。固守而不爲。則法中罪人。無可逃者。使其實無爲人之道。乃欲乘時網名。背理而強爲之。不識罪人之名可免乎。不可免乎。或不可免。則較之固守不爲之罪。亦倍矣。頗知此理。故不敢冒爲也。嘗默究之。住持之要。有三種力。庶幾無敗事。一道力。二緣力。三智力。道力體也。緣力智力用也。有其體而缺其用。尚可爲之。但化權不周。事儀不備耳。使其道體既虧。縱有百千神異。苟欲資之。益不相稱。雖緣智。奚爲哉。或體用併缺。冒焉爲之。使無因果。固不足論。使有因果。寧不懍然于中乎。余於佛祖之道。缺於悟證。尋常形之語言毫楮者。特信解耳。思古人得旨後。復不憚危亡。三二十年。置身爐鞴之側。尚欲屏其悟跡。蕩其證理。然後入眞入俗。不見一法當情。則其通身如利劔。如古鏡。無停機。無剩語。儼臨千群萬衆之上。不知爲尊。不知爲榮。具如是體裁。或遭人天推出。庶幾無忝。斯豈情見未脫者所能假借耶。原夫悟證之跡。或未盡洗。則其能所之見。動輒紛然。謂能所者皆情見也。且悟證之跡。尚不容存於心。何況信解純是情見。其於至道之體。愈親而愈疎。益近而益遠。且自未能會乎道。安有能使人會道之理哉。以此礙之不能自遣故。不敢妄尸大牀。稱弘道之師也。
　客曰。審如是說。古今列刹相望。其握塵柄者。代不乏人。豈皆其[5]不失其體用者乎。

---

[5] Translation follows Noguchi and Matsubara, *Sanbō yawa*, 233 其 = 眞.

幻曰。子問甚詳。爾不聞。各各三昧。各各不知。既不之知。欲竊議其可否。無乃益予之過耶。
客於是相視一笑。

[31] 或問。僕半生。跡寄空寂之場。而情馳聲利之域。方責造物之不我助。偶有以住持之名見任。喜而從之。自負此名字而來。返不若未負之爲安也。何則百務之通塞。群情之喜怒。咸萃於吾方寸。或少有不周於思慮。則禍辱不旋踵而集。豈從上佛祖。果如是耶。
幻曰。爾不思受名之初。乃受責之始也。天下之名。未嘗孤起而忽生。蓋由實而致名。名之與實。猶影之隨形也。猶衣之出於帛縷也。猶飯之本乎米粟也。所云責者。求實之謂也。如稱影之名。必求其形之實。言衣食之名。必求其粟帛之實。當其初負住持之名。必先自責其持任正因。令法久住之實有無也。苟無其實。則不異離形而論影。捨粟帛而議衣食。言說愈多而實效愈遠矣。心機愈密而大用愈乖矣。攀緣愈熾而正因愈廢矣。使吸寒之。猶有可禦之方。或流而忘返。則不至泥犁不已也。且名者何物也。而競尚之。蓋非尚名也。乃所以有我也。以有我故。而生愛見。愛見莫甚於名故。名於五欲居其一也。欲潛乎心。隱微難見。遇緣而動。萬夫莫能敵。千聖莫能制。雖斧鋸在前。鼎鑊在後。將不暇顧。又何畏夫因果哉。然名之至美者。聖賢也。道德也。其次則功利也。又其次則技能也。由是欺聖賢以網之。駕道德以要之。專技能以奪之。竊功利以據之。美名根於心。妄識馳於念。至若舉措言動。惟名是務。至於論其名之實。則掉頭弗之顧也。雖營營終日。逆知。其何所爲而不敗哉。間有報緣適爾。偶中所求。使美名加於百世而不衰。一旦報緣忽盡。即前日之名。乃今日之辱也。名愈多。而辱愈甚。故知罔實之名。乃取敗取辱之具也。原夫聖人洞窺理底。存實于中。惟恐斯須或忘之也。是故於無量刼　專求至道。乃破生死魔而返靈源之實也。精修六度。普運四心。乃興大慈而啟大悲之實也。三百餘會。半滿偏圓。乃觀根應病。利生接物之實也。末後手拈一花。衣付飲光。乃以心印心。以器傳器之實也。至若百千勝行。恒沙功德。靡有一法不自實際理地中流出。是謂純一真實。無所爲於內。無所慕於外。無所矜於已。無所待於人。惟勇健不息。履實踐真之正念。爲當然也。以其誠實之行。具足圓滿。則調御師天人尊優曇華光明藏。種種嘉號。種種美名。曾不約而至矣。使聖人。瞥興一毫念慮。有所慕其名於外。縱滿百千萬億恒沙數刼。堅修衆善。不惟美名之不遂。將見逐妄之譏不可逃也。古人惟患實之不存。不患名之不至。蓋知實乃名之招也。故天下古今。未有無其實而有其名者。所云住持之實。何實也。遠稟先佛之教體。近持諸祖之化權。內存自己之真誠。外起人天之傾信。不以賢而使進之。不以愚而使退之。不以順而愛。不以逆而憎。以平等慈。與物無間。皆所謂代佛揚化。據位稱師之實也。苟力有所不逮。當退而養之。晦而藏之。決不可苟也。或欲假一毫方便以資其實。猶螢光之助太陽也。聖

人惟知實之可踐。踐實之外。復何念於名耶。譬如積聚粟帛之多。則衣食之名。曾不待求而自至矣。自有叢林已來。其住持之美名。若懸的也。其抱聰俊。負才能者。咸以筆舌辯利之矢。得而射之。或不顧其實。皆自中其矢耳。豈能中夫的哉。然化門之翕張。法道之隆替。名乎實乎。蓋不能外於此矣。

[32] 或有以進退爲問。

幻曰。寄四大浮囊於三界海中。眇若太倉之一粟。其驟進勇退。雖日千萬里。何利害云乎哉。良由人情好惡不等。進亦是非。退亦是非。人不能遠鑑至理。動爲是非所惑。一進一退。惟任妄情。卒無所主。聖賢獨不然。其進必以道則思所以濟人。其退必以道則思所以補過。其於進退之頃。雖百折挫。而浩然無憂。較之卒無所主者。何如哉。其或干榮冒寵。孳孳爲一己之謀者。進則與業會。退則爲情轉。是非之跡。動輒紛然。因果之招。凜然莫隱。道人於進退。寧容無擇焉。

[33] 或問。公與私。對私則喻矣。公之爲義何如。

幻曰。我何人也。輒敢妄議之。竊嘗聞之。古人謂。公之一言。乃佛祖聖賢之本心也。至大至明。凜乎獨立。而天地莫能掩。鬼神莫能窺也。揀而辨之。有至公焉。有大公焉。有小公焉。至公者道也。大公者教也。小公者物務也。昔迦文老人。夜覩明星。唱言。奇哉。眾生具有如來智慧德相。於此發明聖凡同稟其靈。俾傳之無窮。乃至公之道。浚源於此也。已而三百餘會。隨機任器。設教殊塗。文字語言。浩如山海。乃大公之教。張本於此也。及其化被五天。光流震旦。僧園資具。徧在寰區。此小公物務之所從生也。非道無以發其教。非教無以任其物務。非物務無以暢其道。是三者。更相成而互相資。蓋均出乎佛祖聖賢本心之公也。且天普覆而地普擎。海普涵而春普育亦已至矣。未若吾公之普又至也。何則語其道則圓裹三界。洞貫十慮。無一含靈而不與同證者也。語其教則三乘十地之階梯。萬行六度之品級。大張宏設。不使一眾生不得其門而入也。語其物務則崇門大殿之開闢。廣堂密室之容受。雖一飯亦必考鐘伐鼓以警其幽顯。俾之均沾而悉被也。人之所以不至佛祖聖賢之域者。蓋不存乎公也。苟不存乎公。靜則蘊乎憂思。動則涉乎禍辱。窮則滯於下愚。達則長其罪惡。已而三塗六趣。纏縛萬生。卒未有自釋之理。良由此心之不存乎公也。如離婁。困踏於暗室之底。負千里神光。不能睹其分寸。是以聖人教化。不得不啟之也。故安樂人之所趣。而不知致安樂者公也。福慧人之所尚。而不知資福慧者公也。聖賢人之所仰。而不知達聖賢者公也。佛祖人之所親。而不知契佛祖者亦公也。公也者與本心而無一毫少間也。以故。聖人指至公之道以明其心。設大公之教以照其心。任小公之物務以正其心。惟心與公異名而同體者也。然公之爲理。不可苟也。不可強也。無作爲也。離種種情偽。是一直之道也。

惟至真至實之心能契之。少涉念慮則不公矣。故聖賢操之履之。趨之向之。未嘗違越其絲髮。凡縱心舉念。不假思惟。渾然至公。不期昭顯而顯矣。世之罔其公者。非罔其公。乃自欺其心爾。苟知心之不可欺。自然動則與公合其明。靜則與公合其照。以至通教道而持物務。舉不失其公矣。所云公者。人或終身無所知而昧之。則亦無如之何也。聞有知之而故背之。返張至公之道。以網其名。假大公之教。以濫其位。竊小公之物務。以濟其欲。深沉重溺而罔思所以效之者。又不止於自欺也。昔朝有欲改某寺為倉。一僧力拒不從。因聞于王。王授劍與使者曰。今再拒則斬之。如不畏死則與免。尋而使者諭旨。僧笑而引頸曰。為佛法死。實甘飴之。彼當引頸之際。了無畏怯。豈苟而強之也。蓋一出於真誠。推原其心。豈直為僧園物務之小公。深有意於教道者也。隋太守堯君素。下令以諸僧登城。固守敢諫者斬。時有沙門道遜。歷階披陳而拒之。君素直視遜曰。此僧膽氣。如是壯耶。遂免。此為大公之教。遽抵鋒冒刃不懼死亡。又豈苟而強之也。東山演祖書略曰。今夏諸莊旱損。我總不憂。室中舉箇狗子無佛性話。無一人會得。此誠可憂。原其所志。於至公之道。拳拳翼戴。不敢斯須忽忘之也。然諸莊旱損而言不憂者。非不憂也。以物務之小者。較之於至道。則物務可略其憂也。僧園物務。本於興教傳道而建立。使教之不振。道之不傳。雖飛樓湧殿。餘金剩粟。充塞大千。不惟無補於公。適足以為教道之累也。公之存亡。係於法道之隆替。可不慎乎。可不慎乎。

[34] 或有以威為問。

幻曰。威之於天下有二。所謂二者。有道德之威。有權勢之威。道德之威出於天。權勢之威出於人。出於天者服其心。出於人者服其形耳。然服其心之威。不特威之閫內。使風行萬里之外亦威之。又不止威之於今日。將聲傳百世之下亦威之矣。何以知其然。如古之道德淳全者。今人挹其遺風。仰其餘烈。莫不意消心醉。而況承顏接辭於當日。而不畏敬者乎。彼服人心之威。一出於至誠。蓋自然之理。不容毫髮念慮加於其間也。夫道德之威。人心感服固無疑矣。使聖賢苟擅其道德而必於服人。則人豈服之哉。且道德之美。聖賢尚不得專擅以服人。而世之昧者捨道德而附權勢。自不知其危。猶瞀瞀終日尤人之不我服。何其謬哉。然權勢之威。縱能服人之形亦頃刻耳。反面則不威矣。其能威之於身後耶。不特不能威之於身後。人將結恨於懷。欲追其威服之跡以報之。則其為禍未易量也。故知。前日之威。鮮有不為後日之禍。幸吾儕遠稟四無量心之大訓於西域聖人之後。威權之柄。宜終身不預焉。

或曰。聞規正天下之心。莫善於賞罰。匪恩莫賞。匪威莫罰。予於世道固遠矣。其僧園資具。或任人之不職。欲不威之。可乎。

幻曰。昭昭因果。實臨爾躬。聖賢垂範。誰敢易也。使威之而不悛。將如之何。當歸求其道德。可也。未見道德在躬。至誠浹洽於內外。而人不之信從也。安用威爲。且海內之威。無日不在。而肆暴習惡者。莫之少畏。豈其威。果不及之耶。苟道德之不充。而靡思退養。惟務持威柄以臨人者。不禍於今。將引其禍於身後者必矣。聞者畏之。

[35] 或問。吾法須外護。然後可行。乃有佛法付囑國王大臣之說。

幻曰。事說則可也。理說則未知其可。何則隋珠絕纇。人將忘重溟之險以求之。卞璧無瑕。世將輕連城之價以易之。理固然也。使吾衣底之珠不具。懷中之玉枵然。雖卑言屈體狎近於人。則人將遠之。又安肯輕連城以易之。忘重溟以求之者乎。故佛祖以道德自任。夷險一致。身世兩忘。曾何意於求外護也。以道德不能自掩。則王臣乃傾誠以待之。世之昧者。不顧己之道德爲如何。必欲干榮冒寵。奔走權門而稱外護。或不遂所欲。則怨嗟之聲。形於言。鬱勃之氣。浮於貌。不至禍辱不已也。豈抱道之器合如是哉。

[36] 或問。僧園物務有所缺漏而忘身補之。可乎。

幻曰。有藥必聚於良醫之門。無貨不投於巨商之肆。樹將茂而鳥集。池既成而月來。昔雪山大沙門。棄萬乘尊榮。受六年飢凍。視大千世界。不翅一漚之輕。曾何有爲於世耶。及萬德功圓之日。則眾寶樓閣。諸莊嚴具。周帀圍繞。雖滅度二千年。遺風餘烈。充塞海宇。是謂出乎爾者返乎爾者也。聞。菩薩成就世間。或不具足。不責彼之不我助。惟精修六度。廣布四心。化機圓熟。而諸施者持以奉獻。或蒙領納。則踊躍歡喜。自利利佗。均名解脫。是僧伽藍成就福田者也。今之苾蒭。於所爲處。動背至理。惟務惡求。如片地之不獲。或多財以壓之。或重勢以臨之。或搆罪以恐之。或挾術以勝之。雖成就於一時。皆煩惱業根。豈福田利益者哉。競以千年常住一朝僧之說爲張本。殊不思。千年常住。苟非定慧資熏。自佗兼利。必何所從而得耶。或罔其所自。是猶捨池而招明月。棄樹以集眾鳥。理豈然哉。理豈然哉。

[37] 或問。說法之儀式。必須雨花堂須彌座爲然乎。否耶。

幻曰。謂儀式則然也。謂說法則豈其然哉。夫法無定相。說亦無定相。其揮白麈拂。播搖唇吻者。事相之說也。如吾佛。不起菩提座。不出那伽定。不動廣長舌。不見一法相。而熾然常說。又豈待四十九年三百餘會爲說邪。如諸菩薩。能捨難捨。以布施爲說法。能持難持。以戒律爲說法。能受難受。以忍辱爲說法。乃至修六波羅蜜四無量心。皆說法也。如觀世音三十二應處。至若天龍鬼神人非人等。即其所現。是說法時。更不待別有所言也。如從上諸祖之擎叉。輥毬。提油。舞笏。隔江招手。立雪安心。豎空拳於草廬。疊雙趺於巖穴。撼木鐸於紫陌紅塵之隙。放絲綸於白蘋黃葦之濱。打地。叩舷。張弓。面壁。孤峯獨宿。狹路相逢。得牛還馬。而道出平常。喚甕作鐘而意居言外。千途萬轍。玉振金聲。豈必皆雨花堂。須彌座為然也。心同乎道。雖形影相弔於巖穴草萊之下。未嘗不是儼臨大眾。播揚宗教之時。苟不同乎道。雖榮披上服。尊據大牀。問若雲興。酬如瓶瀉。口舌相勝。惟益高心。媚悅世情。鈎引時習。謂之說法利生。代佛揚化。甚非予所知也。

[38] 或問。古人得旨之後。或孤峯獨宿。或垂手入鄽。或兼擅化權。或單提正令。或子篝盈室。或不遇一人。或泯絕無聞。或聲喧宇宙。或親嬰世難。或身染沉痾。雖同趣少室之門。而各蹈世間之路者。何也。

幻曰。言乎同者。同悟達磨直指之真實自心也。言乎異者。異於各稟三世之虛幻緣業也。以報緣觀之。非樂寂而孤峯獨宿也。非愛閙而入鄽垂手也。擅化權而非涉異也。提正令而非專門也。雖弟子滿門非苟合也。雖形影相弔非絕物也。其畢世無聞非尚隱也。其聲喧宇宙非搆顯也。至若榮枯禍福。一本乎報緣。以金剛正眼視之。特不翅飛埃之過目耳。安能動其愛憎取捨之念哉。所以龍門謂。報緣虛幻。豈可強為。演祖謂。萬般存此道。一昧信前緣。苟不有至理鑑之。則不能無惑於世相之浮沉也。

[39] 或問。據師位者。代佛揚化。本於得人以續慧命。今五宗之嗣。惟濟北而下。血脉不斷。餘皆絕嗣者。豈授受之際。失於囑累耶。抑貪緣之使然耶。

幻曰。聖人之道。雖隱顯隨時。亦由定分耳。其時代之延促。人物之盛衰。化權之隆替。雖一毫。不能加損於其間。昔吾祖。未離西乾。已受般若多羅預讖。此其可驗矣。當青原南嶽未著之時。其五家已有定分矣。當五家方盛之頃。其脩短之數。安得無定分焉。特彼此昧畧。而不自知也。或謂。臨濟道出常情。為人痛切。機圓語活。其煅煉人物。速如反掌。以故。家聲久遠不墜。自餘反是。宜乎。不永於世也。此說。不惟誣謗先哲。臆斷是非。亦乃昧天理之甚者。然近代之據師位者。不思等心垂化。令法久住。往往急於求嗣。效閭巷庸俗之所為。以勢利相傾。名位相誘。物欲相勝。情妄相欺。似此。雖數千百傳繩繩不墜。何有益於理哉。豈惟無益。實害之至也。故月堂有日中灌瓜之喻。石室有鑽腋插羽之譏。具在典章。不知何所圖。而弗之顧也。如古之雲門。得法於陳尊宿。而宿使其終嗣雪峯。叢林迨今尊之。又如慈受。謁佛鑑於蔣山。室中有奇遇。欲易其所嗣。鑑終却之。叢林尤歸美焉。但恐我之道。不能廣被於人。使異其所嗣。亦何憾焉。譬如分東家之燈而照西室。但取其破幽燭暗為美。又安庸責彼昧吾燈之自來也耶。

[40] 或問。楞嚴經云。我滅度後。菩薩阿羅漢。於末法中。現種種形。與其同事。終不自言我真菩薩。真阿羅漢。泄佛密因。輕言末學。惟

除命終隂有遺付。覩今之據師位者。於人天前稱說悟由。或學者之未信。則伸之以誓。似違古佛之誠言。增後人之妄習。莫知其可否。

幻曰。此說其來有漸矣。如五燈編諸祖之本傳。必先載其領悟之緣。當其悟之之頃。如久忘忽記。如啞子得夢。惟巳自知。非第二人境界。是謂自證三昧。使其絕口不言。安有問野鴨。吹布毛。見桃花。聞畫角之說乎。蓋此說之露亦有由也。或因師詰問。或遇事指陳。或末後表證無偏。或當時遮掩。不及惡聲流布。豈得巳哉。其中亦多有不形所悟者。既預祖燈。寧無證據。蓋覆藏深密。不欲顯露而然也。其真有所得者。雖未嘗以悟之一言掛之唇齒。其如山含玉而草木華滋。淵抱珠而波瀾澄瑩。自然之理也。本色宗匠。但據已所得。與人決擇。政不必引己悟因以求其信。亦不必生心動念。巧設機緣。移換當人。折困來學。但一一隨力展布。學者或不加信。惟任之而巳。苟縱生滅則失正受也。審如是則悟之理。其可秘乎。其可泄乎。

[41] 或問。禪者臨終坐脫。或不能者。不知平昔以何所守而然。

幻曰。無所守也。此多係緣業。不可苟也。夫悟心之士。情消。境寂。見謝。執忘。初不以此爲介。其或臨終不嬰疾苦及諸障難。則了了分明。超然獨脫。因行掉臂。復何爲哉。且世有不學道修行之人。亦間有坐脫者。乃至傾動敬心。光揚末後。此非報緣而何。凡學道之士。不力窮心要。預思末後不能獨脫。恐人譏誚。而孜孜以此爲重者。則有一種外魔。乘其所重而入。令汝預知時節。作種種奇特。殊不知。爲魔所著。流入三途。何益於理。間有真實悟心之士。臨終或中毒。或遇難。或久嬰異疾。至若四體莫支。一語莫吐。而其平昔道力。不能奪者。但只堅持正念。以待其盡。未嘗不與至理契合也。臨此之際。或自照世間不破。或爲生人以言激忤。或強生一念。欲如之若何。則利害不小也。宗門中有尊宿。指期坐脫。體香襲人。飛走哀鳴。草木衰落。火光散彩。舍利流輝。至若種種神異。不測之事。聳動四衆者。此皆世世生生。住善知識位中。以定慧資熏。其勝因不昧。感斯異報。亦非尊宿著意而然。或地位中菩薩。來展化權。現斯勝相。非一生叅學能如是也。係乎報緣之說盡矣。

[42] 或問。諸方說法。無義路與人尋討。乃活語也。子所說者。皆實法繫人。無乃死語乎。

余曰。爾擬於諸方活語中活。而不肯向死語中死。其亦俊矣。爾如肯向死語下死去。久之死中忽自活。將見不勝其活矣。

夜話至此林雞忽鳴。東方漸白。余乃睡去。客亦忘言。少頃睡覺。思終夜所談。竟不記一字。偶童子。收之毫楮。出以示余。因怒而麾之曰。余無是語。此所謂叢林粥飯氣也。宜屏諸

Chinese Text for Translation 4: *House Instructions for Dwelling-in-the-Phantasmal Hermitage* in *Zhongfeng Extensive Record*

(*Gozanban* 9, 350d–356a; CBETA, B25, no. 145, p. 873, b1–p. 877, a13.)

幻住家訓

[1]　幻人一日據幻室依幻座執幻拂時。諸幻弟子俱來雲集。有問。松緣何直。棘緣何曲。鵠緣何白。烏緣何玄。幻人豎起拂子召大衆曰。我此幻拂。豎不自豎。依幻而豎。橫不自橫。依幻而橫。拈不自拈。依幻而拈。放不自放。依幻而放。諦觀此幻。綿亘十方。充塞三際。豎時非豎。橫時非橫。拈時非拈。放時非放。如是了知。洞無障礙。便見。松依幻直。棘依幻曲。鵠依幻白。烏依幻玄。離此幻見。松本非直。棘元無曲。鵠既不白。烏亦何玄。當知此幻翳。汝眼根而生。幻見潛汝意地。起幻分別。見直非曲。指白非玄。徧計諸法執性橫生。曠古迨今纏縛生死。[2]　由是累及雪山大沙門。眼不耐見。方出母胎。便乃周行七步。目顧四方。指地指天。大驚小怪。將過去百千萬億刦所證底第一義諦。向諸人淨潔田地上。狼藉殆盡。審如是奇特建立。要且於幻法。了無加損。老雲門謂。當時若見。一棒打殺。貴圖天下太平。雖則增金以黃。其奈又添一重幻翳。當時四十九年三百餘會。彼以幻問。此以幻答。文彩熾盛。音響沸騰。其幻頓幻漸幻偏幻圓。且置之勿論。末上以幻手拈幻花。謂吾有正法眼藏涅槃妙心。直得。老飲光擘破幻顏。兩肩負荷。自爾一人傳虛萬人傳實。幻幻相因。授受不已。[3]　至少林。面幻壁。安幻心。懺幻罪。解幻縛。問幻姓。書幻偈。磨幻磚。垂幻足。掛幻拂。聾幻耳。摑幻掌。就中引出箇掣風顛漢施一幻喝。如青天怒雷。乃至幻照幻用。幻賓幻主。縱橫交錯。與奪殺活。態千狀萬。莫窺其涯。迨今諸方無面目老比丘。出其門嗣其宗。承虛接響。置一幻於口門。藏諸幻於量外。文其言巧其機。高其風逸其韻。峻其令大其家。更無有一人能出其幻者。[4]　幻乎。其旨圓。其義備。其體大。其用周。與諸佛祖。相爲始終。盡塵沙刦。不可窮盡。間有未能了此大幻於言象之表者。或以某師說禪簡明。或以某師說禪圓活。或以孰爲高古。或以孰爲峭峻。孰爲細密。

孰爲文彩。孰爲粗暴。孰爲不工。尚其優而效之。鄙其劣而棄之。亂真機於巧偽之場。屈要旨於笙簧之域。見聞日博。是非日滋。大義日乖。真風日墜。殊不知。前輩深達大幻之士。凡吐一辭出一令。其簡明也是幻。圓活也是幻。高古也是幻。細密也是幻。至若直捷文彩。粗暴不工等。咸自廣大幻輪中流出。此幻輪一轉。如水就決。似風行空。迥絕安排。了無揀擇。隨機任器。殺活臨時。使古人。存一點分別取捨之情。潛於隨扣隨應之間。則與雜毒無以異也。豈甘露醍醐之謂哉。[5] 更有人將箇禪冊子。廣讀博記。欲契祖師西來意。却成實法流布。豈不立文字。直指人心之道。果如是迂曲耶。若是真實要證此大幻法門。便請全身直入。直下更無一絲毫障礙。苟或脚跟擬議。意地躊躇。切不可隨語生解道。一切是幻。本來見成。我但拍盲坐斷。更別有甚麼工夫可做門路可求。是則固是。爭奈儞依情帶識。墮在草窠。欲較他古人獨脫悟明。不翅天地懸隔。只如香嚴擊竹。靈雲見桃。太原聞角。洞山過水。如此輩皆是偷心泯絕。脫落知解。能所兩盡。得失俱忘。如空合空。似水投水。既非強勉。安許拍盲。乃於不知不覺處。脫落根塵。自然語默動靜。不帶枝葉。此是大解脫門。惟心死識忘情消見謝者。乃能涉入。或半點心意識不盡。縱使透過古今。超越言象。欲與古人握手於真寂之海。何異螢光之附太陽。非其類也。今日既是與諸人。應箇時節。不可只與麼說了便休。[6] 借五須彌筆蘸四大海水。向東弗于逮打箇直落。復於南贍部洲轉箇曲角。徐於北鬱單越著一點。轉向西瞿耶尼亞箇半刀。併作一箇幻字。懸向盡十方虛空之頂。使大地人。有眼者見。有耳者聞。有身者覺。有意者解。乃知過去佛久遠於此已證涅槃。現在佛今各於斯成等正覺。未來佛將於其中開正法眼。以至微塵數諸菩薩。各各不離當處修六度運四心。度衆生斷苦縛。乃至無邊聖賢。更無有一人不依此幻具大神變。而獲自在者。奈何諸人終日。折旋俯仰。動靜語默。觸目無間。剛不自悟。將謂與佗聖賢佛祖。有無邊法界之所間隔。自甘陸沉徒受輪轉。今日特爲你。起模畫樣和盤托出。如前所云。便請全身直入。直教一切處點畫分明。一切處受用成現。與三世佛歷代祖。契理契事同出同沒。更有何物爲障爲礙。而尚存觀聽。猶滯功勳者哉。[7] 古今之下。如有一佛一祖不由此大幻法門。而獲菩提解脫者。無有是處。更教儞知。盡法界內。無古無今。但有情無情等。如有一物不依此大幻法門。而具生住異滅者。亦無有是處。當知。幻無聖凡。幻無彼此。了得此幻。在彼不見有菩提涅槃。在此不見有生住異滅。一切幻幻圓滿無二無二分。無別無斷故。非是強言。法如爾也。苟或於此。未能脫白露淨全機超入。且不要忽忽草草。但辦取一片鐵石身心。拌取一生兩生。[8] 向所爲底無義味話頭上。拍盲立定。丁字脚頭。心憤憤地與之抵捱將去。正當抵捱時。都不要儞向禪道佛法上別求解會。只如撞著銀山鐵壁相似。除却箇齩嚼不破底無義味話頭之外。更無第二念蹲坐。其懸懸之心如措足於百尺竿上。著脚於萬仞崖巔前無可攀。後無可援。但與麼把教定靠教穩。孜孜兀兀只如是去。[9] 當知大幻法門在你腳底。不曾移易一絲毫。只待你情消見盡蹉步踏著。則知太原聞角。洞山過水之時節。不我隔也。到此。更須和箇所入底大幻法門。一踢踢翻。不留聯迹。始是丈夫。脫或乍得入門。苟存一念歡喜之心。依舊與昨日之迷。無閒然也。此事不是說了便休。亦不是見了便休。直須始終丈夫。不受一法籠罩。方堪爲荷負大法之眞實種草。邇來法道不古。人心懈怠。爲師爲徒。彼此只求解會。日夕相誘。築得一肚禪道佛法。其如生死命根。不曾於懸崖撒手處絕後再甦。一回墮在惡毒海中。不自知非。此誠可憫。叅禪學道。何所圖哉。[10] 然本上座固非其人。惟是不肯自昧叅禪正因。而況諸人幸不遭此邪謬。各各是不肯墮人窠臼底端人正士。既來遮裏相從。我此間又非唱導之師。建立門戶。彼此相依。於半間茅屋之下。只圖眞實以辦平生。然此雖曰。大幻法門。苟非神悟。決不可造次而入。只如說箇幻字。今古共知。於中欲覓一人。於此幻中。掉臂而入。橫身而坐。肆足而行。任意而用。放開捏聚。一切自由者。極難乎人。其故何哉。蓋由心存所知。而未甞悟脫。於一切處。明知是幻不待旋踵。而反爲幻所縛。以若所知。則與不知者。何以異也。只如教家道。一假一切假。無中無空而不假。此說之下。了無剩法。惟其不悟。翻成文字語言流布。豈佛法果有教禪之二哉。以其神悟。教即是禪。以存所知。禪即是教。故圓覺謂。末世衆生。希望成道。無令求悟。惟益多聞。增長我見。斯言殆盡之矣。[11] 只如會通和尚。見鳥窠吹起布毛。應時脫略。德山見龍潭吹滅紙燭。當下超宗。今人但見前輩領悟如是之易。而不知其未領悟時之難。苟知其難。則古人之易。亦今人之易也。苟不知其難。欲効古人如此之易。未免爲情識。虛妄引入相似般若中。重生死之根塵。深輪回之陷穽耳。且古人領悟之易。置之勿論。如何是未領悟時之難。只如二祖未悟之頃。立齊腰之雪。不知爲寒。斷娘生之臂。莫知爲痛。只遮一箇樣子。不惟今人之難。在二祖分上亦未甞不難。以其求法之眞。所以忘其難也。自二祖而降。其親師爲道。痛爲生死無常。而有契有證之士。於未領悟時。未有一人不如是之難。當知。古人之生死。即今人之生死也。今人之道業。即古人之道業也。蓋古人負眞誠而忘其難。所以致其易。今人逐虛妄而棄其難。必欲効其易。故於此一法中。雖同知是幻。而其利害優劣所以異也。此是從上佛祖。不易之論。[12] 一時老婆引援及此。在本色道流分上喚作惡口。亦名實法綴人。亦名教壞人。又喚作瞎學人正眼。今日彼此不獲已也。然而遮許多做工夫底露布。在當人爲法之誠。自然步步踏著。豈是起模畫樣。教得人底道理。其或爲法之心。不眞不誠。不苦不切。縱使百千方便。束縛得他。儼然如箇死人。何異吹網欲滿。[13] 又如潙山充典座。雪峯做飯頭。寶壽作街坊。演祖爲磨主。此猥屑之務。豈眞龍象所當爲哉。蓋亦爲道之眞。忘其鄙陋。有如此者。今人稍負聰敏。或叢林補職不稱。則掉臂譏主法者之誤。於此觀之。則古今之真妄判然矣。幻人於幻法。實未曾悟。今日但路見不平。竊論如此。[14] 到遮裏。索性將平昔所解底大幻法門。重爲發露去也。過去是已去之幻。見在是目前之幻。未來是將至之幻。一大藏教依幻而說。千七百則陳爛葛藤由幻而生。菩提涅槃根幻而成。真如般若倚幻而現。慈悲喜捨即幻而興。六度萬行憑幻而立。三乘十地仗幻而等差。戒定慧貪瞋癡煩惱塵勞無常生死等從幻而出。以至明暗色空見聞覺知。未有不稟吾幻而有者。豈但松直棘曲鵠白烏玄是幻。乃至天以幻蓋。地以幻擎。海以幻涵。春以幻育。桃以幻紅。李以幻白。迷以幻難。悟以幻易。我以幻說。爾以幻聞。森羅萬象一幻所印。此大幻印中。固是不留剩法。只如幻人手中拂子。即今與須彌山王眉毛廝結。且道。是幻耶。非幻耶。若謂是幻。帶累幻人。墮在幻網中。萬刼出不得。若謂非幻。請去却語默動靜。出來露箇消息。

Chinese Text for Translation 5: *In Imitation of Hanshan's Poems* in *Zhongfeng Extensive Record*

(*Gozanban* 9, 356b–365d. CBETA 2019.Q3, B25, no. 145, pp. 877b1–886a5.)

擬寒山詩

有客從予而問曰。叢林戶稱爲叅禪。且禪固不可逆測而知。惟叅之一言。莫識所云。請釋之。

　予曰。所云叅者。乃古人咨决心疑。究明己事。不可不由之徑也。如安心懺罪洗鉢盂聞水聲之類耳。蓋生死之心疑未决。如墮網之欲出。若沐漆而求解。望見知識之容。未待卸包脫屨。其胷中岌岌未安之事。遽衝口而問之。一言不契。又復往叩而佗之。或停餐輟飲。廢寢忘勞。至若風雨寒暑之不移。禍福安危之莫奪。其所叅之念。不致洞明不已[1]也。是謂真叅。餘皆似之耳。非叅也。何謂似。如火爐頭禪牀角。領納一言半句相似語。蘊于情識不自知覺。久之遇緣逢境。忽然觸發。是謂知解依通。非叅也。或於方冊梵夾中。以聰明之資博聞廣記。即其所曉處和會祖機一一合頭。乃穿鑿搏量。非叅也。或循規守矩。不犯條章。靜默安舒。危坐終日。乃緣境攝持。非叅也。或搜尋難問。記憶機緣。堂上室中。苦攻逆敵者。乃狂妄時習。非叅也。緫而言之。但胷中。實無爲生死大事之正念。或形影相弔於巖穴之下。或肩駢踵接於廣衆之中。各偏於所向而取著之。非吾所謂叅也矣。

　客又曰。近代尊宿教人起大疑情。看古人一則無義味語。斯可謂之叅乎。

　予曰。傳燈諸祖。各有契證。初未聞有看話頭起疑情而悟者。良由機緣泛出。露布橫生。况是學者胷中。爲生死之心。苦不真切。脚未跨門。咸遭誑惑。由是據師位者。不得已。而將箇無義味話。放在伊識田中。教伊吞吐不行。齩嚼不破。孜孜兀兀。頓在面前。如銀山鐵壁。不許其斯須忘念。日深月久。情塵頓盡。心境兩忘。不覺不知。以之悟入。雖則不離善權方便。亦與叅之之義。幾近矣。或學者不實

---

[1] Note: in the *Gozanban* 9 text of the *Zhongfeng Extensive Record* 㠯 sometimes = 㠯 or 㠯. Here 㠯 = 已. Other instances have not been marked, but they have been taken into consideration in the translation.

以死生大事爲任。則師與資俱成途轍。荊棘祖庭。穢滓佛海。豈叅云乎哉。因往復酬酢。遂引其說。偶成擬寒山詩一百首。非敢自廣。蓋痛心於教外別傳之道。將墜無何。誠欲策發初心之士耳。

　或謂。宗門有活句死句。全提半提。擒縱無偏。與奪自在之理。子何不發明之。此何時。而尚欲以實法綴繫於人耶。

　予曰。世有能跨千里之步。而終身不能自越其閫者。予不信也。彼與奪自在之師。皆由叅之不謬。悟之無垠。蓄養深厚。如千里駒。輕肆其足。便有追風逐日不可及之態。而不自知也。使彼師。苟存其與奪自在之見于胷中。則人法不空。能所交接。與魔外何別哉。當知。真寂體中尚無地可寄。其與奪自在之跡。則其可講而學耶。得不重貽達者之所譏。蓋識法者懼也。道人其鑒諸。

[1]
叅禪一句子　衝口已成遲　擬欲尋篇目　翻然墮水泥
舉揚無半字　方便有多岐　曲爲同叅者　吟成百首詩

[2]
叅禪莫執坐　坐忘時易過　疊足取輕安　垂頭尋怠惰
若不任空沉　定應隨想做　心華無日開　徒使蒲團破

[3]
叅禪莫知解　解多成捏怪　公案播唇牙　經書塞皮袋
舉起盡合頭　說來無縫罅　撞著生死魔　漆桶還不快

[4]
叅禪莫把玩　流光急如鑽　那肯涉思惟　豈復容稽緩
時刻不暫移　毫釐無間斷　撒手萬仞崖　乾坤無侶伴

[5]
叅禪莫涉緣　緣重被緣牽　世道隨時熟　人情逐日添
工夫情未瞥　酬應力難專　早不尋休歇　輪回莫怨天

[6]
叅禪莫習懶　懶與道相反　終日尚偷安　長年事疎散
畏聞廊下魚　愁聽堂前板　與麼到驢年　還佗開道眼

[7]
叅禪莫動念　念動失方便　取捨任情遷　愛憎隨境轉
野馬追疾風　狂猿攀過電　蘸唾捉蓬塵　癡心要成片

[8]
叅禪莫毀犯　動輒成過患　作止誠可分　開遮豈容濫
內外絕安排　自佗俱了辦　突出摩尼珠　光明照天岸

[9]
叅禪莫揀擇　舉世皆標格　曾不間閑忙　何嘗分語默
一念離愛憎　三界自明白　更擬問如何　當來有彌勒

[10]
叅禪莫順己　動須合至理　工夫要徹頭　志願直到底
瞥爾情念生　紛然境緣起　白日擬偸鈴　難掩虛空耳

[11]
叅禪宜自肯　胷中常鯁鯁　不擬起精勤　自然成勇猛
一念如火熱　寸懷若冰冷　冷熱兩俱忘　金不重爲鑛

[12]
叅禪宜退步　勿踏行人路　橫擔一片板　倒拖三尺布
得失豈相干　是非都不顧　驀直走到家　萬象開門戶

[13]
叅禪宜具眼　庸鄙休觀覽　千里辨雌黃　雙輪豈推挽
洞見佛祖心　爍破鬼神膽　搖搖照世光　不受眉毛[匚@贛]

[14]
叅禪宜朴實　朴實萬無失　纖毫若渉虛　大千俱受屈
話柄愈生踈　身心轉堅密　一氣直到頭　捏出秤鎚汁

[15]
叅禪宜努力　真心血滴滴　如登千仭高　似與萬人敵
有死不暇顧　無身未堪惜　冷地忽擡頭　何曾離空寂

[16]
叅禪宜簡徑　只圖明自性　了了非聖凡　歷歷無欠剰
擬向即是魔　將離轉成病　脫略大丈夫　塵塵自相應

[17]
叅禪宜及早　遲疑墮荒草　隙陰誠易遷　幻軀那可保
當處不承當　轉身何處討　寄語玄學人　莫待筭筒倒

[18]
叅禪宜正大　切勿求奇恠　真機絶覆藏　至理無成壞
拽倒祖師關　打破魔軍寨　赤手鎮家庭　塵塵俱出礙

[19]
叅禪宜決定　莫只成話柄　瞥爾墮因循　灼然非究竟
但欲了死生　何曾惜身命　一踏連底空　佛魔聽號令

[20]
叅禪宜捨割　命根要深拔　活計再掃除　生涯重潑撒
十念空牢牢　萬古阿剌剌　放出一毫頭　光明吞六合

[21]
叅禪要明理　理是心王體　每與事交叅　惟有智堪委
法界即其源　禪河以爲底　後園枯樹椿　勿使重生耳

[22]
叅禪要直捷　一切無畏怯　用處絶踈親　舉起無分別
法性元等平　至理非曲折　過去七如來　與今同一轍

[23]
叅禪要到家　不必口吧吧　履踐無生熟　途程非邇遐
寸心常不動　跬步亦何差　踏斷芒鞋耳　門前日未斜

[24]
叅禪要脫略　何須苦斟酌　道理要便行　事物從教却
豈是學無情　自然都不著　更起一絲頭　茫茫且行脚

[25]
叅禪要精進　勿向死水浸　動若蹈輕冰　行如臨大陣
晝夜健不息　始終興無盡　捱到髑髏乾　光明生末運

[26]
叅禪要高古　備盡嘗艱苦　身世等空華　利名如糞土
深追雪嶺蹤　遠接少林武　道者合如斯　豈是誇能所

[27]
叅禪要識破　萬般皆自做　榮辱與安危　存亡并福禍
元是現行招　等因前業墮　如是了了知　世間無罪過

[28]
叅禪要本分　只守箇愚鈍　豈解敘寒暄　何曾會談論
兀兀似枯椿　堆堆如米囤　一片好天真　常不離方寸

[29]
叅禪要孤硬　素不與物諍　白日面空壁　清塵堆古甑
遇境自忘懷　隨緣非苦行　昨夜煮虛空　煨破沙糖甕

[30]
叅禪要深信　豈應從淺近　直擬跨懸崖　不辭挨白刃
橫披古佛衣　高佩魔王印　道源功德山　咸承慈母孕

[31]
叅禪爲生死　豈是尋常事　從始直至終　出此而沒彼
不啻萬劫來　曾無片時止　今日更遲疑　又且從頭起

[32]
叅禪爲成道　丈夫宜自保　雪嶺星欲沉　鼇山話將掃
疾捷便翻身　更莫打之繞　轉步涉途程　出門都是草

[33]
叅禪爲超越　大地無途轍　寸心千丈坑　萬里一條鐵
躍出威音前　坐斷僧祇劫　回首照菱花　銳氣生眉睫

[34]
叅禪爲絕學　擬心成大錯　既脫文字禪　還去空閑縛
拈却死蛇頭　打破靈龜殼　腰間無半錢　解跨揚州鶴

[35]
叅禪爲究竟　直入金剛定　兩端空悟迷　一道融凡聖
澄潭浸夜月　太虛懸古鏡　儞擬著眼看　即墮琉璃穽

[36]
叅禪爲直指　未舉心先委　動足路千條　擡眸雲萬里
安心鑰雜金　懺罪乳加水　棒喝疾如風　暖熱門庭耳

[37]
叅禪爲己事　要明還扣己　得失莫回頭　是非休啟齒
不肯涉蹊徑　直欲探源底　流出自胷襟　孤風絕倫比

[38]
叅禪爲圓頓　豈分根利鈍　草木尚無偏　含靈皆有分
一法印森羅　三藏絕言論　更擬覓端由　道人今日困

[39]
叅禪爲求悟　胷中絕思慮　但欲破疑團　決不徇言路
寢食兩俱忘　身心全不顧　蹉脚下眠牀　絆斷娘生袴

[40]
叅禪爲明宗　道不貴依通　鷲嶺花猶在　熊峯髓不窮
心空千古合　見謝五家同　情識猶分別　門庭是幾重

[41]
叅禪無利鈍　且不貴學問　妙悟在真疑　至功惟發憤
任說佗無緣　直言我有分　一踏桶底穿　蠛蠓吞混沌

[42]
叅禪無古今　但勿外邊尋　席上沉孤影　慁前惜寸陰
志密行亦密　功深悟亦深　打開無盡藏　撮土是黃金

[43]
叅禪無貴賤　各各不少欠　密護在真誠　精操惟正念
廊廟倦躋攀　輿臺忘鄙厭　悟來心眼空　昭然無二見

[44]
叅禪無奇特　惟貴心無惑　對境消佛魔　當機泯空色
問著有來由　舉起無蹤跡　曾不離平常　通身自明白

[45]
叅禪無巧妙　非覺亦非照　將底作光明　以何爲孔竅
佛祖弄泥團　象龍噇草料　海底黑波斯　却解逢人笑

[46]
叅禪無限量　古今稱絕唱　跳下破繩牀　拈起折主杖
祖令要親行　佛亦難近傍　子細點撿來　盡是做模樣

[47]
叅禪無秘訣　只要生死切　心下每垂涎　眼中常滴血
盡意決不休　從頭打教徹　脫或未相應　輪回幾時歇

[48]
叅禪無僧俗　四大同機軸　一念根本迷　萬死常相逐
推開生死門　打破塵勞獄　携手下煙蘿　共唱還鄉曲

[49]
殺禪無愚智　家親自爲崇　智者落妄知　愚人墮無記
拶破兩頭空　轉歸中道義　拈起一莖柴　覆却西來意
[50]
殺禪無靜閙　盡被境緣罩　聞見有兩般　混融無一窖
水底月沉沉　樹頭風浩浩　更擬覓家鄉　路長何日到
[51]
殺禪非義學　豈容輕卜度　拽斷葛藤根　解開名相縛
一句鐵渾崙　千聖難穿鑿　蹉口忽咬開　虛空鳴嚗嚗
[52]
殺禪非漸小　至體絕邊表　難將有限心　來學無爲道
一證一切證　一了一切了　遙觀兔渡河　特地成煩惱
[53]
殺禪非可見　可見墮方便　鳥跡尚堪追　電光還有現
靈鑑寫羣形　體用成一片　擬剔兩莖眉　浮雲遮日面
[54]
殺禪非可聞　敲唱謾區分　語默影搏影　放收雲合雲
石鼓鳴晴晝　煙鐘送夕曛　未能忘口耳　響寂動成羣
[55]
殺禪非勸誘　誘引那長久　超越須自心　出生離佛口
一步跨向前　萬夫約不後　作略解如斯　步步無窠臼
[56]
殺禪非術數　單提第一句　佛祖不能窺　鬼神爭敢覷
靜若須彌山　動如大火聚　遍界絕覆藏　當機無覓處
[57]
殺禪非息念　妙性圖親見　瞥起落緣塵　不續墮偏漸
起滅有蹤由　渾崙非背面　當處悟無生　塵塵離方便
[58]
殺禪非自許　至理通今古　覓處不從佗　得來須契祖
句句合宮商　門門追步武　毫髮若有差　惺惺成莽鹵
[59]
殺禪非杜撰　要了舊公案　擇法任智臆　爲人若冰炭
道本絕踈親　理爭容混濫　一點更留情　自佗何了辦
[60]
殺禪非教外　亦不居教內　兩頭能混融　一道無向背
法法契真宗　處處成嘉會　少存分別心　直入魔軍隊
[61]
殺禪絕所知　有知皆自欺　靈光雖洞燭　當體屬無爲
擉瞎棒頭眼　掃空繩上疑　更來存此跡　節外又生枝

[62]
衆禪絕能所　獨行無伴侶　既不徇涯岸　何曾立門戶
空棒鞭鐵牛　幻繩牽石虎　機関活卓卓　疑殺少林祖

[63]
衆禪絕聖凡　三界沒遮欄　染淨遭佗惑　悟迷還自瞞
倒卓青雲眼　橫趨赤肉團　欲名名不得　今古許誰看

[64]
衆禪絕階級　坦蕩又平直　擬動脚趾頭　直墮心意識
三界鼓狂花　萬里栽荊棘　舉似王老師　堪差[2]又堪惜

[65]
衆禪絕露布　機前莫罔措　喝退趙州無　趁出雲門顧
縛住走盤珠　塞斷通天路　不假拈一塵　兩手都分付

[66]
衆禪絕有無　道人何所圖　空中書梵字　夢裏畫神符
不有何庸遣　非無曷用除　話頭如不薦　徒費死工夫

[67]
衆禪絕真妄　語言難比況　幻名惟兩端　空花非一狀
智者欲掃除　愚人常近傍　舉措似勤渠　於法皆成謗

[68]
衆禪絕修證　生死那伽定　三有金剛圈　十虛大圓鏡
徧界淨法身　極目真如性　動著一毛頭　驢年會相應

[69]
衆禪絕照覺　道人休卜度　擊碎明月珠　剪斷黃金索
拈過赤斑蛇　放出青霄鶴　去就不停機　依前未離錯

[70]
衆禪絕影像　豈許做模樣　象龍徒蹴踏　佛祖謾勞攘
徧界覓無蹤　當陽誰敢向　有人稱悟明　快來噇拄杖

[71]
衆禪最易為　只要盡今時　不作身前夢　那生節外枝
日移花上石　雲破月來池　萬法何曾異　勞生自著疑

[72]
衆禪最簡捷　當念忘生滅　聞見絕羅籠　語言盡超越
昨夜是愚癡　今朝成俊傑　好箇解脫門　惜無人猛烈

[73]
衆禪最成現　元不隔條線　滿眼如來光　通身菩薩面
圓聞聞不聞　妙見見非見　墮此兩重関　入地獄如箭

[2] Translation follows CBETA 2019.Q3, B25, no. 145, p. 883a16: 差 = 嗟.

[74]
| 叅禪最省力 | 不用從佗覓 | 壯士臂屈伸 | 師王[3]影翻鄹 |
| 纖疑或未銷 | 操心來辨的 | 回首望家鄉 | 鐵壁復鐵壁 |

[75]
| 叅禪最廣大 | 一切俱無礙 | 橫亘十方空 | 竪窮三有界 |
| 既不涉離微 | 曾何有憎愛 | 時暫不相當 | 依前入皮袋 |

[76]
| 叅禪最明白 | 太用無軌則 | 揭開三毒蛇 | 放出六門賊 |
| 遍造業因緣 | 都成性功德 | 勿使路人知 | 恐佗生謗惑 |

[77]
| 叅禪最瞥脫 | 不受人塗抹 | 來去赤條條 | 表裏虛豁豁 |
| 喜時則兩與 | 怒來便雙奪 | 觸處不留情 | 是名真解脫 |

[78]
| 叅禪最安樂 | 不被情塵縛 | 真照豈思惟 | 靈機非造作 |
| 一處證無爲 | 千門成絕學 | 窮刦墮輪回 | 由來自擔閣 |

[79]
| 叅禪最枯淡 | 冥然忘毀讚 | 兀兀守工夫 | 孜孜要成辦 |
| 如飲木札羹 | 似嚼鐵釘飯 | 此心直要明 | 不怕虛空爛 |

[80]
| 叅禪最寂寞 | 寸懷空索索 | 四大寄禪牀 | 雙眸懸壁角 |
| 疑團不自開 | 情實徒加鑿 | 但得志堅牢 | 何愁天日薄 |

[81]
| 叅禪不持戒 | 那更存知解 | 弗省是自瞞 | 尚欲添捏怪 |
| 生死轉堅牢 | 輪回無縫罅 | 坐待報緣消 | 且來償宿債 |

[82]
| 叅禪不守己 | 硬要說道理 | 卜度須彌山 | 便是栢樹子 |
| 但只鼓唇牙 | 不肯憂生死 | 禪到眼光沉 | 噬臍無及矣 |

[83]
| 叅禪不合度 | 紛紛徇言路 | 公案熟記持 | 師資密傳付 |
| 世道愈相攀 | 己躬殊不顧 | 十冊古傳燈 | 轉作砧基簿 |

[84]
| 叅禪不解意 | 纔聞便深記 | 兜率有三關 | 曹洞列五位 |
| 楞嚴選圓通 | 雜華宣十地 | 及話到己躬 | 一場無理會 |

[85]
| 叅禪不著物 | 立地要成佛 | 肯將生死心 | 沉埋是非窟 |
| 從古墮因循 | 如今敢輕忽 | 生鐵鑄齒牙 | 一齩直見骨 |

[3] Translation follows CBETA 2019.Q3, B25, no. 145, p. 884a5: 王 = 主.

[86]
叅禪不顧身　直與死爲隣　寸念空三際　雙眸絕六親
門前皆客路　衣下匪家珍　誰共滄溟底　重重洗法塵

[87]
叅禪不可緩　自心須自判　迷悟隔千塗　首尾惟一貫
掇轉鐵圍山　現出金剛鑽　變化不停機　把伊眼睛換

[88]
叅禪不屈己　人天咸讚美　英氣逼叢林　真風振屏几
千聖共擡眸　萬靈皆側耳　一句絕承當　敲出少林髓

[89]
叅禪不求勝　勝爲禪人病　勝乃脩羅心　勝即魔軍令
勝非解脫場　勝是輪廻穽　惟佛無勝心　所以稱殊勝

[90]
叅禪不求名　叅禪不爲利　叅禪不涉思　叅禪不解義
叅禪只叅禪　禪非同一切　叅到無可叅　當知禪亦戲

[91]
叅禪第一義　全超真俗諦　達磨云不識　六祖道不會
古月照林端　高風吹嶺外　兒曹共指陳　呼作西來意

[92]
叅禪欲悟心　該古復該今　仰處如天闊　窮之似海深
名聞三際斷　體露十虛沉　圓湛含空色　奇花秀晚林

[93]
叅禪非戲論　直欲契靈知　積學非佗得　施工是自欺
精金離煅日　古鏡却磨時　或未忘聞見　何曾出有爲

[94]
叅禪禪有旨　旨悟亦無禪　少室空餘月　靈山獨剩天
認聲言直指　對影說單傳　今古尋玄者　區區亦可憐

[95]
叅禪緣底事　獵縣更遊州　但覺千山曉　那知兩鬢秋
工夫增執縛　學問長輕浮　逗到龕幃下　清燈照古愁

[96]
叅禪何太急　東去又西馳　走殺天真佛　追回小廝兒
空中施棒喝　靴裏動鉗鎚　縱有神僊訣　難教出水泥

[97]
叅禪誰作倡　少室有神光　雪重齊腰冷　刀輕隻臂亡
真風陵大法　英氣勵頹綱　孰謂千年後　門前賊獻贓

[98]
叅禪無樣子　樣子在當人　本淨通身白　元無徹骨貧
智襟懸古鏡　懷抱積陽春　不待重開眼　何曾隔一塵

[99]
叅禪作麼叅　切忌口喃喃　擺尾淹蘆甕　低頭入草菴
有言非向上　無句起司南　未解如斯旨　前三復後三

[100]
叅禪叅不盡　叅盡若爲論　鶴放青松塢　牛尋碧水村
雨深苔蘚路　雲掩薜蘿門　更覓禪叅者　歸家問世尊

Chinese Text for Translation 6: *Song of Dwelling-in-the-Phantasmal Hermitage* in *Zhongfeng Extensive Record*

(*Gozanban* 9, 452d–453b. CBETA 2019.Q3, B25, no. 145, p. 949a11–b7.)

幻住菴歌

幻住菴中藏幻質。諸幻因緣皆幻入。幻衣幻食資幻命。幻覺幻禪消幻識。六窻含裏幻法界。幻有幻空依幻立 。幻住主人行復坐。靜看幻華生幻果。放還收。控勒幻繩騎幻牛。時或住。八萬幻塵俱捏聚。時或眠。一覺幻夢居四禪。有時動。幻海波翻幻山聳。有時靜。幻化光中消幻影。可中時有幻菩薩。來扣幻人詢幻法。我幻汝幻幻無端。幻生幻死幻涅槃。淨名室內龜毛拂。龍女掌中泥彈丸。更有一則幻公案。幻證幻修須了辦。莫言了辦幻云無。只此無無名亦幻。學人未達真幻輪。動輙身心自相反。幻心瞥爾生幻魔。幻翳忽然遮幻眼。陽燄空華乾闥城。天堂地獄菩提名。有問此幻從何起。雲月溪山自相委。要見菴中幻主人。認著依前還不是。

Chinese Text for Translation 7: *Cross-Legged Sitting Chan Admonitions (with Preface)* in *Zhongfeng Extensive Record*

(*Gozanban* 9, 460a–d. CBETA 2019.Q3, B25, no. 145, pp. 954b15–955a19.)

坐禪箴并序

夫非禪不坐。非坐不禪。惟禪惟坐。而坐而禪。禪即坐之異名。坐乃禪之別稱。蓋一念不動為坐。萬法歸源為禪。或云。戒定是坐義。智慧即禪義。非情妄之可詮。豈動靜之能間。故知不離四威儀。而不即四威儀也。

乃為作箴。箴曰。

叅禪貴要明死生。死生不了徒營營。至理不存元字脚。有何所說為箴銘。或謂叅禪須打坐。孤硬脊梁如鐵作。如一人與萬人敵。散亂昏沉休放過。或謂叅禪不須坐。動靜何曾有兩箇。楊岐十載打塵勞。險絕祖關俱透過。坐而不坐心外馳。摩裩擦袴空勞疲。釘樁搖櫓消白日。心空及第知何時。不坐而坐志還切。寸懷鯁鯁難教擎。說到無常與死生。眼中不覺流鮮血。如是坐如是禪。不勞直指與單傳。寬著肚皮只麼守。誰管人間三十年。如是禪如是坐。蒲團七箇從教破。拍肓志氣無轉移。肯把身心沉懶惰。禪即是坐坐即禪。是一是二俱棄捐。話頭一箇把教定。休將識鑿并情案。坐禪只要坐得心念死。今日明朝只如此。若是真誠大丈夫。一踏直教親到底。坐禪不怕坐得多。百歲光陰一剎那。老爺喫乳如大海。為要掃空生死魔。坐禪豈可為容易。莫把聰明遮智慧。千七百則爛葛藤。何用將心求解會。坐到坐忘禪亦空。吐詞凌滅少林宗。只箇渾身也拈却。未待口開心已通。有志坐禪須與麼。若不如斯成懡㦬。更拌性命也嫌遲。大事因緣非小可。擬將此作坐禪箴。不特自欺還謗我。

Chinese Text for Translation 8: *Ten Poems on Living on a Boat* in *Zhongfeng Extensive Record*

(*Gozanban* 9, 471a–472b. CBETA 2019.Q3, B25, no. 145, pp. 963a13–964a3.)

船居十首(己酉舟中作)

[1]
世情何事日羈縻　做箇船居任所之　豈是畸孤人共棄　都緣踈拙分相宜
漏篷不礙當空掛　短棹何妨近岸移　佛法也知無用處　從教日炙與風吹

[2]
水光沉碧駕船時　疑是登天不用梯　魚影暗隨篷影動　鴈聲遙與櫓聲齊
幾回待月停梅北　或只和煙繫柳西　萬里任教湖海闊　放行收住不曾迷

[3]
人在船中船在水　水無不在放船行　藕塘狹處拋篙直　荻岸深時打棹橫
千里溪山隨指顧　一川風月任逢迎　普通年外乘蘆者　未必曾知有此情

[4]
太廈何知幾百間　爭如一箇小船閒　隨情繫纜招明月　取性推篷看遠山
四海即家容幻質　五湖爲鏡照衰顏　相逢順逆皆方便　誰暇深開佛祖關

[5]
家在船中船是家　船中何物是生涯　檣栽兎角非干木　纜繫龜毛不用麻
水上浮漚盛萬斛　室中虛白載千車　山雲溪月常圍繞　活計天成豈自誇

[6]
一瓶一鉢寓輕舟　溪北溪南自去留　幾逐斷雲藏野壑　或因明月過滄洲
世波汩汩難同轍　人海滔滔孰共流　日暮水天同一色　且將移泊古灘頭

[7]
散宅浮家絕所營　閑將行色戲論評　煙簑帶雨和船重　雲衲衝寒似紙輕
帆飽固知風有力　柂寬方覺水無情　頭陀不慣操舟術　幾失娘生兩眼睛

[8]
爲問船居有底憑　渾無世用一慵僧　拋綸擲釣非吾事　舞棹呈橈豈我能
轉柂觸翻千丈雪　放篙撐破一壺冰　從教纜在枯椿上　恣與虛空打葛藤

[9]
懶將前後論三三　端的船居勝住菴　爲不定方真丈室　是無住相活伽藍
煙村水國開晨供　月浦華汀放晚氽　有客叩舷來問道　頭陁不用口喃喃

[10]
船無心似我無心　我與船交絕古今　漚未發時先掌柂　岸親到處不司鍼
主張風月篷三葉　彈壓江湖艣一尋　袞袞禪河遊殆遍　話頭從此落叢林

Chinese Text for Translation 9: *Ten Poems on Living in Town* in *Zhongfeng Extensive Record*

(*Gozanban* 9, 474c–475. CBETA 2019.Q3, B25, no. 145, pp. 965b6–966a16.)

鄽居十首(汴梁作)

[1]
古稱大隱為居鄽　柳陌華衢間管絃　畢竟色前無別法　良由聲外有單傳
錦街破曉鳴金轡　繡巷迎春擁翠鈿　覿面是誰能委悉　茫茫隨逐政堪憐
[2]
綠水青山入眼塵　心空何物可相親　既無世務堪隨俗　却有鄽居最逼真
月印前街連後巷　茶呼東舍與西隣　客來不用論賓主　篆縷橫斜滿屋春
[3]
足跡無端遍海涯　現成山水不堪誇　市鄽既可藏吾錫　城郭何妨著我家
四壁虛明連棟月　數株紅白過牆華　見聞不假存方便　只麼隨緣遣歲華
[4]
山居何似我鄽居　對境無心體自如　手版趣傾樓上酒　腰鈴急送鋪前書
沉沉大夢方純熟　擾擾虛名未破除　白日無營貧道者　草深門外懶薅鋤
[5]
起滅循環事若何　萬般粧點苦娑婆　榮膺廊廟三更夢　壽滿期頤一剎那
翫月樓高門巷永　賣花聲密市橋多　頭陀自得居鄽趣　每笑前人隱薜蘿
[6]
鄽市安居儘自由　百般成現絕馳求　綠菘紫芥攔街賣　白米青柴倚戶收
十二時中生計足　數千年外道緣周　苟於心外存諸見　敢保驢年會合頭
[7]
山根水際我嘗諳　特地移居逼闤闠　人影紛紜方雜沓　市聲撩亂政沉酣
千樓燈火為標準　萬井笙歌作指南　却喜頭陀忘管帶　無邊法界是同參
[8]
山居却似苦無緣　既不居山學隱鄽　新縛蒲團侵市色　旋移禪板近人煙
庭華日暖藏春鳥　檻樹風高噪晚蟬　一鉢普通年外雪　與誰同共潤心田

[9]
塵居不費買山錢　溢目風光意自便　逐日驊騮蹄踏踏　弄晴蝴蝶翅翩翩
見忘境不須頻遣　執謝心常合本然　如是住來知幾刦　難將消息與人傳

[10]
市鄽卜築道何親　物物頭頭契本真　微有得心魔所攝　擬存住念鬼爲隣
招提禁夜鐘聲近　閭巷催年鼓吹頻　三世如來諸法相　一回新又一回新

Chinese Text for Translation 10: Selections from *Zhongfeng Dharma Talks* in *Zhongfeng Record B*

(Seventeen excerpts in *Gozanban* 9: 506c; 506c–507a; 507c–d; 512a–513c; 514a–515a; 516d–517b; 517b–c; 518b–d; 519c–520b; 520b–c; 522c–523a; 524a–c; 525b–c; 526b–c; 526c–527a; 530d–531a; 533a–c. CBETA 2019.Q3, X70, no. 1402, p. 729a2 to CBETA 2019.Q3, X70, no. 1402, p. 743b16–17.)

[1] 示禪人

上人若要超生死。日用單提那著子。莫問得力不得力。萬刼千生只如此。提不起處猛提撕。舉不起時須舉起。切莫住輕安。輕安不是西來旨。切莫顧危亡。纔顧危亡迷正理。更須不得坐在靜鬧閑忙中。見聞知覺裏。但只常教一念絕所依。非但忘嗔亦忘喜。等閑和箇忘亦忘。信脚踏飜東海水。非不非是不是。差之毫釐失之千里。

***

[2] 示禪人 (雄藏主)

做工夫。只是一箇信心。信知有此一段大事。提起所參話。晝夜只是與麼參去。政當參時。也無純一不純一。得力不得力底道理。純一得力揔是妄覺。非工夫邊實有此事。提起話參時。只是一箇沒奈何。揔無第二箇境界。今日參不得。今日不奈何。明日參不得。明日不奈何。乃至三十年參不得。三十年只是一箇沒奈何。或未到悟明之際。若有半點奈何之心。皆墮情計。非真工夫也。此事要與生死大事為對。不是世間可學可求可用心之事。參禪如咬鐵橛子相似。政當咬時。有甚奈何處。你若耐得許多沒奈何。便是有力量真辨道人操志也。海東雄上主求語警策。乃筆以告之。

***

[3] 示禪人
參禪並無一切造作。只要一箇為生死大事正念。真切提起所參話
也。不要與精進昏散較量多少。將心較量轉成散亂去也。但去
尋箇穩便處住了。不問年深月遠。但有一日精神。參取一日。
久久不變不異。不知不覺。自然有開悟之時。如未獲開悟。切
不得將心意識。向一切佛法道理上卜度。不怕道業不成也。勉
之。老幻如此說云。

***

[4] 示海東淵首座
工夫上說起疑情。當知疑情初無指授。亦無体段。亦無知覺。
亦無把柄。亦無趣向。亦無方便。亦無做作安排等事。更無別
有道理。可以排遣得。教你起疑。其所謂疑者。但只是你為自
己躬下一段生死大事。未曾明了。單單只是疑此生死大事。因
甚麼遠從無量刼來。流轉迨今。是甚麼巴鼻。又因甚麼。從今
日。流入盡未來際。決定有甚了期。只這箇便是疑處。從上佛
祖。皆從此疑。疑之不已。自然心路絕。情妄消。知解泯。能
所忘。不覺忽然相應。便是疑情破底時節也。在前古人。也不
曾去看話頭。參公案。上蒲團做模樣。只是切切。扵生死大事
上疑著。三千里五千里。撞見箇人。未脫草鞋便驀直問。我為
生死事大。無常迅速。千人萬人都是如此出家。如此行脚。如
此求人。如此學道。初不為第二件事。設有亦不為也。後代以
來。宗門下。不合有許多露布葛藤。往往脚未跨門。便被此一
等語言引誘將去。墮在葛藤窠臼中。喚作佛法。喚作禪道。流
入知解羅網中。不得出頭。惟益多聞乃所知障。扵道實不曾有
交涉。扵是近代尊宿。眼不耐見蓺林中有此一病弊。待你未開
口時。但只把一則無義味話頭。撇在學人面前。只要你放舍一
切身心世間諸緣雜念。并禪道佛法語言文字等。只教你向此話
頭上。起大疑情參取去。正當參時。也不是要明佛法了參。也
不是要會禪道了參。也不是要求一切知解了參。其所用心參
者。單單只是不奈自己有箇生死無常大事何。所以參到話頭破
處。則生死大事。與之俱破。生死大事明處。則一切語言文
字。與之俱明。離死生外。別無話頭。離話頭外。別無生死。
雖則從上古人。只疑生死了悟道。今之人只疑話頭了悟道。
其所疑之事。似或有異。其悟之道。其實無古無今。無雜無
異也。正當疑話頭時。也莫求方便。須信參禪無方便。也莫求
趣向。須知參禪無趣向。也莫求把柄。須知參禪無把柄。其所
言方便者。即箇話頭。便是方便。即箇話頭。便是趣向。便是

把柄。但只要信得及。靠得穩。此生參箇話頭。決定要就此話頭上打徹。如打未徹。初無障礙。只是自家。欠一種猛利。欠一種堅固。欠一種不退轉。欠一種信得及。把得定耳。但能把得箇參話頭底正念住。也莫管它昏沉散乱。也莫管它動靜語默。也莫管它生老病死。也莫管它苦樂順逆。也莫管佗成就不成就等。乃至除却箇參話頭底正念之外。縱是三世佛歷代祖同時現前。以第一義諦。無上法要。傾入我心腹中。亦須當時與嘔却。亦莫管它。盖此事不在佛祖上。不在境緣上。不在文字上。不在知解上。但只在你一箇信得。生死無常大事極處。所以不柰箇生死何。參古人話頭。除却參古人話頭底一念子外。更擬向第二念中尋討。大似撥波求水尒。古人道。密在爾邊。又何曾有一法與人。為見聞為持守。惟今日教你看箇話頭。早是不得已也。更若離此話頭外。別作思惟計較。展轉沒交涉。久後工夫熟。時節至。疑情破。須知疑者參者。乃至和箇話頭。打歸自己。更無一法當情。亦無一法為了為不了。故教中謂。森羅万象。一法之所印。只箇一法。亦無討處。其何話頭之有哉。但辦肯心。決不相賺。海東淵禪人。日居僧堂中。因看話頭處未通。出紙求指示。乃直筆以此答之云爾。

***

[5] 示夫上主
據如所言。十二時中作主不得。不識離却所參話頭外。又喚甚麼作主。當知即箇話頭。便是你主。但常令此所參底話頭。不離心念。便是作得主。亦不可起作得主想。古人大意上。初不曾有作主之說。如溈山謂。強作主宰。莫徇人情。乃一時發人之精進之詞。非道也。

又謂昏沉散亂。是非逆順等上。看話頭之說。此說初無難曉底道理。自是你曉不得。強生知見。且如正看話頭之頃。忽爾昏散順逆等境現前。便當奮起精神。向昏散順逆中看。久久昏散順逆情妄自消耳。有人。見此昏散順逆等現前。便乃瞥生疑妄。謂畢竟別有何方便。可以去此昏散等習。又乃歸咎扵根器宿業及種種境緣。才起此心。則扵昏散上重加昏散。順逆中又添順逆也。所以教你昏沉散乱時只就昏沉散乱上看。也不是別有何物可看。亦不是看昏沉散乱是何物。亦不教你扵昏散順逆等別尋巴鼻。只教你便就昏散等上。單單提起話頭自看。永不放捨。亦不妄起第二念分別。此是昏散順逆等。此非昏散順逆等。大凡做工夫只要悟話頭。不要你排遣昏散等。你但痛念生死無常大事。單單提箇話頭。起大疑情以求正悟。惟是生死念切。自然話頭綿密。扵看話頭綿密處。昏散等自然不現。凡是做工夫時。見有昏散等。即是你念生死之心不切。看話頭之念不密耳。

又言。扵話頭上起疑。恐落思量之說。差矣。古人只為箇生死大事未決。三十年二十年。三千里一萬里。逢人便問。我為生死大事。何曾看話頭起疑来。雖不看話頭起疑。而一箇生死大事未決之心。便是古人疑處。近代參學之士。苦不以生死為事。況是宗門繁盛。語言滋多。脚未跨門先以記持語言為務。把箇為生死之正念一隔隔斷。扵是近代尊宿不得已。將箇沒義味話頭。瞥在你八識田中。教你去却一切知鮮。單單只向此話之所未曉處疑著。其所疑者如撞著箇銀山鉄壁相似。面前更無寸步可進。鋭[1]起第二念便是落思量。但不起第二念即是疑情。其疑情中。自然截斷一切知見鮮會等病。忽尒你扵所疑處觸翻。方知如古人一言半句。真箇是大火聚吹毛劍。不可犯也。但辨信心。無事不了。

***

[6] 示日本元禪人 (住京師真如禪寺。号古先。法嗣扵師。)
此心迷成生死。悟成涅槃。然生死之迷。固是難遭。殊不知。悟之涅槃。猶是入眼金塵。當知般若如大火聚。不許一切湊泊。你做工夫之心。不肯真切。不能扵宼初一念上。拍盲坐斷。十二時中硬剝剝如大死人相似。靠箇所參話。一切斬斷。每扵坐不斷處。而生異計。作難想。作易想。引起差別情妄紛然交接于懷。不能隨處剪斷。立十種重碩。必欲憑此碩力。剪斷浮思幻想。如石壓草。便立千種重碩。也壓不得。轉見疎闊。
你不思生死無常是無始時。一段最大因緣。必欲相應。都無異方便。惟有一箇所參話。直下但辨取。一片不退轉。不改易。不遷變底決定正念。生與同生。死與同死。設使扵未悟之際。千釋迦。萬弥勒。傾出四大海佛法。入你耳根。揔是虛妄塵勞。皆非究竟。但是你一箇正念。靠不穩。其顛倒狂妄。千途萬轍。了無休歇期。子細子細。元禪人勉之。

***

[7] 示聖門哲禪人 (住京師真如禪寺。後号明叟。法嗣于師)
昔僧問馬祖。如何是佛。祖云。即心是佛。此一句話。直是軟頑。一切人是說。箇箇領略得去。及至問伊道。那箇是你心。你便東

---
[1] Translation follows CBETA X70, no. 1402 = 纔.

指西指。認色認空。說道說理。展轉沒交涉也。且心既不可指。
你又喚甚麼作佛。索性沒討頭處。須知此事。端的是悟始得。
你若不曾悟去。任你盡世。認箇即心是佛。及至眼光落地時。
討箇心也不見。討箇佛也不見。甘受輪迴。悔將無及。如是喚作
參禪者。你鄉裏人。比比皆是。爭似將箇趙州因甚道箇無字話。
立定腳頭。一氣拍盲。參向前去。若不親到大徹大悟之地。決定
不休。能如是立志參究。久之頓悟。則知即心是佛。與箇無字。
捻成剩語。聖門哲禪人求語警策。老幻(某甲)書。

***

[8] 示定林了一上人
若了一。萬事畢。且一作麼生了。若要覓箇了處。一切用心。皆是
平地風波。都無你了處。但將一箇趙州因甚道箇無字。頓在胸中。
默默地挼此一生。堅密身心。與之厮捱將去。政當厮捱時。不得你
了會。亦不得你不了會。了與不了。都是妄見。你若住此妄見中。
展轉無你了處。但只將箇所參話。橫于胸中。今日也恁麼參。明日
也恁麼參。扵所參處。應有一切殊勝奇特境界現前。揔是魔恠。更
不得第二念認著及與遣除。乃至分別取捨以為則。但有此心。俱落
意地。要脫它生死根塵。也大難。但是三十年二十年。不獲悟明。
惟加堅密。挼得生與同生死與同死。扵所參話一念子靠教穩怗怗
地。不動不搖。久之異情不起。妄念平沉。扵無所覺知處。驀忽猛
省。方知至一之道。扵未行腳時。已嘗了了。政不待別有所了而
了也。是謂定林。你若不曾恁麼真正悟明一回。便恁麼喚作了也
不得。喚作一。亦不得。更要喚作定林。大遠在。予說不虛。一禪
人。道念綿密。年齒方盛。儘有發越祖道之姿。但辦肯心。決不相
賺。

***

[9] 示因禪人
但信教自己及提起所參話。寬著程限。挼取久遠參去。自然有人
悟入之時。不可扵正參時。生一切疑慮之心。又不可生一切速
求開悟之心。譬如行路。力極則自到了。
正參話頭。做工夫時。但有一切見聞知覺。奇特殊勝應驗等事。
皆是魔緣。但不生心隨逐。久則自解。你若瞥生一念樂著之
情。從此墯入魔境。自謂發明。却成狂亂。

悟道。如人到家。面前物境既是故家。一一自然。穩當明白。更無纖毫疑惑之念。苟存半點疑惑。決定不是故家。便須挼去別參。或不尔則謾成異見矣。

參無字。只要向無字上起疑情。參道趙州因甚道箇無字。十二時中只與麼參。正當參時。不問有思量分別。無思量分別。有思量。無思量。屬妄想。如今只要你單單向所參話上起疑情。乃至捻不要一切境緣上作分別想。但離却所參話外。別起一念。不問是佛念法念。俱是非正念。皆生死種子。

真實做工夫底人。十二時中。念念如救頭然。如一人與万人敵相似。那討閑工夫。向身命世緣上着到。亦有甚工夫。要求人開發。更有甚閑工夫。要問人討言句。覓鮮會。更有一等人。三日不得人開發。便乃心下茫然。無所施其巧。這箇捻是逐妄流轉。不是做工夫底人。大率做二[2]夫底人。如做賊要偷人金帛相似。行時行要偷。坐時坐要偷。閑時閑要偷。忙時忙要偷。更那肯露此要偷之心。要人看見。愈要偷得切。則愈藏機得密。心心尔。念念尔。久之不退。管取到古人地位。豈似伊十二時中。做主不定。只要隨它妄想流轉。強作主宰。走在蒲團做模樣。念念馳求。不肯休歇。那討相應底時節。記取記取。光影如流。速宜自省。

***

[10] 示然禪人

參禪但信得一箇話頭。及便只參一箇。但是正參底也。用趙州因甚道箇無字話。外更有一歸何處話現前。你但莫采它。久之自然忘去也。你如今但挼取一片長遠身心。去參。切不可要求速得成就。若存速成就之念。久久引入知解網中去也。參禪但存了一箇痛為死生大事底正念。守箇所參話三十年二十年。乃至一生只與麼去。永不要起一念要求速悟之心。此心才生即是妄念。永不與道相應也。

你但不要求速悟。你底工夫熟。時節至。譬之行路。雖不期到。但行步。不歇不斷。自然到也。然禪人。但恁麼信去。莫要學別人求速悟底。走入邪路去。你可將此話。就說與你許多鄉中人知之。

---

[2] Translation follows CBETA X70, no. 1402 = 工.

[11] 示英禪人
禪宗。有一等聰利之人。始焉扵師家語言下。鮮會得相似。便尒承當。當時師家。不暇攻其悟不悟。一時放過。扵是一以自己所入處。展轉教人。扵是不要疑話頭。只貴現成領畧。互相帶累。入知見網中。說時似同。行處了無交涉。

有一等初根愚鈍。見說參禪須看話頭。起大疑情。方頓悟入。扵是硬剝剝地。三十二十年靠取箇所參底話頭。首尾一貫。不肯放捨。久之情妄頓消盡。然開悟後来。凡遇學人請益。必欲令人看話頭起疑情做工夫。似此等師家爲人。雖曰難扵進入。却始終不壞人根性。

自有宗門已来。雖云直指人心。其涉入門戶。千途萬轍。各各不同。盖師家據一箇直指之理。徇人根性。及自家悟入之山不同。所以誘引不同。原其至理究竟之處。一皆了脫死生大事爲期。餘無可爲者。衆生識性多差。不能一屙便休。又有悟後又要見人之說。或有得箇入處又要履踐之說。此皆是悟處。不能一蹋到底。尚帶異執。不能與人鮮粘去縛。扵是有見人履踐。若約一悟永悟底。斷無此說也。古人雖不看公案起疑情。但扵未悟時用心。與今人徹底不同。若教今人不做工夫。箇箇都坐在顛倒網裏。

古人有云。依它作鮮障自悟門。圓覺經。末世衆生希望成道。毋令求悟。惟益多聞。增長我見。

***

[12] 示榮藏主
提撕話頭時。言無味。你擬喚甚麼作味。言味且置。你又向何處進取一步。要求味及要進步。皆是根本妄想。你擬存此心要做工夫究明死生。展轉沒交涉。你如今要知味麼。但扵所參話上。綿綿密密去。不要別求方便。做得做不得。只麼參到頭去。即此便是滋味。即此便是進步底道理。除此別要求味求進步。揔是顛倒妄想。萬刧無你了處。古人學道。但只爲箇生死事大無常迅速。也無話頭得參。更問如何。更寬如何。劈脊便棒。欄腮便掌。已是老婆心。更有甚較量分。亦有甚語話分。今時人自信不及。不柰你何。把箇無義味話。與你參究。更嫌沒滋味。更要討進步處。大似開眼說夢。榮上主。隨衆雙徑。向道之心堅篤。出紙求語警策。乃直筆以示之云尒。

***

[13] 示素禪人

參禪。初無方便。只要你拶取一片真實為生死大事底正念。提起箇所參話。不問三十年二十年。一氣不轉頭。疑不得處去疑取。拶不上處去拶取。但疑不得。拶不上。都不要別起第二念。要如何疑。如何拶。原夫疑亦只是疑箇所參底話頭。拶也只是要拶箇所參底話頭。除此箇所參底話頭。更別無甚麼輕安寂靜。奇特殊勝。靈驗等。與你做窠臼。才覺所參話不現前。便又與之密密提起。念念不斷參去。但辨肯心。決不相賺。

***

[14] 示日本中浦居士

父母未生前那箇是本來面目。中浦還直下曾與至中之理相應麼。如其未能。此事不是說了便休。便須單單提起前話。拶取一生。孤寂身心。空閑志氣。默默然如大死人相似。如不致悟。決定不休。但辨此等堅密肯心。則身與心境與緣俱不期中而中矣。復何疑哉。復何疑哉。

***

[15] 示日本平親衛直菴知陟居士

昔。龐居士問馬祖云。不與萬法為侶者。是甚麼人。祖云。待汝一口吸盡西江水。即向你道。此說之下。其直如絃。你擬涉思惟。則當處已不勝其曲矣。又龐居士謂。難難。百石油麻樹上攤。龐婆謂。易易。易似和衣一覺睡。其女靈照謂。也不難。也不易。百草頭上祖師意。三人雖說難說易。而亦不知其當下其直亦如絃也。你擬扵難易邊覓又不勝曲矣。所以毗耶老人。有直心為道場。離諸委曲故。如其扵此至直之理。未能披襟領荷。捻不要別第二念。但只將箇父母未生前那箇是我本來面目話。頓在胸中。默默然參取。孜孜然究取。矻矻然疑取。凜凜然做取。做到情忘識盡處。驀忽猛省。始信迷時也直。悟時也直。得時也直。失時也直。上天堂。下地獄。坐蓮臺。入劍穿。更無有一斯須不與至直之理脗然混合。到此。也無佛可求。也無眾生可弃。直之又直者矣。親衛平居士。號直菴。出紙需予以警策入道之語。乃直筆以酬之。併為說偈。

言直行直心乃直 擬存知解便乖踈 話頭日用參教徹 說箇如絃已涉途

***

[16] 示會庵嘉禪人

死生大事。不是說了便休。不是會了便休。說得底會得底。揔是無始時來輪迴業識。急須吐却。但單單提起箇所參話頭。挵取一生真實身心。向三根椽下坐。如大死人相似。胷中絕氣息。忘見聞泯知解。惟有一箇所參話。立定脚頭。只與麼參去。縱使一生不悟。其所參之正念。不變不易。來世出頭來。管取一聞千悟。此是決定底事。古所謂但辦肯心。決不相賺。會庵嘉禪人。求語警策。乃尒示之。

***

[17] 示玉溪鑒講主

佛法是自心。此心一大藏教。詮註不破。三世諸佛指點不出。千七百祖。仰望不見。尽大地人。追趕不及。從古至今。任有百千玄解。皆是向此心背後叉手。由是曹溪謂。說箇直指。早是迂曲了也。此說之下。如馬前相撲。擬眨眼來。性命已在它人手裏。安許停機佇思。而後領畧耶。或未能向未屙已前和身拶入。切不可匆匆草草。向聲前句後。取次承當。不妨發起一片真實決定信心。向己躬下守箇無義味話。奮平生猛利身心。孜孜兀兀。拍盲做向前去也。不問三十年二十年。但有一日光陰。做取一日。久遠信心堅。立志密。不知不覺。忽尒開悟。方知此道不從人得。如啞子得夢。從上若教若禪多少沒意智者。揔向這裏瞥脫。政當做時。苟存一念外緣。一念取捨。一念愛憎。一念子。任差別情妄隨物流轉。更存一念記持學解等情識。不能應念勦絕。欲望它鑒破光亡。無異却步求前。決無有相應之時也。玉溪講主鑒公。需以警策。乃扶病直筆以告之。

Chinese Text for Translation 11: *Instructions to the Assembly* from *Zhongfeng Talks* in *Zhongfeng Record B*

(*Gozanban* 9, 542b–543a. CBETA 2019.Q3, X70, no. 1402, pp. 716c3–717a6.)

示眾

前日之晚。首座與維那到菴言。結夏在近。請為眾道話一中。本曾許在三兩日有暇。當請以過菴點茶一杯。共語片時。以見遞相警策耳。不謂連值陰雨路滑不便。使更過十二日。則兩山人事又尔交接。不能遂幻人遠避之心。思之合堂大眾皆飽參之士。尋常到菴未曾不蒲團上事相扣。安有結夏解夏之為辨道時節。若以至理言之。最初發心向道時。此夏已曾結了也。十二時中看箇所參底無義味話頭。未即決了。便是坐夏時。三十年二十年推到神消識盡。冷地裏忽尔猛省得著。便是解夏之時。自恣之日。豈以區區九十日為限哉。凡做工夫不靈驗者。往往只是偷心未死。所以虗延歲月。別無佗病。若是偷心死扵今日。則今日便相應。死扵明日。則明日便相應。何謂偷心。但離却ヶ所參底話外。別見有ヶ自己。是偷心。扵所見之自己外。別見有人有我。是偷心。做得純熟時。知道純熟。是偷心。做不純熟時。知道不純熟。是偷心。面前見有昏沉散乱時。是偷心。不見有昏沉散乱。唯有ヶ所參底話頭。與疑情交結不斷時。是偷心。但是看話頭處。瞥生一念子。不問是凡是聖。是真是偽。惚言之皆偷心也。忽有ヶ伶俐人。向予說處惚不相干。別資一路。為道為理。為見為聞。此又是偷心中之偷心。佛亦不可救藥。但盡得許多偷心。只與麼依本分靠取ヶ所參底話。如泥塑木雕底有氣死人。外不見有大眾。內不見有自己。冷冰冰地絕見絕聞。如是守去。久之管取心空及第者必矣。謾書此以當菴中茶話。本上座且過山避人事數日。更不須尋問幻跡在何地。直饒尋見亦不共語。幸首座維那白之。

Bibliography

Araki Kengo. *Hogyō hen*. Zen no goroku 14. Tokyo: Chikuma shobō, 1981.
Backus, Charles. *The Nan-chao Kingdom and T'ang China's Southwestern Frontier*. Cambridge: Cambridge University Press, 1981.
Braverman, Arthur, trans. *Mud & Water: The Collected Teachings of Zen Master Bassui*. Somerville, MA: Wisdom Publications, 2002.
Broughton, Jeffrey L. *The Bodhidharma Anthology: The Earliest Records of Zen*. Berkeley: University of California Press, 1999.
Broughton, Jeffrey Lyle. *Zongmi on Chan*. New York: Columbia University Press, 2009.
Broughton, Jeffrey L., with Elise Yoko Watanabe. *The Chan Whip Anthology: A Companion to Zen Practice*. New York: Oxford University Press, 2015.
Broughton, Jeffrey L., with Elise Yoko Watanabe. *Core Texts of the Sŏn Approach: A Compendium of Korean Sŏn (Chan) Buddhism*. New York: Oxford University Press, 2021.
Broughton, Jeffrey L., with Elise Yoko Watanabe. *The Letters of Chan Master Dahui Pujue*. New York: Oxford University Press, 2017.
Broughton, Jeffrey L., with Elise Yoko Watanabe. *The Record of Linji: A New Translation of the* Linjilu *in the Light of Ten Japanese Zen Commentaries*. New York: Oxford University Press, 2013.
Buswell, Robert E., Jr., and Donald S. Lopez Jr. *The Princeton Dictionary of Buddhism*. Princeton, NJ: Princeton University Press, 2014.
Cahill, James. *Hills Beyond a River: Chinese Painting of the Yüan Dynasty, 1279–1368*. New York: Weatherhill, 1976.
Chao Zhang. "Chan Miscellanea and the Shaping of the Religious Lineage of Chinese Buddhism under the Song." *Kokusai Bukkyōgaku daigakuin daigaku kenkyū kiyō* 21 (2017): 243–282.
Chinese Buddhist Electronic Text Association. http://www.cbeta.org.
Chinese Text Project. https://ctext.org.
Dictionary Department, Institute of Linguistics, Chinese Academy of Social Sciences. *The Contemporary Chinese Dictionary (Chinese-English Edition)*. Beijing: Foreign Language Teaching and Research Press, 2002.
Dufficy, William, trans. *The Illusory Man by Zhongfeng Mingben*. Las Vegas, NV: Independently published, 2022.
Eigen-ji kaisan goroku kenkyūkai, ed. *Eigen Jakushitsu oshō goroku*. 3 vols. Kyoto: Zen bunka kenkyūjo, 2016.
Enomoto Wataru. "Nichi-Chū kōryū shi no naka no chūsei zenshū shi." In *Chūsei Zen no chi*, edited by Sueki Fumihiko, 37–72. Kyoto: Rinsen shoten, 2021.
Eskildsen, Stephen. *Daoism, Meditation, and the Wonders of Serenity: From the Latter Han Dynasty (25–220) to the Tang Dynasty (618–907)*. Albany: State University of New York Press, 2015.
Furuta Shōkin. *Nihon no Zen goroku 11: Bassui*. Tokyo: Kodansha, 1979.
Gōto Kōson, ed. *Hakuin oshō zenshū*. 8 vols. 1934–1935. Reprint, Tokyo: Ryūginsha, 1967. archive.org/details/hakuinoshozenshu04hakuuoft/page/42/mode/2up.
Harada Kōdō. "Chūsei ni okeru genjū ha no keisei to igi." *Komazawa daigaku bukkyō gakubu kenkyū kiyō* 53 (1995): 21–36.
Harada Ryūmon. *Jakushitsu Genkō*. Tokyo: Shunjūsha, 1979.

Hearn, Maxwell K. *How to Read Chinese Paintings*. New York: The Metropolitan Museum of Art, 2008.
Heller, Natasha. "Between Zhongfeng Mingben and Zhao Mengfu: Chan Letters in Their Manuscript Context." In *Buddhist Manuscript Cultures: Knowledge, Rituals, and Art*, edited by Stephen C. Berkwitz, Juliane Schober, and Claudia Brown, 109–123. New York: Routledge, 2009.
Heller, Natasha. "The Chan Master as Illusionist: Zhongfeng Mingben's *Huanzhu Jiaxun*." *Harvard Journal of Asiatic Studies* 69, no. 2 (2009): 271–308.
Heller, Natasha. *Illusory Abiding: The Cultural Construction of the Chan Monk Zhongfeng Mingben*. Cambridge, MA: Harvard University Asia Center, 2014.
Heller, Natasha. "Pure Land Devotional Poetry by a Chan Monk." In *Pure Lands in Asian Texts and Contexts: An Anthology*, edited by Georgios T. Halkias and Richard K. Payne, 540–548. Honolulu: University of Hawai'i Press, 2019.
Henricks, Robert G., trans. *The Poetry of Hanshan: A Complete, Annotated Translation of Cold Mountain*. Albany: State University of New York Press, 1990.
Hirakawa Akira. *Buddhist Chinese-Sanskrit dictionary*. Tokyo: The Reiyukai, 1997.
Ibuki Atsushi. *Chūgoku Zen shisō shi*. Kyoto: Zen bunka kenkyūjo, 2021.
Ide Seinosuke. "Chūhō Myōhon jisan zō o megutte." *Bijutsu kenkyū* 343 (1989): 19–36.
Iritani Sensuke and Matsumura Takashi, eds. *Kanzan shi*. Zen no goroku 13. Tokyo: Chikuma shobō, 2019.
Iriya Yoshitaka. *Gozan bungaku shū*. Shin Nihon koten bungaku taikei 48. Tokyo: Iwanami shoten, 2016.
Iriya Yoshitaka. *Gūdō to etsuraku: Chūgoku no zen to shi*. Tokyo: Iwanami shoten, 1983.
Iriya Yoshitaka. *Nihon no Zen goroku 10: Jakushitsu*. Tokyo: Kōdansha, 1979.
Ishii Shūdō. "Chūgoku no gozan jissetu seido no kiso teki kenkyū 1." *Komazawa daigaku bukkyō gakubu ronshū* 13 (1982): 89–132.
Ishii Shūdō. "*Daie Sōkō to sono deshitachi* (hachi)." *Indogaku bukkyōgaku kenkyū* 25, no. 1 (1977): 257–261.
Kodama Osamu. *Jakushitsu Genkō no shōgai*. Kyoto: Shibunkaku shuppan, 2014.
Kroll, Paul W. *A Student's Dictionary of Classical and Medieval Chinese*. Leiden: Brill, 2017.
Lauer, Uta. *A Master of His Own: The Calligraphy of the Chan Abbot Zhongfeng Mingben (1262–1323)*. Stuttgart: Steiner, 2002.
Lee, Sherman E., et al. *Eight Dynasties of Chinese Painting: The Collection of the Nelson Gallery-Atkins Museum, Kansas City, and the Cleveland Museum of Art*. Bloomington: The Cleveland Museum of Art and Indiana University Press, 1980.
Levine, Gregory, and Yukio Lippit. *Awakenings: Zen Figure Painting in Medieval Japan*. New York: Japan Society, 2007.
McCausland, Shane. *The Mongol Century: Visual Cultures of Yuan China, 1271–1368*. Honolulu: University of Hawai'i Press, 2015.
McCausland, Shane. *Zhao Mengfu: Calligraphy and Painting for Khubilai's China*. Hong Kong: Hong Kong University Press, 2011.
Monier-Williams, Monier. *A Sanskrit-English Dictionary*. 1899. Reprint, Oxford: The Clarendon Press, 1974.
Morrison, Elizabeth. *The Power of Patriarchs: Qisong and Lineage in Chinese Buddhism*. Sinica Leidensia 9. Leiden: Brill, 2010.
Mujaku Dōchū. *Daie Fukaku Zenji sho kōrōju*. Kyoto: Zen bunka kenkyūjo, 1997.
Noguchi Yoshitaka. *Gendai Zenshū shi kenkyū*. Kyoto: Zen bunka kenkyūjo, 2005.
Noguchi Yoshitaka. "Jakushitsu Genkō to Chūhō Myōhon." *Zen bunka* 242 (2016): 28–37.
Noguchi Yoshitaka. "Migo Zen: Tenmoku Chūhō kenkyū." *Kyūshū Chūgoku gakkai hō* 22 (1979): 14–25.

Noguchi Yoshitaka and Matsubara Shinju, trans. *Chūhō Myōhon: Sanbō yawa yakuchū*. Tokyo: Kyūko shoin, 2015.

Parker, Joseph D. *Zen Buddhist Landscape Arts of Early Muromachi Japan (1336–1573)*. Albany: State University of New York Press, 1999.

Protass, Jason. *The Poetry Demon: Song-Dynasty Monks on Verse and the Way*. Studies in East Asian Buddhism 29. Honolulu: University of Hawai'i Press, 2021.

Rouzer, Paul. *On Cold Mountain: A Buddhist Reading of the Hanshan Poems*. Seattle: University of Washington Press, 2016.

Shiina Kōyū, ed. *Gozanban Chūgoku Zenseki sōkan 9: Goroku* 4. Kyoto: Rinsen shoten, 2013.

Siderits, Mark and Shōryū Katsura, trans. *Nāgārjuna's Middle Way: Mūlamadhyamakakārikā*. Somerville, MA: Wisdom Publications, 2013.

Takakusu Junjirō and Watanabe Kaigyoku, eds. *Taishō shinshū daizōkyō*. 100 vols. Tokyo: Taishō issaikyō kankōkai, 1924–1934.

Tanaka Ryōshō, ed. *Zengaku kenkyū nyūmon*. 2nd ed. Tokyo: Daitō shuppansha, 2006.

Tatsumi Nami, ed. *Chū'i yōgo jiten*. Tokyo: Gensōsha, 2020.

Tokyo National Museum's *Preceptor Clam Man* (sometimes called *Reverend Shrimp-Eater*): emuseum.nich.go.jp/detail?langId=ja&webView=&content_base_id=100309&content_part_id=0&content_pict_id=0.

Tsuchiya Taisuke and Yanagi Mikiyasu, trans. *Hōgenroku Mumonkan*, Shin kokuyaku daizōkyō, Chūgoku senjutsu bu 1–6, Zenshū bu. Tokyo: Daizōshuppan, 2019.

Yu Delong, ed. *Chushi Fanqi quanji*. Beijing: Jiuzhou chubanshe, 2017.

Yu Delong, ed. *Zhongfeng Mingben quanji*. Beijing: Jiuzhou chubanshe, 2018.

Wang Youru. *Historical Dictionary of Chan Buddhism*. Lanham, MD: Rowman & Littlefield, 2017.

Watson, Burton, trans. *Cold Mountain: 100 Poems by the T'ang Poet Han-shan*. New York: Columbia University Press, 1970.

Welter, Albert. *The Meaning of Myriad Good Deeds: A Study of Yung-ming Yen-shou and the Wan-shan t'ung-kuei chi*. New York: Peter Lang, 1993.

Welter, Albert. *Yongming Yanshou's Conception of Chan in the Zongjing lu: A Special Transmission within the Scriptures*. Oxford: Oxford University Press, 2011.

Welter, Albert, Steven Heine, and Jin Y. Park, eds. *Approaches to Chan, Sŏn, and Zen Studies: Chinese Chan Buddhism and Its Spread throughout East Asia*. Albany: State University of New York, 2022.

Wilkinson, Endymion. *Chinese History: A New Manual*. 5th ed. Cambridge, MA: Endymion Wilkinson, 2018.

Wu Pei-Yi. *The Confucian's Progress: Autobiographical Writings in Traditional China*. Princeton, NJ: Princeton University Press, 1990.

Xiang Chu, ed. *Hanshan shi zhu*. Beijing: Zhonghua shuju, 2000.

Yamada Kōdō, ed. *Zenmon hōgo shū*. 3 vols. 1921. Reprint, Tokyo: Shigensha, 1996.

Yifa. *The Origins of Buddhist Monastic Codes in China: An Annotated Translation and Study of the Chanyuan Qinggui*. Honolulu: University of Hawai'i Press, 2002.

Yoshizawa Katsuhiro, ed. *Shoroku zokugo kai*. Kyoto: Zen bunka kenkyūjo, 1999.

Yü Chün-fang. *The Renewal of Buddhism in China: Zhuhong and the Late Ming Synthesis*. New York: Columbia University Press, 2020.

Yunqi Zhuhong (雲棲袾宏). *Ming Chan Masters* (*Abbreviated Collection of Famous Monks of the Imperial Ming* [*Huangming mingseng jilüe* 皇明名僧輯略]). CBETA, X84, no. 1581, p. 358, c6.

Index

For the benefit of digital users, indexed terms that span two pages (e.g., 52–53) may, on occasion, appear on only one of those pages.

abbot
    must attract monastery patrons with Way-virtue, not blandishments, 157
    taking on *name* of, 148
    three energies essential to serving as, 146
    Wuzu Fayan as exemplary, 152
accomplishments, stagnation in, 173
admonition (*zhen* 箴) genre, 2–3, 19, 20, 22, 23, 141, 214–15
admonition, self-, 141. *See also* warning whip (*jingce* 警策)
Amitābha as *huatou*. See under *huatou*
"Amitābha Buddha is not anything beyond the confines of *your own mind*," Chan Master Konggu Jinglong (空谷景隆禪師), 57
"Amitābha in your own mind," Chushi Fanqi, Chan Master (楚石梵琦禪師), *Poems of Longing for the Pure Land* (*Huai jingtu shi* 懷淨土詩), 56
Amitābha's Pure Land Sukhāvatī, "going to be reborn in" (*wangsheng* 往生), 100
    little mention of in Linji Ming Chan, 61
    no different from our own world, 102
Ascending-the-Hall (*shang-tang* 上堂) discourses, lack of, in *Zhongfeng Extensive Record*, 21–22
aspiration for awakening, 119, 135–38, 245–46
authority
    two types of, 155
    wielding, as abbot, 156
autobiography within *huatou* Chan
    as Chan sermon, 9
    Dahui Zonggao's, 7
    examples of, 7–9
    as found within Xueyan Zuqin–Gaofeng Yuanmiao–Zhongfeng Mingben lineage, 7–9
    history of, 7
    perseverance emphasized within, 9
    as psychological portraits of *huatou* practice, 9
    of Zhongfeng Mingben, 10–13
    Chinese text of, 13n.50
    chronological not psychological, 10, 13
    no mention of social contacts in, 10, 13–14
    purely chronological tone of, as distinct from predecessors', 7, 10
    as a warning to himself, 10–14
awakening
    at least one time, 64–66, 127
    destruction of *sensation of uncertainty* as tantamount to, 5
    dispersed by master's shout into true awakening, 68–70
    do not order sentient beings of latter age to seek, because they will only increase intellectual learning and reinforce self-view, 176
    do not take a rest even if you fail to bring about, 241
    dying without, while firmly maintaining correct thought 115
    emphasizing by a truly awakened person, 97
    equated with finding of lost pearl, 68–70
    examples of, 172, 174, 175
    as extinguishing *furtive mind*, 172
    a fierce realization, 245–46
    impossible to reach the bottom of in one stride, 239
    is not a truly existent dharma, 125–26
    as *lantern is lantern* (*buddha* is *buddha*), 68–70
    as *lantern light is lantern light* (*mind* is *mind*), 68–70
    likened to
        arriving home, 236
        before you attained awakening, 226–27
        space fusing with space, 172
        throwing water into water, 172

awakening (*cont.*)
  must be awakening on one's own, 115
  not everyone who has attained it reveals it, 164
  remembering what was long forgotten, likened to, 80
  as *single laugh*, 85, 85n.5
  smashing *ball of uncertainty* as tantamount to, 8–9, 28
  talk of *a single awakening is awakening for all time* must be cut off, 239
  teachings *are* Chan with, 175
  as *time of the ending of the summer retreat*, 245–46
  traces of, must not linger in the mind, 32–33
  as *true knowing*, 141
  without any expectation of arrival, spontaneously you will arrive, 238
  you must not seek quick awakening, 238
  Zhongfeng Mingben's self-professed lack of, 10–13, 32–34
    "I also am in the dark about true knowing," 141
    I am certainly not someone who has had a real awakening, 19
    I am lacking in awakening, 146
    I have no more than a confident understanding that comes from ordinary language and books, 146
    I have not yet been able to understand the Way, 146
    interpreted as *upāya* by disciple Tianru Weize, 34
    as very nature of his "not-awakened Zen" (*migo Zen* 未悟禅), 34
axes and saws, 148

"backup"
  discriminations, do not produce, 230
  matter, other than *great matter* of saṃsāra, 227–30
  thought
    as aversion to the medicine of the *huatou*, 77
    engender none apart from *huatou*, 53, 71–72, 174, 227–30, 240–42
    must not acknowledge, 234–35
    must not remove, 234–35
    not producing, that alone *is* the sensation of uncertainty, 232

bad, defined as wanting to benefit self, 130
ball of uncertainty, 50–51, 205. See also *sensation of uncertainty*
  smashing, 9, 28, 89, 108
Ban-la-tuo-yin (般剌脫因). See Layman "Sameness Hermitage"
Bassui Tokushō (拔隊得勝), 53–54, 53n.133
beginner's mind, 125, 135–38, 180–82
being greatly indignant, Gaofeng Yuanmiao's, 4n.12
bell, huge, 89
"big bug," 72–73, 72n.5
bird-tracks in the sky, 96, 104
black lacquer
  bathing in, 179–80
  bucket, 183
Black Mountain, ghost cave of, 51–52, 64n.3, 123n.98
blacksmith, 32–33, 146
blade of grass, 99–100, 102, 241–42
blind
  fellow, 58–59
  one, 23–24
    be diligent and steadfast like, 243–44
    complete *chopping off* shown by, 233
    have the unswerving determination of a, 214–15
    holding a torch in daytime, 141
    stand perfectly still like a, upon the *huatou that has no meaning or taste*, 28–29, 174
  students, 199
blindness, phantasmal, 212–13
Blue Cliff Collection
  cannot add to or subtract from that *ready-made gong'an*, 133
  equivalent to "myriad forms are always speaking dharma," 134
  printing blocks, Dahui Zonggao's legendary burning of, 132–33n.104
  of the *ready-made gong'an*, 134
  removal of from Buddhist canon would not change anything, 134
boat, the. See also houseboats
  anything is life on, 217
  has hawser of tortoise hair, 217
  has mast of rabbit horn, 217
boats
  living on, emphasized in Zhongfeng Mingben's autobiography, 13–14

living on, Zhongfeng Mingben's poems concerning, 216–19
standing with a foot in two, concurrent Chan practice (*canchan* 參禪) and Pure Land *nianfo* (念佛) as, 36–38
Bodhidharma, 19, 72–73, 80–82, 84, 89, 94, 102, 103, 111, 112–15, 127, 162
Chan of
    does not rely on explanations in the sutras, 84
    as *seeing the Nature and becoming a buddha*, 96
    as *separate transmission outside the teachings*, 84
    turns its back on expounding "the *Real*," 96
Daoist *Treatise on Fetal Breathing* falsely attributed to, 83, 83–84n.1, 84
did not possess supranormal powers, 140
did not speak of precepts, 135–38
didn't know while facing a wall for nine years, 58–59
direct pointing of, 83, 83–84n.1, 84, 87, 88, 89, 103, 104, 171, 239, 243–44
direct transmission of, 108
"Externally, cut off all objective supports; internally, make the mind free of panting. With the mind like a wall, it will be possible to enter the Way," 87, 87n.12
facing a phantasmal wall, 24–25
laughs at everyone he meets, 195
meeting Zhongfeng Mingben likened to, 45–46
never gave any instruction, 133
not establishing the written word and direct pointing to the human mind of, 84
people who read widely in Chan books to tally with intention of, 171
personal realization of, as spitting out words until they cease, 214–15
pointed to *one mind is Chan*, 25–26
portraiture of Zhongfeng Mingben possibly as, 15n.55
purport of, 25–26, 112, 135–38
purport of, was not ease, 225
as response-body of Avalokiteśvara Bodhisattva, 140
single lamp flame of, 103
single transmission of, 135–38
taught how to directly clarify your own mind, 87

boulders to press down grass, 233
brambles depend upon phantasm (*huan*幻) to be tangled, 168–178
brow-mite, 194, 194n.15
Budai (布袋)
    big belly of, Zhongfeng Minben depicted with, 14–15n.53, 15–17, 15n.55
    Gaofeng Yuanmiao's generosity in teaching likened to, 138
    legend of, 15–16, 16n.57
buddhadharmas, none outside your mind, 79–80, 243–44
buddha-nature, likened to water and its physical states, 66–68
buddha-nature sea, never freezes, 66–68
buried by other people, 97
Buttressing the Teachings Compilation (*Fujiao bian* 輔教編), Fori Qisong (佛日契嵩), 94, 94n.31

calculation
    cut off, 71–72
    delusive, "how do I do it" as, 225
    you must throw off, 75–76
    you must transcend, 104
    if you produce, other than the *huatou*, 227–30
    strange, 233
    verbalization as, 75
calligraphy
    metaphor of
        "even before brush has hit the paper," 71–72
        using *huatou* **phantasm** (*huan*幻), Zhongfeng Mingben's, 29–30, 172n.6, 173
    willow-leaf style of Zhongfeng Mingben, 14–15, 14–15n.53
Caodong school of Chan
    five ranks of, 112–15
    during Yuan, 2
catch your breath, 71–72
Chan and Pure Land, four alternatives of. *See* Yongming Yanshou
Chan in Yuan dynasty, two geographical spheres of, 2
"Chan is another name for sitting," 214
Chan practice (*canchan* 參禪). *See also* practicing Chan (*canchan* 參禪); *huatou* (話頭)
    beyond one lifetime, 50–51, 112–15, 117–18, 135–38, 165, 174, 225, 243

318 Index

Chan practice (*canchan* 參禪) (*cont.*)
  dullness in, 238
  if you have just one day's worth of spirit for, then practice for one day, 226–27
  incorrectly said to be an effortless dharma method, 117
  likened to
    chewing on an iron spike, 226
    a lone individual facing an enemy of ten thousand, 236–37
    putting out a fire on one's head, 236–37
    a thief who conceals his intentions, 236–37
  no need to practice by coming to understand the Chan Way, 227–30
  no need to practice by seeking for an all-encompassing intellectual knowledge, 227–30
  and Pure Land *nianfo* (念佛)
    both are methods for ending samsara, 35–38, 38n.93, 80–82, 102, 239
    one should practice either but not both, 35–38, 60, 102
  requires no karmic effort, 226–27
  sharpness in, 238
Chan style (禪風), 2–3, 3n.8
Chan Whip, 55–61
Chan/Zen/Sŏn Studies, 2, 2–3n.7
chestnut, burred, *huatou* is like swallowing, 89
chopped off, 233
Chūgan Engetsu (中巖圓月), Japanese Zen poet, 46, 46n.113
Chushan Shaoqi, Chan Master (楚山紹琦禪師), 59
Chushi Fanqi, Chan Master (楚石梵琦禪師), *Poems of Longing for the Pure Land* (*Huai jingtu shi* 懷淨土詩), 56
completely imagined nature arises from phantasmal (*huan* 幻) seeing, 168–69, 169n.2
confidence, 53, 59–60, 66–68, 71–72, 78–79, 108, 112–15, 120, 226, 236
  deep, 190
  great, 174n.9
  only in the single *huatou*, 237–38
  produce a mind of truly resolute, 243–44
  as ultimate locus of the *great matter of samsaric impermanence*, 227–30
correct eye looks on without rejoicing, 73–74

"cosmopolitan Chan," 1–2, 1n.2, 38–40, 38–39n.94, 43–45, 43–44n.106, 44–45n.108
couplet free of involvement with awakening or delusion, 68–70
cross-legged sitting, 26–27, 30, 35, 49, 51, 111, 214–15. *See also* sitting
  do not become attached to in Chan practice (*canchan* 參禪), 183
  dying in posture of, 165
    not connected to *exertion*, 165
    not important, 165
crow depends upon phantasm (*huan* 幻) to be black, 168
cut off, 233

Dadu (Beijing), 2
Dahui Zonggao
  Blue Cliff Collection printing blocks, legendary destruction of, 132, 132–33n.104
  huatou practice of, 28
  huatou practice of, summarized, 5
  huatou-practice Chan of, pervasive in Ming, 60
  intellectual sharpness not conducive to *huatou* practice, 28
  "keep on pressing hard" (*ya jiangqu* 崖將去/*si ya* 去/*si ya* 廝崖), 28
  knowledge not conducive to *huatou* practice, 28
  "mind of samsara will collapse" (*shengsi xin po* 生死心破), 28
  "neither tensed nor slack" (*ji* 急/*huan* 緩 or *jin* 緊/*huan* 緩), 28
  "pass through" (*touqu* 透取/*toude* 透得), 28
  as possible beginning of autobiography within *huatou* Chan, 7
  Recorded Sayings of Chan Master Dahui Pujue (*Dahui Pujue chanshi yulu* 大慧普覺禪師語錄)
    as compared to *Zhongfeng Extensive Record*, 21
  "saving on the expenditure of energy is gaining energy" (*shengli bian shi deli chu ye* 省力便是得力處也), 28
  tasteless (*mei ziwei* 沒滋味) *huatou* of, 28

dead person, breathing, be like, 245–46
dead word, 166–67, 182

death
  cross-legged sitting posture and, 165
  not connected to *exertion*, 165
  not important, 165
  huatou is single *correct thought*, in life same as life and in death same as death, 233, 234–35
  huatou practice and, 77–78
  as transcendent escape alone, 165
deep entrance into one approach, 131
deer a horse, calling a, 75–76
dementia in late life, possible, Yuansou Xingduan's, 5
Deshan's whack of the stick, 73–74
detaching from the phantasmal (*li huan* 離幻)
determination, lack of ancients', in *huatou* practice, 112
dhāraṇī as ultimate principle, 88
dharma talk, Zhongfeng Mingben's autobiography as, 13
diabetes, Zhongfeng Mingben's, 10–13, 12n.45
Diamond Sutra
  Chan Master Jiefeng Ying's (傑峯英禪師) dialogue concerning, 58–59
  Deshan's burning of commentary on, 41–43, 42n.102
  Zhongfeng Mingben's early understanding gained from reading, as "not awakening," 10–13
difficulties of the ancients prior to awakening, 176
  easiness after awakening better noticed by present-day people than, 176
  examples of, 176
direct pointing, Bodhidharma's, 83, 83–84n.1, 84, 87, 88, 89
dithering, 6, 23–24, 171
donkey year, 184, 202, 222
"do not ask whether it will take twenty or thirty years: all you have is the time of a single day: do it for that one day," 243–44
dragons
  and elephants, 104, 177
  Ye Gong's painted, 112–15, 114n.78
dried turd (*ganshijue* 乾屎橛). See under *huatou*
drum
  great, 89, 108
  smeared with poison, 104

Dufeng Benshan, Chan Master (毒峯本善禪師), ***who is this one doing the nianfo*** (念佛) *huatou*, 57
dullness in Chan practice, 238
dust-travails (Sanskrit *kleśa*), 143
  do not emerge from everyday affairs, 143
  in *Huayan Sutra*, 143
  overturned by buddhas and patriarchs, made into buddha-events, 143
  rooted in delusion, 143
Dwelling-in-the-Phantasmal (*huanzhu* 幻住) Hermitages, Zhongfeng Mingben's, 10–13, 23, 175
  genuine state of phantasm is stored in, 212–13
  "here I am not a teacher who preaches and guides others," 175

easiness of ancients, present-day people only focus on, 176
energy, saving on the expenditure of. See "saving on the expenditure of energy is gaining energy" (*shengli bian shi deli chu ye* 省力便是得力處也)
everything is a phantasm
  Jakushitsu Genkō's summary of Zhongfeng Mingben's teaching, 47–48
  as synonym for *ready-made*, 24
exertion of mind
  to avert *torpor* and *distraction* is a mistake, 124
  getting free of dualities not connected to, 80
Extensive Record of Preceptor Tianmu Zhongfeng (*Tianmu Zhongfeng heshang guanglu* 天目中峯和尚廣錄). See *Zhongfeng Extensive Record*
eyelids will fall off, 72–73

failure
  seeing another's, and not questioning our own, 112
  students blaming current decline of *buddhadharma* for, 112
false knowing, as intellectual understanding, 141
famous name and high position, 120
farmer who blames lack of plowing on weather cannot expect autumn harvest, 112–15
fetal breathing, 83, 83–84n.1, 84

fierceness, 227–30
filial piety, 75
finger, burning off, Gaofeng Yuanmiao's *upāya* of, 135–38, 135–36n.109
fire
  burning, to dispel cold, not as good as state of balmy room, 130
  consuming both pieces of wood that kindled it, metaphor of, in *Perfect Awakening* sutra, 26
    Guifeng Zongmi's explication of, 26–27
  great ball of, 104, 232
    prajñā is like, 233
  that burns up wood, 122
  trying to put out, with armful of firewood, 127
  upāyas of Chan patriarchs likened to a ball of, 141
firefly's light added to sun's illumination, 172
fishing net, trying to inflate, 108, 177
"Five Mountains," 1–2, 1n.1
five ranks of Caodong school, 112–15
five schools/houses/lineages of Chan, 103, 104
flip, 8, 36n.91, 64n.6, 107n.63, 122, 134, 191, 196, 203, 232
flour
  grubs infesting, 122
  oil getting into, 89
flower, Śākyamuni's holding up a, 24–25, 68, 104, 141, 148, 169, 193, 212–13
flowers, Zhao Chang's painted, 33, 112–15, 114n.78
Fori Qisong (佛日契嵩), *Buttressing the Teachings Compilation* (*Fujiao bian* 輔教編), 94, 94n.31
four alternatives, Yongming Yanshou's. See Yongming Yanshou
four seasons comprising a year function because they are inseparable, 85
four tenets, none separate from the one buddha vehicle, 85
fox slobber, 89, 90–92n.26
furtive mind
  chopping in two, 120
  as deluded consciousness, 120
  dominated by, present-day people, 120
  extinguishing, as awakening, 172
  inside *furtive mind*, 245–46
  not yet dead, 245–46
  as samsara, 120

as ultimate essence of the Tathāgata's *wondrously bright original-mind*, 122

gaining energy/not gaining energy
  do not ask whether you are, 225
  is a form of false awareness, 226
  no such principle at the moment of practicing, 226
Ganges, numerous as grains of sand in the, 68–70, 143, 148, 170
Gaofeng Yuanmiao (高峰原妙), 4
  autobiography of, 7–8
  great confidence of, 4n.12
  main *huatou*, *to where does the One return* (*yi gui he chu* 一歸何處), 135n.108
  Three Essentials of Chan, 4n.12, 174n.9
  upāya of ordering students to burn a finger, 135–38, 135–36n.109
gaohuang illness, 77–78
ghee, 89, 104, 171
ghosts and spirits, 152
Gōkai Honjō (業海本淨), Japanese Zen disciple of Zhongfeng Mingben, 44
gold dust in the eyes, 89
gong'an (公案), 3n.9, 30–31, 111. See also *huatou* (話頭)
  boring through a string of, 115
  as crucial element for complete transcendence, nothing surpasses, 104
  definition of, 104, 104–5n.59
  employed by buddha mind to reveal, 104
  employed by Chan patriarchal mind to illuminate, 104
  getting *taste* from, Dahui Zonggao's, 64n.3
  just your spreading your lips and teeth, 183
  keeping an eye on, 239
  nianfo (念佛), 55, 60
  old, necessary to be finished with the, 199
  phantasmal, 212–13
  practicing the, 227–30
  prohibition against memorizing as topics of conversation, 104
  ready-made, 49, 133, 133n.105, 134, 222
  ripening, 206
  as a standard, 104
good, defined as wanting only to benefit others, 130
goose, 134
goosefoot vegetable, dining on, 31–32
grass pressed down by boulders, 233

grass roots don't give birth to pine or camelia trees, 117
great confidence, of Gaofeng Yuanmiao, 4n.12
great death, 233, 241, 243
Great Functioning, 38n.93, 97, 148, 204
great matter
   confidence is the ultimate locus of, 227–30
   confidence that there is this, 226
   of impermanence of samsara, you yourself have, 72–73, 227–30, 231–32
   is not something you see and then take a rest, 175
   is not something you speak about and then take a rest, 175
   karmic causes behind, 214–15
   mind of, should never retrogress, 53
   one, of causation, 112–15
   of samsara, 51, 53, 72–73, 80–82, 97, 115, 118, 227–30, 240–41
      ancients and, 232
      called *uncertainty*, 227–30
      Chan practice is only for completely clarifying, 36–37
      escaping from, 239
      is not something you talk about and then take a rest, 243
      lacking the *correct thought* of, 179–80
      original purpose of producing the aspiration for awakening is to settle the, 118
      as part of Chan practice, 35, 237–38, 240–41
      single *correct thought* for, 226–27
      smashed when *huatou* is smashed, 227–30
      take as one's own personal grave responsibility, 30–31, 57, 115, 180–82
      this matter must face off against, 226
      uncertainty is nothing other than, 227–30
      will be smashed when *huatou* is smashed, 227–30
   samsaric impermanence as the, 86, 112–15
   shouldn't be of concern, bear *small matters* one by one, 71–72
great meaning, 171
great phantasm (*huan* 幻), 171. *See also* phantasm (*huan* 幻), phantasmal (*huan* 幻)

accords with karmic propensities of sentient-being vessels, 171
cuts off *logical arranging* and selection process, 171
dharma gate of
   all buddhas and patriarchs have relied upon, 173
   all sentient beings have relied upon for endowment of arising-abiding-changing-ceasing, 173
   give a swift kick to, once awakened, 174
   lies waiting right under your feet, 174
   realize, by entering with your *whole being*, 171, 173
   you should not rush to enter, if you are not after awakening, 175
   teachers who understood, 170
   style of, a phantasm (*huan* 幻), 171
great sameness, 104, 131
Guifeng Zongmi, 25, 93n.28, 142n.126
   explication of *Perfect Awakening* sutra, 26–27, 27n.76
   numinous knowing, as core of Chan, 142n.127
   "red meatball" of, 200n.18
Guyin Jingqin, Chan Master (古音淨琴禪師), 59–60

habit-energies accumulated over eons, inability to discard, 85
hair, sword that severs single, 89
Hangzhou, 1–2
Hanshan's Poems (*Hanshan shi* 寒山詩), 93n.28, 180–82, 181–82n.5, 201n.20, 212–13, 212–13n.1
Head Librarian Ung (雄藏主). *See* Ung, Head Librarian (雄藏主)
Head Seat Yŏn (淵首座). *See* Yŏn, Head Seat (淵首座)
Heart Sutra, 63–64
heavenly crown and dirty sandals, 120
hell is not a real dharma, 140
horse
   calling a deer a, 75–76
   restraining, by restraining a picture of, 86
hot water, unavailability of to blame for decline in practice-work, 112
houseboat living not uncommon in Yuan dynasty, 4

houseboats, Zhongfeng Mingben and, 4, 10–13, 12n.37, 33
how do I do it, thought of, leads to delusive calculation, 226
House Instructions of Dwelling-in-the Phantasmal Hermitage, 28–29
huan (幻). *See* phantasm (*huan* 幻)
huatou (話頭) 3n.9, 5. *See also gong'an* (公案)
  after I'm dead and cremated, what will be my original nature, 52
  A-mi-tā-bha, 36–37
  Amitābha as *huatou*
    Chan Master Chushan Shaoqi (楚山紹琦禪師), 59
    Chan Master Guyin Jingqin (古音淨琴禪師), 59–60
  begging bowl, 108
  beyond samsara no separate *huatou*; beyond the *huatou* no separate samsara, 227–30
  at birth where from and at death where to (*sheng cong he lai si cong he qu* 生從何來死從何去), 8–9
  chewing to pieces a single, 119–20
  constantly make it sever every support you have, 225
  cypress tree in the front of the garden, 104
  definition of, 5
  discern mind in forms, 97
  do not stop keeping an eye on, 227–30
  dried turd (*ganshijue* 乾屎橛), 7–8, 61–62, 103, 104, 104–5n.59, 108
  eliminate anything beyond this correct thought of practicing the *huatou*, 227–30
  examining the old woman, 108
  falling into words, 108
  "functioning as Head" in daily life, the *huatou* is, 230
  in that way keep an eye on, 72–73
  just *in that way* rely on your *original allotment* and rest in the *huatou* you are practicing, 245–46
  keep an eye on the *huatou*, 7–9, 57, 59, 62, 72–73, 78–79, 80, 97, 180, 230–32, 238, 245–46
  in life live together with, in death die together with, 118
  lift to awareness the, 225, 241
  like meeting an enemy, 84, 112–15
  like swallowing a burred chestnut, 89
  mind is buddha, 97
  must not seek out another *upāya* other than, even after twenty or thirty years without awakening, 118
  must stand your ground against, 118
  near to the very meaning of practice, 180–82
  nianfo gong'an (念佛公案; using *nianfo* as a *huatou*) common in Ming dynasty, 55–61
  no *something you can keep your eye on*, 230
  not different from *upāya*, 181
  original face (*benlai mianmu* 本來面目), 29, 52, 111, 112, 241
    Chan Master Xueting (雪庭禪師), 59–60
  periodic changes of, during course of practice, 9
  phantasm (*huan* 幻) calligraphic metaphor, Zhongfeng Mingben, 29–30, 172, 172n.6
  phantasm (*huan* 幻), Zhongfeng Mingben, 29–30
    as phantasmal, 29–30
  press on *huatou* for an entire lifetime, 241
  raise to awareness the *huatou*, 7–8, 36–37, 59, 112, 152, 225, 226–27, 231–32, 236, 240–41, 243
  rally, 225
  reciting out loud, 60
  as *road of no meaning*, 104
  sensation of great uncertainty over, 227–30
  simply focus your uncertainty upon the fact that you do not understand this huatou, 232
  single phrase, 78–79
  as sun of wisdom that melts ice of delusion and turns it back into buddha-nature water, 66–68
  tasteless (*mei ziwei* 沒滋味), 72–73
  that has no meaning or taste, 64–66, 180–82, 227–30, 243–44, 245–46
    as medicine, 77–78
    placed in field of your eight consciousnesses will remove all your intellectual knowledge, 232
  as *that which you can get nothing from another*, 97
  there is no way to inquire into this single dharma: this is the reason why the huatou *exists*, 227–30

three catties of linen thread, 103, 104
to be practiced in daily activities until penetration is reached, 242
to where does the one return (yi gui he chu 一歸何處), 8–9, 237–38
   as Gaofen Yuanmiao's main *huatou*, 135n.108
   today people awaken to the Way via sensation of uncertainty over the *huatou*, whereas the ancients did so via sensation of uncertainty over samsara, 227–30, 232
   uncertainty and practice, in combination with this *huatou*, enact a return to *self*, 227–30
up in a tree, 108
visualization of *huatou phantasm* (*huan* 幻) as calligraphy, Zhongfeng Mingben's, 29–30
what was my original face before my father and mother conceived me, 80–82
what we refer to as *upāya* is precisely the *huatou*, 227–30
when smashed, the *great matter of samsara* will also be smashed, 227–30
when the four elements are falling apart, where is tranquility and stability, 80
when you die, at what locus will you calm your mind down, 52
who is doing the nianfo (念佛), Chan Master Konggu Jinglong (空谷景隆禪師), 57–58
who is this one doing the nianfo (念佛)
   Chan Master Chushan Shaoqi (楚山紹琦禪師), 59
   Chan Master Dufeng Benshan (毒峯善禪師), 57
   Chan Master Tianqi Benduan (天琦本瑞禪師), 58–13
wu 無, 7–9, 234–35, 236, 237–38
huatou (話頭) practice. *See also* Dahui Zonggao; *huatou* (話頭); *sensation of uncertainty*
things that go against you/things that go along with you and, 230
torpor/distraction and, 230
Yuansou Xingduan's apparent avoidance of recommending, 5
Zhongfeng Mingben's instructions on, 28–29
Zhongfeng Mingben's lifelong steadfast teaching of, 5

Huayan Sutra, 89
"every sentient being is endowed with the merits of *tathāgata* wisdom," 134, 134n.106
dust-travails (Sanskrit *kleśa*) deployed by good teachers as *upāyas* in, 143

I am certainly not someone who has had a real awakening, 10–13, 19, 32–34, 141, 146
I merely map out truth/reality to manage ordinary life, 175
"If you have just one day's worth of spirit, then practice for one day," 226–27
ill, Zhongfeng Mingben writing while, 243–44
illness, 148
   is like an illusion, 74
   is opportunity for *huatou* practice, 75–78
"impossible for a buddha to *become* a buddha," 96
In Imitation of Hanshan's Poems. *See* practicing Chan (*canchan* 參禪)
in that way, 99–100, 174, 214–15, 234–35, 245–46
in that way go on maintaining, 245–46
indolent Chan monk, 218
insect venom, 141
instructions to the assembly
intellectual knowledge, 80
   do not use in Chan practice (*canchan* 參禪), 183
   sharpness not conducive to *huatou* practice, 28
   understanding as *false knowing*, 141
iron-and-stone body-mind attitude for a lifetime or two, 174

jade
   of Bian He, 157
   flawless, 112–15
Jakushitsu Genkō (寂室元光), 44–53, 44–45n.108, 45n.110
   preference for secluded life like Zhongfeng Mingben's, 48–50
   summary of Zhongfeng Mingben's teaching as *everything is a phantasm* 47–48
Ten Necessities for Zen, as an echo of Zhongfeng Mingben, 51–53
"the *watō* that has no meaning or taste (*mu gimi watō* 無義味話頭)," 50–51

Index

Japanese disciples of Zhongfeng Mingben, 43–54
jar of water, glibness likened to, 160
Jiefeng Ying, Chan Master (傑峯英禪師), 58–59
Jineng (濟能禪師), Chan Master of the Qing dynasty
    Horned Tiger Collection (*Jiaohu ji* 角虎集), 61–62
    practice of *nianfo* (念佛), singular, as recommended by Zhongfeng Mingben, 61–62
Jingshan, Mt.
    Gaofeng Zonggao and, 8–9
    Old Man of, Wuzhun Shifan, 7–8
    Youansou Xingduan and, 3–4

Kaifeng, 12n.39, 220n.1
karma, accumulation of, shrinks one's Way-power, 63–64
"keep on pressing hard" (*ya jiangqu* 崖將去/ *si ya* 去/*si ya* 廝崖), 28
kettles and cauldrons, 149
knowing
    intellectual knowledge a hindrance to, 227–30
    three kinds of, 141
knowledge not conducive to *huatou* practice, 28
Konggu Jinglong, Chan Master (空谷景隆禪師), 57–58
Korean disciples of Zhongfeng Mingben, 38–40
kudzu, 32, 40–41, 97, 178, 196, 214–15, 218, 227–30

lack of awakening, Zhongfeng Mingben's self-professed, 10–13, 32–34
    "I also am in the dark about true knowing," 141
    I am certainly not someone who has had a real awakening, 19
    I am lacking in awakening, 146
    I have no more than a confident understanding that comes from ordinary language and books, 146
    I have not yet been able to understand the Way, 146
    interpreted as *upāya* by disciple Tianru Weize, 34
    as very nature of his "not-awakened Zen" (*migo Zen* 未悟禅), 34

lamp, holding up in a dark room, not as good as being in a state of brightness, 130
language barriers of Japanese pilgrims visiting Zhongfeng Mingben, 45–47
Lantern Festival, 68, 68n13
lantern is lantern (*buddha* is *buddha*), 68–70
lantern light is lantern light (*mind* is *mind*), 68–70
lantern is the light, 68
lapis lazuli, 70, 103, 192, 192n13
latrine, burning incense to cover the stink of, 130
Layman Pang, on "difficult" or "easy," 241–42
Layman "Sameness Hermitage" (Tong'an 同菴居士 = Ban-la-tuo-yin 般剌脫因; Mongol), disciple, 38–40, 79–80
laziness, as human nature
    once a lack is fulfilled, 125
    whether in teachers or followers, in seeking intellectual understanding, 175
"let go and bring things to closure," 175
lifebuoy, physical body as, 151
lift to awareness the *huatou*, 5
Li Lou, 152, 153n.140
Linji, 24–25
Linji Chan
    dominance of in Yuan, 2, 162–63
    in Five-Mountains system, 2
    in Ming, 55–61
Linji's shout, 73–74
lion cub, 89
live word, 166–67, 182
living in town, 220–24
    as mixing one's traces with differentiated mundane world, 112–15
losing one's life, caring about, 225
Lotus Sutra, 64–66, 89
    laziness of old monk who forgot once ordained the only four fascicles he had memorized previously, 125–26

Mahākāśyapa, 88, 148n.137
"maintain"
    in that way continue to, 245–46
    loosen your belly-skin and simply, 214–15
    nothing to, 165
    practice in order to die in cross-legged sitting posture, 165
Maitreya, 112
Māra sense-objects, do not chase after, 236

Master of Dwelling-in-the-Phantasmal Hermitage, Zhongfeng Mingben, 212–13
matter of self, 134
matter, this. See *this matter*
Mazu, 108
meaningless and tasteless *huatou*, 28–29, 77–78
medicine, 6, 77–78
    "backup thought," as aversion to, 77–78
    buddhas cannot save you with, 245–46
    good, found at residence of good physician, 158
    grasping at becomes a disease, 99–100
    as *huatou that has no meaning or taste*, 77–78
    oral teachings of buddhas and patriarchs as, for curing illness of samsara 120
    simply speaking of will not cure illness, 89
melons, Yuetang's overwatering of, 162–63, 163n.161
mendicant without any plan, 221
"Mind *is* buddha," Zhongfeng Mingben on, 234
"mind of samsara will collapse" (*shengsi xin po* 生死心破), 28
Mind-Mirror Record, Yongming Yanshou's, 93, 93n.28, 94
    as "*dhāraṇī* gate of the written word," 94
    as seawall that protects Chan, 94
mind-substance, 129
Ming Chan Masters, 55, 56–61
Ming-dynasty Linji Chan
    characteristics of, summary, 60–61
    entangled with Pure Land *nianfo* (念佛), 61
    nianfo gong'an (念佛公案; using *nianfo* as a *huatou*) common in, 55–61
    Tianru Weize's Chan style influential throughout, 61
    Zhongfeng Mingben's Chan style influential throughout, 55, 61
Mingjiao, Preceptor. *See* Fori Qisong (佛日契嵩)
Mingzhou, 1–2
mirror, ancient, 146
Mongol legacy, 1–2
moon
    reflection on water of, 104
    seeming to move as viewer moves while remaining in place in sky, 108

mountain, each who goes up makes effort on one's own, 63–64
Mr. Man-in-Charge
    being, to lose secure grip on, 118
    falsely recognizing shadows of six sense-fields as, 99, 115
    Jakushitsu Genkō on, 51–52
    Zhongfeng Mingben on, 51–52, 97
Mr. Phantasm, 38, 83, 168, 178
multiethnic nature of Mongol Yuan, 1–2
mute person, dream of, 127, 164, 243–44
"myriad forms are always speaking dharma," equivalent to *Blue Cliff Collection*, 134
myriad good practices, cultivation of, second after *enlightened mind*, 95
name, 148
    actualities beckon, 148
    actualities behind, 148
    attachment to, most extreme of five desires, 148
    gaining, only possible via practicing actualities behind, 148
    sage practices actualities, not 148
    sincerely carry out actualities behind, 148
    what one says and does is only striving for, 148
    will turn into shame, 148

Naong Hyegǔn (懶翁慧勤), 1–2, 12n.42, 56
native village, fields of, 79, 89
nectar, 171
"neither tensed nor slack" (*ji* 急/*huan* 緩 or *jin* 緊/*huan* 緩), 28
nest
    sitting in a, 63–64
    of stereotyped formulas, 80–82, 84, 97, 108, 171, 175, 240–41
New Year's Eve, 63–64
Ni Zan (倪瓚), 4, 4n.13
nianfo gong'an (念佛公案; using *nianfo* as a *huatou*) common in Ming dynasty, 55–61. *See also* Pure Land *nianfo*/*nembutsu* (念佛)
nianfo/*nembutsu* (念佛), Rinzai Zen bias against in Zen practice, 55. *See also* Pure Land *nianfo*/*nembutsu* (念佛)
nianfo (念佛), two types of, in Ming Chan practice, 60
    as a *huatou* (*nianfo gong'an* 念佛公案 = *canjiu nianfo* 參究念佛 ["probing" or "practicing" *nianfo*]), 60

nianfo (念佛), two types of, in Ming Chan practice (*cont.*)
    as "ordinary *nianfo*" (*pingchang nianfo* 平常念佛), 60
        can be used if *nianfo* as *huatou* is inappropriate/inconvenient (*bu bian* 不便), 61
nianfo (念佛) and Chan, concurrent practice (*jianxing* 兼行) discouraged, 60
Night Conversation, 2–3, 20, 22, 38, 40–41, 83–167
night sitting, 83
nirvana as absence of *furtive mind*, 120
no easiness! argument of the ancients, 177
nosebleeds, Zhongfeng Mingben and, 10–13
no taste, *huatou* and, 239–40
"not awakened," Zhongfeng Mingben as, 10–13, 32–34
"not cutting off bad, not cultivating good," 127–28
nothing-to-do, tiny closet of, 115, 119–20
number of Chan monks active in Yuan, Caodong, 2
numinous knowing, 209
    as core of Guifeng Zongmi's Chan, 142n.127
    possessed by mind from the outset, 141
    as the Way, 141

oil getting into flour, 89
old age and *huatou* practice, 76–78
old and shabby Chan masters of great comprehension, 89
old granny Chan, 177
one day's work accrues one day's results, 63–64
one-house transmission, as incorrect, 104
one-mind dharmadhātu, 127
one-pointedness of mind, 35
only my form and shadow consoling each other, 159, 161, 179–80
ordinary life, rouse a fierce attitude in, 243–44
original allotment, 189, 245–46
origination-by-dependence, time and, 63–64
ox
    getting from student and returning a horse, 104, 159
    iron, whip with empty stick, 200
    look for at Jade-Green River village, 211
    phantasmal, 212–13

Paeg'un Kyŏnghan (白雲景閑), 1–2
"passing through" the barrier of verbalization, 30–31
Pax Mongolica, 1–2, 38–40, 38–39n.94
pearl
    lost, finding of equated with awakening, 68–70
    of the Marquis of Sui, 157
people on duty, 120
Perfect Awakening Sutra, 97
    Gaofeng Yuanmiao and, 135–38
    metaphor of fire consuming both pieces of wood that kindled it, 26
        Guifeng Zongmi's explication of, 26–27, 27n.76
    as probable source of Zhongfeng Mingben's *phantasm* (*huan* 幻) teaching, 25–26
perfect-and-sudden, *Perfect Awakening Sutra* and *Śūraṃgama Sūtra* as essential discourses upon, 135–38
perfect-and-sudden vehicle, 96, 135–38
phantasm (*huan* 幻), 23, 175. *See also great phantasm* (*huan* 幻); *phantasmal* (*huan* 幻); *Song of Dwelling-in-the-Phantasmal Hermitage*
    1,700 Chan standards arise from, 178
    awakening and nirvana come into being rooted in, 178
    bodhisattvas never separated from, 173
    buddhas of the future will open correct dharma-eye in, 173
    buddhas of the past realized nirvana in, 173
    buddhas of the present completing correct awakening in, 173
    dependence upon, 168–78
    as delusion, 178
    entire Buddhist canon speaks in dependence upon, 178
    as equivalent to provisional, 175
    everything is a, 23–25
    has no duality, no dichotomy, 173
    has no sages or common persons, 173
    has no *this* (arising-abiding-changing-ceasing) and *that* (awakening and nirvana), 173
    as *huatou*, Zhongfeng Mingben's, 29–30
    kindness, compassion, joy, equanimity generated by, 178

Linji's successors of, none able to go outside of, 170
other Sanskrit synonyms for, 23n.68
as part and parcel of buddhas and patriarchs, 170
relied upon by limitless sages and worthies, 173
searching for your *single person* in the middle of, 175
six perfections and myriad practices are established in reliance on, 178
as synonym for Sanskrit *māyā*, 23
tathatā and *prajñā* rely on, 178
three vehicles and ten bodhisattva stages rely upon, 178
visualization of character for, as *huatou*, 29–30
Zhongfeng Mingben's teaching of, *Perfect Awakening* sutra as probable source for, 25–27
phantasmal (*huan* 幻), 23, 24–25. See also great phantasm (*huan* 幻); phantasm (*huan* 幻); *Song of Dwelling-in-the-Phantasmal Hermitage*
awakening, 212–13
Chan, 212–13
dependence upon, 168–78
detaching from the (*li huan* 離幻) (*see* detaching from the phantasmal [*li huan* 離幻])
dharmas
all perfect, 63–64
people who have never really awakened in, 177
Śākyamuni's teachings added to the "screen" of, 169
fly whisk, 24, 168, 170
huatous as, 29
ox (*see under Song of Dwelling-in-the-Phantasmal Hermitage*)
seeing, *completely imagined nature* arises from, 168–69, 169n.2
seeing, as discrimination, 168–78
shadows, an entire lifetime's, 31–32
shadows of *numinous luminosity*, 97
stories of buddhas and patriarchs as
Baizhang's shout that deafened Mazu's phantasmal ears, 170
Bodhidharma sitting facing a phantasmal wall, 170

Hongren asking Huike's phantasmal name, 170
Huairang's polishing a phantasmal tile, 170
Huike pacifying phantasmal mind, 170
Huineng composing phantasmal verses, 170
Linji
phantasmal *function* of, 170
phantasmal *giving* and *snatching away* of, 170
phantasmal *guest* and *host* of, 170
phantasmal *killing* and *giving life* of, 170
phantasmal shout of, 170
slapping Huangbo with his phantasmal palm, 170
Shenxiu composing phantasmal verses, 170
teaching methods
dangling phantasmal feet, 170
drooping a phantasmal fly whisk. 170
pilgrimage and *huatou* practice, 78–79
pilgrims, Chan, from all over East Asia, 1–2, 2n.3, 18, 38–40, 38–39n.94, 43–45, 43–44n.106, 44–45n.108
pilgrims, Japanese, language barriers to visiting Zhongfeng Mingben, 45–47
pine tree depends upon phantasm (*huan* 幻) to be straight, 168–178
piss, 239, 243–44
poison pit, 89
pond, discarding, yet expecting moon to shine upon it, 158
porridge
morning, unavailability of to blame for decline in practice-work, 112
smell of, and of pre-noon meal, 167
practice (*can* 參), 179–80
practice after awakening, 126, 179–80
practice-work. *See* Chan practice (*canchan* 參禪)
practicing Chan (*canchan* 參禪) in *In Imitation of Hanshan's Poems*, 182–211
as-soon-as-possible is proper, 187
Chan has an aim, 209
cuts off any instructional materials, 201
cuts off both true and false, 201
cuts off cultivation-and-realization, 201–2
cuts off doer/done, 199–200

practicing Chan (*canchan* 參禪) in *In Imitation of Hanshan's Poems* (cont.)
  cuts off illumination-and-awakening, 202
  cuts off knowables, 199
  cuts off sage/ordinary person, 200
  cuts off stages, 200
  cuts off the two extremes existence and non-existence, 201
  cuts off unreal reflected images, 202
  discarding-and-carving-off is proper, 187
  do not activate thoughts, 184
  do not allow habitual laziness, 184
  do not become attached to cross-legged sitting, 183
  do not engage in choosing, 184–85
  do not go along with self, 185
  do not use intellectual knowledge, 183
  do not violate the precepts, 184
  do not wade through objective supports, 183
  does not guard self, 206
  does not seek fame, 208
  does not seek to be superior, 208
  does not stick to things, 207
  does not take the body into account, 207
  does not try to understand concepts, 206–7
  exerting energy is proper, 186
  has no state or condition, 210
  having the eye is proper, 186
  how does one practice?, 210–11
  impartiality-and-fairness is proper, 187
  involves an unyielding self, 207–8
  is a matter of karmic conditions, 209
  is direct pointing of Bodhidharma, 192
  is for the sake of clarifying the Chan personal realization, 193–94
  is for the sake of completing the Way, 191
  is for the sake of cutting off learning, 192
  is for the sake of jumping over, 191–92
  is for the sake of the matter of self, 193
  is for the sake of perfect-and-sudden, 193
  is for the sake of samsara, 190
  is for the sake of seeking awakening, 193
  is for the sake of the ultimate, 192
  is most efficient in saving energy, 203
  is most pleasureful, 204
  is most simple-and-quick, 203
  is not a matter of exhortations and guidance, 198
  is not a matter of having a high opinion of oneself, 198
  is not a matter of hogwash-talk, 193–99
  is not a matter of outside-the-teachings, 199
  is not a matter of rational study of meanings, 196–97
  is not a matter of stopping thoughts, 198
  is not a matter of strategy-and-tactics, 198
  is not a matter of things that can be heard, 197
  is not a matter of things that can be seen, 197
  is not joke discourse [prapañca], 209
  is not step-by-step trivialities, 197
  is the broadest, 203–4
  is the easiest thing to do, 202
  is the highest meaning, 208
  is the most illumined, 204
  is the most quiescent, 205–6
  is the most ready-made, 203
  is the most withered and pale, 204–5
  is the quickest liberation, 204
  is wanting to awaken to your mind, 209
  it is necessary that the eight consciousnesses be smashed, 189
  it is necessary to arrive home, 188
  it is necessary to be a person of the original allotment, 189–90
  it is necessary to be of high elegance and antique simplicity, 189
  it is necessary to be solitary and obstinate, 190
  it is necessary to clarify principle, 188
  it is necessary to have deep confidence, 190
  it is necessary to have zeal, 189
  it is necessary to shed-and-delete, 188–89
  it is necessary to take the direct-and-quick, 188
  practice the inexhaustible, 211
  resolve is proper, 187
  self-assent is proper, 185
  should not be slack, 207
  should not measure, 206
  simple-and-direct is proper, 186
  simple-and-plain is proper, 186
  stepping backwards is proper, 185
  there are neither monks nor laypersons, 196
  there are neither stupid persons nor wise ones, 196
  there are no limits, 195
  there are no secret instructions [just for initiates], 195
  there is neither stillness nor noisiness, 196
  there is no noble/base, 194

there is no observing the precepts, 206
there is no past/present, 194
there is no rare-and-special, 195
there is no sharp/dull, 194
there is no such thing as skillfulness, 195
who is performing the song-and-dance?, 210
why the big hurry?, 210
prajñā is like great ball of fire allowing nothing to approach, 233
press hard with *huatou*, 174
no need to ask how to, 240–41
proof in texts and sayings, modern-day people constantly seizing upon, 132
Pure Land *nianfo* (念佛)
and Chan (禪) are both mind, 102
and Chan (禪) are one, but in name dual, 102
and Chan practice (*canchan* 參禪) are both methods for ending samsara, 35–38, 38n.93, 80–82, 102
or Chan practice (*canchan* 參禪), one should practice either but not both, 35–38, 60, 102
derivation of *nianfo* (念佛), 35
in *Poems of Longing for the Pure Land* (*Huai jingtu shi* 懷淨土詩) by Chan Master Chushi Fanqi (楚石梵琦禪師), 57
who is doing the nianfo (念佛) *huatou* of Chan Master Konggu Jinglong (空谷景隆禪師), 57–58
who is this one doing the nianfo (念佛) *huatou* of Chan Master Dufeng Benshan (毒峯本善禪師), 57
Pure Land *nianfo* (念佛) and Chan (禪), four alternatives of. *See* Yongming Yanshou (永明延壽)

Qianyan Yuanzhang (千巖元長), 38–40, 39n.95, 43–44
Qing dynasty Linji Chan's concern with Pure Land/Chan practice, as legacy of Zhongfeng Mingben, 61–62

rain, sound of, 89
rational-concept scholars, 83, 85
ready-made
enjoyment is, 173
everything is from the outset, 23–24
ready-made gong'an

every sentient being has underfoot the single, 133, 133n.105
as landscape, 49
Zhongfeng Mingben's dharma approach of *great phantasm* as putting an end to, 24
Real, the
Bodhidharma Chan turns its back on expounding, 96
don't search for, 112–15
students of the Way who don't know, 99–100
wherever you stand is, 141
recluse(s), 48, 79n.22
Great, of the Snow Mountains (Śākyamuni), 158
Great, who lived in town (Śākyamuni), 220, 220n.1
Hanshan's Poems considered to be written by shadowy, 181–82n.5
of mountain, laughable, 222
preserving the high integrity of one's possession of the Way by becoming a, 146
remaining one is not as criminal as reeling in a reputation, 146
in town, training to be a, 223
Zhongfeng Mingben not a total, 4
reclusion, 50, 146, 151, 161
Recorded Sayings of Chan Master Gaofeng Yuanmiao, 7–8
Recorded Sayings of Chan Master Xueyan Zuqin, 7–8
"red meatball," 200, 200n.18
reverse examination, 119–20
Rinzai Zen bias against use of *nembutsu* (念佛) in Zen, 55

Śākyamuni
gave phantasmal (*huan* 幻) answers to phantasmal (*huan* 幻) questions, 169
held up phantasmal (*huan* 幻) flower with phantasmal (*huan* 幻) hand, resulting in Kāśyapa's phantasmal (*huan* 幻) smile, 169
his one transmission of a falsehood became ten thousand persons' transmission of fact, phantasm (*huan* 幻) in turn the cause of phantasm (*huan* 幻), 170
"Sentient-beings are endowed with the merit-characteristics of tathagata wisdom," 152

sameness
    dharma nature has always been, 188
    emerging from and disappearing into, 173
    of a single taste, dharma gate of, 102
    wisdom of, 64–66, 64n.6
"Sameness Hermitage." *See* Layman "Sameness Hermitage"
sameness-practice, 222
"Samsara is the *great matter*." *See great matter and impermanence is swift*, 227–30
    Jakushitsu Genkō, 51
    Zhongfeng Mingben, 51, 97
sandals, straw, 78–79
śarīra, 165
"saving on the expenditure of energy is gaining energy" (*shengli bian shi deli chu ye* 省力便是得力處也), 28
sea of venomous poison, 175
seeds
    of beans don't produce hemp or wheat, 117
    for the Way, 117–18
seeing the Nature, 97
semblance dharma, 120
semblance prajñā, 119, 119n.91, 176
semblance talk as dependent power of intellectual knowledge, 179–80
sensation of great uncertainty. See also sensation of uncertainty (*yi* 疑情)
    of Gaofeng Yuanmiao, 4n.12
    over the *great matter of samsaric impermanence*, 230
    over the *huatou that has no meaning or taste*, 227–30
sensation of uncertainty (*yi* 疑情), 4n.12, 5, 7–9, 28, 59, 60
    at beginning of Chan tradition, no one had heard of keeping an eye on the *huatou* and producing, 180–82
    collapse of (*yiqing po* 疑情破), as synonym for "mind of samsara will collapse" (*shengsi xin po* 生死心破), 28
    in Dahui Zonggao's *huatou* practice, 28
    destruction of, as tantamount to awakening, 5, 28
    involves
        no arranging things, 227–30
        no effortful doing, 227–30
        no guidance, 227–30
        no "handle," 227–30
        no personal inclination, 227–30
        no separate rationale, 227–30
        no specific awareness, 227–30
        no specific posture, 227–30
        no *upāya*, 227–30
    locus of producing, 240–41
    over the *huatou*
        do not seek for any upāya, 227–30
        today people awaken to the Way via sensation of uncertainty over the *huatou*, whereas the ancients did so via sensation of uncertainty over samsara, 227–30
separate transmission outside the teachings, 41, 84, 85, 86, 87, 104, 132–33n.104, 180–82
Shan-da-mi-di-li (善達密的理). *See* Zhaotang Ciji (照堂慈寂)
sharpness in Chan practice, 238
Shi Miyuan (史彌遠), 1n.1, 73–74
shoulder-to-shoulder and heel-to-heel in a vast crowd, 180
sickbed, 73–74. *See also* illness
single laugh, 85, 85n.5
single person, searching for your, right in the middle of this phantasm (*huan* 幻), 175
single phrase. See under huatou
single taste, 7–8
single transmission
    of Bodhidharma, 85, 96, 127, 135–38, 214–15
    of Chan, 100, 220
sitting. *See also* cross-legged sitting
    don't worry if it gains a lot, 214
    immovable for one single thought-moment is, 214
    is another term for Chan, 214
    reach the forgetting of sitting, 214–15
sixteen-foot body of a buddha, 99–100, 102
smashing *ball of uncertainty*, 9, 28, 89, 108. See also *sensation of uncertainty*
snowflake in a flame, 59
snow goose depends upon phantasm (*huan* 幻) to be white, 168, 178
snowy day, three types of Chan monks on a, 66–68
Song of Dwelling-in-the-Phantasmal Hermitage, 179
    as usual is incorrect, 212–13
    "does not exist" of "[*Managing*] does not exist" is phantasmal, 212–13

gong'ans (*huatous*), phantasmal, 212–13, 213n.2
   used to *manage* phantasmal realization and cultivation, 212–13
   "I am phantasmal; you are phantasmal; phantasm is bottomless; phantasmal birth; phantasmal death; phantasmal nirvana," 212–13
   if wheel of true phantasm is not comprehended, 212–13
   phantasmal blindness will impede phantasmal eyes, 212–13
   phantasmal mind will suddenly produce phantasmal Māras, 212–13
   must not say *managing* itself is phantasmal, 212–13
   phantasm of *awakening*, 212–13
   phantasmal bodhisattva, 212–13
   phantasmal dharmas, 212–13
   phantasmal ox [unchecked mind of student] goes to sleep, 212–13
   reined in by phantasmal rope, 212–13
   will become active, 212–13
   will become still, 212–13
   will come to a stop, 212–13
   shadows will die down in light of phantasmal magical-transformations, 212–13
   student will reside in four *dhyānas* upon a single awakening to phantasmal dream of, 212–13
   phantasmal people, 212–13
   phantasmal things
      likened to holding a tortoise-hair fly whisk, 212–13, 212–13n.1
      likened to the Serpent King's daughter's holding a mud-ball in the palm of the hand, 212–13

sound of waterfall, stream, thunder, wind, 134
speaking dharma
   are not only talks given from the high seat in the Dharma Hall, 159
   is outside of verbalization, 159
   non-verbal examples of, from the Chan patriarchs, 159
spirits, monks drinking, 135–38
state of *no-feces-and-urine*, 130
stone woman giving birth to a child, prohibiting, 133
stopping-to-rest, 68–70, 183, 184, 236–37

summer retreat
   rules of, 64–66, 64n.5
   Zhongfeng Mingben's instructions to the assembly prior to, 245–46
sumō, 243–44
sun of wisdom melts ice of delusion to turn it back into buddha-nature water, 66–68
śūnyatā, 186
   phantasmal (*huan* 幻), 212–13
supranormal powers, 138–40
   ordinary persons have always possessed them, 140
Śūraṃgama Sūtra, 21, 61, 87, 89, 97, 97n.39, 99–100, 108, 109n.68, 143, 159, 160n.154, 164, 206
   Gaofeng Yuanmiao and, 135–38
   Zhongfeng Mingben and, 25–26, 122, 122n.97
sword, 73–74, 89, 130, 152, 177, 190, 241–42
   ancients' whole body was like a sharp, 32–33, 146
   Daoxun braving Yao Junsu's, 152
   Gaofeng Yuanmiao's essential of being greatly indignant, likened to wish for vengeance using, 174n.9
   long, wield the, 52
   of old and shabby Chan masters, 89
   sharp, 146
   that severs a fallen feather, 232
Sword, Tai'e, 141, 143n.133

T'aego Pou (太古普愚), 1–2
talking about a meal does not cure hunger, 68–70
talking Chan, present-day teachers' reliance on, 89
tasteless (*mei ziwei* 沒滋味) huatou, 28. See also huatou (話頭)
   Zhongfeng Mingben's, meaningless and, 28
tea, 111, 245
ten bodhisattva stages, 96
"Ten Monasteries," 1–2
Ten Poems on Living in the Mountains, Zhongfeng Mingben's, 49–50
there is not a single dharma
   that confronts your deluded feelings, 227–30
   to give to others, 227–30, 229n.9
   to understand or not understand, 227–30

there's-no-alternative, today, tomorrow, for thirty years if you're not able to practice, 226
thief, person doing practice-work is like, 236–37
thirtieth day of the twelfth month, 63–64, 63n.1
thirty whacks of the stick, 7–8
thirty-years practice, 30, 31
this matter, 4n.12, 7–8, 25–26
   does not lie with
      the buddhas and patriarchs, 227–30
      intellectual knowledge, 227–30
      sense-objects, 227–30
      the written word, 227–30
   lies only in your having sufficient confidence, 227–30
   must face off against the *great matter*, 226
   not a mundane thing that can be sought after, 226
   not a mundane thing that can be studied, 226
   not attained through verbalization, 97
   not something to which one applies the mind/mental effort, 89, 226
this mind, 77–78, 126, 233
   in delusion becomes samsara, in awakening becomes nirvana, 233
"thorn in the heart," 99–100
thorn, level of understanding with a, 141
Three Essentials of Chan, Gaofeng Yuanmiao's, 4n.12
three types of Chan monks on a snowy day, 66–68
thunderclap, 141
Tianmu, Mt., Zhonfeng Mingben succeeding to Gaofeng Yuanmiao's, 4
Tianqi Benduan, Chan Master (天琦本瑞禪師), 58
Tianru Weize (天如惟則), successor of Zhongfeng Mingben, 17–18, 24, 43–44
   Chan style of, influential throughout Ming dynasty, 55
   interpretation of Zhonfeng Mingben's "not awakened" as *upāya*, 33–34
   Pure Land *nianfo* (念佛) or Chan practice (*canchan* 參禪), one should practice either but not both, 36–38
   two boats, standing with a foot in, 36–37
      quoted by Chan Master Konggu Jinglong (空谷景隆禪師), 57

tiger, wanting to paint a, 127
tile striking bamboo, awakening at sound of, 111
time and *origination-by-dependence*, wasting, 63–64
torpor/distraction, 123–24
   do not keep an eye on, 231–32
   do not seek another *upāya* beyond the *huatou* to remove, 231–32
   enters if Chan *huatou* practice is not genuine and earnest, 123
   exerting mind to repel is a mistake, 124
   keep an eye on the *huatou* in the middle of, 231–32
   no need for you to push away, 227–30
   raise to awareness the *huatou* on top of, 231–32
   as *scenery of your native land* (=your *original face*), 123
   seeing, then thinking to ward off, is a mistake, 123
   will fail to appear once *huatou* practice is meticulous, 231–32
tortoise-hair fly whisk, phantasmal things are like holding a, 212–13, 212–13n.1
transmission of the flame of the lamp, 103
"treading onward," 31–32
tree, discarding, but expecting birds to flock to, 158
true mind, 89
True Nature, 142n.127, 143
True Person, 97, 108, 175, 184, 200n.18
true state of being awakened, 68–70
turn the light backwards and take a step back, 134
two boats, standing with a foot in, concurrent Chan practice and Pure Land *nianfo* (念佛) as, 36–37, 57

ultimate standard, 85, 85n.4
uncertainty (yi 疑). See also *sensation of uncertainty*
   about *great matter of samsara*, 227–30
   about samsara, unresolved, 179–80, 227–30
   buddhas and patriarchs all proceeded from neverending, 227–30
   just this is locus of, 227–30
   simply focus your uncertainty upon the fact that you do not understand this huatou, 232

understanding the phantasmal (*zhi huan* 知幻), 23–27
understanding/not understanding are both false views, 234–35
Ung, Head Librarian (雄藏主), Korean Sŏn disciple of Zhongfeng Mingben, 38–40
Unreserved Functioning, 64–66
upāya, 25–26, 30–31, 34, 53, 53n.133, 61–62, 84, 85n.4, 88, 97, 100, 104, 115, 118, 119, 123n.99, 134, 141, 148, 177, 180–82, 184, 197, 198, 217, 221, 227–30, 231–32, 233
    from the outset there are no, 240–41
    Gaofeng Yuanmiao
        on ordering students to burn a finger, 135–38, 135–36n.109
        on receiving the precepts as, 135–38
urgency, 177

vehicle, perfect-and-sudden, 96
verbalization
    incorrectly relying upon, 97
    within wordlessness, deployed as an *upāya* by the buddhas and patriarchs, 104
    vessel giving shape to emptiness which has not fixed shape, 108
Vimalakīrti, 241–42
visualization of *huatou phantasm* (*huan* 幻), 29–30

walking stick, 78–79
warning whip (*jingce* 警策), 13–14, 226, 234, 239–40, 241–42, 243–44, 245
wasting an entire year, 63–64
way home, the, 66–68
Way, the, 31–33, 40, 46–47
    as extreme *impartiality*, 152
    is not something you can get from other people, 243–44
    one who lacks understanding of cannot become abbot, 33
weeds, 96
what was my original face, 52. See *huatou* (話頭)
wheel of true phantasm, 212–13
whip, 29, 59, 112, 127, 180–82, 200
willow-leaf style calligraphy, Zhongfeng Mingben's, 14–15, 14–15n.53
wings, Shishi's installing on his disciples, 162–63, 163n.162
winter-melon seal, 115, 116n.84

wisdom of sameness, 64–66, 64n.6
wu (無). See *huatou* (話頭)

Xiaoyan Debao (笑巖德寶禪師 =Yuexin 月心), 60
Xingyuan Huiming, Chan Master (性原慧明禪師), 59
Xuanjian (玄鑒) of "Nanzhao" (Yunnan), successor to Zhongfeng Mingben, 40–44
Xuedou's Verses on Ancient Standards, 132
Xueting, Chan Master (雪庭禪師), 59–60
Xueyan Zuqin (雪巖祖欽), autobiography of, 7–8

Yama, King, 33, 112–15
Ye Gong's dragons, painted, 112–15, 114n.78
yi ju (一句). See *huatou*
"yoked," 77–78, 89, 236–38, 243–44
Yŏn, Head Seat (淵首座), Korean Sŏn disciple of Zhongfeng Mingben, 38–40
Yongjia Collection, 87, 87n.8
Yongming Yanshou (永明延壽), Preceptor
    four alternatives of Pure Land and Chan practice, 80–82, 100
        have Chan no Pure Land, 81n.27, 100
        no Chan have Pure Land, 81n.27
        have Chan have Pure Land, 81n.27
        no Chan no Pure Land, 81n.27
    Mind-Mirror Record, 93, 93n.28, 94
    Zhongfeng Mingben's high esteem for, 93–95
your old home, 236
Yuan dynasty, 1–2
Yuan-dynasty Chan, 1–2
Yuansou Xingduan (元叟行端), 3
    angry (怒) style of Chan, 5–6
    Chushi Fanqi (楚石梵琦), in lineage of, 56
    dementia in late life, possible, 5
    huatou practice, apparent avoidance of, 5
    as one of two most well-known Linji-Chan masters in Yuan, 3
    "stick and shout" freely applied, 6–7
    successful career, 3–4
yulu (語錄), 7. See also autobiography within *huatou* Chan
Yunmen Kuangzhen, Chan Master (雲門匡真禪師)
    dried turd and, 104–5n.59
    go out and meet glare of, 201
    lofty antiquity of, 104
    "would have struck Śākyamuni dead with one blow of my stick," 169

334 Index

Yunnan School of Chan, Zhongfeng Mingben as founder of, 40, 41, 43
Yunqi Zhuhong (雲棲袾宏), 55, 55n.140
   Chan Whip (*Changuan cejin* 禪關策進), 55–56
   Ming Chan Masters (*Huangming mingseng jilüe* 皇明名僧輯略), 56–60

Zhao Chang's flowers, painted, 112–15
Zhao Mengfu (趙孟頫), calligrapher/painter, disciple and close friend of Zhongfeng Mingben, 38–40
Zhaotang Ciji (照堂慈寂 = Shan-da-mi-di-li 善達密的理; Uighur?), successor to Zhongfeng Mingben, 17–18
Zhejiang, 1–2
Zhongfeng Extensive Record. 4, 5
Zhongfeng Mingben (中峯明本), 2–3, 4
   abbot, refusal to serve as
      owing to disinterest in cultivating fame or reputation, 146, 151
      owing to *lack of awakening*, 146
   on *advancing* (to abbotship) or *retiring* (in reclusion), 151
   as Assistant to the Prior, 10–13
   atypical career of, 4, 10–13, 22
   autobiography, 10–13
      Chinese text of, 13n.50
      chronological not psychological, 10, 13
      no mention of social contacts in, 10, 13–14
      as a warning to himself, 10–14
   avoidance of human affairs, 245–46
   Budai (布袋), depicted as, 14–15n.53, 15–17, 15n.55
      symbolic of freedom from monastic administrative responsibilities, 16–17
   calligraphic metaphor using *huatou phantasm* (*huan* 幻), 29–30
   calligraphy of, willow-leaf style, 14–15, 14–15n.53
   calm and gentle (坦夷) style of Chan, 6–7
   Dharma Talks of Preceptor Tianmu Zhongfeng National Teacher Puying (*Tianmu Zhongfeng heshang Puying guoshi fayu* 天目中峯和尚普應國師法語; abbreviated as *Zhongfeng Dharma Talks*), 17
   Diamond Sutra, early understanding gained from reading as "not awakening," 10–13
   dislike of administrative affairs, 10–13
   disrespectful piece of writing, 245–46
   Dwelling-in-the-Phantasmal (*huanzhu* 幻住) Hermitages, 10–13, 23, 175
   "here I am not a teacher who preaches and guides others," 175
   "everything is a phantasm," 23–25
   Extensive Record of Preceptor Tianmu Zhongfeng (*Tianmu Zhongfeng heshang guanglu* 天目中峯和尚廣錄; abbreviated as *Zhongfeng Extensive Record*), 17–18
      as compared to *Recorded Sayings of Chan Master Dahui Pujue* (*Dahui Pujue chanshi yulu* 大慧普覺禪師語錄), 21
      compiled by devoted disciple Zhaotang Ciji (照堂慈寂 = Shan-da-mi-di-li 普達密的理; Uighur?), 17
      complete contents of (list), 18–21
      contents of, representative, as selected for current volume, 22
      lack of "abbacy *yulus*," 21
      lack of Ascending-the-Hall (*shang-tang* 上堂) discourses, 21–22
      literary cast to, 21
   Gaofeng Yuanmiao, studying with, 4
   Gōkai Honjō (業海本淨), Japanese Zen disciple of, 44
   honesty and humility of, 13, 32–34, 146, 152, 182, 245–46
   houseboats and, 4, 33, 151
   House Instructions of Dwelling-in-the-Phantasmal Hermitage, 28–29
   on *huatou* practice, 28–29
   influence of, in Ming period, 55
   influence on Japanese students who never met him, 53–54, 54n.135
   Jakushitsu Genkō (寂室元光), Zen poet, disciple, 44–45, 44–45n.108, 45n.110, 53
   Japanese disciples of, 43–54
   Kaō Sōnen (可翁宗然), possibly Japanese painter Kaō, disciple, 44–45, 45n.109
   as key figure of Linji Chan in South during Yuan, 2
   Korean disciples of, 38–40
   Layman Feng Zizhen (馮子振), disciple, 38–40
   Layman "Identity Hermitage" (Tong'an 同菴居士 = Dan-la-tuo-yin 般剌脫因; Mongol), disciple, 38–40

little finger missing from left hand in portrait of, 135–38, 135–36n.109
Master of Dwelling-in-the-Phantasmal Hermitage, 212–13
Mr. Phantasm, 38, 83, 151, 168, 178
  Even if you were to see me, we would not talk together, 245–46,
Night Conversations in a Mountain Hermitage, 2–3, 20, 22, 38, 40–41, 83–167
  "not awakened" claims of, 10–13, 32–34
    "I also am in the dark about true knowing," 141
    I am certainly not someone who has had a real awakening, 19
    I am lacking in awakening, 146
    I have no more than a confident understanding that comes from ordinary language and books, 146
    I have not yet been able to understand the Way, 146
    interpreted as *upāya* by disciple Tianru Weize, 34
    lack of claims of awakening do not mean no awakening
      "Chan craftsmen (the *real thing*) do not have to quote the story of their own awakening to convert others," 164
      "Chan craftsmen (the *real thing*) relate the story of their own awakening only at need, as *upāyas*," 164
      "many in the past concealed their awakening, lacking any desire to reveal it," 164
      "many in the past did not give outward form to the content of their awakening," 164
      a teacher's revealing his own awakening could be detrimental to students, 164
    as very nature of his "not-awakened Zen" (*migo Zen* 未悟禅), 34
  as one of two most well-known Linji-Chan masters in Yuan, 3
  one's *own personal grave responsibility* (*ji zhong ren* 己重任), 30–31
  "passing through" the barrier of verbalization, 30–31
  Perfect Awakening sutra as probable source of *phantasm* (*huan* 幻) teaching, 25–26
  personality of, 4, 6–7, 13
  phantasm/phantasmal (*huan* 幻) (*see* phantasm (*huan* 幻), phantasmal (*huan* 幻))
  phantasm as *huatou* (*huan* 幻), 29–30
  portraits of, 14–15n.53, 15–17, 15n.55
  Pure Land *nianfo* (念佛) and Chan practice (*canchan* 参禅)
    both are methods for ending samsara, 35–38, 38n.93
    enter deeply into one gate, 61
    one should practice either but not both concurrently, 35–38
  Purity Rules for Dwelling-in-the-Phantasmal Hermitage, 6–7, 31–32
  Qianyan Yuanzhang (千巖元長), successor, 38–40, 39n.95, 43–44
  reclusion
    ancients did not esteem, even if they lived in anonymity, 161
    having only my form and shadow to console each other, 159, 161, 179–80
    if mind is identical to the Way, even isolation in caves and wastelands is equal to spreading the teachings before an assembly, 160
    if mind is not identical to the Way, no official position or its honors will turn it into "*speaking dharma* to benefit beings," 159
  reclusive tendencies of, lifelong, 4, 10–13, 146
  "stick and shout" of, 6–7
  Śūraṃgama sutra, 25
  Talks of Chan Master Tianmu Zhongfeng Guanghui (*Tianmu Zhongfeng Guanghui chanshi yu* 天目中峯廣慧禅師語; abbreviated as *Zhongfeng Talks*), 17, 23
  Ten Poems on Living in the Mountains, 49–50
  Tianmu Recorded Sayings (*Tianmu yulu* 天目語錄), non-extant possible source for *Zhongfeng Record B*, 22–23
  Tianru Weize (天如惟則), successor, 17–18, 24, 43–44
    interpretation of Zhongfeng Mingben's "not awakened" as *upāya*, 33–34
    Pure Land *nianfo* (念佛) or Chan practice (*canchan* 参禅), one should practice either but not both, 36–38
  "treading onward," 31–32

Zhongfeng Mingben (中峯明本) (cont.)
   Xuanjian (玄鑒) of "Nanzhao" (Yunnan), successor, 40–44
      disciple and Chan pilgrim from Yunnan, 40–43
      Yunnan School of Chan, as founder of, 40, 41, 43
   yearning to "retire and take a rest," 10–13

Zhao Mengfu (趙孟頫), calligrapher/painter, disciple and close friend, 38–40

Zhaotang Ciji (照堂慈寂 = Shan-da-mi-di-li 善達密的理; Uighur?), successor, 17–18